THE INTERNATIONAL MONETARY FUND
1972–1978

Cooperation on Trial

VOLUME I: Narrative and Analysis

Margaret Garritsen de Vries

INTERNATIONAL MONETARY FUND
WASHINGTON, D. C.
1985

© 1985 International Monetary Fund

Library of Congress Cataloging in Publication Data

De Vries, Margaret Garritsen, 1922–
    The International Monetary Fund, 1972–1978.

    Includes indexes.
    Contents: v. 1–2. Narrative and analysis —
v. 3. Documents.
    1. International Monetary Fund—History. I. Title.
HG3881.5.I58D42   1985   332.1'52   85-2352
ISBN 0-939934-40-X (v.1)
ISBN 0-939934-43-4 (set)

The paper used in this publication meets the minimum requirements of American National Standard for Information Sciences—Permanence of Paper for Printed Library Materials, ANSI Z39.48-1984.

Foreword

The International Monetary Fund is again offering to the public a major work describing its history. This new sequel of three volumes covers the period 1972 to 1978. An earlier set of three volumes, published in 1969, recounted the origins of the Fund and the first twenty years of its existence, and an additional two volumes, published in 1976, related the Fund's history from 1966 to 1971.

The seven years covered here, spanning most of the decade of the 1970s, were particularly turbulent for the international monetary system and for the Fund. To help its members deal with the severe economic problems that arose in those years, the Fund initiated many activities, greatly increased its lending, and, following the collapse of the par value system and of negotiations to introduce a fully reformed system in the near future, undertook to supervise a gradually evolving international monetary system. Volume I and Volume II, *Narrative and Analysis*, describe at length these economic problems and the Fund's actions. Considerable effort has been made to explain not only what happened but also why. Volume III reproduces the most important documents published by the Fund from 1972 to 1978 and makes available several papers previously unpublished.

Many problems for which the Fund has had to take on increasing responsibility in the years after 1978, such as those arising out of the heavy external indebtedness of a number of developing members, increasing protectionism, the flow of international capital, and the need for Fund surveillance of exchange rates, originated in the period described here. Hence, in publishing these volumes, the Fund hopes to promote understanding of its present work, as well as its past.

Margaret Garritsen de Vries, the Historian of the International Monetary Fund, who came to the Fund in 1946 as one of its first staff members and who was the author of the History for 1966–71 and part of the History for 1945–65, has written this History. As in the past, she has had full access to the Fund's records and has interviewed governors of the Fund, members of the Executive Board, and colleagues on the Fund staff. While these volumes are once again, as the Forewords to earlier volumes state, "history written from the inside," they are the personal responsibility of the author, and no statement or opinion expressed should be understood as committing the Fund in any way.

August 1985

J. de Larosière
Managing Director
International Monetary Fund

Contents

Volume I: Narrative and Analysis

PART ONE *End of the Par Value System*
(January 1972–March 1973)

Holding the New Rates in Early 1972, 11; Unrest in Exchange Markets in Early 1972, 17; Origin of the European Narrow Margins Arrangement (the Snake), 20; Calmer Exchange Markets in Late 1972, 23

Fund Operations Restored, 27; Use of SDRs for the Fund's Accounts, 29; Arranging for Repurchase by the United Kingdom, 31; New Par Value for the Dollar, 34; Normal Fund Operations Re-Established, 37; Arguments over Inconvertibility of the Dollar, 38; Urging Canada to Adopt a Par Value, 40; Developing Members' Economic Circumstances, 41

Economic Situation of the United Kingdom Prior to June 1972, 45; Crisis of June 1972, 49; Continuation of the Floating Rate, 52; Related Actions by Other Countries, 54; Other Changes in Exchange Rates in Late 1972, 56; Exchange Rates at the End of 1972, 58

Background to the Pressure on the Italian Lira, 61; Reasons for the Italian Dual Market, 63; The Dollar Again Devalued, 64; The Italian Lira Floats, 69; The Japanese Yen Floats, 70; Introduction of Joint Float of EC Currencies, 75

CONTENTS

PART TWO   *Negotiations for a Reformed System*
(September 1972–June 1974)

PART THREE *Atmosphere of Crisis
and the Fund's Responses*
(September 1973–October 1974)

CONTENTS

PART FOUR *The Fund in a Troubled World Economy: The Setting After 1973*

PART FIVE *Increased Use of Resources*
(January 1975–December 1978)

PART SIX *Arranging for an Increased Use of Resources (1974–1978)*

Tables

Illustrations

Following page 360

Volume II: Narrative and Analysis

PART SEVEN   *Resolution of the Gold Problem (1973–1978)*

PART EIGHT *Amending the Articles of Agreement (1974–1978)*

PART ELEVEN   *Resurgence of the SDR in 1978*

PART TWELVE   *Continued Evolution of the Fund as an International Institution (1972–1978)*

CONTENTS

Appendices

Tables

Illustrations

Following page 816

1. H. Johannes Witteveen, Chairman of the Executive Board and Managing Director, September 1, 1973–June 16, 1978

2. Meeting of the Executive Board, December 13, 1976

CONTENTS

□   □   □   □   □   □

Volume III: Documents

Preface

The founders of the International Monetary Fund regarded economic cooperation among nations as the key to securing world peace. Since 1969 the Fund has been publishing histories of its activities, and these histories—now totaling eight volumes—reveal the evolution of that cooperation. Here we see, among other developments, how world economic interdependence has gradually come about and how a multimember economic institution, whose existence has distinguished the international economic scene since World War II, has evolved. The histories trace the alterations and developments in the Fund's policies and activities, with changing economic circumstances and personalities, and the growth of the Fund's influence and authority.

The primary source of information for the histories is the Fund's documents and records, supplemented by recollections of Managing and Deputy Managing Directors, Executive Directors, Fund staff, and other participants in the events portrayed. These persons have had an opportunity to comment on the draft manuscript, and many Executive Directors sent the manuscript to their governments for comment. I myself am a long-standing member of the Fund staff, having come to the Fund in 1946 as one of its first staff members. The Fund, moreover, is its own publisher. For these reasons, these histories are sometimes regarded by outsiders as "official," although it should be emphasized that the text is not formally approved by the Executive Board or by national authorities.

The histories are written in the way just described to provide an authoritative account of the Fund's policies and activities that Fund officials and officials of member governments can regard as accurate, sufficiently complete, and reasonably balanced. The Fund would not grant to an outsider access to the information on which this account has been based. Not wishing to compromise the full and frank consultations and discussions that it holds with members, the Fund scrupulously guards the confidentiality of its records and documents and the secrecy of its discussions with the officials of members and of the minutes of meetings of its Executive Board. Nevertheless, the Fund believes that it is important to make available an authoritative history of its activities for recent years so as to increase public understanding of current international monetary and financial problems and of the Fund's work.

Advantages derive from a history written from the inside. The author had a strategic position from which to view history as it unfolded and had constant access to those who helped to shape events. Factors that might have been overlooked by someone less familiar with the institution and the influence of particular individuals can be better evaluated by an author writing from within. Samuel Eliot Morison, official historian of the U.S. Navy during World War II, understood this when he requested President Franklin D. Roosevelt at the outset of the war to attach him to the Navy so that he could observe naval battles and write what he termed "a shooting history." Not all the shots in the history of the International Monetary Fund were fired within the Fund, however. I have therefore attempted to portray the evolution of the Fund and its activities in the broader setting of contemporary economic developments, and to describe its policies and their evolution against the background dialogue engaged in by professional economists and government officials.

In preparing the present volumes, I am again indebted to numerous participants in the events recounted here, although I cannot mention all their names. Pierre-Paul Schweitzer and H. Johannes Witteveen gave me insight into developments in their periods as Managing Director. Frank A. Southard, Jr. and William B. Dale explained several events that occurred while they were Deputy Managing Director. J. de Larosière and Edwin H. Yeo III gave me a detailed account of their negotiations which led to the amended Article IV, dealing with exchange arrangements. Sir Jeremy Morse and Edward George supplied files, answered queries, provided explanations and interpretations about the work of the Committee of Twenty, and read a draft of Chapters 8–14. Sir Joseph Gold described numerous events of which he has personal knowledge, especially in respect to the drafting of the Second Amendment, read the entire manuscript, and made valuable suggestions. J.J. Polak helped me assess several topics with which he was intimately concerned, particularly the staff sketch of a reformed system written in 1972. L. Alan Whittome and other staff of the European Department enriched the chapters describing the negotiations for the stand-by arrangements for Italy and the United Kingdom in the years 1974 to 1977. Leo Van Houtven suggested persons to interview and generally encouraged me as my work proceeded. Philine Lachman explained several legal issues and questions. J. Keith Horsefield, responsible for *History, 1945–65*, read this sequel, as he did the sequel for 1966–71, and made several suggestions.

Faye L. Olin, my editorial assistant since 1975, helped with editing, prepared statistical tables and Appendix A, assembled the documents for Volume III, and was invaluable in numerous ways. Milton K. Chamberlain carefully guided me to the relevant documents and records and patiently checked innumerable facts. Anne C.M. Salda and other staff of the Joint Fund-Bank Library kept me abreast of relevant new books and articles. David D. Driscoll did an outstanding job of editing the final manuscript of Volumes I and II and oversaw the volumes through to publication. Elin Knotter carefully styled the manuscript and prepared the index. Jennie Lee Carter gave the documents in Volume III a meticulous final editing and saw that volume through to publication. Alva C. Madairy and others in the composition unit of the Graphics Section, under the direction of A. Kenneth Hutcherson, put the manuscript into type and saw the publication of these volumes through to completion. Hordur Karlsson designed the dust jacket.

I am also deeply indebted to Louise T. Pike, Mai Stuart, and D. Mary Windsor, who put countless drafts and redrafts of the manuscript through the word processor.

Although such expression is rare in a volume like this, I must also publicly express my gratitude to my husband, Barend A. de Vries. Writing histories of the International Monetary Fund has been a way of life for me for over two decades, and I owe a great debt to my family for accommodating such a demanding and absorbing task. Barend, also an economist, on the staff of the Fund for 6 years and then of the World Bank for 29 years, has been a continuous sounding board and a frequent stimulator of my thoughts.

Needless to say, any shortcomings, errors, or omissions that remain are my own responsibility.

M.G.deV.

THE INTERNATIONAL MONETARY FUND

1972–1978

Volume I: Narrative and Analysis

*"Further evidence will be furnished
at Bretton Woods that men of
different nationalities have learned
how to adjust possible differences and
how to work together as friends. The
things that we need to do, must be
done—can only be done in concert."*

—Franklin D. Roosevelt, to
the Bretton Woods Conference,
July 1, 1944

Introduction

THE SEVEN YEARS from January 1, 1972 to December 31, 1978 were the most complex and difficult that the Fund had so far experienced. In March 1973 the system of par values, which had been under severe stress for the previous five years, broke down altogether. As a primary function of the Fund was to implement a system of par values, several critics intimated that the Fund had outlived its usefulness.

The collapse of par values and the introduction by nearly all the Fund's members of exchange arrangements contradictory to the Articles of Agreement were only the start of the troubles that the Fund had to face. Beginning in 1973, the Fund's members were plagued with the deepest economic and financial problems of four decades. Inflation reached historically high levels for most industrial countries. Steep increases in prices for crude oil brought on massive balance of payments deficits for all members except for a few oil exporters which were, in turn, suddenly faced with massive surpluses. The most severe worldwide recession since the 1930s ensued in 1974–75, and in a hitherto unknown phenomenon, rising prices coexisted with high unemployment in industrial countries. Even after recovery, economies grew much more slowly than in the 1960s. The new floating exchange rates introduced in lieu of par values underwent wide fluctuations. Intense speculation in gold caused its price to soar to unprecedented levels, obviating its use for settling financial transactions. As non-oil developing members borrowed to finance their huge deficits, several rapidly piled up external debts. International monetary cooperation was sorely tested.

In response to these developments the Fund undertook to reshape its functions and to redirect its activities. In doing so, it became so integrally involved with the newly evolving international monetary system that disentangling developments in the system from developments in the activities and policies of the Fund was impossible. The history of the Fund during 1972–78 is in many respects the history of the international monetary system.

The last Fund History ended with December 1971.[1] January 1972, besides being consecutive, is for many reasons an appropriate starting date for another

---

[1]The earlier volumes of Fund History are *The International Monetary Fund, 1945–1965: Twenty Years of International Monetary Cooperation*, Vol. I, *Chronicle*, by J. Keith Horsefield; Vol. II, *Analysis*, by Margaret G. de Vries and J. Keith Horsefield with the collaboration of Joseph Gold, Mary H. Gumbart, Gertrud Lovasy, and Emil G. Spitzer and edited by J. Keith Horsefield; Vol. III, *Documents*, edited by J. Keith Horsefield (Washington: International Monetary Fund, 1969), hereafter cited as *History, 1945–65*; and *The International Monetary Fund, 1966–1971: The System Under Stress*, Vol. I, *Narrative*, by Margaret Garritsen de Vries, and Vol. II, *Documents*, edited by Margaret Garritsen de Vries (Washington: International Monetary Fund, 1976), hereafter cited as *History, 1966–71*.

episode of Fund History. As the year opened, monetary authorities (including the Governors, the Executive Directors, and the Managing Director of the Fund, assisted by the Fund staff) were attempting to make the pattern of exchange rates agreed at the Smithsonian Institution in December 1971 hold until a reform of the entire international monetary system could be completed. After three years of talking about the need to realign the exchange rates for the currencies of the large industrial countries, monetary authorities had at last achieved that realignment. After a decade of discussion about reform of the international monetary system, full-scale negotiations were about to begin. A new era was in the offing.

December 1978 ends that era. Amended Articles of Agreement had recently come into force, concluding efforts to reform the system. The international monetary arrangements evolving since August 15, 1971, when official convertibility for the dollar was suspended, were now sanctioned by international law. By December 1978, moreover, the disequilibrating effects on the imbalances in international payments immediately following the huge jump in oil prices of 1973 had just about worked themselves through the financial system, which had somehow managed to cope. What was later to be termed "the first round of oil price rises" was regarded as over.

Selecting a framework suitable to narrate the activities and policies of the Fund from 1972–78 and related developments in the international monetary system has been anything but easy. Complicated, interrelated developments took place concurrently. As the Fund tried to solve one problem, it found that the solution depended upon resolution of still another problem. Furthermore, in presenting the history of the Fund, it has been essential to supplement any chronicle or narrative with analysis.

The present approach is topical and chronological. The *Narrative and Analysis* is divided into 12 Parts, each treating a different topic. The Parts are arranged as chronologically as possible, the chronological order is frequently noted, and a detailed Chronology is given at the end of Volume II. To introduce topics and to tie together interrelated developments, several chapters begin with explanatory material.

Part One (Chapters 1–6) relates the events from January 1, 1972 to March 19, 1973 that brought about the final demise of the system of par values and ushered in the new regime of "widespread floating." Carl Sandburg noted that a tree is best measured when it is down; so the par value system, as agreed in 1944, can best be assessed after it was felled. Concluding Part One (Chapters 5 and 6) is a retrospective analysis of the par value system. Part Two (Chapters 7–14) discusses the negotiations for a reformed system, which also started in January 1972 and went on until June 1974. A detailed description of the negotiations, especially those carried on in the Committee of Twenty, is followed by a discussion of the reasons for the failure of the negotiations and an assessment of the results achieved (Chapters 13 and 14).

The continuation of floating exchange rates and, most important, the big jump in oil prices announced in December 1973 and the resulting disequilibria in world

4

payments created an atmosphere of crisis, especially in the context of failure to agree on a reformed system and the end of the Committee of Twenty. Part Three (Chapters 15–19) describes the Fund's response from September 1973 to October 1974 to this crisis, especially the introduction of an oil facility based on borrowed funds, but also the initiation of guidelines for floating exchange rates, establishment of an Interim Committee and of a Development Committee, and the introduction of an extended Fund facility.

Problems persisted, however, as the 1970s unfolded. The world economy continued to be characterized by high rates of inflation, by much slower economic growth in most industrial countries than had prevailed in the 1950s and 1960s, by chronic disequilibria in world payments, and by wide swings in exchange rates. Moreover, there was no agreement on rules for international monetary arrangements. The Fund relied primarily on only one obligation of members under the Articles of Agreement—the obligation of members to collaborate with the Fund (Part Four, Chapter 20).

In these circumstances, from 1974 to 1978 the Fund undertook three activities. First, it took measures that greatly enlarged members' use of its resources. It liberalized its compensatory financing facility and approved many more stand-by arrangements (Part Five, Chapters 21–26) than in previous years. To raise money for these activities, members' quotas were twice enlarged and a supplementary financing facility was introduced. Since the supplementary financing facility, like the oil facility, was based on borrowed funds, the Fund transformed itself into a financial intermediary, borrowing from some members to lend to others (Part Six, Chapters 27–30). Second, to establish agreed rules for international monetary arrangements, the Fund began in July 1974 a comprehensive redrafting of its Articles of Agreement, but before doing so it had to resolve several issues concerning gold that the Committee of Twenty had left unsettled. In resolving these issues, the Fund agreed to sell some of its holdings of gold and to put part of the proceeds from these sales into a Trust Fund for the benefit of the Fund's developing members (Parts Seven and Eight, Chapters 31–39). Third, to help solve world economic problems the Fund instituted intensive periodic analysis of the outlook for the world economy (Part Nine, Chapter 40).

Meanwhile, floating rates for the major currencies became a necessary part of the everyday life of monetary authorities and of the Fund. Floating rates had long been advocated by some economists and opposed by others; now experiences with actual floating rates were beginning to accumulate. Some experiences were unfavorable. Moreover, as it seemed increasingly likely that floating rates would persist and as frequent conflicts occurred between the authorities of different countries over developments in exchange rates, the Fund had to find ways to exercise surveillance over these rates. Part Ten (Chapters 41–44) relates developments in exchange rates from 1973 to 1978.

Still another problem of the 1970s was the continued expansion of international liquidity in the form of national currencies. By 1978 Fund officials, as they had in the

INTRODUCTION

1960s, were seeking ways for the international community to gain greater control over international liquidity. Inevitably attention centered on the SDR, the Fund's own novel reserve asset, whose creation had crowned the Fund's achievements in the 1960s. Beginning in 1978 several further actions were taken to improve the quality of the SDR as a reserve asset. The resurgence of the SDR in 1978 is discussed in Part Eleven (Chapters 45 and 46).

Part Twelve (Chapters 47–53) presents a detailed picture of how the Fund continued to evolve as an international organization in 1972–78. Many of the Fund's regular activities, such as holding consultations with members and providing them with technical assistance, were intensified. In addition, the Fund took on added responsibilities regarding the external debt of its developing members, the access of developing members to capital markets, international trade policy, the provision of information, and its relations with other international organizations. The Fund's relations with commercial banks also grew and became complicated. There were important developments, too, in the Fund's policymaking process. Finally, the *Narrative and Analysis* closes with a discussion of the experiences that the Fund had accumulated in its 33 years and of some lessons to be learned from these experiences.

Whatever period is selected for coverage, it is impossible to begin and end precisely with a given year. Great effort has been made, nonetheless, to make these latest volumes of Fund History self-contained. Readers need not have read the Histories describing events before January 1972, as considerable background material has been included in the present volumes. For the reader who wishes further information, numerous footnotes cite relevant passages in earlier Fund Histories. An effort has been made to adhere strictly to the cutoff date of 1978, otherwise the story would never be finished. Specific results of activities going on at the end of 1978—such as a decision taken by the Executive Board, the introduction of a new facility for use of the Fund's resources, and the completion of sales of gold by the Fund—are, however, noted in footnotes.

Since the history of the Fund is in part the history of meetings and of discussions among financial officials, many officials are mentioned. A few techniques have been adopted for identifying them in a relatively simple way. Those appointed by members as Governors of the Fund and of the World Bank have usually been referred to in these capacities (especially when they were attending meetings of the Fund such as Annual Meetings of the Board of Governors or meetings of committees of the Board of Governors) rather than in their capacities as officials of their home countries, usually ministers of finance or governors of central banks. The Managing Director, who is also Chairman of the Executive Board, is referred to as the Managing Director to avoid the need to distinguish the capacity he may have been acting in at the time. At times the term "Fund management" is used to refer to the Managing Director and Deputy Managing Director. There are many references to individual Executive Directors and Alternate Executive Directors. In general, the practice has been followed of using the full name of an official and his country of nationality the first time he is mentioned and using only surnames thereafter. However, in instances where a series of names includes officials not previously mentioned, it has seemed desirable to deviate from this practice and to repeat given names and countries of nationality or in a few instances to omit the given name of an official.

In the years reviewed here, several appointed Executive Directors were replaced, and following the customary biennial elections of Executive Directors, newly elected Directors took office on November 1 of 1972, 1974, 1976, and 1978. Numerous changes took place as well of Alternate Executive Directors. For ease of exposition, these changes have not been spelled out as the narrative proceeds. A description of the main changes in the composition of the Executive Board from 1972 to 1978 is given in Chapter 51.

In the period reviewed here, the names of some member countries were also changed. For ease of presentation, the names in effect on December 31, 1978 have been used except in a few unusual instances.

PART ONE

End of the
Par Value System

(January 1972–March 1973)

"Achievement of a solution to the problems posed by the current situation urgently requires a collaborative international approach."

—PIERRE-PAUL SCHWEITZER, addressing the Board of Governors in Washington, September 27, 1971

CHAPTER
1

Aftermath of the Smithsonian Agreement

*H*INDSIGHT SUGGESTS that the exchange rate realignment agreed at the Smithsonian Institution in Washington on December 18, 1971 by the Group of Ten, that is, by the finance ministers and central bank governors of Belgium, Canada, France, the Federal Republic of Germany, Italy, Japan, the Netherlands, Sweden, the United Kingdom, and the United States, was doomed from the start. Unrest in exchange markets and disturbing flows of speculative capital persisted throughout much of 1972. Early in 1973 the Smithsonian exchange rates collapsed.

HOLDING THE NEW RATES IN EARLY 1972

That the currency realignment of the Smithsonian agreement would not hold could be seen, however, only after 1972. At the start of 1972, monetary authorities, including the Governors, the Executive Directors, and the Managing Director of the Fund, looking back on nearly five years of recurrent exchange crises and especially on the chaotic exchange markets of the last four months of 1971, aimed to restore order and stability to the international monetary system. They expected that the United States would in a few months declare a new par value to the Fund and that the Fund's financial operations, disrupted on August 15, 1971 when the U.S. authorities suspended the convertibility of officially held dollars into gold or other reserve assets, would resume in a normal way. They expected other countries to follow the United States in declaring new par values and that these par values would pave the way to end the regime of central rates and wider margins that the Fund had established on December 18, 1971 as a temporary alternative to the system of par values and narrow margins.

Their first objective was to develop confidence in the new pattern of exchange rates until these rates had time to reduce the large imbalances in international payments that had existed at least since 1966. These imbalances consisted primarily of a deficit by the United States and substantial surpluses by most other industrial countries. Their second objective was to negotiate a long-term reform of the international monetary system to replace the Bretton Woods system set up in 1944. The objectives of developing confidence in the new exchange rates and of planning a reformed system were interconnected. Confidence in the exchange rates would make it more likely that these rates would correct the chronic payments imbalances. Overcoming these imbalances would in turn facilitate negotiations for reforming the system. Positive steps toward a reformed system would also make the exchange markets more confident of the new rates.

At the same time that monetary authorities were trying to attain these objectives, they were confronted by a recession which began in 1969 in most industrial countries after nearly a decade of continuous and rapid economic expansion. The recession persisted through 1971. From 1969 to 1971 world output grew at an average annual rate of 3–4 percent, compared with an average annual rate of 5 percent from 1960 to 1970. As 1972 began, there was more unused productive capacity in the industrial world than at any time since the recession of 1958. Unemployment of labor and capital was particularly marked in Canada, Italy, Japan, the United Kingdom, and the United States. To make matters worse, efforts to stimulate economic recovery in these countries were frustrated by the highest rates of inflation in many years. In order not to aggravate the inflation, governments were reluctant to take expansionary measures to bring about recovery.

Economic Prospects for the United States

These problems of unemployment and inflation, combined with balance of payments disequilibria, had been at the root of the U.S. suspension in August 1971 of the convertibility of officially held dollars into gold or other reserve assets, an action which had abruptly disturbed international monetary relations and had forced the realignment of currencies. Simultaneous with the suspension of dollar convertibility, President Richard M. Nixon announced a New Economic Policy for the United States, providing for domestic measures unusual for the United States and especially unusual for a Republican Administration. A 90-day freeze on prices, wages, and rents was instituted, to be followed by a more flexible "Phase II" program of controls over prices, wages, and rents. Major fiscal stimuli were also introduced. After the inauguration of President Nixon in January 1969, U.S. authorities, favoring measures that left market forces free, had decried mandatory price and wage controls as unnecessary and undesirable and had refrained from fiscal expansion. Hence, these changes in U.S. policy, like the suspension of dollar convertibility, came as a surprise.

In discussions with the staff as part of the Fund's Article VIII consultation with the United States in early 1972, U.S. officials explained why the New Economic Policy had been introduced. At the start of 1971, they had set as domestic economic goals to be attained by the middle of 1972, an election year, reducing the rate of unemployment from the then existing level of 6 percent to about 4.5 percent and lowering the rate of inflation from about 4 percent to about 3 percent. They believed that reasonable stability of prices and full utilization of productive capacity in the domestic economy would not only benefit the U.S. domestic economy but would produce the longer-run improvement needed in the U.S. balance of payments. Slowing down inflation would help the current account of the balance of payments by reducing imports and expanding exports; higher output would help the capital account by making investment within the United States more attractive than investment abroad. About the middle of 1971, however, it appeared that these goals were not being met. The domestic economy was expanding but not so fast as to produce the desired reduction in unemployment. The rate of inflation had stopped accelerating but there was danger that it would again increase. The balance of payments position was deteriorating rapidly and was of particular concern. Because measures to stimulate employment resulted in greater demand for imports, they carried the risk of further worsening the balance of payments. Moreover, official entities abroad no longer exhibited a willingness to add to their holdings of dollars. For all these reasons, the new, integrated economic plan of August 15, 1971 was decided upon.

The U.S. measures of August 15, 1971 were a watershed in international monetary history. George P. Shultz was at the time Director of the Office of Management and Budget and a participant in the decisions made by President Nixon and other U.S. participants at Camp David on the weekend of August 15, 1971. According to Mr. Shultz, in taking these measures the U.S. authorities gave the highest priority to devaluing the dollar and to solving the balance of payments problem. He explained that devaluation of the dollar was politically unpopular and that linking price and wage controls to devaluation helped to counter any domestic political backlash that devaluation might have caused. The imposition of price and wage controls was regarded as a sign of presidential strength in the fight against inflation and was favored both by the opposition Democratic Party and by businessmen who viewed price and wage controls as more likely to control wage increases than price increases. The imposition of these domestic controls to fight inflation dominated the news and thus "diverted public attention from the mysterious action of 'closing the gold window' and swamped any tendency to regard the devaluation aspect of the August 15 decisions as weakness." Mr. Shultz did not say, however, that price and wage controls were deliberately introduced for this reason. He merely wondered whether such controls would have been introduced if devaluation of the dollar had not been necessary.[1]

In appraising the U.S. situation during the Article VIII consultation earlier in 1972, the Fund management and staff, as well as U.S. officials, were more optimistic than they had been for some years about the prospects for the U.S. domestic economy and for the U.S. balance of payments position. They believed that the introduction of the New Economic Policy and the realignment of currencies under the Smithsonian agreement gave the U.S. Government the policy instruments it

---

[1]George P. Shultz and Kenneth W. Dam, *Economic Policy Beyond the Headlines* (New York: W.W. Norton and Company, Inc., 1978), p. 117.

13

previously lacked to deal effectively with inflation, unemployment, and balance of payments deficits that had plagued the United States since at least 1966. Price and wage controls improved the chances that policies to reduce unemployment would be compatible with slowing down the rate of inflation. The realignment of currencies laid the basis for reconciling a return to full employment with the re-establishment of external payments balance. Unlike other large industrial countries that had devalued in the last several years—notably the United Kingdom in 1967 and France in 1969—the United States devalued at a time of considerable unemployment and substantial underutilization of productive capacity. There was, therefore, room both for an improvement in the current account of the balance of payments (that is, for more exports and less imports) and for an increase in domestic absorption (that is, for more domestic consumption and investment).

While U.S. and Fund officials expected an eventual improvement in the U.S. balance of payments, they expected another sizable current account deficit in 1972. They felt that most of the favorable effects of the exchange rate realignment would not occur until well into 1973 or even later, in line with the experience of other industrial countries that two to three years were required before exchange rate changes had discernible beneficial effects on their balances of payments. In addition, the world cyclical situation was unfavorable to the U.S. balance of payments position: the United States was taking expansionary measures while several other large industrial countries were still in recession. Both U.S. officials and the Fund staff hoped, however, that another *major* U.S. payments deficit in both the capital and current accounts could be avoided in 1972. Avoiding a large deficit required the return to the United States of short-term capital after its massive speculative outflow in 1971.

Foreign official dollar holdings were more than $40 billion at the time of the suspension of dollar convertibility in mid-August 1971, and the Fund staff believed that once capital inflows got under way, reflows into the United States of capital invested abroad could gain tremendous momentum. The staff urged U.S. authorities to do everything possible to make certain that large reflows actually materialized. They particularly urged the U.S. authorities to orient U.S. monetary policy toward achieving overall balance of payments equilibrium in 1972 and to pursue a moderately tight monetary policy during that year, limiting the growth of the money supply and raising short-term interest rates so as to attract interest-sensitive funds from abroad. The staff further suggested that in the interest of achieving overall payments equilibrium for the year the U.S. authorities not yet phase out the controls on capital movements introduced in the 1960s to help curb the U.S. deficit on capital account. Since international banking and investment were closely integrated and highly competitive, controls on capital were unpopular with bankers and businessmen in most industrial countries, and U.S. officials were eager to eliminate U.S. controls that discriminated against U.S. bankers and investors.

When the Article VIII consultation with the United States was held in the Executive Board, most Executive Directors concurred that there were good reasons to be optimistic about the outlook for the U.S. domestic economy and the U.S. balance of payments, especially as the effects of the currency realignment took hold. William B. Dale (United States) took issue, however, with the staff's recommendations for U.S. monetary policy.[2] He explained that while the U.S. authorities agreed with the staff's appraisal and recommendations for the U.S. economy in general, they could not commit themselves to monetary policy in 1972 designed to achieve overall balance in the U.S. external payments for the year. It was essential that U.S. authorities retain a free hand in formulating monetary policy in order to facilitate the expansion needed in the domestic economy.

Economic Prospects for the Federal Republic of Germany and for Japan

Early in 1972 the Fund also reviewed the outlook for the economic situation in other large industrial countries, especially in the Federal Republic of Germany and in Japan, since these two countries had experienced very large trade and current account surpluses for several years, a counterpart to the deficit of the United States. Now that the deutsche mark and the yen had been revalued along with the dollar, officials looked forward to eventual substantial reduction not only of the U.S. deficit but also of the German and Japanese surpluses. German and Japanese authorities reasoned that reduction of their surpluses was in the interest of the world as a whole and could give them more freedom in pursuing their economic policies. Better balance in world payments would help attain fuller employment and more rapid economic growth for the benefit of all countries. Moreover, it would allow the Federal Republic of Germany, Japan, and the United States to pursue stimulative domestic economic policies without having to worry so much about the consequences of these policies on the balance of payments deficit of the United States or on inflation in the Federal Republic of Germany and Japan.

At the beginning of 1972, however, it was clear that correction of the German and Japanese surpluses, like that of the U.S. deficit, would take considerable time. As they explained to the Fund staff in early 1972 in the course of an Article VIII consultation, officials of the Federal Republic of Germany believed that their country's trade surplus for 1972 might be even larger than that for 1971, despite the revaluations of the deutsche mark in 1969 and again in December 1971. Many factors operated to keep the trade surplus large. Widespread rigidities in trade patterns because of cartel arrangements and other international agreements restricted

---

[2]In the text of this History, Executive Directors and Alternate Executive Directors are identified by the country of their nationality. For the Executive Directors who were elected, however, this identity gives only an approximate indication of their constituencies. A complete listing of the Executive Directors, their Alternates, and the members that appointed or elected them (as well as the country of nationality of both the Executive Directors and their Alternates) for the period 1972–78 is given in Appendix A, Tables A–1, A–2, and A–3, to Vol. II of these volumes. The management and senior staff as of the end of 1978 are listed in Appendix B. The same information for earlier years can be found in Appendices A–1, A–2, and A–3 to Vol. I of *History, 1945–65*, pp. 619–40, and in Appendices A–1, A–2, and A–3, and Appendix B to Vol. I of *History, 1966–71*, pp. 655–66.

changes in relative prices following adjustments in exchange rates. Important sectors of industry in the Federal Republic of Germany were heavily geared to exporting. Even if profit margins were reduced, German producers might well continue striving to maintain their share of foreign markets in the hope that, as had happened in the mid-1960s, domestic costs of production would rise less rapidly in the Federal Republic of Germany than in competitor countries, and that German export trade would again become more profitable. Also, a large proportion of exports from the Federal Republic of Germany consisted of highly specialized capital goods for which demand was relatively price-inelastic and highly income-inelastic.

The authorities of the Federal Republic of Germany believed that these considerations did not mean that the revaluation of the deutsche mark would be ineffective. But the authorities did suggest that the conventionally assumed time lags for the effectiveness of exchange rate changes were underestimated. It would take a few years for the effects to develop. German authorities also emphasized that in appraising the likely effectiveness of the change in the par value of the deutsche mark in December 1971, it was not sufficient to look at the trade account alone. The deficit on invisibles, which had tended to rise in line with the increase in the trade surplus, would increase more rapidly in 1972 because of the revaluation of the deutsche mark, and in 1973 the aggregate current account was likely to be in deficit.

The Article VIII consultation held in the Executive Board in February 1972 revealed that Japan's trade surplus for 1972 would also remain substantial despite the revaluation of the yen. The demand for imported manufactures in Japan grew comparatively slowly. Japan's imports consisted largely of raw materials, fuel, and other items used in industrial production, which were affected more by the level of economic activity in the country than by changes in relative prices; the latter usually had larger effects on imports of consumer goods. At the Executive Board discussion, Hideo Suzuki (Japan) stressed that a fundamental transformation in Japan's economic structure involving a shift of resources from exportation to internal consumption was needed to achieve a better equilibrium in Japan's balance of payments position. In the interim the Japanese authorities intended to increase imports through further liberalization of trade and reduction of tariffs.

■　■　■　■　■　■

Realizing that the imbalances in the current accounts of the balance of payments of the United States, the Federal Republic of Germany, and Japan would actually increase in 1972, the Executive Directors, Pierre-Paul Schweitzer as Managing Director, and the Fund staff considered it essential for the stability of the international monetary system that the monetary authorities of the major industrial countries try to instill strong market confidence in the Smithsonian exchange rates until the long-standing disequilibria in international payments could be corrected and measures to reform the system could be developed and implemented. Confidence in the new rates not only would prevent further disruptive movements of capital but would help to induce capital to return to the United States, thus stabilizing the U.S. overall payments accounts. Mr. Schweitzer also believed that it was essential that the authorities of the main industrial countries coordinate their domestic monetary policies, such as those relating to short-term interest rates, that affected flows of short-term capital. Mutually supportive monetary policies were, he was convinced, probably the most important factor likely to channel capital flows in a favorable direction. While Fund officials expected negotiations for full-scale reform of the international monetary system to take about two years, they were very much aware that agreement on reform would help support the new exchange rates. Hence, as described in Chapter 8 below, they started early in 1972 to draw up plans for reforming the system.

UNREST IN EXCHANGE MARKETS IN EARLY 1972

Building confidence in the Smithsonian exchange rates proved to be difficult, especially in the first seven months of 1972. Although nothing was said in discussions between officials of members and the Fund in early 1972 about the adequacy of the exchange rate adjustments agreed at the Smithsonian Institution—for example, whether the depreciation of the dollar in terms of other currencies had been sufficient—unrest in exchange markets suggested considerable uncertainty about the new rates. By February the currencies of most industrial countries had appreciated vis-à-vis the dollar nearly to the limits of the wider margins permitted under the Smithsonian agreement. This appreciation of other currencies produced a pattern of rates that suggested continuing weakness of the dollar. Another symptom of this weakness was the movement of speculators out of the dollar into gold, raising the price of gold in private markets. Within several weeks after the devaluation of the dollar, the price of gold rose to above $47 an ounce, compared with the then official price of $35 an ounce and the planned official price of $38 an ounce. Contributing to uncertainty about the durability of the new exchange rate structure were widespread doubts in February 1972 about the strength of the economic recovery in the United States and about the anti-inflationary effects of Phase II of the price-wage control program, as Arthur F. Burns, Chairman of the Board of Governors of the Federal Reserve System, reported to the Joint Economic Committee of the U.S. Congress.[3] No capital reflow to the United States developed in the first quarter of 1972. Indeed, as the quarter went on, substantial outflows of capital from the United States into the major continental European countries and Japan revived.

By March 1 the situation had become worrisome, especially to European officials. Officials of the Federal Republic of Germany took the unusual step of introducing a cash deposit requirement (*Bardepot*) on certain borrowing by residents from nonresidents (essentially on borrowing abroad by nonbanking institutions). The deposit, set at 40 percent of the liabilities covered, had to be lodged with the

---

[3]Statement published in *Federal Reserve Bulletin* (Washington), Vol. 58 (February 1972), p. 124.

Deutsche Bundesbank in deutsche mark and was non-interest-bearing. This measure increased the cost of foreign borrowing by two thirds and was designed to discourage interest-sensitive inflows of capital. German officials also expected that by reducing interest-sensitive capital inflows, the *Bardepot* was likely to reduce other capital inflows as well, since speculative flows of capital that moved in anticipation of further exchange rate changes were often stimulated by movements of interest-sensitive capital.

On March 3, Valéry Giscard d'Estaing, Minister of Economy and Finance of France, speaking in Versailles to a group of European and U.S. businessmen, warned in unusually frank remarks that "indifference" by the U.S. Government to short-term capital outflows and to the inconvertibility of the dollar posed a threat to a truce with regard to monetary issues in the West.[4] The speech was considered strong and contained the message that the United States *must* take measures to reduce capital outflows until the currency readjustments began affecting payments positions if the United States did not want to be confronted with a maze of controls by European countries severely restricting use of the dollar. European officials were reluctant to accumulate any more inconvertible dollars, and there was talk not only of introducing exchange controls in Europe but also of floating European currencies against the dollar.

Believing that the Fund ought to take at least minimum steps to help preserve the new structure of exchange rates and concerned about what alternative exchange rate systems or controls might develop, Frank A. Southard, Jr., as Acting Managing Director, at a meeting of the Executive Board on March 9 emphasized how important it was that monetary authorities publicly state their determination to maintain an orderly international monetary system. He urged the Executive Directors to relay to their authorities the need for an explicit statement that they would collaborate among themselves and with the Fund to coordinate their domestic monetary policies. Mr. Southard also suggested informally to Under Secretary for Monetary Affairs of the U.S. Treasury, Paul A. Volcker, that the U.S. authorities make a strong statement to the effect that they were ready to collaborate with other countries to support the exchange rate structure. Mr. Volcker's response reflected the atmosphere of the time. Having in mind Mr. Giscard d'Estaing's speech of March 3, he observed that while the U.S. authorities were willing to make statements to engender confidence in the dollar, it was also essential that authorities of other countries refrain from making statements that unsettled exchange markets.

In May, to discourage inflows of speculative capital into French francs, French authorities reorganized the dual exchange market France had introduced in August 1971. Many current transactions were shifted from the financial market to the official market, resulting in the financial market in a premium that acted as a deterrent to capital inflows. In June and July serious speculation broke out again. The price of gold in private markets again began to rise, reaching $65 an ounce in June. Huge

---

[4]*New York Times*, March 4, 1972, p. 33.

speculative capital outflows caused the authorities of the United Kingdom to decide on June 23 to let the exchange rate for the pound sterling float temporarily.[5]

Lack of Capital Inflows into the United States

A number of factors explain the absence of the expected capital inflows into the United States and, indeed, the renewal of capital outflows and the consequent onset of unrest in exchange markets in the first months of 1972. Speculation, especially in Europe, suggested that the United States was planning to raise the official price of gold further than the planned $38 an ounce, to $70 an ounce or even to $140 an ounce, that is, to double or quadruple the then official price of $35 an ounce.[6] Uncertainties about the likely course of U.S. action in the near future fed this speculation. There were intimations that U.S. officials would have preferred a larger devaluation of the dollar in December 1971 and that further devaluation might be undertaken. There was concern that the United States would need to enlarge its gold reserves. These reserves had dipped to $10 billion, a level widely believed to be the minimum that had to be retained. An enlargement of U.S. gold reserves required only a stroke of the pen raising the price of gold. There was fear of inflation and of more dollar devaluation since the U.S. authorities were again in 1972 embarking on expansionary policies, despite the criticism that the United States had received from officials abroad for resorting to inflationary policies since 1966 to finance expenditures in connection with the Viet Nam war.

Concern that the U.S. Congress might not approve the proposed devaluation of the dollar compounded uncertainty about future action by U.S. officials. The offer of the U.S. Administration to change the par value for the dollar had been the key ingredient enabling the Group of Ten to agree on currency realignment in December 1971. At the Smithsonian Institution, John B. Connally, Secretary of the U.S. Treasury, agreed "to propose to Congress a suitable means for devaluing the dollar in terms of gold to $38.00 per ounce as soon as the related set of short-term measures is available for Congressional scrutiny. Upon passage of required legislative authority in this framework, the United States will propose the corresponding new par value of the dollar to the International Monetary Fund."[7] The United States was one of the few members of the Fund for which a change in par value required the approval of its legislature. Private businessmen and bankers both in the United States and abroad were concerned that as the par value bill proceeded through the U.S. Congress, protectionist measures might be added to it, since action by the United States on its par value had been made dependent on other countries taking trade measures, and negotiations on these trade measures had not yet been very successful.

---

[5]The floating of the pound sterling in June 1972 is discussed in Chap. 3.

[6]*New York Times*, January 8, 1972, p. 39.

[7]Communiqué of the Ministers and Central Bank Governors of the Group of Ten, December 18, 1971, par. 5; reprinted in *International Financial News Survey* (Washington: International Monetary Fund), Vol. 23 (December 22–30, 1971), p. 418.

Other factors, too, explain the absence of capital reflows to the United States in the months following the currency realignment of the Smithsonian agreement. Interest rate differentials between the United States and most other major industrial countries were such as to discourage these reflows. Short-term security yields in the United States were lower than at any time since 1963, and U.S. interest rates on long-term bonds, while still relatively high by pre-1969 standards, were well below the corresponding long-term rates in most industrial nations. Also, in the early part of 1972, the United States continued to run a large trade deficit and a sizable deficit in its basic balance of payments; bankers and officials of other institutions with dollar holdings abroad did not sufficiently appreciate the long interval needed before the effects of the new exchange rates could take place and hesitated to return dollar holdings to the United States. Monetary authorities, moreover, seemed to be making little progress in agreeing to the reforms needed to put a new international monetary system into effect. In particular, officials in the U.S. Government had not yet reached consensus on specific objectives for a reformed system and the major countries had not even reached agreement on the forum in which negotiations would proceed.

In these circumstances, not only did capital fail to return to the United States but the antipathy that developed after the suspension of dollar convertibility in August 1971 between U.S. officials and officials of the then six countries of the European Community (EC) (Belgium, France, the Federal Republic of Germany, Italy, Luxembourg, and the Netherlands) continued and even worsened. Officials of countries belonging to the EC accused U.S. officials of not seriously trying to restore a system of par values. As evidence they cited the reluctance of U.S. officials to intervene in exchange markets to support the new rate for the dollar and their indifference to further short-term capital outflows from the United States. Officials of the EC countries viewed as unreasonable the positions taken by U.S. authorities in refusing to reinstitute even limited convertibility for the dollar and in giving priority to the U.S. domestic economy over the U.S. balance of payments. In their view, U.S. officials again seemed ready to inflate the U.S. economy even at the expense of the external payments position. Officials of the EC countries also regarded U.S. authorities as slow to consider measures for reforming the international monetary system. On the other side, U.S. authorities, believing that they had taken sufficient initiative in 1971 with regard to the dollar and the U.S. balance of payments position, waited for further action from the authorities of other industrial countries. U.S. authorities especially expected other countries to take action to liberalize trade so that they would import more from the United States.

ORIGIN OF THE EUROPEAN NARROW MARGINS ARRANGEMENT (THE SNAKE)

Given the circumstances just described, the authorities of the countries of the EC decided that it was in their own best interest to tighten the ties between themselves. They went ahead with plans for a narrow margins arrangement to limit the fluctuations between their own currencies.

Developments Until 1971

One of the principal long-term objectives of the countries of the EC is the achievement of a monetary union. Such a union involves either the adoption of a common currency or, as a minimum, the elimination of fluctuations in the exchange rates between their individual currencies. The countries of the EC discussed the pursuit of uniform exchange rate policies as early as 1962 but could achieve little until they had completed the formation of a customs union, unifying their trade and tariff policies. Once a customs union was achieved toward the end of the 1960s, the heads of state or of government of the six EC members, believing that a new impetus was needed for the further integration and development of the Community, revived the idea of a monetary union. At a meeting in The Hague in December 1969, they agreed to prepare a plan for the establishment of such a union. The Werner report in 1970 concluded that a monetary union, involving the reduction and eventual elimination of exchange rate fluctuations between the currencies of the EC countries and the complete liberalization of capital movements between them, should be achieved in phases during the 1970s. Mutual financial assistance was also to be provided to help the participants adhere to agreed arrangements for their exchange rates.

The determination of the EC countries to achieve monetary union and to limit exchange rate fluctuations between their currencies was demonstrated at the Twenty-Fifth Annual Meeting of the Fund's Board of Governors, held in Copenhagen from September 21 to 25, 1970. The Executive Directors had been studying the possibility of introducing greater exchange rate flexibility into the par value system, and after deliberating for a year and a half, had produced a report, *The Role of Exchange Rates in the Adjustment of International Payments*. They awaited further instructions from the Governors at the Annual Meeting. The Governors of the EC countries, however, emphasizing the firm intention of these countries to harmonize their exchange rate policies and to restrict exchange rate flexibility, made clear their lack of interest in further discussions of ways to make the par value system more flexible.[8] This lack of interest ended further consideration in the Fund of exchange rate flexibility until after the system of par values had collapsed.

Developments in 1971 and Early 1972

On March 22, 1971 the EC adopted a resolution on the establishment by stages of an economic and monetary union. The resolution invited the five central banks involved to keep fluctuations in the rates between Community currencies within

---

[8]These developments were described in *History, 1966–71*, Vol. I, pp. 500–16; the reader is referred particularly to pp. 514–16.

margins narrower than those resulting from the application of margins in force for the U.S. dollar, by means of concerted action vis-à-vis the dollar.[9] These five central banks planned to narrow the margins of exchange rate fluctuation between their currencies from ± 1.5 percent to ± 1.2 percent of parity.[10] The events of 1971, however, hampered progress toward monetary union. First came the floating of the deutsche mark and the Netherlands guilder in May, and then the emergency measures with respect to exchange rates and capital controls that the countries of the EC and other countries introduced following suspension of convertibility by the United States on August 15.

After the Smithsonian agreement in December 1971, the EC countries resumed their move toward monetary union. They saw three possible problems for their currencies as a result of the newly agreed arrangements. The first problem was that the widening of margins of up to 2.25 percent on either side of par values or central rates permitted under the Smithsonian agreement made possible maximum variations of up to 4.5 percent between the rates of exchange of the currencies of EC countries, if central banks continued to intervene in the exchange markets in dollars, still the most frequently used intervention currency. A 4.5 percent difference could occur, for example, if the dollar rate for the currency of one EC country was at the upper intervention point and at the lower intervention point for the currency of another EC country. Over time variations in the rates between currencies of two EC countries of up to 9 percent could result if, for instance, this relationship became reversed. Such large variations would affect competition in trade between the EC countries and would upset the Community's common agricultural policy.

A second problem was that, since the dollar was inconvertible and since monetary authorities outside the United States had undertaken to buy and sell unlimited quantities of dollars when exchange rates reached agreed margins, EC countries might have to accumulate additional dollars with no guarantee of being able to convert them into other reserve assets. Authorities of the EC countries viewed this situation as consecrating the role of the dollar in intra-Community monetary relations and making the Community, willingly or unwillingly, an extension of the dollar area.

A third problem was the possibility that speculative inflows of short-term capital similar to those which had taken place during the previous few years could recur, once more upsetting the exchange rates between the dollar and the currencies of the EC countries.

To help solve these problems the Council of Ministers agreed in March 1972 that the central banks of the EC countries would progressively reduce the existing fluctuation margins between their currencies but would use fully the margins allowed by the Fund for the currencies of countries not belonging to the Community.

---

[9]Although there were then six members of the Community, there were only five central banks because Belgium and Luxembourg had a joint central bank.

[10]Parity is the relationship between two currencies, determined by the ratio of their par values. A par value is the value of a currency in terms of gold or SDRs.

By July 1, 1972, the maximum gap between the currencies of the EC countries was to be 2.25 percent, half the margin of 4.5 percent agreed at the Smithsonian Institution in December 1971. To this end the five EC central banks would intervene in the foreign exchange markets in the currencies of the EC countries, which meant that the five central banks had to accumulate the currencies of the other countries in the Community. Furthermore, these central banks arranged periodically to settle debts and balances resulting from intervention in each other's currencies. They would continue, if necessary, to intervene in dollars to keep the 4.5 percent margins between their currencies and the dollar.

The authorities of the EC countries regarded the introduction of this currency arrangement as an important step toward economic and monetary union. They construed their agreement as in effect establishing an "independent monetary area" for the EC within the international monetary system. Their long-term objective was "the elimination of all fluctuation margins between Community currencies."[11]

This currency arrangement between the EC countries came to be known as the snake in the tunnel, or simply as the snake. The walls of the tunnel were the 4.5 percent margins of the Smithsonian agreement, but the snake within those walls had a maximum width of 2.25 percent. The actual width of the snake was determined by the spread between the exchange rate premiums (or discounts) expressed in percentage of parity with the dollar of the strongest and the weakest currencies of the countries of the Community. There was no common level between the dollar and the currencies of the EC countries, such as might be determined by joint agreement between the participating central banks. The position of the snake within the tunnel was left to market forces. No intervention in dollars was allowed, except under special circumstances, until the snake reached the walls of the tunnel. Imbalances with countries not in the EC were thus entirely absorbed by changes in exchange rates. This arrangement avoided the need for continuous and difficult bargaining among the countries of the Community as to what should be "the Community level of the dollar," and possible conflict between countries with strong and weak currencies.

In addition to the snake arrangement there was another arrangement between the Benelux currencies, "the worm." Belgium, Luxembourg, and the Netherlands agreed in August 1971 to reduce the margins between the Belgian franc and the Netherlands guilder to ± 1.5 percent of the parity between their currencies.

CALMER EXCHANGE MARKETS IN LATE 1972

As monetary authorities had hoped, exchange markets and free markets for gold did progressively stabilize in the last five months of 1972. Rates for the U.S.

---

[11]European Community, *Background Information* (Washington, March 29, 1972); reprinted in *International Financial News Survey* (Washington: International Monetary Fund), Vol. 24 (April 5, 1972), pp. 98–99.

dollar in exchange markets rose appreciably against a number of currencies, particularly against the deutsche mark and the Netherlands guilder. The exchange rates agreed at the Smithsonian Institution seemed more likely to hold than they had in the early months of 1972. Pressure on the U.S. authorities and on the Fund to take measures to help strengthen the new pattern of exchange rates abated somewhat.

Greater stability in exchange markets in the last few months of 1972 was attributable to several factors. A number of monetary authorities publicly reaffirmed their belief in the exchange rates agreed at the Smithsonian Institution. For example, immediately following the floating of the pound sterling on June 23, Mr. Schweitzer made a statement to the effect that he continued to view the general readjustment of exchange rates at the end of 1971 as a major contribution to the establishment of equilibrium in international payments and welcomed the decision of a number of industrial members, including the EC countries, to maintain that structure of exchange rates. On July 20, George P. Shultz, who had succeeded Mr. Connally as Secretary of the U.S. Treasury, met in Washington with Helmut Schmidt, who had succeeded Karl Schiller as Minister of the Economy of the Federal Republic of Germany, and both men pledged their support for the existing pattern of exchange rates.

These statements, intended to allay fears of further changes in exchange rates, were backed up with action. The authorities of the Federal Republic of Germany had on June 29 introduced exchange controls to curb capital inflows. The prior approval of the Deutsche Bundesbank was required for the purchase by nonresidents of domestic bonds (although not of securities). Previously the authorities of the Federal Republic of Germany had used only measures that worked through price-and-cost incentives to restrain capital inflow and had refrained from explicit restrictions on capital movements. The U.S. Federal Reserve System, in July, also undertook operations in foreign exchange markets for the first time since August 15, 1971; the Federal Reserve Bank of New York undertook heavy sales of deutsche mark.

The firming up of plans for reform of the international monetary system in the middle of 1972 also helped stabilize exchange markets. In June it was agreed that an ad hoc Committee of Governors of the Fund would be the forum in which to conduct the negotiations for a reformed system. In September, at the Twenty-Seventh Annual Meeting of the Fund's Board of Governors, Mr. Shultz came forward with a detailed proposal developed within the U.S. Government for a reformed system.[12] The importance to international monetary reform of a constructive initiative from the United States was widely recognized. Also, on the political side, the decisive victory in November by President Nixon in his bid for a second term and the expectation of peace in Viet Nam, after a prolonged war, helped strengthen the U.S. dollar.

In addition, the world economy was now performing better. In 1972 overall output in the seven largest industrial countries grew by nearly 6 percent, again almost approaching the high growth rates of the 1960s. Increases in gross national

---

[12]These developments are described at length in Chaps. 8 and 9.

product were most marked in the United States, Canada, and the United Kingdom; but recovery accelerated as well in France, the Federal Republic of Germany, Japan, and Italy.

Improvements in the U.S. domestic economy and in the U.S. balance of payments began to be apparent in the last months of 1972. For 1972 as a whole, the United States experienced more than a 6 percent economic growth in real terms, the largest since 1966, and under the Phase II policy for restraint of prices and wages, prices had risen only 3 percent, less than in any year since 1966. The restoration of confidence in the U.S. domestic economy, together with a sharp rise in U.S. interest rates, stimulated sizable reflows of short-term funds from Europe to the United States. Also, the controls on capital inflows that European countries had imposed earlier in the year were making the placement of funds in most European money markets increasingly difficult. Moreover, other measures adopted by European countries to deter capital inflows were either raising the costs of foreign capital to domestic borrowers or making yields less attractive to the lenders. As a result of capital inflows, the overall U.S. balance of payments deficit declined considerably in 1972. The aggregate deficit, on an official settlements basis, turned out to be $10.3 billion, a very high figure by previous standards but sharply lower than the $29.8 billion of 1971.

The stability of exchange markets in the last few months of 1972 proved to be short-lived, however. It was a calm before the storm that burst forth in the first three months of 1973.

25

CHAPTER

2

Operating in an Ailing System

WHILE MONETARY AUTHORITIES were trying to make viable the new exchange rates agreed at the Smithsonian Institution, Fund officials were, in the first six months of 1972, adjusting the Fund's policies to the changed international monetary arrangements existing after December 1971. In January 1972 the Executive Board took a decision to permit a temporary resumption of the Fund's financial operations, disrupted since the suspension of convertibility of the dollar. In February the Fund changed the unit in which its accounts were kept from U.S. dollars to SDRs. In April the Fund made special arrangements enabling the United Kingdom to carry out a large repurchase of pounds sterling held by the Fund. In May a new par value for the U.S. dollar was established. Subsequently several other members, whose currencies were closely related to the dollar, also set new par values. Immediately after the new par value for the dollar went into effect, the Executive Board took a decision putting the Fund's operations on a more normal basis, replacing the decision of January. In May the Executive Board made known its views about the continued inconvertibility of the U.S. dollar, and in June Fund officials urged that Canada, which had had a floating rate since May 1970, return to the par value system.

FUND OPERATIONS RESTORED

The suspension of convertibility for the dollar on August 15, 1971 had caused problems in the conduct of the Fund's transactions and operations. Normally, the currencies used in the Fund's transactions and operations were selected in accordance with the principles and procedures set forth in a statement on currencies to be drawn and currencies to be used in repurchasing, approved by the Executive Board in July 1962.[1] Under this decision, subject to other constraints, the currencies

---

[1] *History, 1945–65*, Vol. I, pp. 516–20, and Vol. II, pp. 448–59.

used in purchases and repurchases were to be selected in such a way that the ratio between a member's reserve position in the Fund and its gross holdings of gold and foreign exchange would be roughly equal for each member whose currency was used in the Fund's transactions and operations. Thus, the proportion of reserves held by members in the form of positions in the Fund would continue to be approximately the same for each member.

The Fund normally conducted its transactions and operations on the basis of par values or, in the absence of agreed par values, on the basis of provisionally agreed exchange rates. Certain rules had existed since June 1954 to enable the Fund to make computations and transactions in currencies of members with fluctuating exchange rates. These rules had been used to cope with the effects of the introduction of fluctuating rates by Canada in May 1970 and by the Federal Republic of Germany and the Netherlands in May 1971. More explicitly, after the announcement by Canadian authorities on May 31, 1970 that the exchange value of the Canadian dollar would not be maintained within the prescribed margins around parity, the Executive Board decided on July 14, 1970 to apply these rules to the Canadian dollar. This decision had enabled the Fund to continue using Canadian dollars in its transactions and operations in the General Account in the second half of 1970 and the first half of 1971 and to adjust the valuation of its holdings of Canadian dollars. Similarly, on May 19, 1971, after the exchange rates for the deutsche mark and the Netherlands guilder were allowed to float, the Executive Board took decisions on ways to determine appropriate exchange rates for the Fund's transactions and operations in deutsche mark and Netherlands guilders so that the Fund could continue to use these currencies.

After August 15, 1971, almost none of the currencies that the Fund would use in purchases and repurchases and for other transactions and operations had their exchange rates effectively maintained within the margins around parities. Since the Fund had regularized its operations only for three major currencies without par values—the Canadian dollar, the deutsche mark, and the Netherlands guilder—the exchange rates at which the Fund's transactions and operations in many other currencies would take place suddenly became a widespread problem. Purchases and repurchases through the General Account could no longer be effected on the basis of agreed par values or of provisionally agreed exchange rates, and transactions in the Special Drawing Account could not be conducted on the basis of representative exchange rates. Furthermore, members could not use dollars held in their reserves for transactions and operations with the Fund since the Fund held dollars in excess of 75 percent of the U.S. quota and could not accept more of that currency. Moreover, in the absence of agreed arrangements for convertibility, it was difficult for members to use dollars to acquire from other members currencies for use in transactions and operations with the Fund because few members wanted to accept more dollars. Repurchases of currencies held by the Fund were especially hard to effect, as is explained later in this chapter. Finally, without agreement on the values to be used for currencies and gold, how to value the Fund's assets, which consisted of holdings of members' currencies and of gold, also became a problem.

Once the Smithsonian agreement was arranged and the Fund's temporary regime of central rates and wider margins established, the Fund made temporary arrangements for valuing its holdings of currencies and for determining the exchange rates that would be applicable in its transactions and operations. On January 4, 1972, the Executive Board took a decision that was to apply until the new par value for the U.S. dollar became effective. There were several elements to the decision. Within a reasonable period after a member established a central rate for its currency, the Fund would adjust its holdings of the member's currency in accordance with that central rate. If the member was availing itself of wider margins, the adjustment of the Fund's holdings of a currency involved in a transaction with the Fund was to be based on the ratio of the representative rate for the member's currency in the exchange market to the effective parity relationship between that currency and the member's intervention currency. Participants in the Special Drawing Account that used SDRs were enabled to obtain against SDRs amounts of foreign exchange that corresponded to the prospective par value of the U.S. dollar based on a price for gold of US$38 an ounce, rather than on the par value of the U.S. dollar based on a gold price of US$35 an ounce.

The Fund could again temporarily conduct its transactions and operations.

USE OF SDRs FOR THE FUND'S ACCOUNTS

Two factors coalesced to induce the Fund early in 1972 to change the unit in which it presented its financial accounts and statistics from U.S. dollars, used since the Fund's origin, to SDRs. First, the U.S. dollar, the most commonly held reserve asset, previously regarded as a unique national currency of constant value, had been devalued in terms of gold and was no longer convertible into gold. Second, the Managing Director, the staff, and several Executive Directors were looking for ways to strengthen the SDR as an international reserve asset, and the change in the status of the dollar provided them with a unique opportunity.

The recommendation that the Fund change the unit in which its financial accounts and statistics were expressed from dollars to SDRs came from the staff in February 1972. The change would affect the Fund's General Account (SDRs were already used as the unit of account in the Special Drawing Account). In making the recommendation to the Executive Board, the staff emphasized the obvious necessity of the Fund's having a common standard by which to measure its assets, which comprised many national currencies and gold. The Fund had to present its balance sheet and its financial operations, for example, in some common unit. Under the Articles of Agreement then in force, the Fund had to maintain the gold value of its assets, but this could be achieved whether the Fund's financial accounts were expressed in U.S. dollars specified as a given weight or fineness of gold, in another currency with a defined gold content, in grams of gold, or in SDRs which had a fixed gold content.[2]

Of these possibilities, the staff argued for the use of SDRs. Accounting in SDRs was preferable to accounting in a national currency because SDRs had a fixed value in terms of gold and thus their use would avoid the problems that resulted whenever the value of a national currency was changed. Accounting in SDRs was preferable to accounting in gold because expression of values in weights of gold, such as grams, was awkward and cumbersome. The use of SDRs to present the finances of the General Account would make its presentation consistent with that of the Special Drawing Account. Furthermore, the use of the SDR as an accounting unit would advance the idea that the Fund had its own asset in which to express its balance sheet and other financial statements just as countries used their own national currencies to express their financial accounts. Users of the Fund's accounts might have some initial difficulty in comprehending the value of the Fund's assets or the cost of its operations expressed in SDRs, but the staff believed that this difficulty would diminish or disappear as transactions in SDRs became more frequent and as familiarity with the SDR increased.

The staff considered the possibility that the Fund's accounts could be presented in terms of both SDRs and U.S. dollars but rejected such a dual presentation because it posed several problems. First, in February 1972 a new par value for the dollar had not yet been formally introduced, and until it was, the Fund was still valuing the dollar at the same gold content as the SDR. In other words, SDR 1 = $1. The presentation of accounts in both units would at the time mean merely duplicate figures. Second, after the new par value for the dollar and a higher price for gold in terms of dollars went into effect, a different relationship would exist between the dollar and the SDR (that is, $1.08 would equal SDR 1) and between the dollar and many other national currencies. Two different values for Fund transactions—one in SDRs and another in U.S. dollars—would be confusing. Moreover, the Fund had already been expressing the value of certain operations, such as repurchases and stand-by arrangements, solely in SDRs, a valuation which emphasized the constant gold value of assets and liabilities in the General Account. Third, when the new par value for the dollar was formally introduced, values in the General Account expressed in dollars would increase: financial statements of the General Account before and after the change of the gold value of the dollar would not be comparable. Fourth, presentation of the Fund's financial statements in two accounting units would involve higher administrative costs.

On February 25, 1972 the Executive Board decided to recommend to the Board of Governors that in view of the SDR's fixed gold value, its international character,

---

[2]Unless otherwise specified, references to the Articles of Agreement in this History are to the Articles as they existed after the First Amendment became effective on July 28, 1969 and before the Second Amendment became effective on April 1, 1978. These Articles were in force for all except the last nine months of the period covered here. In subsequent chapters, the numerous references to the Second Amendment, and even to the original Articles, are clearly indicated.

and its role as an international reserve asset, the Fund's By-Laws be changed to provide for the presentation of the accounts of the General Account in SDRs. In the discussion preceding the decision, Claude Beaurain (France) expressed the well-known preference of the French authorities for the use of gold as the appropriate unit of account. If the SDR was to be used, he felt the Fund should emphasize its gold content by using the phrase "units of account expressed in terms of 0.888671 gram of fine gold," rather than using the phrase "in terms of SDRs." He pointed out that the EC countries were already using an accounting unit expressed in gold. Other Executive Directors, however, clearly preferred SDRs to gold as the Fund's accounting unit. Furthermore, they did not like using the awkward phrase expressing the SDR in terms of its gold content. Günther Schleiminger (Federal Republic of Germany) in particular supported the use of the SDR as the Fund's accounting unit. He stressed that SDRs placed the Fund in a unique position compared with other international organizations in that the Fund had its own asset and could use it for accounting purposes. When the decision was taken, Mr. Beaurain formally objected.

The Executive Board's recommendation was approved by the Board of Governors, effective March 20, 1972.[3] The Fund's internal confidential accounts, the accounts and statistics describing the Fund's transactions and operations in its internal reports, and data for the Fund's transactions and operations in its publications have been all subsequently expressed in terms of SDRs.

ARRANGING FOR REPURCHASE BY THE UNITED KINGDOM

The inconvertibility of the dollar after August 15, 1971 caused especially difficult problems in effecting repurchases. Most members had sizable reserves of dollars and wanted to use them to repurchase outstanding drawings from the Fund, especially since their liabilities to the Fund were expressed in terms of gold and they wanted to reduce these liabilities before the price of gold went up further. Likewise, because they expected further increases in the price of gold, they preferred to repurchase with dollars rather than with SDRs whose value was fixed in terms of gold. Until the mid-1960s, members had customarily and with ease used dollars to repurchase their currencies from the Fund. Beginning in 1964, however, it was not always possible for members to use dollars directly in repurchases because the Fund often held dollars in amounts in excess of 75 percent of the U.S. quota and could not accept dollars in repurchases. To help members make repurchases, the U.S. authorities from time to time made drawings on the Fund called turnstile drawings: the U.S. authorities purchased from the Fund currencies that the Fund could accept in repurchase and then sold these currencies at par to countries that wished to use the dollars they held to fulfill their repurchase obligations to the Fund.

---

[3]E.B. Decision No. 3577-(72/16), March 20, 1972, and Resolution No. 27-3; Vol. III below, p. 556.

After the suspension of convertibility of the dollar, however, the U.S. authorities became notably reluctant to use gold-related positions in the Fund or primary reserve assets—gold and SDRs—to facilitate repurchases. Hence, it became impossible for members to effect repurchases in dollars. At the same time, other members whose currencies might be used in repurchase were hesitant to see their creditor positions in the Fund diminished by this use of their currencies. Such repurchases decreased their holdings of assets fixed in terms of gold. Moreover, the repurchasing member was likely to obtain currencies for the repurchase by offering dollars, and many Fund members did not want to accumulate more dollars since dollars could no longer be converted into gold or SDRs.

To enable repurchases to be effected, in October 1971 the Fund staff worked out ad hoc turnstile arrangements. Three members that had creditor positions in the Fund—Canada, France, and the Federal Republic of Germany—agreed to what amounted to a revolving fund using their currencies. Canadian dollars, French francs, and deutsche mark might be used for repurchases to the extent that drawings had been made in these currencies since August 15, 1971, provided that consultation with the member whose currency was being used preceded each repurchase transaction. For the next several months all drawings and repurchases were effected in these three currencies. By these arrangements members avoided any enlargement of their dollar holdings as a result of transactions through the Fund; yet these arrangements allowed repurchases to be effected that might otherwise have had to be postponed. In March 1972 the number of currencies included in the turnstile arrangements was increased to include Austrian schillings, Italian lire, and Japanese yen. In addition, the Fund arranged for the use of pounds sterling in drawings.

Early in 1972 a repurchase problem arose, whose solution became unusually involved and complicated. Citing details of the problem and of its solution reveals how difficult it was for the Fund to carry on its normal operations during this period, how strongly U.S. authorities opposed providing even a very limited convertibility of the dollar following the August 1971 suspension, how the Deputy Managing Director took the initiative in devising a solution, and how in a spirit of international cooperation the Canadian authorities in effect provided the convertibility that U.S. authorities refused.

In March 1972, Derek Mitchell (United Kingdom) advised the Acting Managing Director, Frank A. Southard, Jr., that the U.K. authorities were in a position to repurchase all the Fund's holdings of pounds sterling in excess of 75 percent of the U.K. quota and that they would like to do so as soon as possible. The amount of the repurchase was to be the equivalent of a little more than SDR 1,150 million. This amount was made up of two components, SDR 950 million resulting from the drawings on the Fund by the United Kingdom in 1969 and 1970 under the stand-by arrangement for $1.0 billion approved in June 1969, and SDR 200 million representing payments made by the United Kingdom to the Fund in pounds sterling, mainly for charges on these drawings.[4]

---

[4]The drawings the United Kingdom made under the stand-by arrangement approved by the Fund in November 1967 had already been repaid in 1971. *History, 1966–71*, Vol. I, p. 351.

In asking to make this repurchase, Mr. Mitchell emphasized to the Fund management that the 1969 stand-by arrangement and the Fund's subsequent close surveillance of the U.K. economic situation had received adverse comments in the U.K. press and in the U.K. Parliament. Hence, for domestic political reasons the U.K. authorities were especially eager to repay all their outstanding indebtedness to the Fund and to announce the repayment publicly as soon as possible. Since the United Kingdom was likely to incur a substantial repurchase obligation under Article V, Section 7(*b*), by April 30, 1972, the U.K. authorities wanted to undertake the repurchase *before* April 30, 1972 in order to present it as voluntary.

The turnstile arrangements were, however, inadequate for this large repurchase transaction. The U.K. authorities, frustrated in their desire to repay their debts to the Fund and to reinstate the United Kingdom's gold tranche position, sought advice from the Fund management on how to effect the repurchase. The management proposed an arrangement under which the United Kingdom, the United States, and, acting as a group, eight countries which were then net creditors in the General Account—Austria, Belgium, Canada, France, the Federal Republic of Germany, Italy, Japan, and the Netherlands—would participate in the U.K. repurchase. They would participate with primary reserve assets (gold, SDRs, and Fund positions) to the extent of one third each, the equivalent of about SDR 400 million, for a total of about SDR 1,200 million.

The arrangement would work as follows: (i) the United Kingdom would use SDRs in an amount equal to one third of the Fund's holdings of pounds sterling above 75 percent of quota and for the balance would use U.S. dollars to acquire currencies acceptable to the Fund in repurchases; (ii) simultaneously with the U.K. repurchase, the United States would purchase within its gold tranche pounds sterling in an amount equivalent to one third of the Fund's balances of pounds sterling above 75 percent of the U.K. quota, thereby restoring by one half the creditor positions of members whose currencies were used in the repurchase; and (iii) the eight countries which were net creditors in the General Account and whose currencies the Fund could accept in repurchase would accept the concomitant reductions in their Fund positions. The reduction in the net creditor positions of each of the eight countries would be in proportion to their reserve positions in the Fund.

When the management assembled the Executive Directors of the ten members concerned for informal talks, it became quickly apparent that the proposed three-way equal participation was not acceptable. The U.S. authorities in particular had trouble with it. As Mr. Dale explained to the other Executive Directors, the U.S. authorities considered the arrangement unfair to the United States and believed that it would involve a greater loss of gold than the United States could afford. The United Kingdom would receive a large gold tranche position in the Fund, enhancing its primary reserve assets, that is, gold, SDRs, and positions in the Fund, while the United States would suffer not only a reduction in its primary reserve assets but even in its basic gold reserves. The U.S. authorities noted further that the contribution of the eight net creditors in the General Account would change only the composition of their primary reserve assets and would not reduce these assets. In the view of the

U.S. authorities, the maximum gold tranche purchase of pounds sterling that the United States could afford was the equivalent of SDR 200 million.

An alternative, even more complicated, arrangement was worked out. First of all, it involved a total of SDR 1,150 million rather than SDR 1,200 million. The eight creditor countries mentioned above were willing to increase their participation from SDR 400 million to SDR 500 million. With SDR 200 million from the United States, that still left SDR 450 million to be financed. Of this amount, the U.K. authorities felt that they could pay a maximum of SDR 400 million. The remaining SDR 50 million was forthcoming through an exceptional compromise arranged between the authorities of Canada and Mr. Southard, as Acting Managing Director. The Canadian authorities had indicated a willingness to carry out an operation of up to SDR 50 million with either the United States or the United Kingdom as a means of reaching agreement on the U.K. repurchase. Mr. Southard worked out the details for the Canadian authorities to transfer to the United Kingdom an amount of gold equivalent to SDR 25 million and SDR 25 million (in SDRs) in exchange for pounds sterling. Both the gold and the SDRs were immediately turned over to the Fund by the United Kingdom. The U.K. authorities were thus able to use SDR 425 million in SDRs and SDR 25 million in gold in their repurchase transaction with a net use of only SDR 400 million.

The Executive Board approved these arrangements on April 26, 1972. The next day the Chancellor of the Exchequer, Anthony Barber, publicly announced that the United Kingdom had repurchased all the pounds sterling held by the Fund in excess of the U.K. quota.

NEW PAR VALUE FOR THE DOLLAR

Establishing a new par value for the U.S. dollar in May 1972 was the most important step taken by monetary authorities in 1972 to restore a system of par values after the disturbances of 1971. As mentioned in Chapter 1, the U.S. Congress had to approve any change in the par value for the dollar. Because of the need for Congressional approval, the monetary authorities gathered at the Smithsonian Institution in December 1971 had understood that establishing a new par value for the U.S. dollar would take some time. At the Smithsonian meeting, U.S. monetary authorities had indicated informally to the other participants that they hoped to be in a position to propose the par value to the Fund by April 30, 1972. The Fund and most of its members wished to have the new par value for the U.S. dollar formally put in place as soon as possible. A new par value for the dollar would indicate that the par value system, at least in a limited form, had not yet been abandoned. Also, a new par value for the dollar would enable the Fund again to conduct its financial operations on a more normal basis.

On February 9, 1972 Mr. Connally sent to the U.S. Congress a draft bill "to provide for a modification in the par value of the dollar and for other purposes," known as the "Par Value Modification Act." As Mr. Dale explained to the Executive

Directors seeking clarification about the timing of the U.S. action, two bills had to be passed by the Congress. A par value bill would authorize the change in par value, and a related appropriations bill would enable the United States to make the required payments to the Fund and to other international financial institutions, such as the International Bank for Reconstruction and Development (IBRD), hereafter referred to as the World Bank, the Inter-American Development Bank (IDB), and the Asian Development Bank (AsDB), to maintain the value in terms of gold of dollars held by these institutions. The U.S. authorities had decided not to propose the change in par value to the Fund until Congress had passed the appropriations bill. Mr. Dale assured the Executive Directors that the U.S. authorities intended to take the necessary action in the Fund regarding the dollar at the earliest possible moment so as not to generate any uncertainty about the new par value for the dollar.

Congress approved the par value bill on March 31, 1972.[5] Twice during April, Mr. Dale again explained to the Executive Directors the need for an appropriations bill and indicated that the U.S. authorities were still hoping Congress would approve it by the end of the month. Action was delayed, however, and it was not until May 5, 1972 that Mr. Connally sent a letter to Mr. Schweitzer officially proposing a change in the par value of the dollar, from one thirty-fifth to one thirty-eighth of a troy ounce of fine gold, to become effective at noon on May 8, 1972. The par value for the dollar was to be altered from 0.888671 to 0.818513 gram of fine gold per dollar, or from $1.00000 to $1.08571 per SDR. This change, a 7.89 percent devaluation of the dollar in terms of gold, fell within the terms of Article IV, Section 5(c)(i), of the Articles of Agreement that permitted a member to change the initial par value of its currency up to 10 percent without objection by the Fund. Since the Fund did not have to take any action on a change of this degree in the par value for the dollar, it merely noted the change.

Other Par Value Changes

The establishment of a new par value for the dollar led to several other members changing the par values for their currencies. Some members that had communicated central rates to the Fund now proposed par values, discontinuing their central rates. Others that had maintained their exchange rates with the U.S. dollar since December 18, 1971 now set par values formalizing the relationship between their currencies and the dollar. Members that changed their par values between May 8, when the par value for the dollar was changed, and June 1, 1972 were China, the Dominican Republic, El Salvador, Greece, Guatemala, Honduras, Iceland, Israel, Jordan, Liberia, Mexico, Nepal, Nicaragua, Pakistan, Somalia, and Thailand.[6] The changes in the par values of these 16 members are listed in Table 1.

---

[5]Public Law 268, 92nd Cong., March 31, 1972, 86 Stat. 116.

[6]Between 1949 and April 1980 China was represented in the Fund by the authorities of Taiwan. A letter from the Foreign Minister of the People's Republic of China to the Managing Director dated April 1, 1980, states: "The Government of the People's Republic of China, being the sole legitimate Government of China, is the only Government that can represent China in the International Monetary Fund and in its Special Drawings Rights Department."

Table 1. Changes in Par Values, May 8–June 1, 1972

Member	Currency Unit	Grams of Fine Gold per Currency Unit		Currency Units per SDR		Date Par Value Established
		From	To	From	To	
China[1]	NT dollar	0.0222168	0.0204628	40.0000	43.4286	May 8
Dominican Republic	peso	0.888671	0.818513	1.00000	1.08571	May 9
El Salvador	colón	0.355468	0.327405	2.50000	2.71429	May 8
Greece	drachma	0.0296224	0.0272838	30.0000	32.5714	May 19
Guatemala	quetzal	0.888671	0.818513	1.00000	1.08571	May 10
Honduras	lempira	0.444335	0.409256	2.00000	2.17143	May 15
Iceland	króna	0.0100985	0.00930128	88.0000	95.5429	May 9
Israel	pound	0.211588	0.194884	4.20000	4.56000	May 17
Jordan	dinar	2.48828	2.29184	0.357143	0.387754	May 8
Liberia	dollar	0.888671	0.818513	1.00000	1.08571	May 8
Mexico	peso	0.0710937	0.0654810	12.5000	13.5714	May 10
Nepal	rupee	0.0877700	0.0808408	10.1250	10.9929	May 13
Nicaragua	córdoba	0.126953	0.116930	7.00000	7.60003	May 8
Pakistan	rupee	0.186621	0.0744103	4.76190	11.9428	May 11
Somalia	shilling	0.124414	0.118193	7.14286	7.51881	June 1
Thailand	baht	0.0427245	0.0393516	20.8000	22.5828	May 8

1See fn. 6 on p. 35.

The change in Pakistan's par value was an especially large decrease in the gold value of the rupee, a devaluation of 60.13 percent. Inasmuch, however, as this devaluation was accompanied by the elimination of multiple exchange rates, the effective devaluation of the rupee was much less than 60 percent. It was, nevertheless, about 40 percent for imports and between 15 percent and 25 percent for exports.

Effective May 24, 1972, the Fund also agreed to an initial par value for the rupee proposed by the officials of Mauritius, of Mau Rs 5.55555 = SDR 1. In addition, four other members changed their par values because of the change in the par value for the U.S. dollar, three of them making the changes somewhat ahead of the United States. On April 5, 1972, Guyana proposed a change in its par value, from 0.444335 to 0.409256 gram of fine gold, corresponding to G$2 = US$1, the same relationship between the Guyana dollar and the U.S. dollar that had existed earlier. On April 5, Panama proposed a change in its par value, from 0.888671 to 0.818513 gram of fine gold per balboa, keeping the relationship between the balboa and the U.S. dollar unchanged at B 1.00 = US$1. On April 12, Haiti proposed a change in its par value, from 0.177734 gram of fine gold to 0.163703 gram of fine gold per gourde, keeping the relationship between the gourde and the U.S. dollar unchanged at G 5.00 = US$1. Since these three changes represented changes of less than 10 percent from the initial par values for the currencies of these members, the Fund merely noted the changes. On May 8 Costa Rica announced that the par value of the colón was being changed from 0.134139 to 0.123549 gram of fine gold, although the new par value had not yet been agreed with the Fund.

NORMAL FUND OPERATIONS RE-ESTABLISHED

A decision adopted by the Executive Board on May 8, 1972, the same day the new par value for the U.S. dollar became effective, replaced the temporary decision of January 4, 1972 regarding the exchange rates to be used in the Fund's transactions and operations. The new decision was to apply only to those currencies for which exchange rates were not maintained within the 1 percent margins prescribed by the Articles of Agreement or within the 2 percent margins permitted by the Executive Board decision of 1959.[7] These currencies were to be valued at exchange rates derived from market exchange rates, that is, on the basis of the representative rate for the currency as established under Rule O-3 of the Fund's Rules and Regulations, rather than on the basis of par values or central rates.[8] For all other currencies, including the U.S. dollar, the French franc, and the pound sterling, the Fund again operated on the basis of agreed par values.

---

[7]This decision of 1959 was described in *History, 1945–65*, Vol. I, pp. 469–70.
[8]Rule O-3, as adopted in 1969, can be found in *History, 1966–71*, Vol. II, p. 187.

ARGUMENTS OVER INCONVERTIBILITY OF THE DOLLAR

After the establishment of a new par value for the dollar and the decision to conduct again the majority of the Fund's transactions and operations on the basis of agreed par values, some semblance of order seemed to have been restored to the international monetary system. The element from the previous par value system still missing, however, was convertibility of the dollar. Since August 15, 1971, European officials had been pressing U.S. officials to restore, or at least to promise to restore, some degree of convertibility to the dollar. They regarded as an anomaly a system in which there existed a par value for the dollar but in which there was no mechanism to defend that par value, as indicated by a willingness of the U.S. authorities to convert dollars into reserve assets at that par value. But, as mentioned earlier, European authorities were particularly disturbed at the prospect of having to accumulate more holdings of inconvertible dollars. They viewed as a bad omen the reluctance of the U.S. authorities to restore even the degree of convertibility necessary to enable the Fund to effect repurchases in a normal way. European authorities were especially unhappy, for example, about the position that the U.S. authorities had taken in April on the repurchase by the United Kingdom.

The inconvertibility of the U.S. dollar was often criticized in discussions in the Executive Board during the first months of 1972. The Fund management, wanting to restore the Fund's repurchase operations, tried to help bring about some degree of convertibility. In a speech in February, Mr. Southard, Deputy Managing Director, explained that "it has up to the present time not been possible to work out any arrangements for even the most limited convertibility of the dollar within the Fund."[9] When unrest in exchange markets persisted in March, Mr. Southard, as Acting Managing Director, very aware of the attitude of European authorities, suggested to Mr. Volcker that the U.S. authorities consider giving some degree of convertibility to the dollar. Several weeks later in the course of the staff discussions that were part of the Article VIII consultation with the United States, the staff also raised the same question with the U.S. authorities.

The U.S. authorities felt very strongly on this issue. They were concerned that U.S. gold reserves were already less than one third the value of official holdings of dollars abroad. Officials within the U.S. Government, moreover, were divided over the role of gold in any future international monetary system. Meanwhile, U.S. authorities considered it preferable to hold on to as much gold as possible until reform of the system was worked out. They wanted a large turnaround in the U.S. balance of payments position before they contemplated any commitment to dollar convertibility. For all these reasons, they emphasized in the first months of 1972 that any restoration of convertibility of the dollar would have to be negotiated as part of

---

[9]"The Financial Setting: Current Status and Future Directions—International Finance," remarks by Frank A. Southard, Jr., at Panel Discussion, The Conference Board, New York, February 23, 1972, published in *International Financial News Survey* (Washington: International Monetary Fund), Vol. 24 (March 1, 1972), pp. 57–59; reference is to p. 59.

the reform of the international monetary system. They pointed out, too, that the other participants in the Group of Ten had, as part of the Smithsonian agreement, assented to "nonconvertibility" of the dollar until the system was reformed.

When the Executive Board took up the Article VIII consultation with the United States at the end of May 1972, the issue of dollar convertibility was raised in a rather heated way by most members of the Executive Board from the EC countries. Marc Viénot (France), in particular, regretted what he termed the "intransigent attitude" of the United States toward restoring dollar convertibility. Other members of the Executive Board elected by EC countries, including Pieter Lieftinck (Netherlands), Günther Schleiminger (Federal Republic of Germany), and Heinrich G. Schneider (Austria), wanted to have the Executive Board take a decision calling the attention of the United States to its obligations with respect to convertibility under the Articles of Agreement. They noted that although Article VIII consultations normally did not include decisions, in 1970 decisions were added for some members pursuing practices deviating from their obligations under Article VIII. There had been, for example, decisions on Canada, the Federal Republic of Germany, and the Netherlands with regard to their floating exchange rates. These precedents led many Executive Directors to believe that a decision ought to be added to the consultation with the United States, and they deliberated its nature and wording.

The decision taken reflected to a considerable extent a statement of Mr. Dale that the U.S. authorities intended to collaborate fully with the Fund and with its members and that such collaboration could best occur in the framework of discussions about reforming the system. The Fund noted that the United States did not buy officially held foreign balances of U.S. dollars either under Article IV or Article VIII and welcomed the reaffirmation of the U.S. authorities that they intended to collaborate with the Fund and with its other members to proceed promptly with an appropriate reform or improvement of the international monetary system. Mr. Viénot, emphasizing that he would support a decision only if it clearly urged the United States to comply as soon as possible with the obligations of Article VIII, Section 4 (the obligation pertaining to convertibility), abstained from the decision.

The continuing inconvertibility of the U.S. dollar was to come up on other occasions, too, in the course of 1972. The Italian monetary authorities in particular took the position that, despite the re-establishment of a par value for the dollar, it was preferable for the central rate regime to remain in effect until reform of the system was completed rather than return to the par value system without dollar convertibility. When the Executive Board discussed in May the decision concerning the exchange rates to be used in the Fund's transactions and operations, the staff suggested that the term "central rate" be abolished, implying that the central rate regime be ended. Francesco Palamenghi-Crispi (Italy), however, objected to its discontinuation.

Several European members, including Belgium, the Federal Republic of Germany, Italy, the Netherlands, and Sweden, as well as Japan, were still using central rates. In July Mr. Schweitzer, on a visit to monetary officials of several members in Europe, suggested that an early transition from central rates to par values, even if not all members could participate immediately, would enhance confidence in the new structure of exchange rates. But when Mr. Schweitzer reported to the Executive Board on his talks in Europe, Mr. Palamenghi-Crispi again stressed that the Italian authorities doubted whether a transition from central rates to par values would be of much use. At the 1972 Annual Meeting in Washington in September, Giovanni Malagodi elaborated his Government's position. A par value system without dollar convertibility meant that the burden of defending exchange rates fell on countries that had to finance the U.S. deficit and had to continue to accumulate inconvertible U.S. dollar balances.[10] Thus, despite the establishment of a new par value for the U.S. dollar, the Italian authorities regarded as imperative the continuation of a central rate regime until a reformed system went into effect.

URGING CANADA TO ADOPT A PAR VALUE

That the Fund was still trying in 1972 to preserve a par value system was exemplified not only by its actions vis-à-vis the United States but also by its urging Canada, which had used a floating rate since 1970, to select a new par value. The staff discussions with respect to the annual Article VIII consultation with Canada were held in Ottawa in May 1972 and the Executive Board discussion took place in July. The staff adduced several reasons why Canada should re-establish a par value. First, since wider margins were available under the Smithsonian agreement, the rate for the Canadian dollar could move in a larger range, making it easier for Canada to defend a par value than under the former narrow margins. Second, the argument of the Canadian authorities against setting a par value—that economic and exchange conditions were unsettled—was likely to be valid indefinitely. Since the Canadian dollar had been floating for nearly two years, it was already more than a temporary float, and no substantive change was likely in the near future. Third, Canada had a strong external payments position. Fourth, the international community could not have faith in an international monetary system in which a country as important as Canada remained permanently exempt from the rules.

At the Executive Board meeting, Robert Bryce (Canada) explained why the Canadian authorities believed that the time was not ripe for Canada to commit itself to maintaining a par value even within the wider margins now possible. The international monetary system was seriously disturbed and there was danger that any par value selected for the Canadian dollar might prove inappropriate and unsustainable in the market. Although the continued floating of the Canadian dollar would not prove a source of disruption for other members of the Fund, the choice of

---

[10] Statement by the Governor of the Fund for Italy, *Summary Proceedings of the Twenty-Seventh Annual Meeting of the Board of Governors, 1972* (Washington: International Monetary Fund, 1972), pp. 79–80. (Hereafter cited as *Summary Proceedings, 19–.*)

an inappropriate par value could well prove so. The Canadian situation was also an exception. No other major country's currency was so closely and inextricably linked in trade, in other current transactions, and in capital flows with the United States. At a time such as mid-1972, when the U.S. balance of payments and the U.S. dollar were manifestly in difficulties and in need of substantial adjustments, Canada had good reason to fear the consequences of such difficulties and adjustments.

Mr. Dale stressed that his authorities tended to agree with the Canadian authorities that a par value for the Canadian dollar should not be declared. The U.S. authorities believed that the trade deficit of the United States vis-à-vis Canada in 1972 was abnormally large and still had to be corrected. The par value suggested by the staff for Canada seemed to U.S. officials to undervalue the Canadian dollar.

Australian, European, and Japanese officials, however, were much less willing than were U.S. officials to give up attempts to retain a system of par values. Executive Directors appointed or elected by Australia, by the EC countries, and by Japan all believed that Canada should reconsider its exchange rate policy with a view to ending its floating rate and to setting a new par value. The strongest views were voiced by Lindsay B. Brand (Australia), who emphasized the belief of most Executive Directors that stable exchange rates were far superior to other rates because they reduced uncertainties in an uncertain world and thus facilitated trade. Mr. Lieftinck agreed with the staff view that the arguments used by the Canadian authorities for retaining a floating rate could be used in almost any circumstances. The existing uncertainties in the international monetary system might last for some time and the vulnerability of Canada's economy and balance of payments position to developments in the United States was likely to persist. André van Campenhout (Belgium) and Messrs. Suzuki and Viénot likewise argued that the Canadian authorities were in a position to establish a par value. Interestingly enough, inasmuch as most developing members of the Fund continued to maintain fixed exchange rates and most Executive Directors elected by developing members usually argued for fixed rates, the Executive Directors and Alternate Executive Directors from developing members were most sympathetic with the argument of the Canadian authorities that continued uncertainty about the whole international monetary system induced them to keep a floating rate.

After this discussion, the Executive Board took a decision in which the Fund urged the Canadian authorities "to reconsider its nonobservance of a par value" and noted that Canada's compliance with its international obligations in this respect would contribute to a better functioning of the international monetary system.

DEVELOPING MEMBERS' ECONOMIC CIRCUMSTANCES

When 1972 began, developing members, like industrial members, were suffering from the effects of the slowdown in world economic activity in 1970 and

1971.[11] In particular, their exports had been growing at a slower rate than in the 1960s. Their aggregate current account deficit had been steadily increasing from less than $5 billion a year on average in the mid-1960s to $8 billion in 1970 and $9.5 billion in 1971. These increasing current account deficits derived primarily from higher payments for international services, such as earnings on foreign investment and the servicing of external debt; there was little change in the collective trade deficit of developing members.

The current account deficit of developing members as a whole in 1971, as in the years since the mid-1960s, was not a problem, however. The deficit was more than covered by net inflows of capital and foreign aid so that for developing members as a group, an overall balance of payments surplus existed. In fact, in 1971 developing members shared with several industrial members the payments surpluses that were the counterpart of the large payments deficit of the United States, and capital inflows to developing members rose considerably faster than their aggregate current account deficit. Developing members did, however, experience some payments problems. Most capital inflows were of short-term funds and of unidentified capital, not the type of funds that developing members could confidently count on for any length of time. Moreover, the overall balance of payments surplus of developing members as a group was unevenly distributed. Much of the surplus was that of Middle Eastern countries, which benefited from what was at the time an unprecedented increase of more than 20 percent in the average unit value of petroleum exports.

The position of developing members improved again in 1972. Recovery in the economies of the industrial members strengthened demand for primary products. Also, toward the end of the year there began an unusually large spurt in commodity prices. Commodity prices other than those for petroleum rose from 1971 to 1972 by an average of 13 percent, showing large increases after years of weakness for a number of nonfood agricultural items—such as copra, cotton, jute, linseed oil, rubber, and wool. As a result, the payments positions of developing members in 1972 were considerably bolstered. They had a collective trade surplus of $3 billion, reducing their aggregate current account deficit to less than $7 billion. Furthermore, since international credits were generally more plentiful and interest rates lower

---

[11]The Fund used the following classification of members plus Switzerland in its statistics and reports (but not for purposes of policies) during the period covered by this History:

Industrial countries: Austria, Belgium, Canada, Denmark, France, the Federal Republic of Germany, Italy, Japan, Luxembourg, the Netherlands, Norway, Sweden, Switzerland, the United Kingdom, and the United States.

Primary producing countries in more developed areas or "more developed primary producing countries": Australia, Finland, Greece, Iceland, Ireland, Malta, New Zealand, Portugal, Romania, South Africa, Spain, Turkey, and Yugoslavia.

Primary producing countries in less developed areas or "less developed primary producing countries," often shortened in this History to "developing countries": all other members.

In addition, at times, the less developed or developing countries were subdivided to distinguish 13 "major oil exporters": Algeria, Bahrain, Indonesia, Iran, Iraq, Kuwait, Libya, Nigeria, Oman, Qatar, Saudi Arabia, the United Arab Emirates, and Venezuela. Also in the Fund's statistics, figures for "world" trade, "world" reserves, or "world" output customarily meant Fund members plus Switzerland.

than in the two preceding years, developing members experienced an enlarged capital inflow. Consequently, they had an unprecedented overall payments surplus in 1972 of more than $8 billion, of which $4.5 billion was for countries whose main exports were commodities other than petroleum. Among developing members, Brazil was the largest recipient of capital by far, but relatively large net capital inflows went also to Colombia, Egypt, Iran, Israel, Korea, Mexico, and Venezuela.

In 1972, officials of developing members also began to express a more unified position on international monetary questions. With negotiations on measures to reform the international monetary system about to get under way, they set up their own Group of Twenty-Four, formally the Intergovernmental Group of Twenty-Four on International Monetary Affairs, which held its inaugural meeting at both the ministerial level and at the level of deputies in Caracas in April 1972.

That the financial officials of developing members were beginning to articulate a common position on exchange rates was apparent, too, at the 1972 Annual Meeting. Several of the Governors from developing members, such as Sambwa Pida Nbagui, D.T. Matenje, J.M. Mwanakatwe, Ali Wardhana, David H. Coore, and Mohamed A. Merzeban, underscored their interest in fixed exchange rates and a system of par values by emphasizing the adverse effects for developing members of changes in exchange rates by the main industrial members.[12] Moreover, with a prescience that Governors for industrial members did not express—or did not dare to express for fear of upsetting exchange markets—some of the remarks of the Governors for developing members suggested a serious concern about the viability of the exchange rates established at the Smithsonian Institution.

---

[12]Statements by the Governor of the Fund for Zaïre, the Governor of the World Bank for Malawi, the Governor of the Fund and the World Bank for Zambia, the Governor of the Fund for Indonesia, the Governor of the Fund and the World Bank for Jamaica, and the Governor of the World Bank for Egypt, *Summary Proceedings, 1972,* pp. 31, 88, 98–99, 140, 192, and 196–97.

CHAPTER

3

Floating of the Pound Sterling

STERLING HAD BEEN IN TROUBLE several times after World War II but it had always rebounded, often dramatically. It is not surprising, therefore, that monetary authorities viewed the floating of the pound sterling in June 1972 as only a temporary aberration from the system of par values that they were trying to put back together.

ECONOMIC SITUATION OF THE UNITED KINGDOM PRIOR TO JUNE 1972

After the devaluation of the pound sterling in November 1967, it took about two years for the balance of payments position of the United Kingdom to show any notable improvement. In the meantime, the stand-by arrangement for $1.4 billion that the Fund approved for the United Kingdom at the time of the devaluation was fully drawn and, in June 1969, the Fund approved another stand-by arrangement for $1 billion.[1] By September 1969, the U.K. balance of payments situation was clearly turning around. A large deficit was converted into a large surplus, and in 1970 the United Kingdom achieved a surplus on current account equivalent to $1.9 billion, the largest it had ever experienced. This improvement on current account induced the return of short-term capital, so that in 1970 the United Kingdom had an overall payments surplus of $3.1 billion. The U.K. authorities began to repay the short-term and medium-term external debts incurred since 1964 in their efforts to bolster sterling.

In 1971 the United Kingdom, like several other industrial countries, developed a huge payments surplus as a counterpart to the suddenly swollen deficit of the United States. The U.K. current account surplus rose to $2.8 billion and the overall payments surplus to $6.5 billion, more than twice the surpluses of 1970, already the

---

[1] *History, 1966–71*, Vol. I, pp. 338–51 and 431–37.

45

largest on record. In fact, the current account and overall surpluses of the United Kingdom in 1971 were the largest of any country except Japan. The U.K. authorities continued to repay their external debts, and in the course of 1971 repurchased the sterling that the Fund held as a result of the U.K. drawings under the 1967 stand-by arrangement.

Even after these debt repayments, the official net reserves of the United Kingdom by the end of 1971 totaled over SDR 5 billion, a remarkable increase over the position at the end of March 1969, when official liquid liabilities exceeded gross reserves for a net negative reserve position of SDR 5 billion. The United Kingdom's reserves were, however, still relatively low—equivalent to only two and a half months' worth of imports at their 1971 level—but it was evident that sterling had come through the currency crises of 1971 in better shape than it had been in for many years.

What was regarded by the U.K. authorities at the time of the realignment of currencies in December 1971 as a strong balance of payments and reserve position prompted them to leave the par value of the pound sterling in terms of gold unchanged, a decision which the Fund staff considered justified. A new middle rate between the pound sterling and the U.S. dollar was set at £1 = $2.6057, compared with the former rate of £1 = $2.40, an appreciation in terms of the dollar of 8.57 percent. But the pound sterling was effectively appreciated very little, at most 1 percent, against a weighted average of the currencies of all the United Kingdom's trading partners. The U.K. authorities availed themselves of the new wider margins of up to 2.25 percent permissible under the Fund's temporary regime of central rates, giving a buying rate of $2.6643 and a selling rate of $2.5471 per pound sterling.

The favorable external position also augured well for the entry of the United Kingdom into the European Communities. Negotiations for entry into the Communities had been going on since 1961, when the U.K. Government submitted the first of three applications for admission. After more than ten years, these negotiations were successfully completed and the United Kingdom was scheduled to become a full member on January 1, 1973.

As part of the procedure for the Fund's 1972 Article VIII consultation with the United Kingdom, a staff team went to London in the first week of May 1972 for discussions with the U.K. authorities. This mission arrived within a day or so after the U.K. repurchase in April, discussed in Chapter 2. This repurchase had freed the United Kingdom of all outstanding short-term and medium-term external debts for the first time since 1964.

The consultation held at the Executive Board level in July revealed that economic conditions in the United Kingdom were not so favorable as developments in the U.K. balance of payments and reserve positions in 1970 and 1971 and the repayment of all short-term and medium-term external debts suggested. Underlying the good external performance of the United Kingdom was increasing unemployment of manpower and industrial resources and a further, and by no means wholly welcome, increase in export prices following improvements in the U.K. terms of trade that had already taken place. After a comparatively rapid rate of increase in 1968, the rate of increase in domestic output declined sharply in 1969 and, except for a brief period in 1971, subsequently remained well below the country's productive potential. The expansion in output that did occur had been successfully channeled into improving the balance of payments on current account. At the start of 1972, unemployment, which had been rising steadily for some time, exceeded one million workers, a sensitive figure politically, since this was the first time the number of unemployed in the United Kingdom had reached that figure since 1947. Also, prices were rising fairly rapidly. Specific figures tell the story. Gross national product in real terms rose by only 1.6 percent in 1971, compared with an annual average of 2.8 percent in the 1960s, while the general price level rose by 9 percent, higher than the 7 percent rise in 1970, and more than twice the annual average rise of 4 percent during the 1960s.

Slack domestic demand in 1970 and 1971 had kept imports low, although the Fund staff estimated that even at fuller employment and larger demand, the United Kingdom would still have had a large current account surplus in 1971. The U.K. external position was helped in the short run also by favorable terms of trade and a rapid rise in export prices. But this had its worrisome aspects. Export prices had risen partly because of attempts by entrepreneurs to restore profit margins on their exports. Deliberate increases in export prices, coupled with a high rate of domestic inflation, threatened in the long run to impair the competitiveness of U.K. exports.

In the Fund staff's view, there was no simple explanation for the unexpected slow growth in real output in the United Kingdom after 1968. It appeared that the slowdown resulted largely from the tight monetary and fiscal policies pursued in 1968 and 1969 to improve the balance of payments after the 1967 devaluation. U.K. authorities and officials in the Fund, who under the terms of the 1969 stand-by arrangement kept the U.K. economy under close review, were gratified by the upturn in the U.K. balance of payments that began toward the end of 1969. But they had to face the possibility that the tight macroeconomic policies of 1968 and 1969 that had successfully reversed the external accounts may have unduly depressed the domestic economy for too long or, alternatively, the likelihood that because of the long time lag before the effects of economic policies were felt, policies to curtail domestic expansion should have been introduced several years earlier. Many Executive Directors as well as the staff were inclined to believe that the U.K. policies of 1968 and 1969 had been both "too much" and "too late."

Stimulative Policies in 1972

To stimulate the sluggish domestic economy, at the beginning of 1972 the U.K. authorities, under the Government of Prime Minister Edward Heath, again switched course, undertaking macroeconomic policies that were unequivocally reflationary. The 1972–73 budget was a major exercise in demand management. Aimed at stimulating both consumption and investment, it contained tax concessions and increases in public expenditures. Monetary policy, too, was to be eased so as to augment the money supply by amounts that were high by the standards of previous years. At the same time, because of concern that wage settlements were a major cause of the cost-price spiral, the U.K. authorities hoped also to achieve a progressive de-escalation in the level of wage settlements.

The U.K. authorities wanted especially to stimulate more corporate investment. They wanted to reassure industry that a period of sustained expansion was now feasible, given, among other factors, the strength of the current account of the balance of payments and the improved reserve position. Chancellor of the Exchequer Anthony Barber, presenting the budget to Parliament in 1972, stated explicitly that the U.K. authorities placed domestic employment ahead of concern about the balance of payments or the external value of the pound sterling. In essence, Mr. Barber stated that the lesson of the international balance of payments upsets of the last few years was that it was neither necessary nor desirable to distort domestic economies to an unacceptable extent in order to maintain unrealistic exchange rates, whether they were too high or too low. He emphasized that in the modern world he certainly did not believe that there was any need for the United Kingdom, or any other country, to be frustrated in its determination to sustain sound economic growth and to reduce unemployment.

These words proved to be controversial. Some welcomed his words, likening them to John Maynard Keynes's explanation to the House of Lords in May 1944 that under the new Bretton Woods system the rate for the pound sterling could be determined by internal economic circumstances and not necessarily by external conditions. These observers—noting how exchange rates eventually became rigid in the 1950s and 1960s under the par value system—commented, some of them sarcastically, that U.K. authorities had taken more than 25 years to rediscover that under the par value system they did not have to regard their exchange rate as fixed at the expense of domestic employment. Others criticized Mr. Barber's remarks, believing that his speech contributed to the subsequent large outflow of short-term capital. In the view of these critics, Mr. Barber's remarks suggested that, although re-emerging cost and price inflation and an expected simultaneous rise in domestic demand adversely affected the U.K. external position, the U.K. authorities would not take strong measures to defend the exchange rate.

In its appraisal of the U.K. economy following discussions in London in May 1972, the Fund staff was moderately optimistic that growth would accelerate in 1972 and that a current account surplus in the balance of payments, which was important to enable the U.K. authorities to accumulate further reserves, could also be achieved. Noting, however, that the trade account for the first few months of 1972 had already deteriorated considerably, the staff was concerned about possible adverse effects of three developments. First, industrial unrest was increasing as workers were reacting with greater militancy to policy restraints on their living standards. The coal miners, for example, had been on strike throughout January and February. Second, a new outburst of cost-price inflation was possible and if inflation resumed at a high rate, economic growth and the balance of payments surplus would suffer. Third, foreign markets were manifesting a growing resistance to rapidly rising prices of U.K. exports, and this could inhibit the recovery of U.K. exports when world trade in manufactures revived.

During the Article VIII consultation in July 1972, the Executive Directors pointed out that the problems of the domestic economy of the United Kingdom were the same as those plaguing nearly all industrial countries. Prices, and particularly wages, were rising at a fast pace. Meanwhile unemployment and unused resources were at the highest levels of the postwar period, as both consumption and private investment lagged. The U.K. authorities were in the paradoxical position of trying to achieve economic recovery without reactivating cost-push forces. They were pioneering the solution of the problem of the coexistence of unemployment and inflation, a problem which raised difficult social-economic issues. To hold costs in check meant dealing with strong trade unions, urging acceptance of wage increases less than past increases in the cost of living, thereby lowering workers' real incomes, and facing the prospect of labor unrest. To hold prices in check involved restraining business profits and possibly depressing corporate investment, employment, and ultimately productivity.

In their pursuit of expansionary fiscal policies and controls on wage and price increases, the U.K. authorities, regarded by many Fund officials as having a relatively keen understanding of economic problems, seemed convinced that wage demands were more a cause of the rise in domestic prices than were increases in domestic money supply. The management and staff and several Executive Directors therefore looked to the policies of the United Kingdom for enlightenment on the causes of inflation and on the best methods to deal with the problem of its coexistence with unemployment. After the consultation, the Fund staff studied, for example, whether in an advanced industrial economy, one cause of inflation, such as expansion of the money supply, could be emphasized to the exclusion of other causes, such as demands for higher wages. They also studied the interaction between the private and public sectors during the inflationary process. Staff who emphasized the expansion of money supply as a cause of inflation examined the effect on monetary expansion of attempts by workers to push wages higher in real terms, especially in the context of enlarged government spending to maintain employment.

CRISIS OF JUNE 1972

Meanwhile, between the staff's discussions in London in May and the Executive Board consultation in July, there occurred another of the several sterling crises familiar since World War II. On Friday, June 16, very heavy flows of short-term capital started to leave the United Kingdom, driving sterling below the mid-rate of $2.6057 per pound. In line with the new EC arrangements to maintain margins of no more than 2.25 percent between the currencies of EC member states (arrangements to which the United Kingdom, although not yet a member of the Community, had subscribed from May 1), the weakness of the pound sterling triggered concerted intervention by the Bank of England and by the central banks of the EC countries in the exchange markets in London. The Bank of England started to sell the strongest currencies of the EC countries against swap credits obtained from the central banks of those countries, while the central banks of these countries started to buy pounds sterling in their markets and to sell these purchases forward to the Bank of England. The agreement between the participating European central banks provided that the claims acquired by the EC countries on the United Kingdom would be settled through the transfer of reserves from the United Kingdom to those countries by the end of July.

Thursday, June 22, witnessed the biggest outflow of short-term capital in a single day in the history of the United Kingdom. By the end of the day, purchases of pounds sterling financed by the central banks of Belgium, France, the Federal Republic of Germany, the Netherlands, and Norway since the previous Friday totaled £1 billion (SDR 2.4 billion), about one third of the United Kingdom's net reserves. Exchange markets in London, in other Western European countries, and in Japan were closed. The U.K. authorities decided to let the rate for sterling float and on Friday, June 23, sent to Mr. Schweitzer the standard communication used by members introducing floating rates. They informed the Fund that for the time being the market rate for the pound sterling would not necessarily be confined within announced limits either around the U.S. dollar or around the currencies of the EC countries, but that the Government intended to return, as soon as conditions permitted, to the maintenance of normal Fund margins around parity and to participation in the narrow margins arrangements of the EC.

As a further precaution against fresh outflows of capital, exchange controls on capital transactions were intensified. Specifically, exchange control was introduced between the United Kingdom and the countries of the sterling area other than the Republic of Ireland (the Republic of Ireland took parallel action) and controls were imposed on outflows of resident capital from the United Kingdom to other Overseas Sterling Area countries, including Australia, Ghana, Iceland, India, Kenya, Pakistan, Singapore, and Sri Lanka. Current payments to these countries, however, were not to be restricted. Following these measures, the world's exchange markets were reopened within a week.

Reaction in the Fund

Reaction among officials in the Fund to the sudden float of the pound sterling was tempered by the expectation that the float was to be temporary, as were most existing exchange arrangements, pending reform of the international monetary system. In speeches to Parliament, Mr. Heath and Mr. Barber emphasized the temporary nature of the float. This was further underscored by the planned entry of the United Kingdom into the European Communities on January 1, 1973. To take up its obligations as a member of the European Economic Community, the U.K. authorities would have to return to a par value or at least to a central rate by the end of 1972. Fund officials also considered that the use of exchange controls preventing further outflow of capital from the United Kingdom would limit the duration of the float.

In these circumstances, the staff in its appraisal and the Executive Board in its deliberations and decision accepted the U.K. action as the only sensible response when the underlying balance of payments problem did not call for a straight devaluation. The Executive Board decision was couched in the customary format used when floating rates were introduced. The Fund noted the circumstances in which floating was introduced, welcomed the intention of the authorities of the member concerned to collaborate with the Fund and to resume the observance of margins around parity as soon as circumstances permitted, and called for close consultation with the Fund. Like the decisions taken when the deutsche mark and the Netherlands guilder were floated in May 1971, the decision on the floating of the pound sterling went further than pre-1971 decisions on floating rates by specifically directing the Managing Director to initiate consultations.

Despite the similarity of the Executive Board decision on the pound sterling to the decisions taken when other currencies were floated, the tone of the preceding discussion in the Executive Board was different, especially considering that the currency involved was one of the two national currencies customarily used by other members as reserves. Executive Directors were much less concerned with the implications for the system of par values of the floating of the pound sterling than they had been when Canada in May 1970 and the Federal Republic of Germany in September 1969 and May 1971 introduced floating rates. While they acknowledged that a floating rate for the pound sterling added to the disorder and illegality already prevailing in the international monetary system, several Executive Directors went so far as to commend the U.K. authorities for their quick response to the latest crisis.

The Executive Directors were also interested in the lessons that might be drawn from the U.K. experience for a reformed international monetary system. It was evident that a reformed system should be able to reduce, in one way or another, the disturbing effects on exchange rates of short-term capital flows. An adequate system should permit adjustments in the exchange rates of all currencies, including reserve currencies, such as the pound sterling and the U.S. dollar. Some adjustments in exchange rates might require a temporary use of floating rates. In this respect, the floating of the pound sterling might be more relevant in the future to the experiences of other countries with floating rates than the previous floats of the deutsche mark had been, since the pound sterling was likely to be devalued in exchange markets, the more common situation, while the previous floats of the deutsche mark had been preludes to revaluation.

Another lesson to be learned from the floating of sterling was that a reformed system should not be based on reserve currencies, because changes in the exchange rates of reserve currencies transmitted shocks to other countries. P.S.N. Prasad (India) called attention to the disadvantages for developing members of an international monetary system that relied on national currencies for reserves. He pointed out, graphically, that on 12 of the 14 occasions on which India had changed its exchange rate since 1918, India, as a member of the sterling area, was responding to changes in the rate for the pound sterling rather than to conditions within India.

All in all, in readily agreeing to a floating rate for a reserve currency, the Fund had come a long way in accepting floating exchange rates in the 25 years since 1948 when Mexico, the first member of the Fund to do so, suspended its par value and introduced a floating rate. At that time, the management and staff and the Executive Directors had been concerned almost entirely with the implication for the par value system and for the Fund's authority over exchange rates if the Fund permitted a member to violate the Articles of Agreement.[2] Nonetheless, as of mid-1972 floating rates were still considered the exception, and the Fund took seriously the newly emerging obligation of members with floating rates to hold special consultations with the Fund on their exchange rate policies.

CONTINUATION OF THE FLOATING RATE

To implement the Executive Board decision of June 1972 calling for special consultations between the United Kingdom and the Fund, the Managing Director met with the Chancellor of the Exchequer and a staff team held discussions with other U.K. officials in Washington during the Annual Meeting in September 1972. Sterling meanwhile had declined to $2.44–2.45, a depreciation of about 6 percent from the par value. In October it was to drop to $2.34, thereby falling through the $2.40 level which the market had hitherto considered as some kind of floor.

The Fund staff believed that the U.K. authorities could end the floating rate and set a new par value. Depreciation had improved the U.K. competitive position, higher interest rates in the United Kingdom and exchange controls had strengthened the capital account of the balance of payments, and the reserve position had stabilized. Capital outflow, the reason for introducing the float, had ceased. The staff also believed that terminating the floating rate early would help preserve the currency realignment of the Smithsonian agreement. If the pound sterling should continue to float and was to depreciate significantly before the completion of the balance of payments adjustments that the currency realignment was intended to produce, other changes in exchange rates and further disorder in exchange markets might be precipitated. Moreover, the depreciation of sterling was causing problems for countries that pegged their exchange rates to sterling. The staff also favored repegging the pound sterling rate because, after January 1, 1973, when the United Kingdom entered the European Economic Community, there would be no obvious external pressure on the U.K. authorities to end the float. The temporary float might therefore be extended indefinitely.

---

[2]*History, 1945–65,* Vol. I, pp. 227–28 and Vol. II, pp. 153–54.

The U.K. authorities, on the other hand, considered it premature to repeg a rate which had recently been depreciating in exchange markets. But more significantly, they were much more worried than they had been at the time of the suspension of the par value in June that the rate of domestic inflation in the next year could exceed that of other industrial countries and could start a downward slide of the rates for the pound sterling in exchange markets. Consequently, any par value established at this time might not be sustained for long. Instead of planning for a new par value, the U.K. authorities now emphasized a concerted attack on domestic inflation. Following the failure of tripartite negotiations between the U.K. Government, the Trades Union Congress, and the Confederation of British Industry on voluntary restraints on prices and incomes, the Government undertook a special counter-inflation program, which came into effect in November 1972. Under the program, the Government radically changed its policy by introducing a temporary "standstill" on wage and price increases, to be followed in April 1973 by a second stage of stringent income and price controls.

Following these discussions at the management and staff level, a special consultation with the U.K. authorities on their exchange rate policy was held in the Executive Board in November 1972. This was one of the first special consultations, held between the customary annual consultations, with members that had floating exchange rates. There had also been one with Canada in 1972. These special consultations with the United Kingdom and Canada were prototypes for a regular program of special consultations on exchange rate policies that the Fund was to inaugurate in November 1973.

In the special consultation with the United Kingdom in November 1972, the Executive Directors first expressed their pleasure with the cooperation of the U.K. authorities with the Fund in this new type of consultation. In addition, they were impressed with the comprehensive anti-inflationary program that the U.K. authorities were undertaking. But they did not want to urge the U.K. authorities as yet to end the floating rate. They were mainly concerned that if a new par value for the pound sterling collapsed, all the exchange rates of the Smithsonian agreement would be jeopardized. For these reasons they took a decision welcoming the strong determination of the U.K. authorities to diminish the rate of inflation and to re-establish the conditions for a new par value and indicating that "the Fund considers that such action should be taken at the earliest possible time." The Managing Director was still to initiate consultations.

One month later, on December 15, Peter J. Bull (United Kingdom) informed the Executive Directors that the Chancellor of the Exchequer had that morning announced in the House of Commons the Government's decision not to return for the time being to the maintenance of margins around a fixed parity for the pound sterling. The spot rate meanwhile remained at about $2.35 per pound sterling. By the end of 1972, the pound sterling had depreciated from the level of June 1972 by approximately the same magnitude—about 10 percent on a trade-weighted basis—as the 1967 devaluation had achieved.

RELATED ACTIONS BY OTHER COUNTRIES

A change in the value of the pound sterling has for centuries been an unusually important event in international monetary history. In recent times, the devaluations of sterling in 1949 and 1967 had worldwide repercussions. Indeed, devaluation of sterling in the late 1940s was regarded as the main precondition for achieving the devaluation of other Western European currencies that many experts were then advocating. And when sterling *was* devalued, from $4.03 to $2.80 in September 1949, not only did devaluations of most other European currencies and of the Canadian dollar immediately follow, but the currencies of virtually all members of the sterling area were adjusted to conform to the new rate for the pound. At the time, moreover, the sterling area was extensive, encompassing countries in four continents, and was bound closely together by formal and legal arrangements. Currencies of the members were fixed in relation to the pound sterling and sterling was the currency in which their trade and financial transactions were conducted, in which they intervened in exchange markets to keep their exchange rates stable, and in which they kept their official reserves. Other countries not formally in the sterling area, including Denmark, Norway, Portugal, and Spain, also maintained close trade and financial links with the United Kingdom so that their currencies also had to be adjusted.[3]

In November 1967, more than 18 years after the devaluation of September 1949, when the pound was devalued for the second time since World War II, sterling was a less used currency and the sterling area was a less closely bound group than it had been even 10 years earlier. The dollar had become the principal currency in international finance, as described in Chapter 4. The achievement of external convertibility of the pound sterling in 1958 and the subsequent reduction and virtual elimination of restrictions on both current transactions and capital movements had brought about a loosening of the regulations applied within the sterling area against other areas. All countries, both inside and outside the sterling area, had increased their trade and investment on a worldwide basis. As a result, they were less dependent on markets in the United Kingdom and the rest of the Commonwealth or on capital from the United Kingdom. In addition, with the phenomenal growth of the economies of the Western European nations and of Japan, there had been a decline in the relative economic position of the United Kingdom. Therefore in 1967, when sterling was again devalued, this time from $2.80 to $2.40, or a little less than 15 percent, Fund officials expected fewer devaluations than had occurred following the first devaluation in September 1949. Nonetheless, the Managing Director made

---

[3]The devaluations of 1949 are described in *History, 1945–65*, Vol. I, pp. 234–41 and Vol. II, pp. 96–100. An impression of the size, extent, and diversity of the countries of the sterling area at the end of World War II can be found in Judd Polk, *Sterling: Its Meaning in World Finance* (published for the Council on Foreign Relations, New York: Harper and Brothers, 1956). Additional information on the workings of the sterling area can be found in Philip W. Bell, *The Sterling Area in the Postwar World: Internal Mechanism and Cohesion, 1946–1952* (Oxford: Clarendon Press, 1956). Both Bell (pp. 435–64) and Polk (pp. 270–81) also provide a long bibliography of references to other works on the sterling area.

deliberate efforts to head off potential devaluations. It was critical for exchange rate stability and for the effectiveness of the devaluation of sterling that the U.S. dollar, the French franc, and other Western European currencies not be devalued. In the end, only 14 members with unusually close trade and investment relations with the United Kingdom devalued at this time: Cyprus, Denmark, The Gambia, Guyana, Iceland, Ireland, Israel, Jamaica, Malawi, New Zealand, Sierra Leone, Spain, Sri Lanka, and Trinidad and Tobago. The U.K. Government also effected devaluations on behalf of several nonmetropolitan territories.[4]

By June 1972, when the floating of the pound was announced, sterling area connections had become weaker still. As part of the negotiations for the United Kingdom's entry into the EC, the U.K. authorities had in 1971 eased controls over direct investment outside the sterling area and had begun to take measures to facilitate an orderly and gradual rundown of officially held balances of sterling, held mainly by the central banks of other members of the sterling area. Furthermore, by 1972 many members of the sterling area no longer pegged their currencies to sterling; instead many now pegged their currencies to the dollar. Not only had several countries that were relatively advanced economically, such as Australia, Iceland, and New Zealand, made this switch, but so had a number of developing countries, including Ghana, Jordan, Kenya, Nigeria, Pakistan, Tanzania, Uganda, Western Samoa, and Zambia. In June 1972, when the pound sterling was floated, six more developing countries of the sterling area, Cyprus, Iraq, Kuwait, Malaysia, Oman, and Singapore, joined the switch to pegging to the dollar instead of to sterling.

Although it no longer held the dominant position it had in 1945, sterling was in 1972 nonetheless still widely used as a reserve currency and as a vehicle currency to pay for international transactions. London was still one of the world's principal financial centers. Consequently, the decision of the U.K. authorities to float the pound touched off corresponding action by 18 other Fund members. Seventeen members decided to float their currencies along with sterling: Bangladesh, Barbados, Botswana, Fiji, The Gambia, Guyana, India, Ireland, Jamaica, Lesotho, Malawi, Mauritius, Sierra Leone, South Africa, Sri Lanka, Swaziland, and Trinidad and Tobago.[5] Malta decided to allow its currency to float independently. Almost all these members had previously maintained effective par values or central rates. Sri Lanka, after having pegged to the U.S. dollar since the end of 1971, returned to pegging to sterling. The currencies of a number of what were at the time nonmetropolitan territories, including Antigua, Dominica, Grenada, Montserrat, St. Christopher-Nevis-Anguilla, St. Lucia, St. Vincent, British Honduras, the Cayman Islands, the Falkland Islands, and Gibraltar, also floated along with sterling. The Fund did not resist these decisions to float.

---

[4]See *History, 1966–71*, Vol. I, pp. 437–40. A recent detailed treatment of the devaluations of sterling of 1931, 1949, and 1967 can be found in Alec Cairncross and Barry Eichengreen, *Sterling in Decline* (Oxford: Basil Blackwell, 1983).

[5]At the time that Bangladesh decided to float the rupee along with the pound sterling, it was not yet a member of the Fund. It became a member two months later, on August 17, 1972.

OTHER CHANGES IN EXCHANGE RATES IN LATE 1972

The continued floating of sterling notwithstanding, there was a trend in late 1972 toward the resumption of effective par values. Some members were only tidying up after the Smithsonian agreement and were not making substantive changes in the effective rates for their currencies. Others were setting new effective par values. Burundi, Iran, Jamaica, and to some extent South Africa were in the first category. Effective November 2, 1972, Burundi changed its par value, abolishing the central rate of FBu 87.50 = US$1, but retaining the same relationship with the dollar of FBu 87.50 per dollar. In terms of gold, the par value was changed from 0.0101562 to 0.00935443 gram of fine gold per Burundi franc, which corresponded to 95.000 Burundi francs per SDR. Effective September 6, 1972, Iran converted into a par value the central rate that it had established after the Smithsonian agreement. These actions did not, however, alter the rate for the Iranian rial of Rls 75.75 = US$1, which had prevailed since 1955. In terms of gold, the par value for the Iranian rial was changed from 0.0117316 to 0.0108055 gram of fine gold per rial, which corresponded to 82.2425 rials per SDR.

Jamaica also set a new par value for the Jamaica dollar, effective January 17, 1973. The par value was changed from 1.06641 grams to 0.900364 gram of fine gold per Jamaica dollar, corresponding to J$0.987013 = SDR 1. This rate gave a relationship with the U.S. dollar of J$1 = US$1.10; the fixed relationship with sterling of J$1 = £ 0.50 was terminated, and the Jamaica dollar ceased to float.

Effective October 24, 1972, the South African rand ceased to float along with sterling, and a new par value was set. As South Africa produced more than two thirds of the Western world's gold, its authorities emphasized their firm belief in the principle of par values fixed in terms of gold. After the 1971 currency realignment, South Africa was among those members that changed their par values in terms of gold. South Africa altered its par value from 1.24414 to 1.09135 grams of fine gold, thereby depreciating the rand against the U.S. dollar by 4.76 percent, from R 1 = US$1.40 to R 1 = US$1.33333. The par value set in October 1972 was established at 1.04550 grams of fine gold per South African rand, corresponding to R 1 = SDR 1.17648, equivalent to R 1 = US$1.27732. This represented a change in par value from 28.5000 to 29.7500 rand per fine ounce of gold, a devaluation of 4.202 percent from the par value set in December 1971. The same changes in par values were made by Botswana, Lesotho, and Swaziland, whose currency was also the South African rand.

The par value changes by Australia, Bolivia, and Iceland in the last few months of 1972 represented substantive changes in their exchange rates. In December 1971, the Australian Government had decided, as a result of a hard-fought compromise between parties in the coalition government concerning the rate for the Australian dollar, to retain the previous par value of the Australian dollar in terms of gold. This decision implied an 8.57 percent appreciation against the U.S. dollar; the rate vis-à-vis the U.S. dollar went from $A 1 = US$1.12 to $A 1 = US$1.21600. Australia, which had been in overall balance of payments surplus since 1967, experienced an even larger surplus in 1971 and 1972. The rate of capital inflow had gradually more than doubled, and by 1972 even the current account, which traditionally showed substantial deficits, had swung into surplus. By the last few months of 1972, Australia's reserves had grown to the equivalent of about 120 percent of its annual imports, a ratio between reserves and imports unheard of in Australia, and among the highest such ratios of the countries of the OECD, surpassing even that of Japan. Policies to deal with capital inflows had been a difficult political issue in Australia, but in September 1972 several measures were taken to reduce these inflows, a shift from the traditional Australian policy of welcoming virtually all foreign capital. Following elections in December 1972, Australia proposed a change in its par value, effective December 22, 1972, revaluing the Australian dollar from 0.995310 gram of fine gold per Australian dollar to 1.04360 grams. The new par value corresponded to 0.851544 Australian dollar per SDR, and to $A 1 = US$1.2750, an appreciation vis-à-vis the U.S. dollar of 4.85 percent. The Fund concurred in the change.

Bolivia had established a par value for the boliviano in 1953 but no transactions had taken place at that rate for nearly 20 years. Instead, all exchange transactions had taken place in a single free exchange market. The rate in that market had remained stable since January 1959, and in January 1963 the boliviano was replaced by the Bolivian peso at a rate of Bs 1,000 = $b 1.00. The exchange rates used by the Central Bank on December 31, 1971 were $b 11.875 buying and $b 11.885 selling per US$1. A par value for the Bolivian peso was established, effective October 31, 1972. The new par value (set in terms of gold at 0.0409256 gram of fine gold per Bolivian peso, corresponding to 21.7143 Bolivian pesos per SDR) was equivalent to $b 20 = US$1. The establishment of the par value thus involved a considerable depreciation of the Bolivian peso from the previous rate.

Iceland had changed its par value more times than any other Fund member. After setting an initial par value of I Kr 6.49 per US$1 in December 1946, Iceland changed its par value in 1949, in 1950, in 1960, in 1961, in 1967, and in November 1968, when it set a par value of I Kr 88 per US$1.[6] These changes had devalued the króna by nearly 93 percent. In December 1971, Iceland kept the rate of I Kr 88 per US$1 as a central rate. As we have seen in Chapter 2, after the United States set a new par value in May 1972, Iceland did likewise, changing its par value to 0.00930128 gram of fine gold (I Kr 95.5429 per SDR 1) equivalent to I Kr 88 = US$1. This was a devaluation of 7.89 percent from the par value expressed in terms of gold, the same as that proposed for the U.S. dollar. Nevertheless, Iceland proposed yet another change, effective December 19, 1972. The Icelandic króna was to be equal to 0.00830471 gram of fine gold, a devaluation of 10.7 percent in terms of gold. This par value corresponded to 107.008 Icelandic krónur per SDR 1, equivalent to I Kr 98.56 = US$1.

The Fund concurred in the change for the same reasons that it had concurred in the previous changes in Iceland's par values. Iceland's economy was based almost totally on the fishing industry. Because of the traditional income-sharing arrange-

---

[6]*History, 1945–65*, Vol. II, pp. 117–18, and *History, 1966–71*, Vol. I, pp. 438–39 and 473–74.

ments in Iceland, higher earnings from fish exports entailed a rise in the incomes of fishermen. A rise in fishermen's incomes quickly induced wage increases in other sectors of the economy that had much lower productivity than fishing but were protected by a high tariff. The resulting upward pressure on domestic prices then led to further wage increases for the shore workers whose wages were tied to the cost of living index. The spiral again continued upward as the price paid for fish by the domestic fish-processing industry rose. Such developments, as well as the volatility of world prices for fish and natural fluctuations in the availability of fish, had been at the root of the recurrent problems of external and internal stability in Iceland for over two decades.

EXCHANGE RATES AT THE END OF 1972

Because developments starting in January 1973 led to widespread floating, it is instructive to note here the situation of exchange rates as 1972 ended. By the end of 1972, despite the floating rates of Canada, the United Kingdom, and some developing members that belonged to the sterling area, including India, the prospects for fixed exchange rates seemed by no means dim. The United States had a new par value, although it did not itself undertake to maintain rates for the dollar by interventions in exchange markets. France also had an effective par value. Austria, Belgium, Denmark, the Federal Republic of Germany, Italy, Japan, Luxembourg, the Netherlands, Norway, and Sweden had central rates. These members were maintaining exchange rates for their currencies within agreed margins; for some currencies the wider margins permitted under the Fund's temporary regime of central rates and wider margins applied, while for others the narrow margins arrangements of the EC applied. Several more developed primary producing members, including Australia, Iceland, New Zealand, and Spain, had par values or central rates. Many developing members, including those belonging to the French franc area and those which had fixed their exchange rates in relation to the dollar, such as Jamaica, Kenya, Malaysia, Nigeria, Tanzania, Uganda, and Zambia, also maintained par values or stable exchange rates. Some developing members, such as Bolivia, were even proposing new effective par values after years of not having par values.

The world's monetary authorities faced the future with an unusual mixture of hope and uneasiness. Hope that the Smithsonian exchange rates might hold until the reform of the system was completed, expected by the middle of 1974, stemmed primarily from the improving U.S. domestic economy, the recovery of output in many industrial countries, the reduction during 1972 of speculative capital movements, and from the gradual attainment in exchange markets in the latter part of 1972 of stable rates for the dollar.

Yet there was also considerable uneasiness about the prospects for stability and order in the international monetary system. Exchange crises could erupt suddenly, as they had several times in the previous few years. Exchange rates for the dollar had been under serious pressure in 1972, and prices for gold in private markets had fluctuated widely. The pound sterling had been forced to float and continued to do so. Imbalances in the current accounts of the major industrial countries were even greater in 1972 than in 1971. Most notably the current account deficit of the United States, at $6 billion, was substantially larger than it had been in 1971, and as in 1971 there were again sizable increases in the current account surpluses of several continental European countries, including the Federal Republic of Germany, and in the current account surplus of Japan. The improvement in the U.S. overall payments position resulted entirely from reductions in outflows of short-term capital. The deficit on basic balance—the current account plus net long-term capital—of about $9 billion was still at the level of 1971. Finally, negotiations for a reformed system had gotten off to a slow start.

In these circumstances, it was hard to predict the course of events.

Onset of Widespread Floating

*T*HE CURRENCY DISTURBANCES during the first three months of 1973 that led to the adoption of widespread floating started in Italy when pressure on the lira increased. Capital movements, mainly in the form of "leads and lags," that had begun to be troublesome in the second half of 1972 became so large in January 1973 that the Bank of Italy had to intervene heavily in the market to support the lira.[1] To stem capital outflows and the loss of reserves involved in this intervention, the Italian authorities announced, on Saturday, January 20, when exchange markets were closed, the introduction of a dual exchange market to take effect on Monday, January 22. One market, in which exchange rates were to be maintained within permitted margins, was designated for trade, tourism, and other transactions on current account. Another market, in which exchange rates were to fluctuate freely, was set up for capital transfers. There thus emerged the "commercial lira" and the "financial" or "capital lira."

BACKGROUND TO THE PRESSURE ON THE ITALIAN LIRA

The economic problems in Italy which gave rise to intensified capital flight from the lira in the second half of 1972 and especially in January 1973 had begun late in 1969. In fact, the problems could in some respects be seen as a sequel of events going back to 1963, a turning point in Italy's economic history after World War II. Throughout the 1950s and the early 1960s, Italy experienced rapid economic growth, and the authorities were highly successful in increasing domestic efficiency and

---

[1]Leads are prepayments of obligations before the normal date of payments; lags are the postponement of payments of obligations beyond the normal date of payments. Under fixed exchange rates, prepayments and postponements of payments of international obligations, services, and capital assets were often induced by anticipations of impending changes in rates, thus constituting speculative capital movements. Because of the size of international financial payments, such leads and lags in effecting payments can often be of enormous magnitude. A description of leads and lags and an assessment of their importance in foreign exchange markets can be found in Paul Einzig, "What Are Leads and Lags?" in Banca Nazionale del Lavoro, *Quarterly Review* (Rome), Vol. 20 (December 1967), pp. 376–89 and in his *Leads and Lags: The Main Cause of Devaluation* (London: Macmillan; New York: St. Martin's Press, 1968).

international competitiveness, their main policy objectives. Growth was led by exports, a high level of investment was achieved, employment rose rapidly, and prices were stable. The country became an exporter of automobiles and of small industrial and mechanical products, such as typewriters, and a world leader in shoes and other leather goods, in textiles, and in the fashion industry. Indeed, Italy experienced one of the fastest rates of export growth in the world and continued through the 1960s to be second only to Japan among industrial countries in the rapidity with which it increased its share of world export markets. Economists and public officials spoke of the "Italian miracle."

The maintenance of a fixed exchange rate was found conducive to the attainment of the main policy objectives. Financial policies were cautious and problems of income distribution were deliberately accorded lower priority than economic growth.

In 1963, this postwar boom came to an end. A series of strikes resulted in a sharp rise in wages, reduced profit margins, and lowered investment. In addition, because of a sudden balance of payments deficit, the Bank of Italy tightened credit policies, causing a credit squeeze. These events brought about recession in 1963–64. The Italian economy never again resumed the same rapid rate of growth. Although the real rate of growth remained relatively high, the economy consistently operated below capacity. Moreover, domestic demand rose less than output, and large current account surpluses emerged from 1964 onward, just when there was an urgent need for a higher level of domestic investment.

After 1969, however, Italy's problems became severe. From 1969 to 1971 the country suffered its deepest and most protracted recession since the end of the war. The recession of 1969–71, like that of 1963–64, was brought about by a wave of strikes, which led to large increases in wages and to lower investment. From then on social unrest, recurrent strikes, and frequent government turnovers plagued the country. These developments led to reduced profit margins, a sharp decline in the propensity to invest, and a consequent rise in unemployment. In addition, the growth of private consumption gradually leveled off as continuing economic uncertainty and sagging employment induced consumers to spend more cautiously. Also, price increases accelerated.

It was difficult for the authorities to overcome either the low level of investment or lagging domestic consumption. Stimulating private investment was hard because private entrepreneurs lacked confidence in the country's economic prospects and in the determination of the Government to follow a consistent and coordinated economic policy. Increasing public investment was hard because it required a thoroughgoing overhaul of Italy's fiscal arrangements. In particular, arrangements were needed so that public investment projects essential for the improvement of infrastructure could be planned and carried out. Since these and other obstacles made it difficult to pursue an expansionary fiscal policy, it was difficult also to stimulate domestic consumption through fiscal policy. For these reasons, the authorities turned to monetary policy to stimulate the economy. They also found it hard to take measures to reactivate the economy because they now believed that greater priority should be given to altering the distribution of income and providing social services than to maintaining employment and fully utilizing industrial capacity.

Growing exports and a strong tourist industry provided the country with current account surpluses from 1957 to 1972, except for 1963. Even in the recession years 1969–71, Italy had current account surpluses, averaging more than $2 billion per year in the second half of the 1960s and reaching $2.3 billion in 1971.

Current account surpluses were offset by large net capital outflows, making roughly for overall balance. Capital outflows were due partly to internal factors, such as the attempt to evade taxes by sending funds abroad, and a narrow choice of domestic financial assets. But capital outflows were also partly the result of several years of relatively easy monetary policies, which had produced a high degree of liquidity in Italy. In fact, from August 1971 until the middle of 1972, one of the objectives of Italian monetary policy had been to stimulate capital outflows in order to offset the current account surplus and to keep the payments position in balance. This policy prevented an excessive accumulation of reserves, which would have added to the already swollen levels of domestic liquidity.

An overall external payments deficit emerged in 1972, however, for several reasons. Measures taken since 1969 to stimulate the lagging domestic economy were by 1972 reflected in a rising demand for imports. Price inflation was also quickening, adding to the demand for imports. The wage explosion of 1969, superimposed on the wage increases of 1963–64, raised Italy's labor costs considerably, reducing the competitiveness of Italian exports. Moreover, political uncertainty grew as the government fell and another had to be formed. All these circumstances precipitated an acute lack of confidence in the lira shortly after the floating of the pound sterling in June 1972.

Lack of confidence in the lira was reflected mainly in adverse movements of leads and lags. In addition, more capital flowed out in other forms, particularly as further labor crises seemed likely and continually rising wage costs raised doubts about the Italian trade position. After years of virtual balance of payments equilibrium and despite a continued surplus on current account, Italy experienced in 1972 an overall deficit and a loss of reserves: a current account surplus of $2.4 billion was exceeded by an outflow of capital of over $3 billion. The Italian authorities therefore reversed their policy of stimulating capital outflow. Despite this reversal, a large loss of reserves occurred, and an even larger loss was prevented only because public institutions and commercial banks undertook heavy borrowing abroad, under the direction of the Bank of Italy.

REASONS FOR THE ITALIAN DUAL MARKET

Continued heavy pressure on the lira in January 1973 prompted Italian authorities to introduce the dual exchange market, described at the beginning of this chapter. Early in 1973, the Italian authorities informally explained to the Fund management the considerations governing their decision. First, they wanted to assure exchange traders that they had no intention of changing the par value for the lira. (The same par value, equivalent to Lit 625 = US$1, had been maintained since it was set with the Fund as an initial par value on March 30, 1960. In December 1971, when the realignment of major currencies took place, a central rate for the lira of Lit 581.5 = US$1 had been adopted; this rate represented an upward adjustment of the lira by 7.5 percent with respect to the dollar, but kept the lira rate vis-à-vis Italy's European trading partners virtually unchanged.) In view of Italy's persistent current account surpluses, the Italian authorities believed there was no need to devalue the lira, an assessment shared at the time by the Fund management and staff. In fact, in the staff view, persistent large current account surpluses represented a misuse of Italy's real resources, which went into foreign investment rather than into needed domestic infrastructure. Hence, the staff did not favor devaluation of the lira, which would have fostered those surpluses.

Second, the Italian authorities believed that, with the anticipated ending of the Viet Nam war, Wall Street might prove an irresistible magnet for Italian capital. Third, the basic machinery for enforcing dual market arrangements had been in existence for many years and it was relatively easy to make it function quickly; instituting capital controls would have been more difficult.

Fourth, the Italian authorities believed, as they explained to the Fund management and staff, that dual exchange markets were likely to become an important instrument for controlling unwanted flows of capital. Belgium and Luxembourg had used such a capital market since the 1950s, and France had introduced one in August 1971. Other European officials were increasingly viewing dual market systems as a way to control capital movements. In this context, the Italian authorities considered it possible that their dual market might become a permanent feature of Italian exchange policy. Consequently, as described later in this chapter, when the rate for the commercial lira was floated on February 13, the Italian authorities continued to maintain a second market for capital transactions. Italy had in effect two floating rates.

THE DOLLAR AGAIN DEVALUED

Establishment of a dual market in Italy on January 22, 1973 did not reduce capital outflows; it did not even prevent them from accelerating. No sooner had the dual market come into effect than there were large flows of funds from Italy to Switzerland. Because these capital inflows made it more difficult for Swiss officials to manage domestic liquidity, on January 23 the Swiss National Bank announced a temporary suspension of its intervention in foreign exchange markets. The rate for the Swiss franc vis-à-vis the dollar appreciated to a premium of about 6 percent over the rate set at the time of the Smithsonian agreement.

Once speculative capital movements started, they spread quickly to other markets, especially since other developments indicated that the dollar could soon again be weak. In January the U.S. Government announced the end of Phase II of its mandatory price and wage control program and its replacement by a looser and more voluntary Phase III. Prices of grains and other foods in the United States were expected to rise sharply as China, India, and the U.S.S.R., which had experienced crop failures, began buying grains from the United States. Hence, although the U.S. Council of Economic Advisors was projecting an abatement of inflation, fear increased that the United States would soon again be experiencing further rapid rises in prices.

Still greater concern for the future of the dollar arose when the figure for the U.S. balance of payments for 1972 became available. Despite the reflow of short-term capital to the United States in 1972 and the consequent marked improvement in the aggregate U.S. payments position, the total deficit for 1972 was still three times as large as the highest deficit of the 1960s. Even more worrisome was the U.S. merchandise trade position. In value terms, the trade deficit in 1972 had risen to $6.8 billion, larger by $4 billion than the deficit for 1971 and certainly the largest in U.S. history. By far the biggest loss was in trade with Japan, where the deficit increased to $4 billion, a rise of nearly $1 billion, although the United States also had its first trade deficit with Western Europe in more than 30 years. The U.S. trade deficit was reduced more on a volume than on a current value basis because the exchange rate changes of December 1971 had an initially adverse effect on U.S. terms of trade. The volume of exports, which had declined in 1971, expanded by more than 9 percent, considerably more than the 5.5 percent annual increase during 1960–70. As a result, although the United States had for many years experienced a progressively declining share of world exports, particularly in 1971, its share of the world export market remained stable during 1972. Despite these favorable developments, the U.S. trade position improved less in 1972 than the Fund had estimated. The United States continued to have a large trade deficit, while many industrial countries with trade surpluses, such as Canada, France, and Italy, increased their share of total world exports. The major industrial countries were consequently making considerably less progress toward reducing disequilibrium in their trade positions in 1972 than had generally been anticipated.

By the first few months of 1973, many public officials and economists were beginning to think that further sizable adjustments of exchange rates were needed to correct the U.S. payments position. Mounting distrust of the dollar was reflected in a general weakening of its market position against several continental European currencies. The deutsche mark, just above its central rate on January 19, 1973, rose to a larger premium by the end of January. The rates for the Netherlands guilder and the Belgian and French francs also rose. The Danish krone remained strong and the Swedish krona strengthened.

Further heavy speculative sales of dollars took place in the last week of January and the first week of February, and the monetary authorities of a number of countries had to intervene, buying dollars on a large scale to maintain established margins. In the first ten days of February, the flow of dollars into the official reserves of European countries and Japan approximated $10 billion. The Deutsche Bundesbank alone was forced to take in $5.9 billion in the first nine days of February. The authorities of the Federal Republic of Germany declared their intention not to revalue the deutsche mark unilaterally and adopted measures to tighten their restraints on the inflow of funds. These measures had little effect on stanching the massive inward flow. Market pressures spread to other currencies and to money and security markets around the world were racked by currency speculation and uncertainty. Monetary officials of the major industrial countries were tempted to resort to unilateral defensive action, such as introducing dual markets or reinforcing controls on capital movements. Yet, both European and U.S. officials recognized that such actions would not correct the continuing underlying imbalances of the United States and of other industrial countries. These imbalances were at the heart of the problem of capital movements.

Against this background, Mr. Volcker left Washington on Wednesday, February 7, on a whirlwind trip for a series of meetings in Europe and in Japan, traveling secretly so as not to arouse further speculation in exchange markets. His presence abroad became known publicly only on Saturday, February 10. Most major official exchange markets were closed for the next several days. Conversations between Mr. Volcker and officials of France, the Federal Republic of Germany, Italy, Japan, and the United Kingdom were directed to finding out whether the willingness of the United States again to devalue the dollar would be an acceptable solution. These consultations paved the way for further devaluation of the dollar. U.S. officials agreed to propose to Congress a reduction in the par value of the dollar of 10 percent in terms of the SDR. Officials of France and the Federal Republic of Germany agreed not to change their existing par values, thereby permitting an 11.11 percent appreciation of the French franc and of the deutsche mark against the dollar. Italian officials decided to let the rate for the Italian lira in the commercial market float, and Japanese officials agreed also to let the dollar-yen rate float. U.K. authorities indicated that the pound sterling, which was already floating, would continue to do so.

A new structure of exchange rates for all the countries of the OECD could be identified. The United States would devalue the dollar by 10 percent in terms of the SDR. Australia, Austria, Belgium, Denmark, Luxembourg, the Netherlands, Norway, and Spain, in addition to France and the Federal Republic of Germany, would maintain their existing rates. Finland, Portugal, and Sweden would fix new rates at a smaller appreciation against the dollar. Greece, Iceland, Turkey, and Yugoslavia would depreciate their currencies by the same percentage as the dollar. Italy, Japan, and Switzerland, in addition to Canada and the United Kingdom, would have floating rates for the time being.

On Monday evening, February 12, at 9:45 p.m., while Mr. Volcker was airborne on his return to Washington, Mr. Shultz announced that President Nixon would ask Congress to authorize the proposed change in the par value of the U.S. dollar. The interest equalization tax and the controls of the Office of Foreign

Direct Investment were also to be phased out and terminated at the latest by the end of 1974, and the Board of Governors of the Federal Reserve System was to consider relaxing the voluntary foreign credit restraint program. Thus, mandatory and voluntary U.S. controls on capital would come to an end.

The U.S. Treasury estimated that, expressing currencies in terms of U.S. cents per foreign currency unit and using weights based on the value of trade of the United States with the country in question, the cumulative effect of the two exchange rate realignments (December 1971 and February 1973) together represented an average appreciation against the dollar of the currencies of the OECD countries of 15.5 percent or, excluding Canada, of about 23 percent. At the time, Treasury officials expected that an exchange rate adjustment of this magnitude would bring about a major improvement in the U.S. trade position, although considerable time would be required to achieve this result. This conclusion, based on extensive econometric work by economic experts at the Treasury, was supported by work done by other U.S. Government agencies, by international institutions, and by academic and private research institutions.

In this way, after years in which the world's financial officials had believed that the dollar could not be devalued, there came about the second devaluation of the dollar in 14 months.

Fund Participation

In view of the Fund's guardianship of the par value system, details of the way in which this second change in the par value of the U.S. dollar came about, revealing the extent to which the Fund participated, is of special interest. In the midst of an emergency in exchange markets, the United States quickly and secretly consulted its biggest trading partners about their reactions should the United States propose a devaluation. The part played by the Fund in the process was markedly different from its customary role, in which a member requested the Fund's approval in advance of the change. The United States did not approach the Fund formally. Instead, while Mr. Volcker was visiting European capitals and Tokyo, Mr. Shultz kept Mr. Schweitzer closely informed, on a highly secret basis, on the progress of the consultations. On Monday, February 12, about 7:30 p.m., at the request of Secretary Shultz, Mr. Schweitzer went to the U.S. Treasury and was with Treasury officials for nearly two hours as the drafts of Secretary Shultz's statement for his forthcoming press conference were being completed. Mr. Schweitzer reviewed the statement with Mr. Shultz and informed him that he had no objections to the statement on the matters of direct concern to the Fund. Mr. Schweitzer returned to the Fund before a final decision was reached in the Treasury on the hour for Secretary Shultz's press conference. Mr. Dale informed Mr. Southard shortly before 10:00 p.m. that Secretary Shultz would hold a press conference at 10:30 p.m. Mr. Dale would bring to the Fund copies of the statement and accordingly it would be in order to call the Executive Board into session if Mr. Schweitzer wished to do so. At the Executive

Board meeting convened at 11:00 p.m., which continued until 2:00 a.m., the Executive Directors were formally notified of the U.S. action.

Mr. Dale apologized to the other Executive Directors for the lateness of the hour and for the fact that the Executive Board meeting was being held *after* Mr. Shultz's public statement. He explained the procedural difficulties facing the U.S. monetary authorities in changing the par value for the dollar. Under U.S. law, they could not act directly through the Fund since a change in par value had to be authorized by the Congress. At the moment, the U.S. Congress was not in session and would not reconvene until February 20. In the meantime, the U.S. monetary authorities had to take emergency action to curb the crisis spreading in exchange markets. They had to some extent taken international repercussion into account by consulting several countries in advance. Mr. Dale elaborated that there were to be no further international negotiations, such as those pertaining to international trade measures, as there had been after the Smithsonian agreement. He also called attention to the fact that Mr. Shultz expressed both the old and the proposed par value for the dollar in terms of the SDR, a significant boost for the SDR.

Mr. Dale's explanations notwithstanding, some Executive Directors— Mr. Lieftinck in particular—regretted that the Fund had not received an official request from the United States to comment on or to approve its actions. The Executive Board had only a statement by the Secretary of the U.S. Treasury, which had already been released, informing the Fund of the change in the par value of the dollar. Perhaps for the first time in the Fund's history, the Executive Board did not have for its consideration a paper prepared by the staff. In these circumstances, there was little that the Executive Board could do. The Fund would have to wait until the U.S. Congress had authorized the submission of a proposal to the Fund before the Fund could act on it. The dollar devaluation on the other hand would be reflected immediately in exchange markets, with the result that a new exchange rate structure would emerge without much consultation with or approval by the Fund. Such a situation was far from welcome and made evident the need for a reformed international monetary system.

The Executive Directors from developing members expressed disappointment because developing members were excluded from Mr. Volcker's negotiations and because Mr. Schweitzer, as a representative of the international community, had not been invited to the discussions Mr. Volcker had held in Paris with the authorities of a few countries. They questioned whether the Committee of Twenty was a meaningful body if the "Big Five" (France, the Federal Republic of Germany, Japan, the United Kingdom, and the United States) arranged among themselves changes in the exchange rates of the major currencies, which affected all countries. They agreed, nevertheless, that the way in which this second currency realignment was effected was preferable to the sequence of events leading up to the Smithsonian agreement. Then, officials of the large industrial nations, acting in the Group of Ten and the EC, had taken it upon themselves to establish a new pattern of exchange rates without seeming to recognize the existence of the developing countries or of the Fund.

Apart from the procedure, most Executive Directors welcomed a second dollar devaluation. As stated in a press release issued by the Fund at the time, they believed that another devaluation of the dollar would make an effective contribution to a better balance in the U.S. payments position and in the world payments situation, generally improve confidence in the dollar, and thereby help bring about the reform of the international monetary system then in progress. In informal remarks, Mr. Schweitzer noted that, contrary to the commonly expressed belief, this second devaluation of the dollar demonstrated that the United States could indeed change the par value of the dollar.

Rates in exchange markets promptly reflected the prospective change in the par value of the dollar, although the new par value was not established with the Fund until passage of the relevant U.S. legislation in October 1973. To enable the Fund in the meantime to make calculations on the basis of the new par value, the Executive Directors took a decision on February 16, 1973 permitting calculations for Fund transactions and operations, other than calculations for the dollar, to be made on the basis of a value for the dollar that reflected its prospective par value (US$1 = SDR 0.828948 or a price of gold of $42.2222 per ounce) instead of its existing par value (US$1 = SDR 0.921053 or a price of gold of $38 per ounce). This decision meant that the valuation and adjustment of the Fund's holdings of a currency would be made immediately on the basis of the prospective U.S. par value rather than later when the new par value came into effect. Thus the Fund was able to avoid some of the complications that followed the currency realignment of December 1971 and the setting of a formal par value in May 1972, described in Chapter 2. Calculations for transactions in the Special Drawing Account, except those for the dollar, were made on the same basis. The decision remained in effect until the new par value for the dollar was established with the Fund in October 1973.

On October 15, Mr. Shultz informed H. Johannes Witteveen, who had succeeded Mr. Schweitzer as Managing Director on September 1, that the United States proposed a change in the par value of the dollar to become effective at 12:01 a.m. on October 18, 1973. The Fund concurred in the proposal on October 17. The United States planned to implement the new par value, as it had the previous par value for the dollar, by leaving it up to other countries to intervene in exchange markets to maintain spot rates within margins. In hearings before the U.S. Congress on the bill to change the par value, Mr. Volcker reassured members of Congress that in their understandings with other countries, the U.S. authorities were not obliged to intervene generally in currency markets to maintain given margins around parities or central rates but would intervene only when it was considered necessary and desirable to facilitate orderly market conditions.

THE ITALIAN LIRA FLOATS

As mentioned above, when the dollar was devalued on February 12, 1973, both the Italian and the Japanese authorities decided, for the time being, not to maintain

69

the rates for their currencies in the official exchange markets within announced limits. The lira and the yen began to float. The Italian authorities informed the Fund of their decision on February 13. Since the newly established market for capital transactions was to continue, the Italian lira was floating in two separate markets.

At the time, the Fund management and staff and most Executive Directors were still trying hard to preserve a system of fixed exchange rates, if not in the form of par values then at least in the form of central rates. Because of the importance of the Italian lira, they believed its floating added further uncertainty to the world as a whole and to the Mediterranean area in particular. In appraising the decision of the Italian authorities to float the lira, the staff recognized that, as a second realignment of major currencies took place, the Italian authorities had special problems, such as large capital outflows, in determining a fixed exchange rate for the lira that would be viable for the long run. But they warned the Italian authorities not to overestimate the degree of guidance for a future rate that could be expected from the rates prevailing in the Italian free market. Also, the staff was not convinced that two separate markets with floating rates served any purpose, especially since the Italian authorities intended to intervene in both markets to maintain a narrow spread between the rates. In the staff view, the Italian authorities were unable to separate the markets effectively and, in any event, capital outflows consisted to a considerable extent of leads and lags that affected the volume of transactions in the commercial market. Because of these problems with Italy's exchange rate policy, the management and staff welcomed close contact with the Italian authorities to determine a new fixed rate for the lira and the timing of its introduction.

When the issue of Italy's floating rate came to the Executive Board, the Executive Directors centered much of their attention on setting up for Italy the same type of special consultations that the Fund applied to other members with floating exchange rates—Canada, the United Kingdom, and, as described below, Japan. These special consultations would consist not merely of informal discussions between the authorities of the member and the Managing Director and staff. There would be a report to the Executive Board and discussion in the Board. In its decision, the Executive Board stated that the Fund welcomed the intention of the Italian authorities to collaborate with it, in accordance with the Articles of Agreement, and to resume, as soon as conditions permitted, the observation of margins around the central rate consistent with the decision of the Fund of December 1971 permitting central rates and wider margins in lieu of par values and narrow margins. The Executive Board also stressed that the Fund would remain in close consultation with the Italian authorities on their resumption of margins and that the Managing Director would take appropriate initiatives for those consultations.

THE JAPANESE YEN FLOATS

In April 1949, while Japan was still under U.S. military occupation, the official exchange rate for the yen was set at ¥ 360 per U.S. dollar. This rate was considered advantageous, especially vis-à-vis the dollar, as a rate that would facilitate the recovery of Japanese industries and exports. In May 1953 this rate was agreed with the Fund as the initial par value for the yen, Japan having become a member of the Fund the previous August.

Although Japanese exports grew at a very rapid rate throughout the 1950s and the first half of the 1960s, there was no problem of an exceptionally large overall trade surplus, nor of a large trade surplus with the United States, until 1965. On the contrary, until 1965 Japan ran sizable deficits on current account in many years. Moreover, as late as 1964, the United States, like Japan, was itself experiencing a faster than average expansion in exports of manufactured goods, and both countries succeeded in increasing substantially their share of world export markets. To a large extent the counterpart of their success was the failure of the United Kingdom to maintain its share of world markets.

Late in 1965, stimulated by a sharper than usual increase in exports and by expansionary monetary and fiscal policies, Japan's economy entered a period of exceptional growth. Recession in Japan's major trading partners in 1966 and 1967, however, prevented the current account position from becoming strong until early 1968. By 1968 the upswing in industrial countries and the onset of inflation in the United States began to cause large increases in Japanese exports. These increases in value terms reached 24 percent in 1968, 23 percent in 1969, 21 percent in 1970, and 24 percent in 1971. Hence, Japan's high and sustained rate of economic growth became associated with large and expanding current account surpluses only partially offset by net capital outflows.

By 1971, as the trade position of the United States moved into deficit and its large balance of payments deficit became a world problem, the size of Japan's trade surplus with the United States (from the U.S. point of view, the deficit of the United States with Japan) became a serious issue in the economic relations between the two countries. The U.S. authorities had believed for some time that the Japanese authorities ought to revalue the yen. The Japanese authorities, on the other hand, concerned that revaluation would inhibit the country's export industries, disturb the value of assets, debts, and other financial relations between Japan and its trading partners, and be regarded at home as a defeat for the Government's economic policies, were reluctant to revalue. In addition, the Japanese authorities were not altogether convinced that revaluation was the correct way to reduce Japan's trade surplus. To some extent they viewed the need for revaluation of the yen as temporary and believed that the long-run solution to the trade surplus was for Japan to expand imports. Hence, rather than revalue they preferred such measures as lowering tariff barriers and relaxing controls on imports. If necessary, they might resort to the temporary use of export restraints.

Japan introduced its first "yen-defense" program in June 1971 but, following the suspension of dollar convertibility by the United States on August 15, 1971, had to modify the program. In the wake of considerable speculative capital inflows in the two weeks after the U.S. suspension of convertibility, the Japanese Government allowed the yen to float from the end of August until the Smithsonian agreement, by which time it had appreciated by about 12 percent. On December 20, 1971, the authorities adopted a central rate equivalent to ¥ 308 per U.S. dollar—a 16.88 percent appreciation vis-à-vis the dollar—and availed itself of wider margins. Throughout 1972 a series of bilateral negotiations were held between the United States and Japan aimed at increasing imports into Japan from the United States.

Executive Directors Consider the Float

Since the Executive Directors in February 1973 took up the communication from Japan stating that the yen would be allowed to float temporarily, along with their consideration of the Article VIII consultation with Japan, they were provided with a comprehensive review of the country's domestic economic and balance of payments positions and of the developments leading to the floating of the yen. After the Smithsonian agreement, the initial exchange rate for the yen had been set near the upper intervention limit of ¥ 314.93 per dollar, but during the first six months of 1972, it moved steadily to the lower intervention level of ¥ 301.07 per dollar. During the second half of 1972, it remained at this level but its maintenance required the Bank of Japan to make large purchases of dollars in the Tokyo exchange market.

In mid-1972, the Japanese authorities proposed a second yen-defense program, but failed to obtain the approval of the Diet. In October 1972 the Government announced a third yen-defense program. In addition to a more expansionary budget policy, aimed at increasing the demand for imports, the program aimed at reducing the protracted balance of payments surplus directly by restraining exports, promoting imports, and encouraging a net outflow of capital, and indirectly by stimulating the movement of resources from the external sector to the production of consumer goods and of social overhead capital, such as housing. Among measures to promote imports were the removal of quantitative restrictions on some imports, an increase in the quotas of imports still subject to residual import restrictions by 30 percent or more, and a 20 percent across-the-board reduction in tariffs on mineral, industrial, and processed agricultural products.

The Japanese authorities emphasized to the Fund staff that, in their view, import liberalization in Japan compared favorably with that in other industrial countries. The restrictions on imports still remaining were essential to protect agriculture, fisheries, and a limited number of manufacturing industries. While further progress would be made in relaxing Japan's restrictions on imports, such progress would have to be gradual and accompanied by adjustment assistance to the industries affected. In any event, it would be a mistake to expect relaxation of import restrictions to effect major changes in Japan's balance of payments position.

The Japanese authorities explained further that these measures formed part of a policy to reduce Japan's current account surplus and to increase its capital outflow so that the basic balance in the external accounts would be close to zero. They emphasized to the Fund staff that in the course of 1972, even after the revaluation of the yen in December 1971, they had introduced export controls on 20 major export items in order to slow down the rate of export expansion in response to complaints from abroad about disruption of domestic markets by Japanese goods. The export of many other items was also subject to restraint, either because of formal or informal agreements with foreign governments or because of export cartels involving agreed quantitative targets for particular export markets.

Despite a strong economic recovery in 1972, which fostered imports, and despite direct action to reduce its trade surplus, Japan's surplus in 1972 was $9 billion, even larger than the record surplus of 1971. The current account surplus reached $7 billion, about $1 billion larger than in 1971. As a result of liberalization of transactions to encourage outward capital movements and the introduction of other measures to stimulate investment abroad by Japanese businessmen and to deter inflows of short-term funds, the Japanese authorities managed, however, to turn the more than $4 billion net inflow of capital of 1971 into a net outflow in 1972 of similar magnitude. This $8 billion shift in the capital account reduced the overall balance of payments surplus of Japan to $2.9 billion in 1972, much below the surplus of 1971.

In explaining to the Executive Directors the decision of the Japanese authorities to float the yen in February 1973, Kaichi Kawaguchi emphasized that his authorities welcomed the second devaluation of the dollar. The Japanese authorities temporarily floated the rate for the yen instead of immediately setting a new par value because they had yet to find an appropriate level for the par value. Apparently the floating of the yen was a compromise, necessitated by the reluctance of the Japanese authorities to choose a fixed rate at a level primarily designed to accommodate U.S. authorities. On other occasions the Japanese authorities had emphasized their strong bias for fixed exchange rates, and on this occasion Mr. Kawaguchi stressed that the Japanese authorities intended to return to the maintenance of normal margins around parity as soon as possible.

Mr. Kawaguchi explained that the unparalleled growth of the Japanese economy since the second half of the 1940s had resulted in some imbalance in the allocation of resources between the private and public sectors and that building social infrastructure and caring for social welfare needs had fallen behind economic growth. A strong external payments position and rapid economic growth, however, gave the Japanese "elbow room" for the management of the economy, and they were reorienting their policies, especially budget policies, to give greater importance to the resource allocation function and less importance to the demand-management function. Accordingly, the Japanese authorities expected that economic growth in their country would be slower in the future. They agreed with the Fund staff that reduction of the balance of payments surplus remained Japan's most critical problem but expected that the floating of the exchange rate would have an appreciable effect on this problem. Moreover, they stressed that they would continue to take other measures as well.

Most interested in a reduction in Japan's surplus was, of course, the United States, with whom Japan had its biggest bilateral surplus. At the Executive Board meeting, Mr. Dale emphasized that appreciation of the Japanese yen against other currencies, particularly against the dollar, was an essential condition for movement toward equilibrium in world payments. But appreciation of the yen alone was not sufficient. Because of the structure of the Japanese economy, the elasticities of both exports and imports with respect to changes in the exchange rate were unusually low. Making for low trade elasticities were a large heavy industry sector largely oriented toward exports, high rates of capital formation, rapid increases in productivity, and imports greatly weighted toward primary products. It was essential, therefore, that changes in the rate for the yen be accompanied by other policies to alter the allocation of resources in Japan if the trade balance was to shift toward a sustainable and reasonable surplus. Specifically, private consumption needed to be substantially increased. To this end, determined efforts were needed to improve the distribution of products throughout Japanese society and to change consumers' habits in favor of imported goods, particularly durable consumer goods, such as refrigerators, dishwashers, and clothes washers and dryers. The percentage of gross national product devoted to consumption was much lower in Japan (only about 52 percent) than in other industrial countries, where consumption absorbed close to two thirds of gross national product.

Other Executive Directors, too, observed that Japan had experienced remarkable economic development, characterized by expanding productive capacity and an aggressive foreign trade policy. A real growth rate of over 10 percent a year had made per capita income in Japan one of the highest in the world. As a consequence of the large investment program, the economy had developed both the ability to grow at a high rate and the need to do so in order to absorb excess productive capacity and maintain relatively high employment. Such excess capacity exerted pressure on the export sector and caused continuous large surpluses in the balance of payments. Japan's surpluses had attracted international attention. If excess capacity was to be absorbed and the growth of exports checked while the growth of imports was encouraged, development policy in Japan would have to place more emphasis on domestic consumption. That, in turn, would require a reorientation of productive facilities toward internal markets. The backlog in social infrastructure was especially apparent in residential construction, which still accounted for a small share of real gross national product, especially for such a prosperous economy.

The Executive Directors, therefore, welcomed what they considered a reorientation of Japanese policies toward growth for the domestic market and toward social improvement rather than toward growth based on exports. They also expressed a strong preference for import promotion over export control as a way to restore better equilibrium in Japan's trade accounts without reducing the level of world trade and urged that capital exports, including development assistance, be given priority. They also welcomed the decision of the Japanese authorities to allow the yen to float temporarily as an additional contribution to exchange rate adjustment beyond what was provided by the change in the par value of the U.S. dollar.

Although Executive Directors did not directly refer to policies the Japanese authorities might follow in intervening in the market, they did so by innuendo. Anthony K. Rawlinson (United Kingdom), for example, hoped that the Japanese authorities would manage the exchange market and related exchange control policies in such a way that the movement of the rate would be allowed to play its proper role in the adjustment process. Mr. Kawaguchi stressed that in principle the float was to be a "clean" one, that is, one in which the authorities did not intervene in the market, as distinct from a "dirty" one, in which the authorities intervened in order to influence the rate.

As in other instances where rates were floating, the Executive Directors specified in their decision that the Managing Director would take the initiative in arranging consultations between the Japanese authorities and the Fund. As there were now to be special consultations on floating exchange rates with four members (Canada, Italy, Japan, and the United Kingdom), the Executive Directors began to be concerned about the substance of these consultations. Mr. Dale, for example, stressed that members consulted on floating rates ought to provide full and up-to-date information, preferably on intervention practices, and certainly on foreign assets and liabilities of official agencies in order that the Executive Directors could judge what had been happening in their reserve positions. It might also be necessary to have information on government policies and measures that affect the foreign assets and liabilities of nonofficial bodies. It was difficult to judge whether a float was clean or not until adequate information was available.

Developments in the Rate

By the end of February, the rate for the yen in exchange markets had risen to approximately ¥ 265 per dollar, a level, according to press reports, somewhat more appreciated than Japanese officials had planned, but presumably less appreciated than U.S. officials had in mind. (It seems that the United States had in mind a rate of about ¥ 260 to the dollar.) The yen remained at about ¥ 265 = $1 for several months, while the Bank of Japan sold about $1 billion a month from reserves to prevent depreciation. Intervention by the Bank of Japan was needed mainly because of large increases in imports and net long-term capital outflow. The rate of ¥ 265 per dollar represented a revaluation of 35 percent of the yen vis-à-vis the dollar since May 1971, before the major exchange rate adjustments began.

INTRODUCTION OF JOINT FLOAT OF EC CURRENCIES

Because of the events of January and February 1973, some members of the Executive Board, such as Mr. Viénot and Robert van S. Smit (South Africa), on February 12, expressed concern about the number of currencies now floating and the increasing trend of major countries away from par values. Their concern for the future of the par value system was amply justified. Only nine days later, still more crises were to erupt that resulted in toppling the system altogether.

75

On Wednesday, February 21, there were again signs of pressure on the dollar in several markets. One week later on Wednesday, February 28, intense pressure on the dollar in the Netherlands market prompted the Dutch authorities to buy up large amounts of dollars. On Thursday, March 1, speculation spread to the Federal Republic of Germany and the Deutsche Bundesbank had to purchase $3.7 billion in dollars, the largest amount ever bought or sold by a central bank in a single day up to that time. On Friday, March 2, after having taken in $580 million in 90 minutes, the Bank of France closed the Paris exchange market. Then exchange markets in other countries were closed. This breakdown in exchange transactions was the most severe in more than three decades. Although business was still transacted, all central bank intervention was suspended.

In an attempt to resolve the crisis, the finance ministers of the now nine countries belonging to the EC (Denmark, Ireland, and the United Kingdom had joined the EC two months earlier) announced that they would meet on Sunday afternoon, March 4, in Brussels. In an unusual move, the Chairman of the Council of Ministers, Willy De Clercq, Finance Minister of Belgium, invited the Managing Director of the Fund to attend. Mr. Schweitzer accepted. It seemed likely that the European authorities were considering a joint float of the EC currencies against the dollar, but such a float was by no means certain. The U.K. authorities, preferring to float separately, were advising against a joint float. The Italian authorities also preferred an independent float. The French authorities were reluctant to abandon fixed rates. The authorities of the Federal Republic of Germany, who had wanted to arrange a joint float of the EC currencies in May 1971, were not optimistic that it could be arranged even now. Meanwhile, in view of the urgency of the situation, Mr. Schweitzer, before leaving for Europe, met in Washington, on Friday, March 2, with Mr. Volcker to see what action the U.S. authorities were prepared to take to defend the newly established par value for the dollar or to retain a fixed rate system.

Mr. Schweitzer Opposes Floating

Mr. Schweitzer explained his views on the crises to Mr. Volcker on March 2 and to the finance ministers of the EC countries on March 4. As he saw the situation, the second devaluation of the dollar and the floating of the Japanese yen created a satisfactory pattern of exchange rates for the major currencies. This pattern seemed to be sustainable and could provide the basis for the gradual achievement of a better balance in external transactions between the United States and Japan, which had by far the largest bilateral imbalance. The current crisis was much more serious than preceding crises because it was caused entirely by unjustified speculative flows of capital. Past crises had stemmed at least in part from belief in the exchange markets that certain exchange rates would shortly have to be adjusted anyway. In the present crisis, no exchange rate adjustment was needed. In these circumstances, a joint floating of the EC currencies would, he thought, lead to uncertainty about all exchange rates, with no knowledge as to what pattern of rates might emerge.

Mr. Schweitzer was also concerned about the potential division of the world into currency blocs—a dollar bloc, an EC bloc, and a yen bloc.

As an alternative to a joint float of the EC currencies, Mr. Schweitzer tried to persuade both Mr. Volcker and the European finance ministers to undertake a concerted defense of the newly set relationships between the dollar and the currencies of the industrial countries that continued to have fixed exchange rates. This defense would consist of massive joint intervention, tight restrictions on credit expansion, and cooperation to control capital movements. The staff put together a proposal for collective intervention. At issue was how the exchange risk should be distributed among the major countries. In the staff proposal, countries that established a par value or a central rate would share jointly the burden of intervention between the country acquiring dollars and the United States. To Mr. Volcker, the Fund management suggested that the United States might make use of the Fund's resources.

Mr. Volcker responded that the U.S. authorities would accept a system of floating rates. In fact, although not all U.S. authorities were in agreement that floating rates were acceptable—Mr. Burns, in particular, did not like them—Mr. Volcker took the position that general floating might be appropriate, because the Canadian dollar, the Italian lira, the Japanese yen, and the pound sterling were already floating, because the exchange markets did not seem to be convinced that the existing pattern of fixed rates would hold, and because many European officials inclined toward floating against the dollar.

At their March 4 meeting, the finance ministers of the EC countries decided that, because of the international character of the crisis, a meeting should be arranged that included not only the EC countries but also the other principal countries involved. It was imperative, of course, that the United States and Japan attend. Therefore, it was agreed that officials of the EC countries and of the Group of Ten, then under the chairmanship of Valéry Giscard d'Estaing, would meet in a joint session in Paris on Friday, March 9. Before the March 9 meeting, Mr. Schweitzer, accompanied by Mr. Southard, met again with Mr. Volcker. Mr. Volcker was increasingly skeptical about the participation of the United States in a concerted defense of existing par values. He stressed that the U.S. Congress would not appropriate funds for any losses involved in supporting the rate for the dollar. For example, Representative Henry Reuss, who was carefully monitoring developments, favored limiting the use of the swap network and of other arrangements that carried exchange risks. Mr. Volcker stressed also to Mr. Schweitzer that there had been a great deal of talk, both before and after the February 12 exchange rate adjustments, about a joint European float. Speculators were ready to shoot at any fixed target (par value or central rate) presented by the authorities. It was probably already too late for a substantial collective intervention. Moreover, European officials who inclined toward floating might not welcome efforts by the United States to prevent a general float.

Despite the general inclination of major industrial countries toward floating rates, at a meeting of the Executive Board just before Mr. Schweitzer left for the combined meeting of the officials of the countries of the EC and of the Group of Ten, Alexandre Kafka (Brazil), Carlos Massad A. (Chile), P.S.N. Prasad (India), Mohammed Yeganeh (Iran), and Lindsay B. Brand (Australia) urged Mr. Schweitzer to take positions strongly supporting a stable international monetary system and the existing structure of exchange rates.

Both Mr. Schweitzer and Ali Wardhana (Indonesia) attended the Paris meeting. Mr. Wardhana had been invited as Chairman of the Committee of Twenty in a deliberate effort of the representatives of industrial countries to include a representative of developing countries. The finance ministers of the EC countries and the deputies of the Group of Ten held prior, separate meetings.

The meeting on March 9 of the deputies of the Group of Ten was chaired by Rinaldo Ossola of Italy. The Fund's Economic Counsellor, J.J. Polak, attended, as he usually did, as a representative of the Managing Director. Authorities of the EC countries expressed their belief that the causes of the latest exchange crisis were the declarations by the U.S. authorities that they would not defend the par value of the dollar and were planning to terminate capital controls by the end of 1974. The U.S. deputies disagreed. Nevertheless, they avoided at the level of deputies any confrontation on these issues which they felt would be dealt with more appropriately at the ministerial level.

At the ministerial meeting of the Group of Ten and the EC, Mr. Schweitzer made a strong appeal to give the existing set of agreed exchange rates a reasonable chance to work. He emphasized that he was expressing the point of view held by the Executive Directors elected by members of the Fund not represented at the Paris meeting. He was convinced that the currency crisis was not justified on the basis of the existing exchange rate structure. The crisis had, in fact, occurred immediately *after* a substantial realigning of the exchange rates of the major currencies and the setting of par values and central rates considered by all concerned adequate to correct, over time, the continuing imbalance in international payments. He noted that some officials had even expressed the view that the latest exchange rate adjustment went too far and that the dollar was now possibly undervalued. The currencies for which a reasonable rate could not be set with confidence at the time— the yen, the pound sterling, the lira, the Canadian dollar, and the Swiss franc—were floating. Mr. Schweitzer stressed that he was, therefore, not calling for the maintenance of a deficient exchange rate structure. On the contrary, the structure was reasonable, certainly more reasonable than any set of exchange rates that market forces would produce, at least in the near future. There was consequently a solid basis for a collective effort to defeat the latest speculative attack on a number of currencies. He warned, too, that if the attack could not be dealt with effectively, serious doubts would arise about the feasibility, at least for a considerable period ahead, of any structure of agreed rates once that structure came under pressure. The reform efforts then in progress in the Committee of Twenty were, therefore, also in jeopardy.

A Joint Float Agreed

After Mr. Schweitzer's appeal for a defense of existing fixed rates, officials of the Group of Ten and of the EC still could not agree on what action to take. Officials from EC countries listed a number of measures, including intervention in markets, to keep the system stable. But Mr. Shultz, speaking for the United States, stated that it was unclear from the statement of Mr. De Clercq, Chairman of the EC finance ministers, whether the officials of the EC countries were considering exchange intervention to defend par values and central rates or to help keep a newly arranged joint float orderly. In the absence of agreement, it was decided to formulate proposals during the forthcoming week and to meet again in Paris the following Friday, March 16.

On Monday, March 12, in a separate meeting of the EC, six members of the Community—Belgium, Denmark, France, the Federal Republic of Germany, Luxembourg, and the Netherlands—decided to maintain arrangements limiting fluctuations between their currencies to 2.25 percent, but no longer to ensure that exchange rates for the U.S. dollar would be kept within the previously agreed margins. In effect, they established a joint float against the dollar. The EC Council agreed that close and continuing consultation on monetary matters should be maintained among the national authorities involved. To assist the orderly adjustment of exchange markets to the joint float, the authorities of the Federal Republic of Germany revalued the deutsche mark in terms of the SDR by 3 percent. Four days later, on Friday, March 16, the Group of Ten and the EC finance ministers met again in Paris, but they had little to do except to note the decision by the EC.

Reactions in the Fund

Once the EC countries had introduced a joint float against the dollar but not against each others' currencies, it was purely a philosophical question whether the European currencies were floating or, since they floated only against the dollar, whether the dollar was floating. Whichever view one took, the economic consequences were the same. The difference was meaningful for the Fund, however, since the Fund had to decide how to respond to virtually identical communications from the authorities of Belgium, Denmark, France, the Federal Republic of Germany, Luxembourg, and the Netherlands. These communications stated that from March 19, 1973 each of these countries would maintain a maximum margin of 2.25 percent for rates for exchange transactions in its official market only between its currency and the currencies of each of the other countries, and that in so acting each considered that it was fulfilling, "in present circumstances," its obligations under Article IV, Section 4, of the Articles of Agreement and the decisions of the Fund. (Article IV, Section 4, obliged each member "to collaborate with the Fund to promote exchange stability, to maintain orderly exchange arrangements with other members, and to avoid competitive exchange alterations," and to maintain exchange rates within permitted margins.) The Belgian and Dutch authorities agreed to maintain the margin between the franc and the guilder within the narrower margins on which they had previously agreed. Sweden, not a member of the EC, also informed the Fund that it, too, would be joining the common float; Norway joined the arrangements on March 20. The authorities of Ireland, Italy, and the United Kingdom notified the Fund that for the time being there would be no change in their exchange systems. Their currencies were to continue floating independently, but they intended to join the common float as soon as possible.

The Managing Director and the staff believed that the six countries of the EC and Sweden which were floating jointly only against the dollar should be treated differently from Canada, Italy, Japan, and the United Kingdom which had floating rates vis-à-vis all currencies. The EC countries and Sweden had par values or central rates which, though not necessarily observed within established margins, were considered reasonable; the use of floating rates was not a technique to find new fixed rates. They also maintained margins between their own currencies. The Managing Director and the staff wanted to establish as a basis for treating these seven countries differently that it was these countries that had floating rates vis-à-vis the dollar and that it was not the dollar that was floating against European currencies. Moreover, they believed that consultations on floating rates ought to be held with the seven countries as a group, rather than individually. The joint float might then be construed as a step toward the restoration of a system of adjustable parities, operating within such margins as might be considered adequate. If, on the other hand, the Fund held consultations with each country individually, the new floating arrangements would be regarded as a floating of the dollar and hence widely interpreted as a total breakdown of the par value system.

At the Executive Board meeting, the Executive Directors appointed or elected by EC members, emphasizing that European countries were trying to preserve a stable system, supported this position of the Managing Director and staff. They pointed out that any other country willing and able to undertake the necessary obligations was welcome to join the common float. The Executive Directors elected by developing members, concerned that the par value system was becoming entirely unhinged, also favored an Executive Board decision that stressed the need to maintain order and stability in the international monetary system. In the decision taken, therefore, the Fund noted the communications received and called on all members to collaborate with it to restore and maintain orderly exchange arrangements, including exchange margins consistent with the decisions of the Fund.

Reactions Elsewhere

Despite the decision of the Fund to treat the new arrangements as a joint European float, the arrangements were universally interpreted as the onset of floating exchange rates. Thus, despite the efforts of Fund officials to prevent it, a new era of widespread floating dawned. Soon, both European and U.S. officials were taking credit for the new era. European officials, thinking in terms of the sequence of events just related, believed that the initiative for floating rates lay with them. For example, Otmar Emminger, then Deputy Governor of the Deutsche Bundesbank and later its President, has written that "in March 1973 the Deutschemark, together with a number of other EEC currencies and two associated Scandinavian currencies, went over to a 'joint float' in relation to the dollar and other currencies."[2] Yet Mr. Shultz, himself an advocate of floating exchange rates, was to consider the introduction of floating rates as one of his major achievements while he was Secretary of the U.S. Treasury.

■　■　■　■　■　■

This account relates the events immediately preceding the introduction in 1973 of the regime of floating rates. It was, however, only the last episode in a lengthy odyssey. In the previous several years, as crises in the par value system had occurred, an increasing number of prominent economists, especially but not solely in the academic community, had come to favor flexible rates. Indeed, some had been suggesting flexible rates for a long time. One academic economist, for example, had been recommending flexible rates for more than two decades, and a few others had also been putting forth arguments for floating rates nearly that long. Because of the frequent exchanges of views since the early 1960s between economists outside government and public officials on problems of the international monetary system, economists outside government who favored flexible rates had a direct influence on the thinking of public officials in the United States and Europe who took the decisions just described.

The reasons many prominent economists advocated flexible rates are summarized in Chapter 6 as part of the analysis of the factors that brought about the collapse of the par value system. But first Chapter 5 presents a retrospective analysis of the achievements of the par value system.

---

[2]Otmar Emminger, *On the Way to a New International Monetary Order* (Washington: American Enterprise Institute for Public Policy Research, 1976), p. 3.

CHAPTER

5

The Par Value System in Retrospect: Achievements

*M*ARCH 19, 1973, when generalized floating was introduced, is a historic date for it marks the demise of the par value system.[1] The par value system had been buffeted by recurrent crises in exchange and gold markets ever since flights from the dollar into gold began in January 1968, shortly after the devaluation of sterling in November 1967. (The devaluation of sterling was a less serious crisis in that it did not shake the international monetary system as a whole.) Previous to the crises of 1972 and 1973 caused by the floating of the pound sterling, the Italian lira, and the Japanese yen, by the second devaluation of the U.S. dollar, and by the joint float of the currencies of the EC countries described in the two preceding chapters, crises from 1968 to 1971 included abandonment of a single fixed price for gold in March 1968, disagreements over the exchange rates for the French franc and the deutsche mark through most of 1968, culminating in the meeting of the Group of Ten in Bonn in November 1968, subsequent changes in the rates for these currencies in the second half of 1969, floating of the Canadian dollar in 1970, crises in European exchange markets in May 1971 leading to the floating of the deutsche mark and the Netherlands guilder, and suspension of convertibility into gold of officially held dollars by the United States on August 15, 1971.[2]

Most U.S. monetary officials date the collapse of the system as August 15, 1971, when the United States suspended official convertibility of the dollar. Certainly that date ended the convertibility feature of the Bretton Woods system. But U.S. officials generally view that date as the end of par value arrangements as well since the par values for the dollar and for other currencies were inextricably connected to convertibility of officially held dollar balances. Most European officials contend that the par value system did not finally come to an end until the introduction of the joint

---

[1]The system agreed in 1944 is customarily referred to as the par value system since par values were at the heart of that system. The broader term, the Bretton Woods system, usually refers to three main elements of the arrangements—par values, convertibility of currencies, and freedom from payments restrictions.

[2]These earlier crises are described in *History, 1966–71*, Vol. I, pp. 403–409, 449–64, 476–82, and 519–30.

float of European currencies against the dollar in March 1973. As is discussed in the following chapter, these differences of view about the particular crisis which signalled the end of the par value system reflect deeper differences of view about how the system functioned and why it collapsed.

Rather than pinpointing the date of collapse, it seems preferable to regard the collapse of the par value system as a gradual process occurring between January 1968 and March 1973. Bit by bit, as the crises just enumerated occurred, pieces of the system were given up. The process was completed on March 19, 1973, because after that date officials made no further attempt to patch up or hold together the par value system, even temporarily, as they had for about a year after the Smithsonian agreement in December 1971. Instead, they looked toward a wholly reformed system.

By August 1971, public officials and economists in and out of government had been examining the functioning of the par value system for at least a dozen years. Several had made recommendations for major change, and important innovations— notably the introduction of the SDR in the Fund—were instituted.[3] After the U.S. suspension of convertibility of the dollar, an even more intensive examination of the system was undertaken, partly in the context of discussions to reform the system. This examination went on until January 1976, when agreement was finally reached on very different international monetary arrangements. This nearly two-decade-long scrutiny, involving discussions of the way in which the par value system performed and of the features needed in a reformed system, gave public officials and economists, by the middle of the 1970s, after the system had collapsed, a much better understanding of the system than they had had while it was in operation, although they by no means agreed on how well it had performed or on its major strengths and weaknesses. Through the use of this improved understanding of the par value system and of the causes of its collapse, this chapter presents a retrospective analysis of the achievements of the par value system and of the Fund's role in implementing it. The next chapter presents a retrospective analysis of the causes of the collapse of the system.

INITIAL PURPOSES AND OBJECTIVES

Assessment of the par value system best starts with the purposes of the system as originally conceived by its architects. Inasmuch as over 40 years have elapsed since the Bretton Woods Conference, fairly general agreement might be supposed to prevail on the original purposes of the par value system. Such is not the case, however. Assessing the intentions of the negotiators at Bretton Woods has been one of the favorite pastimes of economists, lawyers, and other specialists in recent years. As international monetary arrangements evolved in ways different from those that

---

[3]See *History 1966–71*, Vol. I, particularly Chaps. 1–9 and Chap. 24.

seemed to have been initially planned, what actually was originally planned or what developments were anticipated have been much discussed. This discussion persists particularly since those best qualified to know precisely what "the Bretton Woods planners" had in mind and why—John Maynard Keynes on the U.K. side and Harry Dexter White on the U.S. side—died in 1946 and 1947, respectively, virtually right after the Bretton Woods Conference. The writings of the main economist on the U.S. side, Edward M. Bernstein, however, shed some light on the thinking underlying the formation of the par value system. What follows is a conception of the purposes and objectives of the par value system, based partly on conversations with Mr. Bernstein.

The par value system was to serve two purposes. It was to introduce for the period after World War II international monetary arrangements that would shield the large industrial countries from the economic stagnation and high unemployment that had plagued them between the two World Wars and thus foster prosperity for the world as a whole. The second purpose was to substitute international consultation through the Fund on exchange rate policy and the use of restrictions on international payments for unilateral governmental decisions. Unilateral decisions, particularly from 1931 to 1935, had led to exchange rate instability, competitive depreciation, extensive use of exchange controls, inconvertibility of currencies, and bilateral payments arrangements.

Studies of the interwar period had demonstrated an integral connection between depressed national economies and unstable exchange rates and the self-defeating nature of efforts of countries to kindle domestic economic recovery by changing exchange rates on an uncoordinated national basis or by imposing restrictions on imports.[4] The classical gold standard had also become discredited. With its emphasis on an automatic price-specie-flow mechanism for balance of payments adjustment, it was identified with domestic deflation and unemployment. Yet, in its absence, the international monetary disorder of the 1930s had prevailed. To solve these problems, efforts to secure agreement among countries on techniques for stabilizing exchange rates had already begun in the mid-1930s.[5]

The founders of the par value system at the Bretton Woods Conference were thus undoubtedly looking backward, trying to correct the mistakes of the past, but as men of vision they were also planning for the future, aiming to devise an

---

[4]A study by the League of Nations on the experiences of countries with exchange rates and exchange controls in the 1920s and 1930s was published just about the time of the Bretton Woods Conference. This study became an immediate classic. The book, *International Currency Experience: Lessons of the Inter-War Period* (Geneva: League of Nations, 1944), was written mainly by Ragnar Nurkse. Chapter 9, stating his conclusions, had considerable influence on the thinking of economists at the time and for many years to come.

[5]The agreements on exchange rate arrangements which were forerunners to agreement in 1944 on a par value system administered by the Fund were briefly reviewed in *History, 1945–65*, Vol. I, pp. 4–10. A more recent examination of the efforts at exchange rate stabilization in the 1930s can be found in Stephen V.O. Clarke, *Exchange Rate Stabilization in the Mid-1930s: Negotiating the Tripartite Agreement*, Studies in International Finance, No. 71, Princeton University (Princeton, New Jersey): Princeton University Press, 1977).

international monetary system that would expand economic well-being for all countries once World War II was over.

Reasoning of U.K. Negotiators

In planning an international monetary system, officials from the United Kingdom were deeply concerned about unemployment. Led by John Maynard Keynes, they were dedicated to the pursuit after World War II of domestic policies to maintain full employment in line with the "new school" of Keynesian economics. They were eager to avoid balance of payments constraints on their contemplated full employment policies and favored an international monetary system that permitted national authorities to change exchange rates in order to correct disequilibrium in a country's external payments. In his famous speech to the House of Lords on May 23, 1944, commending acceptance of the proposals for an international monetary union, Keynes made explicit that "we are determined that, in future, the external value of sterling shall conform to its internal value as set by our own domestic policies, and not the other way round."[6] The desire of the U.K. negotiators to have a free hand in dealing with possible balance of payments deficits resulting from full employment policies also explains Keynes's proposal that the new international monetary agency have the power to issue its own currency—his often-cited proposal for bancor—and the strong preference of the U.K. negotiators at Bretton Woods and in the early years of the Fund for virtually automatic rather than conditional use of the Fund's financial resources.[7]

Reasoning of U.S. Negotiators

The U.S. negotiators at Bretton Woods were also looking forward. They reflected the thinking of President Franklin D. Roosevelt, who, in the course of his third administration, began to plan the establishment of a series of international arrangements and institutions, most notably the United Nations, to come into effect after the end of World War II to keep the peace and promote economic progress. In planning these institutions, the United States assumed an appropriate leadership role, in contrast to its isolationist response to efforts at international cooperation after World War I.[8]

U.S. officials at Bretton Woods tended to think in more pragmatic terms and less in terms of a general economic philosophy than their U.K. counterparts. But

---

[6]*Hansard*, House of Lords, 5th Series, Vol. 131, Cols. 838–49.

[7]The negotiations that brought about the par value system were described at length in *History, 1945–65*, Vol. I, Chaps. 1–5. For an exposition of the particular positions taken by U.K. authorities mentioned here, see pp. 67–77.

[8]A description of the general environment in the U.S. Government in which the Bretton Woods institutions were conceived can be found in Richard N. Gardner, *Sterling-Dollar Diplomacy: The Origins and the Prospects of Our International Economic Order* (New York: McGraw-Hill, rev. ed., 1969), and in Alfred E. Eckes, Jr., *A Search for Solvency: Bretton Woods and the International Monetary System, 1941–71* (Austin: University of Texas Press, 1975).

they, too, wanted an international monetary system that would maximize the use of the world's productive capacity and enhance real world income. The U.S. Government, like that of the United Kingdom, was committed to full employment policies for the postwar period, as exemplified two years after the Bretton Woods Conference by the U.S. Employment Act of 1946. The U.S. delegation at Bretton Woods was not so sure, however, that unemployment would be the major economic problem after the war. In a commentary written in 1977, Mr. Bernstein has explained that while Keynes in 1943–44 expected a substantial economic depression after the war, other economists at the conference, including Mr. Bernstein, saw the postwar period as one of prolonged expansion and inflation, and that before his death in 1946, Keynes had changed his mind from expecting economic depression to expecting economic expansion.[9] Therefore, rather than singling out the employment issue, U.S. negotiators aimed at four goals: full employment, economic growth, price stability, and balance of payments equilibrium.

To achieve these goals, the Bretton Woods system and the newly established International Monetary Fund were only part of the postwar international economic arrangements or what in more recent years has come to be referred to as the world economic order. The world economic order planned for after World War II was to include other international economic organizations, inter alia, the International Bank for Reconstruction and Development (IBRD)—the World Bank—to encourage international investment; the International Trade Organization (ITO), which was never established but in lieu of which the CONTRACTING PARTIES to the General Agreement on Tariffs and Trade (GATT) was created, to ensure liberal commercial policies; and the Food and Agriculture Organization (FAO) to foster stable prices for foods and other agricultural commodities.

In planning this world economic order, U.S. negotiators were convinced that an orderly and stable international monetary system that permitted maximum freedom for international financial transactions, together with a liberal regime for international trade, was the appropriate basis for attaining their economic goals. They were particularly interested in international economic arrangements that would help create a large world market to which all countries had equal access. They also had in mind obtaining the benefits of an international division of labor, especially the more refined and complicated division of labor which the spread of industrial techniques tends to develop. At the same time, although they believed in relying on market-oriented principles and on a free private enterprise system, they believed that some governmental and intergovernmental monitoring of international monetary and trade arrangements was necessary. The international monetary system could no longer be left to arrangements determined primarily by private bankers and private financial institutions, as it had been during the nineteenth century and the first 40 years of the twentieth century. The International Monetary

---

[9]Edward M. Bernstein, "The History of the International Monetary Fund, 1966–71," *Finance & Development* (Washington), Vol. 14 (December 1977), p. 17.

Fund was to administer the system, explicitly to administer a "code of fair practices" in respect to exchange rates and international financial transactions.[10]

U.S. officials at Bretton Woods, keenly aware that the United States was the only country at the start of the postwar period with the financial resources needed to start the Fund's operations, wanted to predetermine and limit that country's financial responsibility. U.S. officials consequently rejected Keynes's suggestion that the Fund be empowered to create reserves through bancor, favoring instead the payment by members of subscriptions in gold and their currencies for the whole of the Fund's resources, and insisted, contrary to the arguments of U.K. officials, that conditions be applied to the use of those resources.

The desire to minimize U.S. Government financing of other countries' balance of payments deficits also explains why U.S. officials favored a system allowing changes in exchange rates. By devaluing their currencies, other countries could reduce their balance of payments deficits, thereby reducing the balance of payments financing that the United States would have to provide. U.S. officials used the same reasoning when they agreed to relatively advantageous exchange rates for the deutsche mark and the Japanese yen shortly after the end of World War II. This reasoning was reflected again in the positions taken by the U.S. Executive Directors (Harry Dexter White, Andrew N. Overby, and Frank A. Southard, Jr.) from the opening of the Fund in 1946 through the end of the Marshall Plan in 1952. For example, in setting initial par values in 1946, the U.S. Executive Director, reflecting views then strongly held in the U.S. Government, emphasized the need for countries, especially in Western Europe, to set their exchange rates at levels that would substantially boost their exports and their capacity to produce goods for export and thus lessen their dependence on U.S. aid. Again in 1948, when it appeared that the currencies of many countries might be overvalued vis-à-vis the dollar, U.S. authorities pushed for the devaluation of many currencies that eventually took place in September 1949. And throughout the Fund's first decade, the U.S. authorities not only permitted but encouraged numerous and relatively large devaluations against the dollar.[11]

The System as an Experiment

The par value system was an innovation. National authorities were to be free to direct their macroeconomic policies, mainly monetary and fiscal policies to achieve domestic goals, provided they abstained from competitive exchange depreciation and from restrictions on current international payments to promote domestic

---

[10]For a study, written at the time, of the aims of the United States in planning its international economic policy for the period after World War II, see Irving S. Friedman and Margaret M. Garritsen (later de Vries), *Foreign Economic Problems of Postwar United States* (New York: American Institute of Pacific Relations, 1947).

[11]A description of the events cited in this paragraph can be found in *History, 1945–65*, Vol. I, pp. 234–42, and Vol. II, pp. 96–100 and 111–14.

employment at the expense of employment in other countries. To avoid deflating domestic economies excessively as the way to correct external payments deficits, a number of policies for balance of payments adjustment were available. For temporary disequilibrium and to ease the execution of domestically painful policies for balance of payments adjustment, recourse could be had to financing from the Fund. In the event of fundamental disequilibrium, there could be changes in exchange rates. In the event of capital flight, controls over capital movements could be used. If necessary other restrictions, such as exchange restrictions or even restrictions on imports, could be used, with the approval of the Fund or the GATT.

The significant advance of the Bretton Woods agreement was thus that nations surrendered some sovereignty, especially with regard to exchange rates, in return for the benefits of membership in the Fund. The system of par values accordingly can be construed as much as an attempt to subject exchange rate changes to international agreement as an attempt to institute fixed exchange rates. Indeed, contrary to instituting fixed rates, the Fund's Articles of Agreement allow a country, subject to international approval, to choose devaluation over deflation to overcome a balance of payments deficit.

That the par value system and the International Monetary Fund were bold new experiments and that no one was certain how the new arrangements would work in practice is exemplified by the questions that leading economists raised at the time. Whether the simultaneous pursuit by several industrial countries of domestic policies to achieve full employment or price stability would be consistent with a satisfactory array of balance of payments positions was unknown. As is evident from his *Proposals for an International Clearing Union*, Keynes saw the problem primarily as how to avoid insufficiencies in aggregate demand: "if active employment and ample purchasing power can be sustained in the main centres of the world trade, the problem of surpluses and unwanted exports will largely disappear, even though, under the most prosperous conditions, there may remain some disturbances of trade and unforeseen situations requiring special remedies."[12] It was considered particularly important for the maximization of world real income that the United States and the United Kingdom, "the main centres of the world trade," maintain full employment.

Some economists questioned whether a system based on free trade and multilateral payments would actually maximize world trade. They argued that the international exchange of goods might possibly be larger if countries applied discriminatory restrictions to imports from the United States, where productivity was much higher than in Europe. Thomas Balogh of Oxford University argued that a multilateral trade and payments system based on free trade principles would work primarily to the advantage of the United States, the country with the largest and strongest economy, and would not maximize real income for the poorer and smaller

---

[12]*History, 1945–65*, Vol. III, p. 28.

members of the system.[13] In a pioneering study Professor James Meade of Cambridge University began to treat adjustment of the balance of payments as a policy problem, examining the kinds of economic policies that a country might pursue to attain simultaneously full domestic employment and equilibrium in the external balance of payments.[14]

ACHIEVEMENTS OF THE SYSTEM IN THE FIRST 25 YEARS

The achievements in the world economy during the first 25 years of the existence of the Fund and the Bretton Woods system have to be regarded as nothing short of remarkable. As is well documented elsewhere, from 1946 until the early 1970s, when the par value system was in operation, the Western industrial countries and Japan experienced unparalleled economic growth and unprecedented levels of prosperity and consumption. The developing countries also made far greater economic strides than did the industrial countries in comparable stages of their economic growth.[15]

In fact, the 1950s and the 1960s may well prove to have been the period of greatest worldwide economic expansion in history. During this expansion, moreover, the world was able to overcome the most serious postwar international economic and financial problem, the "chronic world dollar shortage." This term described the persistent inability, from 1945 to about 1958, of countries to export enough goods and services to earn dollars to pay for their large imports of goods and services from the United States. By 1958 the dollar shortage had been eliminated and there were already signs of the impending dollar glut.

The Fund's Role in the Economic Expansion

Critics contend that the Bretton Woods system and the Fund had little to do with these remarkable economic and financial achievements. They point out that the system as originally envisaged, with freedom from restrictions on international payments and convertibility of currencies, did not become established until the end of 1958, and that by 1965 it was already beginning to encounter serious difficulties.

---

[13]See, for example, his "The International Aspects of Full Employment," in *The Economics of Full Employment*, Six Studies in Applied Economics prepared at the Oxford University Institute of Statistics (Oxford: Basil Blackwell, 1946) and his "The United States and International Economic Equilibrium," in Seymour E. Harris, ed., *Foreign Economic Policy for the United States* (Cambridge, Mass.: Harvard University Press, 1948), pp. 446–80.

[14]See his *The Balance of Payments: The Theory of International Economic Policy*, Vol. 1 (London: Oxford University Press, 1951). For this study, together with related pioneering studies of international economic policy, Professor Meade was to receive the Nobel Prize in Economic Sciences in 1977.

[15]The reader interested in specific figures is referred to David Morawetz, *Twenty-Five Years of Economic Development, 1950–75* (Washington: World Bank, 1977).

These critics maintain that if the Bretton Woods system was fully operational for only seven years, it could not have been responsible for the economic expansion of the postwar period.[16]

These critics, however, are in the minority. The general consensus is that the international environment, including the international monetary system as implemented by the Fund, contributed appreciably to postwar economic growth. The prime movers in the economic recovery of Western Europe and of Japan were the expansion of their exports and of world trade, "the golden girdle of the globe." Trade through the 1960s grew even faster than world production, and there were huge increases in international investment, mainly by rapidly growing multinational firms. Trade and investment, in turn, were stimulated by the progressive attainment of the objectives of the Bretton Woods system. At the start of the postwar period restrictions on trade and payments had been extensive, including discriminatory restrictions on imports requiring payments in dollars. Except for the U.S. dollar, the Canadian dollar, and the currencies of the Central American countries, no currencies were convertible. The gradual lifting of restrictions is often cited as the vital factor which stimulated European exports and gave impetus to Western European recovery. Much of the lifting of restrictions can be attributed to the trade liberalization policies of what was then the Organization for European Economic Cooperation (OEEC), later converted into the Organization for Economic Cooperation and Development (OECD). But the policies of the International Monetary Fund also encouraged the expansion of exports of all its members, not just those in the dollar area.

The Fund's particular role in fostering world economic prosperity after World War II was to help its members attain realistic exchange rates and to push its members toward the progressive liberalization of trade and payments and the attainment of currency convertibility. The Fund fulfilled this role in a number of ways. For example, it used the effect of the proposed par value on exports as its main criterion in judging the adequacy of the initial par values set in 1946. When a few years later it appeared that conditions in Western Europe were ripe for increased exportation, the Fund advocated changes in exchange rates that helped bring about the devaluations of 1949. Throughout the 1950s and in 1960 and 1961, the Fund especially endeavored to ensure that improvements in countries' balance of payments positions were accompanied by an appropriate lessening of their restrictions on trade and payments, by reduced discrimination against their purchases from the United States and other countries in the dollar area, and by adequate steps toward convertibility of their currencies. The Fund developed policies relating use of its financial resources to a member's progress in the removal of its restrictions. The Fund also directed the use of its financial resources toward helping countries refrain from reimposing restrictions when they were again confronted with balance of payments deficits.

---

[16]This argument has been put forward, for example, by W.M. Scammell in his *International Monetary Policy: Bretton Woods and After* (New York: John Wiley & Sons, 1975), pp. 123–69.

The Fund's emphasis in the 1950s on the reduction of multiple currency practices, used primarily by developing members, helped to bring about more realistic exchange rates for these members so as to improve their trade positions. At a time when developing members were using multiple exchange rates and other restrictions to encourage import-substitution strategies of economic development, the Fund was emphasizing the need for realistic exchange rates that would orient their economic growth more toward exports.[17]

Although its policies were directed toward the elimination of restrictions on current transactions, the Fund considered the lifting of controls on capital transfers desirable as well. Not only were long-term investment flows expected to increase, but freely moving capital was expected to help equilibrate payments positions. In time, to an extent undreamed of by the Fund's founding fathers, restrictions on both current transactions and capital transfers were eliminated.

In fact, as short-term capital movements became freer of restriction and came to be a disturbing element in countries' balances of payments, the Fund in 1961 took one of its most important decisions on the use of its resources. In 1946 the Fund had taken a decision interpreting its Articles of Agreement virtually to preclude the use of the Fund's resources by a member whose balance of payments difficulties arose from a deficit on capital account. But in 1961 this decision was reversed. Capital movements could be taken into account when a member requested use of the Fund's resources.[18]

The Fund had yet another role in stimulating the growth of world trade and investment that prompted world economic expansion as a whole in the 1950s and 1960s. The major economic problem of the postwar years proved to be inflation rather than deflation. Since its establishment, the Fund's policies were directed to helping countries deal with this problem. The first Annual Report of the Fund in 1946 already identified inflation as a general world economic problem and by 1948 the Fund was encouraging governments to take appropriate measures for its prevention.[19] This early and continuing emphasis by the Fund on anti-inflationary measures was aimed at countries strengthening their external payments positions so that they could lift restrictions on trade and payments and attain currency convertibility.

The Fund was also in the forefront of analysis relating countries' macroeconomic policies, and later more specifically their monetary policies, to developments in their balances of payments. On the occasion of the exchange rate devaluations of 1949, Fund staff were among the first to stress that countries had to accompany depreciations of their exchange rates with tight monetary and fiscal

---

[17]The policies of the Fund referred to in these two paragraphs are described at length in *History, 1945–65*, Vol. II. See particularly pp. 52–54, 122–46, and 249–316.

[18]These decisions on use of the Fund's resources and capital transfers have been described at length in *History, 1945–65*, Vol. I, pp. 503–506, and Vol. II, pp. 34–35, 384, 410–16, 539–41, and 568.

[19]*Annual Report of the Executive Directors for the Fiscal Year Ended April 30, 1948* (Washington: International Monetary Fund, 1948), pp. 15–20. (Hereafter cited as *Annual Report, 19—.*)

policies in order to make the devaluations effective. The relation between exchange rate changes and macroeconomic policies was developed as early as 1948 in the Research Department, under the guidance of Edward M. Bernstein.[20] After several years of experience with countries' balance of payments problems, the Research Department staff presented an overview of how balance of payments adjustment worked, taking into account domestic macroeconomic policies and exchange rate changes.[21] At about the same time, staff working with Latin American members started to develop criteria based on data for monetary aggregates, such as data for money in circulation and credit outstanding, to judge the domestic situation of a member and to relate these criteria to developments in the member's balance of payments situation. This early work was the forerunner of more formal theoretical models developed by the Fund staff from 1957 to 1974 for analyzing the relations between monetary policy and the balance of payments of a country.

Above and beyond these achievements, the major contribution of the Fund was to facilitate among its members the development of harmonious cooperation on monetary and financial policies. Cooperation among the monetary authorities of members, of course, took place in many forums, and especially in the informal contacts established by the central bankers of the ten large industrial nations.[22] But the Fund, too, was an important instrument in the growth of international cooperation among the world's monetary policymakers. As officials of member countries worked together in the framework of the Fund, they came to know each other personally and gradually established a trust that enabled them to disclose confidential information about the payments and reserve positions of their countries, their exchange restrictions, and the prospects for these positions and restrictions. They were able to discuss fully and frankly not only their mutual balance of payments policies but also their domestic monetary and fiscal policies.

This cooperation was facilitated by the absence from the Fund between 1954, when Czechoslovakia ceased to be a member, and 1972, when Romania was admitted to membership, of members from the Eastern European bloc. (Yugoslavia was, of course, an original Fund member and continued to be a member in good standing.) Because the U.S.S.R. and the other members of the Eastern European bloc were not members, the Fund was spared the divisive arguments and political controversy that characterized the United Nations almost from its beginning. Despite the heterogeneity of its members, which differed economically in level of gross national product, degree of industrialization, population density, per capita income, extent of dependence on international trade, and which ranged politically

---

[20]See, for example, J.J. Polak, "Depreciation to Meet a Situation of Overinvestment" (unpublished, International Monetary Fund, September 10, 1948), and *Annual Report, 1950*, pp. 23–24. A further paper related changes in a country's trade balance to changes in its total consumption and investment; Sidney S. Alexander, "Effects of a Devaluation on a Trade Balance," *Staff Papers*, International Monetary Fund (Washington), Vol. 2 (April 1952), pp. 263–78.

[21]E.M. Bernstein, "Strategic Factors in Balance of Payments Adjustment," *Staff Papers*, Vol. 5 (August 1956), pp. 151–69.

[22]Charles A. Coombs, *The Arena of International Finance* (New York: John Wiley & Sons, 1976).

from countries committed to "free world objectives" to those regarding themselves as nonaligned, the Fund was able to mobilize considerable collaboration among members. This collaboration can be attributed primarily to the efforts of Fund officials to stress technical rather than political elements in reaching understandings on international monetary topics.

In some respects international cooperation among all Fund members can be said to have reached an especially high point at the Twenty-Second Annual Meeting in Rio de Janeiro in September 1967 when monetary authorities agreed to establish a facility within the Fund for creating SDRs. By this action, the Fund was empowered to create reserve assets, a power denied to it at its founding.

In their 1970 report, *The Role of Exchange Rates in the Adjustment of International Payments*, the Executive Directors affirmed that the objectives of the Bretton Woods system and of the Fund were fulfilled along the lines originally hoped for. That report credited the outstanding postwar economic record to the determination of governments to take responsibility for the economic performance of their countries, that is, to pursue active modern stabilization policies. It noted further that, as had been seen by the founders of the Fund, national authorities had to combine active domestic economic policies with active international economic collaboration, and that the Bretton Woods structure was the cornerstone of this collaboration.

In sum, as initially envisaged under the Bretton Woods system, Keynesian macroeconomic policies had been pursued in most industrial countries and had succeeded through the cooperation of all Fund members. The Bretton Woods system, moreover, had succeeded despite the tensions of the Cold War, the strains accompanying the emergence of many new nations from colonial status, the upheavals produced by rapid social and technological change throughout the world, and the conduct of two major—the Korean and the Viet Nam wars—and several other conflicts.

HOW THE SYSTEM WORKED

While the par value system worked smoothly for nearly 25 years, it had not necessarily worked as initially envisaged. In fact, the system evolved in four ways that had not been foreseen.

Passive Role of the United States in Exchange Markets

The first was the way exchange rates were implemented under the system. The United States assumed an essentially passive role in exchange markets and in the determination of rates for the U.S. dollar. The exchange rates of other currencies vis-à-vis the dollar were determined by the actions of the central banks of other countries. The initiative for exchange rate change was left to countries other than the

United States and, indeed, until the second half of the 1960s, nearly all exchange rate changes were depreciations against the dollar. In effect all countries, including the major industrial countries, were free to change their exchange rates, including rates between their currencies and the dollar, to correct their balance of payments positions without being concerned about the consequences for the trade or financial transactions of the United States.

An implementation of the par value system that assumed a passive role for U.S. authorities in exchange markets grew directly out of the Fund's original Articles of Agreement. Under the original Articles, each member undertook to permit within its territories exchange transactions between its currency and the currencies of other members only within prescribed margins. The maximum and the minimum rates for exchange transactions between the currencies of members taking place within their territories were not to differ from parity for spot exchange transactions by more than 1 percent and for other exchange transactions by a margin which exceeded that for spot exchange transactions by more than the Fund considered reasonable.

The Articles recognized, however, the unique position of the United States. At the time, the monetary authorities of the United States neither customarily intervened in foreign exchange markets nor held currencies of other countries as reserves. The United States did, however, hold over 70 percent of the world's gold reserves. Hence, the drafters of the Fund's original Articles provided that the United States could fulfill its exchange rate obligations in the Fund differently from other members. A provision was inserted by which a member whose monetary authorities freely bought and sold gold at a fixed official price for the settlement of international transactions was deemed to be fulfilling the undertaking with regard to fixed exchange rates.

Other members fulfilled the requirement to keep spot exchange rates between their own and other currencies within prescribed margins around parities mainly by market interventions, a technique with which they were familiar. Their central banks entered exchange markets to buy and sell currencies so as to keep spot rates fixed. For its part, the United States fulfilled its exchange rate obligations under the Articles by its willingness to convert into gold freely and without limit dollars held by foreign monetary authorities. In this way, the dollar had a fixed relationship with gold, and hence also with the currencies of other members.

This implementation of the par value system, in which all members of the Fund other than the United States were prepared to intervene in exchange markets, also meant that an intervention currency was necessary. As the strongest convertible currency after World War II, the dollar was already the principal vehicle or transaction currency—the currency in which most international transactions were conducted—and it soon became the intervention currency as well. Margins around parities also came to be defined in terms of the intervention currency, making the U.S. dollar, rather than gold, the unit in terms of which all other currencies were expressed.

The Role of the Dollar

Because the U.S. dollar was the currency of intervention, the basis was laid for a second important development in the Bretton Woods system: a special role for the U.S. dollar. For a number of reasons, after World War II countries wanted to accumulate reserves. Because the supply of gold did not keep pace with the demand for reserves, the dollar became not only the main transaction and intervention currency but also the principal reserve currency, that is, the currency in which countries kept their foreign exchange reserves. Since other countries wanted to build up their holdings of dollars, the United States was able to finance balance of payments deficits by accumulating dollar liabilities abroad as well as by the drawing down of its gold stocks. Moreover, other countries were more willing to permit an expansion of liquidity in their own economies through the growth of reserves than to pursue domestic monetary policies that would enhance their domestic liquidity. Hence, the financing by the United States of its payments deficits through an enlargement of dollar liabilities abroad permitted an expansion in the supply of international liquidity to accommodate the growth of international trade and capital transactions and also an expansion in the domestic liquidity of countries with payments surpluses. For a long time, this arrangement suited the objectives both of the United States and most other Fund members. But the Bretton Woods system, originally envisaged as a gold-exchange standard, in which both gold and national currencies (the pound sterling as well as the dollar) were used in international settlements and held as reserves, evolved into a gold-dollar standard, and eventually into a virtually pure dollar standard.

Exchange Rate Rigidity

A third important development in the par value system was the eventual association of the system not with exchange rate change but with exchange rate rigidity. Except for a floating rate for the Canadian dollar from 1950 to 1962, a devaluation of the French franc at the end of 1958, and the revaluations of the deutsche mark and the Netherlands guilder in 1961, the par value system operated from September 1949 until November 1967 with no changes in the par values for the major currencies. By the mid-1960s the major industrial countries developed considerable resistance to changing their exchange rates.

A disposition by the large industrial countries to effect balance of payments adjustment without changing their exchange rates resulted at least in part from their success from about 1950 to 1965 with using macroeconomic policies to correct balance of payments disequilibria without undue repercussion on domestic employment. The Federal Republic of Germany, for example, in 1950 and again in 1965 and 1966, was able to turn a payments deficit promptly into a surplus without devaluation. Italy, in 1963 and 1964, corrected a payments deficit without a change in the value of the lira. On several occasions prior to 1968, Japan was also able to manage its balance of payments by the use of monetary policy alone. The United States, too, after developing an overall balance of payments deficit for part of 1950 and then from 1952 onward, increased its merchandise trade balance from $1 billion in 1959 to $8 billion in 1964 by use of domestic fiscal and monetary policies. That the remarkable increase in the trade balance was offset by an enormous rise in U.S. foreign investment does not discount the achievement of balance of payments adjustment through domestic economic policies.[23]

There were several reasons why, as the system evolved in practice, countries used demand-management policies rather than exchange rate changes to correct external payments imbalances, contrary to what had been expected when the par value system was planned. The postwar period was characterized almost from its beginning by inflationary pressure rather than by the economically depressed conditions that had marked the 1930s. Hence, controlling inflation became an objective of postwar domestic financial policy. Countries with balance of payments deficits were especially receptive to the use of anti-inflationary policies, involving monetary and fiscal restraint, to correct their deficits. Countries with payments surpluses were more reluctant to resort to expansionary policies. In addition, economic analysis, much of it originating in the Fund, and the experience of countries were already suggesting by 1948 that devaluation or the use of import restrictions to correct balance of payments deficits had to be supplemented by measures to curb aggregate demand. Devaluation of the exchange rate alone was not sufficient. Rather than devalue *and* use anti-inflationary measures, countries came to prefer anti-inflationary policies alone as an instrument of balance of payments policy.

Accordingly, the initial philosophy underlying the Bretton Woods system—that monetary and fiscal policies should be directed toward the attainment of full employment while exchange rate changes were used to maintain balance of payments equilibrium—gradually changed. External as well as internal equilibrium came to be considered a legitimate objective of domestic economic policy, particularly of monetary policy. Gradually, too, the Fund's consultations with members were extended to internal economic policies, although attention to internal economic policies had not been explicitly mentioned in the Fund's original Articles.

Not only were industrial countries willing to depend heavily on anti-inflationary policies to correct external payments disequilibria and not to change their exchange rates, but unusual circumstances prevailing until about 1965 enabled them to correct balance of payments disequilibria without changing their exchange rates. First of all, existing exchange rates were on the whole appropriate, especially for the European currencies and the yen. After the 1949 devaluations, exchange rates for the Western European currencies and the Japanese yen, particularly vis-à-vis the dollar, could even be regarded as advantageous. In fact, many economists and public officials came to believe, even by 1952, that the magnitude of the devaluations

---

[23]An analysis of the balance of payments adjustment of industrial countries in the period after 1949 until about 1963 by the Fund staff can be found in J. Marcus Fleming, "Developments in the International Payments System," *Staff Papers*, International Monetary Fund (Washington), Vol. 10 (November 1963), pp. 461–84; and Anne Romanis (later Anne Romanis Braun), "Balance of Payments Adjustment Among Developed Countries," *Staff Papers*, Vol. 12 (March 1965), pp. 17–34.

of 1949 may have been excessive and that the deliberately favorable exchange rates set for the deutsche mark and the Japanese yen after World War II to stimulate the economic recovery of the Federal Republic of Germany and of Japan may have been too favorable from the point of view of other industrial countries, especially the United States.

In addition, trade was being progressively liberalized. Hence, markets for goods and investment were continuously being enlarged so that industrial countries could increase their exports all the more readily without changing their exchange rates.

The United States was also willing after 1952 to run payments deficits year after year and even to initiate large transfers of foreign aid and investment, which greatly enlarged the deficits. To finance these deficits, the United States was willing also to lose much of its gold reserves in favor of a better distribution of world gold reserves and, in order to help nations abroad acquire still further reserves, to increase its dollar liabilities abroad. For many years the U.S. balance of payments deficit was not considered a problem even by European authorities. On the contrary, they, as well as U.S. authorities, focused on European countries achieving balance of payments surpluses and sufficient productive capacity to enable them to accumulate the reserves that the United States was losing.

Another factor favored easy balance of payments adjustment by industrial countries for some years after World War II. Economists became fully aware of its significance only in the sharply altered circumstances of the 1970s. Throughout the industrial world of the 1950s and the first few years of the 1960s, a tremendous expansion of output was possible without severe pressure on prices from wage costs. Expansion of output was possible because most economies experienced considerable unemployment and underemployment. Hence, economic slack could be taken up; there were ample opportunities to shift manpower from low to high productivity sectors of the economy. There were also rapid increases in the labor force. Special long-run factors, such as differential rates of growth between the industrial countries in technology and productivity, also were at work to help production expand. Technology and productivity increased quickly, both absolutely and relatively, especially in the Federal Republic of Germany and in Japan. All these factors made for ready increases in output which could go either into expanded exports or into domestic substitutes for imports, thereby facilitating correction of trade deficits.

Last, attention to balance of payments disequilibria meant attention to balance of payments deficits. All the circumstances just described were particularly helpful for correcting deficits. There was little concern at the time with the need to correct payments surpluses. The uniqueness of the prevailing circumstances and their implications for balance of payments adjustment through use of macroeconomic policies instead of through changes in exchange rates was not sufficiently appreciated at the time. As a consequence, industrial countries came to view the par value system as a system of virtually fixed exchange rates.

Circumstances for developing members were, of course, vastly different. Developing members found it difficult to rely on anti-inflationary policies to cure their balance of payments deficits, and had to devalue their currencies. Some devalued because they were vigorously pushing exports. Others devalued because they were trying to curtail excessive imports in the interest of encouraging domestic production of substitutes. As a result, under the par value system, the Fund's developing members during the period 1950–65 used the mechanism of exchange rate change much more commonly than did industrial members. Many underwent exchange depreciation even in excess of their relatively higher rates of inflation.[24]

Freedom for Capital Movements

The fourth important development in the par value system was that, as already mentioned, movements of capital, even on short term, were gradually made much freer of controls than had been expected when the liberal trade and payments regime was planned. Restrictions on capital movements were accepted at the Bretton Woods Conference, although restrictions on trade and current transactions were not, because the gains from expanded and integrated trade were considered likely to be far greater than the gains from expanded and integrated capital markets. As trade expanded, however, demand developed for a readily available international means of payments and for an extensive network of credit facilities. In addition, as giant multinational companies undertook production on a worldwide basis, they too needed to raise and transfer capital easily. Banking operations consequently grew tremendously and became integrated across national boundaries. This financial integration was facilitated and encouraged by the gradual removal of controls on capital movements. But once capital markets became closely integrated, national authorities found it difficult to reimpose controls on capital movements.

■ ■ ■ ■ ■ ■

The par value system thus evolved through roughly the first half of the 1960s as a system in which exchange rates vis-à-vis the dollar were determined in the markets of other countries. The United States was willing to accept the resulting rates, and the dollar had a unique role as a reserve currency which most countries were willing to accept. In addition, industrial countries effected balance of payments adjustment primarily through demand-management policies rather than by changing their par values. Finally, capital movements were gradually made virtually free of controls. Although these developments permitted the par value system to function smoothly for many years, they were eventually to bring about the collapse of the system.

---

[24] A study of the magnitudes of exchange rate changes by developing members from 1948 to 1967 can be found in Margaret G. de Vries, "Exchange Depreciation in Developing Countries," *Staff Papers*, International Monetary Fund (Washington), Vol. 15 (November 1968), pp. 560–76.

CHAPTER

6

The Par Value System in Retrospect: Problems

C OLLAPSE OF THE BRETTON WOODS SYSTEM in the 1970s came as a shock, but it was like the shock of the death of a family member who had been ill for a long time. Several economists in the academic community had recognized dangers in the system for years, and by the late 1950s U.S. officials, too, became concerned at the persistence of U.S. balance of payments deficits and their seeming inability to do much about them.

EARLY SUGGESTIONS FOR CHANGE

Since the introduction of the par value system, academic economists were more critical of it than were public officials and more inclined to suggest changes in it. Some questioned whether exchange rates had to be fixed. Professor Milton Friedman, of the University of Chicago, was the first to advocate flexible exchange rates.[1] His advocacy of flexible rates in the early 1950s was based mainly on the grounds that it was difficult, if not impossible, for governments to determine par values which would produce the exchange rates needed for balance of payments equilibrium and that exchange rates which were free to move in accordance with demand and supply would be more satisfactory.

Shortly afterward, Professors Gottfried Haberler of Harvard University and James Meade of Cambridge University also wrote what have become classic articles advocating flexible rates.[2] Professor Haberler's position in the mid-1950s was that

---

[1]"The Case for Flexible Exchange Rates," in *Essays in Positive Economics* (Chicago: University of Chicago Press, 1953), pp. 157–203. Professor Friedman had already been making the case for flexible rates a few years before publication of these essays.

[2]Gottfried Haberler, *Currency Convertibility* (Washington: American Enterprise Association, Inc., 1954), and J.E. Meade, "The Case for Variable Exchange Rates," *Three Banks Review* (Edinburgh, September 1955), pp. 3–27. Other relatively early academic advocates of flexible rates

greater flexibility was needed than the par value system allowed if dismantling exchange controls and restrictions was to occur and be sustained. Always a staunch advocate of floating rates, Professor Haberler in recent years has questioned the 1944 study of the League of Nations, concluding that the years from 1931 to 1936 were not really characterized by excessive exchange rate instability and competitive depreciation.[3]

Around 1960 changes were proposed in the way the Bretton Woods system provided liquidity and reserves to the Fund's members. These proposals were independently advanced in 1958 and 1959 by Robert Triffin, of Yale University, who published his new proposals, and in a seminar on international economics at Harvard University by Edward M. Bernstein, then recently resigned from the Fund staff. More proposals for changing the system of reserve creation were soon put forward.[4]

The difficulty of devaluing the dollar in the par value system was also made clear to U.S. officials in the late 1950s. During the second administration of President Dwight D. Eisenhower, Robert Anderson, the Secretary of the Treasury, believing that a devaluation of the dollar—that is, an increase in the dollar price for gold— would probably be followed by corresponding changes by other countries in the price for gold in terms of their currencies, informally asked the U.S. Executive Director, then Frank A. Southard, Jr., how the dollar could be devalued vis-à-vis other currencies. When Mr. Southard explained that effective devaluation of the dollar could be brought about only by breaking the link between the dollar and gold, U.S. authorities realized that such action would pull out the linchpin of the par value system, and so were disinclined to consider it.

Signs of possibly serious problems with the par value system became more generally recognized. U.S. authorities were worried that stimulating domestic employment would result in larger balance of payments deficits. As John F. Kennedy assumed office in January 1961 he confessed that the U.S. balance of

---

include Professor George N. Halm, of the Fletcher School of Law and Diplomacy at Tufts University, Professor W.M. Scammell, of McMaster University in Hamilton, Ontario, and Professor Egon Sohmen, of the University of Chicago. Early in the 1950s Professor Scammell, for example, wrote "What Sort of Exchange Rates?" *Westminister Bank Review* (London, May 1954), pp. 1–4. The fullest explanations of the views of Professor Halm and Professor Sohmen can be found, respectively, in *Approaches to Greater Flexibility of Exchange Rates: The Bürgenstock Papers*, arranged by C. Fred Bergsten, George N. Halm, Fritz Machlup, and Robert V. Roosa, and edited by George N. Halm (Princeton, New Jersey: Princeton University Press, 1970), and Egon Sohmen, *Flexible Exchange Rates: Theory and Controversy* (Chicago: University of Chicago Press, 1st ed., 1961); rev. ed. entitled *Flexible Exchange Rates* (1969).

[3]Gottfried Haberler, *The World Economy, Money, and the Great Depression, 1919–1939*, Foreign Affairs Study, 30 (Washington: American Enterprise Institute for Public Policy Research, 1976). In addition to the study by Professor Haberler, other studies examining countries' experiences with floating rates in the interwar period have also cast doubts on the conclusions of the study by the League of Nations. One such study by Fund staff is that of S.C. Tsiang, "Fluctuating Exchange Rates in Countries with Relatively Stable Economies: Some European Experiences After World War I," *Staff Papers*, International Monetary Fund (Washington), Vol. 7 (October 1959), pp. 244–73.

[4]These proposals were all described in *History, 1966–71*, Vol. I, pp. 17–20.

payments deficit was one of his two greatest worries; the other was the threat of nuclear war.[5]

PROBLEMS OF LIQUIDITY, ADJUSTMENT, AND CONFIDENCE

In 1963–64 a group of 32 academic and public economists identified three basic problems of the Bretton Woods system: liquidity, adjustment, and confidence in reserve media.[6] For the next decade discussions of the shortcomings of the Bretton Woods system centered around these three problems. It was generally realized that these problems were not inherent in the Bretton Woods system as it had been designed but were closely connected with how it worked.

Nature of the Problems

The liquidity problem was this. Once Keynes's proposal for bancor was rejected at Bretton Woods, there was no adequate provision for enlarging world reserves to keep pace with expansion in international trade and investment. The supply of gold was insufficient to accommodate the demand for reserves and although an extensive network of international lines of credit had been established, access to this credit involved decisions by monetary officials on an ad hoc basis. The Fund developed policies that increased use of its resources, especially between 1956 and 1958, but even after the quota increases of 1959 and 1966 its holdings of gold and members' currencies were too small for countries to regard this secondary line of reserves as adequate. Moreover, countries wanted access to reserves that they could use without conditions imposed by the Fund. As was described in Chapter 5, in the absence of a good reserve asset, most countries used the dollar. This method of compensating for the deficiency of the par value system, however, put the United States in the position of having to run, or of being able to run, continuous balance of payments deficits. Should the United States try to reduce its payments deficit, the growth in world reserves would be slowed. Reliance on the dollar also encountered the risk that the par value system could unravel any time if the monetary authorities of other countries ever lost their confidence in the dollar and decided to convert their accumulated dollar holdings into gold.[7]

The adjustment problem was this. By the mid-1960s, although industrial countries found it increasingly difficult to correct payments imbalances, either deficits or surpluses, through the use of demand-management policies, they were

---

[5]Arthur M. Schlesinger, *A Thousand Days* (Boston: Houghton Mifflin Co., 1965), pp. 652–65.

[6]Fritz Machlup and Burton G. Malkiel, eds., *International Monetary Arrangements—The Problem of Choice: Report on the Deliberations of an International Study Group of 32 Economists* (Princeton, New Jersey: Princeton University Press, 1964).

[7]Discussion of the liquidity problem as it was seen early in the 1960s can be found in *History, 1966–71*, Vol. I, pp. 13–32.

not willing to make changes in their par values. Consequently, no instrument was available for correcting payments imbalances. Demand-management policies no longer sufficed because of changes in domestic economic conditions in most industrial countries toward the end of the 1950s. These changes first became evident when macroeconomic policies failed to provide the requisite stimulus to overcome recession in the United States and the United Kingdom in 1958. The cost-push phenomenon counted more than it had before in determining price levels. Economists began to refer to a trade-off between the rate of unemployment and the rate of inflation (the more of one, the less of the other) along the lines of the "Phillips curve."[8] The use of macroeconomic policies gradually became more difficult not only for managing the domestic economy but also for adjusting balances in external accounts. Countries with balance of payments deficits began to avoid deflationary policies because they aggravated unemployment, while countries with balance of payments surpluses began to avoid expansionary policies because they produced unwanted inflation.

An inability or unwillingness to change par values made correction of payments imbalances through use of this other major instrument of balance of payments policy virtually impossible. U.S. authorities found it especially difficult to change the par value for the dollar since rates for the dollar in terms of other currencies were determined by monetary authorities abroad rather than by U.S. actions. Moreover, as the 1960s progressed, political considerations entered ever more insistently into exchange rate decisions. Regarding the most chronic payments imbalances of all—the U.S. deficit and the corresponding surpluses of Canada, several Western European countries, and Japan—there was a particularly sharp difference of opinion as to whether the dollar should be devalued or other currencies revalued. Countries with payments surpluses were reluctant to revalue their currencies against the dollar because this would reduce the profitability of their export industries, which had been responsible for much of their economic growth, and would increase competition from imported products, particularly agricultural commodities. The par value system offered no way to assign relative responsibility for devaluation or revaluation.

Increased international mobility of capital also made balance of payments adjustment more difficult because it restricted the effectiveness of demand-management policies. Attempts by a country in payments deficit to stimulate domestic investment by lowering interest rates induced an outflow of capital that worsened the deficit. Attempts by a country in payments surplus to reduce inflation by raising interest rates caused capital inflows, which exacerbated its difficulties in controlling increases in its money supply. Capital mobility also made large discrete changes in par values difficult: once a par value for a major currency was altered,

---

[8]A.W. Phillips first used the concept of a curve relating the rate of increase in nominal money wages to the level of unemployment in "The Relation Between Unemployment and the Rate of Change of Money Wage Rates in the United Kingdom, 1861–1957," *Economica* (London), Vol. 25 (November 1958), pp. 283–99. The term "Phillips curve" quickly came into vogue to describe the relation between unemployment and the rate of increase in prices in general.

speculative capital was likely to move into other currencies in anticipation of further par value changes. Such capital movements often forced the very changes in par values that the monetary authorities were trying to avoid or resulted in par value changes that had little relation to the size of the exchange rate alteration required.[9] These difficulties became apparent for the first time when the U.K. authorities tried to manage their balance of payments deficit from 1964 to 1967.

The third problem was confidence in reserve media. As dollars accumulating in the hands of central bank authorities outside the United States began to exceed the value of the gold holdings of the United States, there was fear of a crisis of confidence in the dollar. A reluctance by banks and enterprises abroad to increase their dollar holdings further could lead to a shortage of international liquidity, which would be deflationary for the world economy. This had happened in 1931 when a collapse of confidence in the pound sterling wiped out much liquidity and imposed severe deflation on the rest of the world.[10]

In addition, flight from the dollar into other currencies or into gold, as holders sought conversion of their dollars by the U.S. Treasury, would jeopardize the stability of other currencies, or more likely, prompt the sudden suspension of the convertibility of official dollar holdings into gold, forcing an end to the par value system, as eventually happened on August 15, 1971.

Reactions

Economists wrestled with possible solutions to these problems, a growing number suggesting flexible exchange rates, others a large increase in the official price for gold, and still others new arrangements in the Fund for reserve creation. But public officials who were devoted to the par value system or at least to some system of fixed rates did not respond quickly to recommendations for change.

The devotion of the world's monetary authorities and of most private traders and bankers at the time to the par value system has to be seen in context. Successful international cooperation in monetary and financial affairs had been achieved under the par value system, world trade and international banking services had expanded greatly, and world economic growth had been phenomenal. Public officials, businessmen, and bankers the world over were eager to preserve that cooperation which they had come to associate with stability and order in the international monetary system. Stability and order, in turn, had come to be identified with a

---

[9]The implications of the enhanced international mobility of capital for the par value system were described by Sir Eric Roll, *International Capital Movements—Past, Present, Future*, the 1971 Per Jacobsson Lecture (Washington, September 26, 1971).

[10]Concerns that a crisis of confidence could cause deflation were expressed, for example, by Robert Triffin in *Gold and the Dollar Crisis: The Future of Convertibility* (New Haven: Yale University Press, 1960) and by Peter B. Kenen in "International Liquidity and the Balance of Payments of a Reserve-Currency Country," *Quarterly Journal of Economics* (Cambridge, Mass.), Vol. 74 (November 1960), pp. 572–86.

system of par values. Monetary authorities were aware, moreover, that as various suggestions for changing the par value system were made around 1960, the goals of the par value system themselves had not yet been fully realized. Not until February 1961, when the Western European countries accepted the convertibility obligations of Article VIII of the Fund's Articles of Agreement, were the Bretton Woods goals of par values or fixed exchange rates, convertible currencies, and freedom from restrictions actually achieved. Policymakers had toiled for many years to make these objectives a reality and were unlikely to change readily the system that was just coming into effect.

Public officials also had confidence that the par value system could continue to work effectively, although possibly with changes. For a short time, from about 1960 to 1962, public officials and technicians, including the Fund staff, hoped that the development of more refined techniques of demand management might enhance mobility of capital to facilitate rather than to frustrate balance of payments adjustment. The Fund staff discovered a new relationship between macroeconomic policies and their balance of payments consequences: though monetary and fiscal policies had similar effects on domestic economies and on the current account in the balance of payments, they had opposite effects on the capital account in the balance of payments.[11] Fiscal policy might therefore be directed to internal stability while monetary policy was directed to external stability. A country suffering simultaneously from payments deficits and unemployment, for example, could reflate its domestic economy either by reducing taxes or by increasing public expenditure and raising interest rates (rather than the traditional lowering) so as to attract funds from abroad. For a while after this discovery, economists placed considerable emphasis on finding the appropriate fiscal and monetary "policy mix" to achieve a capital surplus or deficit equal to the current account deficit or surplus at full employment.

THE LIQUIDITY PROBLEM GIVEN PRIORITY

Despite interest in the policy mix, public officials experienced a growing realization in the early 1960s that the changes taking place in the international economic environment had significant implications for the par value system and that the system needed fundamental change. In 1963, the Group of Ten and the Fund began to address the need for fundamental change by tackling the liquidity problem. Official discussions began in September 1963 and a facility for creating SDRs was introduced in the Fund in July 1969.

Resolution of the liquidity problem and introduction of a new mechanism for reserve creation, however, proved insufficient to prevent the collapse of the system only four years later. Even at the 1968 Annual Meeting, while the establishment of

---

[11]Robert A. Mundell, "The Appropriate Use of Monetary and Fiscal Policy for Internal and External Stability," *Staff Papers*, International Monetary Fund (Washington), Vol. 9 (March 1962), pp. 70–79.

the SDR facility was being hailed, many officials, including Mr. Schweitzer, expressed anxiety about the future of the international monetary system.[12] Critics, accordingly, have subsequently suggested that attention in the mid-1960s to the problem of liquidity was misdirected or excessive. They contend that policymakers should have directed their efforts to solving the problem of adjustment, particularly by devising ways by which par values could be more easily altered. Exchange rate changes that industrial countries needed could then have been made without all the subsequent crises. Other critics contend that policymakers should have solved the problem of confidence. Their contention is that officials should have concentrated less on creating new forms of reserves and more on ways to gain international control over existing reserves. This would have prevented the large-scale expansion of dollar liabilities and the subsequent flight from the dollar into gold that prompted the U.S. suspension of convertibility.

In view of these criticisms, it is worthwhile to look back and to examine why monetary officials focused on liquidity in the 1960s. There were three principal reasons.

First, in trying to improve the par value system by working on the liquidity problem, officials were looking for a way to build on, and not to alter, existing arrangements. In announcing the studies of international liquidity to be undertaken after the 1963 Annual Meeting of the Fund's Board of Governors, the Group of Ten specified that these studies were to be based on the two assumptions that fixed par values would continue to form the crux of international monetary arrangements and that the price of gold in terms of dollars would remain unchanged. They thereby ruled out what were viewed as excessive proposals for instituting flexible rates or for returning to the gold standard at a higher official price for gold.

Improving the liquidity mechanism instead of changing the exchange rate mechanism or raising the price of gold seemed in line with the direction in which the system was moving. The most important development in the Fund's implementation of the par value system, especially after 1956, had doubtlessly been the Fund's provision of financial assistance to members undertaking balance of payments adjustment. It was also primarily in providing financial assistance that the central banks of large industrial countries had been cooperating informally from 1961 onward, through swap and similar credit arrangements, to keep the system functioning smoothly. Moreover, the idea that the Fund might be given power to create reserve assets had already been considered—and rejected—when the Fund was created. So, in the mid-1960s this concept could rightly be regarded as an addition to the Bretton Woods system, as an idea whose time had come.

Second, public officials were convinced that the liquidity problem was at the root of the other two problems, adjustment and confidence. The supply of liquidity, that is, of reserves and credit facilities to finance balance of payments deficits, determined what policies governments employed to manage their balance of

---

[12]*History, 1966–71*, Vol. I, pp. 483–84.

payments. Inadequate liquidity could, for example, force deficit countries to adopt deflationary policies, which would cause unemployment, or to impose controls, which would restrict trade.

Officials regarded as critical solving the chronic disequilibria in world payments, that is, the persistent deficit in the balance of payments of the United States, the recurrent deficits of the United Kingdom, and the recurrent surpluses of most continental European countries, without reducing economic activity in the major industrial countries. As noted earlier in this chapter, for the first time since the end of World War II, by the early 1960s balance of payments considerations were limiting the pursuit of stimulative macroeconomic policies in the United States, as they had in the United Kingdom for some years. Recession in these two countries, at the time the world's largest importers, would depress the world economy.

The Fund staff was becoming more cognizant of the special circumstances that had facilitated balance of payments adjustment in the early postwar period. They realized that industrial countries had reached the limits for relatively easy balance of payments adjustment through the use of deflationary demand-management policies without causing unemployment. Furthermore, two factors that had also facilitated balance of payments adjustment in the past could no longer be relied on. One was the willingness of U.S. authorities to lose reserves. As U.S. reserves were becoming depleted, U.S. authorities felt that their further outflow had to be stopped. The second was that trade had expanded in large part because restrictions had gradually been lifted. Now that trade was virtually free of restriction, the scope for further trade expansion from the lifting of restrictions was minimal. Inasmuch as balance of payments adjustment was becoming more difficult, the staff began to look for new ways for industrial countries to achieve adjustment that would still permit expanding levels of trade. Increasing world liquidity seemed to be the most appropriate way.

In turning attention to the problem of liquidity, the staff also believed that a new reserve asset in the system would permit Western European countries to accumulate reserves in this form, rather than in dollars. At the time, many were convinced that in the interest of payments surpluses and reserve accumulation, as well as of internal price stability, European countries deliberately pursued policies of monetary restraint. These policies, in turn, forced the United States into payments deficits. A source of reserves other than U.S. dollars would enable or even induce the United States to reduce its deficits.[13] Moreover, the staff believed that the new SDR would alleviate the threat of flight from the dollar or from other currencies by providing an alternative form of reserves. In brief, at least the Fund staff regarded

---

[13]Milton Gilbert, Economic Advisor of the Bank for International Settlements (BIS), an advocate of a large rise in the price of gold, especially used the argument that more liquidity in the system (through a revaluation of existing gold stocks) would enable the United States to reduce its payments deficits. See, for example, his "The International Monetary System: Status and Prospects," presented to the Swiss Institute of International Studies in Zurich on December 6, 1971, and Bank for International Settlements, *Forty-Second Annual Report, April 1, 1971–March 31, 1972* (Basle, 1972), p. 32.

reserve creation as a new policy instrument to be added to the international monetary system and consciously used to improve world economic welfare.

Third, changes in par values by the major industrial countries were not at this time considered imperative or even necessary. A relative handful of economists, looking mainly at the large outflows of U.S. long-term investment capital into Canada and Western European countries in the 1950s and 1960s, considered at the time that the dollar was overvalued, making the acquisition of European assets relatively cheap for U.S. investors. But, with the exception of French President Charles de Gaulle, virtually no public officials called for changes in par values to redress either the U.S. payments deficit or the large European surpluses. The development after 1958 of large overall U.S. balance of payments deficits, large overall European balance of payments surpluses, and a dollar glut seemed to result from the continuation of the same economic trends that had ended the dollar shortage earlier in the 1950s. Postwar U.S. foreign economic policy had succeeded gradually in strengthening the European economies. European industrial productivity had increased well beyond expectations, exports had greatly expanded, balance of payments positions had gone from substantial deficit to substantial surplus, and reserves had increased sharply. Now the countries in surplus should encourage greater imports of goods and services, especially from the United States, and share more of the burden of spending for mutual defense and financial aid for developing countries. This process would take time. The idea that trade measures were preferable to changes in exchange rates to reduce the U.S. payments deficit and European surplus was exemplified also by developments in the trade field. Thus, concurrent with the liquidity exercise, the Kennedy Round of trade and tariff negotiations was begun in 1963. These negotiations were explicitly intended to stimulate imports into European countries by reducing tariffs and other trade barriers.

Furthermore, changes in par values, at least for the dollar, were not considered imperative because of the nature of the U.S. deficit, which arose primarily from outflows of private long-term investment and from public aid and military expenditures abroad. The U.S. merchandise trade surplus had actually increased from 1959 to 1964. To curtail the private outflow of capital, U.S. authorities took direct action, introducing, for instance, an interest equalization tax in 1963. If the dollar was devalued, public expenditures abroad were more likely to increase than to decrease.

There was even some debate within the United States as to whether *anything* needed to be done about the payments deficits. For example, in 1963 a group of highly respected economists forecast a sizable U.S. surplus or at worst a small deficit by 1968.[14] Some believed that the U.S. payments deficit on capital account did not reflect disequilibrium. The United States was lending on intermediate and long term and borrowing on short term and hence supplying needed financial intermediation.

---

[14]See the report by Walter S. Salant, Emile Despres, and others, *The United States' Balance of Payments in 1968*, The Brookings Institution (Washington, 1963).

The general public in Western Europe had a penchant for maintaining financial assets in liquid form, chiefly as deposits with commercial and savings banks. European banks accordingly tended to stay liquid with their central banks; and the central banks in turn tended to stay liquid with the rest of the world, for example, by holding dollars in liquid form. Since such attitudes caused long-term interest rates in Europe to be relatively high, European enterprises in need of long-term funds tended to float bonds in U.S. capital markets where they could borrow larger amounts on long term at lower rates of interest than they could in capital markets in Europe. Differences in liquidity preferences of U.S. nationals and of Europeans thus created scope for trade in financial assets, just as differing comparative costs create the basis for mutually profitable trade in goods.[15]

It is also worth recalling that the large and persistent current account surpluses of Canada, the Federal Republic of Germany, Italy, Japan, and some smaller industrial countries developed only in the latter half of the 1960s and, for the most part, only after 1968 when the bulk of negotiations for the creation of the SDR had already been completed.

Monetary authorities both in the United States and in Europe were consequently not disposed until well into the 1970s to consider changes in par values for the major currencies. The evidence for this is strong. For example, the 1966 report on balance of payments adjustment of Working Party 3 of the Economic Policy Committee of the OECD contained little reference to exchange rates. U.K. authorities resisted devaluation of sterling for three years prior to 1967. At the Bonn meeting of the Group of Ten in November 1968, monetary authorities were unwilling to face up to the need to change the rates for the deutsche mark or the French franc. When the Executive Directors began a review of the mechanism for changing exchange rates under the par value system in 1969, they did so in a seminar format, off the record. In 1970 most Governors of the Fund were still in no mood to amend the Fund's Articles of Agreement to provide for greater flexibility of exchange rates: the attempted reform of the exchange rate mechanism proposed by the Executive Directors failed.[16] Meanwhile, under its existing Articles, the Fund had no authority to take the initiative to propose changes in exchange rates and could do relatively little about effecting adjustment through changing the par value mechanism.

In judging the priority given by the world's monetary authorities to the question of liquidity in the mid-1960s, it should also be said that they did not anticipate that the negotiations to establish a new reserve-creating mechanism would be so prolonged. Nearly seven years were to pass from the time they first

---

[15]This argument of Emile Despres, Charles P. Kindleberger, and Walter S. Salant was first presented in an article, "The Dollar and World Liquidity—A Minority View," in *The Economist* (London, February 5, 1966), pp. 526–29. Professor Kindleberger of the Massachusetts Institute of Technology subsequently elaborated the argument in his "The Euro-Dollar and the Internationalization of United States Monetary Policy," in Banca Nazionale del Lavoro, *Quarterly Review* (Rome), No. 88 (March 1969), pp. 3–15.

[16]The events mentioned in this paragraph have been described in *History, 1966–71*, Vol. I, pp. 36, 38, 96–98, 431, 450–53, 500–503, and 514–15.

became concerned about reserve-creation arrangements in 1963 until the first allocation of SDRs in January 1970.

CAUSES OF COLLAPSE: DIFFERING INTERPRETATIONS

For many years U.S. and European officials have espoused conflicting explanations as to when and why the par value system collapsed. These conflicting views have affected their conceptions of the features to be incorporated in a reformed system.

U.S. officials have regarded the suspension of the convertibility of officially held dollars into gold or other reserve assets on August 15, 1971 as the end of the par value system and have placed primary emphasis on why suspension was necessary. U.S. Government reports published in 1973, for example, stressed that the suspension of convertibility, which broke the link between the dollar and gold, "gave public recognition to the fact that the postwar international monetary arrangements, known as the Bretton Woods system, had become untenable" and lauded President Nixon's "bold initiatives" in formulating a new economic policy and in bringing the system to an end.[17] Even U.S. experts outside the Nixon Administration who, in fact, were sharply critical of what they termed "Nixon shocks" to the international monetary system, pinpoint the action of August 15, 1971 as crucial in ending the par value system.[18] Several U.S. experts even took the view that the Bretton Woods system had effectively come to an end before 1971 inasmuch as central bank authorities abroad since 1968 had by agreement refrained from converting dollars into gold. Indeed, the emphasis of C. Fred Bergsten on the status of convertibility arrangements for the dollar prompted him to divide the evolution of the international monetary system from 1946 to 1971 into four phases depending on the convertibility status of the dollar. In the first phase, which lasted through 1958 (the "dollar shortage" period), the dollar was the *only* major convertible currency. In the second phase, from 1959 until 1967–68, *all* major currencies were convertible. In the third phase, from 1967–68 until August 1971, the dollar's convertibility became increasingly nominal. In the fourth phase, starting in August 1971, the dollar was the only major currency *not* convertible.[19]

Once convertibility of the dollar had been suspended, the par value system could no longer function as it had in the past. Other members of the Fund had to decide whether to accumulate dollars despite the inconvertibility, that is, to be

---

[17]*Economic Report of the President Transmitted to the Congress, January 1973* (Washington: Government Printing Office, 1973), p. 120; and *International Economic Report of the President Transmitted to the Congress, March 1973* (Washington: Government Printing Office, 1973), p. 1.

[18]See, for instance, C. Fred Bergsten, "The New Economics and U.S. Foreign Policy," *Foreign Affairs* (New York), Vol. 50 (January 1972), p. 216; and Charles A. Coombs, *The Arena of International Finance* (cited in fn. 22 of Chap. 5 above), pp. 208–20.

[19]See his *The Dilemmas of the Dollar: The Economics and Politics of United States International Monetary Policy* (New York: New York University Press, 1975), p. 5.

entirely on a dollar standard, or to let their exchange rates fluctuate, since they could no longer guarantee their intervention in exchange markets to keep the rates between their currencies and the U.S. dollar within the prescribed margins around the par values. Considered in this light, the U.S. decision in August 1971 brought to an end the gold-exchange standard, that in many respects had come to be a dollar standard, and can be regarded as analogous in international monetary history to the U.K. decision almost exactly 40 years before, on September 21, 1931, to leave the gold standard, which in many respects had been a sterling standard.

U.S. officials regarded the suspension of convertibility as necessary to realign the exchange rates of the major industrial countries. Countries with surplus payments positions, such as the Federal Republic of Germany and Japan, were reluctant to revalue. Unilateral action by the United States to change the par value for the dollar in terms of gold, they believed, would have induced other countries to make corresponding changes in the relationship between their currencies and gold. The relationship between the dollar and other currencies would thus remain effectively unchanged.

U.S. officials, accordingly, have faulted the par value system for its lack of an adjustment mechanism, that is, for its failure to trigger changes in exchange rates. In their view, the system had a devaluation bias: pressure on countries in deficit to devalue their currencies was much greater than pressure on countries in surplus to revalue. Moreover, strong demand-management policies by the United States aggravated domestic unemployment but did not correct the U.S. payments deficit. In the large U.S. economy, imports, at least in the 1960s, formed a relatively small proportion of gross national product. Deflationary policies caused only small decreases in imports. Decreases in imports, in turn, were partly offset by decreases in exports. Hence, substantial declines in production and income, involving undue unemployment, were necessary to induce relatively small improvements in the net balance of payments position. Such declines in U.S. output were bad for the world economy as well as for that of the United States. They believed, therefore, that under the par value system there was no way that the United States could correct its balance of payments deficits.

European Interpretation

European officials, especially in the Federal Republic of Germany, on the other hand, date the end of the par value system March 19, 1973, when the six EC members arranged a joint float against the U.S. dollar. These officials did not, even before 1971, accept the argument that U.S. authorities were unable to adjust the par value for the dollar or that they had to suspend convertibility of the dollar. Later on they cited as evidence the changes in the par value of the dollar of December 1971, as part of the Smithsonian agreement, and of February 1973. As evidence that the par value system did in fact continue until March 1973, they point to the substantial effort during late 1971 and 1972 to retain par values.

112

European officials have stressed that the par value system broke up because EC countries needed to protect themselves from the imported inflation to which the system subjected them. In their view, the par value system proved to be "an engine of inflation" for two reasons. First, since other countries held U.S. dollars as reserves, the United States could pursue inflationary policies virtually without limit, continuing to run payments deficits and to let billions of dollars pile up in the hands of authorities abroad. Second, in keeping the rates for their currencies fixed in relation to the dollar, as required under a system of fixed rates or par values, European monetary officials, especially in the Federal Republic of Germany, had to buy all excess dollars offered; these purchases created large amounts of their own local currency, inflating their own money supplies. In order to gain control over their own domestic monetary policies, European countries had to stop intervening in exchange markets to support fixed relationships between their currencies and the dollar and organize a common float of their currencies against the dollar. Otmar Emminger, then Deputy Governor of the Deutsche Bundesbank, frequently stated this view after March 1973.[20] Mr. Emminger has also often talked and written about the struggle of the monetary authorities of the Federal Republic of Germany with imported inflation.[21]

The authorities of the Federal Republic of Germany had tried to introduce a joint float in May 1971. Although German officials, particularly Mr. Emminger, like central bankers in other countries, had long favored fixed exchange rates, partly under the influence of academic economists, they had come to view floating as the only way out of their dilemma. Academic economists, both in Germany and in the United States, such as Professor Herbert Giersch of the Institut für Weltwirtschaft at Kiel and Professors Milton Friedman and Gottfried Haberler, were urging German officials, especially Karl Schiller, then Minister of the Economy, to float the deutsche mark.[22]

The attempt of German authorities to get agreement on a joint float of European currencies in May 1971 was unsuccessful. But in March 1973 the joint float did materialize. In the European view, the par value system was now at an end since European authorities no longer used dollars to intervene in their exchange markets and they no longer expected to use the dollar as a reserve currency. In the European view, the par value system continued to work as long as U.S. monetary authorities issued dollars only up to the amounts central bank authorities of other countries were willing to hold. Once U.S. authorities issued dollars in excess of these amounts, the system collapsed.

---

[20]Otmar Emminger, *Inflation and the International Monetary System*, the 1973 Per Jacobsson Lecture (Basle, June 16, 1973), and *On the Way to a New International Monetary Order* (Washington: American Enterprise Institute for Public Policy Research, 1976), p. 3.

[21]See, for instance, his *The D-Mark in the Conflict Between Internal and External Equilibrium, 1948–1975*, Essays in International Finance, No. 122, Princeton University (Princeton, New Jersey: Princeton University Press, 1977).

[22]See *Kieler Diskussionsbeiträge zu aktuellen wirtschaftspolitischen Fragen*, Institut für Weltwirtschaft (Kiel, June 1971), p. 11.

Both U.S. and European authorities have criticized the par value system for "asymmetry." But they view asymmetry differently. U.S. authorities contend that the system was asymmetrical because the dollar, unlike other currencies, could not be devalued, a distinct handicap. Another asymmetry was that the system was biased toward devaluation. Revaluation to correct surpluses was rare. European authorities argue that the system was asymmetrical because the dollar enjoyed a special advantage—President de Gaulle used the words "exorbitant privilege"—by virtue of its being a reserve currency.

CAUSES OF COLLAPSE: THE AUTHOR'S PERSPECTIVE

The official interpretations of the causes of collapse of the par value system suggest that, by the end of the 1960s, the major industrial countries no longer benefited from prevailing international monetary arrangements. In the 25 years since the system was created, the conduct of international trade and investment had changed radically. The rise of giant multinational corporations, large-scale flows of capital, technological advances, the spread throughout the world of similar consumption habits and of cultural and recreational tastes as a result of communication, television, and travel, the growth of new, expanding markets and suppliers as additional countries entered more fully into the world economic community, greatly increased international mobility of labor, and intensified competition between nations had profound effects on the structure of world production and on patterns of international trade. Industrial countries especially had become "economically interdependent." (Such interdependence was later also to include the developing countries.) Economic interdependence meant that economic conditions and policies in one country quickly affected those in other countries. The changed circumstances meant also that governments began to find external obligations increasingly in conflict with domestic objectives.

Although these developments only started trends that were to continue, and even to accelerate later in the 1970s, by 1971 they had already made the economic cost of adhering to the Bretton Woods system excessively high for the industrial countries. For the United States, the economic cost of domestic unemployment and lack of freedom to pursue stimulative macroeconomic policies had become burdensome. For the first time in many years trade deficits meant that U.S. exports were being edged out of markets abroad and, even more seriously, that imports of consumer goods were displacing U.S. products in the domestic market. The economic cost for the United States of controlling the transfer of funds abroad by U.S. businessmen and banks had also become burdensome. The banks and business enterprises of the United States were handicapped in a competitive, financially integrated world in which banks and business enterprises of other industrial countries seemed to be winning the race. The U.S. Government was especially unwilling to tolerate such cost against the background of U.S. generosity in the conduct of its foreign economic policy in the previous two decades. U.S. officials believed that it was time for Western European countries and Japan to share responsibility for world leadership by lifting remaining barriers to imports, fostering growth within their own economies, underwriting mutual defense costs, and increasing their financial aid to developing countries.

For Western European countries, the economic costs were the need to cope with rising inflation in the United States and the accumulation of larger balances of inconvertible dollars, involving some loss of management of their own monetary policies. Officials of Western European countries—most notably the Federal Republic of Germany, because of the hyperinflation it experienced after World War I—were concerned about the dangers of inflation. Western European countries were especially unwilling to pay these costs in a context in which they, as a group, had become economically coequal with the United States. In addition, many Western European officials resented economic penetration of Europe by the United States, especially through large direct U.S. investment. They were annoyed that the United States could follow a policy of "benign neglect" under which it need not take measures to reduce its balance of payments deficits on the grounds that these deficits were beneficial to the rest of the world.[23] European officials did not want to be part of the "dollar area" and wanted instead to advance their own monetary and economic union.

After 1968, moreover, industrial countries were more reluctant to adjust their payments disequilibria—deficits or surpluses—since such adjustments meant a further slowdown in economic growth or greater unemployment. In the absence of such adjustments, any system was bound to collapse.

Yet another factor operated to cause the par value system to collapse. By 1971, the existence of an interdependent world economy altered basic assumptions about the formation of economic policy. In 1944 it was assumed that each government could resolve the conflict between the pursuit of full employment and of balance of payments equilibrium by demand-management policies or by changes in the exchange rate. The "fundamental disequilibrium" concept of the Fund's Articles of Agreement was a disequilibrium that a country, although in consultation with others, could correct by its own action. In terms of economic theory, the models used were of "closed national economies." The international economy was where national economies intersected and interacted.

By the 1970s, however, a global or world economy had emerged, qualitatively different and infinitely more complex than the interactions of various national economies. National economies had become interdependent and their financial systems interconnected to an extent never previously imagined. Consequently, major industrial countries could no longer correct their disequilibria unilaterally. The question that had been only academic three decades earlier, whether the pursuit of full employment by all industrial countries would produce a satisfactory array of

---

[23]The suggestion for a strategy of benign neglect is usually said to have first come from Professor Gottfried Haberler, although Professor Haberler has denied authorship. See his *Money in the International Economy* (London: Institute of Economic Affairs, 2nd ed., 1969).

balance of payments positions, had become a live policy question. For industrial countries to attain their economic objectives it was increasingly necessary that their economic policies be worked out in unison. Exchange rates had to be determined on a multilateral basis to arrive at a suitable *pattern* of exchange rates, as distinct from an exchange rate for a single currency. Macroeconomic policies of industrial countries had to be coordinated so that cyclical swings in one industrial country would not offset policies in another. Monetary policies had to be harmonized in order to avoid movements of interest-sensitive capital that could upset the payments position or exchange rate of any industrial country. Policies with respect to trade and capital movements had to be formed on a multicountry basis. Although for the first time in history monetary officials of the ten largest industrial countries had sat together to negotiate their exchange rates at the Smithsonian Institution in December 1971, they were not yet prepared for close coordination of their economic policies. In the absence of coordinated policies, balance of payments disequilibria persisted. Given the magnitude of capital and its international volatility in the 1970s, the Bretton Woods system could not endure in the face of prolonged unadjusted disequilibria.[24]

THE FUND IN A COLLAPSING SYSTEM

Inasmuch as the par value system collapsed basically because industrial countries were unable or unready to coordinate their policies, it would seem that the Fund would have served as a made-to-order forum for mutually determining exchange rates and coordinating policies affecting international transactions. What was the Fund doing as the system collapsed? Its most profound action to modify the functioning of the weakening par value system was the establishment of the SDR. Efforts to solve the problem of global liquidity and to introduce the SDR absorbed the bulk of the Fund's efforts during the 1960s. Fund officials believed that the solution to the problem of international liquidity was the introduction of the SDR, as was explained earlier in this chapter. Rightly or wrongly, Fund officials believed at the time that the introduction of the SDR was a significant step toward the correction of the prolonged imbalances in international payments that were later to cause the system's collapse. They regarded SDRs as the first major reform of the par value system since its creation, a reform of such scope as to require the first amendment of the Articles of Agreement since the Fund was established 25 years before, a step that Fund officials as recently as 1965 were not sure would be acceptable to its members.

As late as 1970, Fund officials were well aware that the monetary authorities of major industrial members were not yet willing to give the Fund effective control over

---

[24]One U.S. monetary expert has described the reasons for the breakdown of the par value system in somewhat similar terms, explaining that the three policies that came to be associated with the par value system—fixed exchange rates, free capital movements, and independent monetary policy—were not compatible; a country could have any two of these three arrangements but not all three. See Henry C. Wallich, C.J. Morse, and I.G. Patel, *The Monetary Crisis of 1971—The Lessons to Be Learned*, the 1972 Per Jacobsson Lecture (Washington, September 24, 1972), especially pp. 5–7.

world reserves, such as might be achieved by members' depositing in the Fund their gold and foreign exchange reserves or by agreeing to use their traditional reserves only in conjunction with SDRs. While the Fund staff was advancing suggestions for such arrangements, monetary authorities were by no means ready to make the Fund in this way a "supranational central bank." In the absence of such arrangements, Fund officials hoped that the availability of SDRs as a supplement to traditional reserves would be a beginning toward eventual control by the Fund of the volume of international liquidity. They envisaged a par value system and a gold-exchange standard which included the SDR.[25] They based their vision on the expectation that the SDR would become an increasingly larger component of total world reserves. They did not foresee that the first allocations of SDRs between 1970 and 1972 would coincide with a sharply worsened U.S. payments deficit and an increase in world reserves that exceeded the aggregate increase in world reserves in all previous history, reducing the SDR to a minute portion of world reserves.

Apart from the SDR, could Fund officials have done more to help the major industrial members change their exchange rates and thus have prevented collapse of the par value system? The Fund's actions must be judged in the light of circumstances. For one thing, the authorities of the EC countries were unwilling to consider making the exchange rate mechanism more flexible. By early in 1971, moreover, changing the exchange rates for the dollar and other major currencies had already become controversial.

Even among the Group of Ten, debates about exchange rates were so acrimonious that another technique—consultation among the "Big Five"—was used to effect the currency realignment of February 1973. Negotiations on exchange rates had to be conducted in secret so as not to unsettle exchange markets further. Under these circumstances, it is difficult to envisage the Fund, then an organization of 130 members, as the scene of such bitter and secret negotiations.

Other considerations, too, limited the Fund's involvement in the events from 1971 to 1973 that shook the foundations of the par value system. Prior to the suspension of convertibility, U.S. authorities believed they would not receive a fair hearing in the Fund and were not inclined to suggest currency realignments through the Fund. Convinced that the par value system, including dollar convertibility, jeopardized U.S. interests, they believed that Fund officials, nonetheless, were likely to make every effort to preserve that system. Measures needed to rectify the U.S. balance of payments deficits involved liberalization of trade restrictions and nontariff barriers as well as changes in exchange rates. Since many of these measures went beyond the Fund's jurisdiction, U.S. officials were convinced that bilateral negotiations would be more effective.

Strong differences of view between EC and U.S. officials had, moreover,

---

[25]See, for example, J. Marcus Fleming, "The SDR: Some Problems and Possibilities," *Staff Papers*, International Monetary Fund (Washington), Vol. 18 (March 1971), pp. 25–47, and Fred Hirsch, "SDRs and the Working of the Gold Exchange Standard," *Staff Papers*, Vol. 18 (July 1971), pp. 221–53.

already developed. French officials especially believed the United States was destroying the par value system and was no longer willing to undertake its international obligations under the Fund's Articles of Agreement when these obligations required tight measures to bring the U.S. balance of payments into equilibrium. The United States should take the measures needed to correct its chronic payments deficits and return to par values and convertibility. In taking this view, Western European officials tended to discount the frustration of U.S. officials in negotiating measures by other countries to help correct U.S. payments deficits. They tended to discount, too, the conviction of U.S. officials that the U.S. economy was no longer much stronger than other industrial economies and that the United States could no longer afford to be as lenient in its international economic and financial relations as it had been in the past.

Given these differing views, U.S. officials were inclined to think that Fund officials were more receptive to the arguments of officials of the EC countries. After all, Mr. Schweitzer had at the 1970 Annual Meeting in Copenhagen publicly called on the United States to use only reserve assets for the settlement of its deficits rather than enlarge its dollar liabilities. The Governors at that Annual Meeting had agreed not to consider exchange rate flexibility any further, a position contrary to that of U.S. officials. Mr. Schweitzer had suggested on television in September 1971 that the dollar be devalued, which U.S. officials believed compromised their ability to negotiate an appropriate realignment of currencies. Finally, as described in earlier chapters, several Fund officials had suggested late in 1971 and in 1972 that some convertibility of the dollar be reintroduced.

In the middle of 1972, there were reports that the U.S. authorities preferred not to have Mr. Schweitzer reappointed for a third term as Managing Director of the Fund when his term expired in August 1973. Against this background, as the crises of February and March 1973 developed, Mr. Schweitzer assumed a relatively low profile.

These factors help to explain why the Fund seemed to be more buffeted by than in control of events taking place outside the Fund. Nonetheless, as each crisis ensued, the Managing Director took a stand, trying hard to preserve the par value system. After the devaluation of the pound sterling in 1967, Mr. Schweitzer believed that his most useful contribution was to restore confidence to the system in order to prevent further crises. There are several illustrations of his efforts to restore confidence in the system following a crisis. After the devaluation of the pound sterling, he publicly expressed confidence not only in its new rate but also in the continued soundness of the rate for the U.S. dollar. After the introduction of the two-tier market for gold in March 1968, he interpreted it as an indication that the monetary authorities of the large industrial countries were determined to keep an official fixed price for monetary gold; it was a sign that the system would continue to be based on an official price for gold. At the Bonn meeting of the Group of Ten in November 1968, Mr. Schweitzer expressed the view that because of its unsettling effects on exchange markets, it would be unwise to call a conference of the Group of Ten on exchange rates as some monetary authorities were suggesting. When the

Canadian authorities introduced a floating exchange rate in May 1970, the Managing Director and the Executive Board asked them to reinstitute a par value as quickly as possible in the interest of helping to keep the system from collapsing. Again in May and August 1971, Mr. Schweitzer made several efforts to retain features of the par value system.[26] After the United Kingdom floated the rate for the pound sterling in June 1972, Mr. Schweitzer again attempted to inspire confidence in the exchange rates agreed in December 1971, and as late as March 1973 he tried hard to support the new structure of exchange rates that emerged after devaluation of the dollar in February 1973 so as to prevent the emergence of floating rates.

Mr. Schweitzer and other Fund officials were not rigidly attached to the par value system. Despite a belief that some type of par value arrangement provided the best hope for international cooperation on exchange rate policy, over the years the Fund had developed considerable flexibility in its policies toward floating exchange rates. Nevertheless, by the late 1960s, the Fund's developing members had become strong advocates of fixed rates and Mr. Schweitzer undertook to make the position of developing members heard. Fund officials believed, furthermore, that floating rates would divide the world into currency blocs and would not produce a more satisfactory pattern of exchange rates. In the circumstances of the first months of 1973, when negotiations for a reformed international monetary system were still seriously under way and when many members of the Fund favored a reformed system based on par values, Fund officials feared that abandonment of the actual use of par values would diminish the prospects for agreement on a reformed system. In believing that the events of 1971 to 1973 would indeed be the death knell not only for the Bretton Woods system of par values but also for a reformed system based on par values, they proved to be correct, as will be shown in Part II.

Despite these explanations of why the par value system collapsed and of the Fund's actions while the system was collapsing, it is essential to reiterate that, although crises in exchange and gold markets had been going on for more than five years, the final collapse in March 1973 was unexpected. As late as the middle of February when the dollar was again devalued, the world's monetary authorities gave little indication that they thought that the end of the system was at hand.

---

[26]See *History, 1966–71*, Vol. I, pp. 520–21 and 538–41.

PART TWO

Negotiations for a Reformed System

(September 1972–June 1974)

"We are at present entering a new
period in the history of the
international monetary system . . .
We seem to have reached a point of
no return when we can only go
forward in search of new avenues
and horizons."

—ALI WARDHANA, addressing the Board of Governors
in two speeches, in Washington, September 1972

CHAPTER
7

First Report on Reform

*R*EFORMING THE INTERNATIONAL MONETARY SYSTEM presented monetary officials with an unusual challenge. They sensed that they were entering
a new era and that, like those who had planned and negotiated the Bretton Woods
system three decades earlier, they had an unusual opportunity to write a new
monetary constitution for the world.

EXECUTIVE BOARD'S MANDATE

The Executive Board and the Fund staff planned the first steps toward a
reformed system. They had been directed to study a "reform of the international
monetary system" by a resolution adopted by the Board of Governors at the 1971
Annual Meeting. In Part III of the resolution the Governors addressed themselves to
long-term reform of the system.[1] The Governors requested the Executive Directors
to do three things. They were to report without delay on measures to improve or
reform the international monetary system. They were to study all aspects of the
international monetary system, including the role of reserve currencies, gold, special
drawing rights, convertibility, the provisions of the Articles of Agreement with
respect to exchange rates, and problems caused by destabilizing capital movements.
If possible they were to include in their report texts of any amendments of the
Articles of Agreement necessary to give effect to their recommendations.

The response was the report on reform of the international monetary system
transmitted to the Board of Governors on August 18, 1972.

STAFF SKETCH

The origin of the report was a "sketch" of a reformed international monetary
system which the Fund staff prepared in the first few months of 1972 to give some

---

[1]Resolution No. 26-9, October 1, 1971; Vol. III below, pp. 55–56. The debates attending the
drafting of this resolution and the actions taken by the Fund in response to Parts I and II of the

direction to the discussion of the Executive Directors.[2] At the time no one was certain what features a reformed system ought to have or what features could be negotiated among financial officials. Monetary officials were still trying to hold together the system of par values and expected to maintain successfully the new realigned exchange rates for at least a few years to give them time to construct a reformed system. Officials of Western European countries were trying to persuade U.S. officials to re-establish some degree of convertibility for the dollar and were eager to achieve a reformed system that contained convertibility obligations. U.S. officials were focusing on reducing or even turning into surplus the U.S. balance of payments deficit before they agreed on any new international obligations.

Clearly after August 15, 1971, "reform" of the international monetary system meant something quite different from what it had meant before. In the second half of the 1960s and through 1970, reform meant improving the Bretton Woods system by, for example, introducing a new reserve asset (the SDR) or by making relatively minor modifications in the par value system so that large industrial countries could more easily change the par values for their currencies. After August 15, 1971, reform meant radically altering the Bretton Woods system by constructing a wholly new international monetary system with arrangements for convertibility, reserves, and reserve currencies different from what had existed in the Bretton Woods system, as well as a substantially altered exchange rate mechanism.

The sketch was innovative and exploratory. It provided suggestions for four components of a reformed system: improvement of the exchange rate mechanism; reduction of the use of reserve currencies, mainly the dollar; introduction of measures to treat the dollar the same as other currencies in financing balance of payments deficits and surpluses; and the possible replacement of the dollar as the most used intervention currency in exchange markets by some other intervention system. The sketch also described the interrelations between these four components and certain other changes, such as in the characteristics and uses of the SDR required to make a reformed system more complete.

The staff's suggestions for each of the components of the reformed system were the following.

An Exchange Rate Mechanism Based on Par Values

In considering ways to improve the exchange rate mechanism in a reformed system over that of the Bretton Woods system, the staff took up where the

---

resolution, which dealt with the immediate difficulties for the exchange rate system resulting from the suspension of dollar convertibility by the United States on August 15, 1971, were described in *History, 1966–71*, Vol. I, pp. 547–51.

[2]"Reform of the International Monetary System—A Sketch of Its Scope and Content," dated March 7, 1972, and two supplementary notes, "Possible Fund Financing of Short-Term Capital Movements" and "Gold Purchases by the Fund," both dated May 2, 1972, are in Vol. III below, pp. 3–17.

discussion of the Executive Directors had left off in August 1970 when they finished their report, *The Role of Exchange Rates in the Adjustment of International Payments.*[3] The 1970 report had been extremely cautious. Its most radical feature was its title, which explicitly recognized that somehow exchange rates had to become more of a policy instrument in correcting balance of payments disequilibria than they had been in the Bretton Woods system. The report itself in a sense sidestepped this problem. The Executive Directors, fully reflecting the position of their governments at the time, supported continuation of the par value system, based on stable but adjustable par values at realistic levels. They accepted only some relatively minor techniques for making the par value system more flexible, rejecting any very different exchange rate arrangements, such as floating rates or much wider margins around parities.

Following this line of thought, the staff sketch prepared early in 1972 suggested that a reformed system, like the Bretton Woods system, be a par value system, but a modified one. There were to be (i) prompter and smaller changes in par values, with the Fund initiating proposals for change if necessary; (ii) use of wider margins around parities; and (iii) an escape clause which legalized temporary deviations from par values in unusual circumstances.[4] These modifications in the par value system, so the staff believed as of 1972, would mitigate the problem of disequilibrating capital movements, recognized as the main factor making it virtually impossible for officials of large industrial members to maintain par values for their currencies.[5] Permitting changes in the par value of the U.S. dollar was given especially high priority.

The Research Department suggested a reconstructed par value mechanism for the reformed system partly because the staff of that department thought that, because of the development of a multilateral exchange rate model (MERM) and a world trade model (Project Link), it was at last possible to compute exchange rates for several countries simultaneously that would meet such criteria as the elimination of payments imbalances between the countries. The calculations made for the currency realignment agreed at the Smithsonian Institution in December 1971 had demonstrated the feasibility of these computations which could be supplemented by analytical evaluation. These members of the staff were hopeful that a reformed system could provide for multicountry consultations in which officials would consider the concurrent need for devaluation and revaluation of the main currencies and that these consultations would yield agreed appropriate patterns of exchange rates. The staff's belief that discussions based on calculations resulting from economic models could provide satisfactory exchange rates was based partly on their expectation that several simultaneous adjustments in par values on the scale of the

---

[3]This report was discussed in *History, 1966–71,* Vol. I, pp. 512–14 and reproduced in Vol. II of that work, pp. 273–330.

[4]This part of the staff sketch was based on a staff memorandum that the Fund later published. (Fred Hirsch, "The Exchange Rate Regime: An Analysis and a Possible Scheme," *Staff Papers,* International Monetary Fund (Washington), Vol. 19 (July 1972), pp. 259–85.)

[5]This situation has been described in *History, 1966–71,* Vol. I, particularly pp. 13–15, 350, 449, 476, 496–500, 502, and 525.

realignments of December 1971 would probably not again be needed in the near future. The changes in the exchange rates of the major currencies considered essential since 1968, especially devaluation of the U.S. dollar, seemed at last to have been made. Another major realignment seemed unlikely, particularly if individual countries promptly made further necessary adjustments in their par values. Although the senior staff of some other departments, especially the European and Western Hemisphere Departments, did not agree with this reasoning, the Research Department was primarily responsible for drafting the sketch.

The belief of the Research Department that a reconstructed par value system would be workable reflected their euphoria and that of the Secretariat of the OECD immediately after the Smithsonian agreement. To them the exchange rate realignment appeared as a triumph. Not only had exchange rates been successfully negotiated for the first time in history between the countries of the Group of Ten, but the Fund staff and the Secretariat of the OECD had made major contributions. For its part, the Research Department had calculated the new pattern of rates and produced estimates of the payments imbalances to be corrected which jibed well with estimates made by the Secretariat of the OECD. Although the estimates of the Fund and the OECD differed substantially from those of the U.S. Government, the Fund staff viewed the discrepancies as "understandable."[6] Did not all countries exaggerate how much their balances of payments ought to improve or minimize how much their surpluses ought to be reduced? It was, accordingly, the responsibility of international organizations to put together a total picture. The staff was euphoric because the Fund had won a victory in now having exchange rates as a discussable topic between the Fund and officials of large members. Consequently, as the Smithsonian Institution meeting ended, the staffs of the Fund and the OECD were looking forward to a period of international cooperation, especially on exchange rates, in which the multinational institutions would play a sizable role. Under these circumstances the Fund staff envisaged a reformed international monetary system, based on fixed exchange rates or par values, in which effective consultations, guided by calculations for exchange rates, would decide on further adjustments in par values.

Arrangements to Reduce Use of the Dollar

To reduce the use of national currencies, especially the dollar, as reserves, the sketch discussed "consolidation arrangements." Large outstanding balances of dollars held by central banks as reserves would be consolidated in the Fund or somehow converted into an alternative asset, such as the SDR. This would reduce liquidity in the international monetary system. That liquidity, widely regarded as excessive, was heavily in the form of dollars.

---

[6]The calculations and estimates of the Fund staff and the differences in the estimates of the U.S. Government were discussed in *History, 1966–71*, Vol. I, pp. 537–38 and 543–44.

The sketch described arrangements for the Fund to distribute special issues of SDRs against balances of reserve currencies tendered to it by its members. (Later on, the term "substitution account" was used to describe arrangements of this type.) In this way the SDR would become the primary reserve asset of the international monetary system. Questions still to be settled concerned the scope of such consolidation—whether all existing holdings of dollar balances would be exchangeable for SDRs—and the changes needed to make the SDR a sufficiently attractive reserve asset, such as increasing its rate of interest, enlarging the number of official bodies that could hold SDRs, broadening the transactions in which SDRs could be used, and relaxing the rules for reconstitution so that financial officials would be willing to exchange dollars for SDRs.

In the sketch the staff also suggested considering making the SDR, rather than gold, the numeraire of the reformed system. In an international monetary system the numeraire is the unit used to express par values and to measure the degree of currency devaluation and revaluation. Since the Fund's creation, it is also the unit in terms of which the value of the Fund's financial assets are maintained. The staff pointed out that the SDR was already to some extent the de facto numeraire. The decision of the Executive Board of December 18, 1971, for instance, provided that members could communicate central rates expressed in terms of SDRs.[7] Early in 1972, the Fund introduced the SDR as the unit for all its accounts. The staff recommended that when the Articles of Agreement were amended, the SDR should become the de jure numeraire.

The staff advised against deciding at this time either that the Fund change its practices for the valuation of gold or that the Fund abolish a fixed official price for gold. In other words, beyond suggesting that the SDR become the numeraire of the reformed system, the staff did not tackle the question of the role of gold in a reformed system nor suggest special measures to induce members to replace their holdings of gold with holdings of SDRs. A supplementary note to the sketch, circulated two months later, dealt with the possibility that SDRs might become so much more attractive than gold that members might offer substantial amounts of their gold holdings for sale to the Fund. Under the Articles of Agreement, the right of members to sell gold to the Fund and the Fund's duty to purchase the gold offered were uncertain.[8] Envisaging the possibility that members might want to sell gold to the Fund on a large scale, the staff explained that the Fund would either be obliged to purchase it or, having a choice, would want to purchase it either to prevent members from selling it in the free market or to avoid putting members in the position of being unable to sell it legally. Some provision to deal with this contingency would probably have to be considered in discussing a reformed system.

---

[7] *History, 1966–71*, Vol. I, p. 559.

[8] The question of the legal duty of the Fund to purchase gold offered by its members had come up in 1968 and 1969 when South Africa wanted to sell gold to the Fund. At that time the Fund decided that as a matter of policy, as distinct from its legal obligation, it would purchase gold from South Africa in certain specified circumstances. See *History, 1966–71*, Vol. I, pp. 409–16.

To make the treatment of the dollar and of other currencies symmetrical in financing balance of payments deficits, the staff developed the concept of "asset financing." This concept had first been mentioned by the Managing Director at the 1970 Annual Meeting in Copenhagen and had created a stir among U.S. officials.[9] (It was later to become known as "asset settlement.") Rather than building up liabilities in a national currency, a reserve center country, that is, a country whose currency was used as reserves by other countries, would periodically convert any increases in other countries' balances of that currency. For this conversion, the reserve center country would use its holdings of reserve assets—SDRs, gold, or reserve positions in the Fund—or draw on negotiated credits, for example, by borrowing from the Fund or by using the swap network established by the central banks of the major industrial countries.

Asset financing, or asset settlement, in the reformed international monetary system would replace the Bretton Woods system's feature of convertibility. The latter was often termed "on demand convertibility," or "demand convertibility." Monetary authorities holding balances of a given currency had a right to convert these balances into reserve assets *upon demand*, but they did not have to exercise this right. The staff argued that demand convertibility was no longer suitable either for the dollar, which was not convertible after August 1971, or for other currencies then beginning to be used as reserve currencies and showing a dangerous potential for expanding reserve liabilities. Asset settlement would require countries, such as the United States, whose currencies were held by others as reserves to pay more or less on a current basis for their balance of payments deficits just as countries whose currencies were not held by others as reserves were required to do. The dollar would thus become equivalent to other currencies for financing balance of payments deficits. Asset settlement would also ensure that fluctuations in the amounts of reserve currencies outstanding would no longer affect the amount of world reserves. The burden of regulating the level of world reserves would then fall more heavily on international arrangements for the SDR, which was the idea agreed on in 1968 when SDRs were established.

The central place of the dollar in the existing international monetary system also derived from its use as the principal intervention currency in exchange markets. Indeed, even if other currencies, such as pounds sterling or French francs, were used for intervention, they were themselves pegged to the dollar, so that the dollar ranked as the ultimate intervention currency. Use of a single ultimate intervention currency was one factor making it difficult to secure for the issuer of that currency sufficient freedom to adjust its exchange rate. Use of a single intervention currency also made it difficult to secure for other countries sufficient safeguards against undue fluctuations in reserves.

Accordingly, the staff came up with a solution for the problem of a single intervention currency in the most complicated innovation of the reformed system, a

---

[9]*History, 1966–71*, Vol. I, pp. 491–92.

system of multicurrency intervention. Each of a number of countries would buy or sell each other's currencies in exchange markets, under agreed arrangements, with a view to influencing their relative exchange rates. Any resulting acquisition or loss of another country's currency would be settled more or less simultaneously by direct transfer of primary reserve assets between the countries in question. The staff proposed the introduction of multicurrency intervention because they believed it would provide several features desired in a reformed international monetary system. It would completely eliminate the special position of the dollar for countries participating in a multicurrency intervention regime. It would make the exchange rate of the dollar more flexible. Because margins around parities would no longer be expressed only in terms of the dollar, countries would not necessarily try to keep the rates between their currencies and the dollar stable, as under the previous system. A multicurrency intervention arrangement would also bring about automatic asset settlement for participating countries, including the United States, and would leave no practical option other than consolidation of existing balances for the totality of these countries' holdings of dollars. The staff, nonetheless, recognized that the introduction of multicurrency intervention would constitute a sharp break from the past practice of dollar intervention and might not yet be attainable.

Other Changes Suggested in the Sketch

Recognizing conflicting views about controlling capital movements, the staff did not go into detail in the sketch on measures to restrain excessive short-term flows of capital. They suggested, however, that a partial solution to the problem might lie in financing capital flows, perhaps through a new facility in the Fund. A supplementary note to the sketch on possible Fund financing of short-term capital movements posed a number of questions that would have to be considered should such a facility be created. Which members would be eligible to draw upon a capital-financing facility? How large would such a facility be? What conditions would govern its use?

Finally, in the sketch, the staff raised, but left open, the question of how a reformed international monetary system might provide more financial resources for developing members of the Fund. The staff recognized that developing members might regard as relatively disadvantageous a number of features of a reformed international monetary system, such as the replacement of holdings of reserve currencies by SDRs and a higher rate of interest on SDRs, which would benefit mainly the large industrial members with substantial reserves. In fact, as net users of SDRs, developing members would have to pay the higher interest rate on SDRs. Tighter rules for effecting balance of payments adjustment and allowance for more frequent changes in the exchange rates of industrial members could also adversely affect developing members. Moreover, officials of developing members, as compensation for their agreement to these features of a reformed system, might again press for a "link" between allocations of SDRs and the provision of development finance, or for other special arrangements to make additional funds available for financing development.[10]

REACTIONS OF EXECUTIVE DIRECTORS

To consider the staff sketch and to discuss the components of a reformed international monetary system, such as the replacement of existing reserve currencies with special issues of SDRs (that is, consolidation), the nature of a revised exchange rate mechanism, a multicurrency intervention system, and the designation of a numeraire for a reformed system, the Executive Directors met time and again in early 1972. From January to March 1972 they held 11 informal seminars in which they exchanged personal views and 4 formal meetings in which they expressed the positions of their authorities. They were aware that producing a report on reform of the international monetary system in time for the 1972 Annual Meeting in September would place the Fund, and the Executive Board in particular, in the forefront of negotiations to reform the world monetary system and, consequently, in a leadership position. But they were clearly far from agreed on the specific content of their report or of the various features in the staff sketch. The views the Executive Directors expressed in these informal seminars and formal meetings reflect the differences and uncertainty of position on most features of a reformed system prevailing among the world's financial authorities in the first few months of 1972.

Positions Favoring the Staff's Suggestions

The Executive Directors' consideration of the staff sketch can be regarded as a prenegotiation stage of a reformed international monetary system. In the first few months of 1972, only Mr. Mitchell and his Alternate, Ronald H. Gilchrist (United Kingdom), on the Executive Board were sure of what features they favored. Their assurance resulted from the advanced position taken by Anthony Barber at the 1971 Annual Meeting. Officials in the Bank of England and the U.K. Treasury had been discussing the elements of a reformed system since 1968, partly in conjunction with Paul A. Volcker, Under Secretary for Monetary Affairs in the U.S. Treasury since January 1969 when President Nixon took office. Hence, at the 1971 Annual Meeting, right after the unexpected suspension of convertibility of the dollar, Mr. Barber put forward a number of concrete suggestions for a reformed system based on earlier discussions in the United Kingdom. Many regarded Mr. Barber's points as novel and significant, and financial officials reacted favorably to what was construed as his advanced position. Interestingly enough, although U.K. authorities were pleased at

---

[10]The subject of the link, that is, a relation between allocations of SDRs and the provision of development finance, had been discussed and dropped earlier, from 1966 through 1969, during the negotiations that led to the establishment of the SDR. See *History, 1966–71,* Vol. I, pp. 61, 72, 84–85, 110–11, 197, 219–20, and 245–46.

this favorable response, they were also surprised by it since they regarded his points as not being all that new.

Mr. Barber proposed reducing the use of national currencies as reserves and making the SDR the basis of the reformed system. The SDR would be the numeraire of the system and the main asset in which countries held their reserves. World liquidity would be subject to controls to provide for adequate, but not excessive, liquidity without reliance on the balance of payments deficits of one or more countries. According to Mr. Barber, such a reformed international monetary system would remove some faults of the Bretton Woods system, yet would revive some of the system's best elements. It would strengthen international control over the creation of new international liquidity. Because the par value of the dollar, just as any other currency, would be expressed in terms of SDRs, the U.S. Government could, if it wished, change that par value relatively easily. The unique problem of the Bretton Woods system, that the par value of the dollar was hard to change, would thus be eliminated.[11]

Following Mr. Barber's lead, when the Executive Board began discussions of a reformed system, Messrs. Mitchell and Gilchrist spoke confidently of the need for a reformed system that included consolidation arrangements involving the exchange of reserve currencies for SDRs, a creditable scheme for the settlement of payments imbalances by the use of primary reserve assets other than national currencies, international control over the volume of world liquidity, and severe limitations on the further accumulation by central banks of balances of other countries' currencies. Sensing that the Fund management and staff might try to put the Fund in a controlling, supervisory position in a reformed system, Mr. Mitchell, however, maintained that strict control of the new system by the Fund was not essential. While the Fund would occupy an important position in the reformed system, particularly in supervising all forms of short-term financial assistance, the Fund did not need to supervise the settlement of all international payments or to harmonize holdings of reserve assets, provided that there was control in the system over the accumulation of reserves.

Mr. Schleiminger and his Alternate, Lore Fuenfgelt (Federal Republic of Germany), and Mr. Lieftinck, like Mr. Mitchell, accepted several features of the reformed system suggested in the staff sketch. In Mr. Schleiminger's view the heart of the reform exercise concerned the future financing of balance of payments deficits. He was receptive particularly to the staff proposals for asset settlement, namely, periodic compulsory conversion by the reserve center country of any increase in balances of its currency that might arise from its overall payments deficits.

Noting the succession of international monetary standards, from the gold standard to the gold-exchange standard of the Bretton Woods system, to the existing but unacceptable inconvertible dollar standard, Mr. Lieftinck made a strong appeal

---

[11]Statement by the Governor of the Fund for the United Kingdom, *Summary Proceedings, 1971*, pp. 32–35.

for an SDR standard. Because of the unsettled conditions in exchange markets in the first months of 1972, he favored the quick introduction of a reformed system to restore confidence in exchange rates and in the major currencies. He shared with other Executive Directors and the Fund management and staff concern that an unplanned system might arise, separating the world into a number of currency blocs, such as a dollar bloc and a bloc of EC currencies. To distinguish a system based on currency blocs from a reformed system, Executive Directors began to speak of a "one-world" system, which most of them preferred.

Positions Questioning the Staff's Suggestions

Other Executive Directors had difficulties with the features of the reformed system contained in the staff sketch. Mr. Bryce queried the need to consolidate into SDRs the billions of dollars held by the central banks around the world, which would involve a huge increase in SDRs. Also, governments would have to give up, in a relatively short time, the kind of reserves they were familiar with and accept as a large fraction of their reserves an asset that seemed to require a great deal of explanation. The SDR, still a novel unit in international finance, was not yet ready to be put to such an unreasonable test. Furthermore, the Canadian authorities saw serious problems in using SDRs for refinancing liabilities of reserve center countries; it was not up to the Fund to refinance existing dollar liabilities with SDRs. In place of consolidation, the holders of excess dollars could make direct bilateral arrangements with the United States, or with the United Kingdom should they be holding pounds sterling.

Mr. Beaurain explained that the French authorities wanted narrow margins on either side of parity or of a central rate set for the time being at a maximum of 2.25 percent. Eventually they should be narrower. The French authorities believed that the Fund should not have too forceful a role in suggesting to an individual member a change in par value. Its par value remained the primary responsibility of the member concerned. The French authorities continued to attach importance to "fundamental disequilibrium," especially as a way to distinguish between current transactions and capital movements as sources of balance of payments difficulties. If its competitive trading position did not justify such action, a member should not be obliged to revalue its currency because of an inflow of short-term capital. Capital controls, including the dual market mechanism, rather than exchange rate manipulations were the appropriate remedy for dealing with destabilizing inward and outward capital flows. The French authorities also wanted consolidation arrangements to be limited to no more than a small part of the outstanding balances of reserve currencies. Moreover, they did not want consolidation to take the form of special issues of SDRs. Consolidation should rather be effected by a detailed schedule of amortization of existing balances and by bilateral arrangements between the reserve center country and the holders of reserve currency balances.

Mr. Kafka, too, was skeptical of the features suggested for a reformed international monetary system. He doubted whether the Fund would be able to persuade countries to accept certain criteria as to when to change their exchange rates or would be able "to push both surplus or deficit countries into following them." He also believed that, even with consolidation arrangements, some reserve currencies would remain and that rules about their use would be necessary. He questioned the need for convertibility of national currency balances by reserve center countries and whether the obligation to convert forced reserve center countries to exercise more discipline over their payments deficits, as was argued by French officials. In his view, reserve center countries could always find ways to borrow from the rest of the world. If the reserve center country was to finance its deficits through primary reserve assets, such as gold or SDRs, it would have to earn those assets through such means as a trade surplus. He asked the Executive Directors point blank whether they were prepared to face the international deflationary impact likely to result if the main reserve center country, that is, the United States, was substantially to reduce its balance of payments deficits.

Mr. Dale, however, had the most problems with the staff's suggestions for a reformed system. He asked the Executive Directors to think through the implications of the broad objectives of reforming the international monetary system that they seemed to be taking for granted. Objectives such as the "replacement of existing reserve assets by special issues of SDRs," "international control over the quantity and the composition of global reserves," and "fully symmetrical financing of balance of payments situations" all sounded attractive. But they involved the assumption of difficult new obligations and commitments, particularly by the United States. In his view, and here Mr. Dale was expressing a position U.S. officials would repeat many times in the next two years, it was vital to pay special attention to the process by which balance of payments disequilibria ought best to be adjusted. Explicitly, the United States, a country in which the foreign sector of the economy made up only a small proportion of gross national product, needed to tilt its policies for adjustment of balance of payments deficits heavily in favor of changes in exchange rates and away from reliance on deflationary macroeconomic domestic policies.

Noting that the staff sketch called for a "slightly modified par value system," Mr. Dale circulated his own list of appropriate objectives for an exchange rate system. Exchange rates had to be judged in relation to how well they enabled equilibrium in the trade and current accounts and in the overall balance of payments to be attained. The many considerations influencing the flows of merchandise trade and of short-term and long-term capital had to be taken into account in deciding the appropriateness of a country's exchange rate policy. Among these considerations were the need for structural changes in an economy, internal demand-management policies, trade policies, and the use of restrictions and discriminatory arrangements by major trading partners. Discussions on reforming the world monetary system, he emphasized, had not yet taken up these considerations.

Mr. Dale was not in a position, however, to put forward alternative proposals for a reformed system. U.S. officials were still uncertain what features they wanted. There were, at the time, two points of view among U.S. officials. One view was held by Mr. Burns, Chairman of the Board of Governors of the Federal Reserve System. In common with the heads of central banks of most other industrial countries, Mr. Burns believed that the reformed system ought to be based on par values, as was the Bretton Woods system. However, to improve on the Bretton Woods system, proponents of this view wanted the reformed system to include prompt adjustments in par values, guidelines and consultative machinery for determining when par values needed to be changed, and greater responsibility for countries with payments surpluses to change the par values for their currencies. Mr. Burns also expected gold to continue to have some role, although a reduced one, in any future international monetary system.[12]

Mr. Shultz, Secretary of the U.S. Treasury, had a different view. Prior to joining the U.S. Administration, Mr. Shultz had been associated with the economists at the University of Chicago who favored floating exchange rates and considered himself less conventional in money matters than most central bankers. He favored a reformed system that provided considerable flexibility of exchange rates, especially for the U.S. dollar, and virtually no role for gold.[13] Not only were U.S. monetary authorities inclined to have differing views on the features of a reformed system but, in addition, Mr. Shultz had been Secretary only since May 1972 and was just beginning to develop his proposals for a reformed international monetary system. Members of the U.S. Congress, such as Henry S. Reuss, Chairman of the Joint Economic Subcommittee, although eager for the authorities of the Administration to come forward with specific proposals for a reformed system, had also not yet made up their minds about what features they preferred.[14]

Meanwhile, U.S. Treasury officials, concerned about the prolonged debates that had gone on in 1971 as to whether deficit or surplus countries were responsible for correcting their disequilibria, took the view that there was little point in negotiating proposals for a reformed system until a firmer consensus had developed on the causes of the breakdown of the previous system. To some extent, too, U.S. authorities believed that they could not enter into productive negotiations on a reformed system until after the U.S. elections in November 1972.

PROBLEMS IN DRAFTING THE REPORT

Because of the wide range of reactions of Executive Directors to the suggestions for a reformed system contained in the staff sketch, the staff suggested, and the

---

[12]Mr. Burns's views were expressed in a speech at the American Bankers Association International Monetary Conference in Montreal, Canada, on May 12, 1972. This speech was reprinted with the title "Some Essentials of International Monetary Reform," in *Monthly Review*, Federal Reserve Bank of New York, Vol. 54 (June 1972), pp. 131–34, and in *Federal Reserve Bulletin* (Washington), Vol. 58 (June 1972), pp. 545–49.

[13]See Shultz and Dam, *Economic Policy Beyond the Headlines* (cited in fn. 1 of Chap. 1 above), pp. 119–21.

[14]U.S. Congress, House, Committee on Banking and Currency, *International Monetary Reform* (Hearings Before the Subcommittee on International Finance on Defining Objectives of the United States in the Area of International Monetary Reform), 92nd Cong., 2nd Sess., June 22, 1972 (Washington: Government Printing Office, 1972).

Executive Board agreed, that the required report should aim at identifying and examining the major issues on which further study and discussion would be required, at both technical and policy levels, and at laying out the options available, but should not draw conclusions about the desirable shape of a reformed system. Even on this basis it proved difficult to write the report on reform.

U.S. officials were still making up their minds about the features they preferred in a reformed system and were shaping the proposals that Mr. Shultz was to present to the Board of Governors at the 1972 Annual Meeting. In the meantime, Mr. Dale was in an awkward position. He was uncertain about the usefulness of producing a report which described options available for a reformed system but which omitted options more in line with the thinking of his authorities. He had particular difficulty with the major option, an improved par value system coupled with an asset settlement mechanism centering on the SDR. He questioned whether such a system was practicable if the United States, the largest industrial country, was not prepared to agree to such unrealistic commitments. He pressed for an "open re-examination" of the conclusions of the 1970 report on exchange rates. He asked for fuller discussion of "objective indicators," such as changes in the levels of reserves held by countries, which would point to the need for changing an exchange rate, especially by countries with balance of payments surpluses. He urged that the report on reform say that many industrial countries had pursued policies involving undervalued exchange rates for their currencies and that a future problem for the reformed international monetary system would be the forestalling of "competitive undervaluation." He suggested consideration also of an arrangement for *partial* asset settlement. To meet his objections, Mr. Dale suggested that the planned first chapter of the report, describing the historical background of the negotiations for a reformed international monetary system, the need for such a system, and the broad objectives to be attained, be made the substantive part.

Most Executive Directors disagreed with Mr. Dale's suggestion. They did not want the report to concentrate mainly on the weaknesses of the former Bretton Woods system. Moreover, they were convinced that the concepts put forward by the staff, such as a modified par value system, asset settlement, and an improved and stronger SDR, were indeed components of any reformed system. Yet, despite the split in views, no one was in favor of a report that identified majority and minority opinions.

The report was also to emphasize the need for countries to make changes in par values more frequently and more promptly when such changes were required. Yet, Mr. Suzuki, as well as Mr. Dale, was troubled that an exhortation to countries to make par value changes could, in the unsettled exchange market conditions of 1972, be interpreted as a sign of lack of confidence in the exchange rates agreed at the Smithsonian Institution. Hence, the report itself could contribute to the undoing of the Smithsonian exchange rates, just when officials were trying hard to make these rates viable. (As early as August 1972, Mr. Dale was suggesting at Executive Board meetings that in changing the par value of the dollar in December 1971, U.S. officials had been prepared to go further, and needed to go further, than other countries had been willing to accept.)

A few Executive Directors were also interested in preserving a key role for gold in a reformed system. Mr. Brand, who was elected also by South Africa, protested that the drafting of the section on gold by the staff represented "a psychological war against gold." He was supported by Messrs. Viénot and Beaurain. They favored a substantive role for gold and an increase in the fixed official price so as to narrow the gap between the official price and the prices prevailing in private markets. Mr. Viénot also wanted the report to stress that failure of the United States to adjust its par value unduly passed the burden of balance of payments adjustment to other countries.

The Executive Directors elected by developing members, most notably Mr. Prasad, were disappointed that the problems of developing members were not treated more fully in the sketch and wanted the report to remedy this lack. They were concerned also that if the Fund was to have more power to apply pressure or sanctions on members to change their exchange rates, such pressure was more likely to be used against developing than against developed members. Byanti Kharmawan (Indonesia) called attention to the danger for members of a future international monetary system if many industrial members wanted to achieve current account surpluses in order to export capital; developing members would be in perpetual deficit on current account vis-à-vis industrial members.

All these views had somehow to be reflected in the report. As a result, the staff prepared more than two dozen drafts, which the Executive Directors considered in 40 meetings for two months, from June 19 to August 18. Included in these 40 meetings was a final marathon series of 11 meetings in 6 successive days so that the report could be published in August, prior to the 1972 Annual Meeting.

The drafting was ultimately successful because the Executive Directors and the staff cooperated closely. For example, though Mr. Dale frequently criticized drafts prepared by the staff, he was willing to have his own points redrafted by the staff so that they harmonized better with the rest of the report. As time went on, most Executive Directors also wanted features of the reformed system described in such a way that they would be more realistic and workable. Hence, they went along with many of Mr. Dale's concerns, agreeing, for instance, on a gradual phasing in of full asset settlement or voluntary participation in asset settlement by countries other than reserve center countries. References to asset settlement could be made more conditional, and there could be less firm commitments than envisaged in some of the staff drafts to a system of multicurrency intervention, to a substitution account, and to a Fund facility for financing flows of short-term capital.

Members of the Executive Board were thus in the end reasonably flexible. In fact, the Executive Directors for the EC countries and for other countries in the Group of Ten seemed to have been more willing to compromise on the features of a reformed system than were some of their higher-level authorities. At the time, some of the highest ranking officials of the EC countries, especially of France, seemed to be turning increasingly conservative about the features of a reformed system, favoring par values that were not often changed and wanting gold to be an important reserve asset of the system. They favored controls to restrict capital flows. These concepts implied an international monetary system that was less flexible and even tighter than the original Bretton Woods system had been. These concepts were also far removed from the features of the reformed system that many other officials, especially of the United States, envisaged. Consequently, it seemed that officials at the highest levels were developing positions that would be hard to reconcile. Yet, the Executive Directors produced a report with which they all more or less agreed.

THE FINISHED REPORT

The final report was transmitted to the Governors on August 18, 1972, in time for them to read it before the Annual Meeting.[15] The report contained many innovative ideas of the staff sketch, but they were advanced in a tentative way. Arguments for and against each suggestion were spelled out. The report was put out on the assumption that considerably more discussion was required and that the highest financial officials of the Fund's members would have to familiarize themselves with the complex and technical subjects under discussion.

Chapter I, "The Need for Reform," briefly explained the reasons for the reform effort. After describing the three principal characteristics of the Bretton Woods system, the chapter explained the difficulties that had arisen in the functioning of the system, much as has already been explained in Chapter 6 above, and the aims of a new system. These aims, however, were written in the most general of phrases.

Chapter II, "The Exchange Rate Mechanism," repeated most of the reasoning and conclusions contained in the 1970 report of the Executive Directors, *The Role of Exchange Rates in the Adjustment of International Payments*. Emphasis was still placed on the need for stable but adjustable par values, reflecting a continued belief by monetary authorities that prompt adjustments of par values would enable the international monetary system again to function smoothly without the disruptive effects of speculative capital movements. The report on reform, however, unlike the earlier 1970 report on exchange rate adjustment, now recognized that the United States would have to be able to change the par value for the dollar more readily than in the past; that the Fund might have to be able to take the initiative in suggesting par value changes to members; that substantially wider margins around parities than in the Bretton Woods system might well have to be accepted; that some kind of objective indicators to suggest the need for changes in par values might have to be introduced; and that the Fund should have more power to approve the temporary use of floating rates.

---

[15]*Reform of the International Monetary System: A Report by the Executive Directors to the Board of Governors* (Washington: International Monetary Fund, 1972), reproduced in Vol. III below, pp. 19–56.

Chapter III, "Convertibility and the Settlement of Imbalances," contained the newest ideas in the report. There was the first public airing of the concepts of "asset settlement" and of a "substitution account," with elaborate explanations of both concepts. Three possible ways in which asset settlement might be effected were explained, together with an appraisal of how each way could achieve full asset settlement and leave members free as far as possible to determine the composition of their reserves. One way was for the reserve center country to undertake to convert an amount equivalent to any net increase in balances of its currency outstanding in official hands by transferring a corresponding amount of reserve assets (gold, SDRs, reserve positions in the Fund, or currencies of other members) to official holders in exchange for its currency. The countries which would have to accept the reserve assets and the amounts they would have to accept would be determined under the administration of the Fund by procedures possibly analogous to the methods used by the Fund to designate recipients of SDRs. This way would ensure full asset settlement of reserve center surpluses and deficits (except insofar as there was international agreement on the need for some increase in balances of a particular reserve currency) but would accommodate asset preferences of individual members only to the extent that this could be done through a designation or similar procedure.

In a second way of implementing asset settlement, each country would agree not to let its holdings of any reserve currency diverge from a previously specified level, perhaps equal to reserves needed as working balances. Countries would be obliged to present to the reserve center countries for conversion into reserve assets any foreign exchange holdings which accrued to them above these levels and, to the extent that they fell below these levels, to reconstitute their balances by selling primary reserve assets to the reserve center countries. The total of all reserve currency balances outstanding would thus remain approximately constant over time, thereby achieving full asset settlement, but countries would not have much freedom in determining the composition of their reserves.

A third way relied to a greater extent on voluntary action. A substitution facility in the Fund would allow members to convert reserve currency balances into SDRs at any time or, alternatively, at specified times. Settlement of imbalances by a reserve center country would then be achieved through the Fund: when in deficit a country that was a reserve center would buy from the Fund, in exchange for reserves, an amount of its currency equivalent to the increase in its liabilities outstanding to official holders, and when in surplus would sell its currency to the Fund in the amount of any decline in its liabilities outstanding to official holders. This procedure would give countries a high degree of freedom in the determination of the composition of their reserves and would achieve full asset settlement as long as the cumulative total of currencies sold to the Fund for substitution into SDRs permitted the Fund to sell the required amount of its currency to a reserve center country that was in deficit.

This third way was interesting in another respect. By suggesting the possibility of a substitution account to accept reserve currency balances from members and to issue SDRs in exchange, the Fund itself had come around to suggesting the most extreme of the ideas Professor Triffin put forward 14 years earlier, which the Fund had then rejected as too radical.[16]

Another idea published for the first time in the report, also in Chapter III, was that of shifting from an intervention system in which all currencies were directly or indirectly pegged to the dollar to a system in which intervention was somehow made much more symmetrical. In other words, a multicurrency intervention system was described.

Chapter IV of the report, "The Roles of Various Assets in Reserves," was concerned with the respective roles in a reformed system of reserve currencies, gold, and SDRs. The staff and several members of the Executive Board had long been interested in enhancing the role of the SDR in the international monetary system and the report provided them with the chance to explain how it might be done. This chapter started out by noting that adoption of asset settlement could well mean that increases in global reserves would be in the form of SDRs rather than in the form of reserve currencies, as they had been in the past. Not only would the relative role of currencies in global reserves decline over time but so would the absolute amounts of reserve currency holdings. Much of the remainder of the chapter was devoted to explaining how these developments could be brought about, that is, how a substitution facility in the Fund could work, and how the features of the SDR could be changed so as to enhance its attractiveness and use as the primary reserve asset of the international monetary system. The chapter also contained some explanation of the role of gold in a reformed system, but it did not offer solutions for controversial problems concerning gold, particularly what to do about the large existing holdings of gold in official hands.

Chapter V, "The Problem of Disequilibrating Capital Movements," explained the causes and consequences of the growth of disequilibrating capital flows and examined the means of offsetting and accommodating short-term flows. It then considered the "wide range of possible measures available to countries to influence capital flows." These included using wider margins around parities, harmonizing interest rate policies, administratively controlling capital movements, relying on separate markets for capital transactions, and restraining official holders of currencies from switching the composition of the currencies being held. The chapter briefly discussed, too, the possibility of introducing into the Fund a facility for financing short-term capital flows.

The last chapter, Chapter VI, "International Monetary Reform and the Developing Countries," described some of the special interests of developing countries in a reformed system. Developing countries had been emphasizing how the disruption in the Bretton Woods system, especially in the second half of 1971, had affected them adversely and why it was essential for them to participate fully in the formulation and negotiation of any proposals to reform the system and in any

---

[16]*History, 1966–71*, Vol. I, pp. 21–22.

associated proposals relating to international trade. This chapter of the report gave recognition to these needs and noted that officials of developing countries favored some of the particular features in a reformed system, such as a system of par values with maintenance of narrow margins around parities. In addition, it pointed out that the developing countries continued to be especially interested in a link between the creation of SDRs and the provision of finance for development purposes and spelled out four possible ways in which some such link could be established. This chapter also put the public on notice that a study of the link was already under way in the Fund.

Significance of the Report

In commending the report to the Governors at their 1972 Annual Meeting, Mr. Schweitzer stressed that its scope was comprehensive. It reviewed the need for reform of the international monetary system against the background of experience with the Bretton Woods system. It set out the aims of a reformed system. It provided many suggestions about the directions that further work on international monetary reform might take. It gave attention to the vital interest of developing members in the functioning of the international monetary system and considered the possibility of increased flows of resources for development purposes in a reformed system. Mr. Schweitzer also stressed that the report did not gloss over the differences in attitude among members or minimize the diversity of members' positions and interests on many particular issues of reform.[17]

Although the final report was warmly received by the Governors at the 1972 Annual Meeting, the decision had already been taken to create a special Committee of Twenty to negotiate a reformed system, as is discussed in Chapter 8. The report was significant, nonetheless. It contained most of the themes that dominated the discussions and the work of the Committee of Twenty in the next two years. In fact, as the Fund staff responsible for helping the Executive Board draft the report, particularly the Economic Counsellor, examined the outcome of the work of the Committee of Twenty, they believed that the Executive Board's own report had held up well. The staff observed, for instance, that no new features of a reformed system emerged from the negotiations of the Committee of Twenty and that all the features described in the report, such as a substitution account and the emergence of the SDR as the central reserve asset of the system, remained on the agenda for further discussion at some future time. Nonetheless, by 1978, if not earlier, the Executive Board's report of 1972, like the *Outline of Reform* in 1974 that resulted from the Committee of Twenty, had a distinct air of unreality or of having been an academic exercise. Reform of the international monetary system either along the lines of the report on reform or of the *Outline* of the Committee of Twenty was not achieved. The exercises of both the Executive Board and the Committee of Twenty in that sense, therefore, failed. Some reasons for that failure are offered in Chapter 13.

---

[17]Opening Address by the Managing Director, *Summary Proceedings, 1972*, pp. 27–28.

CHAPTER
8

Creation of the Committee of Twenty

OFFICIALS OF THE UNITED STATES wanted the reform of the international monetary system to be undertaken by a forum other than the Group of Ten or the Fund, the two bodies that had worked out the agreement that led to the establishment of the SDR. Agreement was reached in the middle of 1972 on a special committee of Fund Governors, called the "ad hoc Committee of the Board of Governors on Reform of the International Monetary System and Related Issues." Because it comprised 20 Fund Governors, reflecting the then 20 constituencies of the Executive Directors, this committee was usually referred to as the Committee of Twenty. Although during the negotiations leading up to agreement on this committee the proposed body was sometimes referred to as the Group of Twenty, because of the undertone of exclusiveness of the word Group associated with the Group of Ten, the Committee of Twenty, or C-20, became the accepted sobriquet.

The idea of setting up a committee of the Board of Governors of the Fund evolved gradually. Only in 1972 were governmental officials ready to agree. Thus, the Committee of Twenty had a prehistory in many respects transcending its importance as a committee. This prehistory reveals, for example, that discussions about setting up *any* committee of Fund Governors touched off a struggle over which officials and which countries were going to have authority over the management of "international money." What powers would the select group have? Would the group make recommendations only, or would it take decisions binding on all Fund members? What would be its relations with the Fund's Executive Board? Which Fund members would be represented in the group and how would they be determined? Would there be voting in the group and, if so, would it be the weighted voting determined by members' quotas in the Fund, like the weighted voting in the full Board of Governors and in the Executive Board?

Only after acceptable answers to these sensitive questions were found was agreement reached on a temporary Committee of Twenty. Once a formula was found for that Committee, the same model was used for a permanent Council planned to be set up following amendment of the Articles of Agreement. In the meantime, an Interim Committee, based on the same model, was to serve. Even then, however, the struggle over setting up a high-level group to decide on international monetary arrangements was not at an end. Despite initial expectation that the Council might come into being shortly after the Second Amendment went into effect, as of the end of 1978 it seemed that disagreement over the desirability of setting up the Council might indefinitely postpone its formation.

This chapter first summarizes the attempts to set up some committee of Governors before 1972. It then explains why the Committee of Twenty was created in 1972, the debates that preceded agreement on this particular committee, the way in which the Committee was organized, and how its meetings were conducted. The discussions and negotiations about reforming the international monetary system carried on in the Committee of Twenty are described in the following five chapters.

REASONS FOR CONSIDERING A COMMITTEE OF GOVERNORS

The Managing Director, Pierre-Paul Schweitzer, and the staff first thought in the middle of the 1960s that a subgroup of the Board of Governors would be a useful addition to the Fund's policymaking machinery. By then the issues relating to the international monetary system were becoming complex and officials of member governments disagreed on how to resolve them. Agreement and compromise at the political level were needed to resolve controversial issues. Governors of the Fund are usually considered the "political" level.[1] The "political" level refers to persons with cabinet or subcabinet rank, such as finance ministers, who report directly to heads of state or government and whose office accordingly depends on political considerations.

It was clear by the 1960s that the full Board of Governors was not a suitable forum for discussion and negotiation. First, the Governors met only at Annual Meetings where it was hard to hold discussions. Governors came to Annual Meetings primarily to make speeches, to perform their legal duties of formally voting on resolutions prepared in advance by the Executive Directors, to meet with each other, and to do business with private bankers and financiers attending the meetings as invited guests or visitors. It was difficult to get Governors to attend plenary sessions. Second, the number of Governors was becoming too large: by September 1963 it had reached more than 100.

In these circumstances, the idea found favor with the Fund management and staff that a small group of Governors, meeting two or three times a year between Annual Meetings, could discuss key questions of policy and take interim recommendations later to be put to the full Board of Governors. The work of the Executive

---

[1]See Joseph Gold, "'Political' Bodies in the Fund," in his *Legal and Institutional Aspects of the International Monetary System: Selected Essays* (Washington: International Monetary Fund, 1979), pp. 238–91. (Hereafter referred to as Gold, *Legal and Institutional Aspects.*)

Directors and of the Fund management and staff on questions requiring approval of the Board of Governors could meanwhile proceed on the basis of the interim recommendations of the smaller group of Governors.

The thinking of the management and staff about the need for a political body as part of the Fund was also influenced to a large extent by the existence and activities of the Group of Ten. The Group of Ten (the finance ministers and central bank governors—two officials from each country—of Belgium, Canada, France, the Federal Republic of Germany, Italy, Japan, Netherlands, Sweden, the United Kingdom, and the United States) was a unique and influential political group and not a body of the Fund.

The Group of Ten originated in 1961 in the course of discussing the establishment of the General Arrangements to Borrow.[2] Beginning about 1963, it began to meet frequently to examine the prospective need for additional liquidity in the international monetary system. To study more deeply the technical issues involved, the Group designated deputies, who also began to meet regularly. These officials of the ten largest industrial countries met separately on the premise that because their common interest in and responsibility for the international monetary system sharply differentiated them from the less industrial and developing members, they should have their own forum in which to consider and coordinate their positions. Indeed, they wanted the Group of Ten to be the *major* forum for negotiation on international monetary subjects in which they could consider subjects prior to, or simultaneous with, discussions going on in the Fund. The authorities of the United States in 1963, 1964, and 1965 particularly urged that assessment of the adequacy of international liquidity and the possible need for a new reserve asset in the international monetary system be discussed in the Group of Ten. U.S. officials insisted that discussions of reserve creation take place in the Group of Ten because at the time, like other officials of the Group, they favored arrangements in which any new reserve asset would be distributed only among the ten largest industrial countries, in other words a limited group approach to reserve creation.

Because of its power and influence, the Group of Ten played a decisive role in the series of negotiations from 1963 to 1968 that eventually led to the establishment of SDRs in the Fund. The Executive Board often waited to take decisions until the Group of Ten had formulated an agreed position. In an unprecedented move by the Fund to coordinate its actions with those of the Group of Ten, joint meetings between the Executive Directors and the deputies of the Group of Ten were held in 1966 and 1967.

Executive Directors, however, became sensitive to the encroachment of the Group of Ten on the Fund's business. One Executive Director, Ahmed Zaki Saad (Egypt), went so far as to refuse to attend the joint meetings of Executive Directors and the deputies of the Group of Ten. One of Mr. Saad's arguments against these

---

[2]The events summarized in this section were discussed at length in *History, 1966–71*, Vol. I. See especially pp. 28, 67–82, 88–89, 95–108, 119–27, 134–37, 141–43, 150–58, 162–65, 170–75, 292–95, 543–45, 551–53, 617–18, and 626.

joint meetings was that the Executive Board of the Fund customarily met as an organ of the Fund, that is, as a unit that had decision-making power and the right to vote as did the Board of Governors, and that under the Fund's Articles, the deputies of the Group of Ten had no legal right to participate in Executive Board meetings. However, in the view of the General Counsel, who assisted Pierre-Paul Schweitzer and Otmar Emminger (then Chairman of the deputies of the Group of Ten) in working out the procedures for the joint meetings, the Executive Directors were not meeting as an organ of the Fund but were holding informal discussions and exchanges of views as individuals; Executive Directors were merely attending meetings with another group by virtue of their office. Another argument of Mr. Saad's against the joint meetings and the argument that most influenced him to boycott these meetings was that the Fund alone was the appropriate forum for considering international monetary arrangements. Mr. Saad had participated at Bretton Woods in the founding of the Fund and after the Fund's establishment had been one of the first 12 Executive Directors. Since 1946 he had consistently taken strong positions aimed at building up the influence and authority of the Fund. Hence, when the possibility of meetings of the Executive Directors with the deputies of the Group of Ten was being considered in 1966, Mr. Saad took the position that the Fund had been created especially for multinational discussions of international monetary policy and that no other group should be allowed to usurp this function.

The influence of the Group of Ten in discussions of international monetary arrangements increased. By 1969, the Group of Ten was deliberating on subjects directly related to the Fund that had previously been the sole prerogative of the Fund, most notably the increase in 1970 in members' quotas under the Fifth General Review of Quotas. Other Executive Directors, including even some, such as Mr. Lieftinck, from countries participating in the Group of Ten, also began to be bothered by the seeming takeover of some of the Fund's main responsibilities by the Group of Ten. Several Executive Directors were annoyed especially by the activities of the deputies of the Group of Ten.

By 1971, the Group of Ten was taking actions on international monetary questions without the Fund's participation. The most prominent such action was the realignment in December 1971 of the exchange rates for the currencies of their ten countries. Although in the last months of 1971 officials of the Fund's developing members were urging the Group of Ten to agree on exchange rates for the currencies of the large industrial countries so that these exchange rates would again be stabilized after the disorder created by the suspension of dollar convertibility in August 1971, they deeply resented being excluded from participation in the discussions. The nine Executive Directors elected exclusively by developing members requested another joint meeting of the Executive Directors with the deputies of the Group of Ten. In order to have a forum in which officials from all Fund members could participate, such a joint meeting was held in December 1971. Moreover, because they felt excluded from the Group of Ten, officials of developing countries, toward the end of 1971, took steps to set up their own Group of Twenty-Four.

FRUSTRATED EFFORTS BEFORE 1972

Prior to the Committee of Twenty in 1972, efforts to establish a committee of Fund Governors were unsuccessful. Nevertheless, these efforts, despite their failure, provided valuable experience. They made it apparent that only a relatively large committee based on the constituencies represented on the Executive Board would be acceptable and they foreshadowed the debates, repeated in recent years in respect to a permanent Council, over the powers and voting system of special bodies of Governors.

The first attempt came in 1966 in the course of the deliberations concerning creation of a new reserve asset. As a way to broaden participation in the deliberations beyond the Group of Ten, U.S. officials proposed a Governors' advisory committee on reserve creation for consideration at the Annual Meeting in September 1966. The committee was to comprise the Group of Ten and Fund Governors from several other members, with voting in accordance with the Fund's weighted system. This proposal was rejected. The Managing Director suggested instead an advisory committee on reserve creation composed of the deputies of the Group of Ten and the Executive Directors, partly because such a committee would make use of the ready-made geographical representation embodied in the Executive Board. There was to be no voting in this committee. The Executive Directors and the deputies of the Group of Ten strongly preferred this solution.[3]

The next attempt came in 1968 while the amendments to the Articles later known as the First Amendment were being drafted. Under discussion was Article XVIII, which provided that questions of interpretation of the Articles could be decided by simple majority of the Executive Directors and on appeal by the same majority of the Board of Governors.[4] Officials of the EC countries proposed, inter alia, as a condition for accepting the SDR facility a change in Article XVIII: an external tribunal of three arbitrators would be introduced as a court of last appeal if a member was dissatisfied with a decision interpreting the Articles taken under the existing procedures.[5]

French officials, concerned about legal matters in the Fund from the beginning, believed that interpretations of the Articles had been more in accord with the views of officials of the United States and the United Kingdom than with their own views. Hence, as the Articles were being amended they sought to amend Article XVIII so as to diminish the effect of weighted voting. Since the provisions of Article XVIII(c) for an external tribunal already existed for the resolution of disagreements between the Fund and a member which has withdrawn, or between the Fund and any member during liquidation of the Fund—provisions which specified already accepted

---

[3]See *History, 1966–71*, Vol. I, pp. 100–103.

[4]Article XVIII of the original Articles of Agreement is in *History, 1945–65*, Vol. III, p. 205.

[5]The other proposals have been described in *History, 1966–71*, Vol. I. See especially pp. 131–33, 155, and 253–60.

procedures—it seemed easy to apply them also to disagreements concerning interpretations of the Articles.

Although on the surface the proposal seemed esoteric and minor, it had potent consequences. At issue was the authority of the Fund to interpret its own charter, an authority that had been a prime factor in enabling the Fund to adapt to changing circumstances and to be flexible in its actions.[6] This flexibility could be jeopardized if a member could at any time appeal to an outside arbitral tribunal, whose decision would be final.

Mr. Schweitzer's position was that any change in the way the Fund interpreted its Articles was unnecessary but, if French officials insisted on some change, the Fund should use procedures based on its own policymaking organs, rather than some external body. He proposed a standing Committee on Interpretation of the Board of Governors, which would be a strong body. If a member wished to refer a question of interpretation to the Board of Governors under Article XVIII, the question would have to be considered first by the Committee on Interpretation, which would make formal recommendations to the Board of Governors, the recommendations being made without voting.

This committee also never materialized. Briefly, what happened was the following. When the Group of Ten met in Stockholm in March 1968 to discuss unsettled issues in the draft amendments, U.S. officials, eager to obtain agreement on the SDR facility, seemed willing to consent to all the French proposals, including the one with regard to Article XVIII.[7] To help save Article XVIII, Mr. Schweitzer put forward the compromise idea of a Committee on Interpretation of the Board of Governors, and, to gain the support of French officials, he proposed that each member of the committee have only one vote. This idea was accepted.

Accordingly, under the amended Article XVIII, the Executive Board was to take decisions on questions of interpretation of the Articles and any member government could appeal to the Board of Governors, as in the original Articles, but the appeal would be to the special committee, which would have power to vote and make decisions, rather than merely give advice. The idea that each member cast a single vote represented a basic change from the Fund's usual weighted voting procedures. Moreover, it would take a special high majority of 85 percent of the voting power to overrule the committee.

Strenuous efforts were made in 1969 and 1970 to get agreement on a By-Law for setting up the committee. While the size and composition of the committee were discussed by the Executive Board on several occasions, and the staff circulated a number of papers projecting alternative committee sizes and group formations and the corresponding percentages of quota and voting power that would be involved, it

---

[6]Joseph Gold has discussed interpretation of its Articles by decisions of the Executive Board as one of the Fund's "techniques of response" to changing circumstances in *History, 1945–65*, Vol. II, pp. 567–73.

[7]Other issues resolved at the Stockholm meeting have been described in *History, 1966–71*, Vol. I, pp. 170–75.

proved impossible for the Executive Directors to agree. Hence, while the provision for such a committee remains in the Articles, even after the Second Amendment, it has never been implemented.

The main reason why the Committee on Interpretation has never been established was disagreement over its size. When the Administration of President Lyndon B. Johnson put the proposed First Amendment to the Articles before the U.S. Congress, as required by U.S. law, Henry S. Reuss, Congressman from Wisconsin and a member of the Committee on Banking and Currency of the House of Representatives, was especially concerned about the proposed amendment of Article XVIII. He emphasized that the power to interpret the law exceeds the power to write the law. The verbal exchanges between Mr. Reuss and Frederick L. Deming, Under Secretary of the Treasury for Monetary Affairs, suggest that Mr. Reuss objected to the surrender by the United States of its proportion of weighted voting power in the Committee on Interpretation because it would lose its influence over interpretation of the Fund's Articles. Mr. Reuss was particularly concerned that the scarce currency clause in the Fund's Articles could be interpreted adversely for the United States. He therefore extracted from officials of the U.S. Treasury an understanding, tantamount to an assurance that, when the Committee on Interpretation was established in the Fund, the United States would retain the same proportion of voting power as it had under the system of weighted voting.[8] Since the United States had approximately 20 percent of the voting power in the Fund, this understanding meant that the membership of the Committee on Interpretation could not exceed about six persons. In any event, U.S. officials probably preferred a small committee to ensure an efficient committee.

While U.S. authorities wanted the committee to be small, the authorities of other Fund members also wanted to be represented. To meet their needs, the committee would have to be relatively large. Because of this conflict, the efforts made in 1969 and 1970 to establish the committee were not successful.

Further Unsuccessful Efforts at Creating a Governors' Committee

Despite the failure of efforts to establish the Committee on Interpretation, the staff, also early in 1969, engaged in further efforts to get a standing committee of the Board of Governors introduced. Many officials, including Mr. Schweitzer and the Economic Counsellor, Mr. Polak, who attended the meeting of the Group of Ten in Bonn in November 1968, were struck by the disorderly and unrepresentative character of the meeting. Although the meeting had been called to consider changing the exchange rates of the main currencies, especially the deutsche mark and the French franc, little was accomplished.[9] These officials believed that an

---

[8]U.S. Congress, House, Committee on Banking and Currency, *To Establish a Facility Based on Special Drawing Rights in the International Monetary Fund*, Hearings on H.R. 16911, 90th Cong., 2nd Sess., May 1 and 2, 1968 (Washington: Government Printing Office, 1968), pp. 170–72.

[9]See *History, 1966–71*, Vol. I, pp. 450–53.

alternative high-level body might be more effective than the Group of Ten in bringing about a currency realignment and possibly a change in the whole exchange rate mechanism.

These circumstances, plus the dissatisfaction of officials from developing countries and from Australia at being excluded from the meeting of the Group of Ten, prompted the General Counsel, in January 1969, to draft a paper outlining a possible procedure for setting up a standing committee of the Board of Governors. The timing seemed appropriate since a new U.S. Administration was taking office.

In May 1969 the General Counsel prepared a revised paper for discussion by the Executive Directors as part of their informal examination of the need for introducing greater flexibility into the exchange rate mechanism.[10] The paper suggested a standing committee of the Board of Governors modeled on the composition of the Executive Board; the staff was convinced that the model of the 20 constituencies of the Executive Board was the only acceptable arrangement. Whatever faults the representative character of the Executive Board might have, it was an established model, acceptable in concept and in structure to all Fund members.

While the paper received a great deal of sympathetic consideration, Executive Directors feared a loss of authority, and the proposal for a standing committee of Governors came to nothing when the discussions about revising the exchange rate mechanism petered out.

It was against this background that discussions for some committee, possibly of the Board of Governors, began in 1972.

THE COMMITTEE OF TWENTY FORMED IN 1972

In the last several months of 1971, the decade-long predilection of officials of the industrial countries for the Group of Ten changed. Paradoxically, in view of the earlier role of the United States in strengthening the Group of Ten, it was the officials of the United States who became most disenchanted with the Group of Ten. Mr. Connally was the Secretary of the U.S. Treasury at the time, and his dissatisfaction with the Group of Ten was widely reported. The not dissimilar but more mildly expressed views of his successor, Mr. Shultz, who assumed office in May 1972, have been conveyed in his own writings.[11] According to Mr. Shultz, he, Mr. Connally, and U.S. officials responsible for international monetary policy came to feel that the Group of Ten was excessively weighted in favor of the EC countries. Not only were there five EC members—Belgium, France, the Federal Republic of Germany, Italy, and the Netherlands—among the ten industrial countries making

---

[10]These informal discussions have been described in *History, 1966–71*, Vol. I, pp. 500–503.

[11]Shultz and Dam, *Economic Policy Beyond the Headlines* (cited in fn. 1 of Chap. 1 above), pp. 121–22.

up the Group of Ten, but after about 1966–67 officials of the EC countries usually met separately in advance of Group of Ten meetings to discuss their positions on upcoming issues. At times the EC countries disagreed among themselves so that at meetings of the Group of Ten debate was complicated and agreement could not be attained. At other times, the five EC countries took a common line at meetings of the Group of Ten. In this event, since protocol at meetings of the Group of Ten allowed each of the ten participants to speak, the EC countries had a chance to repeat the same position several times, while the United Staes could state its views only once. U.S. officials felt frustrated as they found themselves faced by EC countries either with diverse and discordant views or in a solid phalanx.

U.S. officials were also concerned that with the entry into the EC of the United Kingdom at the beginning of 1973 a majority of the Group of Ten would belong to the EC. The other three members of the Group of Ten—Canada, Japan, and Sweden—expressed independent views, which, U.S. officials noted, were more often opposed to the views of U.S. officials than in accord with them. For these reasons, according to Mr. Shultz, "the United States wanted a forum in which its inherent economic and financial power could not be offset by procedural conventions."[12]

When Mr. Connally, at a meeting of the Group of Ten in November 1971, made apparent his extreme discontent with the Group of Ten as the group that would negotiate the forthcoming reform of the international monetary system, the Fund management and staff saw an opportunity to press for a committee of the Board of Governors as the body to consider reform. With the approval of the Deputy Managing Director, early in January 1972 the General Counsel sent to some of the delegations of the Group of Ten, including the U.S. and the Canadian delegations, copies of his paper of May 1969 describing such a committee. Two weeks later, the staff circulated to the Executive Directors a short paper, An Advisory Committee of the Board of Governors: Outline of an Illustrative Plan, which had as an attachment the detailed paper of 1969.[13]

This paper was the start of an intensive series of discussions on the appropriate group in which to discuss reform of the international monetary system. The deputies of the Group of Ten were not eager to take on the task of negotiating a reformed system. Their experience in the 1960s with the deliberations on international liquidity and the establishment of the SDR had been exhausting for them and offensive to nonparticipants in the Group of Ten. As officials of some developed countries and all developing countries objected to the exclusivity of the Group of Ten, the experience had been painful to the Group of Ten as well. It was theoretically possible that the Executive Board could be the body to negotiate reform, but U.S. authorities were strongly opposed to that solution.

---

[12]Ibid., p. 122.

[13]These papers, plus two supplements that were prepared in March 1972 to take into account the views of the Executive Directors on this illustrative plan, are in Vol. III below, pp. 129–49.

U.S. Preference for Reform Discussions Outside the Fund

As a group other than the Group of Ten to negotiate a reformed system was first being considered in early 1972, Paul A. Volcker, Under Secretary of the U.S. Treasury for Monetary Affairs, in talks with his counterparts in other industrial countries and with Fund management, on behalf of U.S. authorities, proposed a body that was only loosely connected with the Fund. In those first few months of 1972, U.S. authorities would probably have preferred a body not associated with the Fund in any way. In general terms, U.S. authorities argued that the Fund could not reform itself, but they also had specific objections to the Fund's participation. First of all, they regarded the Fund as having authority to deal only with subjects relating to the international monetary system, such as exchange rates, arrangements for convertibility, the role of gold in the system, and the future of SDRs. However, they wanted to be sure that the proposed group could discuss not only strictly monetary issues, but also other issues, such as trade policy, fiscal policy, financial aid to developing members, sharing military expenditures, and international investment. Since the middle of 1971, U.S. authorities had been taking the position that correction or elimination of U.S. balance of payments deficits required negotiations that went beyond the monetary subjects of rates, convertibility, SDRs, and other currency arrangements into other areas of international economics. U.S. officials especially wanted to negotiate new arrangements for international trade. They particularly wanted to avoid the recurrence of the situation after August 1971 when the Group of Ten insisted on discussing changes in exchange rates and new arrangements for convertibility of the dollar but refused to consider questions relating to trade restrictions and other matters that U.S. officials regarded as equally or even more important.

But beyond this consideration, U.S. officials insisted that Fund officials, who they thought would be excessively influenced by the history and past operations of the Fund and excessively biased in favor of a system of par values, not be closely involved in the negotiations. In an informal meeting at the end of March 1972 between Mr. Volcker and Mr. Schweitzer, at which Mr. Dale, as the U.S. Executive Director, and Mr. Gold and Mr. Polak were also present, Mr. Volcker explained that he did not want the General Counsel and the Economic Counsellor to dominate the negotiations. He also conveyed his belief that the staff sketch of a reformed system then being discussed in the Fund was unjust to the United States. The staff, he thought, was emphasizing the mechanics of a reformed system, such as ways to effect convertibility and asset settlement and methods for adjusting exchange rates, and was giving little thought to the real issues, that is, to the changes in international payments positions needed before these mechanics could be instituted. The staff was paying virtually no attention to the objectives of a reformed system, to the underlying reasons for the payments problems of the United States, or to the views of U.S. officials on how to change the chronic imbalance in world payments.

Indeed, in retrospect, events suggest that the U.S. authorities were in fact having great difficulty in getting their views recognized in the Fund. For example, there was Mr. Schweitzer's call at the 1970 Annual Meeting for the United States to engage in asset settlement; the views of the Fund management and staff expressed from August 1971 to the time of the Smithsonian agreement on how to restore some degree of convertibility and obtain new par values; the Deputy Managing Director's request early in 1972 to the United States to consider re-establishing some degree of convertibility; the pressure by the Fund on the United States for arrangements to facilitate the U.K. purchase of April 1972; the 1972 staff sketch of a reformed system, and the subsequent pressure of Fund officials on U.S. authorities to go along with the report on reform of 1972. A careful reading of these events confirms that the complaints of U.S. officials late in 1971 and early in 1972 that the Fund management and staff were not giving enough sympathetic consideration to U.S. problems and views had some basis.[14]

Mr. Volcker also objected to a large role for the Executive Directors in any group set up to consider a reformed system. In his view, the Executive Directors could be regarded as functionaries or officials of the Fund who had a vested interest in preserving "the traditional functions of the Fund." Also, Executive Directors were closely allied with the staff through daily contacts.

Mr. Volcker's views on the nature of a new group to negotiate reform collided with the ideas of the Fund management and staff. The Fund management and staff were convinced that the best way to organize a high-level group was to establish a committee of 20 Fund Governors based on the 20 constituencies that made up the Executive Board so that all Fund members would be able to regard themselves as represented. To include officials who would represent all the numerous developing members of the Fund was especially important since developing members were becoming an effective force in international monetary affairs and their consent to the shape of any reformed system was indispensable. Reform would require amendment of the Articles of Agreement, and collectively the developing members had more than enough votes to prevent ratification of any amendments they did not endorse.

The Fund staff also proposed that the preparatory and technical work to be considered by the committee of Governors be done by the Fund staff under the direction of the Managing Director, who could be chairman or co-chairman of whatever related group of deputies for the committee of Governors was chosen. The Executive Board would discuss this preparatory work and related questions of policy before recommendations were passed on to the committee of Governors. The staff suggested this procedure as a result of the Fund's experience with the discussions of international liquidity and the negotiations for the establishment of SDRs. While the discussions and negotiations pertaining to international liquidity had started out in the Group of Ten in 1963, they ended up in the Fund after about 1965 when the Group of Ten could not agree among themselves. The procedure of having the

---

[14]The expression of views by the Fund management and staff mentioned in this paragraph have been described in *History, 1966–71*, Vol. I, pp. 491–92, 531–41, and 549–51, and in Chaps. 1, 2, and 7 above.

preparatory and technical work done by the Fund staff and then holding discussions in the Executive Board was used also in 1969 and 1970 when financial officials wanted to re-examine the exchange rate mechanism. In the staff view, the most appropriate way of implementing this procedure under a committee of the Board of Governors was to have the Executive Directors serve as the deputies of the committee.

U.S. officials also considered it essential that any countries not in the Group of Ten be included in the contemplated group. While the Group of Ten could continue, its existence should not mean that it would engage in parallel negotiations with whatever new body was established. U.S. officials especially thought that it would be useful to involve officials of "intermediate countries," such as Australia and Spain, and of developing countries in any high-level policymaking group. They wanted to include more countries in a new group partly to provide various viewpoints but also in the hope that officials of countries other than those in the Group of Ten might lend support to U.S. positions.

Mr. Volcker's idea was to set up some permanent group of high-level officials, probably other than a committee of Fund Governors. It would be a high-level steering group of at most 20 officials, possibly patterned on the constituencies in the Fund's Executive Board, but in any event independent of the Fund. This permanent steering group would have a small permanent staff of its own who could draw on the expertise of officials of individual countries and on the staff or the secretariat of other international organizations, such as the BIS, the EC, the GATT, the OECD, the World Bank, and the UNCTAD, as well as on the staff of the Fund. While he recognized the primacy of the Fund in monetary matters, Mr. Volcker did not want to be totally dependent on the Fund for "direction, staff, or discussion by the Executive Directors." It was, he argued, essential to promote contrasting views.

A permanent committee of officials who were at the same time Fund Governors but who acted independently of the Fund, with a level of deputies to do technical and preparatory work and with its own staff to assist in that work obviously did not appeal to those in the Fund who feared a distinctly lesser role for the Fund not only in the reform exercise but in other problems. Both Executive Directors and Fund staff were concerned about the possible creation of a new separate body.

Officials of industrial members other than the United States were inclined to prefer a committee of the Board of Governors associated with the Fund. Officials of some EC countries, particularly of the Federal Republic of Germany, favored a committee of the Board of Governors allied with the Fund, because they were concerned that the United States might dominate the discussions and therefore wanted to strengthen the Fund's part in the negotiations. Japanese officials, who had assumed a low profile in the negotiations for SDRs in the 1960s, began to take more positive positions in the discussions for a reformed international monetary system. Japanese officials were inclined to regard a committee of 20 officials, however selected, as too large and initially sought to support some smaller group.

Officials of developing members were strong supporters of the establishment of a committee of the Board of Governors. As has been mentioned, they felt very much slighted by the Group of Ten. But, in addition, they realized that representatives of developing members would have to be included on any committee of the Board of Governors, and that because there were more developing members than industrial and relatively more developed members, representatives from developing members were likely to make up more than half of such a committee.

In any event, most officials from both developed and developing members considered it desirable to set up some body composed of "political" functionaries. At the time, the negotiation of a new treaty for international monetary cooperation, that is, an arrangement that went well beyond amending the Articles of Agreement of the Fund to involving a wholly new Fund, seemed possible. There was a powerful case, therefore, for instituting a high-level political body to do the negotiating.

A Committee of Governors Agreed

Discussions about the forum for negotiating a reformed system continued through the first five months of 1972. U.S. officials continued to be reluctant to agree to a committee of the Board of Governors modeled on the composition of the Executive Board, while officials of France and the Federal Republic of Germany, wanting to get on with the reform exercise, accused U.S. officials of dragging their heels. Several Executive Directors, though favoring creation of a committee of the Board of Governors modeled on the Executive Board, remained opposed to creation of a related group of deputies unless the Executive Directors served as these deputies. To help overcome the concern of Executive Directors with the creation of an alternative group of deputies, Mr. Lieftinck proposed that the committee of Governors be an ad hoc committee, to last only through the negotiations for a reformed system. A committee of Governors who served temporarily to plan a new international monetary system would be comparable to the one-time event of the Bretton Woods Conference. A temporary committee, however it worked and whoever were the deputies, would be less of a threat to the Executive Board than a permanent body. The idea that any committee of Governors would be temporary was quickly accepted and the proposed committee was called a special advisory committee to indicate that it would exist only for a limited time, only for negotiating a reformed system, and only to make recommendations.

In April, prior to attending a meeting of the deputies of the Group of Ten in London at which the subject of the forum was to be discussed, the Economic Counsellor set out for the Fund management the concessions that the various parties would have to make if a committee of the Board of Governors was created; the Fund management could thus decide what reactions to have to the resulting features of the committee. U.S. officials would accept a committee of Fund Governors with a membership of 20, based on the constituencies in the Executive Board. Officials of other members would accept terms of reference for the committee that were broader than reform of the international monetary system and a level of deputies composed of officials other than the Executive Directors, and would accept as chairman of the committee a Governor, not the Managing Director. No position by the Fund management on these features of a committee of the Board of Governors was needed or appropriate. On his own initiative, Mr. Schweitzer had already suggested that since he was not in favor with U.S. officials at the time, it was preferable for him not to be the chairman. In addition, the General Counsel had advised him not to press for or accept the position of chairman of the new committee of Governors because of a possible conflict between that role and the usual role of the Fund's Managing Director as Chairman of the Board of Executive Directors and head of the Fund staff.

Fund officials had a strong vested interest in the features still to be worked out, however, for the chairmanship of the deputies, for the relationship between the deputies and the Executive Directors, and for the staff work. The Fund management and staff continued to favor a procedure by which the Executive Directors served as deputies to those on the committee of Governors and in which the Fund staff did the preparatory work. This procedure was what the Managing Director and the staff regarded as a bona fide committee of Fund Governors. Meanwhile, some Executive Directors elected by developing members, who believed that they themselves were likely in any event to be selected by their governments as deputies, began to support the idea of deputies who might be separate from the Executive Board.

A committee of the Board of Governors modeled on the Executive Board was gradually agreed upon at a meeting of the deputies of the Group of Ten held in London late in April 1972 and at an informal gathering held in May 1972 when several of these officials attended an International Monetary Conference in Montreal. Although at the meeting in London in April the deputies of the Group of Ten generally agreed that a new Group of Twenty, a special committee of the Board of Governors of the Fund, should be the main forum for negotiating reform, they did not agree that this group would necessarily be made up of the 20 constituencies that composed the Fund's Executive Board. The deputies also agreed to discuss the subject of the forum again in May at the conference in Montreal.

In Montreal, officials from Canada, Japan, the United Kingdom, and the United States, most of whom also served as deputies of the Group of Ten, met informally to discuss the forum with Mr. Emminger, a deputy from the Federal Republic of Germany, who had meanwhile consulted officials from Belgium, France, and Italy. Mr. Gold and Mr. Polak attended the meeting to present the Managing Director's views on a bona fide committee of the Board of Governors. Most officials present, especially Canadian officials and Mr. Emminger, criticized Mr. Volcker sharply for continuing to talk about a "rump group," not fully representative of all Fund members. Mr. Volcker was also attacked for suggesting that if a committee of Fund Governors was created as a committee of the Board of Governors modeled on the constituencies of the Executive Board, the committee take into account the weighted voting power of the members of the Fund. Mr. Gold objected on legal grounds to voting in the committee. The Articles of Agreement contained no express authority for voting in committees or for voting by any unit other than the Board of Governors or the Board of Executive Directors. Some officials on the committee might be neither Fund Governors nor Executive Directors, but even officials of the committee who were Governors or Executive Directors would not be serving on the committee in those capacities. Hence, it was not possible to have voting in the committee.[15] But authorities from Canada and the United Kingdom also stressed with Mr. Volcker that weighted voting in the committee had deep political connotations and that the committee need not dwell in a formal manner on the differences in power among Fund members.

After these at times bitter exchanges, it was agreed that the Fund staff would prepare a complete draft resolution for the Board of Governors to consider, taking into account the observations made during this informal meeting. The draft resolution was to be made available to all countries in the Group of Ten through the Executive Directors. The staff indicated that at the same time it would also give copies informally to all the other Executive Directors.

George P. Shultz, who was shortly thereafter to become Secretary of the Treasury, provided another reason why U.S. authorities may have finally agreed to a committee of Fund Governors modeled on the Executive Board. The Secretary of the Treasury was traditionally the Governor for the Fund for the United States and from the time of the creation of the Fund, the Department of the Treasury had been the agency within the U.S. Government that dealt with the Fund. Treasury officials in 1972 wanted to be sure to retain this responsibility.[16]

Efforts now turned to drafting a resolution establishing a special committee of 20 Fund Governors based on the constituencies of the 20 Executive Directors.

TERMS OF REFERENCE OF THE COMMITTEE OF TWENTY

The Executive Board agreed to the draft of the final Resolution establishing the ad hoc committee of Governors on June 23, 1972 and approved it for transmittal to the Board of Governors in a decision dated June 28. It was adopted by the Board of Governors on July 26 by mail vote. The substance and wording of this resolution reflected the way in which the disputed procedural arrangements were settled.[17] The arrangement contained a number of features designed to satisfy the authorities of the United States, particularly Mr. Volcker, so that the Committee was not precisely what the Fund management and staff had been pressing for. The Committee was to be made up of 20 Governors based on the constituencies of the 20 Executive Directors, so that all members of the Fund could regard themselves as being represented. The preamble to the resolution, in fact, stated that "decisions relating to the reform should be taken with the full participation of both developed

---

[15]For further information on voting in committees of the Fund, the reader is referred to Gold, "Weighted Voting Power in the Fund: Some Limits and Some Problems," in *Legal and Institutional Aspects*, pp. 306–13.

[16]See Shultz and Dam (cited in fn. 11 above), p. 123.

[17]Resolution No. 27–10; Vol. III below, pp. 151–53.

and developing member countries," the first overt reference by the Board of Governors to developed and developing members. The terms of reference of the Committee were, however, to be broader than the reform of the international monetary system alone so that trade and other international economic issues could also be discussed. The term "and Related Issues" was added to the name of the "ad hoc Committee of the Board of Governors on Reform of the International Monetary System" to take this broader frame of reference into account.

The Governors of the Fund of the five members that appointed an Executive Director—France, the Federal Republic of Germany, Japan, the United Kingdom, and the United States—would each appoint one member of the Committee and each group of members that elected an Executive Director would select in any way they chose a Governor to serve on the Committee. Nine Governors would thus be from industrial or more developed primary producing members and eleven from developing members. Each member of the Committee could appoint two associates also entitled to speak at the Committee's meetings. This provision was designed to permit participation in related issues by ministers of trade or other officials with domestic responsibilities. But a member of the Committee had full freedom in his choice of associates and if he wished could, and some later did, appoint associates who had responsibilities on monetary matters in other members of the electorate that appointed him. The Chairman was to be a member selected by the Committee, but was not to be the Managing Director.

The problem of safeguarding the role of the Executive Directors was resolved in a number of other ways in addition to making the Committee an ad hoc committee. The Managing Director and the Chairman of the deputies were to "establish appropriate arrangements to bring about an effective coordination of the work of the Executive Directors," who were then themselves also working on reform of the international monetary system in response to the resolution of the Board of Governors at the 1971 Annual Meeting, and the work of the deputies.[18] The Committee was to take into account the reports and recommendations of the Executive Directors on reforming the system. The Executive Directors were also entitled to attend ministerial meetings of the Committee as advisors and to participate in the meetings of the deputies. The expression "entitled to participate" meant that the Executive Directors had the right to speak if they wished. Other officials at the meeting, who were observers, could only attend and had no right to speak.

It was agreed that, while the Fund staff would be involved in the Committee's work only in a very limited way, and while the Executive Directors would not serve as deputies of the Committee, the Committee would not have a permanent secretariat or staff. The Governors elected to serve on the Committee and the deputies whom they appointed would decide just how preparatory work was to be done. They could make any arrangements considered necessary "for studies by

---

[18]Ibid., par. 4(a).

qualified persons or for furthering the work of the Committee or of the deputies in any other way." This qualification was put into the resolution to satisfy U.S. officials that studies done for the Committee of Twenty would not be confined to studies done by the Fund staff.

No provision was made for voting by the Committee. The Chairman of the Committee was to seek to establish the sense of the meeting without voting. There was a political compromise, nonetheless, between those officials who wanted voting, and a fortiori weighted voting, and those who did not. In the absence of unanimity of views expressed in the Committee, all views were to be reported to the Board of Governors with an identification of the members of the Committee holding the various views. With that information, the Board of Governors would be able to make an appropriate calculation of the voting power behind particular views if they were to be put to a vote in the Board of Governors.

The Committee members were each to appoint two deputies to do the major part of the technical work and were to select a Chairman of the deputies. The Managing Director was to participate in the meetings of the Committee of Governors and could designate a representative to take his place at any meeting he did not attend. He could also designate not more than two members of the Fund staff to represent him at meetings of the deputies. This last arrangement was based on the model developed early in the 1960s in which the Economic Counsellor and the General Counsel customarily represented the Managing Director at meetings of the deputies of the Group of Ten. These two representatives usually accompanied the Managing Director to ministerial meetings of the Group of Ten and would also accompany him to ministerial meetings of the Committee of Twenty. Otherwise, staff attendance at meetings of the deputies of the Committee of Twenty was restricted to a few technicians and staff supplying supporting secretarial services.

The arduous debates preceding the formation of the Committee of Twenty added to the agenda of that Committee the topic of how a more permanent high-level political body of financial officials might be instituted.

INAUGURAL MEETING AND FUNCTIONING OF THE COMMITTEE

By the time of the 1972 Annual Meeting the Committee of Twenty was constituted and ready for its inaugural meeting. Generally the member of the Committee was the minister of finance of the largest country in the constituency; in a few instances he was the governor of the central bank. There were also two associates for each Fund Governor on the Committee, making for 60 Governors and associates in all. The use of two associates for each Fund Governor on the Committee permitted each of the countries with the five largest quotas to designate its central bank governor as well as its deputy to the finance minister as associates and permitted the other 15 delegations to include as associates ministers of finance or central bank governors from other countries in the constituencies. Thus, as it turned out, the two associates were usually also monetary officials rather than officials with responsibility for trade or other matters. Associates were entitled to participate in the ministerial meetings of the Committee.

Since the Committee of Twenty was a body of the Fund, the Secretary of the Fund, as the Secretary of the Board of Governors, was notified of all appointments to the Committee and of all meetings planned by the Committee. He made arrangements for distributing documents, for holding meetings, and for preparing a summary record of each meeting, just as he did for all other Fund meetings.

The Committee of Twenty held its inaugural meeting in Washington on September 28, 1972, while the Twenty-Seventh Annual Meeting of the Board of Governors was in progress. This inaugural meeting was an organizing meeting convened by Ali Wardhana, the Minister of Finance of Indonesia and Governor of the Fund for that member. As Chairman of the Board of Governors for 1972, Mr. Wardhana convened the first meeting of the Committee of Twenty. He was ending his assignment as Chairman of the Board of Governors and was selected Chairman of the Committee of Twenty, a position he retained throughout the two years the Committee existed. In addition to the 60 Governors and associates, the Managing Director attended the meetings of Governors of the Committee of Twenty, as did the Executive Directors and Alternate Executive Directors who were included among the advisors for each constituency. Also present were senior-level observers from the Swiss National Bank and from six international organizations—the BIS, the EC, the GATT, the OECD, the World Bank, and the UNCTAD—and a limited number of Fund staff. The Committee of Twenty was thus something of a misnomer. Despite strict limiting of the attendance, about 200 people in all attended the inaugural meeting at the ministerial level, and this number attended the subsequent five ministerial meetings.

The deputies, two from each of the Fund's constituencies, were senior officials of finance ministries and central banks with high-level responsibility in their countries, and in some cases, governors of central banks. They held their inaugural meeting one day after the meeting at ministerial level, on September 29, 1972, also in Washington. The Committee of Twenty selected C. Jeremy Morse, of the United Kingdom, as Chairman of the deputies. At the time Mr. Morse was an Executive Director of the Bank of England and Alternate Governor of the Fund for the United Kingdom and had served in these capacities since the mid-1960s. Rinaldo Ossola, as Chairman of the deputies of the Group of Ten, had been the front-runner for the post. Mr. Ossola had also chaired the group that produced the often-cited "Ossola Group report" of 1965 and had been a leading participant in the negotiations for SDRs. Since 1967 he had been Chairman of the deputies of the Group. [19] Mr. Ossola was supported by U.S. officials, partly because he was not hostile to floating exchange rates. For this reason, however, he was less acceptable to some of the European authorities. There was secret, written polling for the post of Chairman of

---

[19]These contributions of Mr. Ossola have been described in *History, 1966–71*, Vol. I, pp. 37, 52, 58–61, 115, 120, 156, 157, 166, 292, 371, and 541.

the deputies of the Committee of Twenty. On the first polling, taken at a dinner of the members of the Committee of Twenty a few evenings before the inaugural meeting of the deputies, Mr. Morse and Mr. Ossola each received ten votes. There was then intensive lobbying on behalf of Mr. Morse by some of the members of the Committee of Twenty from the countries that were not in the Group of Ten. These officials argued that Mr. Morse's involvement in sterling area affairs at the Bank of England would make him more sympathetic to the concerns of developing countries. In this lobbying, using the words expressed informally by Mr. Morse, "the French authorities outgunned the authorities of the United States."

The second decisive polling was taken and the outcome announced during the meeting of the Committee of Twenty on September 28. The vote went in Mr. Morse's favor, 12 to 8. According to Mr. Morse, the French, Indonesian, and presumably the British members of the Committee of Twenty voted for him, while the U.S., Australian, and presumably the Italian members of the Committee voted for Mr. Ossola. How other members of the Committee voted has not been disclosed. After the polling, Mr. Ossola generously walked across the room to shake Mr. Morse's hand. The two men remained good friends thereafter, Mr. Ossola playing an important part in the work of the deputies of the Committee of Twenty.

Although some bankers and financial officials continued to regard Mr. Morse as an officer of the Bank of England, such was not the case. To become Chairman of the deputies of the Committee of Twenty, Mr. Morse resigned from the Bank of England, and as Chairman of the deputies, he was paid by the Fund. In fact, after his assignment with the Committee of Twenty finished, Mr. Morse did not return to the Bank of England but joined a leading London bank, Lloyds Bank Ltd., of which he later became Chairman.

The number of persons attending meetings of the deputies was only somewhat smaller than the number attending ministerial meetings. The Governors and associates did not attend deputies' meetings nor did the Managing Director. But in addition to the 40 deputies, the Executive Directors and their Alternates and other advisors, observers from six international organizations, and a small number of Fund staff were present. Hence, at the deputies' meetings about 180 people were in the room, although most had no right to speak unless recognized by the Chairman.

In other words, even at the working level of deputies, the Committee of Twenty was a large and clumsy structure, but given its origin, it was no larger than it had to be in the circumstances. The large number present at meetings of the Committee of Twenty, at ministerial level and at the level of deputies, did not, moreover, in the view of nearly all participants, hamper the proceedings. More than half were observers who did not speak; and, as the next several chapters will show, various means other than general sessions were used—executive sessions, division into small groups, and working parties—to permit debate and negotiation.

The deputies met every seven or eight weeks, about twice as often as the ministers. Six of their twelve meetings were at the Fund's headquarters in Washington and three were at the Fund's office in Paris; one, the inaugural meeting, was at the Sheraton Park Hotel in Washington, one was in Nairobi, and one was in Rome. Deputies' meetings typically lasted three days, although their length varied from one to five days.

Deputies submitted numerous papers that they had themselves prepared or that were prepared by member governments. In addition, the Chairman of the deputies asked the Fund staff to prepare some papers. Several papers on topics of particular concern to the six international organizations with senior-level observers at the meetings, papers prepared by the staff or secretariat of these organizations, were also submitted for consideration by the deputies. However, most documents for the deputies' meetings were prepared by six persons who made up the Bureau.

The Bureau consisted of the Chairman of the deputies, Mr. Morse, four Vice-Chairmen, Edward George of the Bank of England, Personal Assistant to Mr. Morse, and a secretary. That the Committee of Twenty was necessarily involved in questions of political significance, whose resolution needed as wide agreement as possible was reflected in the composition of the four Vice-Chairmen. The Vice-Chairmen, selected by the deputies, were chosen so as to give a wide geographical representation and differing viewpoints. They were Jonathan H. Frimpong-Ansah, Governor of the Bank of Ghana; Alexandre Kafka, Executive Director elected by several Latin American members, a Brazilian national; Robert Solomon, Adviser to the Board of Governors of the Federal Reserve System of the United States; and Hideo Suzuki, Executive Director appointed by Japan. In order to give the Bureau a somewhat more varied viewpoint, efforts were made to find a Vice-Chairman from one of the French-speaking African countries, but when none was available, Mr. Frimpong-Ansah was selected and agreed to serve. The members of the Bureau were thus all accustomed to think and write in English, and although French officials naturally regretted the failure to find a francophone Vice-Chairman, in Mr. Morse's view, the common background of the six members of the Bureau helped them to work efficiently together. The four Vice-Chairmen acted as representatives of their geographic areas. They consciously presented the points of view of the member or group of members from which they came, although they did not receive instructions from the authorities of member governments. Moreover, the Chairman of the deputies and the four Vice-Chairmen reached decisions by consensus. Specifically, the Chairman did not impose his will on the Vice-Chairmen. Mr. George, the sixth member of the Bureau, assisted the Chairman and the four Vice-Chairmen.

Although an instrument of the Fund, headquartered in Washington, the Bureau did most of its work between deputies' meetings in London, making use of a suite of rooms provided by the Bank of England. Mr. Morse selected this location partly for a personal reason: he did not want to move his family to Washington. But another reason for the Bureau's working in London was Mr. Morse's desire to avoid excessive influence on the Bureau's work either by the U.S. Government or by the Fund. As was made clear earlier in this chapter, at the time relations between the U.S. Government and the Fund were not good, and U.S. officials wanted to dilute the influence of the Executive Directors and the Fund staff on the reform exercise.

Mr. Morse believed that working in England would give the Bureau of the Committee of Twenty more independence.

For its part, the Fund staff did not want to be closely identified with the work of the Bureau. The Economic Counsellor and the General Counsel were, for example, invited to and attended one session of the Bureau in London. They could have attended other sessions but preferred not to because they believed that the Chairman of the deputies and the Vice-Chairmen were politically oriented and in the interest of reaching consensus were "intent on their own compromised solutions or watered-down positions."

In the course of their work, the deputies of the Committee of Twenty set up seven Technical Groups to consider important disputed issues at greater length than was possible in the full deputies' meetings. These groups, chaired by the Chairman or one of the Vice-Chairmen of the deputies, contained one representative of each constituency, usually the Executive Director or his Alternate, and one or two advisors from each constituency, plus those observers from international organizations who wished to participate. As it did for the ministers and for the deputies of the Committee, the Secretary's Department of the Fund supplied support services for the Technical Groups.

The start of the Committee of Twenty augured well for its future work. The potential areas of conflict did not prove to be as troublesome as might at first have been expected. After considerable discussion, it did prove possible to reach agreement on the structure of the Committee and for monetary authorities to agree on the necessary personnel. As will be seen in Chapter 9, it was possible also to agree quickly on an agenda of the major issues to be resolved. These agreements all suggested that monetary authorities were serious about their efforts to plan a reformed international monetary system.

CHAPTER
9

Exploring the Issues of Reform

*H*OPES RAN HIGH IN SEPTEMBER 1972. At the Annual Meeting there was an aura of excitement and expectation, much in contrast to the gloom and sense of disaster that had been pervasive at the Annual Meeting of the year before. Setting up the Committee of Twenty was a momentous step, and despite their conflicting views, officials anticipated productive negotiations for a reformed system.

SCOPE AND PLAN OF WORK

The assignment of the Committee of Twenty was a challenge. The Committee was to undertake the most ambitious attempt ever to work out a many-faceted reconstruction of the international monetary system. Complex and highly technical monetary issues would have to be discussed. In addition, full attention was to be given to the interrelation between monetary topics and the "existing or prospective arrangements among countries, including those that involve international trade, the flow of capital, investment, or development assistance." The Committee was also to make suggestions on strengthening the Fund's decision-making process. U.S. officials wanted to give the Fund more authority in convincing a major industrial country of the need to change its exchange rate or to take other policy action to correct its payments imbalance. The aim was to have the Fund's decisions elevated from the level of the Executive Directors to the level of finance ministers or governors of central banks, that is, to political appointees rather than civil servants. Noting that the Group of Ten and the EC assessed balance of payments performance at the ministerial or subministerial level, U.S. officials believed that a comparable change in the structure of the Fund would give the Fund added clout in the international community.

The work was to be completed within two years, by the 1974 Annual Meeting, since two years seemed to be as long as so large an exercise could be kept going. Most members of the Committee were reasonably confident of success and of accomplishing their task within the specified period. The communiqué following the inaugural meeting expressed "determination to make rapid progress toward agreement on reform of the international monetary system."[1] The speeches of Messrs. Shultz, Barber, and Schmidt at the 1972 Annual Meeting also suggested that they expected to achieve agreement on the main features of a reformed system by the time of the next Annual Meeting, in Nairobi in September 1973.[2]

In October 1972, Mr. Morse, as Chairman of the deputies, planned a work program in which one year would be devoted to settling the major issues and to preparing a preliminary outline in time for the 1973 Annual Meeting. The second year was to be devoted to technical elaboration and to putting the ideas agreed in the preliminary outline into the necessary legal language. Mr. Morse's minimum aim was to push the infant reserve asset, the SDR, one stage further and to resolve the controversy about the relative roles of fixed and floating rates in any new arrangements. His maximum aim was to redesign completely the international monetary system, as had been done at Bretton Woods. With an optimism based on his own experience in previous negotiations, he considered some reform along these lines realistic and achievable. He had played a part in three successful multicountry negotiations on international monetary issues in the past, the agreement on sterling balances in 1968, the launching of the SDR from 1966 to 1969, and the entry of the United Kingdom into the European Communities in 1970–71. He believed that the reform of the international monetary system was also an achievable assignment.

His optimism was, nevertheless, tempered with caution, as the assignment was clearly difficult. Members of the Committee, like their governments, held opposite views on many features of a reformed system. For their part, U.S. officials attributed much of the unusual U.S. merchandise trade deficit to the intense desire of European countries and of Japan to expand their exports and to run large trade surpluses, primarily to keep up domestic employment. U.S. officials accordingly gave priority to designing an adequate mechanism to adjust balance of payments disequilibria. They believed that the reformed system ought to contain some method of inducing, or even forcing, countries with large and persistent balance of payments surpluses to take action, especially by changing the exchange rate, to reduce these surpluses. For them the most crucial provisions of a reformed system were how exchange rates would be altered and what pressures would be applied against countries that failed to correct undervalued exchange rates or to liberalize their trade policies so as to permit more imports from the United States. They also favored a system that included relatively more floating of exchange rates than had been possible under the par value system.

Officials of EC countries, convinced that the U.S. payments deficits were caused by relatively easy U.S. money policies and the resulting inflation and that the special role of the dollar in international payments encouraged these deficits since

---

[1]See Vol. III below, p. 197.

[2]Statements by the Governor of the Fund and the World Bank for the United States, the Governor of the Fund for the United Kingdom, and the Governor of the World Bank for the Federal Republic of Germany, *Summary Proceedings, 1972*, pp. 44, 53, and 71.

the United States did not need primary assets or borrowed credits to finance them, stressed their unwillingness to accumulate inconvertible dollars indefinitely. They resented the transformation of the gold-exchange standard into a dollar standard. The provisions of a reformed system with respect to convertibility or some equivalent, such as asset settlement, were for them in the words of Valéry Giscard d'Estaing, "the touchstone of reform."[3]

Officials from over 100 developing members of the Fund fully participating in the negotiations had still another emphasis. They came to the negotiating table determined to ensure that any reformed system took account of the special interests of their own countries, particularly by providing for the transfer of real resources from industrial to developing countries.

BALANCE OF PAYMENTS ADJUSTMENT AND A PROPOSAL BY THE UNITED STATES

The deputies held their first meeting dealing with substantive issues in the Fund's headquarters in Washington on November 27–29, 1972. The Bureau grouped the monetary issues to be explored (apart from issues on trade or on restructuring the Fund) under five major headings: (i) balance of payments adjustment; (ii) the settlement of payments imbalances, such as through asset settlement or convertibility; (iii) the volume and composition of reserve assets, including the positions of gold, the dollar, and the SDR, in the system; (iv) disequilibrating flows of capital; and (v) the special problems of developing countries.

The deputies began with balance of payments adjustment, following a procedure which carried through their next several meetings. Numerous documents were distributed prior to the meeting. Many deputies themselves submitted written proposals for discussion and also circulated detailed comments on the proposals of other deputies. During the first several deputies' meetings, however, discussion centered around annotated agendas prepared by the Bureau. These were relatively short papers designed especially to identify points on which officials agreed and to clarify the points on which they differed. They described agreements so far reached, listed questions that might further advance agreement, and asked the deputies for views on these questions.

The annotated agenda circulated for the November 1972 meeting sought deputies' positions on how to assess the need for balance of payments adjustment, particularly for changes in par values; what inducements, sanctions, or pressures the international community—presumably the Fund—should use to force countries to promote balance of payments adjustment; the possible legalization of temporary floating rates; the use of controls including multiple exchange rates to restrain

---

[3]Statement by the Governor of the Fund and the World Bank for France, *Summary Proceedings, 1972*, p. 74.

inflows and outflows of capital; and the use of restrictions on trade and on other current account transactions for correcting balance of payments disequilibria. These topics were to be brought up at deputies' meetings throughout the next two years. The deputies agreed readily on the list of issues that had to be explored and resolved.

At the end of the first day, U.S. deputies Paul A. Volcker and J. Dewey Daane distributed a paper spelling out the details of a U.S. proposal, subsequently known as the Volcker plan.[4] The U.S. proposal had been foreshadowed in President Nixon's address to the Governors on the opening day of the 1972 Annual Meeting and described a day later by Secretary Shultz.[5] It was to play a major part in the Committee's discussions for the next year for three reasons.

First, because of the key position of the United States in any international monetary arrangements, monetary officials had waited for nine months in 1972 for the U.S. Administration to state its views on reforming the system. Believing that nothing would happen on international monetary reform until the United States presented a proposal, many were irritated at the delay. Hence, most greeted the U.S. initiative of September–November 1972 with enthusiasm. Second, the United States was the first and eventually the only country to come forward with comprehensive suggestions for a reformed international monetary system. Although the U.S. proposal was not nearly so precise or all-encompassing as had been the U.S. proposals for a Stabilization Fund in 1942 that were the basis for the Bretton Woods system and the creation of the International Monetary Fund, it dealt with more features of the reformed system than those of any other constituency on the Committee of Twenty. Third, it appeared that U.S. officials who had previously opposed an asset settlement system might ultimately agree to it provided the reformed system included a satisfactory adjustment mechanism and procedures for asset settlement that had sufficient flexibility.

The principles underlying the U.S. proposal, enunciated by Mr. Shultz at the 1972 Annual Meeting, were similar to those guiding the U.S. negotiators at Bretton Woods 28 years earlier. The system of international monetary arrangements should be designed for market-oriented economies, as free as possible of governmental intervention, interference, and regulations. It should be combined with free trade and unrestricted investment. There should be a common code of conduct for all countries governing trade, monetary, and investment relationships, as embodied in the original Articles of Agreement of the Fund and in the GATT. As in the past, national governments should have a choice between policy instruments for bringing about balance of payments adjustment. As the negotiators at Bretton Woods had

---

[4]"The U.S. Proposals for Using Reserves as an Indicator of the Need for Balance-of-Payments Adjustment," in Appendix A, Supplement to Chap. 5, *Annual Report of the Council of Economic Advisers*, in *Economic Report of the President Transmitted to the Congress, January 1973* (Washington: Government Printing Office, 1973), pp. 160–74.

[5]Address by the President of the United States and Statement by the Governor of the Fund and the World Bank for the United States, *Summary Proceedings, 1972*, pp. 2–4 and 34–44.

emphasized, success of the system depended on the pursuit, particularly by the large industrial countries, of effective domestic policies for economic growth and price stability.

There was, however, an important difference between the philosophy of the United States in 1944 and in 1972. In 1972 U.S. officials, including President Nixon, worked from the premise that basic changes in the economic positions of the major industrial countries and hence in their relative political power had made the Bretton Woods system obsolete. In Mr. Volcker's words: "With the resurgence of Europe and Japan, a monetary structure which assumed and was based on a single predominant currency—the dollar—became untenable. The implicit assumption that a dominant United States with immense reserves and an impregnable competitive position could play a relatively passive role in the adjustment process, while in effect underwriting the stability of the system as a whole, simply no longer fits the elementary facts of the distribution of economic and political power in today's world."[6]

In 1972, accordingly, U.S. officials stressed the inability of a country, even as large as the United States, to achieve balance of payments adjustment on its own. They emphasized the need for symmetrical standards and procedures to guide adjustment, especially among the major industrial countries.

Features of the U.S. Proposal

At the 1972 Annual Meeting, Mr. Shultz made it clear that the United States would accept an exchange rate regime based on central or par values if provision was made for fairly wide margins around these values and for countries to float their currencies and if appropriate criteria were used to bring about changes in exchange rates, including changes for countries with balance of payments surpluses. The United States would also agree to making the dollar again convertible into primary reserve assets, although within defined limits. Part of the existing holdings of dollars by the central banks of other countries might also be exchanged for a special issue of SDRs at the option of the holder. The United States, moreover, would accept the SDR as the numeraire of a reformed system and would agree that the SDR could be made free of encumbrances, such as reconstitution obligations, designation procedures, and holding limits, which detracted from its use. In all these respects, the United States seemed to have accepted the proposals put forward by Mr. Barber a year earlier.

Mr. Shultz had other suggestions which U.S. officials were to push in the deliberations of the Committee of Twenty. Gold should assume a diminishing role in the reformed system. Controls on capital movements should not be allowed. The

---

[6]Remarks of Under Secretary of the U.S. Treasury for Monetary Affairs, Paul A. Volcker, at the Annual Meeting of the Minnesota Economic Association at the College of St. Thomas, St. Paul, Minnesota, October 27, 1972, reprinted in U.S. Treasury Department, *News* (S-71), October 27, 1972, pp. 6–7.

Fund, with responsibility for monetary matters, should closely harmonize its policies with those of the GATT, which had responsibility for trade matters.

The paper distributed by Messrs. Volcker and Daane to the deputies in November 1972 gave specific details. There should be introduced a system of objective indicators, based on changes in the levels of countries' reserves that would signal the need for countries to change their exchange rates. A norm, or base level, for the reserves of each country would be established. Recognizing that the setting of norms would be controversial, U.S. officials offered several suggestions on how they might be determined. Norms might be in proportion to members' quotas in the Fund or determined by the past level of reserves of a country. The sum of all norms was to be roughly equal to total world reserves. As more SDRs were allocated by the Fund, countries' norms would increase. The reserve norm was to be surrounded by two warning points and beyond that by an outer point and a low point. Disproportionate increases or decreases in a country's reserves causing reserves to reach these indicator points would signal the need for balance of payments adjustment. If a country's reserves passed one of the warning points, there would be a strong presumption that the country should take action to adjust its balance of payments. In fact, there were to be virtually mandatory triggers for action. If a country's reserves moved toward the outer point or the low point, the country would be expected to apply adjustment measures of progressive intensity. If its reserves reached critical levels, a country would be subject to sanctions or graduated pressures, such as the loss of scheduled SDR allocations, an authorization by the Fund or some other international agency for other countries to impose surcharges on the country's exports, or the imposition of a tax on excess reserve holdings to be applied by the Fund. Provision was, nonetheless, made for overriding any signals for adjustment if on further examination changes in reserves did not seem to suggest the need for action to correct balance of payments disequilibria.

Convertibility of the dollar into primary reserve assets would take place when the U.S. reserve position, including the position of dollar liabilities abroad, was strong enough and a reserve indicator system was in operation. Convertibility was to be circumscribed, however, by what were called "convertibility points," later called "primary asset holding limits" (PAHL). Each country was to have a limit set at a fixed proportion above its reserve norm; if its reserves exceeded its limit, it would cease to be eligible to convert additional reserves into primary reserve assets. (The convertibility point was really an inconvertibility point in that no further conversions were to be allowed above the point.) The term "asset settlement" was deliberately avoided in the U.S. paper. Primary reserve assets meant in practice SDRs, since in the U.S. view gold was eventually to be phased out of the system.

The third feature of the reformed system as envisaged by the United States, though less emphasized than reserve indicators and provision for convertibility, was the introduction of multicurrency intervention, in which the authorities of central banks used several currencies for intervening in exchange markets, rather than only the U.S. dollar. U.S. officials favored a system of multicurrency intervention because it would give the dollar the same degree of flexibility within the margins around parities as other currencies. A multicurrency intervention system was thus in line with the thinking of U.S. officials that the reformed system should be symmetrical. U.S. officials preferred a multicurrency intervention system based on ceiling intervention. In such an arrangement, each participant agreed to intervene in exchange markets to buy another participant's currency whenever its own currency was at the ceiling against the other currency, that is, at parity plus the margin.

A Vice-Chairman of the Committee of Twenty, Robert Solomon, noting that the U.S. proposal explicitly acknowledged that one of its major purposes was to make the adjustment process more evenhanded than in the past in the treatment of balance of payments surpluses and deficits, has subsequently likened it to the Keynes plan of 1943. In Mr. Solomon's view, the U.S. plan of 1972 and the Keynes plan of 1943 were similar in respect to the rules for adjustment of payments imbalances, since both plans prescribe specific actions that countries in deficit or surplus might take as their creditor or debtor positions cumulated.[7]

Mr. Solomon has found similarities, too, between the concerns of the United States in the 1970s and those of the United Kingdom in the 1940s. In the 1940s, Keynes and other U.K. officials feared that after World War II the United States would emerge as a permanent creditor and that the full force of balance of payments adjustment would fall on European countries. At Bretton Woods, Keynes, therefore, sought an adjustment mechanism that would work symmetrically while it permitted the restoration of currency convertibility and relatively free multilateral trade. In the 1970s, Mr. Volcker and other U.S. officials, concerned about the weak U.S. balance of payments position, accepted what U.S. officials had rejected three decades earlier. Now they, too, wanted to ensure that countries that had maintained persistent surplus positions would be required to do some of the adjusting.[8]

FEATURES OF A REFORMED SYSTEM PREFERRED BY DEPUTIES FROM OTHER COUNTRIES

The reaction of the deputies from other countries to the U.S. proposal needs to be seen against a discussion of the features of a reformed system that they desired. Even prior to the exploratory discussions of the issues by the deputies in November 1972, it was evident that some sort of compromise would have to be found between those officials, primarily French and Belgian, who argued for stable exchange rates and fixed par values, and those who had come to favor more flexibility in the

---

[7]See his *The International Monetary System, 1945–1976: An Insider's View* (New York: Harper & Row, 1977), p. 242.

[8]Ibid., p. 243. John Williamson has also noted the similarities between the U.S. proposal in 1972 and the U.K. position at Bretton Woods in 1944: "both called for penalties to force surplus countries to adjust, no circumscribing of the reserve-currency role and ample international liquidity." See his *The Failure of World Monetary Reform, 1971–74* (Sunbury-on-Thames, England: Thomas Nelson and Sons, Ltd., 1977), p. 89.

exchange rate mechanism, primarily U.S. officials. Like the sketch of the Fund staff and the Executive Board's report of 1972, the Committee of Twenty started from the premise of a new par value system, which most monetary officials continued to favor. But since its members recognized that a par value system could be implemented to permit lesser or greater degrees of flexibility, the issue concerned the degree of flexibility to be permitted. As Mr. Morse had expressed it at the lecture meeting of the Per Jacobsson Foundation in September 1972, "we continue, as we did unsuccessfully before, to search for a place on the slippery scale between too much fixity and too much flexibility of exchange rates, a place on which we can stand with recovered confidence."[9] At the time, there was no inclination among officials, including those of the United States, to advocate that the reformed system be a floating rate system or any other than a system of par values.

By 1972, most officials, whether from the EC countries or from the United States, were ready to concede that in a reformed system changes in par values would have to be prompter than they had been in the previous par value system. Agreement even on the need for prompter par value changes represented an advance over the thinking of two years before. At the 1970 Annual Meeting officials of only the Federal Republic of Germany, Italy, and the United States favored greater rate flexibility; officials of the other EC countries, especially of France, were opposed. By November 1972, they agreed that par value changes ought to be made more promptly but held very different views on how often par values ought to be changed and on how much emphasis ought to be placed on changes in par values, as against other corrective actions, to effect balance of payments adjustment.

French Attitudes

The strongest views about the need for par values or for fixed rates were held by French officials. At the meeting of deputies in November 1972, the deputies from France, Daniel Deguen and Claude Pierre-Brossolette, took strong exception to the need for frequent par value changes. Mr. Pierre-Brossolette, who was to present the French position at the deputies' level throughout the life of the Committee of Twenty, insisted that the concepts of fixed par values, fundamental disequilibrium, and exchange rate stability "that had been the foundations of the Bretton Woods system" be retained in the reformed system. Positions on exchange rates (and on gold, as described in later chapters) similar to those expressed by Mr. Pierre-Brossolette in the Committee of Twenty had been advocated by French officials in discussions of international monetary questions in the 1960s.[10] In fact, the persistent advocacy in the 1960s and the 1970s by French officials of fixed exchange rates and of a key role for gold in the international monetary system was in line with their

---

[9]Henry C. Wallich, C.J. Morse, and I.G. Patel, *The Monetary Crisis of 1971—The Lessons to Be Learned*, the 1972 Per Jacobsson Foundation Lecture (Washington, September 24, 1972), p. 55.
[10]See *History, 1966–71*, Vol. I, pp. 40, 61–63, 132, 171–72, and 195.

position since the 1920s. Indeed, France had formed the nucleus of the gold bloc in the 1930s.[11]

Apart from a long-standing preference for gold and fixed exchange rates, French attitudes on these subjects in the 1960s and 1970s were deeply and openly political. Policies on these matters were formed first by President Charles de Gaulle and then by President Georges Pompidou, who opposed a strong position for the dollar in world finance. In their view, dollar domination had brought the United States to political domination, especially of Western Europe. The first way to reduce the influence of the United States was therefore to "attack" the dollar. The rest of the French position—such as resurrecting some kind of a gold standard or of enhancing the role of gold in the international monetary system and tying the dollar to gold through a par value—followed. A substitute asset for the dollar was needed, and gold was the best available substitute.

After President de Gaulle and President Pompidou died, political considerations continued to underlay the French position on fixed exchange rates and on gold. After 20 or 25 years of being the dominant economic and political power in the world, the United States had to share its power with other countries. Increased multipolarity distributed economic power among the United States, the nine EC countries, Japan, and some Third World countries. In the view of French officials, the new equality of economic strength among nations ought to be reflected in international monetary arrangements. The United States ought to be subject to the same balance of payments discipline as were other countries. It could not, alone among nations, keep on inflating its economy and adding to world liquidity by issuing more and more dollars to cover the resulting balance of payments deficits. If the U.S. authorities did not impose restraints upon themselves, some external mechanism had to do so. Otherwise, other countries would have little control over their own monetary and fiscal policies within their own national boundaries.

The attitudes of French officials on exchange rates and gold also have to be seen in the context of French aims and initiatives for the political and economic integration of Western Europe. After World War II, French officials had had a large part in planning a new Europe. Jean Monnet and Robert Schuman, then the French Foreign Minister, together with Paul-Henri Spaak of Belgium and others believed that hope for abiding peace in Europe lay in building new economic relationships between Western European countries. These men had been instrumental in devising new forms of economic unity in Western Europe.

After the rapid economic integration of Western Europe in the 1950s and the 1960s, officials of the EC countries recognized that the pace of European integration was slowing down in the early 1970s. In fact, they began to worry that the golden

---

[11]The long-standing position of French officials in favor of gold and fixed exchange rates going back to the Napoleonic era and the reasons for it have received considerable attention by writers on financial subjects. An exposition of the French viewpoint is given in Guillaume Guindey, *The International Monetary Tangle: Myths and Realities*, trans. by Michael L. Hoffman (White Plains, New York: M.E. Sharpe Inc., 1977).

opportunity of real integration might have been missed. Further progress required their devoting the 1970s to the achievement of monetary union and by 1980 of possibly attaining a common European currency. Distinguished French experts firmly believed that the future of the EC itself hung on the creation of a common European currency. Accordingly, as described in Chapter 1, European officials had taken a number of steps toward monetary union and were in the midst of these steps as the discussions in the Committee of Twenty started. Since achievement of European monetary union and of a common European currency would be expedited by a reduction in the use of the U.S. dollar in European financial transactions, French officials had still another reason for taking positions at the meetings of the Committee of Twenty favoring fixed exchange rates and a reduced role for the dollar in the international monetary system. This represented a further bid to challenge the economic and political position of the United States.

French authorities had still other reasons for wanting to enhance the role of gold in the monetary system and for favoring relatively infrequent use of par value changes. The Bank of France held large stocks of gold reserves and the private sector of the French economy continued to hoard gold in large amounts. With regard to exchange rates, French officials believed what was needed to avoid instability were timely, orderly, and infrequent changes in par values rather than frequent small changes. Also, French officials had long been emphasizing that taking internal measures was an important, if not *the* most important, action to rectify balance of payments deficits and had been urging U.S. authorities to take adequate anti-inflationary measures to eliminate U.S. balance of payments deficits.

Views of Deputies from Other Industrial Countries

Although officials of other EC countries also favored only infrequent changes in par values, their stand was not as extreme as that of the French deputies. Changes in par values should, they said, be "a late, if not a last resort," as an adjustment measure. They argued, especially after exchange rates floated, that there was danger of a switch from underuse of exchange rates in the late 1960s to overuse in the 1970s. Like French officials, they wanted to retain fundamental disequilibrium as a precondition for the Fund to approve of exchange rate action. Retention of the concept of fundamental disequilibrium ensured that both the internal and external causes of a country's balance of payments disequilibrium would be taken into account when the Fund assessed the need for a change in a country's exchange rate. At the meeting of deputies in November 1972, the deputy from Belgium, Georges Janson, the deputy from the Netherlands, C.J. Oort, and the deputies from the Federal Republic of Germany, Otmar Emminger and Dieter Hiss, like the French deputies, Messrs. Pierre-Brossolette and Deguen, all expressed the view that taking internal measures, rather than changing exchange rates, was the way to correct payments imbalances. Like the French deputies, the deputies from other countries also had difficulty with the idea of legalizing the use of floating exchange rates even temporarily. When this topic was raised, the deputy from Belgium, the deputies from France, and the deputies from Japan, Koichi Inamura and Hitoshi Yukawa, objected to any use of floating rates.

OBJECTIONS TO USE OF RESERVE INDICATORS

Even the many deputies who favored frequent and prompt par value changes in a reformed system were unsure of the U.S. proposal for reserve indicators. While there was some sympathy for a limited use of quantitative indicators to suggest the need for balance of payments adjustment, at the November 1972 meeting no constituency other than that of the United States was willing to commit itself to using a single indicator in as rigid a way as Mr. Volcker's plan advocated. Mr. Volcker favored reserves as a single indicator on the grounds that they were a neutral statistical measure, minimizing the scope for different assessments that contained political as well as economic considerations. It would be far easier politically, he maintained, to change the par value for the dollar under an agreed system of neutral indicators than in response to the collective judgment of the international community, which suggested political pressure.

Other deputies, however, doubted that it would be easier politically to accept the need for exchange rate adjustment determined by statistical indicators rather than by assessment by the international community. Their main objection to the use of reserves as a single indicator was that changes in reserves alone were not a satisfactory guide to the need for exchange rate adjustment. Capital movements owing to speculation or in response to interest rate differentials, for example, affected the level of reserves. Changes in reserves could be caused by cyclical developments, such as variations in primary product prices, for which exchange rate adjustment would be inappropriate. Another objection to the use of reserves as a signal for exchange rate adjustment was that there was no way to decide fairly when the reserve-gaining rather than the reserve-losing country should do the adjusting. Many deputies thought too that the adjustment process was too complex to be governed by one or two indicators more or less universally applied. Furthermore, they feared that impending indicators, such as changes in reserve levels, would be known to the market and would therefore increase speculation on exchange rates, although they recognized that this danger existed to some extent in any system in which officials assembled to discuss payments imbalances.

Deputies from developing members were especially opposed to the use of reserve indicators. Mr. Saad, whose constituency included oil exporting members that had prolonged balance of payments surpluses and were recognized to be in unique circumstances, had the strongest case. The surpluses of these countries represented the proceeds of sales of exhaustible natural resources and the countries concerned had only the foreign exchange reserves resulting from their surpluses with which to restructure their economies. Reserve accumulation should not in the instance of these countries suggest the need for changes in exchange rates.

Manmohan Singh (India) and deputies from other developing members also set forth reasons why inflows or outflows of reserves should not be taken as indicative of the need for exchange rate adjustment by developing countries. They cited the contingencies to which developing countries were traditionally subject, such as crop failures and wide fluctuations in world market prices for the primary products that they customarily exported, and explained how accumulated reserves could help developing countries through balance of payments deficits resulting from these contingencies. They argued further that reserve accumulation by developing members would strengthen the hands of these countries in seeking loans from private commercial banks, enhance their credit ratings with private bankers and international financial institutions, and allow them freedom and flexibility in timing development projects. Mr. Singh also reminded the deputies from industrial members of the many studies suggesting that changes in exchange rates were not always effective in adjusting balance of payments disequilibria in developing countries; price elasticities of demand and supply were usually low in these countries.

Because of the favorable balance of payments positions then experienced by many developing members, deputies from developing members put forward even stronger objections to the use of reserve indicators than they might otherwise have done. Developing members were concerned that the use of reserve indicators would not permit them to enjoy the full benefits of favorable circumstances, such as favorable terms of trade or relatively large inflows of foreign capital when such circumstances did occur. Many also feared that, in any indicator system, the discipline imposed by the international community would be more rigorous than under the previous par value system and that developing members might be subject to stricter discipline than the major industrial members of the Fund. Thus, the deputies from developing members spoke out emphatically against the U.S. proposal, at least as applied to developing members. They were particularly opposed to the use of pressures on, or sanctions against, developing members that were accumulating reserves.

Alternative Proposal by Italy

The country that made the most effort to obtain compromises for a reformed international monetary system as the negotiations of the Committee of Twenty proceeded was Italy. Italian financial officials came up with suggestions on how to handle asset settlement (described later in this chapter) and what to do about the link between allocations of SDRs and development finance (described in Chapter 11), and proposed an alternative to the reserve indicator technique advocated by the United States. Their proposal, using the concept of basic balance in a country's balance of payments, was spelled out in November 1972 by the Italian deputies, Rinaldo Ossola and Silvano Palumbo. Basic balance was the concept developed within the Fund in 1969–70 as the preferred measurement of members' balance of payments positions; it was defined as the balance on goods, services, and private transfers—that is, the current account—plus net long-term capital. Under the Ossola-Palumbo proposal, the basic balance would be adjusted to diminish the influence of cyclical circumstances. In addition, use of the basic balance as a quantitative measure of a country's payments position would be combined with a thoroughgoing qualitative analysis of the country's current balance of payments situation and a forecast of developments in its payments position to form a combined presumptive indicator of the need for exchange rate action. Arguing in favor of this proposal, Mr. Ossola explained that a country's basic balance was less subject to manipulation than was its level of reserves and less subject to distortion by cyclical and speculative influences. Unlike changes in reserves, it would be easier to agree on why a country's basic balance was too large or too small.

The Italian proposal for a basic balance indicator broadened the notion of the term indicator. Under the U.S. proposal, the term was purely a statistical measure; under the Italian proposal, the term combined a statistical measure with a large element of analysis and assessment. Mr. Ossola's alternative indicator was endorsed by Mr. Oort and by other deputies who emphasized the impossibility of avoiding interpretation and assessment of a country's balance of payments position whatever indicator was used.

Mr. Emminger also suggested alternative indicators. His position was that serious effort should be made to reach a consensus on presumptive indicators for balance of payments adjustment, since such indicators would shift the burden of proof of the need for adjustment from the country's trading partners or from the Fund to the country with the payments imbalance. But like Messrs. Ossola and Palumbo, Mr. Emminger advocated that the reserve position should be only one element in any quantitative indicator, which should also include the underlying balance of payments position, cost-price comparisons, and structural shifts in the capital accounts.

A Successful Meeting

Mr. Morse and several other officials regarded the November 1972 meeting of the deputies, which was really a preliminary meeting on the issues, as a success. Proposals were made and so were counterproposals. Consideration of proposals still took the form of what Mr. Morse characterized as "multilateral monologue" with each deputy presenting his own position. Further meetings were needed for the deputies to progress to actual dialogue and eventually to debate. Nonetheless, at the November 1972 meeting, by listening carefully to each other's viewpoints and suggestions they engendered hope that major differences might be resolved.

Further Consideration of the U.S. Proposal for a Reserve Indicator

In an effort to evaluate the choice between the U.S. proposal for a reserve indicator and the Italian proposal for a basic balance indicator, the Fund staff, in

January 1973, prepared a paper entitled "Reserves and Basic Balances as Possible Indicators of the Need for Payments Adjustment."[12] The staff paper maintained that in order to choose between the two indicators, distinction had to be made between flow disequilibrium and stock disequilibrium. Flow disequilibrium is reflected in the financial flows constituting a member's balance of payments, a disequilibrium analogous to fundamental disequilibrium. Stock disequilibrium is disequilibrium in the optimal distribution of reserves among countries. The basic balance indicator was more suitable for flow disequilibrium while the reserve indicator was preferable for stock disequilibrium. The staff paper also maintained that different uses affected the type of indicator preferred. Indicators could be used, for instance, to identify the existence of balance of payments disequilibrium, to determine the division of responsibility among countries for action to adjust payments disequilibrium, and to discipline countries through sanctions if they did not take the appropriate action. Specificity of the context in which indicators were to be used would be helpful in selecting types of indicators.

Further discussion of the U.S. proposal for a reserve indicator took place at the third deputies' meeting, held at the Fund's Office in Paris on January 23–25, 1973. Views were now more clearly divided on the adjustment process and the exchange rate mechanism. U.S. officials continued to be strongly attached to the idea that reserve indicators should create a presumption of the need for corrective actions by countries with payments imbalances, including countries with surpluses. If action were not forthcoming, graduated pressures or sanctions should be applied by the Fund or the GATT. Deputies from other members, however, would agree only that indicators should be used to trigger consultations between the member and the Fund; they should not be regarded as presumptive of the need for action, and no pressures or sanctions should be used to force action. In general, deputies were not favorably disposed to the use of indicators and until March 1973 were unwilling even to set up a Technical Group to study them.

RESERVE ASSETS

Reserve assets and asset settlement or convertibility were taken up by the deputies of the Committee of Twenty when they assembled for their third meeting.

The annotated agenda for this meeting contained a complex web of questions in which the answer to one question depended on the answer to another. First, there was the question whether the SDR was to be the standard of the reformed system. Then, assuming that the deputies were able to agree on an SDR standard, they had to consider the more difficult questions of how to achieve an SDR standard.

The SDR was far from being the standard of the existing system. The unexpected collapse of the dollar in August 1971 and the determination of U.S.

---

[12]Vol. III below, pp. 57–67.

officials to demonetize gold had suddenly catapulted the SDR into the position of the prospective prime reserve asset of the international monetary system. It was, however, a brand new reserve asset, introduced only in 1970. It was initially intended only to supplement other reserve assets, especially gold, still regarded as the basic reserve asset of the international monetary system. In fact, the SDR had been deliberately valued in terms of gold to make it "as good as gold." The SDR was subject to several limitations on its use, made explicit by the Fund's Articles of Agreement. It could be held only by official monetary authorities. Because it was not transacted in private markets, its liquidity, or conversion into currencies used in transactions, depended on designation procedures of the Fund. Even many central bank officials, especially in developing members, were still unfamiliar with the SDR and unaccustomed to holding and using it, although they were very much at ease with holding and using reserve currencies. Moreover, the amount of SDRs outstanding was minuscule compared with the vast amount of gold and reserve currencies in existence. Establishment of a link between SDR allocations and development finance was also unresolved. In thinking about an SDR standard for the reformed international monetary system, the deputies of the Committee of Twenty therefore had a dual task. They had to develop some concept of the shape of the SDR standard that might ultimately emerge and they had to consider the problems of the transition to such a standard.

The transition involved questions of how to improve the characteristics of the SDR and how to extend its uses. Beyond these questions were questions of what to do about gold and reserve currencies. Achieving a consensus to reduce the role of gold in a reformed system would not be easy. Gold had had a central role in the international monetary system for centuries, and the existing stock of monetary gold was large. Since France held large gold reserves and South Africa produced more than two thirds of the Western world's output of gold, officials of these members were dedicated to retaining an important place for gold in the international monetary system. Officials of the United States, on the other hand, wanted to reduce the monetary uses of gold. They were supported by the developing members, which did not hold much gold. Most developing members had formerly been colonies of European countries, and the central banks of those countries kept the gold reserves of their political empires or currency areas in central pools. After gaining independence, developing members rarely acquired gold, preferring to hold any reserves they might accumulate in foreign exchange, usually dollars, pounds sterling, or French francs. Officials of developing members were not therefore inclined to favor increases in the official price of gold or other changes for gold which would enhance its monetary status, since improvements for gold, far from benefiting them, in fact made them relatively worse off compared with industrial members with large holdings of gold.

Questions about the relative role of reserve currencies in the reformed system were even more difficult to resolve. Reserve currencies were widely used. The world was effectively on a dollar standard and had been for several years. How to reduce use of the dollar and other national currencies had to be decided. Should there be limitations on the accumulation of reserve currency balances by central banks? What form and degree of settlement into primary assets or convertibility should there be? What should be done about past accumulations of dollar balances held by central banks abroad, that is, about the "dollar overhang?" Should some kind of substitution account be set up in the Fund whereby officials of central banks could exchange balances of reserve currencies for SDRs?

Areas of Agreement

The deputies were able to agree relatively readily at their meeting in January 1973 that the SDR should become the principal reserve asset of the reformed system. This agreement was quite an achievement in that the first SDRs had been allocated only three years before. Acceptance of the SDR as the principal reserve asset of the reformed system, however, resulted in large part because of the absence of any suitable alternative. Only G.W.G. Browne, the deputy from South Africa, and Mr. Pierre-Brossolette were willing to make any case for gold. And all deputies, even those from the United States, were willing to agree, or at least concede, that no national currency, such as the dollar, could be the prime reserve asset.

The deputies were also able to agree quite readily that reserve creation and the volume of international liquidity ought to be subject to international control. Otherwise the supply of global reserves would continue to be affected by the injection of reserve currencies into the system when reserve centers had deficits or by the withdrawal of reserve currencies from the system when they had surpluses. But this alternative was unacceptable: all the deputies agreed that global reserves should not be influenced to any significant extent by the balance of payments positions of reserve center countries. Deputies from Western European members used the word "control" of reserve creation to stress that the creation of dollar liabilities as a source of reserves should be done away with in the reformed system. The deputies from the United Kingdom, Christopher W. McMahon and Derek J. Mitchell, suggested the word "management" of reserve creation, leaving the way open for some use of dollars as reserves. All deputies agreed, too, that international control or management of reserve creation should be achieved primarily through decisions to allocate or cancel SDRs.

Most deputies also realized that if the SDR was to be the principal reserve asset of the reformed system, it should command sufficient confidence and strength for monetary authorities to prefer it to alternative reserve assets in the composition of their reserves. They therefore agreed that allocations of SDRs should not be excessive, but be adequate to permit members to achieve reasonable rates of reserve growth. There was fairly wide agreement, too, on the need to relax some of the rules governing the use of the SDR. The limits on participants' obligations to accept SDRs might be raised; the number of institutions that could hold SDRs might be increased to include more than central banks and the Fund itself, then the only legitimate holders of SDRs; and the reconstitution obligations might be liberalized.

Areas of Disagreement

The implications of these general propositions on the SDR were different, however, for different deputies. Deputies from developing members believed that even with an SDR standard and an international management of reserve creation, it would still be possible for allocations of SDRs to be linked in one way or another to the provision of development finance. Deputies from industrial members on the other hand were very much concerned about the dangers of excessive allocations of SDRs.

The deputies also differed about the way to change the valuation of the SDR so as to disconnect its value from that of gold and about the need for a higher rate of interest on the SDR so that central banks would be induced to hold SDRs. Deputies from EC countries favored valuation of the SDR in terms of a group or basket of major currencies and an interest rate for the SDR closely related to the market rates of interest prevailing on foreign exchange balances of the currencies included in the basket. Japan, as a major creditor country which expected to remain a creditor country, favored an SDR that was a high-yielding asset. The Japanese deputies therefore supported a "strong SDR" that was valued in terms of the strongest currency or currencies in the system and that would increase in value as that currency or currencies appreciated. The U.S. deputies were reluctant to agree to these features for the SDR. The U.S. authorities were pursuing monetary policies in which interest rates for dollar-denominated assets were relatively low, and higher interest rates for the SDR could draw funds from dollar assets and weaken the dollar. Deputies from developing members also were not eager to have the interest rate on the SDR raised from the then very low rate of 1.5 percent a year, since they represented the largest single group of users of SDRs.

There was no agreement either about how to assess the appropriate level of global reserves. The deputies recognized that it would not be satisfactory simply to aggregate the reserve aims or targets of individual members; the sum of these reserve aims would clearly exceed an acceptable world total. At the same time, a number of deputies pointed out the need to take account of the demand of individual members for reserves. Again, as they did on other occasions, the Italian deputies, Messrs. Ossola and Palumbo, came forward with a compromise proposal, suggesting that the level of global liquidity needed to be evaluated by relating it directly to the value of world trade.

Even stronger differences of view separated the deputies on the question of how far to carry the reduction in the role of national currencies. While the deputies of the United Kingdom and of the United States, the two principal reserve centers, were willing to agree to a reduced role for reserve currencies, many European deputies, especially from Belgium, France, and the Netherlands, pressed for total elimination of the use of national currencies as reserves; dollars should be held by central banks only in those amounts needed for working balances. Illustrative of the strongly expressed positions were those of Mr. Oort and Mr. Pierre-Brossolette. Mr. Oort, recognizing that while there would be a transitional stage for phasing out reserve currencies and gold, argued that the transitional stage be short. Mr. Pierre-Brossolette objected even to the order in which the questions were being discussed, since the deputies were considering first the question of what to do about reserve currencies and then formulating the provisions for convertibility in the reformed international monetary system. The dollar ought to be adapted to whatever new rules were agreed for the international monetary system; the reformed system ought not to depend on the degree of convertibility that could be agreed upon for the dollar.

Deputies from developing members advocated what they called "freedom of choice in the composition of reserves of developing members," which implied keeping a large proportion of their reserves in dollars. Muhammad Al-Atrash (Syria), Ernesto Fernández Hurtado (Mexico), Paulo Pereira Lira (Brazil), and Luis Ugueto (Venezuela), among others, explained that an increasing number of developing members had in the last several years adopted more aggressive policies with regard to the management of their reserve portfolios. They shifted between reserve assets to take advantage of expected yields, including the effects of changes in the exchange rates for the major currencies; at times they shifted into nontraditional reserve assets. They valued the additional income produced by these portfolio management policies. Mr. Fernández Hurtado also explained that debtor countries, as were most developing members, and creditor countries used reserve currencies differently. Creditor countries could perhaps convert most of their reserve assets into SDRs without affecting their main financial relations with the rest of the world. The reserve currencies held by debtor countries, however, constituted a vital part of their overall financial situation. They often used the largest portion of their reserve currency holdings to induce private commercial banks abroad to grant them loans.

Developing members thus supported the United States in advocating that the dollar should continue to have a large role in any international monetary system.

ASSET SETTLEMENT AND CONVERTIBILITY

The deputies of the Committee of Twenty differed most, however, on asset settlement and convertibility. At one end of the spectrum were the deputies from Belgium, France, and the Netherlands who pressed for a regime under which central banks effectively converted into primary reserve assets on a mandatory basis all national currency holdings beyond working balances. Certainly newly acquired balances (sometimes referred to as "new" dollars) had to be fully convertible, on a mandatory basis, with convertibility achieved through the Fund so that it did not depend on the willingness of the United States to convert balances of its currency. These European officials also wanted to find some way of converting "old" dollars, that is, the dollar overhang.

At the other end of the spectrum were U.S. officials. They considered it a concession even to discuss making the dollar again convertible before the U.S. balance of payments deficit was eliminated. They believed that achievement of a balance of payments surplus by the United States would alleviate the problem of the dollar overhang since other countries would have to use their accumulated dollars to pay for the deficits vis-à-vis the United States which a U.S. surplus would imply. Moreover, the willingness to restore convertibility of the dollar gave the United States its main bargaining power in the negotiations for a reformed system, just as its threat to suspend convertibility had been its major bargaining weapon prior to August 15, 1971. U.S. officials did not wish to make this major concession until they had achieved their objectives with regard to the adjustment mechanism and changes in par values. As for the technique by which convertibility might be arranged, U.S. officials preferred convertibility on a voluntary bilateral basis. Convertibility (e.g., of new dollar balances) into SDRs would be effected, when circumstances permitted, within limits by the issuer of the currency when central banks presented balances for conversion. This kind of convertibility was similar to the on demand convertibility that prevailed under the Bretton Woods system.

Two questions concerning asset settlement or convertibility were thus posed: (i) whether the arrangement should be mandatory or voluntary, and (ii) whether the arrangement should be carried out directly and bilaterally, that is, by the holder of the reserve currency presenting balances to the issuer of the currency, or indirectly and collectively, that is, through the Fund. There was also a difference in view among the deputies as to whether any substitution of dollars for SDRs should be once-for-all or continuously available. The United States was concerned that a continuously available substitution account would enable members to shift reserves out of dollars into SDRs whenever the dollar was weak.

Four Proposals

Asset settlement, convertibility, and consolidation continued to be explored not only by the deputies of the Committee of Twenty at their meeting in January 1973 but also by the Executive Directors in the first few months of 1973. "Consolidation" was the term used to refer to any operation by which the holders of reserves in the form of short-term currency assets, such as U.S. dollars, would exchange these assets for an alternative form of asset that did not constitute a liquid claim on the reserve center, such as SDRs or gold, or positions in the Fund. The idea of consolidation was that holders of reserves would consolidate the various reserve assets that they held in the form of national currencies and gold into one principal reserve asset, such as the SDR. The term "consolidation" was more general than "substitution." Consolidation might be achieved in two ways. The first way, known as substitution, involved the replacement of liquid reserve currency claims (e.g., dollars) by liquid claims on the international community (e.g., SDRs), in the portfolios of reserve holders (e.g., central banks' reserve holdings). The second way, known as funding, involved the replacement of liquid reserve currency claims by illiquid reserve currency claims (e.g., some type of securities) in a bilateral deal between the reserve holder and the reserve center.

The discussion in the Executive Board centered around four proposals, by the United States, the Federal Republic of Germany, the United Kingdom, and Italy.[13] All four proposals envisaged the creation of a substitution account in the Fund through which the Fund could engage in three types of transactions. In one type, the Fund could exchange especially created SDRs against outstanding holdings of reserve currencies. In a second type, the Fund might engage in transactions with reserve centers to secure asset settlement of the reserve currency countries' imbalances, buying the country's currency in exchange for SDRs when the country was in surplus, and selling the country's currency in exchange for SDRs when the country was in deficit, in amounts that resulted in the reserve center gaining or losing a quantity of reserve assets equal to its surplus or deficit. In a third type, the Fund might use the substitution account to provide currencies in exchange for SDRs to countries with a balance of payments need or to restore their working balances of certain currencies.

The U.S. proposal for convertibility envisaged the creation of a substitution account in the Fund limited to the first of these three possible types of transactions, that is, to permit a once-for-all conversion of a part of existing reserve currency holdings into SDRs at the option of the holder. However, a country whose holdings of primary reserve assets exceeded a convertibility point would lose the right to request conversion of holdings of foreign exchange in excess of that point. In addition, the issuing country (e.g., the United States) would have the right to limit or prohibit other countries from adding to their holdings of its currency. U.S. officials envisaged these arrangements operating in conjunction with a system of multicurrency intervention, in which ceilings for intervention were established. Under this system the participating countries (possibly 10 to 20), when in surplus, might acquire the currencies of whichever participants were in deficit. This system would tend to bestow reserve currency status on all the intervention currencies. The currency acquired could be used in one of three ways: (i) to acquire holdings of participants' own currency held by other participants, (ii) to hold in their reserves, provided the issuers acquiesced, and (iii) to acquire primary reserve assets from the country whose currency was bought.

The proposal of the Federal Republic of Germany, presented by Karl-Otto Pöhl to the deputies of the Committee of Twenty at their meeting in January 1973, contained ideas for tight settlement arrangements. It envisaged that all countries would agree to keep the main part of their reserves in primary reserve assets and to restrict foreign exchange reserves to a specified maximum needed as working balances. These maximum limits, which were to be narrow, were to be determined by the Fund according to uniform principles. Countries would have an obligation to present foreign exchange in excess of these limits for conversion into primary reserve assets; they would have no right to request conversion of foreign exchange holdings as long as their holdings were below the limits. Existing reserve currency holdings in

---

[13]These four proposals were described and compared in an annex to a paper by the Fund staff discussed by the Executive Directors in February 1973. See Vol. III below, pp. 99–119.

excess of these working balances would be consolidated. Insofar as monetary authorities desired to change only the composition and not the level of reserves, they could exchange (or substitute) reserve currencies for SDRs in the Fund. Any substitution facility created for this purpose would be limited to the first of the three possible roles of a substitution account described above.

What came to be called the U.K. proposal for asset settlement was, in effect, the second of the three approaches to asset settlement described in the report on reform of 1972. This proposal tried to reconcile the desire of European countries to bring the supply of reserve assets under international control and to have the SDR play an increasingly dominant role in the reformed system, the desire of the United States to avoid large demands for conversion of existing reserve currency holdings, and the desire of developing countries to have some freedom in determining their reserve composition. It envisaged that each country would agree to limit its holdings of each reserve currency to a prespecified level. In normal cases the limit would initially be set at no more than the country's holdings of reserve currencies immediately before the scheme came into operation. Countries would be obliged to present any accretion of foreign exchange above these limits to the reserve center, which would be obliged to convert it into primary reserve assets. On periodic settlements, countries would have the option of either restoring their holdings of reserve currency by purchase against SDRs, or of accepting a new and reduced level of reserve currency holdings which would become the new limit for future settlement. Countries were to be permitted to exchange their reserve currency holdings for SDRs from a substitution account, either directly or indirectly through the reserve center. The account would thus perform the first two of the possible roles of a substitution account. In effect, this proposal amounted to putting a ceiling on countries' holdings of reserve currencies, with amounts above the ceilings to be convertible by reserve centers.

The Italian deputies, Messrs. Ossola and Palumbo, presented the major compromise proposal to the deputies of the Committee of Twenty. They too tried to come up with a proposal that might be acceptable to all. Their proposal was along the lines suggested earlier by Giovanni Malagodi, the Minister of the Treasury of Italy, at a meeting of the finance ministers of the EC countries in July 1972. It combined voluntary action, as wanted by the United States, with multinational settlement through the Fund rather than bilateral conversion as in the past, as wanted by continental European countries. The Italian proposal envisaged the creation of a substitution account in which all three transactions listed above took place. Instead of conversion being a bilateral matter between reserve currency holders and reserve centers, countries requesting conversion of reserve currencies would obtain SDRs from the substitution account. Countries requiring foreign exchange for intervention in exchange markets or for financing a payments deficit might obtain it from the account in exchange for SDRs. Settlement of imbalances by a reserve center would then be achieved through the Fund. The United States would, for instance, periodically pay to, or receive from, the Fund an amount of SDRs equal to its balance of payments deficit or surplus, thus securing full asset settlement as long as the cumulative total of currencies sold to the Fund for substitution into SDRs permitted the Fund to sell the required amount of its currency to a reserve center in deficit. There would not normally be any restriction on the composition of the reserve portfolio of individual countries, except by way of a gentlemen's agreement by the major reserve holders to a limited initial substitution of SDRs for reserve currencies.

Comparison of the Four Proposals

The four proposals thus attempted to resolve the main problem that developed in the Bretton Woods system during the 1960s that convertibility of the dollar into gold depended in part on the deliberate decision by authorities abroad whether or not they would tender dollar holdings to the U.S. Treasury for conversion. The Italian proposal sought to prevent a repetition of this problem by making asset settlement mandatory and by making it take place through the Fund. The proposals of the Federal Republic of Germany and of the United Kingdom sought to avert repetition of such a problem by placing an obligation on countries to seek conversion of additional balances. Under the proposal of the United States, convertibility depended on whether a custom or convention was established to the effect that conversion of dollar holdings would be expected in normal circumstances.

In assessing the four proposals, the Fund staff concluded that the U.K. and Italian proposals would both achieve full asset settlement by employing the substitution account for this purpose. The proposal of the Federal Republic of Germany would achieve something close to asset settlement, but variations in working balances within the permitted limits left scope for some deviation. It was not fully clear to what extent the U.S. proposal would achieve asset settlement. If, in practice, the countries that participated in the multicurrency intervention scheme normally presented for conversion any balances of any currency acquired under that scheme, the U.S. proposal would achieve asset settlement at least to the extent that any imbalances occurred among countries participating in multicurrency intervention. How far this arrangement would produce overall asset settlement would depend on the extent of participation in multicurrency intervention and on the size of imbalances with the rest of the world. If, on the other hand, there was no presumption of conversion of balances acquired (e.g., because the countries that acquired balances in various currencies preferred to hold them rather than to acquire SDRs), operations under the U.S. proposal would not bring about asset settlement.

The staff noted that the four proposals also differed with respect to the freedom countries would have in choosing the composition of their reserves, the objective emphasized by officials from developing members. The proposal of the Federal Republic of Germany closely specified the composition of each country's reserve portfolio and required full initial consolidation. The U.K. proposal placed a one-way constraint on the freedom of reserve composition; it involved no compulsory initial consolidation and provided freedom to switch into SDRs whenever desired, but any rundown of foreign exchange holdings would be irreversible and countries would be prohibited from switching their reserves into new forms. The Italian proposal provided substantially greater freedom of portfolio choice than either the German or U.K. proposals; it relied on voluntary initial consolidation and included freedom for monetary authorities to switch into SDRs whenever they so desired. Under the U.S. proposal the freedom of choice of reserves would depend very much upon the customs or conventions that were established; if countries were not normally expected to request conversion, freedom of choice would be maximized.

The proposal of the Federal Republic of Germany provided maximum control by the Fund over the volume of international liquidity, while such control was hardest to obtain under the Italian and U.S. proposals.

Continued Controversy

The very existence of four proposals for ways to achieve asset settlement and convertibility suggests the controversy and conflicting opinions among the deputies of the Committee of Twenty and among the Executive Directors and other officials on this subject. Officials from EC countries emphasized the need for a fully convertible dollar in order for the reformed system to be symmetrical (i.e., virtually the same for all) with respect to the way in which countries had to finance their balance of payments deficits. The dollar was no longer to have a special role. Officials from the United States emphasized equally firmly that the United States could not undertake "extreme and unrealistic" convertibility obligations, and certainly could not undertake any convertibility obligations until the U.S. payments imbalance was rectified and there was assurance that the reformed international monetary system would contain adequate procedures for obtaining balance of payments adjustment.

As the topic of asset settlement and convertibility was considered at length in the Executive Board in the first several months of 1973, the same division of views appeared among the Executive Directors as existed among the deputies of the Committee of Twenty. The Fund staff tried to facilitate agreement by concentrating on techniques, rather than on the four alternative proposals as a whole, a modus operandi learned in the course of discussions on SDRs. The staff had learned that agreement could sometimes be attained by extracting techniques common to the various proposals. The staff prepared a paper entitled "Technical Choices Involved in Arrangements Regarding Consolidation, Convertibility, and Asset Settlement," which was circulated to the Executive Board in April 1973 and revised a month later after discussions in the Executive Board.[14] The paper explained that asset settlement could be achieved through a system of multicurrency intervention in exchange markets or through a system of predominantly dollar intervention operated in a specified way, partly through the Fund. Members could also still have a large degree of freedom in choosing between SDRs and reserve currencies for the composition of

---

[14]See Vol. III below, pp. 120–23.

their reserves. The staff paper explained, too, that consolidation could be effected rather simply through the creation of a substitution account in the Fund.

While the Executive Directors expressed interest in these techniques, it was clear from their discussion that resolution of the problem of reserve currencies, asset settlement, and convertibility would have to be preceded by a thorough consideration of what was going to happen to the SDR in the reformed international monetary system. Conversion of national currencies into ultimate reserve assets meant in practice conversion into SDRs; asset settlement meant settlement in SDRs. Yet the ways in which SDRs were to be treated in the reformed system were as yet undetermined, and a number of questions concerning the SDR remained unanswered. Would a substitution account for the substitution of foreign exchange for SDRs be established in the Fund? Would a link between allocations of SDRs and development finance be created? To what extent was there a danger of an excess of SDRs as a result of their being substituted for dollars or linked with development finance? By what criteria would more SDRs be allocated in the future? What would be the basis for valuing the SDR when it was no longer valued in terms of gold? Should it bear an interest rate higher than the existing 1.5 percent a year? Would financial institutions other than the Fund or members' central banks be authorized to hold SDRs? How would the characteristics of the SDR be altered and its uses broadened so as to enhance its attractiveness?

There seemed to be little point in discussing ways to reduce the use of gold and national currencies in the international monetary system in favor of the SDR and ways to convert national currencies into SDRs until the issues attending the SDR were resolved. Officials seemed to be on a merry-go-round on these topics.

CHAPTER

10

Impact of Floating Rates on Reform Efforts

*A*T THE CONCLUSION of the inaugural meeting in September 1972, Messrs. Wardhana and Morse expected to call a second meeting of the Committee of Twenty before the end of the year so that ministers might endorse any conclusions reached by the deputies. Although the deputies' meeting in November was considered successful, Messrs. Wardhana and Morse subsequently decided to put off until March 1973 the ministerial meeting in the hope that with more time the deputies might reach consensus on the main features of the reformed system. The January 1973 meeting of the deputies, however, was not as successful as their November 1972 meeting had been. The meeting in January took place just as a number of disturbing events were occurring in exchange markets—pressure on the Italian lira, introduction of a dual exchange market in Italy, and a floating of the Swiss franc—and many deputies believed that the fixed rate system put together in December 1971 was beginning to collapse. They were thus less inclined to reach conclusions. Consequently, while the deputies had made some progress since September 1972 in identifying the issues in reform of the international monetary system and in clarifying the positions of different countries, they had not come so close to agreeing on the features of a reformed system as anticipated by Messrs. Wardhana and Morse when they started their work.

In this environment at the end of January 1973, Mr. Morse was unclear just how the Bureau should proceed. Should the Committee of Twenty continue to design a new international monetary system? Or should it rather now try to devise ways to manage the system that seemed to be evolving in practice? While the members of the Bureau decided to go ahead with planning a reformed system, as initially intended, the papers prepared in February and the first few weeks of March 1973 suggest that they were reviewing this strategy. Members of the Bureau wanted, for example, to add to the mandate of the Committee of Twenty working out rules for floating rates so that countries could avoid the trouble that had beset floating rates in the 1930s. The sensitivity of officials from Belgium, France, and the Netherlands on the question of floating rates, however, prevented Mr. Morse from adding this topic to the agenda for the next meeting of the deputies. Consequently, the Bureau continued in February and the first part of March to work toward a reformed system on the basis of stable but adjustable par values even as events were bringing floating rates into being.

DEPUTIES' AND MINISTERS' MEETINGS OF MARCH 1973

The meetings of the deputies and ministers planned for March 19–20 had to be postponed and proved exceedingly difficult to arrange because these officials were tied up in emergency meetings brought on by the exchange crisis of March 1973. Hence, when the deputies met next, on March 22–23, 1973, again at the Fund's headquarters in Washington, floating rates had already erupted onto the scene. A meeting of ministers was scheduled for March 26–27 at the Pan American Union Building in Washington.

Insistence on Par Values

Despite the onset of floating rates a few days before, most of the deputies wanted to press hard for agreement on a reformed system, presuming it still would be based on par values or at least on fixed exchange rates. This position was advanced by the deputies of most EC countries, except the Federal Republic of Germany, by the deputies from Japan, and by those from most developing countries. Mr. Ossola, then Chairman of the deputies of the Group of Ten as well as Italy's representative to meetings of the EC, emphasized that the finance ministers and central bank governors of the Group of Ten attending the meetings in Paris at which the decisions about floating rates had been taken had agreed to floating rates only in order to allow exchange markets to be reopened on March 19. They regarded generalized floating as temporary. In their communiqués of March 9 and of March 16, they stated explicitly that they regarded the recent disturbances as underlining "the urgent need for an effective reform of the international monetary system" and that they wanted the Committee of Twenty to accelerate and expedite its work on reforming the system.[1]

Mr. Pierre-Brossolette and Mr. Inamura also stressed that the new floating rate regime had to be considered transitional and that a reformed system based on par values and fixed rates was imperative. Mr. Pierre-Brossolette reflected the position taken by EC officials just prior to the March 22–23 meeting of the deputies of the Committee of Twenty. Meeting right after the introduction of floating rates, members of the EC Monetary Committee reiterated that they wanted to preserve as

---

[1]Joint communiqués of the Group of Ten and the European Economic Community, March 9, 1973, par. 7, and March 16, 1973, par. 11; Vol. III below, pp. 630–31.

much of the Bretton Woods system as possible and that it should not be too readily presumed that exchange rate adjustment was the appropriate action to correct payments imbalances. Mr. Inamura's position reflected the view of Japanese officials that it was dangerous to leave balance of payments adjustment to the free play of market forces; with major currencies floating, competitive devaluations and pro-liferating restrictions could recur as in the 1930s.

These positions of officials of EC countries and Japan were articulated again a few days later in the meeting of the ministers of the Committee of Twenty on March 26–27. Mr. De Clercq, Mr. Giscard d'Estaing, and R.J. Nelissen (Netherlands) insisted that the reformed system be based on fixed exchange rates, with Mr. Giscard d'Estaing emphasizing that the introduction of floating rates was by no means to be taken as "the reform of the monetary system." These European officials argued that if the existing situation was permitted to endure for too long, the world would split into separate currency blocs, such as a dollar bloc, a deutsche mark bloc, and a yen bloc, which would make trade and investment on a worldwide basis much more difficult than it had been under the Bretton Woods system. Mr. Malagodi was less strict than French officials regarding changes in par values as only a last-resort measure. He argued that par values could be changed in accordance with the objective and composite indicator—the basic balance indicator—which he and other Italian officials had proposed at previous meetings of the Committee of Twenty.

Kiichi Aichi elaborated the Japanese position favoring a par value system. Japanese officials believed strongly that the best international monetary system was one based on adjustable par values, although they admitted the reformed system would have to permit greater flexibility of par values than did the previous system. As a general rule, the use of floating rates ought to be avoided. Objective indicators could be useful but should be used only to diagnose a need for adjustment. Supporting the position of French officials, Mr. Aichi argued also that exchange rate adjustment should be a "late, if not a last resort" among the alternative policy measures available to cope with a disequilibrium in a country's balance of payments. The SDR should be made the principal reserve asset of the reformed system, and for this reason its attractiveness should be enhanced. Convertibility of the dollar into primary reserve assets was a precondition for a workable system and the problem of the dollar overhang ought to be solved. Finally, short-term credit facilities could be developed to deal with disruptive flows of capital.

Officials from developing members, too, argued both at the deputies' meeting and at the Committee of Twenty meeting in March 1973 that rapid progress on getting the reformed system into operation was essential. They objected strongly to generalized floating because floating rates for major currencies caused uncertainty in their own exchange rates. They objected, moreover, to being excluded from the decisions taken earlier in March by officials of the Group of Ten and the EC. They made it clear that, despite the presence of Mr. Wardhana at the joint meetings of the Group of Ten and the EC, they deplored the tactics of the officials of industrial countries in going ahead and introducing floating rates for major currencies without adequate consultation with officials of developing countries. When the ministers of the Committee of Twenty met, the nine Fund Governors from developing members on the Committee, Y.B. Chavan (India), Antônio Delfim Netto (Brazil), Bensalem Guessous (Morocco), Menasse Lemma (Ethiopia), Hugo B. Margáin (Mexico), Sambwa Pida Nbagui (Zaïre), Ali Wardhana (Indonesia), Jorge Wehbe (Argentina), and Abdul Hassan Zalzalah (Iraq), were unanimous in their view that the reformed system ought to be introduced as soon as possible and that it ought to have ways of dealing with crises in which there was "true cooperation among all members of the Fund."

The push for a reformed system by these officials even after the emergence of floating rates in March 1973 reflected long-standing anxieties about floating rates. At the time, most public officials, as well as bankers and businessmen, looked upon the emergence of floating rates as an unfortunate development with potentially harmful consequences for international trade and investment and for monetary and financial relations between countries. As Mr. Volcker subsequently said, "many feared that resort to floating without clearly defined rules of behavior would undermine international economic integration and interfere with trade and investment. Some went further. They felt that what they saw as a total breakdown of the monetary order was responsible for much of the instability in the world economy and carried the seeds of political and economic chaos."[2] Even in the most favorable light at the time, floating rates represented a vast departure from the fixed rates of the Bretton Woods system that had performed so well since World War II and were historically untested except in the hyperinflation period of the 1920s and the deep depression of the 1930s.

Doubts About a Reformed System Based on Par Values

While officials of Belgium, France, and the Netherlands, of Japan, and of developing countries continued in March 1973 to press hard for early agreement on the reformed system based on par values, other officials of the Committee of Twenty began to question the wisdom of proceeding with discussions looking to a reformed system based primarily on par values. The introduction of generalized floating caused many officials to doubt whether par values would be feasible in the near future. They began to feel that the work of the Committee of Twenty might be academic: there would be no easy or early return to a par value system. Thus at the deputies' meeting in March 1973, R.W. Lawson (Canada), Mr. Mitchell, Mr. Volcker, and, to some extent, H.G. Lang (New Zealand) all argued that it would be appropriate to delay any decision on the exchange rate mechanism for the reformed system until it became clearer whether the floating rate regime was operating satisfactorily. Officials of Canada and of the United Kingdom were inclined to take this position because their own countries had had to resort to floating rates. U.S.

---

[2]"Priorities for the International Monetary System," remarks before the National Foreign Trade Council, New York, November 17, 1975, in *Monthly Review*, Federal Reserve Bank of New York, Vol. 58 (January 1976), p. 3.

officials, having experienced considerable difficulty in changing the exchange rate for the dollar in terms of other currencies under the previous par value system, were now also willing to try floating rates at least for a while.

Officials of the Federal Republic of Germany had also gradually become more reconciled to floating rates. At the deputies' meeting in March, Mr. Emminger explained that the experiences of the past few years, and especially of the first few months of 1973, had conditioned his long-held views that fixed exchange rates were essential. There seemed to be no quick remedy for the difficult problem of capital flows. In his words, "As long as the dangerous combination of a big U.S. payments deficit and a huge volume of liquid funds existed, a larger measure of exchange rate flexibility might have to be accepted on a temporary basis as a defensive device to safeguard orderly conditions in exchange markets." In defense of his change in position, Mr. Emminger, then Deputy Governor of the Deutsche Bundesbank, noted that Mr. Burns, Chairman of the Board of Governors of the Federal Reserve System, another central banker who believed ardently in the par value system, had reported in a U.S. Congressional hearing a few days before that even central bankers looked upon floating rates either with equanimity or as a necessity under current conditions. Mr. Pöhl, the other deputy of the Federal Republic of Germany, also doubted whether it was realistic for the deputies to discuss the reformed international monetary system on the assumption that the existing floating rate arrangements were transitional.

At the Committee of Twenty meeting itself a number of ministers, notably Mr. Barber, Kjell-Olof Feldt (Sweden), Alberto Monreal Luque (Spain), Mr. Schmidt, and John N. Turner (Canada), also believed that large industrial countries, including the United States, might rely on floating rates for the next several years and, therefore, questioned whether the reformed system could any longer proceed on the basis of par values. It was, they believed, unrealistic to assume that a regime of par values might be workable again within a reasonable time. While Mr. Schmidt agreed with Mr. Giscard d'Estaing that a return to fixed but adjustable parities was eventually needed, he argued that until the U.S. balance of payments deficit was eliminated, or at least sharply reduced, floating exchange rates might have to be taken as an acceptable alternative. Mr. Turner did not even pay lip service to the par value system, pointing out that the greater part of world trade was conducted, as of March 1973, on the basis of floating exchange rates and that there could be no return to pegged rates until the existing uncertainties were dispelled.

By March 1973, several financial officials thus began to doubt that the reformed system could in the near future be built on a single dominant exchange rate mechanism such as par values. For the first time, some officials questioned the basic assumption on which they had all been proceeding, namely, that it was possible to reintroduce a system of par values. Some also came to the conclusion as early as March 1973 that the reform exercise of the Committee of Twenty could not therefore succeed.[3]

---

[3]Mr. Emminger, for instance, writing in 1978 and recalling the events of March 1973, stated that "we knew already then that under a system of de facto floating (whatever its official name) most

Emphasis on Coping with Capital Movements

Some of the Fund staff had been convinced for several years that disruptive capital movements were the single most important cause of the collapse of the Bretton Woods system and had been studying ways of controlling such capital movements in the reformed system.[4] The staff sketch had also included a discussion of ways to deal with capital movements. These views and studies were, of course, at the technical level. With the emergence of floating rates in March 1973, officials at the political level also became more deeply concerned about the problem of capital flows and were convinced that the reformed system would have to include ways to handle such flows. The experiences of March 1973 had demonstrated that speculative flows of capital could suddenly undo what seemed to be an adequate structure of exchange rates for the major currencies. Officials now recognized that they could no longer proceed on the hypothesis underlying their earlier work on the reformed system that prompt changes in par values, effected as soon as balance of payments disequilibria appeared to be chronic, would be sufficient to prevent speculative capital movements.

Because of this heightened interest in ways to handle capital flows, the finance ministers and central bank governors of the Group of Ten, recognizing that the large Eurocurrency market was not subject to regulation by any country, asked the deputies of the Committee of Twenty to answer some specific questions about the role of that market in capital movements. Did the Eurocurrency market make capital flows more volatile? Should limits be imposed on the placement of official reserves in the Eurocurrency market? Should reserve requirements comparable to those applied on national banks be imposed on Eurocurrency deposits? They also asked about ways to control the aggregate volume of international liquidity. How could the funding or consolidation of official currency balances, in particular of holdings of dollars and sterling, be achieved so as to lessen the amount of funds available for short-term flows?

The views of officials on the desirability of controls on capital in the reformed system had also changed. Most of them now regarded controls on capital as even more essential than they had hitherto. Although Japanese officials had favored leaving responsibility for capital controls in the hands of each country, Mr. Yukawa now argued for finding ways to control Eurocurrency markets. European officials, pointing to the success of Belgium, France, and Italy with dual exchange markets, were more inclined than before to espouse separate markets for capital transactions as the best way for dealing with large, sudden, and unexpected inflows or outflows of capital. Even Mr. Volcker, who had adamantly opposed controlling capital

---

of the goals pursued in the Committee of Twenty would become a purely theoretical exercise without any practical meaning." See his "The International Monetary Arena Seen From Two Different Angles," *Journal of Monetary Economics* (Amsterdam), Vol. 4 (April 1978), p. 403.

[4]See, for example, J. Marcus Fleming, "Dual Exchange Rates for Current and Capital Transactions: A Theoretical Examination," in his *Essays in International Economics* (Cambridge: Harvard University Press, 1971), pp. 296–325; and "Towards a New Regime for International Payments," *Journal of International Economics* (Amsterdam), Vol. 2 (September 1972), pp. 345–73.

movements, acknowledged that provisions in the reformed system permitting countries to impose capital controls, as against requiring them to do so, might be necessary. Because controls on capital introduced by different countries might proliferate or conflict with each other, however, several deputies favored an international code in the reformed system to govern national practices on capital controls.

DECISION TO DRAFT AN OUTLINE

Because of the new problems resulting from the onset of floating rates for the major currencies and despite the opinion of some officials that it was illusory to continue to think about restoring a par value system, the deputies of the Committee of Twenty decided at their March 1973 meeting to proceed urgently with the preparation of a draft "Outline of Reform," listing the main features of the reformed system. Their decision was supported by the Committee of Twenty at its March 1973 meeting.[5] There Mr. Barber in particular encouraged other members of the Committee to believe that some outline of a reformed system was still possible, despite the new floating rates.

The idea of an Outline of a reformed system derived from the successful use of an Outline when SDRs were created. In that instance, an Outline setting out the basic principles of an SDR facility was prepared by the Fund staff in the first few months of 1967, agreed by the Executive Directors and by the Group of Ten at ministerial level in July and August 1967, and then agreed by the Board of Governors at the 1967 Annual Meeting in Rio de Janeiro. Thereafter, the Outline was developed into specific amendments to the Fund's Articles of Agreement. In this way, agreement on the SDR facility was reached progressively. Because of the success of this procedure, nearly all financial officials took it for granted that a similar procedure would be used for the reform of the international monetary system.

Mr. Morse was confident that the deputies could meet their timetable for completing an outline and securing agreement for it by the Committee of Twenty at ministerial level, for review by the full Board of Governors at the Annual Meeting in Nairobi in September 1973, six months later. To meet this goal the deputies would have to hold more meetings and do more work between meetings than had so far been the case. Mr. Morse's optimism was based on his belief that consensus or near consensus on a number of features of the reformed system seemed to be forming among the deputies and that by their communiqué the members of the Committee of Twenty, too, seemed to approve of these features.

In Mr. Morse's view there were several features on which consensus seemed to be emerging. Officials seemed to be reaching agreement on greater use of objective indicators, at least to signal payments imbalance and to trigger consultation in the

---

[5]Communiqué of Committee of Twenty, March 27, 1973, par. 6; Vol. III below, p. 199.

international community, presumably in the Fund. Most seemed to favor improved procedures for consultation and surveillance in the Fund so as to make international consultation more effective than in the past. Most wanted surplus and deficit countries to take equal responsibility for making the adjustment process work. Views were converging also on several requirements of a new exchange system. Inappropriate par value changes should be discouraged, the United States should be free to change its par value, and temporary floating rates should be legalized in particular situations. Most officials favored better management of global liquidity through a reduction in the use of reserve currencies and use of the SDR as the principal reserve asset of the system. Most believed that there should be a presumption against use of trade controls for balance of payments purposes and exemption as far as possible of developing members from the trade and capital controls imposed by developed members. Deputies from the developing members had frequently stated that this last feature of the reformed system was essential.

To facilitate their work, the deputies in March 1973 set up two Technical Groups to study two main topics of persistent debate, the precise use to be made of objective indicators and ways to deal with disequilibrating capital flows. These groups, formally called the Technical Group on Indicators and the Technical Group on Disequilibrating Capital Flows, were to report to the deputies at their fifth meeting, which was to be an extraordinary five-day meeting, May 21–25, 1973.

Thus, the introduction of floating exchange rates in March 1973 was not the culprit which frustrated agreement by the Committee of Twenty on a reformed system. The work of the Committee of Twenty, and especially of the Bureau, recovered very quickly and even proceeded more intensely.

A Confident Decision

Looking back at the decision of March 1973 to push even harder toward an Outline of Reform, one must marvel at the optimism of the members of the Bureau, the other deputies, the members of the Committee of Twenty, the Executive Directors, and the Managing Director and staff of the Fund, who supported the Bureau's efforts in March 1973 to draft an outline of the reformed international monetary system. Members of the Bureau took on this task despite the recent emergence of a floating exchange rate regime, which ended all semblance of par values for the major currencies, and despite a growing division of opinion on the feasibility of stable and adjustable par values for the reformed system, which they had hitherto assumed would be the exchange rate mechanism. They started to draft an outline although a long list of critical questions remained unanswered. What, if any, sanctions or graduated pressures should the Fund apply to its members to induce, or enforce, adjustment action? Under what conditions would floating exchange rates be permitted, and to what type of surveillance would the Fund subject them? What provisions should govern the settlement of imbalances by the use of primary reserve assets? Should a substitution account be established in the Fund in which balances of reserve currencies would be exchanged for SDRs? If not, what other consolidation arrangements should be introduced in order to reduce the volume of reserve currencies? How should the SDR be developed into the principal reserve asset? More specifically, what changes should be made in the way in which the SDR was valued and what rate of interest should be placed on the SDR? What treatment should be given gold in the reformed system? What measures should be taken to reduce disequilibrating capital flows? What, if any, controls on capital movements should be permitted? Should a new facility for financing capital movements be established? Should a link between SDRs and development finance be introduced?

Despite these difficulties in agreeing on a draft outline, members of the Bureau remained confident that the reformed system might be worked out. They were encouraged by the willingness of the financial officials of the major countries who held divergent views to continue to discuss features of the reformed system. In particular, U.S. financial officials were still willing to discuss the resumption of par values, provided their conditions were accepted, and were still willing to discuss at least some degree of convertibility for the dollar. They also seemed open to suggestions of alternative ways of achieving their objectives. Mr. Shultz and Mr. Volcker were willing to consider these features of the reformed system partly because of the strong desire expressed by officials of most other countries for a return to a system of par values and to dollar convertibility. Moreover, Mr. Volcker had some partiality for fixed exchange rates, if they could be made to work in a way that enabled U.S. officials to change the rate for the dollar. The willingness of the highest-level U.S. officials to continue to seek agreement on a reformed system was a source of encouragement to Mr. Solomon, the U.S. official on the small Bureau that had to draft and redraft various features of the reformed system.

For his part, Mr. Morse had reason for optimism. Since most financial officials wanted agreement on a reformed system, perhaps some broad compromise might be worked out among the disagreeing parties. In such a compromise, the developing members would get the link, the United States would get reserve indicators, and the European countries would get asset settlement.

The hope of the members of the Bureau for eventual success in drafting a mutually agreeable outline was based in part on their experience six years earlier in negotiating the "Outline of a Facility Based on Special Drawing Rights in the Fund." Then, although agreement had proved elusive as late as May 1967, the Outline had been finished and approved by September 1967. The same convergence of views could, they reasoned, happen again.

Looking back at agreement on the SDR scheme, members of the Bureau realized too that although an ideal reformed system might not come into operation for some time, it was nonetheless worthwhile to get the features of such a system agreed and "on the books." Although the SDR scheme had not been used after the initial allocations of SDRs in 1970–72, the SDR *was* in existence and negotiations for the reformed system benefited from its being part of the international monetary system. Likewise, a plan for the reformed international monetary system, once agreed, might remain as a long-run goal until such time as circumstances permitted it to come into operation. These thoughts enabled the members of the Bureau and the deputies to carry on, despite their lack of consensus on many questions.

CURRENT SITUATION ALSO RECEIVES ATTENTION

The communiqué of the Committee of Twenty following the March 26–27 meeting directed the attention of the deputies "to those aspects of reform which have an important bearing on the current situation" and explicitly recognized that with regard to the current situation the Executive Board of the Fund, as well as the Committee of Twenty, had a role.[6] This directive both to the deputies of the Committee of Twenty and to the Executive Directors to discuss measures to deal with the international monetary regime that was evolving in practice, as distinct from the reformed system, gave a shift of emphasis to some of the work of the Committee of Twenty. It also enabled the Executive Directors, the Managing Director, and the staff to become more involved in designing measures to deal with the international monetary regime that was actually emerging. Mr. Morse had not wanted to involve the deputies of the Committee of Twenty too closely in the problem of how the international monetary system would work in the period before the reformed system could be agreed and brought into being. He reasoned that discussion of current problems would distract the deputies from their primary task and could deepen the divisions of opinion among them.

Given the somewhat unreceptive or even critical attitudes of U.S. officials toward the Fund at the time, Fund officials tended to keep a low profile as floating rates were introduced. Hence, neither the Committee of Twenty nor the officials of the Fund had been taking much responsibility for the emerging international monetary regime.

At the Committee of Twenty meeting in March 1973, however, several members urged that attention be paid to current problems. Mr. Turner, for instance, stated that the Committee of Twenty should concentrate on making the existing system work, giving attention to problems of reserve assets and international flows of capital, and should not press for premature agreement in controversial areas. He urged, too, that the Fund manage the emerging system and suggest adaptations of that system. Mr. Monreal Luque, likewise convinced that what was most needed was international regulation of the current situation, suggested that the Fund be asked to devise rules to guide existing international monetary arrangements while the Committee of Twenty concerned itself with the long-run system.

These suggestions for the Fund to involve itself in the current situation were endorsed by Mr. Shultz. Because U.S. officials had been eager for the Fund to be somewhat detached from the reform exercise, the suggestion of Mr. Shultz in March 1973 that the Fund might begin to devise rules for the existing international

---

[6]Ibid.

monetary arrangements meant that the Executive Directors, the Managing Director, and staff felt freer than they had for nearly a year and a half to take some initiative in formulating rules for floating exchange rates and for valuing the SDR. They began to consider these topics immediately. The discussions of these topics in the Executive Board starting in 1973 were to culminate in June 1974 in a number of measures for the interim period.[7]

---

[7]These discussions of the Executive Board are described in Chap. 16.

CHAPTER
11

The Link Reconsidered

*T*HE DEPUTIES OF THE COMMITTEE OF TWENTY still had one
unexplored topic on their agenda—the special interests of developing members in the reformed system. This topic had been scheduled for the deputies'
meeting in March 1973, but because of the urgency of discussing the impact on their
work of floating rates it had been postponed. The deputies took it up at their fifth
meeting in May 1973. The following section provides the reader with some
introduction to the topic.

BACKGROUND ON DEVELOPING
MEMBERS' SPECIAL CONCERNS

Developing members wanted to take the occasion of reforming the international monetary system and amending the Fund's Articles to raise several concerns
of particular importance to them. Partly, they felt that the existing system and
Articles did not adequately recognize their special needs. Although 27 developing
countries had been among the 44 countries represented at Bretton Woods, little
consideration was given to what was subsequently known as economic development.[1] The Fund's original Articles of Agreement, moreover, did not distinguish
between developed and developing members despite the attempts of the Indian
delegation to make development a purpose of the Fund and, failing that, to have the
introductory article take cognizance of the needs of economically backward
countries.[2] Officials of industrial countries had feared that a reference to developing
countries might imply that economic development was a purpose of the Fund, with

---

[1]Representatives from 19 Latin American Republics, China, Egypt, Ethiopia, India, Iran, Iraq,
Liberia, and the Philippines were at Bretton Woods. The 19 Latin American Republics were Bolivia,
Brazil, Chile, Colombia, Costa Rica, Cuba, Dominican Republic, Ecuador, El Salvador, Guatemala,
Haiti, Honduras, Mexico, Nicaragua, Panama, Paraguay, Peru, Uruguay, and Venezuela. See
*Proceedings and Documents of the United Nations Monetary and Financial Conference, Bretton
Woods, New Hampshire, July 1–22, 1944,* Vol. I, U.S. Department of State Publication 2866,
(Washington: Government Printing Office, 1948), p. 5.
[2]Ibid., pp. 23 and 184.

the result that the Fund's resources would be overtaxed. Furthermore, both the Keynes and White plans emphasized the need to distinguish between monetary stabilization and economic development and the advisability of having separate international organizations for the two purposes.[3]

During the 1950s and 1960s, developing countries had experimented with trade and exchange policies within the existing framework to ascertain which policies seemed most likely to expedite their economic development.[4] They also began to influence international organizations to take more of their special needs into account. The first United Nations Conference on Trade and Development (UNCTAD I) was held from March to June 1964 to consider proposals for dealing with the special trade problems of developing countries; UNCTAD was thereafter set up on a permanent basis and periodic conferences were held. The GATT worked out various exceptions to its rules to accommodate the special needs of developing countries. In 1963, with the advent of the compensatory financing facility, the Fund for the first time introduced a policy intended to benefit *especially* its developing members. In 1969, the Fund introduced a buffer stock financing facility.[5] But developing countries remained deeply disappointed that when the SDR had been established in 1969 they had been unable to get agreement on a link between allocations of SDRs and the provision of financing for economic development.[6]

By the 1970s, many developing members had come to view the existing monetary system as even detrimental to their interests. This view had been expounded in a pioneering work in 1951 by Raul Prebisch, the Argentinian economist who was Executive Secretary of the Economic Commission for Latin America (ECLA). Mr. Prebisch had distinguished trade furnished by the "centers" (the industrial countries, which produced manufactures) and by the "periphery" (the developing countries, which produced raw materials) and concluded that the terms of trade and the benefits of trade almost always worked against the periphery and in favor of the centers.[7]

---

[3]*History, 1945–65*, Vol. III, pp. 20 and 39. The Articles of Agreement of the International Bank for Reconstruction and Development (the World Bank) were drafted at the same time as the Fund's Articles with the explicit purpose of "the encouragement of the development of productive facilities and resources in less developed countries." See Articles of Agreement of the International Bank for Reconstruction and Development (December 27, 1945), Article I.

[4]The shift of views from 1945 to 1965 on trade and exchange policies regarded as most appropriate for economic development has been traced by Margaret G. de Vries in "Trade and Exchange Policy and Economic Development: Two Decades of Evolving Views," *Oxford Economic Papers* (Oxford), Vol. 18 (March 1966), pp. 19–44.

[5]How the Fund adapted its policies in the 1950s and 1960s to help its developing members is described in *History, 1945–65*, Vol. II, pp. 122–46, 167–70, 293–95, 417–27, and *History, 1966–71*, Vol. I, pp. 261–86, 343, 358–68, 576, 578–79, 600, and 610–15.

[6]See *History, 1966–71*, Vol. I, pp. 84, 85, 110–11, 219, 220, and 245–46.

[7]United Nations, Economic Commission for Latin America, *Theoretical and Practical Problems of Economic Growth*, UN Document E/CN-12/221 (Mexico, May 1951). Another innovative study on the situation of developing countries in world trade and investment done about the same time was that of Hans W. Singer, "The Distribution of Gains Between Investing and Borrowing Countries," *American Economic Review, Papers and Proceedings of the Sixty-Second Annual*

Consequently, developing countries concluded that the whole structure of economic relations between developing and developed countries had to be altered, especially since international aid from industrial to developing countries was declining. In 1974 they called for a "new international economic order," that is, for sweeping changes in the entire structure of international trade and the international monetary system in ways that would redistribute world income in their favor.[8]

It was against this background that discussions reforming the international monetary system took place. Working closely together, developing members pressed for three major objectives in a reformed system. First and foremost, financial resources for the development of developing members should be enlarged and made easier to obtain; particularly, there should be ways in which transfers of real resources from developed to developing members were effected through the international monetary system. Second, developing members should have preferential access to the markets of industrial members for their manufactured products. Third, rules placed on industrial members regarding correction of their balance of payments disequilibria or accumulation of reserves should not be applied to developing members. Most discussion was to center on the first of these objectives.

LINK BETWEEN ALLOCATIONS OF SDRs AND DEVELOPMENT FINANCE

To transfer real resources from developed to developing members—the first of the three objectives—officials of developing members participating in the discussions on a reformed international monetary system focused mainly on the establishment of a link between allocations of SDRs and the provision of development finance. In fact, this link became a primary objective of officials from developing members in all subsequent discussions of the transfer of real resources to developing members.

Suggestions by the Fund Staff

The link between allocations of SDRs and development finance was a topic to which the Executive Directors, the Managing Director, and the staff directed their attention almost as soon as the Committee of Twenty started their deliberations in September 1972. Although the link had been discussed, and rejected, in the latter

---

Meeting of the American Economic Association (Nashville, Tennessee), Vol. 40 (May 1950), pp. 473–85. More recently, W. Arthur Lewis, in his *The Evolution of the International Economic Order* (Princeton, New Jersey: Princeton University Press, 1978), has described at some length how the trade arrangements that evolved in the nineteenth and early twentieth centuries have worked against developing countries.

[8]The evolution of demands for a new international economic order has been traced in Jagdish N. Bhagwati, ed., *The New International Economic Order: The North-South Debate* (Cambridge, Massachusetts: MIT Press, 1977); see especially "Introduction," pp. 1–24.

half of the 1960s when SDRs were established, Fund officials recognized that developing members retained a keen interest in a link arrangement and that the topic would have to be thoroughly examined in the discussions of reform. Chapter VI of the Executive Directors' report on reform of 1972 had also contained some discussion of it and had reported that further study was already under way in the Fund.

In September 1972, the staff prepared a paper for discussion by the Executive Directors. After this discussion, the paper was revised to take account of Executive Directors' positions and reissued in February 1973.[9] The paper described five types of arrangements, called schemes, by which a link between SDR allocations and development finance could be effected.

Type A schemes were those under which the Fund would allocate SDRs directly to international or regional institutions which provide development finance, such as the World Bank and its affiliate, the International Development Association (IDA), and the various regional development banks.

In type B schemes developing members would be given a larger share of SDR allocations than corresponded to their share in Fund quotas. (Under existing arrangements, SDRs were allocated to all Fund members in proportion to their Fund quotas.) Members could be divided into two categories (developed and developing) or into three or more categories based on the degree of their development or the level of their per capita income. The ratio between the amounts of SDRs allocated and quotas could be different between the categories of members, with developing members having a higher ratio than developed members. Alternatively, the relation between SDR allocations and quotas in the Fund could be entirely severed and some formula could be arranged to produce a country distribution of SDR allocations more favorable to developing members than that based on quotas in the Fund.

In type C schemes the share of developing members in total Fund quotas, and hence in SDR allocations, was raised. Such schemes gave developing members access to a higher proportion of the Fund's resources and greater voting power in the Fund as well as more SDRs.

In type D schemes some or all national governments receiving SDR allocations from the Fund contributed predetermined proportions of their SDR allocations, or the equivalent in currencies, to development finance institutions. Schemes of this type were called an indirect link; development finance institutions received currencies instead of SDRs from the countries themselves rather than from the Fund.

Type E schemes depended on the establishment of a new substitution account in the Fund, as part of the reformed international monetary system. Any excess amounts of interest that the Fund received as a result of operations in such a substitution account would be contributed to development finance institutions or to developing countries as grants, and any amortization paid by reserve center countries to the Fund would be allocated to development finance institutions. Under

---

[9]See Vol. III below, pp. 69–97.

type E schemes, the additional resources for financing development through a link arrangement would come from the existing supply of world reserves; in all other schemes such resources would come from net additions to the stock of world reserves.

Types A, B, and E schemes required changes in the Articles of Agreement; types C and D did not.

In addition to describing these schemes, the staff paper also appraised them according to their effects on the economic development of developing members, such as the amount of net additional real resources for development that they might provide, and their effects on the international monetary system, such as on aggregate demand in the world as a whole, on the decisions to allocate SDRs, and on confidence in the SDR and the operation of the SDR arrangement. The staff concluded that all the schemes were technically operable. Some schemes would probably increase the amount of financial assistance available for development without harming the SDR arrangements, while other schemes, particularly those that might be most helpful to developing members, might, if applied on too ambitious a scale, impair the willingness of other members to accept allocations of SDRs or even to continue to participate in the SDR arrangements. In the view of the staff, the direct repercussions of any of the schemes on aggregate world demand, and hence on inflation, were not likely to be sizable. The effect of link arrangements on total allocations of SDRs over the years was more likely to be on the timing of allocations than on their cumulative total. Beyond this assessment, the staff paper was deliberately neutral.

DISCUSSIONS OF THE LINK IN THE EXECUTIVE BOARD

Discussions of the link in the Executive Board in November and December 1972 and in February 1973 quickly revealed that the world's financial officials were not ready to establish a link between SDR allocations and development finance. A link would be at least as difficult to achieve in 1972–74 as it was when the SDR facility was negotiated in the late 1960s. While the staff had assumed in its paper that some link between SDR allocations and development finance could be agreed and had proceeded to examine possible arrangements, the Executive Directors made no such assumption. Mr. Dale, for instance, was cautious since the U.S. authorities had not yet taken a stand on the link and pointed out that the staff's assumption was a serious misreading of the stage that discussions about a link had reached. Governments were still deciding whether to lend support to any scheme that would forge an explicit connection between SDR allocation and economic development.

The officials of the Federal Republic of Germany already seemed to have decided that they did not want to support a link arrangement. Mr. Schleiminger pointed out that his authorities believed that a link was not compatible with preserving and improving the status of the SDR as a viable monetary instrument and a good reserve asset. Confidence in the SDR was a necessary prerequisite to getting central bankers and other monetary officials to accept it as the primary reserve asset of a reformed international monetary system and to hold SDRs in their reserves in place of gold, dollars, or pounds sterling. Financial officials, he noted, were already doubtful that the SDR would be created in ways and amounts that were any more rational than the ways in which other reserve assets, such as U.S. dollars, had been created. Therefore, if the SDR was to have a chance of becoming the primary reserve asset of the reformed system, it should not have to suffer the burden of attachment to schemes, such as the link, that had little if anything to do with the need for further reserve assets and liquidity in international payments arrangements.

Several Executive Directors from industrial and relatively more developed members agreed that there was need for concern about the implications of any link arrangement on the SDR as a reserve asset. Despite assurances by spokesmen from developing members that, even after the establishment of a link, allocations of SDRs would still be determined by the global need for reserves and not by the need for development finance, it was difficult not to be concerned about the prospect that SDR allocations would be influenced by the need for development finance. This concern was all the greater since financial officials were unsure about how to assess the global need for reserves. Some officials were suggesting that the reserve requirements or reserve aims of individual members ought to be taken into account; it was only a small step further to take into account the development needs of individual members. Some Executive Directors feared, too, that because the link would affect the levels of reserves of members with balance of payments deficits, it might have adverse consequences for the working of the adjustment process. Other Executive Directors, especially Mr. Dale, queried whether a link scheme would actually result in greater amounts of development finance; a link might give developed members an excuse to reduce development aid in other forms.

Mr. Brand and Mr. Lieftinck also doubted the wisdom of any link arrangements, putting forward some of the same arguments expressed when SDRs had been established. The provision of development assistance and the provision of international liquidity were distinct functions exemplified by the creation at Bretton Woods of two institutions, the Fund to provide international liquidity and the World Bank to provide development finance; the two functions should not be merged. Mr. Lieftinck also expressed serious reservations about the distribution among members of the burden of furnishing financial aid to developing members if development aid was to be forthcoming through SDR allocations. It could well be that not only developed members, as proposed in one of the staff schemes, but also members at an intermediate stage of development would have to forgo SDR allocations, or be called upon to make without compensation contributions out of newly allocated SDRs.

Some of the Executive Directors from industrial and relatively more developed members took the view that any changes in the SDR, including the possibility of a link, had to be considered in the light of the reform of the entire international monetary system and were therefore up to the Committee of Twenty to decide.

Among the Executive Directors appointed or elected by developed members, only Mr. Palamenghi-Crispi supported the link. He pointed out that the Italian authorities not only favored the link but had been making specific suggestions for one since 1968. A few other Executive Directors elected by members other than developing countries, while not outright supporting a link were at least inclined to view the possibility sympathetically. Mr. Bryce, for instance, did not regard quotas as a fair basis of SDR allocations. Mr. van Campenhout recalled that André Vlérick had adopted a positive attitude toward the establishment of a link in his speech at the 1972 Annual Meeting.[10] Erik Brofoss (Norway) indicated that the Nordic countries in his constituency, except for one, were inclined to accept one or the other of the schemes suggested by the staff.

The nine Executive Directors elected exclusively by developing members all spoke out resolutely in favor of a link of some kind. Mr. Prasad, in particular, emphasized the determination of officials of developing members to press for a link. They insisted that the international monetary system provide for economic growth as well as for monetary and exchange rate stability. The Fund's purposes were broad, aiming at full use of world resources to achieve full employment and higher standards of living. While balance of payments equilibrium was an objective, it was not to be obtained at all costs. The Fund, in his view, seemed to have lost sight of its basic purposes and to have become excessively concerned with mechanisms and systems.

Most of these Executive Directors took the position that as long as the aggregate amount of SDRs allocated remained the same, it was difficult to see how the monetary or reserve character of the SDR would be impaired. Only the distribution of a given amount of SDR allocations would be affected. Mr. Kharma-wan argued that since SDRs were intended to promote world trade and thus the development of productive resources, the share of SDRs allocated to developing members, members with especially large undeveloped productive capacity, should be increased. Some of the Executive Directors tried to come up with still new arguments for the link. S.B. Nicol-Cole (Sierra Leone), for example, argued that the link would promote balance of payments adjustment by developing members. His argument was that while balance of payments adjustment in developed economies was a short-term phenomenon, it was a medium-term or long-term process for developing members and structurally related to economic development. Therefore, any measure that helped development promoted medium-run or long-run balance of payments adjustment. Antoine W. Yaméogo (Upper Volta), noting that the compensatory financing and buffer stock facilities had not resulted in the drawing of much money from the Fund by developing members, thought that the Fund had to find some way to fill the gap between the needs of the "less favored Fund members" and the amount of resources available; if the link were not forthcoming, the Fund should alter some of its policies with regard to the use of its regular resources.

---

[10]Statement by the Governor of the World Bank for Belgium, *Summary Proceedings, 1972,* p. 230.

The Extended Facility Conceived

From the Executive Board's discussion of the link, it was apparent to the Managing Director and the staff that, whether or not a link arrangement was agreed, the Executive Directors supported liberalization of some of the Fund's policies on the use of its resources so as to enable developing members to draw more from the Fund. The Managing Director and the staff were seriously interested in finding some way for the Fund to channel greater financial resources to developing members. The staff paper on the link had included a small paragraph which suggested that the Fund might institute new arrangements for use of its resources by developing members. It noted, for example, that drawings could be repayable over a longer period than the customary three-to-five-year period and might be made available in support of comprehensive programs of economic stabilization and restructuring of developing members' economies.

Following the cool reception to the link by many Executive Directors, the staff revised the paper on the link, elaborating the idea of a new type of drawing from the Fund, and referring to it as a "link within the Fund." Rather than giving additional SDRs directly to members or to other international organizations, the Fund might administer some arrangement under which members might be able to improve the foundations for their development programs. For instance, drawings from the Fund could be part of medium-term financial programs in which members would be required to agree with the Fund on certain conditions to be implemented over several years instead of on a year-to-year basis, as was done in existing stand-by arrangements.

By January 1973, the idea of a facility in the Fund to assist members in implementing macroeconomic policies to further economic development was well advanced within the staff. The revised staff paper of February 1973 on the link between the allocation of SDRs and development finance contained a fairly detailed suggestion for what was being referred to as an extended facility. The suggested extended facility would provide assistance to developing members directly from the Fund, either from SDRs or from the Fund's regular resources, for a longer term than the usual Fund drawings and stand-by arrangements.

This suggestion aroused considerable interest among the Executive Directors, who immediately agreed that it should be studied further. Thus, in the course of discussions of a possible link between allocations of SDRs and development finance the idea of the extended facility was conceived. The facility was to be introduced in 1974.

DEPUTIES OF THE COMMITTEE OF TWENTY DISCUSS THE LINK

When the deputies began their fifth meeting, May 21–25, 1973, they devoted their opening day to discussions of the special interests of developing countries. The morning session was on the link.

The deputies expressed the same range of views as had the Executive Directors. Lal Jayawardena (Sri Lanka), Chairman of the Working Party on the Link set up by the Group of Twenty-Four, presented the consensus of the officials of developing countries contained in a report on the link prepared in the Group of Twenty-Four. Specific measures for the transfer of real resources to developing countries ought to be an integral part of the reform of the international monetary system. No consideration other than the requirements of the world economy for liquidity should govern the volume of SDR creation. Developing countries agreed that they preferred the form of a link in which developing members would receive a greater proportion of newly created SDRs than they would be entitled to on the basis of allocation in proportion to quotas in the Fund, with the least developed members receiving a still more generous share than other developing members. Explicitly, they preferred the type B schemes described in the paper by the Fund staff. Officials of developing members emphasized that this form of the link had the merit of retaining in principle the present system of SDR allocations: SDRs would still be allocated by the Fund directly to the participating members on the basis of members' quotas in the Fund. Yet developing members would receive a share of SDR allocations proportionately larger than their share in total Fund quotas. Mr. Jayawardena urged that the deputies of the Committee of Twenty agree forthwith to the principle of the link and that they set up their own working party to consider how it should be implemented.

As had happened in the discussion by the Executive Directors about the link, when the deputies of the Committee of Twenty took up this topic, officials of developing members advanced strong arguments in favor of the link and undertook to counter the various arguments that had been presented against it. Mr. Al-Atrash, for example, put forward a paper indicating (i) it was unimportant to regard the provision of liquidity and of development finance as two separate functions since money created by any source in an economy circulated throughout the economy, (ii) since officials of developed members controlled the decision to allocate SDRs, it was inevitable that the size of SDR allocations would be determined solely by the long-term global need of the world economy for reserves and not by considerations of development finance, and (iii) because the relative increase in the world demand for goods and services resulting from the link would be small, its inflationary impact was likely to be minimal.

Several deputies from developing members emphasized that in accepting the principle that the amount of SDRs to be created should be based on the liquidity needs of the world economy, officials of developing members had shown their concern for the necessity to ensure confidence in SDRs and to refrain from excessive SDR creation. Officials of developing members, they stressed, were just as concerned as officials of industrial members that the SDR remain a creditable reserve asset and that world reserves not be excessive. If a link was established, they were not likely to try to ruin the SDR by pressing for excessive SDR allocations.

As had Mr. Prasad in the Executive Board, Mr. Diz in the meeting of the deputies of the Committee of Twenty stressed that officials of developing members were determined to press for some mechanism for transferring real resources to developing members. He pointed out that the deputies from developed members should understand that, while acceptance of a reformed international monetary system that included a link might be politically difficult in some developed members, acceptance of a reformed system which did *not* include a link would be politically difficult in many developing members.

Deputies from developed members expressed the same mixture of views as did the Executive Directors from those members. In line with the previously stated positions of Italian officials, Mr. Ossola voiced the strongest support for a link. A certain amount of sympathy for the link was expressed also by Jacques de Larosière (France), J.G. Littler (United Kingdom), and Georges Janson (Belgium). Opposition was expressed most strongly by William C. Hood (Canada), Mr. Inamura, Mr. Pöhl, Hermod Skånland (Norway), Mr. Volcker, and R.J. Whitelaw (Australia). Once again, as in past discussions of the link, the major argument against it was that the SDR was still untried and that introduction of a link between SDR allocations and development finance ran the risk of weakening confidence in the SDR as a reserve asset and reduced its chances of becoming the primary reserve asset of the reformed system. A second objection was the risk of its inflationary consequences.

Mr. Pöhl explained that he and other officials of his country were especially concerned about the potentially inflationary consequences of any link arrangement. The existing arrangements made it possible to create SDRs ex nihilo because they were designed to meet the growing need for reserves to be held. SDRs were to be used only in the event of temporary balance of payments deficits. If, under revised arrangements, SDRs were to be used to finance regular ongoing demand, their major rationale would be lost. The authorities of the Federal Republic of Germany were not convinced by the argument that the amounts in question would be small compared with the gross national product of industrial countries or with some other measure. The amounts were likely to grow and, in the course of time, confidence in the SDR might well be shaken. Also, Mr. Pöhl was not sure that the link would have no effect on decisions to allocate SDRs. On the contrary, should the link be established, economic development considerations would have a definite influence on such decisions.

Officials of the United States had four major difficulties with the link. First, agreement on a link would not contribute to prompt agreement on a reformed system. Second, while the U.S. authorities appreciated that those who favored the link had pointed out that the effective operation of the international monetary system had priority and that the link should not affect, among other things, the amount of SDRs allocated, they doubted that it was actually possible to have a link without reducing confidence in the SDR. Third, balance of payments adjustment would be adversely affected. SDRs allocated to developing members would end up in the hands of industrial members that already had large trade surpluses. Fourth, U.S. authorities were not convinced that introduction of a link would measurably increase the transfer of real resources from developed to developing members.

Mr. Whitelaw, like Mr. Pöhl, questioned the realism of officials of developing members when they assured other officials that, if a link was instituted, SDRs would still be issued only in amounts compatible with the world's need for liquidity. Nobody knew what the need for liquidity was, and points of view about this need inevitably reflected national interests. Faced with a link arrangement, officials neither of developing nor of developed members could ensure that they would in no way be influenced by the allocation of SDRs to finance development. It would be impossible to make decisions for SDR allocations objectively when SDRs constituted substantial receipts of aid.

Some of the deputies from developed members, including Messrs. de Larosière and Littler, who were at least somewhat inclined to favor a link, suggested that further study be given to the topic. Accordingly, the deputies of the Committee of Twenty agreed in May 1973 to set up a Technical Group on the SDR/Aid Link and Related Proposals.

Discussion of Developing Countries' Other Special Interests

The deputies of the Committee of Twenty devoted their plenary session on May 21, 1973 to a discussion of problems of special interest to developing countries other than the link. These problems were mainly financial, such as access by developing members to capital markets and to international credit and the structure of members' quotas in the Fund. The deputies from both developed and developing members supported an extension of the Fund's financing facilities, such as easing access to compensatory financing, extending the financing of buffer stocks, and making the Fund's resources available for longer periods than under traditional policies. The discussion of quotas revealed substantial agreement that the quota structure of the Fund should not be altered simply to help promote economic development.

There was also discussion of the difficulties that developing members faced in raising capital and of ways to alleviate such difficulties, such as the untying of aid. The deputies also discussed possible surveillance by the Fund of the capital controls of developed members and the encouragement of capital outflows to developing members through the use of tax incentives. In addition, the deputies discussed trade problems of developing members, stressing the importance of adequate export outlets for developing members. It was agreed, however, that this topic could not be usefully pursued by the Committee of Twenty and should be taken up in the multilateral trade negotiations to be conducted in the GATT.

TECHNICAL GROUP ON THE SDR/AID LINK AND RELATED PROPOSALS

The Technical Group on the SDR/Aid Link and Related Proposals, established in May 1973, met in Washington on June 21–22 and July 5–6, under the chairmanship of Mr. Suzuki. The starting point for the work of the Technical Group was the general agreement, affirmed in the March 1973 communiqué of the Committee of Twenty, on "the desirability on the occasion of the reform of promoting economic development and the flow of real resources from developed to developing countries."[11] The Technical Group considered at length the arguments for and against establishment of a link. Arguments in favor concentrated on the improvement in the volume and quality of development assistance that might result from a link. Opposing arguments stressed fears that a link would lead to excessive allocations and a weakening of confidence in the SDR mechanism.

The Technical Group also examined the merits and demerits of the various types of link arrangements suggested by the Fund staff and narrowed its preference to schemes involving direct allocation to development finance institutions (type A schemes), direct allocations to developing countries (type B schemes), and indirect allocations to development finance institutions (type D schemes). Type C schemes, which involved enlarging the share in total Fund quotas of developing countries, and type E schemes, which involved establishing a substitution account in the Fund, were regarded as likely to provoke too much opposition, not necessarily to the link but to changing the quota structure of the Fund or to introducing a substitution account. The Technical Group also reported that officials of developing countries strongly opposed type D schemes on the grounds that they would lead to smaller allocations of SDRs and less total development assistance.

The Technical Group on the SDR/Aid Link and Related Proposals also carefully examined a number of technical issues, should a link be instituted. These technical issues concerned such matters as how to determine the amount, timing, distribution, and use of link allocations and the obligations associated with link allocation.

■　■　■　■　■　■

The link was to remain a live issue, despite the many reservations officials of industrial countries continued to harbor. The Committee of Twenty considered it at ministerial level in July 1973. Governors from developing members again raised the subject at the next three meetings of the Committee of Twenty, in September 1973, in January 1974, and in June 1974. And the final *Outline of Reform* of the Committee of Twenty included a section indicating the status of discussion of the link.

---

[11]Communiqué of Committee of Twenty, March 27, 1973, par. 5; Vol. III below, pp. 198–99.

CHAPTER

12

Toward an Outline of Reform

*I*N *DECIDING IN MARCH 1973* to draft an Outline of Reform in time for the
1973 Annual Meeting, the Committee of Twenty moved from exploration to
negotiation. Attempts to reach agreement on specific features of the reformed
system were now to supersede broad discussion of the issues.

To facilitate agreement, the Bureau began at the end of March 1973 to work
intensively on a draft preliminary Outline for the deputies to consider at their
meeting on May 21–25. At that meeting, the deputies were to try to reach a
consensus on as many features of the reformed system as possible, to narrow any
remaining differences of position, and to agree on a preliminary Outline. The
preliminary Outline was then to be presented to the Committee of Twenty in July to
resolve any conflicts that still existed. After that, it was to be revised and presented
as the First Outline of Reform to the Board of Governors at the Annual Meeting in
September.

When the deputies met in May for their longest meeting of the Committee of
Twenty's two-year existence, a change in procedure signalled the change from
exploration to negotiation. The deputies met in plenary session, the usual procedure
for their previous meetings, only on the first and the last days. On the other three
days, they separated into working groups so as to exchange views more informally
and to come to agreement more readily on principles to be included in the Outline.

In these smaller groups, the deputies returned to the basic topics of the
reformed system which they had explored earlier: balance of payments adjustment,
disequilibrating capital movements, asset settlement and convertibility, consolidation of reserve assets, development of the SDR, the role of gold in the reformed
system, and international trade. This time, however, the deputies were to focus on
those areas on which they could agree.

RE-EXAMINATION OF BALANCE OF PAYMENTS ADJUSTMENT

When the deputies in a working group chaired by Mr. Morse returned in May
1973 to the subject of how balance of payments adjustment among industrial

countries could most appropriately be induced, they had before them the report of the Technical Group on Indicators, which had been set up in March.

Technical Group on Indicators

The Technical Group on Indicators was the first of seven technical groups set up by the Committee of Twenty. The Group met in Washington on three occasions in April and May 1973 under the chairmanship of Robert Solomon. With the exception of the United Kingdom and the United States which appointed persons from the Bank of England and the U.S. Treasury, constituencies were represented by their Executive Director or by an Alternate Executive Director.

The officials who served as technicians on the Technical Group on Indicators hoped that they might resolve some of the difficult questions about the use of objective quantitative indicators for balance of payments adjustment that the deputies working in a less technical way had been unable to resolve. The members of the Technical Group on Indicators were aware that if they did resolve these problems, they would greatly facilitate agreement on the reformed international monetary system. Consequently, they carefully examined a wide range of related questions. They studied all the indicators that might possibly be used: the reserve indicator proposed by the U.S. deputies, the basic balance indicator proposed by Mr. Ossola, the use of domestic prices and costs as indicators of international competitiveness, composite indicators used by some countries, notably the Federal Republic of Germany and Japan, as an aid in diagnosing business cycle movements, and a set of unconnected short-term economic indicators such as were used by EC officials to identify domestic or balance of payments developments in EC countries. They discussed definitional questions such as whether gross or net reserves should be used for the reserve indicator, the norm or base from which changes in reserves ought to be measured, and how a basic balance indicator could be constructed.

Detailed papers were prepared on many topics. For example, Sam Y. Cross and Thomas B.C. Leddy from the U.S. Treasury, representing the United States on the Technical Group, presented papers to show how reserve indicators would work in the international monetary system as a whole and how a gross reserve indicator could be applied to an individual country. Guenther Schleiminger, the Executive Director serving on the Technical Group as the representative of the Federal Republic of Germany, submitted a paper illustrating the importance of using net rather than gross reserves. Simultaneously Fund staff independently reviewed several proposals made since the Bretton Woods Conference in 1944 for introducing objective or quantitative criteria as a supplement to the judgmental concept of fundamental disequilibrium contained in the Fund's original Articles of Agreement.[1]

---

[1]This study was later published as Trevor G. Underwood, "Analysis of Proposals for Using Objective Indicators as a Guide to Exchange Rate Changes," *Staff Papers*, International Monetary Fund (Washington), Vol. 20 (March 1973), pp. 100–117. See also J. Keith Horsefield, "Proposals for Using Objective Indicators as a Guide to Exchange Rate Changes: A Historical Comment," *Staff Papers*, Vol. 20 (November 1973), pp. 832–37.

They also studied how various indicators would have worked in past exchange rate crises and how frequently some kind of assessment would have been needed instead of reliance on indicators. The staff also looked into the question of how relevant reserve data could be reported to the Fund. These staff papers were available to the Technical Group.

In addition to types of indicators, the Technical Group on Indicators discussed a number of policy questions concerning the use of indicators. Were indicators to be used to trigger consultations, to induce policy actions by individual members, or to serve as the basis for the application of graduated pressures by the international community to countries in persistent imbalance? What criteria would be used to suggest that indicators did not signal the need for adjustment action, that is, what criteria should override indicators?

With regard to these policy questions, however, the same differences of view were expressed in the Technical Group as had been expressed at meetings of the deputies. The technicians seemed to be no closer to resolving differences than had the higher-level financial officials.

Deputies' Discussion of Balance of Payments Adjustment

When the deputies, working in smaller groups, discussed the mechanism for achieving balance of payments adjustment, they were well aware that they still had to answer the key question of how, under a par value system, eliminating balance of payments disequilibria, especially of the major industrial members, could be made more effective. They knew that reliance on member governments of the Fund to assess fundamental disequilibrium in their external payments position and to change the par values for their currencies accordingly, as provided in the Bretton Woods system, had not worked satisfactorily. Nevertheless, they rejected the use of any objective quantitative indicators that would signal, like a traffic light, the need for adjustment without an accompanying analysis of a country's balance of payments situation. At most, they could agree that indicators be used only to trigger a consultation between the member and the international community, presumably the Fund.

At the same time they recognized that consultation with the international community had not in the past been fully effective in achieving balance of payments adjustment. More to the point, the Fund's consultations with its members had not provided a framework through which the Fund could suggest changes in exchange rates to its members, certainly not to its largest industrial members. Nor had these consultations prevented the large and chronic payments imbalances that had led to the breakdown of the Bretton Woods system. Most deputies realized that consultations between countries and the international community would have to be much more effective in the future. To this end most deputies favored continuing regular annual consultations between the Fund and its members and supplementing these regular consultations with some form of special consultations. Such special consultations could be brought about by developments in objective quantitative indicators.

To give them added importance they could be held at a high political level, for example, between the member and such financial officials as those serving as the deputies of the Committee of Twenty.

As the deputies discussed the adjustment process at this meeting in May 1973, some, especially those of the United States, were less concerned than they had been earlier about ways to effect changes in exchange rates inasmuch as floating rates for the major currencies now existed. Adjustment through the use of exchange rates had become much easier; it could take place readily in accordance with market forces. Moreover, floating rates meant that the topic of exchange rates was no longer forbidden at international gatherings of financial officials as in the past. Hence, the topic of indicators had become much less important to U.S. officials than it had been before March 1973. The question remained, however, of how to bring about changes in exchange rates in the event of a return to par values in the reformed system. Furthermore, since the exchange rate mechanism of the reformed system was also to permit floating exchange rates in some situations, the Committee of Twenty had to decide on rules regarding floating rates.

CONTROL OF DISEQUILIBRATING
CAPITAL MOVEMENTS STUDIED

A second working group of deputies, under the chairmanship of Mr. Kafka, returned in the third week of May to the topics of controls on capital movements, the rules for floating exchange rates, margins around exchange rates, and arrangements for currency intervention in exchange markets. These deputies had before them the report of the Technical Group on Disequilibrating Capital Flows, set up in March.

Technical Group on Disequilibrating Capital Flows

The Technical Group on Disequilibrating Capital Flows had met three times in April and May at the Fund's Office in Paris, under the chairmanship of Mr. Morse. The participants were all members of ministries of finance or treasuries or of central banks. The Group had as its terms of reference to define and analyze (i) sources of disequilibrating capital flows, (ii) technical problems involved in the use of measures to influence these capital flows, whether the measures were applied by countries individually or by countries working together collectively to control Eurocurrency markets, and (iii) measures to finance or offset disequilibrating capital flows.

The experts on this Technical Group examined first the various flows of short-term private capital. They discussed, for instance, leads and lags in commercial payments, the movement of funds through the banking system, and the actions of multinational corporations in initiating capital flows, taking up both the magnitudes of these flows and the reasons they occurred. They examined at length the attempts of several countries to control flows of private capital. For instance, they looked at

214

the experiences of Belgium and France with separate markets for current and for capital transactions. They also examined the experiences of Australia, the Federal Republic of Germany, Japan, the Netherlands, the United Kingdom, and the United States with other types of controls imposed directly on the movement of funds by banks and business enterprises. This examination included direct administrative controls used by the United Kingdom, the direct investment and voluntary credit restraint programs and the interest equalization tax used by the United States, the *Bardepot* of the Federal Republic of Germany, the exchange controls used by Japan against the outflow of resident capital, and the administrative controls used by Belgium and France to ensure the separation of the market for capital transactions and the market for current transactions.[2]

The Technical Group on Disequilibrating Capital Flows also examined the possibility that the Eurocurrency market added significantly to private capital flows and discussed the problems involved in having reserve requirements, which many countries applied to their banks' domestic currency liabilities, imposed on banks' foreign currency operations, that is, on their Eurocurrency deposits. The Group discussed the possibility of coordinated action by groups of countries to stem disequilibrating flows of private capital and then turned to a brief study of the flows of official funds and possible ways to limit them. It considered, too, what was involved in new arrangements for financing capital flows or in trying to offset them.

Deputies' Discussion of Capital Flows

Despite all this technical discussion of capital flows, when the deputies turned again, at their meeting in May 1973, to the problem of what to do about capital movements, the big question still remained whether controls on capital transactions should be included among the measures that countries should use in the reformed system to adjust their balance of payments positions. The U.S. deputies were still opposed as a general rule to the use of controls on capital but were now alone in this position.

Mr. Emminger suggested a compromise. When the Fund conducted consultations with members with serious imbalances in their payments positions, it should be able to recommend that the member either impose or, in some instances, abolish controls on capital movements. By adding the prospect of the abolition of controls on capital movements, Mr. Emminger hoped to win support of U.S. officials for a provision in the reformed system allowing the possible imposition of capital controls.

---

[2]The experiences of countries with various forms of controls on capital movements were also studied at the time by the Fund staff. See, for example, John Hewson and Eisuke Sakakibara, "The Impact of U.S. Controls on Capital Outflows on the U.S. Balance of Payments: An Exploratory Study," *Staff Papers*, Vol. 22 (March 1975), pp. 37–60; and Anthony Lanyi, "Separate Exchange Markets for Capital and Current Transactions," *Staff Papers*, Vol. 22 (November 1975), pp. 714–49.

OPPOSITE POSITIONS PERSIST ON
ASSET SETTLEMENT AND CONSOLIDATION

At their meeting in May 1973, the deputies, in two working groups, one chaired by Mr. Kafka and the other by Mr. Solomon, tried to come up with some principles on which they could agree with regard to asset settlement, the role of reserve currencies in the reformed system, and possible consolidation arrangements. The discussion revealed, however, that they remained poles apart on these subjects. Mr. Pierre-Brossolette continued to advocate the French position that any settlement system had to be mandatory to a significant degree. He reiterated that the uncontrolled growth of reserve currency balances had played an important part in the breakdown of the previous international monetary system. Even if the existing overhang of dollar balances was effectively removed through some kind of consolidation arrangement, a purely voluntary asset settlement system would run the risk that more currency balances, that is, dollar balances, might be accumulated in the future, again threatening the stability of any future international monetary system.

At the other extreme, Mr. Volcker questioned whether asset settlement was desirable at all and, if so, for what purposes. Noting that the currency component of world reserves since the early 1960s had grown from one fourth of total reserves to two thirds in 1972, he agreed that reserve currencies should play a much smaller role in the reformed system. He agreed further that SDRs should become a more important component of total reserves. But he questioned whether the use of national currencies could be eliminated entirely, as some officials of EC countries proposed. He argued also that future large accumulations of reserve currency balances could be avoided without direct regulation.

Mr. Volcker elaborated the U.S. position that some elasticity was needed in any settlement or convertibility system. Elasticity referred to settlement obligations that could be temporarily relaxed for countries with balance of payments deficits, thereby allowing the volume of world reserves to expand correspondingly. Allowance for some increase in official holdings of foreign exchange from time to time was necessary if countries with balance of payments surpluses held a large proportion of the reserves in other forms, such as gold, SDRs, or positions in the Fund. While a buildup in foreign exchange holdings should not be encouraged as a part of the basic structure of the reformed system, the effective operation of the system did not require banning all holdings of foreign exchange in amounts larger than what might narrowly be defined as working balances. The reserve mechanism needed flexibility to cope with periods of strain, especially when the level of international transactions was high compared with the level of world reserves. The United States wanted such elasticity in the supply of reserve currencies to occur quasi-automatically by permitting whatever increase in reserve currencies that resulted if countries did not convert all their currency balances. Mr. Volcker also repeated the U.S. position that asset settlement could not be considered independently from other aspects of the reformed system. Effective balance of payments adjustment based on reserve indicators was needed to ensure that the issuer of the currency to be converted would acquire the primary assets with which to meet future conversions. He did agree, however, that an asset settlement system was not inconsistent with the general beliefs of U.S. officials who were willing to consider some degree of settlement and convertibility, and even consolidation of past dollar balances, if the right terms could be agreed upon.

The issue of asset settlement and consolidation was basic. Most of the deputies from EC countries continued to regard control over the accumulation of reserve currencies as essential to reform. They regarded even the introduction of asset settlement for currently earned dollar balances as insufficient, since it coped with only part of the problem of excess liquidity. The large volume of dollar balances already existing also had to be reduced.

So strongly held were the extreme positions of the French and the U.S. deputies that Mr. Pierre-Brossolette, declaring that U.S. officials had reverted to their earlier positions and were not prepared to compromise, considered it fruitless for the deputies to proceed with developing an Outline of the reformed system. He stated to Mr. Morse, as Chairman of the deputies, that "we have reached an impasse." Mr. Morse, however, trying hard to advance some degree of consensus, replied that it was "the duty of the deputies to reach impasses." By this he meant that the statement of deputies' positions crystallized points of difference, so that the members of the Committee of Twenty, at ministerial level, would know what issues had to be resolved and could break the impasse.

The deputies then went on to examine a number of possible consolidation arrangements. They discussed a substitution account in the Fund by which dollars held by central banks and other official agencies would be exchanged for SDRs. They also discussed bilateral funding in which official dollar balances would be exchanged by the U.S. Government for some kind of securities that would not be as liquid as dollar balances. Here again, the deputies held different views on arrangements they preferred. Deputies from Belgium, France, and the Netherlands favored mandatory and substantial consolidation of existing balances and a limit on the size of working balances in reserve currencies that countries might hold. Deputies from Italy and from some developing members favored voluntary consolidation through a substitution facility of the Ossola-type, possibly with bilateral funding when countries held a substantial volume of excess reserves. In an interesting but unexpected statement, the deputy from India opposed the substitution of SDRs for existing balances of dollars on the ground that an overhang of SDRs would replace the overhang of dollars, possibly causing officials to be less willing in the future to allocate additional SDRs.

AGREEMENT ON DEVELOPMENT OF THE SDR

The deputies of the Committee of Twenty, like other financial officials, were almost unanimously agreed that the SDR was to be the principal reserve asset of the new international monetary system. They had also almost agreed that the SDR could be the common denominator of the system—that is, the unit of account, numeraire, standard or yardstick, whatever the term used—to serve as the common expression of exchange rates and the common measure of the value of reserve assets. Although it was not necessary to use a particular reserve asset as the unit of account for international transactions—theoretically, an abstract unit was possible—it was convenient to do so, and the SDR was the best primary asset to use. As described in Chapter 2, the Fund's accounts were already being expressed in terms of SDRs.

Most deputies agreed, too, that as the principal reserve asset the SDR had to be sufficiently attractive so that they and their successors would hold it in their reserves, yet not so attractive that they would be reluctant to use it to finance payments imbalances. They agreed quickly that certain features assigned to the SDR when it was first established ought to be liberalized. For example, they all supported widening the scope for transactions in SDRs between willing partners without the need for designating members obliged to receive SDRs. Most favored abolishing the limits placed on the acceptance of SDRs by monetary authorities and thought that the General Account of the Fund should be allowed to accept and use SDRs in place of gold or national currencies. A smaller number favored abolishing the reconstitution provisions. In addition, except for the French deputies, all the deputies agreed that the list of institutions that could hold SDRs should be expanded. Most of them, however, did not want private institutions to hold SDRs. They had in mind letting the various development finance institutions, such as the World Bank, the various regional development banks, and the BIS, become permissable holders of SDRs.

DISAGREEMENT ABOUT GOLD

Despite the obvious importance of provisions concerning gold in the reformed international monetary system, gold received little attention in the discussions of the Committee of Twenty until early 1973, when its price in private markets reached $90 an ounce, compared with the official price of $42.22 an ounce following the second devaluation of the dollar in February 1973. The large discrepancy between the market price and the official price meant that gold reserves held by central banks and other official agencies were not being used in international financial transactions. Central bank authorities did not want to sell gold to each other at the lower official price, nor did they want to depress the prices in private markets by offering their large supplies of officially held gold in those markets. Consequently, the use of gold as a reserve asset was immobilized.

There was considerable disagreement about how to solve "the gold problem," that is, the problem of what to do about the large stocks of gold held by central banks and other official agencies. The authorities of European central banks, especially the French authorities, who held very large amounts of gold, wanted to be able to sell gold to other monetary authorities at prices close to those prevailing in private markets. To effect such sales required that monetary authorities agree either to raise the official price of gold or to abolish the official price and the two-tier market arrangement set up in March 1968, letting all sales of gold, private and official, take place in a unified market. The authorities of European central banks were eager to have either of these actions agreed to even before the reformed international monetary system came into existence.

Accordingly, when the deputies of the Committee of Twenty took up the subject of gold at their fifth meeting, in May 1973, Mr. Pierre-Brossolette complained that the preliminary Outline of Reform prepared by the Bureau did not provide enough options about gold. There should be options to raise its official price or to abolish its official price. Mr. Browne of South Africa, which also had a particularly strong vested interest in any actions taken concerning gold, favored retaining gold as the numeraire of the system. He expected that even if the SDR became the principal reserve asset of the reformed system, over time gold would, and should, have a continuing important role. To win the support of the deputies from developing members for an increase in the official price of gold, Mr. Browne suggested that any increase in the official price be accompanied by arrangements to offset the resulting enlargement of the reserves of members with large amounts of gold and the resulting "maldistribution of liquidity." Such arrangements would involve diverting to developing members part of the profits resulting from the revaluation of gold.

All deputies other than those from France and South Africa, however, opposed raising the official price of gold. Officials of the United States had been opposed for the past few years since they wanted to phase gold out of the monetary system. They argued that an international monetary system based on gold or on other commodities had inherent instabilities and tensions. Speculative pressure in a thin and volatile commodity market readily led to prices for gold as a commodity, that is, for nonmonetary uses, that were much higher than the official price. This inevitably led to demands that the official price be raised. The greater the demand for gold, including for hoarding, the more unstable the official price.

Deputies of the United Kingdom, of several other developed members, and of most developing members also viewed an increase in the official price of gold as inimical to their objective of moving to an SDR-based international monetary system. With an increase in the official price of gold, the value of the world's total gold reserves would be greatly enlarged, and by virtue of its magnitude, gold would inevitably become the principal reserve asset of the system. Deputies from developing members, which held little or no gold, were concerned, moreover, about the inequity of an enlargement of gold reserves. They feared that a great increase in the value of gold reserves would substantially reduce the need for future allocations of SDRs.

Many deputies from both developed and developing members also doubted that a new official price could be found which could be held for any length of time. There was no way to determine a "correct price" and little prospect that any price selected would remain satisfactory for very long. Even with an enlarged value for their gold holdings, countries would continue to raise their reserve targets so that there could again be demands for another increase in the official price of gold. There would still be speculation of further increases in the official price. Hence, in the future no official price could last for over three decades, as had the previous official price of $35 an ounce. Most deputies were also uncertain whether the practical and political problems associated with sharing the profits from a revaluation of gold could be solved.

Deputies opposed to raising the official price had a number of alternative ways to deal with stocks of gold held by central banks. The U.S. and Canadian deputies wanted to retain the existing official price in terms of the SDR but to permit sales by central banks of their official holdings in private markets. In this way, gold would gradually flow out of reserves. Other deputies favored both abolishing the official price and permitting sales by monetary authorities in private markets. They had varying views, however, as to the timing and extent to which monetary authorities should be permitted to deal with each other at any price and to buy gold from private holders. Some favored limitations on official transactions in private markets so as not to upset private markets. Some deputies suggested different steps for the transitional period and for the reformed system. For example, in the transitional period before the reformed system came into effect, the March 1968 agreement could be modified to permit official sales in private markets, but on the introduction of the reformed system, the official price would be abolished.

DISCUSSIONS OF MEASURES AFFECTING TRADE

The Committee of Twenty was also asked, mainly at the instigation of U.S. officials, as described in Chapter 8, to consider trade questions and prospects for closer cooperation between the Fund and the GATT in supervising trade controls. The United States had insisted on the presence of the Director-General of the GATT and the Secretary-General of the OECD at the Committee of Twenty's deliberations on the grounds that since the Committee of Twenty was a temporary body, more permanent organizational arrangements had to be found and existing institutions reshaped to harmonize monetary and trade policies.

Discussion in the Fund

Realizing the importance to the United States of some permanent arrangement to coordinate monetary and trade policy, the Fund staff took an initiative on this subject toward the end of 1972, shortly after the Committee of Twenty began its deliberations. The staff circulated to the Executive Board a paper on multilateral surveillance of trade measures used for balance of payments purposes. The paper contained the conclusion that despite reviews by both the Fund and the GATT of numerous types of trade restrictions, tariffs, and the like, some important trade measures virtually escaped international surveillance. The staff, therefore, made the bold suggestion that the Fund's jurisdiction be extended to include trade measures used for balance of payments purposes and that much greater coordination be instituted between the Fund and the GATT with regard to trade measures.

The discussion of this staff paper in the Executive Board demonstrated that many member governments, as in the past, had great difficulty with any extension of the Fund's authority into trade. Consistent with the position of Australian authorities since the origin of the Fund and the GATT to resist "excessive" incursion into trade and exchange policies by international organizations, Mr. Brand objected that the suggestion for extending the Fund's jurisdiction into trade came from the staff of an international organization itself. The initiative would have been more appropriate, he thought, had it come from national governments. Mr. Viénot, too, had several objections to the extension of the Fund's authority to trade matters. In keeping with what other French officials were saying in the Committee of Twenty, he disliked the staff's presumption that emphasis ought to be given to balance of payments adjustment, as was implied when possible restrictions on trade and how to deal with them were considered. Mr. Kawaguchi, who had succeeded Mr. Suzuki as Executive Director for Japan on November 1, 1972, was concerned that because of the difficulty of separating trade measures used for balance of payments purposes from trade measures used for other purposes, such as for the protection of domestic industries, the Fund would have to engage in multilateral surveillance of all trade measures. Japan's officials were worried that there would be little, if anything, for the GATT to do.

Mr. Dale welcomed the staff's initiative on this topic and Mr. Lieftinck, agreeing with the staff that multilateral surveillance of trade measures had been inadequate, urged members to consider seriously whether the Fund should be permitted to extend its jurisdiction into trade. Nevertheless, because of objections to involvement by the Fund in trade, there was no further consideration in the Executive Board from 1972 to 1974 of the staff's proposals relating to the Fund's authority over trade measures.

Discussion in the Committee of Twenty

When the deputies of the Committee of Twenty discussed the topic of restrictions on trade for balance of payments purposes at their meeting in May 1973, they readily agreed that there would be a strong presumption in the reformed system against the use of restrictions on trade, or on any other current account transactions, to facilitate balance of payments equilibrium. Financial officials of all members continued to adhere to the philosophy that restrictions on imports or payments for invisibles to curb balance of payments deficits ought definitely to be shunned. Deputies from developing members argued that developing countries ought to be exempted from any restrictions on trade or on capital flows imposed by industrial countries for balance of payments reasons. They argued that larger exports would give developing countries more rapid economic growth and that industrial countries ought to solve payments imbalances, especially payments deficits, without reducing their development aid or tying aid to procurement in the donor countries and without reducing their imports from developing countries.

Although, in general, there was support for closer cooperation between the GATT and the Fund regarding surveillance over restrictions on trade, most deputies warned against blurring the lines of jurisdiction between the two institutions. Financial officials of nearly all members were still interested in keeping the functions and authority of the Fund and the GATT distinct and in ensuring that both institutions, while strengthened, had the same roles to perform as they had for the previous two decades.

DEGREE OF CONSENSUS ATTAINED

Because the deputies still disagreed on so many features of the reformed system even after their fifth meeting in May 1973, to most officials it seemed impossible to find general principles to be included in an Outline. But Mr. Morse was uniquely up to his task. Among his most estimable qualities was an ability to extract from a discussion, however divergent the views and however complex the issues, points on which agreement seemed possible and to ascertain the most promising directions in which to guide further discussions. Hence, in summarizing the deputies' positions he was able to find consensus emerging on a number of topics. With regard to balance of payments adjustment, he thought that the gap had narrowed between the position of the deputies of the United States with their emphasis on presumptive indicators and the position of most other deputies for heavy reliance on assessment of a country's balance of payments position. The need to make consultations on payments adjustment more effective in the future was also generally accepted. Additionally, most deputies envisaged some provision in the reformed system for "pressures" or "sanctions" by the international community to induce members to take action to reduce or eliminate disequilibria in their balance of payments. Mr. Morse believed that positions on asset settlement and consolidation and the management of currency reserves in a reformed system were also converging. The crucial question with regard to asset settlement was the degree of constraint which the reformed system should impose on reserve centers and on other countries.

Mr. Morse hoped, too, that some kind of trade-off might be arranged between officials of the United States and France who held the extreme positions. U.S. officials might agree, for example, to some kind of asset settlement system in exchange for acceptance by the officials of the EC countries of a reserve indicator system.

After the fifth meeting of deputies, Mr. Morse believed that progress had also been made on the development of the SDR. Almost all deputies favored making the

SDR the numeraire of the reformed system and many had been interested in cutting its link with gold. Only the French and the South African deputies argued for a rise in the official price of gold. With regard to the issue of a link between SDR allocations and development finance, the deputies would await the report of the Technical Group set up to examine this subject.

Seeing this degree of consensus on several principles of the reformed system, Mr. Morse believed that a more advanced version of the Outline of Reform could be produced in a few weeks. He planned that the deputies would meet again in July 1973, when the Committee of Twenty would also meet, to consider that version of the Outline and to resolve any differences still remaining.

ATTEMPTS AT COMPROMISE BY THE DEPUTIES

In June the Bureau prepared the revised version of the Outline. In June and July, the Technical Group on the SDR/Aid Link and Related Proposals met twice and gave its report to the deputies, who were meeting for the sixth time on July 11–13, 1973, at the Fund's headquarters.

Status of the Link

Participants in the Technical Group on the SDR/Aid Link and Related Proposals included representatives from central banks and from ministries of finance, who were referred to as officials from capitals to indicate that they worked full time in their home governments, as well as Executive Directors and Alternate Executive Directors of both the Fund and the World Bank. The Group reviewed the main arguments for and against the link. It also examined the main types of possible link arrangements, based on schemes developed by the Fund staff, and the technical issues involved in these schemes, such as how the amount, timing, distribution, and characteristics of SDRs would be affected by their introduction.

As the Technical Group held discussions, the same national positions that had been expressed several times before were repeated. As in the past, representatives of developing members unanimously favored the link. In close association with the nine Executive Directors elected exclusively by developing members, they had studied the various schemes for link arrangements described by the Fund staff. They agreed that the interests of developing members would be best served by type B schemes, which would change the formula for allocating SDRs so that developing members would receive a share of allocations larger than their share in Fund quotas. All developing members should benefit, but the distribution of SDRs should be relatively more favorable to the least developed members. The proposed extended facility and possible changes in the Fund's arrangements for the compensatory financing of export fluctuations and for buffer stock financing, which would increase access of developing members to the Fund's financial resources, were viewed not as a substitute for a link but as "welcome supplements."

Representatives of industrial members and of relatively more developed members held divergent views. Those of Belgium, France, Italy, and the United Kingdom favored a link and preferred schemes of types A or B, although representatives of France liked type B schemes better. Those of Australia, the Netherlands, and Japan were willing to go along with a link, if others agreed, but preferred type D schemes, in which developed members agreed to transfer to development finance institutions either part of the SDRs allocated to them or the equivalent in currencies. Representatives of the United States and of the Federal Republic of Germany remained skeptical of any link arrangement, although it began to appear that officials of the Federal Republic of Germany might go along with a link arrangement if other parts of the reformed system could be agreed.

A French Proposal for Pressure on Surplus Countries

Optimism that agreement might be reached on the main elements of the reformed system was suddenly renewed at the deputies' sixth meeting on July 11–13, 1973, when the French deputies came forward with an alternative proposal to that of the U.S. deputies for bringing some kind of pressure on countries with persistent balance of payments surpluses. The French paper started from the admission for the first time by French officials that to some extent the traditional systems of convertibility were "not perfectly symmetrical as to the constraints which bear on both the surplus and deficit countries." Pressure on "creditor countries" (the term customarily used by French officials for countries in surplus payments positions) to adjust appeared somewhat less strong than on "debtor countries" (that is, countries with payments deficits) which had to adjust when their reserves or borrowing prospects disappeared. French officials, however, did not like the U.S. proposal for remedying this asymmetry. The U.S. proposal envisaged the determination of convertibility points on either side of a base level of reserves for each country beyond which countries accumulating reserves could no longer offer holdings of national currencies for conversion. French officials had three main objections to this proposal. First, since it would still make possible an accumulation of reserves in national currencies, it did not fulfill the objective of limiting the outstanding amounts of national currencies used as reserves. Second, it would not make the system symmetrical since debtor countries (the United States in particular) whose currency was widely used in international payments could eventually finance their deficits through an accumulation of debts rather than through a loss of reserves. Third, it would not satisfactorily solve the adjustment problem, the objective sought by U.S. officials, because it did not induce either creditors or debtors to correct their payments imbalances.

The alternative put forward by the French deputies in July 1973 was that, while debtor countries would have strict convertibility obligations, creditor countries would not be authorized to convert foreign exchange holdings beyond a certain amount if they held "very large amounts" of foreign exchange holdings. As an indication of "very large amounts," the French officials suggested a magnitude ten times the amount of a country's quota in the Fund. Rather than being permitted to convert their excess holdings of foreign exchange (which like other holdings were to be remitted to the Fund) officials would be subjected by the Fund to negative interest rates on such holdings. These negative interest rates would be progressive, increasing with the amount of such excess holdings. In brief, the French proposal was to have the Fund tax excess accumulations of reserves held by countries with prolonged balance of payments surpluses.

This suggestion from the French deputies could be considered a proposal for a strong sanction against creditor countries and was intended as an important concession to the U.S. position. Hope emerged among many other deputies, Executive Directors, and the Fund management and staff that agreement might be reached on one of the most difficult issues in the reformed system: whether countries with persistent balance of payments surpluses would be subject to pressures imposed by the international community and what the nature of the pressures might be. In contrast to their previous stance, French officials now agreed that pressures could be applied against creditors. Not only did the French proposal yield a basis for compromise, but it indicated that officials had not yet given up hope that a reformed system might be achieved. The Bureau seemed justified in its decision to continue to push ahead even after the introduction of a floating rate regime a few months earlier.

Status of Consolidation Arrangements

After their sixth meeting on July 11–13, 1973, the deputies passed along to their ministers (the Committee of Twenty) six questions on which they themselves were unable to reach consensus; these questions are listed in the section directly below. The deputies' discussion of consolidation arrangements, which they did not try to get the Committee of Twenty to deal with further at the time, is of particular interest since it suggested that countries, even with large reserves, were not ready to press for substantial reduction of their dollar balances. What came out for the first time in their discussions of consolidation arrangements—whether through a substitution account in the Fund or through some bilateral funding arrangements between the holders of dollar balances and the governments—was that the magnitude of dollar balances likely to be submitted for consolidation was as important an issue as the types of consolidation arrangements. Excess reserves were to be consolidated, but officials of most countries were unlikely to regard their countries as having excess reserves. Yet, for any consolidation operation to succeed in reducing the amount of excess liquidity in the monetary system, virtually all countries would have to participate to a significant degree. Mr. Emminger expressed doubts that the Federal Republic of Germany would be willing to enter into any large-scale consolidation because of his country's need for reserves to meet possible reversals of capital inflows and to convert foreign-held balances of deutsche mark.

Hence, after this discussion by the deputies of consolidation arrangements, the topic of a substitution account was more or less dropped, although officials generally expressed support for some type of voluntary substitution facility in the future.

ENCOURAGING TONE AT THE
COMMITTEE OF TWENTY MEETING

The third meeting of the Committee of Twenty was held on July 30–31, 1973, in Washington, in the Eugene R. Black Auditorium of the World Bank. The meeting was to be a working session aimed, like the deputies' meeting three weeks before, at achieving agreement. No communiqué was to be issued, although there was a brief press release.

The Committee had the following six questions to answer.

First, should a reserve indicator be the main factor used to determine a presumption of need for action to adjust a payments disequilibrium, unless the international community was to decide otherwise? Or should general assessment of the payments position be the main technique, with reserve movements being one of several factors considered in the assessment? Since the proposal by the United States for the use of reserve indicators had been put forward in November 1972, monetary authorities had come to agree that a disproportionate movement in official reserves was a good indicator and might be even the best single indicator for identifying an instance of payments imbalance and for setting a consultation in motion. They also seemed to have reached agreement that, even with the use of a reserve indicator, there would have to be a thorough assessment of the causes and nature of any country's balance of payments position before any decision was made by the international community. Now, officials had to decide the precise role to be played by a reserve indicator as against a general assessment. U.S. officials still wanted an objective quantitative neutral signal of the need for balance of payments action that did not require international "argument" about the need for action.

Second, should the reformed system provide for application of restrictions on trade and other current transactions as one of the possible pressures used against countries that failed to take adequate corrective measures for persistent balance of payments surpluses? A large majority of financial officials had come to accept the need for some pressures in the reformed system, some of which could be financial pressures. Even French officials had come to accept this idea. But whether pressures should extend in extreme cases of persistent surplus to the imposition by other countries of restrictions on trade and current account transactions against countries with surpluses—the position taken by the United States—was still far from accepted.

Third, should reserve currency countries be subject to mandatory convertibility, or should convertibility be voluntary as in the Bretton Woods system? A considerable number of officials, particularly those from EC countries and from Japan, insisted on a tight convertibility system in which all countries, including reserve centers, would be required to settle their payments deficits fully by giving up reserve assets rather than by increasing their liabilities. In such a system there would be some limitation on the rights of other countries to accumulate new reserve currency balances. In sharp contrast, U.S. officials and the officials of developing members preferred a more elastic settlement or convertibility system, in which reserve centers would be required to settle payments deficits by giving up reserve assets only to the extent that other countries requested them to do so.

Fourth, how should the SDR be valued and what interest rate should prevail on it? The relatively ready agreement by the deputies of the Committee of Twenty on a number of liberalizations of the SDR to enhance its status as the principal reserve asset of the reformed system was paralleled by agreement on these liberalizations by the Executive Directors. Hence, by July 1973, a number of changes in the SDR were fairly generally accepted, although debate still attended the question of how the SDR still valued in terms of gold should be revalued. A change in valuation and a determination of a rate of interest were needed not only for the reformed system but also for the use of SDRs in current transactions. At their July 1973 meeting, the Committee of Twenty was to consider the question of the valuation of the SDR and a rate of interest for it.

Fifth, should transactions in gold between central bank authorities be effected only at the official price for gold or should the official price be abolished and central bank authorities be permitted to buy and sell gold at a market-related price? French and South African officials wanted decisions both with regard to gold in the reformed system and for the use of gold in current transactions. Officials of most other members, however, believed that action with regard to gold could wait. Hence, some decision was needed on the priority to be given the question of gold.

Sixth, should a link be established between SDR allocations and development finance?

Compromises Suggested by Committee Members

The Committee of Twenty met in working session in July 1973 but answered none of these six questions. However, as there had been in the deputies' meeting, three weeks before, there was a widespread search for compromise. Mr. Aichi suggested, for instance, that ample credit facilities might be made available to reserve centers if a tight convertibility system was to be agreed. Mr. Giscard d'Estaing repeated the French suggestion that members be required to deposit their excess reserves in the Fund and that these reserves be subjected to progressive negative interest charges. Mr. Schmidt repeated the suggestion of the officials of the Federal Republic of Germany made at the meeting of deputies that a formal obligation be adopted stating that reserves had to be maintained within a specified band, thus limiting the degree to which surplus countries would accumulate reserves. He also pursued a suggestion made by the Fund staff that asset settlement be restricted to the currencies within the multicurrency intervention system. Mr. Shultz indicated that the United States would be prepared to abandon the reserve indicator proposal in the form originally suggested, provided that other ways could be found to put backbone into the adjustment process, and indicated that the French alternative proposal might indeed be acceptable. Mr. Turner proposed detailed arrangements for the combined use of reserve indicators and general assessment to determine the need for adjustment.

On the question of convertibility, several compromises were suggested. Some officials, like Mr. Aichi, would introduce elasticity into the arrangements for convertibility by the provision of additional credit facilities, by possible relaxation through international agreement of the normal settlement obligations, and by the introduction of convertibility or inconvertibility points. Another suggestion was for a mixed convertibility system. Under this system, a sufficiently large number of countries would undertake, in the context of multicurrency intervention, to settle imbalances among themselves fully in reserve assets. Other countries would have the right, but not the obligation, to present currency balances for conversion either bilaterally or multilaterally through the Fund. In this way, countries whose currencies were held as reserves would be participants in a symmetrical intervention system with full asset settlement and at the same time could have some elasticity in their settlements with the rest of the world. Fund surveillance would be necessary to prevent excessive use of such elasticity.

Mr. Barber, Guido Carli (Italy), W.F. Duisenberg (Netherlands), Mr. Feldt, and Shehu Shagari (Nigeria) all put forward compromise suggestions on the issue of adjustment. One proposal was that the amended Articles of Agreement contain a provision under which members would be obliged to maintain equilibrium in their balance of payments and the Fund would be charged with enforcing this provision. A similar, more specific proposal was for a provision to oblige members to keep their official reserves within limits agreed by the Fund.

With regard to the question of pressures, there was widespread acceptance in principle that some form of pressures should be available, and some willingness to accept financial pressures, as in the French proposal. But differing views were expressed with regard to other types of pressures. Messrs. De Clercq, Delfim Netto, Feldt, and Turner were willing to go along with the U.S. proposal for the imposition of restrictions on imports from countries in persistent payments surplus as a pressure of the last resort, but other ministers, including Mr. Carli and Janko Smole (Yugoslavia), were against the use of restrictions as pressures. Mr. Chavan, José López Portillo (Mexico), Alfredo Gómez Morales (Argentina), and Tan Siew Sin (Malaysia) again pleaded for the exemption of developing members from any pressures and sanctions that might be imposed. They were worried not only about trade sanctions but even about the prospect of the publication of a Fund report criticizing the balance of payments position or policies of their countries.[3]

With regard to the valuation of the SDR and its yield, members of the Committee still held divergent positions. The majority supported a valuation of the

---

[3]Additional descriptions of the discussions in the Committee of Twenty of pressures in a reformed system can be found in Gold, "'Pressures' and Reform of the International Monetary System," in *Legal and Institutional Aspects*, pp. 182–216.

SDR based on a basket of some 15 or 20 currencies (more currencies than those traditionally held as reserves) and an interest rate related to the market rates of interest on holdings of those currencies. French, Japanese, and South African officials supported a "strong SDR," a basket made up of only the strongest currencies, and a high interest rate for the SDR.

U.S. officials wanted the SDR expressed as an average of virtually all currencies in such a way that devaluations and revaluations would cancel each other out, giving a constant value. They also favored a low interest rate on the SDR. Mr. Shultz explained why. A high rate of interest on the SDR would induce capital outflow from the United States. He reasoned that if the rate of interest on the SDR was the average of market rates of interest for a selected group of currencies, as proposed by the Fund staff and favored by financial officials of several other members, the rate of interest on some currencies would be above and on other currencies below the rate of interest given to the SDR. Since 1945 interest rates in the United States had tended to be lower than in other countries and might well remain below the world average in the future. Thus, the average rate of interest on the SDR would be above the rate prevailing in U.S. capital markets. Central bankers would then be induced to borrow in U.S. capital markets at comparatively low rates of interest in order to obtain SDRs, which carried a higher rate. The result would be a continuous outflow of dollars and a perpetual balance of payments problem for the United States, created at least in part by a higher interest rate on the SDR. To make matters worse, the more successful the U.S. authorities were in curbing domestic inflation and holding down interest rates, the greater would be the outflow of capital and the larger the U.S. balance of payments deficit. The same problem would exist for any country with a major capital market in which interest rates were below the world average. Mr. Shultz believed, therefore, that the rate of interest on the SDR should be below the level in any country which had major capital markets open for borrowing by officials abroad.

It was essential that the issue of the valuation of the SDR and of the rate of interest be resolved even for the conduct of current international transactions. The issue was to come up again at the next three meetings of the Committee of Twenty, and agreement was finally reached in June 1974.

With regard to gold, the members of the Committee of Twenty took the same view as had the deputies at their meetings earlier in July. U.S. officials still preferred any measures that phased gold out of the system, while F.D. Crean (Australia) and others cautioned that members of the Committee ought to be realistic: gold would in any event continue to be a part of official reserves in the immediate future. Since gold reserves were presently immobilized, a situation which could not continue indefinitely, speculation about the future of gold was inevitable and unsettling to the international monetary system. Tension should be reduced by permitting official transactions at market-related prices and by abolishing the fixed official price and the two-tier arrangement.

With regard to the link, U.S. officials continued to oppose any arrangement. At the July 1973 meeting of the Committee of Twenty, Mr. Shultz declared that the United States still had grave reservations about the link and introduced Mr. Burns to state why. In effect, he was suggesting that U.S. opposition to the link was primarily that of Mr. Burns who argued that the link would undermine confidence in the SDR and would not be in the best interests of the developing members, since it would give the U.S. Congress an excuse not to vote for aid appropriations. Officials of the Federal Republic of Germany also continued to be against the link, although Mr. Schmidt did state that it would be possible for him to consider a link if satisfactory arrangements were made for all other aspects of the reform, especially the establishment of control over international liquidity.

Although none of the six questions were resolved by the Committee of Twenty, financial officials were more optimistic than ever that the Committee of Twenty's deliberations were proving fruitful. As he closed the meeting, Mr. Wardhana called attention to the constructive spirit in which the members of the Committee had faced these difficult questions and their general willingness to consider workable solutions. In a press conference after the meeting, Mr. Volcker stated that he thought that the Committee would be able to publish a written document—an Outline of Reform—by the time of the Annual Meeting in September. Cabling the results of the meeting to the staff in the Fund's offices in Paris and Geneva, Mr. Schweitzer reported that the tone of the meeting was encouraging, with most members of the Committee showing a willingness to compromise on the long-standing questions of the balance of payments adjustment mechanism and asset settlement.

CHAPTER

13

Reform Efforts Collapse

B UOYED BY THE PROSPECT OF AGREEMENT following the various compromise suggestions made at the July 1973 meeting of the Committee of Twenty, the six men making up the Bureau appreciably stepped up their efforts in July and August. The deputies planned to have their seventh meeting at the Fund's office in Paris on September 5–7, just ahead of the 1973 Annual Meeting scheduled for later that month in Nairobi. The Bureau saw the deputies' meeting as crucial. The time had come when the deputies would have to decide whether to put the key issues to their finance ministers for resolution. More explicitly, it was now time to test whether U.S. and French officials, who had been taking opposite positions on exchange rates, on asset settlement, and on gold, were willing to adapt their positions in order to reach agreement.

All along members of the Bureau had considered themselves not only in a servicing or technical role, but also in a negotiating role, attempting to reconcile the positions of U.S. and European officials. They characterized the extreme positions as "automatic," and "discretionary." As they saw it, U.S. officials wanted payments adjustment to be virtually automatic—exchange rate changes should be more or less automatically touched off by some kind of quantitative objective indicator—but also wanted convertibility or asset settlement to be discretionary—to depend on the circumstances of the member concerned. European officials, in contrast, wanted asset settlement to be virtually automatic—convertibility was to be virtually assured—but they wanted balance of payments adjustment to be discretionary—to depend on the circumstances of the country concerned. Until the middle of 1973, the Bureau tried hard to move both U.S. and European officials away from these extreme automatic or discretionary features and toward more presumptive features. Presumptive features were those in which actions, such as a change in an exchange rate or the conversion of dollar balances, would be presumed necessary. Necessary actions would then be taken, unless the Fund were to decide otherwise. In other words, there could be international consultation on whether the presumed actions should be allowed to take place.

The members of the Bureau hoped that by the time the deputies met in Paris in September 1973 Mr. Volcker and Mr. Pierre-Brossolette, who held the two extreme positions, would agree to put to their finance ministers the tough political decisions needed to reconcile their differences. In an attempt to get the deputies to agree on specific mechanisms for adjustment and for convertibility or asset settlement, the Bureau worked for days drawing up models to illustrate how presumptive features in a reformed system could work. One model explained how adjustment might work and the other how a system of convertibility or asset settlement might work.

MODELS FOR ADJUSTMENT AND FOR CONVERTIBILITY

The model for adjustment was an attempt to integrate the position advanced by U.S. officials with the positions taken by officials of other countries. It was criticized as leaning excessively toward the U.S. position, and one member of the Bureau later admitted that it probably did.[1]

It would appear, however, that the model provided a good deal less than U.S. officials sought, at least originally. In the model, countries would commit themselves to pursue policies which would keep their official reserves within limits, or "reserve points." These limits would be agreed from time to time presumably by the Fund. Thus, in effect, a "reserve indicator structure" would be established. There would be special examination of countries with payments imbalances that individually or collectively had significant international repercussions, but only if a disproportionate movement of reserves had occurred, or if the Managing Director suggested such an examination. In other words, movements of reserves could trigger consultation. The special examination would involve, however, assessment of all relevant factors in the country's balance of payments, though the movement of reserves compared with the established reserve limits would be considered of major importance. Policies that the country had already adopted would also be included in the assessment. Following this assessment, the Executive Board might call upon the country to adopt or reinforce policies to correct its payments imbalance.

The model also provided for the application of pressures. Thus if after a consultation a country's reserves remained for some time in excess of the given indicator point, the country would be subjected to graduated financial pressures, unless the Executive Board decided otherwise. If the country's reserves still remained beyond this given point, and if the Executive Board decided that the country had failed to take adequate corrective action, the Executive Board might recommend to a committee of Governors that stronger pressures be applied. In any event, if a country's primary reserve assets reached a predetermined point, the country would be required to deposit further accruals of currency reserves with the Fund and to pay negative interest on them.

While the adjustment model leaned toward the U.S. position, the model for a convertibility or asset settlement system leaned toward the European position. But

---

[1]Robert Solomon, *The International Monetary System, 1945–1976: An Insider's View* (cited in fn. 7 of Chap. 9 above), p. 256.

this model too was a compromise. Presumably it provided less than European authorities wanted, if their hostility against the model is any indication.

The model was for a mixed system, blending the basic objectives emphasized in the Committee of Twenty's earlier discussions of convertibility. There were three such objectives. First, convertibility obligations would be symmetrical, that is, the same obligations for conversion of currency balances should apply to reserve centers and to other countries. Second, management of the volume of global liquidity would be improved. The uncontrolled growth of reserve currency balances was especially to be avoided. Third, elasticity would be adequate so that the volume of world reserves could grow as international financial transactions increased. Consistent with these objectives, countries would have maximum freedom to choose the composition of their reserves.

To meet these objectives the model provided that a sufficiently large group of countries would establish a system of multicurrency intervention in exchange markets, similar to the narrow margin arrangements in the EC snake. These countries would settle payments imbalances among themselves fully in reserve assets. Other countries, which would still use primarily dollars to intervene in exchange markets, would have the right but not the obligation to present currency balances for conversion either bilaterally (directly to the reserve center that issued the currency) or multilaterally (to the Fund). The choice would be subject, however, to a procedure in which the Fund could request countries to convert balances.

Complete convertibility, as European officials wanted, would thus apply between countries participating in the multicurrency intervention system. Convertibility between other countries would be less strict, however, permitting developing countries the freedom they wanted in their reserve composition and providing elasticity to the system. The arrangements for convertibility for countries not in the multicurrency intervention system would allow the further accumulation of some balances in national currencies if countries wanted to have such additional balances, a feature U.S. officials favored. Because the system provided for future growth of reserve currencies, provision was also needed to avoid the undue growth of global liquidity in the form of reserve currency balances about which European officials had been concerned. To this end, the model specified that the Fund could require countries to present currency balances for conversion into primary reserve assets; by such action the Fund could prevent aggregate holdings of particular reserve currencies from rising above an internationally agreed level.

In permitting elasticity in convertibility arrangements, the convertibility or asset settlement model developed by the Bureau even used the idea put forward by U.S. officials of a convertibility point beyond which no further balances could be presented for conversion into primary reserve assets. However, to take account of the objections of European officials to the convertibility point or convertibility limit, the model suggested that the convertibility point be presumptive rather than automatic. In other words, rather than an automatic limit on convertibility, convertibility would be stopped unless the Fund decided otherwise.

233

The model also allowed for a possible substitution facility in the Fund. It included a provision that if no arrangement was made for a large initial consolidation of the overhang of existing reserve currency balances, some mechanism would be needed for dealing with "old" balances. A substitution facility would enable reserve centers faced with conversion demands to purchase SDRs from the Fund. It could enable countries to present currency balances to the Fund for conversion rather than directly to the country of issue. Later settlement would be made between the Fund and the country of issue. The substitution facility could be used, too, for consolidation of currently earned reserve currency balances.

CONTINUED DISAGREEMENT ON ADJUSTMENT AND ON CONVERTIBILITY

When the deputies met in Paris in September 1973, they fully realized that their willingness to come to agreement was now being put to a final test. Nevertheless, agreement seemed unlikely from the outset. While several deputies supported the two models prepared by the Bureau, others rejected them. Hence, disagreement on adjustment and on convertibility continued. Discussions were heated and intense. Deputies favoring the Bureau's models were Messrs. Hood, Brown, Mitchell, and Volcker and, with some reservations, Svend Andersen (Denmark). In Mr. Volcker's view, the Bureau succeeded in catching the essence of what he thought a workable and satisfactory solution to the adjustment problem through proposals reflecting the spirit of the understanding reached at the meeting of the Committee of Twenty in July. In Mr. Volcker's words, there was "just no possibility of the United States accepting mush on the adjustment side and good red meat on the convertibility side, the sort of balance some deputies seemed to be envisaging." Mr. Volcker pointed out, too, that the pressures contained in the Bureau's model were, in his view, "rather mild."

In contrast to Mr. Volcker's position, the deputies from the EC countries and from Japan had considerable difficulty with both models. Deputies from the EC countries criticized the adjustment model as too biased in favor of the U.S. position. They objected especially to the use of reserve indicators to be applied in a presumptive way to trigger policy actions and to serve as a basis for graduated pressures. Mr. Ossola, for instance, tried to redraft the description of the models and in effect change their substance, bringing them closer into line with the basic balance indicator proposed by the Italian authorities and presented to the deputies months before, which in his view was already a compromise solution. He objected that the convertibility model used a system of multicurrency intervention, which was really a technical device designed for intervention in exchange markets, to loosen the convertibility obligations of countries with deficits.

Mr. Oort raised several questions about the adjustment model which showed that he, too, was troubled by the idea of relating movements in reserves to the application of graduated pressures to induce adjustment. In his view, the measurement of reserves to be used for reserve limits, or reserve points, was too simple because it did not take into account the important questions, such as whether to use net or gross reserves, considered in the Technical Group on Indicators.

Mr. Pöhl objected to the adjustment model because it dealt more with pressures to be applied to countries with balance of payments surpluses than with measures to be taken by countries with balance of payments deficits. He disliked the convertibility model for a similar reason; it contained many ways of adding elasticity to the convertibility system, which suited countries with balance of payments deficits, but which were unsatisfactory for countries that maintained discipline and stricter internal policies and hence were in balance of payments surplus.

Mr. Pierre-Brossolette concentrated his attention on the convertibility model, again emphasizing, as had French officials all along, that convertibility would play a far more fundamental role in achieving balance of payments equilibrium among the major industrial countries than would the establishment of a system of indicators or improvement in the consultation procedure, which was what assessment amounted to. Mr. Pierre-Brossolette made explicit that the French position directly opposed the U.S. position. French officials were convinced that tight convertibility arrangements would lead to balance of payments adjustment; U.S. officials were convinced that adjustment arrangements had to be sufficiently strong so as to make convertibility feasible. In the view of French officials, the only alternative to strict convertibility was floating exchange rates: countries that failed to reimburse their creditors would cease to defend their currencies on exchange markets and would let their currencies float instead. Blaming U.S. officials for failure to compromise, Mr. Pierre-Brossolette argued that in the course of the deliberations of the Committee of Twenty over the previous nine months, many members had modified their views, some substantially; only officials of the United States continued to adhere to their original positions. Hence, compromise acceptable to all had not been possible. Noting that a stronger balance of payments position for the United States had developed during 1973, Mr. Pierre-Brossolette expressed hope that it would enable U.S. officials to feel more comfortable about re-establishing convertibility for the dollar.

Mr. Inamura joined the deputies of France, Italy, and the Netherlands in expressing doubt about both the adjustment and the convertibility models that the Bureau had prepared. He disliked the provision in the adjustment model for the application of pressures on countries that had what were considered excess reserves. The need to adjust should rather be determined by assessment of the country's entire balance of payments position. With regard to the model for convertibility or asset settlement, Japanese officials believed, and Mr. Inamura emphasized, that convertibility ought to involve a multicurrency intervention system and asset settlement through the Fund. The model provided for such an arrangement. However, Japanese officials considered, and the model lacked this stipulation, that whether or not they participated in a multicurrency intervention system, all countries should be obliged to carry out full and mandatory settlement through the Fund of any increases in the balances of their respective currencies held as official reserves by other countries. The Japanese position, however, still distinguished countries that participated in a multicurrency intervention system and those which did not. A participant would be required to demand settlement of the full amount of increases in its holdings of other countries' currencies; a nonparticipant with a balance of payments surplus would have the right, but not the obligation, to request settlement. Any elasticity needed in the system could come through a collective decision by the international community.

Japanese officials also doubted the wisdom of applying negative interest rates on the currency reserves deposited with the Fund, as proposed by the French deputies. Following up the suggestion made by Mr. Aichi at the Committee of Twenty on July 1, Mr. Inamura repeated that Japanese officials would go along with new types of credit facilities to assist countries in deficit to meet their mandatory settlement obligations.

Although deputies from developing members supported the adjustment and convertibility models, they were interested primarily in pointing out that certain exemptions from the usual rules should be made for developing members. As before, Mr. Prasad stated that any mechanism or technique to facilitate balance of payments adjustment or to enforce convertibility ought to be consistent with the broader goals and objectives of economic policy, as stated in the original Article I of the Fund's Articles of Agreement. External payments of Fund members were not merely supposed to be balanced; they were to be balanced at high and rising levels of employment and real economic growth. Any adjustment process which did not serve these broader goals was excessively concerned with mechanisms and would be regarded as unsatisfactory by developing members.

Adolfo C. Diz (Argentina) welcomed two features of the models that he considered new and important. First, attention would be focused exclusively on those instances of payments imbalance which "individually or collectively had significant international repercussions." Presumably, the payments positions of developing members did not have "significant international repercussions." Second, account would be taken of the special difficulties that developing members faced in achieving prompt balance of payments adjustment without severely damaging their long-term development programs.

Anwar Ali, from the Saudi Arabian Monetary Agency, noted that the deputies had accepted the unique situation of the major oil producing countries. They recognized that it would not be appropriate to apply the adjustment process to these countries whenever they had balance of payments surpluses or to regard reserve accumulations by these countries in the same way as reserves of other countries with payments surpluses.

Thus, deputies from developing members looked upon the models for adjustment and for convertibility almost entirely from the point of view of how the arrangements would affect developing members.

An Opportunity Missed

Although officials hoped that the September 1973 meeting of the deputies would be decisive, it proved inconclusive. The deputies still did not agree on how to make adjustment work more effectively through the use to be made of indicators, consultations, pressures, or controls on capital flows and still did not agree on whether convertibility or asset settlement arrangements should be mandatory or voluntary, centralized in the Fund or effected bilaterally between countries. Neither did they agree about the form of any short-run elasticity needed in the asset settlement system, nor about the nature and degree of international surveillance and management of such elasticity.

Realizing that this meeting was probably his last opportunity to get agreement on the reformed system, Mr. Morse appealed to the deputies to reach some kind of compromise. He reminded the deputies that in July the Committee of Twenty had requested them to prepare for another Committee of Twenty meeting in Nairobi in September and that they were obliged to reach common ground at least on the two issues of adjustment and convertibility. Mr. Morse emphasized that failure to agree would mean that the work of the Committee of Twenty could not go forward. He pointed out that there could be adverse public reaction to a failure to agree, which would disturb existing exchange markets and damage still further the already disrupted international monetary system.

To facilitate consensus, Mr. Morse defended the two models as being as balanced as one could reasonably hope. He pointed out that the adjustment model was in line with the viewpoints that members of the Committee of Twenty and the deputies had expressed in July. Although use was to be made of a structure of reserve indicators, there was to be an assessment by the Fund before the need for adjustment would be established. Within this assessment, major importance would be attached to movements of reserves, but all other relevant indicators and factors would be taken into account. Graduated financial pressures on both surplus and deficit countries would be applicable only after the Fund had assessed the situation and requested the member to act. Such pressures would be mild at first and only as the situation deteriorated would more severe financial pressures of the type suggested by the French deputies be applied.

Mr. Morse also defended the convertibility model as being in accord with views expressed by members of the Committee of Twenty at their July meeting. The general objective of the Committee of Twenty was to return to a system of convertibility under which balance of payments deficits would normally be settled in reserve assets, and global liquidity would not be increased by enlarging holdings of reserve currencies. Although the deputies had debated at length how much elasticity should be in the settlement system, it seemed that the deputies had agreed that some elasticity was needed to take account of the capital movements which could be expected even in a better functioning international monetary system. Without some elasticity, there would be little chance of maintaining an exchange rate regime based on par values. While some elasticity might be provided by credit in the form of central swaps and of drawings on the Fund, additional elasticity was needed to cover secular growth in the holdings of reserve currencies. As world trade grew, it was not unreasonable to assume that working balances should grow correspondingly. Ways to achieve elasticity would, of course, be subject to international control.

Mr. Morse's appeals to the deputies for consensus failed to produce agreement. Although the models were revised during the meeting, the deputies were unable to resolve the basic issues of adjustment and convertibility. Other outstanding questions that the deputies had considered at their earlier meetings, such as the nature of consolidation arrangements for existing dollar balances, how to value the SDR, what to do about gold, and whether and how to transfer real resources to developing countries through the international monetary system also remained unsettled.

In a perceptive statement, Mr. Whitelaw took the view that the best outcome was that the international monetary system would reform itself. As time progressed, the deputies might be able, in Mr. Whitelaw's words, "to divine what was practical and what was not, rather than to reason it out around a conference table." He underscored his point by noting that Australian authorities saw adjustment of the disequilibria in world payments at the heart of the reform exercise and that in practice such an adjustment was currently taking place as a result of the changes in exchange rates. Accordingly, the major change needed in the international monetary system would soon occur even without reform negotiations.

The plan of the Bureau to get agreement among the deputies of the Committee of Twenty by working out models on adjustment and on asset settlement thus failed. According to Mr. Morse the two principal parties, Mr. Volcker and Mr. Pierre-Brossolette, seemed to have decided not to put the hard issues to their political superiors, Mr. Shultz and Mr. Giscard d'Estaing, for final resolution. In effect, further efforts at compromise were ruled out.

Additional concessions by the French authorities were probably impossible at the time. At the political level, President Pompidou, like President de Gaulle before him, still held the views that only fixed exchange rates could be accepted, that the U.S. dollar could no longer be an inconvertible reserve currency, and that some way had to be found to value gold reserves at a higher price. Mr. Pierre-Brossolette, according to Mr. Morse, was cooperative and understanding about the need to work toward a mutual compromise, but had little room to maneuver. In addition, at the September 1973 meeting, the French deputies were deliberately leaving some key questions open so that Mr. Giscard d'Estaing might, if he wished, make additional proposals in Nairobi.

Circumstances also made concessions by the U.S. authorities difficult. Once floating rates had come into existence, Mr. Shultz, who was ideologically in favor of them, wanted to give them a chance. Other officials in the U.S. Administration seem to have taken little interest in a reformed international monetary system. President Nixon was beset by the Watergate scandal. Henry A. Kissinger had just been nominated as Secretary of State and, as he recalls in his book, *Years of Upheaval*, was mainly interested in trying to consolidate the peace in Indochina and to solidify a Moscow-Washington-Peking triangle. In any event, Mr. Shultz's inclination to give up the negotiations in favor of floating rates was bound to be acceptable both to U.S. officials and to the banking and business community. He himself was an economist and had started the negotiations for reform from a conciliatory position inclined toward par values and some dollar convertibility.

According to Mr. Kafka, Vice-Chairman of the deputies of the Committee of Twenty, at the meeting in Paris in September 1973 officials first surmised that the U.S. authorities wanted "absolute freedom to float." For example, when the discussions turned to the subject of defining some possible objective conditions or guidelines to be used for floating exchange rates, Mr. Volcker maintained that it was impossible to define these terms. He argued further that so long as a country did not engage in "disruptive exchange practices," such as competitive depreciation or exchange rate manipulation, it should be free to float its currency. This position came as a shock to the other deputies, especially since they were still thinking about the possibility of agreeing on a system based on stable but adjustable par values.

Mr. Morse believed that compromise with European officials by U.S. officials could also have been difficult because Mr. Shultz and Mr. Volcker held different views. While Mr. Shultz was not inclined toward fixed exchange rates or a link between SDRs and development finance, which Mr. Volcker might have accepted, Mr. Volcker wanted some mechanism for inducing balance of payments adjustment by countries in surplus and wanted to phase gold out of the system. Since the positions of Mr. Shultz and Mr. Volcker covered the four major issues of reform, there was little room for compromise.

Still another possible reason for the failure of the deputies in September 1973 was that Mr. Emminger and other deputies were increasingly resigned to the inevitability of floating rates and had given up on trying to push for a reformed system based on adjustable par values. Yet they knew that French officials remained insistent on par values. In these circumstances, it seemed pointless to keep on arguing.

Financial officials thus missed their best and perhaps only opportunity to agree on a reformed international monetary system. The meeting of the Committee of Twenty at ministerial level in Nairobi a few weeks later was an anticlimax.

Just before the 1973 Annual Meeting in Nairobi, Mr. Wardhana, as Chairman of the Committee of Twenty, sent his first report to the Board of Governors together with what was called the First Outline of Reform. The report emphasized that "important issues have not yet been resolved," and that "further consideration and study must be given to many matters, including the operational provisions of the reformed system."[2] The report tried to show enthusiasm for the accomplishments that had been made but also explained why further agreement had not been possible: reform involved changes in countries' long-standing patterns of behavior.

---

[2]The report and the First Outline of Reform are in Vol. III below, pp. 155–63.

The implication was that while countries wanted a reformed international monetary system, they resisted any change in their existing practices or attitudes. They wanted reform, but not change.

The First Outline of Reform was fairly general. The reformed system would have an effective and symmetrical adjustment process. The exchange rate regime would be based on stable but adjustable par values, but floating rates would be recognized as providing a useful technique in particular situations. There would be an appropriate degree and form of convertibility for the settlement of imbalances with symmetrical obligations on all countries. There was to be cooperation among countries in dealing with disequilibrating capital flows. Global liquidity was to be better managed, with the SDR becoming the principal reserve asset and the role of gold and of reserve currencies being reduced. The system was also to promote the flow of real resources to developing countries. None of these principles were new. They had been well understood by financial officials even before the Committee of Twenty began its deliberations. The First Outline of Reform did include, however, some additional specifications resulting from the year's work. Countries were to direct their policies toward keeping their official reserves within internationally agreed limits, and for this purpose a reserve indicator structure would be established. The Fund would introduce new procedures for special consultations to which a member would become subject if there had been a disproportionate movement in its official reserves or if the Managing Director suggested such a special consultation. Graduated pressures would be applied both to members with payments surpluses and to members with payments deficits. The Outline stated, however, that the implementation of these general techniques required further study.

This First Outline of Reform was indeed preliminary. Yet, even this preliminary Outline was presented to the Board of Governors as a document by the Bureau not necessarily endorsed by the deputies.

Fourth Meeting of the Committee of Twenty

After the disappointing results of the deputies' seventh meeting in Paris a few weeks earlier, not much was expected from the fourth meeting of the Committee of Twenty held at the Kenyatta Conference Center on September 23, 1973, the day before the opening of the Twenty-Eighth Annual Meeting. The meeting of the Committee of Twenty produced few results. The Governors of the Big Five, Messrs. Aichi, Barber, Giscard d'Estaing, Schmidt, and Shultz, tried to counter the complaints of the nine members of the Committee from developing members that the industrial members lacked political will to make progress toward reforming the international monetary system. The Governors from developing members complained that failure to reach agreement on a new international monetary system within a reasonable time would lead to worldwide recession. They explained that the industrial members, facilitated by floating exchange rates, were pursuing highly inflationary policies and that when these members applied the brakes to such policies the worst recession since World War II would occur. The officials on the Committee of Twenty from developing members, as well as those from Japan and several EC countries, were concerned, too, about the continuation of floating rates. Despite these concerns, there was little or no opposition to the transmission of the First Outline of Reform to the full Board of Governors.

In this atmosphere, Mr. Giscard d'Estaing suggested that the Committee set itself a deadline of July 31, 1974 to reach agreement and meanwhile agree to hold another meeting early in 1974 and a final one a few months later. Other members of the Committee agreed that setting a deadline would be a good way for the Committee to discipline itself to reach whatever agreement might be forthcoming and to finish its work.

Since the interconnection of controversial issues inhibited further progress even on technical questions, ways of overcoming these difficulties were suggested. Mr. Shultz agreed to accept certain assumptions, such as mandatory convertibility, as working hypotheses. Mr. Turner suggested that officials try to reach agreement on some issues that could be solved without necessarily solving other issues. In this regard, he welcomed the suggestion of the new Managing Director, Mr. Witteveen, that the valuation and rate of interest of the SDR were appropriate subjects on which agreement might be possible. Mr. Giscard d'Estaing suggested that the structure of the Fund, in which high-level discussions might proceed once the Committee of Twenty went out of existence, could also be a topic for potential agreement separate from other features of the reformed system.

When the deputies gathered for their eighth meeting a few days later, on September 27, 1973, at the Kenyatta Conference Center, it was apparent that the Committee of Twenty was not going to produce a reformed international monetary system. Furthermore, not only did deputies disagree on the reform but some also feared that sharp increases in the price of crude oil were imminent. In these circumstances, Mr. Morse feared that even the minimum objectives of the Committee of Twenty might be lost. Not only would he have failed to achieve his objective of resolving the fixed versus floating rate debate but he would have failed in the other objectives at which he had aimed—of pushing forward the SDR as a reserve asset, of having consultations in the Fund to facilitate balance of payments adjustment, and of improving relations between developed members and developing members. As a result, the end of September 1973 was a very low point in the life of the Committee of Twenty.

In order to save as much as possible of their work, Mr. Morse and the other five members of the Bureau decided to set up a series of technical groups. These technical groups could then proceed with some of the lesser matters so as to avoid a comprehensive failure of the Committee of Twenty.

Four such technical groups were set up. A Technical Group on Adjustment was to study a reserve indicator structure and graduated financial pressures. A Technical Group on Intervention and Settlement was to study the settlement of payments imbalances, particularly the possibility of linking settlement with a multicurrency intervention system. A Technical Group on Global Liquidity and Consolidation was to examine ways of controlling the volume of dollar balances to be created and of reducing the existing volume. A Technical Group on the Transfer of Real Resources was to examine specific suggestions other than those concerning a possible SDR/aid link and an extended facility in the Fund for longer-term balance of payments finance for developing members.

On this basis, the Board of Governors passed a resolution on September 28, 1973, urging the Committee of Twenty to complete its work as soon as possible.[3] The Committee planned to hold a short meeting in January 1974, mainly to take up the topics related to the current international monetary regime, especially the valuation of the SDR and its rate of interest.

DECISION IN JANUARY 1974 TO ABANDON REFORM EFFORTS

When the Committee of Twenty next met, at the Palazzo dei Congressi in Rome, on January 14–15 at the deputy level and on January 17–18 at the ministerial level, a substantial increase in the price of crude oil had occurred and huge imbalances were expected in the payments positions of all countries. None of the large industrial countries was ready to commit itself to a par value or a fixed exchange rate in the face of uncertainties in its future balance of payments position. In fact, most officials had come to the conclusion that a large measure of floating was unavoidable and even desirable. As a minimum, they all agreed that if the system of par values had not broken down earlier it would have surely succumbed to the payments problems engendered by the new oil crisis. Even French officials, who had been adamantly in favor of fixed rates and against floating rates in all but the most extreme emergencies, conceded that the current regime including floating exchange rates might well have to continue. Indeed, on January 19, a few days after the Committee of Twenty's meeting in Rome, France itself floated the franc temporarily. French officials notified the Fund that during the next six months and on a provisional basis the interventions of the Exchange Stabilization Fund would no longer aim at limiting the exchange rates between the franc and certain other currencies within predetermined margins. In effect, the franc was withdrawn from the EC snake arrangements to float freely "for six months."

In these circumstances the Committee of Twenty in effect decided to shift to a step-by-step, or evolutionary, approach to changing the international monetary system. In other words, instead of the reformed international monetary system coming into being all at once, or even having the features of the reformed system agreed all at once, a new international monetary system would be permitted to evolve out of existing arrangements. What the members of the Committee said in their communiqué following their Rome meeting was that "priority should be given to certain important aspects of reform . . . with a view to their early implementation.

---

[3]Resolution No. 28-5 is in Vol. III below, p. 164.

Other aspects of reform could be agreed with the understanding that their operational provisions would be developed and implemented at a later date."[4] What they were saying was that reform was not being given up; rather a reformed system was to evolve on a piecemeal basis. For its remaining months, the Committee of Twenty would turn to the topics needing early implementation. By concentrating on these topics monetary authorities hoped that existing international monetary arrangements might evolve without excessive disorder. While the members of the Committee of Twenty and their deputies were to discuss these topics, the Executive Board of the Fund was to take decisions, assisted in the usual way by the Managing Director and the staff. The Fund's regular policymaking bodies were thus brought back into the fold on the discussions and decisions concerning the international monetary system.

In March 1974, Mr. Morse was to call the change in the work of the Committee of Twenty from working on a reformed system to working on steps requiring early implementation a "new direction." But in every sense, in January 1974 the Committee of Twenty abandoned its efforts to negotiate a reformed international monetary system.

Disappointment of Developing Members

Just before the Committee of Twenty meeting, officials of developing members had also met as the Group of Twenty-Four in Rome on January 16, 1974, at the Palazzo dei Congressi, under the chairmanship of Ismail Mahroug, Minister of Finance of Algeria. As in the past, the meeting of the Group of Twenty-Four at ministerial level was preceded by a meeting of their deputies, chaired by Rachid Bouraoui, also of Algeria. Realizing that the Committee of Twenty was about to give up its efforts to reform the international monetary system, officials of developing members, disappointed with such an outcome, pressed hard to obtain what they could in the way of early agreement on issues which they regarded as crucial to their countries. At the meeting of deputies of the Group of Twenty-Four, they repeated that they wanted an early agreement on all issues of reform, including not only an improved international trading system but also an improved system for transferring real resources from developed to developing countries. However, since prospects for full reform looked dim, these officials stated their positions on a number of immediate issues. Arrangements should be made to facilitate use of the SDR in official settlements, even prior to its becoming the principal reserve asset of the reformed system. There should be changes in the structure of members' quotas in the Fund and in the voting power of members in the Fund so as to give developing members more equitable shares. A Council of Governors could be established on a permanent basis to help run the Fund, and developing members should have representation on that Council that was at least as large as their representation in the Committee of Twenty; there should also be a strong resident Executive Board.

---

[4]Communiqué of Committee of Twenty, January 18, 1974, par. 3; Vol. III below, p. 200.

Officials of developing members believed especially that some kind of link arrangement should be established without further delay. They expressed special interest, therefore, in the Technical Group on the Transfer of Real Resources, which they had suggested be set up at the time of the Annual Meeting in Nairobi. And they expressed concern over the implications of the recent large increases in oil prices for the economies of those developing members who were oil importers.

REPORTS OF THE TECHNICAL GROUPS

The four Technical Groups set up at Nairobi continued working even after the January 1974 meeting of deputies and ministers when the reform efforts were given up. Prior to the tenth meeting of the deputies, on March 27–29, 1974, three of the four Technical Groups completed their reports. The fourth Technical Group finished its work at the end of April. The work of each of these Technical Groups is described in turn.

Technical Group on Intervention and Settlement

The Technical Group on Intervention and Settlement studied how an intervention system might be used to effect asset settlement. How to develop a more symmetrical intervention system in exchange markets to replace dollar intervention had interested financial officials, including the Fund management and staff, since the beginning of 1972. The possibility of a multicurrency intervention system had been included in the Executive Board's report on reform in 1972. Multicurrency intervention (MCI) was also one of the three features of the U.S. proposal for a reformed system submitted to the Committee of Twenty at the end of 1972. After this report was completed, the Fund staff continued to study the topic, including ways in which adoption of MCI by industrial members would affect the interests of developing members.

By the middle of 1973, the Fund and the U.S. Government had given considerable thought to MCI arrangements. Some deputies of the Committee of Twenty also seemed to support a system of MCI; at least support for new intervention arrangements seemed to be greater than the support generated for most other features of the reformed system. Some officials, as well as the Fund staff, therefore hoped that a carefully prepared suggestion for MCI might be accepted by the members of the Committee of Twenty. Agreement on an MCI system would provide a welcome breakthrough in the impasse reached on most topics of reform. More importantly, since some proposed asset settlement schemes were tied to MCI arrangements, agreement on an MCI system might provide the basis for resolution of the issue of asset settlement. In fact, some Fund staff, after the meeting of the Committee of Twenty in July 1973, were sufficiently confident that focus on MCI arrangements might bring about agreement among the deputies on asset settlement and even on consolidation and substitution that they were critical of the Bureau's attention to general models for adjustment and convertibility. The Fund staff wanted the Bureau to develop more technical schemes in precise detail, especially for MCI arrangements.

It was thus still in a spirit of optimism about the prospects for agreement that the Technical Group on Intervention and Settlement, under the chairmanship of Mr. Morse, met four times between October 1973 and February 1974. Their undertaking was ambitious. Several papers were requested, submitted, and discussed. Representatives of Belgium, France, the Federal Republic of Germany, and the Netherlands jointly prepared a paper describing in connection with the arrangements of the European countries the operation of the European Monetary Cooperation Fund, especially the keeping of accounts and the handling of settlements. Since it was important to know how intervention arrangements were affected when margins could not be kept for one of the currencies, this paper also explained how the crisis in the pound sterling in June 1972 had affected the snake arrangements. Representatives of the Nordic countries provided a paper on the position of Denmark, Norway, and Sweden in the EC intervention and settlement arrangements.

Representatives from Italy and the United States submitted papers elaborating how their proposals for MCI might bring about asset settlement. Jorge González del Valle, Executive Secretary of the Central American Monetary Council, presented a paper describing multilateral settlement arrangements in the Central American common market (Costa Rica, El Salvador, Guatemala, Honduras, and Nicaragua) through the Central American Clearing House (CACH) and among the 11 members of the Latin America Free Trade Association (LAFTA). Representatives of the United Kingdom prepared a paper describing the need for elasticity, that is, for adding to the supply of reserve currencies in an MCI system and how such elasticity might be provided. Representatives of Japan submitted a paper on the rules that would be acceptable to Japanese officials if Japan was to join an MCI system. Mr. Prasad and Choi Siew Hong (Malaysia) prepared a paper describing the safeguards which they considered essential for nonparticipants in an MCI scheme.

The Fund staff prepared three papers. One paper explained members' obligations with respect to exchange rate margins in the post-Smithsonian regime and how they might be adopted under an MCI system. A second paper explained how Fund surveillance over intervention and settlement might work. A third paper provided factual information on the currencies quoted and traded regularly in the exchange markets of 24 Fund members.

When these papers were considered by the Technical Group on Intervention and Settlement, the Group tended to prefer the MCI technique for achieving a more symmetrical intervention system rather than the dollar intervention technique of the Bretton Woods system. The MCI system was generally considered technically feasible for the 10–20 countries considered likely to participate in it. Countries not in the MCI system would keep their spot rates within agreed margins around parity by intervening in one or several currencies of the MCI system. Most participants favored

245

an MCI system in which there would be three groups of countries: (i) an inner group practicing reciprocal intervention and fairly tight asset settlement, but with greater scope for intramarginal intervention than in the EC snake; (ii) an intermediate group maintaining similar margins through unilateral intervention with fairly tight asset settlement; and (iii) an outer group practicing unilateral intervention with one or more of the MCI currencies with greater scope for variation in their holdings of individual national currencies.

The Technical Group on Intervention and Settlement also considered an alternative way of achieving more symmetrical intervention, namely a system using the SDR as an intervention medium, a possibility examined by the Fund staff early in 1972. Under this technique, more symmetrical margins could be achieved if the value of the SDR was based on par values and if a sufficient number of members undertook to buy and sell SDRs within prescribed margins (of say, 2¼ percent) on either side of par value. The staff envisaged that such a system might be established in the longer run on the basis of buying and selling SDRs in the market and that the mechanism of market arbitrage would be relied on to ensure that exchange margins between two currencies did not exceed twice that amount (i.e., 4½ percent on either side of cross parity). Arrangements of this sort would, however, require that the SDR should no longer be confined to official operations and settlements but should be widely traded in and held by private markets.

The idea for an SDR intervention scheme was suggested again late in 1973 by one of the participants in this Technical Group from the United Kingdom. Under the scheme proposed by the United Kingdom, central banks would not be obliged to intervene in exchange markets but would achieve the same result by standing ready to deal in SDRs against their own currencies with commercial banks on condition that the SDRs would be transferred directly to and from other central banks. Alternatively expressed, central banks would sell for domestic currency at a fixed margin promises to deliver SDRs to other central banks and would buy rights to receive SDRs from other central banks in deals arranged for profit through the private market. The arbitrage operations of the market would keep exchange rates within limits determined by the SDR margins.

Toward the last of the meetings of the Technical Group on Intervention and Settlement, the SDR intervention scheme advanced to further prominence. The interest of the officials of the Technical Group in an SDR intervention system surprised the Fund staff. The staff had considered such a system a mere technical possibility, new and strange. SDRs, moreover, were not owned and traded by private persons, and views differed about the desirability in the longer term of developing the SDR as a private asset in this way. Inasmuch as both types of intervention schemes and the SDR scheme were based on a par value regime and inasmuch as officials had by this time come to realize that floating rates might last for several years, a certain air of unreality surrounded the discussions.

The Technical Group on Intervention and Settlement also elaborated and compared the two alternative asset settlement schemes discussed by the deputies of the Committee of Twenty, the more mandatory system and the on demand system. It concluded that, while there were some important differences between the two systems, the differences were not so wide as to be unbridgeable.

Technical Group on Adjustment

The Technical Group on Adjustment held four sessions from October 1973 to February 1974 in Washington under the chairmanship of Robert Solomon. In many respects, this Technical Group took up where the Technical Group on Indicators had left off in May 1973. Now the technicians aimed especially at reconciling the continued differences of view on indicators and on pressures. U.S. participants presented a paper entitled "A Proposed Adjustment System Based on a Blend of Assessment and Reserve Indicators." The U.S. paper made several concessions. Norms for reserve levels in reserve indicators could be based on Fund quotas. Assessment would play a part in determining when reserve indicators should be overridden. Currency balances made ineligible for conversion because of primary asset holding limits (PAHL) should be netted out of the reserves of the issuing country for purposes of determining reserve indicators. Because of these concessions, the U.S. paper received a sympathetic reception from a number of European participants in the Technical Group.

Wolfgang Rieke, of the Deutsche Bundesbank, submitted a paper entitled "A Simplified Reserve Indicator Model." Having in mind the distinction made in an earlier staff paper about indicators based on stocks of reserves (the absolute level of reserves of countries at different times) as against flows of reserves (the accumulation or decrease in a country's reserves over time), Mr. Rieke's paper argued for use of flows in reserves in making up any reserve indicator. Other deputies conceded that flows in reserves were important but preferred to let changes or trends in reserves be a factor in an assessment of the country's situation rather than to try to adapt the reserve indicator. The most important point of the paper of the Deutsche Bundesbank, however, was that it continued to put forward the German position that objective indicators be used only to trigger consultations and not to determine pressures.

Several notes were also submitted to the Technical Group on Adjustment, including one prepared by the Fund staff, on the financial pressures that ought to be used as part of the measures to induce adjustment action. The members of this Technical Group on Adjustment discussed all these questions at length, but little agreement was reached.

Technical Group on Global Liquidity and Consolidation

The Technical Group on Global Liquidity and Consolidation, chaired by Mr. Kafka, held four sessions in Washington between October 1973 and February 1974. Under its terms of reference, this Technical Group was to examine four topics

247

in detail and to report on them to the deputies. The topics were the volume and composition of global liquidity; the extent to which it might be desirable to consolidate reserve currency balances; appropriate procedures for the determination of global reserve needs; and appropriate methods for deciding allocations and cancellations of SDRs. In effect, this Technical Group was to look again into the problems related to global liquidity (consolidation, funding, and substitution) and to examine how to measure global liquidity and how to decide on allocations of SDRs.

This Technical Group also worked intensively. Many papers were submitted. Messrs. Palamenghi-Crispi and Vittorio Barattieri submitted a note explaining the interrelationship between consolidation and asset settlement under the Italian plan for asset settlement. This note emphasized again that asset settlement would have to be achieved in full and through the Fund, especially since consolidation of existing currency balances in the reformed system would only be partial. They also submitted a note outlining a possible method of determining allocations of SDRs. The method was in line with earlier Italian suggestions for determining global reserve needs by using value figures for international trade. Since there had been some doubt whether the Federal Republic of Germany would participate in any consolidation scheme to the extent of surrendering its official holdings of reserve currencies to the Fund in exchange for SDRs, Eckard Pieske submitted a note on the scope of consolidation for his country. Mr. Schneider submitted a statement putting forth the views of officials of Austria, Belgium, Luxembourg, and Turkey on global liquidity, consolidation, and the criteria by which to measure the need for SDR allocations.

Mr. Massad submitted a quantitative study of how to determine the need for SDR allocations. This study placed much greater emphasis on factors important to developing members, such as their aggregate imports, their service of foreign indebtedness, and the distribution of reserves among Fund members. Alfredo Phillips O. (Mexico), Guillermo Bueso (Honduras), and Francisco Suarez (Mexico) prepared a note explaining why developing members needed to maintain a significant part of their reserves in the form of currency balances.

The French participants in this Technical Group—Mr. Beaurain, Jean Foglizzo, and Jacques Wahl—submitted a paper elaborating the French arguments as to why substitution of SDRs for dollars had to be obligatory instead of voluntary, and why it should be progressive, over time, rather than an initial full-scale substitution. At one of the Technical Group's sessions Mr. Wahl explained the reasons for the French position. Voluntary substitution would encourage speculation and thus endanger the stability of exchange markets. Because weak currencies would be deposited with the substitution facility in exchange for SDRs, the marginal utility of the SDR would gradually decline to that of the weakest currency and the SDR would become "the worst reserve asset of central banks." In effect, French officials were trying to achieve mandatory substitution of dollars for SDRs but without weakening the SDR.

Luiz Marinho de Barros (Brazil) submitted a paper to show how a substitution facility in the Fund might be operated to provide a transfer of real resources to developing members and at the same time solve the conflict over the rate of interest to be paid on SDRs.

The U.S. participants submitted a paper on the profits and losses of a substitution account. The United States had been concerned about changing the method of valuing the SDR and increasing its rate of interest partly because of the implications for the United States in maintaining the value of its liabilities to the Fund. Should a substitution account be established in which SDRs were exchanged for dollar balances outstanding, a certain loss would be involved for the Fund and monetary officials expected that the U.S. Government would reimburse the Fund. The U.S. paper came up with three alternative ways of covering profits and losses in a substitution account. The Fund staff submitted notes on how the liabilities of reserve centers to a substitution account in the Fund might be amortized over time and on the possible secondary effects of substitution of SDRs for reserve currencies in Eurocurrency markets.

In the sessions of the Technical Group on Global Liquidity and Consolidation, the French suggestion for a substitution facility, especially as modified by the Canadian participants, received considerable support from the participants from developed and some developing members, although there was still substantial support for the Italian proposal for a voluntary open-ended substitution facility. According to the French suggestion, substitution would be achieved in annual installments that would be negotiated but would be subject to revision to be approved possibly by the Board of Governors. Some limitations on foreign exchange holdings of Fund members might also be involved. Countries holding less than a specified amount of foreign exchange would not be required to participate in the substitution facility; thus, most developing members would not be affected by the mandatory features of the scheme. The Canadian representative proposed a similar scheme whereby countries would select an amount of currency holdings to be substituted for SDRs and a time path over which this substitution would occur. Once a country had decided on a substitution amount and time path, it would be bound by its decision. Developing members would not be obliged to place reserve assets with the substitution facility since they could initially declare that they had no reserves available for substitution.

This Technical Group came to the topic of global liquidity in January 1974, following the increases in oil prices of late in 1973 and the expectation of very large payments deficits by most oil importing countries. In these circumstances, virtually no official thought that his country had "excess" reserves. Not only did total global liquidity suddenly seem inadequate but there was also much less talk about the need to reduce the supply of past accumulation of dollars. On the contrary, there was considerable concern that there could well be a shortage of world reserves.

The Technical Group did not discuss gold, although the U.S. participant insisted that when the Technical Group's report discussed the desired decline in the role of reserve currencies in the future, it should note that a decline in the role of gold was also desired. The participants still disagreed about gold, especially about any changes in its valuation. Participants from developing members again made the point that a revaluation of monetary gold would exacerbate the current maldistribution of reserves and some suggested that if gold was to be revalued, a special allocation of SDRs should be made to developing members to redress the worsened maldistribution.

It was thus difficult for the members of the Technical Group on Global Liquidity and Consolidation to come to any conclusions. They were in the midst of rapid change in world payments positions. In addition, they were still uncertain as to what arrangements would prevail for convertibility and adjustment, what characteristics the SDR would have in the future, and what would happen to gold in the reformed system.

Technical Group on the Transfer of Real Resources

The Technical Group on the Transfer of Real Resources held four meetings in Washington, from the beginning of November 1973 to the end of April 1974, under the chairmanship of Mr. Frimpong-Ansah of Ghana. Many officials of developing members wanted this group to go into the full range of topics involving international trade and monetary arrangements—investment, development aid, capital flows—and their relation to the economic development of the world's developing countries, arguing that there should be a fundamental re-examination of all aspects of the transfer of real resources between the developed and developing world. Mr. Pereira Lira, for instance, referred to the long list of suggestions to improve the position of developing members made at the 1973 Annual Meeting by Mr. Delfim Netto. Mr. Delfim Netto had suggested, for example, that some international forum ought to review such topics as official development assistance, project and program financing, the untying of bilateral aid, the impact of inflation on funds committed by the international community to developing members, the access of developing members to the capital markets of developed members, and the external indebtedness of developing members.[5] Carlos Rafael Silva, then Chairman of the deputies of the Group of Twenty-Four, had sent to Mr. Frimpong-Ansah a memorandum prepared by the deputies of the Group of Twenty-Four setting forth detailed questions to be examined under the various categories listed by Mr. Delfim Netto. Other officials of developing members wanted to add the topic of commodity price stabilization to the agenda.

Participants from most of the developed members held a much narrower concept of the mandate of the Technical Group on the Transfer of Real Resources. In their view, voiced especially by Mr. Schleiminger, the Technical Group's responsibility was to consider a short list of questions on resource transfers specifically tied in with the features expected in a reformed international monetary system. For example, given the greater effectiveness of the adjustment process under the reformed system, could industrial and relatively more developed members be obliged to apply policies to correct their payments deficits or surpluses in a manner which would protect capital flows to developing members and which would be

---

[5]Statement by the Governor of the Fund and the World Bank for Brazil, *Summary Proceedings, 1973*, pp. 166–68.

consistent with the achievement of internationally accepted targets for resource transfers? In a scheme of pressures to be applied to industrial members and to relatively more developed members with large and persistent payments surpluses, could such measures be included as asking countries with surpluses to attain agreed targets for official development assistance, to untie bilateral aid flows, to raise their contribution to multilateral lending agencies, or to take selective trade measures of particular interest to developing members? In developing formulas for the allocation of SDRs among members (other than a link arrangement), could account be taken of the special reserve needs of developing members and the particular difficulties encountered by those members in earning or borrowing reserves?

Because officials of developed and developing members viewed the scope of the work of the Technical Group on the Transfer of Real Resources differently, Mr. Frimpong-Ansah returned to the deputies of the Committee of Twenty in January 1974 for clarification of the Technical Group's terms of reference. The deputies decided that since the Committee of Twenty was winding up its work, the Technical Group on the Transfer of Real Resources should limit itself to questions immediately concerned with arrangements for the international monetary system. However, a broader committee, at ministerial level, to parallel the Interim Committee, described in Chapter 16, could be recommended to carry on the study of the problems of developing members.

Within this framework, the Technical Group confined its examination to the relationship between international monetary arrangements and the transfer of resources to developing members. The Group studied this relationship thoroughly. Papers were submitted, for example, by the Commission of the European Communities (CEC), describing access by developing members to the capital markets of the nine countries belonging to the Community. The Fund staff prepared a detailed survey of the status of the controls on capital movements used by ten of its large developed members. G. Arthur Brown (Jamaica) submitted a paper explaining how tax havens in developed members had undermined both the foreign exchange reserves and tax revenues of developing members by providing an easy opportunity for persons with incomes or assets in developing members to hold resources in these havens.

The participants of the Technical Group came to a number of conclusions. They concluded, for instance, that a better process of balance of payments adjustment would enable industrial members and relatively more developed members to eliminate their payments imbalances by corrective policies which would not involve reductions in the aid which they furnished to developing members or the imposition of restrictions on imports from developing members for balance of payments purposes. Hence, developing members, like developed members, had a vested interest in a smoothly working adjustment process. Participants of the Technical Group concluded, too, that developed members should deliberately try to apply corrective policies so as not to disrupt the development programs of developing members. They also looked into other specific features of the reformed international monetary system and their implications for developing members: the exchange rate mechanism and the effect on borrowing by developing members, the consolidation of currency reserves and the effect on transfers of resources to developing members, and the implications for developing members of the ways in which the relative role of primary reserve assets was changed in a reformed monetary system.

The Technical Group also examined how oil importing developing members could finance swollen payments deficits resulting from the new higher prices for oil. For example, a special note on the oil situation as it affected developing members, based on papers by the staff of the Fund and the World Bank, was prepared. Mehdi Garadaghipour (Iran) submitted a brief note on Iran's proposal for a development fund to help oil importing developing members. The Italian participants, Messrs. Palamenghi-Crispi and Barattieri, submitted a note on how the oil deficits of developing members might be financed.

Finally, participants in the Technical Group on the Transfer of Real Resources went into detail on the "establishment of new institutional arrangements for the study of the broad questions involved in the transfer of real resources to developing countries." Here, taking up the idea discussed earlier that a new committee might be formed, they recommended the establishment of a joint Fund-World Bank ministerial group to consider the transfer of real resources. The subsequent introduction of such a group—the Development Committee—is discussed in Chapter 16.

■　■　■　■　■　■

The work of the seven Technical Groups of the Committee of Twenty, in which both officials from capitals and Executive Directors and Alternate Executive Directors participated, might well be regarded as the most useful results produced by the Committee of Twenty. The seven Technical Groups helped to identify the specific problems involved in implementing a reformed international monetary system based on generally agreed principles. They also considered alternative solutions for these problems and weighed the merits and demerits of these solutions. Their work was to furnish the basis for further discussions in later years on such topics as multicurrency intervention arrangements, which were involved in the European Monetary System, and for a possible substitution account in the Fund.

CHAPTER
14

Final Outline of Reform

*P*REPARATION OF A FINAL OUTLINE OF REFORM made up most of
the work of the Committee of Twenty in its last five months, from January to
June 1974.

At their last three meetings, held on March 27–29, 1974 at the Fund's
headquarters in Washington, on May 7–9, 1974 at the Fund's Office in Europe in
Paris, and on June 10–11, 1974 again at the Fund's headquarters, the deputies
concentrated on getting an agreed text of an Outline. At their March meeting, as
they considered a revised version of the First Outline that had been prepared by the
Bureau, they debated whether the Outline should be endorsed by ministers. Some
deputies favored a document that was the responsibility only of the Bureau as the
First Outline had been. In fact, the deputies from France, André de Lattre and
Mr. Pierre-Brossolette, and those from several developing members, especially
Victor E. Bruce (Trinidad and Tobago) and Eduardo J. Tejera (Dominican Republic),
were not convinced that any Outline ought to be prepared. The French deputies
believed that consensus on an Outline of a reformed system was beyond the
attainment of officials in their existing state of disagreement. Deputies from
developing members objected to an Outline because none of the specific ideas that
they had insisted were in the interest of developing members were being
incorporated. Deputies from Canada, the Federal Republic of Germany, Italy, Japan,
the United Kingdom, and the United States, however, all supported Mr. Morse in
his desire to aim for an Outline agreed upon by the Committee of Twenty and
explicitly endorsed at ministerial level. Mr. Volcker particularly pushed for an
Outline on the grounds that it was important for financial officials and for the world
to have an Outline as "an agreed vision" of the course in which the international
monetary system should gradually evolve. The majority of deputies were persuaded
that an Outline officially endorsed by the Committee of Twenty was a good idea.

At their meeting in May, the deputies prepared the final text. All except the
French deputies regarded this text as having been agreed upon by the Committee of
Twenty at the deputy level. Since the French deputies had participated closely in the
drafting, Mr. Morse hoped that they, too, would accept the final text. At their

meeting in June, the deputies finished their work and were ready to turn over the Outline to their ministers.

When the members of the Committee of Twenty assembled for their sixth and last meeting in Washington, on June 12–13, 1974 at the Eugene R. Black auditorium of the World Bank, many members, especially from the large industrial countries, had changed. Several ministers of finance had moved on to become heads of state. Indeed, the large number of finance ministers who rose to political prominence and who became heads of government or state in the 1970s indicates the great political importance which economic and financial affairs had in the world of the 1970s. By June 1974 Valéry Giscard d'Estaing, who had attended the previous five meetings of the Committee of Twenty, had become President of France, and Jacques de Larosière, Director of the Treasury, Ministry of Economy and Finance, was designated representative of France to the Committee of Twenty's final meeting, representing Jean-Pierre Fourcade, the Minister of Economy and Finance of France; Helmut Schmidt, who had attended four of the Committee of Twenty meetings (missing only the first one in September 1972) had become Chancellor of the Federal Republic of Germany, and Hans Apel was now Minister of Finance and attended the last Committee of Twenty meeting. Other individuals who had been members of the Committee of Twenty had left public service. George Shultz, who had attended all the previous meetings of the Committee of Twenty, had been succeeded as Secretary of the U.S. Treasury by William E. Simon. Anthony Barber, who had also attended all the meetings of the Committee of Twenty since its inaugural meeting in September 1972, was succeeded as Chancellor of the Exchequer of the United Kingdom by Denis Healey when the Labour Government came into power early in 1974. Antônio Delfim Netto, who had been Finance Minister of Brazil for many years, was succeeded by Mario Henrique Simonsen. Bensalem Guessous, Minister of Finance of Morocco, who had attended all meetings of the Committee of Twenty except the first, was succeeded by Abdel-Kader Benslimane.

There were other changes in the attendance of the Committee of Twenty at the final meeting in June 1974. Willy De Clercq, who had attended all meetings of the Committee except the first, as Minister of Finance and then as Deputy Prime Minister and Minister of Finance of Belgium, did not come to the sixth meeting; Hannes Androsch, Federal Minister of Finance of Austria, represented the constituency. Menasse Lemma, Governor of the National Bank of Ethiopia, who had attended all previous meetings did not come to the sixth meeting; the constituency was represented instead by Shehu Shagari, Federal Commissioner for Finance of Nigeria. John N. Turner, Minister of Finance of Canada, who had attended all previous meetings, was not present at the last meeting; the constituency was represented by David H. Coore, the Deputy Prime Minister and Minister of Finance of Jamaica. Japan had already had a change of Finance Minister at the fifth meeting of the Committee of Twenty, in January 1974; Takeo Fukuda succeeded Kiichi Aichi on the latter's death.

As a result of these changes, only a few ministers—Y.B. Chavan, Minister of Finance of India; Kjell-Olof Feldt, Minister of Commerce of Sweden; and

Ali Wardhana, Minister of Finance of Indonesia—attended all six meetings of the Committee of Twenty. Positions taken by various constituencies on the issues facing the Committee of Twenty were national rather than personal, however, and despite the change of faces, the views expressed remained largely the same.

The meeting began with a statement by Ismail Mahroug on behalf of the Group of Twenty-Four, in which he stressed once more the disappointment of officials from developing members in the results of the reform efforts. They felt also that the Outline of Reform represented an unbalanced approach, which gave much more attention to the problems of the developed than of the developing members. Even the immediate steps for the current situation spelled out in Part II of the Outline were inadequate. Any package of interim measures ought to include a link between SDR allocations and development finance; a solution to the gold problem which neither jeopardized the SDR/aid link nor strengthened the role of gold in the monetary system; an extended Fund facility; an increase in the relative share of developing members in the quotas of the Fund; and establishment of a joint Fund-World Bank committee of Governors, a Development Committee, to parallel a proposed Interim Committee.[1]

To help meet these points, the 11 Governors from industrial and relatively more developed members noted that the extended Fund facility was on the verge of being established and that the question of quotas in the Fund was to be looked into. They also agreed to the idea of forming a Development Committee. Nothing was agreed about gold, however, and the link between SDRs and development finance was rejected. One of the reasons for this final rejection of the link by the Committee of Twenty was that by the middle of 1974 the volume of world liquidity was clearly excessive and the world was in the throes of the highest rates of inflation since World War II. It was unrealistic, therefore, to expect further allocations of SDRs for some time. In these circumstances, a link between SDR allocations and development finance was not likely to produce additional funds for developing members, and officials of developed members, especially of the United States and the Federal Republic of Germany, more easily won their case against the link.

On this basis, the Committee of Twenty approved a final report to be transmitted to the full Board of Governors, together with an Outline of Reform and accompanying Annexes. This report and Outline were made public on June 14, 1974.[2]

FINAL REPORT AND OUTLINE

The report of the Committee to the Board of Governors first explained why the Committee switched its priority from planning an overall reformed international

---

[1]Communiqué of Group of Twenty-Four, June 10, 1974; Vol. III below, pp. 636–38.

[2]Reproduced in Vol. III below, pp. 165–96, together with the final communiqué of the Committee of Twenty. pp. 200–205.

monetary system to working out immediate measures under which existing international monetary arrangements would evolve into a system. Essentially, "the uncertainties affecting the world economic outlook, related to inflation, the energy situation, and other unsettled conditions" had increased since the Nairobi meeting. The world's balance of payments structure was changing radically, and it was not yet clear to what extent the positions of individual countries would be altered or how adjustment would be achieved. It might be some time before there would be a return to a system based on stable but adjustable par values or to general convertibility. Nor would the full arrangements for management of the adjustment process and of global liquidity necessarily be feasible in the period immediately ahead. At the same time, the Committee regarded it "as of the highest importance that immediate steps should be taken to begin an evolutionary process of reform." There was, for example, a particular need to maintain close international consultation and surveillance of countries' balance of payments policies in the Fund and to develop orderly means of financing imbalances, including means of meeting the financial needs of many developing countries.

Both the report of the Committee of Twenty and the Preface to the *Outline* verified that the *Outline* was the work of the Committee and not just of the Bureau. The report stated explicitly that the *Committee* was presenting "its final report, together with an *Outline of Reform*." The Preface stated that the Reformed System (that is, Part I of the *Outline*) "records the outcome of the Committee's discussion of international monetary reform and indicates the general direction in which the Committee believes that the system could evolve in the future." The Preface to the *Outline* made it clear, however, that the Annexes—which treated more fully than the *Outline* a number of topics on which agreement was not yet reached—were the work of the Chairman and Vice-Chairmen of the deputies. These Annexes recorded the state of the discussion reached by the Committee of Twenty on controversial topics and on which it did not seem useful to pursue discussion further since events had made it impossible to give immediate effect to any full-scale reform even if one could have been negotiated. The Annexes also presented illustrative schemes and operational detail of how the system could operate. The Bureau envisaged that arrangements in these controversial areas, if and when they were agreed, should be implemented as and when the Fund judged it feasible to do so. The Fund might in some cases introduce such arrangements initially on an experimental basis with a view to subsequent agreement on full implementation.

Part I. The Reformed System

The Introduction to Part I of the *Outline of Reform* stated that there was need for a reformed international monetary system, based on cooperation and consultation within the framework of a strengthened International Monetary Fund, "that will encourage the growth of world trade and employment, promote economic development, and help to avoid both inflation and deflation." This wording gave explicit recognition to a role for the Fund in fostering economic development and in countering inflation and deflation, purposes not specified in the Fund's original Articles of Agreement.

The reformed system was to be characterized by six main features:

(i) an effective and symmetrical adjustment process, including better functioning of the exchange rate mechanism, with the exchange rate regime based on stable but adjustable par values and with floating rates recognized as providing a useful technique in particular situations;

(ii) cooperation in dealing with disequilibrating capital flows;

(iii) the introduction of an appropriate form of convertibility for the settlement of imbalances, with symmetrical obligations on all countries;

(iv) better international management of global liquidity, with the SDR becoming the principal reserve asset and the role of gold and of reserve currencies being reduced;

(v) consistency between arrangements for adjustment, convertibility, and global liquidity; and

(vi) the promotion of the net flow of real resources to developing countries.

While the first five features could be regarded as purposes of the Fund after the First Amendment in 1969, the sixth feature had never been regarded as one of the Fund's primary functions.

The *Outline* also recognized that attainment of the purposes of reform of the international monetary system depended not only on satisfactory principles to govern the system but also on satisfactory and consistent arrangements for international trade, capital, investment, and development assistance, including the access of developing countries to markets in developed countries.

The *Outline* also elaborated arrangements in the reformed system for each of a number of specific topics. The section on adjustment was the longest. Countries would take such prompt and adequate adjustment actions, domestic or external, as might be needed to avoid protracted payments imbalances. Also, countries would "aim to keep their official reserves within limits which will be internationally agreed from time to time in the Fund and which will be consistent with the volume of global liquidity." For this purpose, reserve indicators would be established in whatever way that could be agreed in the Fund.

The Fund was to hold consultations concerning adjustment measures and to exercise surveillance over the adjustment process. These consultations and surveillance were to be conducted at two levels, by the Executive Board and by a proposed ministerial Council. Members would become subject to consultation if there had been a disproportionate movement in their official reserves or if in the judgment of the Managing Director, following informal soundings among Executive Directors, there was prima facie evidence that the country was facing significant imbalances. There would then be an assessment in the Fund which took into account a wide range of factors. While the choice of particular policies was to be left as far as possible to the member concerned, the Fund was to see that a member adopted or reinforced efficacious policies to correct its imbalance. Provision was made for the application of graduated pressures. Floating rates could be adopted in particular situations, subject to Fund authorization, surveillance, and review.

There was a strong presumption in the reformed system against the use of controls on current account transactions or payments for balance of payments purposes, and the Fund and the GATT were to coordinate their positions closely. To control capital flows, countries could use a variety of policies, such as prompt adjustment of inappropriate par values, use of wider margins, the adoption of floating rates in particular situations, and the use of administrative controls, including dual exchange markets and fiscal incentives. They could also harmonize their monetary policies. But they were not to use controls over capital transactions for the purpose of maintaining inappropriate exchange rates or, more generally, of avoiding appropriate adjustment, but otherwise, with certain other qualifications, capital controls were to be allowed. Countries were to cooperate to limit disequilibrating capital flows and to help finance and offset them.

Like many other sections in the *Outline*, the section on adjustment was full of references to the special position of developing countries and the need to protect and promote their interests. Developed countries were to apply adjustment measures in a manner designed to protect the net flow of resources to developing countries and to help in reaching any targets that were internationally agreed for the transfer of resources. Specifically, as countries with balance of payments deficits took measures to reduce these deficits including reducing outflows of capital, they were, nonetheless, to seek as far as possible not to reduce the access of developing countries and international development finance institutions to their financial markets, or to reduce the volume of official development assistance, or to harden the terms and conditions of that assistance. As countries with balance of payments surpluses, particularly those that were not reaching internationally agreed targets for the transfer of resources, took measures to reduce these surpluses, they were to stimulate capital outflows. Thus they were to seek as far as possible to increase development aid and to relax any restrictions on access to their domestic markets by developing countries and to their financial markets by international development finance institutions.

Developing members were also to receive other special considerations when the rules for adjustment were applied. The Executive Board's assessment of a member's need for adjustment action was, in the instance of a developing member, to take into account those characteristics that made it difficult for developing members to achieve prompt balance of payments adjustment without seriously damaging their long-term development programs. A "limited number of countries with large reserves deriving from depletable resources and with a low capacity to absorb imports," that is, oil exporting countries, were not to be subject to the usual adjustment procedures. Whenever possible, developing members were to be exempt from controls imposed by other members, particularly from import controls and controls over outward long-term investment. Finally, developed members were to try to remove legal, institutional, and administrative obstacles to the access of developing members to their financial markets; for their part, developing members were to avoid policies which would discourage the flow of private capital to them.

The first four of the ten Annexes spelled out rather concretely how some of the principles for the adjustment process might be implemented. Annex 1, using the material of the Technical Group on Adjustment, described how a reserve indicator system might operate. Annex 2 listed all the important forms of graduated pressures that had been proposed and the various methods suggested for activating pressures. While the pressures were not listed in order of increasing rigor, there were comments on what was considered to be the mildness or severity of the pressures. The most extreme form of pressure on a member in large and persistent surplus was the application of "discriminatory trade and other current account restrictions" against it by other members. Annex 3 presented, as illustrative schemes, the two new systems of currency intervention in exchange markets, multicurrency intervention and SDR intervention, discussed by the deputies and explored by the Technical Group on Intervention and Settlement. Annex 4 described criteria and procedures to guide the Fund when members adopted floating exchange rates.

Convertibility, Consolidation, Management of Currency Reserves, and Primary Reserve Assets

The basic objectives of convertibility to be accommodated in the reformed system were stated to be "symmetry of obligations on all countries including those whose currencies are held in official reserves; the better management of global liquidity and the avoidance of uncontrolled growth of reserve currency balances; adequate elasticity; and as much freedom for countries to choose the composition of their reserves as is consistent with the overall objectives of the reform." The Fund was to keep the aggregate volume of official currency holdings under international surveillance and management. Just how the Fund was to do this, however, still had to be decided. All countries maintaining par values were to settle in reserve assets those official balances of their currencies presented to them for conversion. The Fund was to establish appropriate arrangements to ensure sufficient control over the aggregate volume of official currency holdings. In effect, after many months of debate, no consensus had been reached on which of the two settlement systems—the mandatory or the "on demand" type—ought to prevail. How these two settlement systems could work was described in Annex 5. Reflecting the work of the Technical Group on Intervention and Settlement, Annex 5 also had a third suggestion for a settlement system, developed by the Bureau, which was a middle position between the two extremes.

Elasticity in the settlement system "could be provided" by credit facilities to finance disequilibrating capital flows. Annex 6 repeated, without much advance, the alternative forms of elasticity in addition to credit facilities that had been discussed, including the proposal of the United States for a primary asset holding limit, that is, an upper limit to convertibility. The Fund was to make provision for the consolidation of reserve currency balances to protect the future convertibility system against net conversion of any overhang of such balances. For this purpose, the Fund could establish a substitution account. Annex 7 enumerated ways in which a substitution account could be established. Annexes 6 and 7 were based on the work of the Technical Group on Global Liquidity and Consolidation.

Countries were to cooperate in the management of their currency reserves so as to avoid disequilibrating movements of official funds. Three novel provisions for achieving this objective were listed, but it was noted that these ways of dealing with capital movements were not universally accepted. Countries should respect any request from a country whose currency was held in official reserves to limit or convert into other reserve assets further increases in their holdings of its currency. Countries should periodically choose the composition of their currency reserves and should undertake not to change it without prior consultation with the Fund. Countries should not add to their currency reserve placements outside the territory of the country of issue except within limits to be agreed with the Fund.

The *Outline* also specified that the SDR was to become the principal reserve asset of the reformed system and that the role of gold and of reserve currencies was to be reduced. The SDR was also to be the numeraire of the system. The Fund was to allocate and cancel SDRs so as to ensure that the volume of global reserves was adequate and was "consistent with the proper functioning of the adjustment and settlement systems." In assessing global reserve needs and making decisions for the allocation and cancellation of SDRs, the Fund was to continue to follow the principles set out in the existing Articles of Agreement. The methods by which the Fund assessed global reserves were to continue to be studied, however. Annex 8 listed factors suggested, mainly by officials of developing members, for additional emphasis in the Fund's assessment of global reserve needs in the future, such as the foreign indebtedness of members, the level of their external debt service payments, and the possibility that the low degree of modernization of the economies of many developing members might lead to an underestimation of their reserve needs.

While the effective yield on the SDR was to "be high enough to make it attractive to acquire and hold, but not so high as to make countries reluctant to use the SDR when in deficit," the *Outline* contained no concrete statement as to how the SDR was to be valued or how a rate of interest on the SDR was to be determined. Annex 9 listed four techniques for determining the value of the SDR. Consideration was given also to relaxing the existing constraints governing use of the SDR, and seven suggestions for such relaxation were listed.

The *Outline* observed that appropriate arrangements for gold were yet to be made. Officials agreed that the role of gold should be reduced, but they recognized that gold reserves were currently an important component of global liquidity and should be usable to finance balance of payments deficits. The three solutions for the gold problem considered by the Committee of Twenty were enumerated. Under one solution (advocated mainly by officials of the United States), monetary authorities, including the Fund, would be free to sell but not to buy gold in the market at the market price; they would not undertake transactions with each other at a price different from the official price, which would be retained and not be subject to a uniform increase. Under a second solution (advocated mainly by French officials), the official price of gold would be abolished and monetary authorities, including the Fund, would be free to deal in gold with one another on a voluntary basis at mutually acceptable prices and to sell gold in the market. A third solution (advocated mainly by officials of South Africa) would permit monetary authorities also to buy gold in the market.

Other Arrangements

As described above, the sixth feature of the reformed system was that it was to contain arrangements to promote an increasing net flow of real resources to developing members. The *Outline* contained a separate section on the link and credit facilities in favor of developing countries. Two forms that a link between SDR allocations and development finance might take were explained. Annex 10, based on the work of the Technical Group on the Transfer of Real Resources, spelled out several of the special concerns of developing members in international monetary arrangements and the need for consistency of arrangements in other economic areas. In the field of monetary arrangements, the Annex discussed adjustment, global liquidity (including the equitable distribution of official reserves and access to official credit facilities), some degree of freedom for developing members to choose the composition of their reserves, and the link.

Finally, Part I of the *Outline* called for a permanent Council of Governors with one member of the Council appointed by each Fund constituency. The Council would have "the necessary decision-making powers to supervise the management and adaptation of the monetary system." The Managing Director was to participate in the Council's meetings.

Characterization of the Reformed System

In an address to the International Monetary Conference in Williamsburg, Virginia, on June 7, 1974, Mr. Morse, the main expert on the reformed system, described what he regarded as its main characteristics.[3] Classified by the nature of its exchange rate mechanism, the reformed system was "a more flexible par value system." While it provided for floating rates in particular situations—because the U.S. dollar might continue to float for a time and the floating of the dollar was likely to lead to widespread use of floating rates for other currencies—the reformed system was to be based upon stable but adjustable par values and was to be equipped with intervention and convertibility arrangements for defending par values. In this way, the reformed system differed substantially from the existing regime in which there was use of floating rates.

---

[3]Reprinted in *Finance & Development* (Washington), September 1974, pp. 13–16.

A system can be characterized by its principal reserve asset or assets, such as the gold standard, the gold exchange standard, and the dollar standard. The reformed system was to be the SDR standard.

A system can be characterized by the degree to which it is a market system, a managed system, or a mixed system. The reformed system was an internationally managed system. It was managed in that it depended on consultation, assessment, and cooperation within the international community. It was even more a managed system in that there were also to be principles and procedures, implemented through the Fund, to govern the adjustment process, the convertibility system, the management of global liquidity, and the transfer of real resources to developing countries.

Finally, characterized by the extent of its internationalism, the reformed system was one in which members had to give up a greater degree of autonomy to the Fund than they had in the past. In Mr. Morse's words, the reformed system "aims to take a step forward to greater international authority in all the main areas, but not a frighteningly large step." Under the reformed system, the Fund had the right to call on members to adjust, and in extreme cases, to reinforce the call with pressures. The Fund was to control, more or less tightly, the aggregate levels of different reserve assets. Moreover, in an unusual display of international cooperation, the reformed system envisaged an adequate aggregate flow of real resources to developing countries.

Another characteristic of the reformed system should be added to those described by Mr. Morse. Classified by whether the system was to be universally applicable to all members as was the par value system or whether the system made distinctions between categories of members, the reformed system, in many of its provisions, explicitly took account of the circumstances of developing members. In other words, there were enough exceptions for developing members that the initial principle of uniformity of the Fund's code of conduct and policies on use of its resources would no longer hold.[4]

Part II. Immediate Steps

It was well understood that the reformed system would not come into being immediately and that in the meantime action by the international community was urgently needed on a number of fronts. There was first of all the problem of how to conduct the Fund's work, especially taking decisions at high political levels, after the

---

[4]According to Joseph Gold, the Fund's General Counsel at the time, the *Outline of Reform* "would probably involve departures from the principle of uniformity if the Articles were amended to give effect to all the conclusions of the Committee." See Joseph Gold, "Uniformity as a Legal Principle of the International Monetary Fund," *Law and Policy in International Business* (Washington), Vol. 7 (1975), p. 796.

Committee of Twenty went out of existence. The SDR was not being used in international transactions, partly because of the "outmoded" way in which it was valued. Floating rates were not subjected to any rules or guidelines. Steeply higher prices for oil, after January 1974, were causing massive current account deficits for most countries. Officials of developing members were eager that the Fund enlarge its financial assistance to them, and it seemed likely that the Fund would do so, but the Fund would have to introduce some new facilities.

The Committee of Twenty worked in close conjunction with the Executive Directors and the Managing Director and staff in the last months of its existence (from January to June 1974), and a number of "immediate steps" were agreed upon by the middle of June, after the Executive Board took the necessary decisions. These immediate steps were described in Part II of the *Outline of Reform* and were fully endorsed by the Committee of Twenty. These immediate steps and the decisions taken by the Executive Board are described in Chapter 16.

WHY THE COMMITTEE OF TWENTY FAILED

As we have seen in earlier chapters, most officials had begun their negotiations for a reformed international monetary system in 1972 filled with hope and optimism for success. There were good reasons for their optimism. Only three years before, after prolonged debate, they had been able to agree on and introduce the SDR as a reserve asset. At the end of 1971, after months of disagreement, they had been able to agree on a realignment of the major currencies, the first such multilateral determination of exchange rates in history. After more than a decade of discussion about reforming the international monetary system, they had identified the weaknesses of the previous system and the basic changes needed in a new system: the adjustment process had to work better; par values had to be changed more frequently; global liquidity had to be brought under more effective international control; the use of currencies should be made more symmetrical and reliance on the dollar reduced; use of the SDR should be increased; and the system should work so as to help promote the economic development of developing members. Moreover, there was a genuine willingness of nearly all officials to negotiate a reformed system. Although many officials had complained earlier that U.S. officials were reluctant to enter into negotiations for a reformed system, most of them regarded Mr. Shultz's statement at the 1972 Annual Meeting as paving the way for serious deliberations. Finally, after years of frequent international meetings and gatherings, officials of the more than 120 members of the Fund had gradually come to know each other personally. Their mutual acquaintance made international cooperation easier, as compromises through informal contact could readily occur.

With all these advantages, why then did the Committee of Twenty fail in its mandate to draw up the reformed system? One can only conjecture. This conjecture is discussed under four headings—end of the old world economic order, different circumstances from Bretton Woods, lack of political will, and weakening of governmental authority.

End of the Postwar World Economic Order

Negotiations for reforming the international monetary system undoubtedly had to begin, as they did, in late 1971. After the events earlier in the year, most officials considered it imperative to get on quickly with planning a reformed system. As shown in Chapter 1, they believed that progress toward a reformed system would help maintain the exchange rates agreed at the end of 1971 and thus keep the par value system from collapsing entirely. The Managing Director and the Fund staff were keen to have a reformed system in place so that as the old system fell apart, members would continue to collaborate with the Fund as they substituted new exchange rate arrangements for the arrangements used under the Bretton Woods system. They feared that in the absence of any agreed system, it might be hard to persuade members to continue this collaboration. In addition, officials wanted to start reform negotiations quickly because they believed that their efforts might well be successful.

In retrospect, however, it would seem that if ever a committee proved to have been badly timed, it was the Committee of Twenty. By the end of the 1970s, it was possible to see that the Committee of Twenty, meeting in 1972–74, operated in an environment in which virtually the entire world economic order known since the end of World War II was just starting to crumble. The par value system, which in 1972 looked as if it might still be preserved, was to collapse entirely less than six months after the Committee began its discussions. Toward the end of 1972 worldwide inflation began to spiral and was shortly to become a major economic problem. The importance of inflation as a problem for the world economy was underestimated by the Committee of Twenty, as it was by most other economists and officials at the time. In addition, the most difficult economic circumstance to which the world had to adjust in the last quarter of the twentieth century—higher prices for oil and other fuel—occurred in the midst of the discussions of the Committee of Twenty, upsetting all expectations of a return to equilibria in international payments for the next several years. Higher oil prices not only presented a problem in themselves but the accompanying energy shortage immediately focused world attention for the first time on the potential exhaustion of the world's supplies of natural resources. Concern about the exhaustion of natural resources, together with new concerns about the pollution of air and water resources and of the environment generally, led to intensive discussion among economists about the limits to economic growth itself.

In these circumstances, plans for a reformed system proved too ambitious and too abstract and required unrealistic commitments by governments. It became hard for officials and economists to envisage the introduction for some years to come of orderly, stable, and systematized international monetary arrangements. Meanwhile, it seemed futile for them to wrangle over features of a system that was unlikely to be put into operation for a decade, if not longer.

Different Circumstances from Bretton Woods

Since the Bretton Woods agreement was successfully negotiated when the world was in a disturbed state, some experts have concluded that the unsettled state of the world does not explain the failure of the Committee of Twenty's reform exercise.[5] There are, however, critical differences in the circumstances attending the two exercises. The Bretton Woods negotiators could prescind from the unsettled state caused by World War II, because it was temporary, and could concentrate on planning for the postwar world. Thus, the prevailing international monetary arrangements had no impact on the positions of the Bretton Woods negotiators on international monetary arrangements to be introduced after the war. In contrast, in the 1970s current events affecting international monetary arrangements decidedly influenced the negotiating positions of the members of the Committee of Twenty. For example, once exchange rates floated early in 1973, U.S. officials wanted to try them. Moreover, after the jump in oil prices and emergence of huge payments deficits, developing members centered their efforts on the need for current balance of payments financing.

In 1944 public officials and economists of different countries agreed both on the broad objectives of economic policy and on the policies needed to achieve these objectives. Chapter 5 showed that on the domestic side there was a new commitment to full employment and that most governments agreed that, if necessary, they should use macroeconomic policies to achieve it. On the international side, after the adverse experiences of the 1930s of competitive exchange depreciation, exchange controls, protectionism, and bilateralism, most allied governments were ready to support a new era of orderly arrangements based on convertible currencies, multilateral payments, and stable exchange rates designed to create a large world market to which all countries would have equal access. In effect, there was a universal rejection of past arrangements in favor of an agreed code of conduct.

In the 1970s, officials agreed neither on economic objectives nor on policies. Some stressed controlling inflation; others stimulating employment. Some continued to believe in Keynesian policies; an increasing number strongly advocated monetarist policies. From the outset they had opposing views about the priorities to be given to different features of a reformed international monetary system.

Years of planning preceded the Bretton Woods Conference. The "White Plan"

---

[5]See, for example, John Williamson, *The Failure of World Monetary Reform* (cited in fn. 8 of Chap. 9 above), pp. 165–66.

had roots dating back to 1940 and the "Keynes Plan" went back at least to the summer of 1941, and the ideas encompassed in both these plans had precedents in stabilization arrangements tried in the 1930s. Both the Keynes and White plans, moreover, went through a number of drafts before they were made public early in 1942. In 1943 the plans were reshaped, as Keynes and White and their respective colleagues exchanged views, and other plans, including those put forward by the French and by the Canadian authorities, were reviewed. U.S. officials also consulted representatives from a number of countries on the draft plans. From September 15 through October 9, 1943, as part of a broader series of meetings covering proposals for postwar international investment, commodity policy, and commercial policy, nine meetings on the monetary plans were held in Washington between a U.S. group, headed by White, and a British delegation, headed by Keynes. Out of these meetings emerged "The Joint Statement by Experts on the Establishment of an International Monetary Fund." Even this Joint Statement went through several drafts before the final text was produced in April 1944. Then, prior to the full-scale conference at Bretton Woods, a limited but still numerous group of countries (16 plus the United States) was invited to send representatives to a preliminary drafting conference at Atlantic City in the second half of June 1944.

In the 1970s, apart from the Executive Directors' report on reform of 1972, there were really no "plans" for reform. Only the U.S. delegation offered specific proposals.

At Bretton Woods the team of technicians was small and could make compromises and concessions that would hold. They regarded it as their duty to arrive at an agreement and determined to do so. In contrast, negotiations in the Committee of Twenty were handled by finance ministers with political considerations in mind. For many of them, compromises were difficult or impossible since they had to refer crucial questions to their heads of state or government. In effect, to some extent a struggle for political power was going on that was largely absent from Bretton Woods.

At the same time there was no one country, or small group of countries, that had sufficient leadership to influence the positions taken by other countries. At Bretton Woods, the United States and the United Kingdom had dominated the negotiations. By the 1970s not only had the role of the United Kingdom in world economic affairs been considerably reduced but the role of the United States, the single most dominant economy after World War II, had been weakened. The loss of the leadership role of the United States was due primarily to the diffusion of economic power among the large industrial nations. But confidence in U.S. leadership had been badly shaken also by the Viet Nam war and in 1973–74 by the Watergate crisis. The nine EC countries were not united enough, or ready, to take up responsibility for world leadership. The negotiations in the Committee of Twenty included full participation by representatives from many more countries than the negotiations conducted at Bretton Woods, but reconciliation of the positions taken by 20 different constituencies proved in the end impossible.

Lack of Political Will

Recalling the drive and determination of a handful of leaders in 1944 to bring about a brave new economic world, officials of developing countries complained at the Annual Meeting in Nairobi in 1973 that officials of industrial countries did not have the political will to cooperate in bringing about a reformed international monetary system. Mr. Morse himself attributed the failure of the Committee of Twenty to lack of political will.

It is certainly fair to conclude from the discussions of the Committee of Twenty that none of the officials was in a compromising mood. There was endless repetition of national positions. Some observers, citing the French proposal for negative interest charges on excess reserves, the Italian efforts at alternative proposals for indicators and asset settlement, and the apparent German willingness to agree to a link, blamed the lack of compromise on the United States. Attributing the failure to compromise mainly to the United States, however, overlooks the important fact that the United States had by far the most serious balance of payments problem and the most at stake in the negotiations, and officials of other countries were not prepared to hold earnest discussions on how the U.S. balance of payments problems might be solved, or at least mitigated, through mutual action.

In these circumstances, U.S. officials and others were inclined to experiment with the floating rate regime that had developed. Members of the U.S. Congress, as well as some high-ranking officials in the Administration, wanted to try out a period of floating the dollar in the expectation that the U.S. payments deficit might be corrected. Officials of the Federal Republic of Germany wanted to try a floating rate for the deutsche mark in the expectation that it would be easier to manage German monetary policy. Officials of other European countries also believed at the time that floating rates would enable them to follow relatively independent domestic monetary policies without concern for international repercussions.

Because of the lack of compromise on the basic issues, officials of developed countries, especially at the technical level, spent most of their time seeking mechanical ways—objective indicators, settlement systems, multicurrency intervention arrangements, substitution accounts—to ensure that international monetary arrangements were consistent with their national positions and failed to offer proposals for coming to grips with the basic economic problems of the day.

Officials of developing countries, eager to shape the world monetary system to the benefit of their own countries, concentrated on a few matters of interest only to them and on making sure they were protected from any arrangements proposed by the industrial countries.

Weakening of Governmental Authority

Another factor in the failure of the Committee of Twenty to bring about a reformed system was the relative weakening of governmental authority. The Bretton

Woods system had been based on the supposition that governments could take, and enforce, decisions concerning their exchange rates and their exchange policies. The Bretton Woods Conference was held at a time when governments were exercising most pervasive control over their economies. By 1974 when the Committee of Twenty was finishing its work, however, the ability of governments to regulate the international monetary system was notably declining. A number of factors made effective control of the international monetary system by governments, or by an international agency such as the International Monetary Fund, much more difficult than before. Liquidity in the international monetary system had grown phenomenally. A worldwide network of multinational corporations and of private commercial banks had developed. Private international banking had grown exceedingly rapidly. Eurocurrency markets seemed beyond the regulations of any government. Close personal relations between bankers and business executives in different countries were made possible by the development of easy worldwide communications and travel. Instant transfers of funds were now possible because of the computerization of banking operations allowing entrepreneurs readily to switch funds from one currency to another or from one country to another when differences in interest rates, exchange rates, taxation requirements, or political situations made it profitable to do so. It was, for instance, much more difficult for officials in central banks, treasuries, or other government agencies to fix and maintain exchange rates, enforce controls on capital movements, or to run any kind of exchange control system than it had ever been before. In these circumstances, it was hard for financial officials to conceive of a reformed international monetary system subject to regulation or control or even coordinated by the international community as the Bretton Woods system had been. Paradoxically, most of the developments integrating the world economy and world financial markets were the result of the Fund's success but not within the scope of the Fund's jurisdiction.

Another factor relating to governmental authority also held back agreement on the reformed international monetary system. Although countries were being pushed toward ever greater economic integration by technological advances and by economic forces, national officials still wanted autonomy over their country's economic policies. Interdependence and the desire for independence came into conflict. The reformed international monetary system as conceived by the Committee of Twenty, and earlier by officials in the Fund, was consistent with and tried to fill the needs of the economic interdependence developed by 1970. Most countries were determined, however, to retain sovereignty over their exchange rate policies, their monetary policies, their trade policies, and their policies vis-à-vis capital transactions. Thus, although the Fund had since its birth been moving in directions in which the reformed system was to go—toward greater flexibility of exchange rates, but under Fund surveillance, more initiative and pressure from the Fund to induce members to change their exchange rates and to adopt other adjustment measures, more effective consultations between members and the Fund, more management of the supply and composition of liquidity by the Fund—the world was not yet ready for the degree of international authority and management involved in the reformed system.[6]

Lack of Emphasis on Techniques Not a Factor

One of the reasons sometimes mentioned for the failure of the Committee of Twenty is that the members of the Bureau of the Committee did not concentrate sufficiently on technical issues or did not devise the most appropriate techniques.[7] The line of reasoning is this. As seen in Chapter 13, the members of the Bureau conceived of their role as a negotiating one. They tried to help close the gap between opposing positions taken by various officials. To this end, for example, they tried to dissuade both U.S. and European officials from demanding extreme features in a reformed system. Some economists, including some of the Fund staff, however, have taken the view that had the members of the Bureau concentrated instead on getting agreement on the specific techniques to be used in a reformed system—a technique for asset settlement and a technique for currency intervention, for instance—officials might have been able to agree on these techniques. These techniques could then have been combined to form an overall system. These economists, especially those on the Fund staff, favored an approach which concentrated on techniques since that approach had been successful in the 1960s in getting agreement on the features of the SDR.

The Bureau of the Committee of Twenty unquestionably does seem to have searched for ways to obtain agreement on broad features of a reformed system while the Fund staff, for example, worked out detailed descriptions of the several techniques that we have read in earlier chapters. Nonetheless, given the circumstances described above, it seems unlikely that agreement on techniques in the reformed system would have ultimately yielded agreement on a reformed system. The difficulties that financial officials had in coming to agreement in 1975 and 1976 on techniques for resolution of the exchange rate problem, of the gold problem, and of other problems described in subsequent chapters, suggest fundamental differences in viewpoint that had to be resolved at the political rather than at the technical level. Even with political agreement for the resolution of these problems and agreement on techniques and eventual agreement on a Second Amendment to the Articles of Agreement, as described below, it was the existing system and not the reformed system that was given legal sanction.

Especially striking several years after the report on reform of 1972 and after the Committee of Twenty finished its work are the discrepancies between the plans for

---

[6]For a description of the ways in which the Fund had gradually been evolving in the direction of the reformed system, see Margaret Garritsen de Vries, "Steadily Evolving Fund Lays Foundation Stones of the Emerging System," *IMF Survey* (Washington), Vol. 3 (September 30, 1974), pp. 305 and 307–309.

[7]See, for example, John Williamson, *The Failure of World Monetary Reform* (cited in fn. 5 above), pp. 181–84.

the reformed system and the actual circumstances at the end of 1978, the close of the period reviewed here. The Executive Directors in their 1972 report and the Committee of Twenty aimed at a fixed exchange rate system; as of the end of 1978, major currencies were continuing to float with wide fluctuations taking place. The reformers planned for a convertibility system; at the end of 1978 the dollar remained inconvertible. They worked toward an SDR standard; as of 1978 the world was still fairly much on a dollar standard. They aimed at control of global liquidity; as of 1978 the creation of greater amounts of dollar reserves and of larger amounts of liquidity was continuing. In every respect actual circumstances differed from the planned reformed system. It seems likely, therefore, that an approach relying on getting agreement on technical pieces of a system would not have brought about agreement on any of the big facets of a reformed system. There is even some question of whether the various technical pieces would have produced an operable system.

■　■　■　■　■　■

In sum, while the conventional explanation of the failure of the Committee of Twenty is that it was "overtaken by events," that is, by the emergence of high rates of inflation in 1973 and by the prospect of unprecedentedly large balance of payments disequilibria in international payments following the increases for oil at the end of 1973, this explanation seems by no means complete or accurate. By the time of the 1973 Annual Meeting in Nairobi, the prospect for successful negotiations was already dim. The emergence of accelerating inflation and the jump in oil prices gave the Committee an excuse for concluding negotiations that were not getting anywhere.

Given all the reasons why officials were unable to construct a reformed international monetary system in 1972–74, while their predecessors had succeeded 30 years earlier, the wonder is *not* the failure of 1972–74, but that the original Bretton Woods Conference was successful. It took very special circumstances to bring the Bretton Woods system and the Fund itself into being.[8] Such unique circumstances plainly did not exist in the years 1972–74.

A FINAL WORD ON THE COMMITTEE OF TWENTY

Although it did not reform the international monetary system, the Committee of Twenty represented a major and intensive effort on the part of financial officials to devise new arrangements and to reconcile opposing views. For the officials involved, the planning, drafting, meetings, informal exchange of views, and hopes for success were serious and exhilarating, as well as frustrating. These were exciting times, as there was a genuine attempt at international negotiation about a vital matter.

---

[8]The factors underlying the success of the Bretton Woods Conference are described in Margaret Garritsen de Vries, "40th Anniversary of Historic Conference Commemorates Birth of the Fund and Bank," *IMF Survey* (Washington), Vol. 13 (July 2, 1984), pp. 193–97.

Despite its failure to effect reform, the Committee of Twenty served a number of positive purposes. Primarily, it provided an opportunity for officials from all Fund members to air their grievances with the former Bretton Woods system and to make proposals for what they wanted in the reformed system. Officials were able to learn firsthand the positions of their counterparts from other countries and how strongly they held these positions. This familiarity with each other's views came at a time when international monetary arrangements were extremely fluid. Consequently, financial officials could better understand each other's positions for the next several years as international monetary arrangements continued to evolve.

The work of the Committee of Twenty also was crucial in facilitating agreement later on pieces of the evolving international monetary system. The *Outline*, especially the Annexes, helped to furnish the basis for agreement on a number of points subsequently developed and incorporated into the Second Amendment of the Articles of Agreement. After the amendment went into effect, some of the features described in the Annexes, such as a substitution account, were brought up for consideration again.

In addition, the Committee of Twenty proved its usefulness as a body for policymaking in the Fund and as a forerunner to other Committees of the Board of Governors—the Interim Committee, the Development Committee, and the Council specified in the Second Amendment. Through use of these Committees, especially the Interim Committee, the policymaking machinery of the Fund was to be significantly altered.

Another significant achievement of the Committee of Twenty, as it ended its work, was turning its attention to current developments and working in conjunction with the Fund's other bodies. After the end of the work by the Bureau and by the Committee of Twenty there was a smooth transition of the work on international monetary questions back to the Executive Board and the Fund management and staff. Within two years after being pushed out of the discussions on reform, as described in Chapter 8, by June 1974, the Executive Directors the Managing Director and staff were back in the picture, making decisions on the international monetary system that would have been impossible earlier when relations between the Fund and the United States were strained. In January 1974, the Committee of Twenty started to work on the immediate steps needed, such as guidelines for floating rates, the valuation of the SDR, and the oil facility. By June 1974, as will be shown in Part Three, the Executive Board was so thoroughly involved in these topics that it was difficult to see where the recommendations of the Committee of Twenty ended and the decisions of the Executive Board began.

PART THREE

Atmosphere of Crisis and the Fund's Responses

(September 1973–October 1974)

"The problems and uncertainties that now confront the world economy call for international cooperation of rare quality."

—H. JOHANNES WITTEVEEN, addressing the Board of Governors in Washington, September 30, 1974

CHAPTER

15

Preparing for
an Evolving System

*T*HE ADOPTION OF FLOATING RATES by several members in February and
March 1973 presented the Fund with several questions. What attitudes should
the Fund take toward floating rates? How could it involve itself with the individual
members that had introduced floating rates? Should the regime of central rates and
wider margins that the Fund had introduced in December 1971 as a temporary
device be abolished? Further questions arose with regard to the Fund's operations
and policies because the link between the U.S. dollar and gold had been severed and
it appeared unlikely that gold would again have a prime place in a reformed system.
How should the SDR be valued since its valuation in terms of gold was no longer
appropriate? Should the SDR receive a higher rate of interest so as to make it a more
attractive reserve asset? How should that interest rate be determined?

The Committee of Twenty, as noted earlier, purposely avoided dealing with
questions such as these relating to the existing system until after September 1973
when it seemed fairly certain that they would be unable to agree on a reformed
system. In the meantime, beginning in April 1973, while the Committee of Twenty
was deliberating a reformed system, the Executive Directors, together with the
Managing Director and staff, started to consider the questions arising out of existing
international monetary arrangements. For the next several months, however, they
were unable to provide answers. Progress on these matters depended on the
outcome of the negotiations in the Committee of Twenty, since agreement on the
features of a reformed system would make unnecessary or override any decisions
taken with respect to the existing system.

After September 1973, H. Johannes Witteveen, the new Managing Director,
returning from the Annual Meeting just held in Nairobi, came forward with
suggestions to help resolve some of the problems in existing international monetary
arrangements. In November and December 1973, the Executive Board took decisions
on certain questions that they had been discussing earlier in 1973. These decisions
permitted participants in the narrow margins arrangements of the EC to use their
holdings of SDRs among themselves, pending a more basic decision on a new

method for valuing the SDR, inaugurated a program of special consultations with selected members on their external policies, and ended the temporary regime of central rates and wider margins. These decisions, described in the present chapter, were in effect a holding operation until more basic decisions could be agreed. In this sense, they can be construed as measures preparatory to an evolving system. More basic decisions relating to existing international monetary arrangements were taken in June 1974. They are discussed in the next chapter.

SPECIAL CONSULTATIONS INAUGURATED

From May 1970 to February 1973 the Fund had initiated special consultations with four members—Canada, Italy, Japan, and the United Kingdom—that had already introduced floating rates. These consultations were supplementary to the annual consultations either under Article XIV that the Fund had been holding with its members since March 1952 or under Article VIII that had been initiated early in the 1960s. They were intended to make concrete the provision of the Executive Board decisions taken when these four members introduced floating rates. These decisions stated that the member would remain "in close consultation with the Fund with a view toward an early return to a par value and the maintenance of agreed margins." Financial officials of each member were to discuss with Fund officials the actions being taken to facilitate resumption of par values.

After the breakdown of the par value system and the adoption of floating rates by most of the Fund's largest members in February and March 1973, it was no longer sensible for the Fund to hold special consultations in order to urge members with floating rates to return to the par value system. If the Fund was to have any influence on exchange rates in the emerging system, the floating rates not only of Canada, Italy, Japan, and the United Kingdom, but now also of the United States, and the joint float of Belgium, France, the Federal Republic of Germany, the Netherlands, and other countries should be kept under review.

Taking its legal basis from the provision of the Articles of Agreement stating that members were obliged to collaborate with the Fund to promote exchange stability (Article IV, Section 4(a)), Mr. Schweitzer and the staff had as early as February 1973 begun to discuss how special consultations on exchange rate policy, supplementary to the usual annual consultations, might be held with all members with floating rates. As had occurred when the annual consultations on exchange restrictions under Article XIV were inaugurated in 1952, attention centered on developing a procedure that would elicit the kind of cooperation from members for consultations to be sufficiently frank and effective. The right procedure was by no means obvious. Although Fund staff could more readily and more frankly than in the past bring up the topic of exchange rates in their discussions with officials of members, these officials still considered discussions of their interventions in exchange markets highly confidential and sensitive. Officials of Western European members were willing to discuss exchange rate policy *only* on a confidential basis with the Managing Director or the Deputy Managing Director and one or two senior members of the staff. They explicitly stated their unwillingness to disclose their exchange rate policies to officials of other countries, including those on the Executive Board. Officials of Japan were reluctant to discuss exchange rate policy in any depth. Officials of the United States liked floating rates precisely because floating left determination of exchange rates in the hands of market forces; they believed that there was little to discuss with officials of the Fund.

These considerations implied that the Fund should use an informal and voluntary procedure for holding special consultations. The Managing Director, for example, might initiate discussions with officials of a member when he considered them necessary, and only one or two staff members would be included. Such informal and voluntary procedures, however, might put the Managing Director in the awkward position of having to negotiate holding special consultations. The very member whose policies the Fund believed were most in need of examination might reject participation in such consultations, leaving the Fund in an embarrassing and ineffective position. On the other hand, too formal a procedure for special consultations that mandated periodic consultations was likely to produce perfunctory discussions and convey the impression that the Fund wanted to arrange consultations only for their own sake.

Another procedural problem was that in making exchange rate decisions the authorities of members were heavily influenced by rapidly changing developments in other members and by exchange rate decisions taken by officials of other members. Hence, the Fund might have to conduct special consultations with several members concurrently, or even with officials of several members present at the same meeting.

In August 1973, when the Executive Directors discussed holding special consultations, they were unable to resolve these procedural problems. Although most Executive Directors recognized the vital importance of keeping the Fund active in the surveillance of exchange rates, few were ready to support the extension of special consultations to the major industrial members. Some Executive Directors, particularly those appointed or elected by Western European members and by Japan, objected that additional consultations with the Fund would impose a heavy burden on officials of members as well as on the staff of the Fund and would duplicate the regular annual consultations. Other Executive Directors objected that the Fund had no criteria by which to judge floating exchange rates and the Executive Board would consequently have considerable difficulty in evaluating the appropriateness of a member's exchange rate policies. Mr. Beaurain explained that the French authorities objected to special consultations for France and the Federal Republic of Germany on the grounds that these members *were* observing the Articles of Agreement and did not need to be subjected to special discussions on their exchange rate policies. Because some kind of consultations on exchange rate policy more frequent than the usual annual consultations was essential to keep the Fund in the exchange rate field, Mr. Southard, as Acting Managing Director, suggested that the

Executive Board return to the subject of special consultations later. The staff meanwhile should discuss informally with individual Executive Directors procedures that might be acceptable.

When Mr. Witteveen took over as Managing Director on September 1, 1973, he immediately explored ways of instituting consultations on exchange rate policy with the major industrial members. After two months of discussions with the staff and of informal discussions with a number of Executive Directors, Mr. Witteveen proposed to the Executive Board on October 31, 1973 that a few senior staff under his close direction periodically hold informal discussions for two or three days with high officials of each of a number of members that had a major impact on international currency relations. Staff would go to these members simultaneously. The list of members to be consulted in these special discussions would not be fixed. The first round, to begin in November 1973, would be held with nine members: Belgium, Canada, France, the Federal Republic of Germany, Italy, Japan, the Netherlands, the United Kingdom, and the United States. The results of the discussions would be summarized in a general way, without revealing the discussions with any individual member, in the world economic outlook papers, a semiannual review that was becoming a regular feature of the work of the Executive Board. At that time, the Managing Director would sum up for the Executive Directors the results of these discussions, "with due care to safeguard the confidentiality of information and views on matters of a particularly sensitive nature."

The Executive Directors, increasingly aware that the Fund ought to take some action on the exchange rate policy of its larger members, welcomed the Managing Director's proposal, commending him for his leadership and for finding a positive way for the Fund to play a crucial role in the exchange rate field "during the transition to the reformed system." They took a decision concurring with his statement on the procedures to be used.[1] Thus there was inaugurated a program of special consultations with members whose external policies had important repercussions on international currency relations. The term "external policies" was more encompassing than exchange rate policies, and included policies that had a direct impact on the balance of payments and thereby on exchange rates, such as controls on capital movements.

In the last two weeks of November 1973, one or two senior staff went to each of the nine members listed above and held confidential discussions with high-ranking financial officials. These discussions were in accordance with detailed guidelines worked out by the Managing Director and the senior staff of the various Area Departments, the Exchange and Trade Relations Department, and the Research Department. The results of the discussions were incorporated, in a general way, in the world economic outlook discussed by the Executive Board in the first week of January 1974.

A second round of special consultations with members whose external policies were of importance to other members was held in the same way in March and April

---

[1]E.B. Decision No. 4076-(73/101), October 31, 1973; Vol. III below, pp. 484–85.

1974. In this second round, Belgium and the Netherlands were omitted and four developing members—Brazil, India, Iran, and Nigeria—were added. The subsequent world economic outlook review incorporating in general terms the results of these special consultations was taken up by the Executive Board early in June.

In this way a series of special consultations began which were held periodically, more than once a year. From 7 to 12 members were usually involved, although the members varied on each occasion. Canada, France, the Federal Republic of Germany, Japan, the United Kingdom, and the United States were always on the list. In the next few years—in addition to Brazil, India, Iran, and Nigeria—Algeria, Egypt, Kenya, Korea, Kuwait, Indonesia, Ivory Coast, Malaysia, Mexico, Pakistan, the Philippines, Saudi Arabia, Singapore, the United Arab Emirates, Uruguay, Venezuela, Yugoslavia, and Zambia were among the nonindustrial members with which special consultations were held.

The way in which special consultations were instituted parallels the way in which the annual consultations under Article XIV were instituted in 1952. The Fund began cautiously, confining its procedures and discussions to what it believed officials of member governments were ready to accept. Only a few members were involved initially, but gradually their number grew. The first round of discussions was experimental, but under the persuasion of the Managing Director and staff, discussions broadened.

Special consultations, referred to within the Fund as miniconsultations or as special "visits" in connection with the world economic outlook exercise, continued after 1978. Although they did not become a primary instrument by which the Fund carried out its operations and implemented its policies in the years covered here, special consultations greatly assisted the staff in preparing the *World Economic Outlook*. With up-to-date information on the economic situation of as many as a dozen members whose economies were critical the staff could much better evaluate the outlook for the world economy.

CENTRAL RATE DECISION REVISED

One of the Fund's more formal responses to the evolving system was to revise in November 1973 the central rate decision that it had taken in December 1971.[2] At that time, the Fund introduced the concept of a central rate because many members were not yet ready to establish effective par values but wanted nevertheless to maintain exchange rates within specified margins. Central rates were intended to be a de facto, although not a de jure, temporary substitute for par values, that is, in the period before observance of par values and maintenance of appropriate margins were resumed either in accordance with existing Articles of Agreement or with some amended Articles. An advantage of central rates was that they obviated the need for

---

[2]The central rate decision was described in *History, 1966–71*, Vol. I, pp. 557–59.

members to go to their legislatures for their establishment, since these rates were not par values agreed upon and fixed in relation to gold as a common denominator. It was thought that this advantage would be especially important for the United States.

After the introduction of widespread floating in the first three months of 1973, central rates for many members had become ineffective. Some members, such as Italy and Japan, that had declared central rates to the Fund no longer maintained margins around these rates. Several other members which had central rates and continued to maintain margins maintained these margins in relation to an intervention currency (namely, the U.S. dollar), but margins were no longer being maintained by the country issuing the intervention currency (that is, by the United States). Prescribed margins did not therefore result in exchange rate stability. The decision of a number of European members to maintain rates within margins only for transactions among their own currencies also resulted in deviations from the initial concept of central rates. In brief, members were deviating not only from the par value system specified in the Articles of Agreement but also from the alternative concept of central rates.

In July 1973, the legal staff recommended to the Executive Board that the central rate decision be revised so that members that wished to do so could have a meaningful central rate. For some members there was a psychological advantage in regarding themselves as maintaining a central rate rather than having no fixed rate at all. These members wanted the Fund's central rate decision to be revised so that their currencies could continue to be regarded as following a central rate even if the intervention currency was floating. More explicitly, some of the members that used U.S. dollars to intervene in their exchange markets still wanted to be regarded as having some kind of fixed exchange rate. Under the revisions recommended by the staff, a member would be able to establish a new central rate, with or without wider margins, if it maintained a stable rate in terms of its own intervention currency or currencies. Moreover, a member maintaining narrow margins against an intervention currency would be deemed to be acting consistently with the central rate decision even if its intervention currency was the currency of a member that did not maintain rates within margins consistent with the decision.

When the Executive Board discussed these revisions in August 1973, most Executive Directors had no firm opinions. Mr. Wahl, however, stated that the proposed revision was unacceptable to the French authorities. The original central rate decision, he stressed, was meant to encourage stable exchange rates. The revisions now proposed by the staff would permit use of the term "central rate" even when a country's intervention currency was floating, thereby making the concept of a central rate less meaningful. This diluted concept of a central rate, moreover, was to apply to participants in the European narrow margins arrangement, putting the arrangements for the French franc, which the French authorities regarded as consistent with the Articles of Agreement, in the same category as the dollar and the pound sterling, which the French authorities regarded as inconsistent with the Articles. Because of these objections and because of the intense debates going on in the Committee of Twenty in the last several months of 1973 over the desirability of fixed versus floating rates, it took two months before the Executive Board was able to take a decision even on this seemingly minor question. But in November 1973, the Executive Board approved the decision revising the central rate regime in the ways that the staff recommended.[3]

WHY THE SDR NEEDED TO BE REVALUED

When the SDR was created, its value was guaranteed and stated in terms of gold. It was made equivalent to 0.888671 gram of fine gold, the same as that of the U.S. dollar on July 1, 1944, when the original Articles of Agreement were drafted. (This continued to be the gold content of the dollar until May 8, 1972.) A link between the SDR, gold, and the U.S. dollar was thus established; an ounce of gold was equivalent to SDR 35, just as it was equal to $35. Transactions in SDRs, however, were made in currency rather than in gold: in exchange for SDRs, participants made available currency that was "convertible in fact." It was therefore necessary for the Fund to have a method of translating the gold value of the SDR into values in terms of currencies. In other words, the SDR had to have a transactions price as well as a price in terms of gold. The Articles of Agreement, as amended in 1969, moreover, provided that a participant using SDRs should receive the same value in terms of currency regardless of the particular currency it received in exchange for SDRs. This provision was called the "principle of equal value."[4] To implement this provision, the exchange rates at which currencies were provided against SDRs had to be taken into account, and the Articles provided that the Fund establish a procedure for determining the relevant exchange rates.[5] The Executive Board was to specify the procedures in the Rules and Regulations of the Fund. This arrangement meant that while the value of the SDR in terms of gold could not be changed without amending the Articles, the Executive Board could determine the method of valuing the SDR in terms of currencies.

Inasmuch as the relevant exchange rates needed to be determined before the start of operations in SDRs, the Executive Board in 1969 adopted Rule O-3 of the Rules and Regulations. Rule O-3(i) provided that the exchange rate in terms of SDRs for the U.S. dollar was to be the par value of the dollar, SDR 1 was to equal $1. Rule O-3(ii) provided that for other major currencies representative rates would be used, rates selected from spot rates for the U.S. dollar actually prevailing in exchange markets and agreed between the member issuing the currency concerned and the Fund. In 1970 and 1971, the Executive Board took decisions on representative rates for a number of currencies.[6] Since the rates for other currencies in exchange markets

---

[3]E.B. Decision No. 4083-(73/104), November 7, 1973; Vol. III below, pp. 485–87.

[4]Article XXV, Section 8(*a*) of the Articles of Agreement as amended in 1969. These Articles are in *History, 1966–71*, Vol. II, pp. 97–141. Article XXV, Section 8(*a*) is on p. 127.

[5]Article XXV, Section 8(*b*).

[6]Rule O-3, as adopted on September 18, 1969, can be found in *History, 1966–71*, Vol. II, p. 187. The representative rates agreed were described in *History, 1966–71*, Vol. I, p. 226.

were fixed in relation to the par value of the dollar, the par value of the dollar was thus the base for determining the price, or value, of the SDR in terms of currencies.

When Rule O-3 was adopted, use of the par value of the U.S. dollar as such a base seemed entirely appropriate. The dollar was at the center of the international monetary system as it operated in practice. The United States legally maintained the value of the dollar at 0.888671 gram of fine gold by standing ready to convert dollar balances into gold. The majority of other Fund members maintained market rates within 1 percent either side of the par value of the dollar. In these circumstances, there was no important difference between a value for the SDR in terms of currencies based on par values and a value in terms of currencies based on actual exchange rates.

Basing the currency value of the SDR on the par value of the dollar was also based on the assumption, regarded as realistic in the mid-1960s when the features of the SDR were being considered, that the actual exchange rate for the U.S. dollar would at all times be equal to its par value. Should the United States decide to change the par value in terms of gold, the value of the SDR in terms of dollars and hence in terms of other currencies would accordingly change. The gold guarantee for the SDR ensured that the value of the SDR would be protected against a devaluation of the dollar; in the event of a devaluation, the SDR would be equal to more dollars than before the devaluation. When the new par value for the U.S. dollar was set in May 1972, the SDR became equal to $1.08571. When the second devaluation of the dollar took place in February 1973, the SDR became equal to $1.20635; (the reciprocal was $1 = SDR 0.828948, which was the way in which the Fund expressed the value of the SDR in terms of currencies for its operational and accounting purposes). Revaluations of currencies with respect to gold, which would make each SDR equal to fewer units of the revalued currency, were expected to be rare events; there had been only two revaluations of major currencies (of the deutsche mark and the Netherlands guilder in 1961) since the Fund was created, and in the mid-1960s there was little indication of further revaluations.

Another reason for basing the currency valuation of the SDR on the dollar was that such a single currency method of valuing the SDR was convenient and easy for the Fund to use. The alternative of valuing the SDR in terms of several currencies was complicated and at the time offered no special advantages.

When the SDR was created, it was assigned a rate of interest, but this was not regarded as one of its crucial features. The crucial features of the SDR concerned arrangements for its allocation, the amounts participants would hold and how they would transfer them, the Fund's part in such transfers, and the uses the Fund itself would make of the SDR. No one was much concerned about the rate of interest.

The original rate of interest on the SDR was set at a low 1.5 percent a year, a rate already in effect in the Fund's transactions and operations. It had been established in 1961 as the rate of interest that the Fund paid to claimants under the General Arrangements to Borrow and was the rate of remuneration paid to members on their net creditor positions, that is, on their super gold tranche positions in the

Fund. (A super gold tranche position was defined as the difference between the Fund's holdings of a member's currency and 75 percent of the member's quota when those holdings were less than 75 percent.) The rate of interest on the SDR was thus determined primarily in terms of its relation to the yields on other Fund-related reserve assets—the readily repayable claims arising out of borrowing by the Fund through the General Arrangements to Borrow and the super gold tranche. In addition, officials of the United States preferred a low rate of interest on the SDR in order to minimize its competition with the dollar as a reserve asset, since. U.S. officials tried to follow low interest rate policies on dollar-denominated assets.

A low rate of interest on the SDR was also regarded as adequate since nominal rates of interest on holdings of money instruments denominated in currencies were relatively low at the time, and it was assumed that the SDR, like gold, would maintain its value better than would holdings of currencies. The only reason for any rate of interest on the SDR (since gold bore no interest) was that Mr. Schweitzer and the staff and most Executive Directors believed that some rate of interest would offer central bank authorities a financial inducement to hold SDRs, rather than gold, in their reserves, thereby helping to launch the SDR as a reserve asset. Another provision of the Articles was that the rate of interest on the SDR had to be equal to the charges each participant had to pay on its net cumulative accumulation of SDRs. (The rate of interest and the charges paid were made the same so that a participant holding more SDRs than its net cumulative allocation *received* a net payment, and one holding less *made* a net payment.) The Fund wanted to keep these charges low.

The rate of interest on the SDR of 1.5 percent a year was specified in the Articles, but the Executive Board could raise or lower this rate, provided that it did not exceed the rate of remuneration and that an increase above 2 percent a year or a reduction below 1 percent a year was approved by a three-fourths majority of the total voting power.

Another Method Needed After Par Values Collapsed

The eruptions in the international monetary system which began on August 15, 1971 raised questions about the validity of the initial method of valuing the SDR. The United States no longer converted dollar balances into gold, raising the question of whether the gold value of the dollar was sufficiently meaningful for the SDR to be based on a fixed relationship with the dollar. From August 15, 1971 until the realignment of currencies four months later, narrow margins were not observed for most major currencies, market rates for several currencies floated, and several currencies began to appreciate vis-à-vis the dollar. These developments revealed clearly that a stable value for the SDR in terms of currencies based on par values, and especially on a par value for the U.S. dollar, did not necessarily mean a stable value for the SDR in terms of currencies based on their actual rates in exchange markets. Then with the onset in February and March 1973 of widespread floating, the value of the SDR, fixed in terms of the U.S. dollar, fluctuated widely in terms of other currencies. Such fluctuations in the currency value of the SDR occurred from one week to the next, as the value of the SDR in terms of currencies moved up or down depending on the strength of the dollar in exchange markets.

In addition, after August 15, 1971 some European financial officials increasingly opposed linking the value of an internationally created reserve asset to an individual currency and to the policies of its issuer, and many officials wanted to provide the SDR with stability of value in terms of currencies in general rather than in terms of only one currency. Those in the Fund were motivated by the belief that a stable value for the SDR in terms of currencies would help to get the SDR established as the main reserve asset of the reformed system.

After it became apparent that the SDR, as originally designed, did not necessarily have a stable value in terms of currencies, many officials came to center their attention on the interest rate on the SDR. They began to believe that this rate of interest should have some relation to market rates of interest. One consideration was that interest rates had risen substantially in the years since SDRs were established and 1.5 percent a year was now relatively very low. Beginning in early 1973, several Executive Directors urged that attention be given to raising this rate. It had also become evident that the SDR would have to have a higher rate of interest when, in the course of the Executive Board discussions for the reformed international monetary system in 1972, serious thought was given to the possibility of a substitution account, in which SDRs would be substituted for balances of reserve currencies. Schemes making mandatory the exchange of reserve currency holdings, on which members received higher rates of interest, for SDRs, which bore a lower rate of interest, would involve a severe loss of income for Fund members. A substitution facility could therefore never be adopted unless the rate of interest on the SDR was raised to be more comparable with the higher rates of interest prevailing on currency balances.

By early 1973, management and staff saw the necessity of relating the interest rate on SDRs to the interest rates prevailing for currencies. This led the staff to rethink the method of valuing the SDR. If the interest rate on the SDR was to be a function of market rates of interest on currencies, it seemed logical to value the SDR itself in terms of currencies. Indeed, the interest rate and the value—in effect the capital value—of the SDR together made up the effective yield on the SDR. By early 1973 the management and staff and several Executive Directors thus regarded the effective yield on the SDR as important. They believed that this yield was the crucial determinant of the willingness of central bank authorities to hold SDRs and that if the rules for holding and using SDRs were relaxed, as seemed likely, it would become even more critical.

Executive Directors Reject a Valuation Based on a Basket of Currencies

The management and staff suggested to the Executive Board in May 1973 that the valuation of the SDR be based on a specified package, or basket, of currencies, in which a number of currencies were combined with given weights, and that the interest rate on the SDR be linked to the average rate of interest on the currencies in the package. In suggesting to the Executive Board a basket of currencies for valuing the SDR, the management and staff were initially more influenced by the need to change the rate of interest on the SDR and to give this asset a satisfactory effective yield than by the need to change the valuation of the SDR itself. The need for an average rate of interest was based on the reasoning that it would not be desirable to make the yield on the SDR higher than that prevailing on any individual currency. Yet, it was also necessary to ensure that the effective yield on the SDR normally compared favorably with that on currencies in general. This was to avoid putting on members undue strain resulting from the rules for holding SDRs and to ensure that SDRs would eventually become the main reserve asset held in adequate amounts by central bank authorities.

The management-staff approach to the question of the interest rate for the SDR stressed comparability rather than equality: the interest rate on the SDR should be comparable to that on currencies but not necessarily equal. Since the SDR would fluctuate less vis-à-vis any currency than currencies did among themselves meant that the SDR was relatively attractive as a reserve asset and thereby could bear a somewhat lower interest rate than a holder could theoretically earn on a comparable portfolio of individual currencies.

The staff suggestion in May 1973 that the SDR be valued in terms of a basket of currencies met with immediate disagreement by the Executive Board. Several Executive Directors were concerned that any change in the method of valuing the SDR might prejudice the work of the Committee of Twenty with regard to the features of the SDR for the reformed system. Messrs. Dale and Wahl were, moreover, opposed to a valuation of the SDR using a basket of currencies. As the Executive Directors took up this subject on several occasions in the last six months of 1973, Mr. Dale expressed the same position in the Executive Board as Mr. Volcker was expressing in meetings of the deputies of the Committee of Twenty and Mr. Shultz in ministerial meetings of the Committee of Twenty. While the negotiations for reform were going on, U.S. officials did not seem to want to take any overt action that would break the tie between the dollar and the SDR or imply that the dollar was no longer the sole major currency of the international monetary system. Revaluation of the SDR in terms of a basket of currencies would inevitably cast doubt on the existing relationship between the dollar, gold, and the SDR and make other currencies virtually co-equal with the dollar.

Mr. Wahl, like French officials at meetings of the Committee of Twenty, did not want any valuation of the SDR which was not based on par values or which suggested that gold would have a reduced role in the reformed system. Mr. Kawaguchi, also taking the position adopted by Japanese officials at meetings of the Committee of Twenty, argued for an SDR valuation based only on "the strongest currencies," defined as those which were appreciating in world markets.

Executive Directors also held different opinions on whether the rate of interest ought to be raised on the SDR, as did officials in the Committee of Twenty. While officials of European members and of Japan favored considerably higher rates of interest on the SDR than the existing 1.5 percent a year, officials of the United States and of developing members resisted any substantial increase in this rate of interest.

SPECIAL ARRANGEMENTS CONCERNING SDRs
FOR EUROPEAN PARTICIPANTS IN THE SNAKE

Meanwhile, fluctuations in the value of the SDR in terms of currencies were beginning to cause problems. Intervention in exchange markets by participants in the narrow margins arrangement of the EC, effective in April 1972, entailed the accumulation by the central banks of these participants of the currencies of the other members. Thus these central banks had to settle their accumulated balances. Under the scheme, settlement of balances customarily occurred on the last day of the month following the month in which the balance appeared, and was to be made either in the currency of the creditor country or in gold, SDRs, reserve positions in the Fund, and foreign currencies. The scheme for settlements on this basis, however, almost immediately encountered operational difficulties. The sharp rise in the free market price for gold made deficit countries unwilling to use gold reserves to settle their net intra-European currency balances. They preferred to use SDRs. However, they were disturbed by the value at which they transferred SDRs among themselves. Their accumulated balances were expressed in units of account of the European Monetary Cooperation Fund and valued at the central rates or par values of the European countries concerned. The SDR continued to be valued on the basis of the par value for the U.S. dollar, that is, on the basis of the prospective par value of the dollar of $42.22 per ounce of gold following the second devaluation of the dollar in February 1973.

When officials of the EC countries raised the matter with the Fund in March and April 1973, their specific problem was this. EC currencies were being exchanged at fairly large premiums of 6–9 percent over the prospective par value of the dollar. Settlement of net balances in intra-European accounts through use of SDRs valued on the basis of the prospective par value of the dollar hence meant an overpayment by the EC debtor to the extent of this premium. France, in particular, was considerably in debt to the Federal Republic of Germany in intra-European accounts, and French officials were eager not to have to buy French francs with SDRs valued in this way. Hence, officials of the countries adhering to the EC snake arrangement requested the Fund to exempt them from the normal arrangements so far as transactions in SDRs between one another were concerned and to permit them to transfer SDRs on the basis of values determined by their own central rates or par values rather than by the par value of the dollar.

The Executive Directors debated the request on a number of occasions during the following months. U.S. officials opposed the change so as to avoid the implication that the par values or central rates for currencies of EC countries provided a better yardstick for measuring the value of SDRs than did the par value of the dollar.

Toward the end of 1973, a temporary solution was found to enable the countries in the snake arrangement to use SDRs in intra-European settlements while a new method for valuing the SDR was debated. On November 5, the Executive Board decided to permit a participant in the Special Drawing Account that used SDRs to purchase balances of its own currency held by another participant to employ the par value or central rate of the currency involved as an alternative to the valuation method under Rule O-3. All transfers of SDRs other than those in this category were to continue to take place at exchange rates based on market rates in accordance with Rule O-3.

This decision involved for the transactions concerned the suspension of the equal value provision of the Articles for 120 days starting November 6, 1973. (A period of 120 days was the maximum period for which the Executive Board could suspend the Articles.) This period was subsequently extended by the Board of Governors for an additional 240 days.[7] This period enabled transactions in SDRs among the EC countries to take place at their par values or central rates until October 31, 1974, well beyond the deadline of July 31, 1974 that the Committee of Twenty had set for itself for agreement on the reformed system, including agreement on a new method for valuing the SDR. Until then, officials of the EC countries could make settlements among themselves in SDRs at what they considered a fair valuation for the SDR without violating the Articles of Agreement. This solution was accepted, but not without opposition. Some Executive Directors opposed it because they did not want to endorse departures from the principle of equal value, considered almost sacred, and because the solution involved the suspension of the operation of a provision of the Articles of Agreement. Nevertheless, this experience was to be a forerunner of the considerable liberalization of the provision for suspending the operation of provisions of the Articles made at the time of the Second Amendment.

The suspension of the equal value principle was a temporary, technical, and limited solution to the problem of the valuation of the SDR that the U.S. authorities could support. It preserved the existing role of the dollar as the link between the value of SDRs and the value of currencies in a broad area of transactions both in SDRs and in the Fund's General Account; in particular, it did not affect the method by which the Fund determined the value of its holdings of gold and currencies. No doubt was cast on the validity of the existing relationship between the dollar, the SDR, and gold. No one could draw the conclusion that the par values or central rates of currencies of EC countries provided a better yardstick than the par value of the dollar for measuring the value of the SDR. Because the suspension was temporary, the action was not prejudicial to the outcome of negotiations on the question of how the SDR should be valued in the future. As an added safeguard, the Fund did not issue a press release announcing the decision so as to prevent the public, especially bankers and the financial press, from drawing wrong conclusions.

---

[7]Resolution No. 29-2, effective March 4, 1974; Vol. III below, p. 284

CHAPTER
16

The System Starts to Evolve

L *ATE IN 1973,* about the time of the Annual Meeting in Nairobi, an
atmosphere of crisis clouded international monetary affairs. It was apparent
that the negotiations of the Committee of Twenty for a reformed system were not
going to be fruitful. The Committee was pressing ahead to complete its work before
it went out of existence, and there was no alternative high-level group of financial
officials to take its place. There were wide swings in the exchange rates for the main
currencies, but no international rules for exchange rates. World economic conditions
were worrisome. Commodity prices were booming and primary commodities were
undergoing price advances on a scale unprecedented since the Korean war two
decades earlier. Speculative stockpiling of all commodities was rampant, further
driving up their prices. These commodity price advances, together with expansionary policies in industrial countries, were causing inflation to accelerate worldwide.
Some industrial countries were experiencing an inflation rate of 10 percent, the
highest since the price boom brought on by the Korean conflict in the early 1950s.
While developing countries as a group benefited from a steep increase in their export
earnings, they realized that the situation was exceptional and temporary and were
concerned about rapidly rising prices for their imports. This unease was evident
during the 1973 Annual Meeting.

It was in this atmosphere of crisis that the Executive Directors resumed
discussions that led in November and December of that year to the decisions
described in the previous chapter and that the Committee of Twenty agreed to
consider existing international monetary arrangements and to work out some
immediate steps to be taken in lieu of a reformed system. In December 1973, the
crisis grew even more pervasive when unexpected, steep rises in the prices for crude
oil were announced, adding fuel to the fires of inflation and throwing the balance of
payments of all oil importing countries into unprecedented deficit. Some immediate
action by the international community seemed imperative.

For these reasons officials of the Fund, including those of the Committee of
Twenty, began to seek solutions for current international monetary problems that

went beyond the holding actions described in Chapter 15. After months of discussion, the Executive Board took several decisions, which were endorsed by the Committee of Twenty at its final meeting on June 12–13.

The decisions of June 1974 and their endorsement by the Committee of Twenty provided a new method for valuing the SDR, raised the rate of interest on the SDR by what was then regarded as a considerable increase, made corresponding changes in the rate of remuneration and in the Fund's charges for its drawings, set forth guidelines for floating exchange rates, made provisions for a voluntary declaration against restrictions on trade, established two new committees of the Board of Governors to succeed the Committee of Twenty, and introduced a temporary oil facility in the Fund. A few months later, in September 1974, the Executive Board decided to introduce yet another new facility in the Fund, the extended facility.

These decisions of 1974 provided the foundations for an evolving international monetary system, determining the course of the Fund's history for the next several years. The decisions relating to the SDR, to the Fund's charges and rate of remuneration, to the guidelines for floating rates, to the declaration against restrictions on trade, and to the new committees of the Board of Governors are described in the present chapter. The decisions relating to the oil facility and its operation are treated separately in Chapters 17 and 18. The decisions relating to the extended Fund facility and its operation through the end of 1978 form the subject of Chapter 19.

A NEW METHOD FOR VALUING THE SDR

At the Annual Meeting in Nairobi, Mr. Witteveen, looking for some subject on which the Committee of Twenty might reach agreement, suggested that it consider a new method for valuing the SDR and for determining its rate of interest. He mentioned to Anthony Barber, Governor of the Fund for the United Kingdom, that a great step forward might be made if the Committee of Twenty, at an impasse in its negotiations, could reach agreement on just one issue. The method of valuing the SDR might be that issue. Mr. Barber supported this suggestion in the meeting of EC finance ministers held during the same week as the Annual Meeting. At the meeting of the Committee of Twenty, Mr. Witteveen also put forward the idea.

Determining the method of valuation of the SDR required discussion by the Executive Board in addition to any discussions the Committee of Twenty might hold. Right after his return from the Annual Meeting, Mr. Witteveen consequently led the Executive Board in these discussions. The Executive Directors considered at length a number of techniques for valuing the SDR that the staff had worked out. Among these techniques were a "standard basket" of currencies, the technique finally adopted, an "asymmetrical basket," an "adjustable basket," and a "par value" technique. Other than to the standard basket, the staff and the Executive Directors gave most attention to the asymmetrical basket. This differed from the standard basket in that a decline in the value of a currency in the basket as a result of a devaluation or a downward float would not be allowed to lower the value of the SDR in terms of other currencies. For each devaluation, the number of units of the devalued currency would be increased to offset the decline in its par value. For a downward float, the number of units of the currency floating downward would be continuously adjusted; the effect of this adjustment would be the same as removing the floating currency from the basket with an offsetting increase in the amounts of the other currencies in the basket. Two other alternatives—stabilizing the SDR in terms of commodities and tying the SDR to the strongest currency in some base period—were not deliberated extensively because they had major drawbacks or were too complicated.[1]

Because the Executive Directors had in late 1973 debated at some length the relative merits of various techniques for valuing the SDR, they had advanced considerably in their appraisal of a more permanent method of valuing the SDR by the time the Committee of Twenty held its next meeting, in Rome, in January 1974. The Executive Board's discussion, however, had been couched primarily in terms of a valuation of the SDR for the reformed system, that is, with an SDR valuation appropriate on the assumption that most members used stable but adjustable par values and only a few used floating rates. Since the Committee of Twenty decided in January 1974 to give up working toward a reformed system, it was necessary to agree on a method for valuing the SDR on an interim basis so that the SDR could be used as the existing system continued to emerge. The Committee of Twenty therefore agreed on a basket of currencies as the interim method of valuation for the SDR and asked the Executive Board to work out the details.

Standard Basket of Currencies

Agreement on a technique of valuation to be used while floating rates were still in use for major currencies proved relatively easy. Only the standard basket of currencies fitted these circumstances. The standard basket was based entirely on market rates of exchange so that the value of the SDR was well defined whether all currencies had effective par values, or whether a few, many, or all currencies floated. The standard basket technique could operate without the maintenance of par values but could also continue to operate if a par value system was restored.

The Executive Board took a decision on June 13, 1974 providing for an interim method for determining the value of SDRs in transactions against currencies based on a standard basket of currencies. The SDR was to be equal to a total of specified amounts of the currencies of the 16 countries that had a share in world exports

---

[1]The alternative methods of valuing the SDR that were considered in the Fund in 1973–74 are explained in J.J. Polak, *Valuation and Rate of Interest on the SDR*, IMF Pamphlet Series, No. 18 (Washington: International Monetary Fund, 1974), especially pp. 12–16. The various baskets of currencies that could be used for valuation of the SDR are also described in Annex 9 of the *Outline of Reform*, Vol. III below, pp. 193–94.

of goods and services in excess of 1 percent on average over the five-year period 1968–72. The amounts of the currencies in the basket were derived from relative weights, beginning with 33 percent for the U.S. dollar—a figure selected to reflect the approximate commercial and financial importance of the dollar—and then lower percentages, broadly proportionate to the countries' share in international transactions, for the 15 other currencies. Rule O-3 was amended to enable the Fund to use spot exchange rates in the exchange markets in London, New York, or Frankfurt as the representative rates for the determination of the equivalents in dollars of the currencies in the basket. The actual composition of the basket in terms of amounts of each currency used, shown in Table 2 below, was announced on July 1, 1974, when the new method went into effect.

The calculations necessary to convert the weights agreed for each currency in the basket into actual currency units were done so as to ensure that the exchange rate for the SDR in terms of any currency on Friday, June 28, 1974, the last day of the old method of valuation, was the same whether calculated by the new or the old method, thus providing a smooth transition from the one to the other. Thereafter, the value of the SDR in terms of all currencies, including the dollar, was to fluctuate from day to day in response to changes in exchange rates in exchange markets.

While the value of the SDR in terms of currencies fluctuated, the number of currencies in the basket and their proportional composition of the basket were expected to produce a reasonably stable value for the SDR in terms of a broad group of currencies; movements in the rates for some currencies were moderated or offset by movements for other currencies.[2]

Coincidentally the announcement of the new basket on July 1, 1974 was made 30 years to the day after the beginning of the Bretton Woods Conference, a day singled out in the original Articles of Agreement in the expression "in terms of gold as a common denominator or in terms of the United States dollar of the weight and fineness in effect on July 1, 1944."[3]

Beginning on July 1, 1974, the Fund also modified its own accounting practices in accordance with the interim valuation of the SDR. The Fund's holdings of each member's currency, as recorded on the Fund's books, were to be revalued periodically on the basis of the representative exchange rates used for valuing the SDR, and the resulting currency balances to maintain the gold value of the Fund's assets were to be settled periodically. For this purpose, the Fund subsequently established representative rates for the currencies of over 100 members.

---

[2]How the Fund calculated the value of the SDR each day using the basket of 16 currencies was described in *IMF Survey* (Washington), Vol. 3 (July 22, 1974), p. 235, and ibid., Vol. 4 (September 15, 1975), p. 280; and by David S. Cutler and Dhruba Gupta in "SDRs: Valuation and Interest Rate," *Finance & Development* (Washington), Vol. 11 (December 1974), pp. 18–21.

[3]Original Articles of Agreement, Article IV, Section 1(a). These Articles are in *History, 1945–65*, Vol. III, pp. 185–214. Article IV, Section 1(a) is on p. 189.

Table 2. Composition of SDR Currency Basket, July 1, 1974

Currency	Weight (*In percent*)	Amount (*In units of* *each currency*)
U.S. dollar	33.0	0.40
Deutsche mark	12.5	0.38
Pound sterling	9.0	0.045
French franc	7.5	0.44
Japanese yen	7.5	26.00
Canadian dollar	6.0	0.071
Italian lira	6.0	47.00
Netherlands guilder	4.5	0.14
Belgian franc	3.5	1.60
Swedish krona	2.5	0.13
Australian dollar	1.5	0.012
Danish krone	1.5	0.11
Norwegian krone	1.5	0.099
Spanish peseta	1.5	1.10
Austrian schilling	1.0	0.22
South African rand	1.0	0.0082
	100.0	

HIGHER INTEREST ON THE SDR AND RELATED CHANGES IN REMUNERATION AND CHARGES

On June 13, 1974, following a decision by the Executive Board, the Fund announced a rise in the rate of interest on the SDR from its original 1.5 percent to 5 percent a year. The interest rate on the SDR was now to reflect changing market rates of interest. Since the value of the SDR was to be determined by the standard basket of currencies, it was logical that changes in the interest rate on the SDR be linked to changes in the interest rates on money instruments denominated in the currencies in the basket. In practice, however, members' reserves were held and invested in only a handful of the 16 currencies in the basket. Hence, the Executive Board decided that a suitable link between the interest rate on the SDR and market rates of interest could be established by averaging the daily interest rates on the 5 currencies with the largest weights in the basket—the U.S. dollar, the deutsche mark, the pound sterling, the French franc, and the Japanese yen. The market instruments indicative of the market rates of interest for these 5 currencies were three-month U.S. Treasury bills, three-month interbank deposits in the Federal Republic of Germany, three-month U.K. Treasury bills, three-month interbank money against private paper in France, and unconditional call money in Japan. The weights to be used in calculating an average of these interest rates were to reflect the relative shares of these 5 currencies in the standard basket, namely 47 percent for the U.S. dollar, 18 percent for the deutsche mark, 13 percent for the pound sterling, and 11 percent each for the French franc and the Japanese yen.

The average money rate on these instruments in June 1974, when the 5 percent a year rate of interest for the SDR was selected, was 10 percent a year; the interest rate on the SDR was thus half the relevant market rate. The Executive Board was to review the interest rate on the SDR every six months and could, by a three-fourths majority of total voting power, change the rate.[4] There was concern, however, that the Executive Board might not be able to agree on a new rate of interest and so a formula was devised that could be used in the event of disagreement. If the weighted average interest rate on the 5 currency instruments over the previous three months did not exceed 11 percent or was not less than 9 percent, the rate of 5 percent on the SDR would remain in force; if the combined average interest rate was below 9 percent, the interest rate on the SDR would be reduced below 5 percent by three fifths of the difference between the combined rate and 9 percent; in a similar manner, if the combined rate was above 11 percent, the rate of interest on the SDR would be increased by three fifths of the amount by which the combined rate exceeded 11 percent.

Ironically, although the initial staff idea of valuing the SDR in terms of currencies was based on resolving the problem of choosing an interest rate for the SDR, in the end this was not an important consideration in choosing a method for valuation. Considerations governing SDR valuation and those governing its rate of interest became separated.

The Executive Board decisions of June 13, 1974 on valuing the SDR and on the rate of interest on the SDR were considered to be of an interim nature. The *Outline of Reform* stated explicitly that the valuation of the SDR was to be "in present circumstances, and without prejudice to the method of valuation to be adopted in a reformed system," the present circumstances referring to the widespread use of floating rates. The Executive Board's decision of June 13, 1974 also contained explicit provision for review after two years of both the valuation of the SDR and its rate of interest.

These decisions of June 13, 1974 were subsequently reviewed, and the basket of currencies used in valuing the SDR was changed effective July 1, 1978. The interest rate on the SDR was also reviewed by the Executive Board several times between July 1974 and the end of 1978. These developments are taken up in Chapter 46 below.

Related Changes in Remuneration and Charges

The Articles of Agreement, as amended in 1969, related the rate of interest on the SDR to the rate of remuneration paid to members on their super gold tranche positions. The interest rate on the SDR was not to be greater than 2 percent or the

---

[4]Total voting power refers to the votes of all members of the Fund at a given time. This total may exceed the number of votes that can be cast in the Executive Board at that time because, on occasion, a few members have not participated in the election of an Executive Director. Hence, there has not been an Executive Director to cast the votes of these members.

rate of remuneration, whichever was higher, or smaller than 1 percent or the rate of remuneration, whichever was lower.[5] The Executive Board could change the rate of remuneration, thereby permitting a change in the rate of interest on the SDR. To enable the interest rate on the SDR to become 5 percent a year, the Executive Board, on June 13, 1974, also decided to raise to 5 percent a year the rate of remuneration paid for the period July 1 to December 31, 1974. However, in order not to raise the Fund's expenses for remuneration unduly and to avoid the need to raise the Fund's charges to undesirably high levels, after considerable debate the Executive Directors agreed to a staff suggestion that for the next two years a lower rate of remuneration would be paid on the segment of the super gold tranche corresponding to the Fund's holdings of a member's currency between 75 and 50 percent of quota. This "split rate of remuneration" was to be reviewed after two years and to lapse in the absence of a further decision.

At this time, in June 1974, the Executive Board also decided to revise the schedule of charges that the Fund applied to use of its resources. The previous schedule of charges had prevailed since May 1, 1963 and, as it had been subject to only minor revisions since 1954, in practice had existed for 20 years. Charges started at zero for amounts outstanding for up to three months and then progressed from 2 percent a year for amounts outstanding from three months to one and a half years to 5 percent a year for amounts outstanding from three to five years. There was also a service charge of ½ of 1 percent a year of the amount purchased on all credit tranche purchases, and a commitment charge of ¼ of 1 percent on the amount approved under a stand-by arrangement, credited against the service charge if the stand-by arrangement was drawn upon. This schedule of charges is given in Table 3 below.

Since 1963 a number of developments had substantially affected the Fund's income and operational expenses. The Fund's facilities for use of its resources had been expanded, use of the gold tranche had been made automatic, the SDR had been created, and payment of remuneration on net creditor positions had been instituted. All these considerations, together with the sharp increases in commercial rates of interest that had taken place from 1963 to 1974, suggested that it was time for the Executive Board to undertake a thoroughgoing review of the Fund's schedule of charges. Two other factors in the first part of 1974 also made a review of the Fund's charges imperative. First, to enable the Fund to pay the higher rates of remuneration resulting from the increase in the rate of interest on the SDR, it was essential to raise the Fund's charges so as not to enlarge still further the Fund's already large budgetary deficit. Second, in order to finance the proposed oil facility (described in Chapter 17), the Fund was planning to borrow from oil exporting countries, and this borrowing was expected to be at interest rates close to market rates. The Fund's charges on members for using the oil facility would therefore have to be closely related to the rates of interest that the Fund would have to pay to the lending countries. However, if the Fund was going to establish relatively high charges on

---

[5]Article XXVI, Section 3 in *History 1966–71*, Vol. II, pp. 127–28.

Table 3. Charges on Transactions Effected
May 1, 1963–June 30, 1974

Charges in percent a year[1] for period stated and for portion of holdings in excess of quota by

More than But not more than (percent of quota)	0 50	50 100	100
Service charge[2]	0.5	0.5	0.5
0 to 3 months	0.0	0.0	0.0
3 to 6 months	2.0	2.0	2.0
½ to 1 year	2.0	2.0	2.5
1 to 1½ years	2.0	2.5	3.0
1½ to 2 years	2.5	3.0	3.5
2 to 2½ years	3.0	3.5	4.0[3]
2½ to 3 years	3.5	4.0[3]	4.5
3 to 3½ years	4.0[3]	4.5	5.0
3½ to 4 years	4.5	5.0	
4 to 4½ years	5.0		

[1]Except for service charge, which was payable once per transaction and expressed as percentage of amount of transaction.
[2]No service charge was payable in respect of any gold tranche purchase effected after July 27, 1969.
[3]Point at which consultation between the Fund and the member became obligatory.

drawings under the oil facility, it seemed it ought to raise the relatively low charges still prevailing on other drawings.

Consequently, the Executive Board decided, also on June 13, 1974, to revise the Fund's schedule of charges on use of its regular resources. The revised schedule, to be applied to transactions effected after July 1, 1974, not only did this but also provided for two simplifications of the previous schedule. The increments in the charges were to take place on an annual rather than a semiannual basis. The charges were to be made uniformly applicable to all holdings of a member's currency in excess of quota rather than being differentiated by the percentage by which the Fund's holdings of a member's currency exceeded the quota. The service and commitment charges were retained.

The revised schedule is given in Table 4.

Table 4. Charges on Transactions Effected After July 1, 1974

Charges in percent a year,[1] payable on holdings in excess of quota, for period stated

Service charge	0.5
Up to 1 year	4.0
1 to 2 years	4.5
2 to 3 years	5.0
3 to 4 years	5.5[2]
4 to 5 years	6.0

[1]Except for service charge, which was payable once per transaction and expressed as percentage of amount of transaction.
[2]Point at which consultation between the Fund and the member became obligatory.

CONSIDERATION OF GUIDELINES FOR FLOATING RATES

In June 1974 the Executive Board also established guidelines for the management of floating rates, following the request of the Committee of Twenty in January 1974. The Executive Directors could legally adopt rules for floating rates and take action to see that such rules were observed without an amendment of the Articles under what was becoming called informally within the Fund the collaboration provision, Article IV, Section 4(a).

Rules Drafted by the Staff

In drafting a possible code for floating exchange rates early in 1974, the staff deemed it desirable that the central bank authorities of members with floating rates take three kinds of actions: (i) smooth out very short-run fluctuations in market rates; (ii) offer a measure of resistance to market tendencies in the slightly longer run, particularly when these tendencies were leading to unduly rapid movements in the rate; and (iii) where possible, resist and even reverse movements in market rates that appeared to be deviating substantially from any reasonable estimate of a medium-term norm. In the staff view, adherence to such a code would provide adequate safeguards not only against competitive depreciation, the most relevant concern at the time the Fund was founded, but also against "competitive non-devaluation," a concern which arose after the middle 1960s. Competitive non-devaluation was the term used to characterize the reluctance of many members to devalue their currencies or to allow them to depreciate.

The staff also had three considerations in mind in implementing any code. First, national policies should not be subjected to greater constraints than were clearly necessary in the international interest. Second, a degree of uncertainty necessarily attended any estimate of a medium-term normal exchange rate; such uncertainty was particularly great in the circumstances of widespread inflation and unprecedented balance of payments disequilibria prevailing in 1974. On occasion, the market view of an exchange rate might be more realistic than any official view either of the country concerned or of an international body. Third, in view of the strength of short-term market forces, it might often be necessary to forgo or curtail official intervention desirable from the standpoint of maintaining exchange rate stability if this intervention involved an excessive drain on a member's reserves or an impact on its money supply that the member found difficult to neutralize.

On the basis of this code and of these considerations, the staff drew up for the Executive Board's review six rules for floating rates.

Rule 1 was to govern very short-run intervention. A member with a floating exchange rate should intervene in the foreign exchange market to maintain orderly conditions, that is, to prevent or moderate sharp and erratic fluctuations in the rates for its currency from day to day and from week to week.

Rule 2 was to govern short-run intervention of a somewhat longer period. A member with a floating exchange rate might intervene to moderate movements in its exchange rate from month to month and quarter to quarter and should do so when well-accepted factors, such as seasonal factors, were at work. However, a member was not to intervene aggressively, that is, was not to accumulate reserves when its exchange rate was falling or reduce them when its effective rate was rising. (The exchange rate of a country was said to be falling if the number of units of foreign currency exchanged for its currency was decreasing. It was said to be rising if the number of units was increasing.)

Rules 3 and 4 were for "stabilizing intervention." A member with a floating rate was to endeavor to agree with the Fund on an estimate of the zone within which the medium-term norm for its exchange rate probably lay (the "normal zone") and to adapt this estimate to changing circumstances. When the exchange rate of the member was outside the normal zone, the member was to refrain from intervening to moderate movements in its exchange rate toward the normal zone, but would be free to intervene aggressively to move the rate toward the normal zone.

Rules 5 and 6 applied to the use of balance of payments policies other than intervention that a member might use to influence its exchange rate. A member with a floating exchange rate was to refrain from introducing restrictions for balance of payments purposes on current account transactions or current payments and should progressively remove existing restrictions of this kind. A member with a floating exchange rate was also to endeavor to apply other policies affecting its balance of payments, particularly those designed to influence capital flows, in a manner consistent, insofar as the effect on its exchange rate was concerned, with the foregoing rules for intervention policies. Specifically, when the effective exchange rate was falling or was below the normal zone, the member was to be free to take measures discouraging capital outflows and encouraging capital inflows, but should not take or maintain measures having the opposite effect. Where the rate was rising or was above the normal zone, the member should be free to take measures discouraging capital inflows or encouraging outflows, but should not apply measures having the opposite effect.

Discussion of These Rules in the Executive Board

The Executive Board held more than a dozen meetings from March until mid-June to consider these rules for floating rates, and the initial staff paper went through eight revisions before the Executive Directors finally reached agreement. Prevailing circumstances help to explain why these discussions were so prolonged. The end of the discussions on reforming the system had left many questions unanswered. Hence, as of the first six months of 1974, basic questions about exchange rates were still unsettled. For example, whether fixed or floating rates were appropriate policies for members was a contested issue and European officials opposed any action by the Fund that might imply it was giving legal sanction to floating rates. When the staff's draft rules for floating rates were discussed in the Executive Board in March 1974, Jacques de Groote (Belgium) and to a greater extent Mr. Beaurain were therefore concerned that the adoption by the Fund of a code of conduct for floating rates might "institutionalize floating." While Mr. de Groote believed that the Fund ought to devise and possibly enforce some code of conduct or rules for floating rates, Mr. Beaurain did not want the Fund to do so. Some Executive Directors also had not yet given up hope that the dollar might still become convertible. Mr. Kawaguchi, for example, preferred to avoid between members and the Fund controversial discussions about their exchange rate policies and about specifying guidelines for floating rates until the subject of asset settlement was resolved.

Executive Directors, like other financial officials, had also just been through debates in the Committee of Twenty about the use of reserve indicators in which changes in the levels of members' reserves would be used to judge the need for exchange rate adjustments. Consequently, when the staff proposed that changes in reserves be one of the criteria used in the rules for managing floating rates, Messrs. Kawaguchi and Schleiminger were especially adamant in their rejection of reserve criteria. The Executive Directors had likewise just been through extensive debates in the Committee of Twenty about whether or not capital movements ought to be restrained by controls and had not reached a consensus. Hence, they found it difficult to agree on the function of capital controls in influencing the course of floating exchange rates.

Not only did the prevailing circumstances make agreement on rules for floating rates among the Executive Directors difficult but so did many of the concepts involved in the staff's draft code and the fear that the Fund might be extending its authority too far. To remove the mandatory tone of terms like "rules" for floating of rates, or a "code of conduct," and to make it clear that they might be altered from time to time, all Executive Directors preferred the phrase "guidelines for the management of floating rates." Mr. Brand was concerned that the Fund would be entering into discussions with members about their reserve policies, which would compromise the freedom of members to use their reserve currency holdings as they wished. Many Executive Directors were concerned about how such concepts as "normal zones" or "medium-term norms" for exchange rates were to be determined and whether the Fund and members would be able to agree on what constituted normal zones for exchange rates. Many Executive Directors also questioned whether members could be asked to direct their policies toward the attainment of normal zones and whether the Fund was asking, in effect, for surveillance over the whole range of a member's balance of payments policies. A number wondered even how changes in exchange rates could be measured in circumstances in which the rates for several currencies were changing concurrently. Because of these misgivings, Messrs. Brand, Bryce, Prasad, and Schneider, among others, considered the staff's recommendations overambitious. In contrast, others, including Knut J.M. Andreassen (Norway), Mr. Massad, H.R. Monday, Jr. (The Gambia), and Mr. Palamenghi-Crispi, believed that the staff's suggestions were not sufficiently strong as to make any difference to the policies that the major members were likely to be pursuing anyway.

Executive Directors from the large industrial members using floating rates were understandably most concerned with the precise way in which any rules, or guidelines, would be applied to their countries. Mr. Cross, appointed Executive Director for the United States only a few weeks earlier and a participant in many meetings of the Committee of Twenty in which the desirability of floating rates as against fixed rates had been acrimoniously debated, emphasized that U.S. officials favored floating rates precisely because floating permitted greater exchange flexibility for the dollar than had been possible under the par value system. He was concerned that U.S. officials might find themselves again in a position of having relatively little freedom in exchange rate policy, while other members were fairly free. Such a situation could arise, he explained, if a member whose currency was used as an intervention currency was frustrated from floating by the intervention policies of other members. Yet, the rules or guidelines for floating rates mainly involved policies for intervention.

Mr. Bryce, pointing out the long Canadian experience with floating, believed that the staff paper was largely normative (that is, dealing with standards to be attained) and did not come to grips with the practical problems actually confronting central bank authorities in the management of exchange markets. He preferred a discussion of the actual experiences of individual countries with floating rates to a discussion of rules or guidelines for floating. Mr. Bryce believed that the particular rules suggested by the staff, stated in terms of norms or agreed zones or targets, were also unrealistic. Exchange rate targets or the objectives and commitments of the central bank authorities would have to be known to those who operated in the market; yet such knowledge would give operators a clear advantage if they believed that the authorities could not meet their objectives. In addition, like Mr. Cross, Mr. Bryce stressed that use of targets or zones and advance commitments to the Fund would run contrary to the very objective of floating, to allow exchange markets to determine exchange rates.

GUIDELINES FOR FLOATING RATES DECIDED

Despite the stance of some Executive Directors which made agreement on any guidelines difficult, the Executive Directors finally reached a decision, mainly because they knew they had to. The deputies of the Committee of Twenty at their eleventh meeting in Paris on May 7–9, 1974 had made it clear that they expected a detailed text on guidelines for the management of floating rates agreed by the Executive Directors for presentation to the Committee of Twenty in June. Agreement was also facilitated because Messrs. Bull, de Groote, and Kafka emphasized that any guidelines would inevitably have to be applied in a flexible and experimental manner and made strong appeals to their colleagues to come up with agreed guidelines. Also, the Executive Directors were willing to meet time and again to clarify points and to suggest alternative phrasing and wording on which they could all agree.

Elements of the Decision

On June 13, 1974 the Executive Board took a decision agreeing to a lengthy memorandum which set forth and explained "Guidelines for the Management of Floating Exchange Rates."[6] The memorandum contained an introduction explaining the basis on which the Fund was issuing such guidelines, that is, widespread agreement that exchange rates were a matter of international concern and a matter for consultation and surveillance by the Fund and that members were legally obliged to collaborate with the Fund on their exchange rate policy. This introduction also set forth the assumptions on which the guidelines were based and the considerations taken into account. These assumptions and considerations had been stated in the original staff paper. At the same time, it was essential to recognize that national policies were not to be unduly constrained, that there was considerable uncertainty with regard to what might be normal exchange rates, and that members might not be able to intervene in accordance with the guidelines if the required intervention affected their reserves or money supply unduly adversely.

Six guidelines were set forth, together with commentary on them. While in some respects they were similar to the rules drafted by the staff, they clearly revealed the Executive Board's preference for guidelines that gave members considerable latitude. For example, the introduction of target zones, a main feature of the staff's rules, was eliminated. Other guidelines were couched in more general language than that suggested by the staff. A member with a floating exchange rate was to intervene to prevent or moderate sharp and disruptive daily or weekly fluctuations, and might act, through intervention or otherwise, to moderate monthly or quarterly movements. Indeed, when temporary factors were involved, the member was encouraged to do so. But a member was not normally to act "aggressively," that is, the member should not so act as to depress its exchange rate when it was falling or to enhance the rate when it was rising.

Moreover, if a member with a floating rate wanted to bring its exchange rate within, or closer to, some target zone of rates, it was to consult with the Fund about the target. If the Fund considered the target rate reasonable, the member would be free to act aggressively to move its rate in that direction. If the exchange rate of a member with a floating rate moved outside what the Fund considered the range of reasonable norms to an extent that the Fund considered likely to harm other members, the Fund was to consult with the member.

Furthermore, a member with a floating exchange rate was to be encouraged to discuss with the Fund its broad objective for the development of its reserves. If the Fund considered this objective reasonable, the member was to be encouraged to follow certain exchange rate policies. A member with a floating rate, like other members, was also to refrain from introducing restrictions for balance of payments purposes on current account transactions.

---

[6]The decision and the attached memorandum—E.B. Decision No. 4232-(74/67)—are in Vol. III below, p. 487.

The guidelines were to be reviewed from time to time and adjusted as appropriate.

Implementing the Guidelines

In the months after June 1974, the staff held internal discussions on how to implement the guidelines. Decisions were needed, for instance, on how to classify members with respect to their exchange rate regimes, on what statistical and qualitative information to request of members, and how to proceed in the special consultations on exchange rates. Staff members did not hold unanimous views. Some were ready to talk to officials of members about normal or target exchange rates, while others wanted the Fund to proceed extremely cautiously, working primarily toward developing closer contact with officials of members with regard to exchange rate policy, but not pressing them toward particular exchange rates.

Early in 1975 the staff recommended to the Executive Board procedures for implementing the guidelines, but most Executive Directors did not like the recommendations. Messrs. Cross, Gérard de Margerie (France), Kafka, Palamenghi-Crispi, Rawlinson, and George Reynolds (Ireland) argued that the Fund should not treat members with floating currencies differently from members with pegged currencies; there should be equal surveillance of all members. Mr. Reynolds objected that, under the recommended procedures, members with floating currencies would be asked to provide the Fund with more information than members whose currencies were not floating, to submit to more consultations with the Fund than other members, and to submit to Executive Board scrutiny on the basis of concepts, such as effective exchange rates, which they regarded as of doubtful value. On the other hand, Per Åsbrink (Sweden) and Messrs. Kharmawan and Lieftinck believed that the Fund should in one way or another exercise surveillance over exchange rates and the balance of payments adjustment process.

No Executive Board decision was taken, and the Managing Director considered it unproductive to push for one. Meanwhile, the staff, mainly in the five Area Departments, working with individual Executive Directors and with officials of members in conjunction with the special consultations, tried to keep alive interest in these guidelines.

DECLARATION ON TRADE

In its communiqué after its last meeting in June 1974, the Committee of Twenty listed as an immediate step to assist the functioning of the international monetary system a provision for members to pledge themselves on a voluntary basis not to introduce or intensify "trade or other current account measures" without a finding by the Fund that there was balance of payments justification for such measures. To make this invitation more specific, Part II, Immediate Steps, of the *Outline of Reform* contained an appendix specifying this declaration on trade measures.[7]

As a follow-up, the Executive Board took a decision on June 26, 1974, concurring in the transmission to members of a letter from the Managing Director requesting that members inform the Fund whether they subscribed to the declaration.[8] In subscribing to the declaration a member was to represent that, in addition to observing its obligations with respect to payments restrictions under the Articles of Agreement, it would not on its own discretionary authority introduce or intensify trade or other current account measures for balance of payments purposes that were subject to the jurisdiction of the GATT or recommend them to its legislature without a prior finding by the Fund that there was a balance of payments justification for such measures. The declaration was to become effective among subscribing members when members having 65 percent of the total voting power in the Fund had accepted it and, unless renewed, was to expire two years from the date on which it became effective.

NEW COMMITTEES OF THE BOARD OF GOVERNORS

In September 1974 the Executive Board also took decisions approving draft resolutions for approval by the Board of Governors establishing an Interim Committee of the Board of Governors on the International Monetary System and a Joint Ministerial Committee of the Boards of Governors of the Bank and the Fund on the Transfer of Real Resources to Developing Countries (commonly referred to as the Development Committee). At its meeting in June 1974, the Committee of Twenty had agreed to these changes in the structure of the Fund. These draft resolutions were approved, together with a resolution ending the Committee of Twenty, in a composite resolution by the Board of Governors at the Twenty-Ninth Annual Meeting in early October 1974.[9] As of October 2, 1974, the Committee of Twenty thereby ceased to exist and the Interim Committee and the Development Committee came into being. These Committees were both structured along the lines of the Committee of Twenty. The 20 members of the Interim Committee were to be Governors of the Fund, ministers, or others of comparable rank. Each member of the Fund that appointed an Executive Director and group of members that elected an Executive Director was entitled to appoint one member and up to seven associates. Executive Directors, or in their absence their Alternates, were entitled to attend the meetings of the Committee, and the Managing Director was entitled to participate in the meetings. The Committee was expected to last only until the Articles of

---

[7]Communiqué of Committee of Twenty, June 13, 1974, par. 3(e) and *Outline of Reform*, Vol. III below, pp. 201, 176–77.

[8]E.B. Decision No. 4254-(74/75). This decision and the Managing Director's letter to members are in Vol. III below, pp. 554–55.

[9]Resolutions Nos. 29–7, 29–8, 29–9, and 29–10; Vol. III below, pp. 208, 213–15, 575–78, 208–210.

Agreement were amended when provision would be made for a permanent Council of Governors. This accounts for its title of Interim Committee. Mr. Witteveen had suggested that, pending establishment of a Council with decision-making powers, an Interim Committee be created with an advisory role and with the same composition and procedures as the proposed Council. The issue of how to revamp the Executive Board of the Fund or to change the Fund's structure, which had been on the original agenda of the Committee of Twenty, was thereby abandoned.

The Development Committee was also made up of 20 persons who were to be Governors of the World Bank, Governors of the Fund, ministers, or others of comparable rank, appointed alternately for a term of two years by members of the World Bank and members of the Fund. There could be up to seven associates for each member on the Committee. The Executive Directors of the Fund and the World Bank, or in their absence their Alternates, as well as the President of the World Bank and the Managing Director of the Fund, were entitled to participate in meetings. (The terms of reference of the Interim Committee and the Development Committee are described in Chapter 50.)

The evolving system was beginning to take shape.

CHAPTER
17

An Oil Facility Introduced

*U*NDOUBTEDLY, THE QUICKEST of the Fund's responses to crises in the international monetary system in the 1970s was its response to the most urgent economic problem of the times—"the oil crisis." On January 3, 1974, only 11 days after oil exporting countries announced on December 23, 1973 that prices of crude oil were to be steeply increased effective January 1, 1974, Mr. Witteveen proposed that a special temporary facility to finance oil deficits be set up in the Fund. His action propelled the Fund into a leadership role in helping its members cope with the new crisis.

The announcement in December 1973 evoked the specter of worldwide economic havoc. Massive price increases for oil confirmed what had been only hinted at before: supplies of crucial raw materials were finite. For industrial countries a key factor in much of their economic growth in the previous 25 years—the availability of abundant and cheap energy—was suddenly removed. For most developing countries, there was danger that economic development, heavily dependent on imported fuel and on chemical fertilizers made from petroleum, would appreciably slow. The possibility that "economic limits to growth" would soon be at hand began to be taken seriously.[1] Virtually everyone realized that all countries would have to introduce effective methods to conserve energy and to develop alternative energy sources.

These problems, however, would have to be addressed over several years. Immediate and pressing were the financial implications of the steep increases in oil prices. Imbalances in international payments on an unprecedented scale were expected at once. Public officials feared dire consequences because they saw no adequate way to finance the anticipated current account deficits of oil importing countries. Nothing short of war had ever before brought about the need for such sudden and immediate global external financing.

These payments imbalances were Mr. Witteveen's concern when he proposed in January 1974 that the Fund introduce an oil facility. Mr. Witteveen's innovative

---

[1]Donella Meadows, Dennis L. Meadows, Jørgen Randers, and William W. Behrens III, in *The Limits to Growth* (New York: Universe Books, 1972), had warned of this prospect at the beginning of the 1970s.

idea was conceived independently of the staff, and he took upon himself the responsibility for convincing officials of the need for an oil facility and for raising the money. Thus, Mr. Witteveen personally devoted an enormous amount of time and effort to the oil facility.

INCREASES IN OIL PRICES AND
THEIR ANTICIPATED IMMEDIATE CONSEQUENCES

Prices for crude oil had been low and stable since World War II. Saudi Arabian light crude oil, the standard for setting the prices of other grades of oil in the Middle East, for instance, had in January 1955 a posted price, or tax reference price, of $1.93 per barrel.[2] The price remained at about this level for the next 16 years. During this period, officials of oil exporting countries, concerned about big international oil companies posting prices for crude oil that were too low, had been negotiating with these companies to fix a minimum price of $1.80 per barrel. To this end and to forge a common strategy for oil exports, representatives of the Governments of Iran, Iraq, Kuwait, Saudi Arabia, and Venezuela, meeting in Baghdad in 1960 at the initiative of Venezuelan officials, had established the Organization of Petroleum Exporting Countries (OPEC). In 1971 and 1972, crude oil prices were raised somewhat. Saudi Arabian light crude, for instance, went to $2.18 per barrel on January 15, 1971, to $2.48 per barrel on January 20, 1972, and to $2.591 on January 1, 1973.

The era of low prices for crude oil then came to an end. OPEC had grown to 13 members as Algeria, Ecuador, Gabon, Indonesia, Libya, Nigeria, Qatar, and the United Arab Emirates joined the original 5 members and had become a more powerful and effective organization. A concession by the international oil companies to Libya's demand for higher prices for crude oil touched off demands for higher prices by other oil exporting countries, so that by October 1973 the price for Saudi Arabian light crude oil was $3.01 per barrel. Meanwhile on October 6, hostilities broke out, involving Egypt, Syria, and Israel. In the middle of October, the Arab members of OPEC, using oil as a political weapon to help induce the Governments of the United States and the Netherlands to temper their "pro-Israel policies," voted to embargo exports of crude oil to the United States and to the Netherlands. In addition to the embargo, members of OPEC unilaterally raised the price for crude oil, this time to $5.119 per barrel for Saudi Arabian light crude, a 70 percent boost.

About two months later, on December 23, 1973, six oil exporting nations—Iran, Iraq, Kuwait, Qatar, Saudi Arabia, and the United Arab Emirates—stunned the world by announcing a doubling of the price of their crude oil effective January 1, 1974. Saudi Arabian light crude oil, for example, was to have a posted price of $11.651 per barrel. This price was established in light of a decision by the oil

---

[2]Posted or tax reference prices were administratively determined nominal prices used as the basis for payments of royalties, income taxes, and the like by international oil companies to the governments of the exporting countries.

ministers of the six states that the government "take" at the beginning of 1974 should be increased from $2 per barrel on average in 1973 to $7 per barrel. Other OPEC members followed this lead soon thereafter, raising their prices on the basis of the prices fixed by the six. The price increases from October 16, 1973 to January 1, 1974, together with changes in other agreements between oil exporting countries and international oil companies, meant a more than fourfold effective increase in the price of crude oil in less than three months. (Meanwhile, the temporary embargo was lifted.)

In reply to complaints by officials of industrial countries about these price increases, particularly the suddenness of such large jumps, and to cries of "price gouging" by an "organized cartel," officials of oil exporting countries offered three principal reasons.

The first was the devaluations of the U.S. dollar that had occurred since December 1971. Since prices for crude oil were expressed in dollars and nearly all payments for oil shipments were invoiced in dollars, the two formal devaluations of the dollar in terms of gold in December 1971 and February 1973, followed by further depreciation of the dollar in terms of other major currencies after the introduction of floating rates in March 1973, reduced the receipts of oil exporting countries expressed in terms of gold or of other major currencies by as much as 15 percent.

A second, and principal, reason was the extraordinary rise in the market prices of most other primary commodities in 1972 and 1973. By the middle of 1973 prices of cotton, wool, rubber, and other agricultural materials were double what they were at the start of 1972. Prices of foodgrains during this 18-month period increased by 50 percent and those of metals by 30 percent. Prices of rice, sisal, wheat, free market sugar, and zinc went up more from January 1972 to December 1973 than did prices for crude oil, even allowing for the fourfold increases in oil prices. This upsurge in commodity prices had no parallel with earlier peacetime experience; commodity prices had not risen so much, or so fast, since the Korean war in 1950–53. In these circumstances, officials of countries exporting crude oil decided that their prices were abnormally low compared with prices of other primary products.

Because oil exporting countries were also importers of primary products, especially of foods, high prices for wheat and rice meant high prices for their imports. In addition, prices of imported manufactured goods had been rising for several years, a rise which was rapidly accelerating with the intensification of inflation in industrial countries in the 1970s. As a result, the terms of trade of oil exporting countries deteriorated steadily between 1960 and 1970, averaging about 2 percent a year, while industrial countries and non-oil developing countries experienced an improvement in their terms of trade averaging about ½ of 1 percent a year. Although the terms of trade of oil exporting countries greatly improved in 1971 and 1972, oil exporters raised the prices for oil in 1973 to help improve further their terms of trade in an inflationary situation.

A third reason cited by officials of exporting countries for raising oil prices was that oil was a depletable asset. Because it was by far the primary economic asset of their countries, officials of a number of oil exporting countries stressed that these countries had to earn enough from their oil exports in the next decade or two to finance economic development to provide employment and income in the longer term. If oil could not be replaced by alternative income-earning assets, they had a responsibility to future generations to limit oil production so as to extend the economic viability of their countries beyond the next few decades.

Consequences for International Payments

The announcement on December 23, 1973 of the steep increases in prices for oil coincided with the completion by the staff of the paper on the world economic outlook for 1974, as described in a later chapter. The impact of the rise in oil prices on the current account balance of payments positions of the Fund's members expected in 1974 was so great that the staff hurriedly revised all their estimates for the coming year. A massive and startling disequilibrium in international payments was expected for 1974. This imbalance, moreover, was imposed on a situation already characterized by sizable imbalances among the industrial countries, since the imbalances of 1970 to 1973 had not yet been corrected following the currency realignments of 1971 and 1973. In 1973 the United States had achieved a $3.3 billion surplus on current account (goods, services, and private transfers) in contrast to its record current account deficit of $7.1 billion in 1972; and the current account surplus of Japan, $7.2 billion in 1972, had virtually disappeared in 1973. Disequilibria among the Western European countries had increased, however; the current account surplus of the Federal Republic of Germany soared to $6.6 billion in 1973 from $2.8 billion in 1972, while the current account surpluses achieved by Italy and the United Kingdom in 1972 turned into deficits in 1973.

The combined balances of payments of industrial countries with other countries both on current account and on capital account had remained relatively stable in 1973. The traditional current account surplus of industrial countries rose moderately in 1973 to some $10 billion, compared with $9 billion in 1972. The current account and overall balances of other large groups of countries were also stable from 1972 to 1973; developing countries that were not oil exporters continued to have a combined current account deficit of $8.0–8.5 billion, and the more developed primary producing countries continued collectively to have a small surplus. The main exception to the stable pattern of balance of payments developments among nonindustrial countries was a more than doubling of the current account surplus of the nine major oil exporting countries (Algeria, Indonesia, Iran, Iraq, Kuwait, Libya, Nigeria, Saudi Arabia, and Venezuela). The surpluses of these countries increased from $2.0 billion in 1972 to $4.8 billion in 1973.

The developing countries as a group continued to do well in 1973, as they had in the previous few years. Inflows of capital and of development aid continued to rise, totaling $15.5 billion, compared with $14 billion in 1972 and $12 billion in 1971. This increased inflow of capital in a year in which the combined current account deficits of developing countries remained unchanged increased their collective overall balance of payments surplus by about $1.5 billion, to $7.5 billion.

The quadrupling of oil prices was expected to turn this international balance of payments situation completely around. The balance of payments deficits of the United States of 1971 and 1972 and the surpluses of many industrial countries, the counterpart of these deficits, had been the largest in history and had brought about the suspension of dollar convertibility and the introduction of widespread floating. They were nevertheless expected to be dwarfed as oil importing countries experienced even larger current account deficits and oil exporting countries developed huge surpluses. The Fund staff estimated in January 1974 that the combined current account surplus of the nine major oil exporting countries would increase in 1974 to perhaps $65 billion, more than 13 times the surplus of 1973, which, as just noted, itself had been more than double the 1972 level. This anticipated increase would have its counterpart in a deterioration of similar magnitude for all other countries combined. The staff estimated that two thirds of this deterioration would be incurred by the industrial countries, shifting them from their current account surplus of $10 billion in 1973 to a deficit of $22 billion in 1974, and that one third of the deterioration in balance of payments positions would be by what the Fund was now calling the "non-oil primary producing countries." This group of countries could incur current account deficits in 1974 aggregating perhaps $27 billion, $20 billion larger than they had been experiencing. Unusually severe balance of payments problems were foreseen for the less developed non-oil primary producing countries, which were expected to have enlarged current account deficits possibly totaling more than $20 billion in 1974.

As Mr. Witteveen explained in a speech early in 1974, these marked shifts in the pattern of world payments radically altered the concept of what constituted a sustainable international balance of payments structure.[3] In the past, a satisfactory position for most industrial countries involved a modest surplus on current account sufficient to cover outflows of aid and capital to the developing world. The counterpart of this surplus was a current account deficit in the developing world, reflecting the natural flow of capital to countries in earlier stages of development. Instead, in the new situation, the overwhelming majority of countries, industrial as well as developing, would have big current account deficits while oil exporting countries would have unprecedented surpluses. The low price elasticities of demand in the short run for petroleum products and of the supply of alternative sources of energy meant that oil importing countries would continue to import large quantities of oil despite higher prices. At the same time, given the concentration of enlarged oil incomes in a small number of oil exporting countries, such as Kuwait, Libya, Qatar, Saudi Arabia, and the United Arab Emirates, which had very small populations, it was expected that only a small proportion of the incremental income of oil exporting countries would be reflected in substantially higher imports. Saudi Arabia, espe-

---

[3]See "Recycling the Oil Billions," an address to the Economic Club of Detroit, May 6, 1974; excerpts reprinted in *IMF Survey* (Washington), Vol. 3 (May 6, 1974), pp. 129 and 133–36.

cially, one of the largest oil exporters, was expected to be a "low absorber of imports."

In these circumstances, the current account surpluses of the oil exporting countries could be considered structural rather than financial. Their genesis did not lie in inappropriate macroeconomic policies or in unrealistic exchange rates. They could not be eliminated by the usual changes in monetary or fiscal policy or in exchange rates, either by countries in surplus or by countries in deficit. Instead, elimination of the payments surpluses of oil exporting countries required basic changes in the patterns of consumption and production of both oil exporting and oil importing countries, that is, in the structure of their economies. These changes would take several years, possibly a decade or two, to accomplish.

Meanwhile, there would be a mammoth swelling of the foreign liquid assets held by oil exporting countries. Accumulations of reserves by the OPEC possibly totaling as much as several hundred billion dollars by 1980 were predicted.[4] Apart from the size of such accumulations, there was the question of the extent to which reserves might be invested in short-term banking instruments or in long-term assets instead of merely being held as deposits of foreign exchange reserves. It was unpredictable, however, to what extent these assets would take the form of long-term investments, banking funds, or the accumulations of foreign exchange reserves. As Mr. Witteveen stressed, there was surely no reason to expect that the country distributions of any capital flows that might take place from the oil exporting countries would match the country distributions of the expected current account deficits.

Implications for Inflation and Recession

Because of the higher cost of fuel, the oil price increases were expected also to cause further price inflation. This prospect was considered alarming as 1974 opened, since inflation, which had been accelerating almost steadily since the mid-1960s, was by 1973 the dominant problem of economic policy for most Fund members. By the second half of 1973, as the rate of increase in general price levels annually exceeded single digits in most industrial countries, the term "double-digit inflation" emerged in the public lexicon. Price increases of 10 percent a year or more in Canada, in the United States, and in Western European countries were extremely high in compari-

---

[4]A number of estimates of the buildup of OPEC funds were made by intergovernmental agencies, by private bankers, and by other experts in 1974 and 1975. There was also considerable discussion of these estimates and subsequent downward revisions. See, for example, Hollis B. Chenery, "Restructuring the World Economy," *Foreign Affairs* (New York), Vol. 53 (January 1975), pp. 242–63; Rimmer de Vries, "The Build-Up of OPEC Funds," *World Financial Markets* (New York), Morgan Guaranty Trust Company (September 23, 1974), pp. 1–10, and "Oil: Looking Back and Looking Ahead," ibid. (January 21, 1975), pp. 1–8; Walter J. Levy Consultants Corporation, "Future OPEC Accumulation of Oil Money: A New Look at a Critical Problem" (New York, June 1975); and Organization for Economic Cooperation and Development, *Energy Prospects to 1985* (Paris: OECD, 1974), and OECD, *Economic Outlook* (Paris), Vol. 17 (July 1975), pp. 78–85.

son with the price increases of the recent past; price increases in the industrial countries from 1960 to 1965, for example, had averaged only 2.5 percent a year, and from 1965 to 1970, 4 percent a year.

The inflationary upsurge in 1973 was by no means confined to industrial countries. The average rate of price increase in the more developed primary producing countries reached over 13 percent, almost three times higher than the 4.9 percent rate of the 1965–70 period. In developing countries, too, the acceleration of price advances was sharp and pervasive. As measured by consumer price indices, the increases in developing countries' domestic prices from 1972 to 1973 amounted, on average, to about 25 percent, nearly double the annual average from 1965 to 1970.

The increases in commodity prices already referred to, of course, added to inflation. Increases in prices of primary products were of such magnitudes as to be important elements in the higher costs—and, hence, higher prices—confronted by importing countries, as well as elements in the larger export earnings by the producing countries. But other factors also aggravated worldwide inflation. In 1973, as a new economic phenomenon, an unusually high degree of coincidence appeared in the phasing of expansion (and later of recession) in industrial countries. Inflation in one industrial country coincided with inflation in other industrial countries. No longer was the United States the prime mover of the rest of the world economy, as it had been for several decades; instead, levels of economic activity and aggregate demand in several industrial countries moved up (and later down) simultaneously. Aggravating inflation further was a pervasive inflationary psychology. With expectations of more inflation to come, it was more difficult for governments and business enterprises to hold down demands for wage and price increases and to curb speculative purchases of commodities, all of which caused costs and prices to spiral still more. Such was the degree and nature of the inflation in 1973 that made the members of the Committee of Twenty, in January 1974, cite it along with the payments consequences of the rise in oil prices as a reason why they had to abandon their efforts to reform the international monetary system.

In one of the frequent paradoxes in economics, it was feared that the rise in oil prices might result not only in higher inflation but also in deep world recession. Higher prices for oil could be thought of as a tax that oil importing countries would have to transfer to the oil exporting countries. To pay this tax, oil importing countries might have to cut back heavily not only on imports of oil but also of other products. Since oil exporting countries were not expected to increase their own demands for imports sufficiently to compensate for the cutback by other countries, there could be a substantial drop in world demand for goods and services. In Keynesian terms, quadrupling the price of oil shifted income to a group of countries having, as a whole, an exceptionally high propensity to save, thereby raising the propensity of the world to save. Since an increase in savings did not lead automatically to higher investment, larger savings had the potential for serious deflation. The problem was complicated further because the higher savings were concentrated in a few countries that were not expected to increase their own domestic investment promptly.

311

Like added inflation, any additional decline in world demand was also regarded as unusually serious in the context of the circumstances prevailing late in 1973 and expected for 1974. Most industrial countries were already experiencing rates of economic growth much below the high annual growth rates of 4.5 to 5 percent which they had enjoyed throughout the 1960s. After the economic slowdown in most industrial countries in 1969–71, there had been a resurgence of economic expansion in industrial countries in 1972 and the first half of 1973, but the recovery proved unsustainable. Growth of real gross national product in industrial countries dropped from the high rate of 8 percent a year in the first half of 1973 to an annual rate of only 3 percent in the second half.

Exacerbating the twin problems of inflation and slow economic growth, macroeconomic problems no longer responded to demand-management policies by national governments. The frustration of trying to stimulate economic growth and greater employment through expansionary demand-management policies without causing increases in the general price level, first manifested in the United Kingdom and the United States in the recessions of 1966–67 and 1970–71, was becoming familiar to all industrial countries and even to some countries, such as Australia, whose economies depended mainly on primary products. Many governments were thus finding it almost impossible to reconcile their objectives for economic growth and full employment with price stability.

PROPOSALS BY THE MANAGING DIRECTOR

The Managing Director was among the first financial officials to address the problems of massive international balance of payments disequilibrium, the aggravation of high worldwide inflation, and the threat of severe recession in nearly all industrial countries. Although the December 1973 announcement of the steep oil price increases was received in Washington just before Christmas, Mr. Witteveen immediately concluded that the Fund ought to take some kind of action and started to formulate a plan. He reasoned that while the world might have been able to cope fairly well with the enlarged current account deficits brought about by the increases in oil prices effected through October 1973, the new round of price increases for 1974 would produce problems of an altogether different dimension. Mr. Witteveen regarded it as fortunate that the Committee of Twenty was scheduled to meet a few weeks later in Rome. Hence, on January 3, he cabled Mr. Wardhana to ask him to suggest to the members of the Committee that at their forthcoming meeting they consider the changes in the world payments situation.

Meanwhile Mr. Witteveen proceeded to form his own proposals against the background of staff advice that the Fund had unlimited powers to borrow and to make its resources available. In a speech to the World Banking Conference in London, on January 15, 1974, he warned that the international monetary system was facing its most difficult period since the 1930s.[5] The combination of higher oil prices, which would give a sharp twist to the serious inflationary spiral, and of energy shortages, which would accentuate the slowdown in economic activity, would place strains on the international monetary system "far in excess of any that have been experienced since the war." Given the regime with floating exchange rates and the lack of agreed rules for international behavior, there was real danger of the introduction of beggar-my-neighbor policies, such as the competitive exchange depreciation and escalation of trade restrictions that had characterized the 1930s. Governments might also adopt deflationary policies, such as tighter monetary and fiscal policies, in order to curb payments deficits. The imposition of restrictions or of deflationary policies could bring on a serious international recession. Mr. Witteveen, along with Mr. Morse, working with the Committee of Twenty, and Emile van Lennep, Secretary-General of the OECD, and other financial officials, was concerned that efforts by major industrial countries to cut back on their imports of oil or other commodities or to curb their external payments deficits in other ways, superimposed on the slowdown in economic growth already occurring in the latter part of 1973, would reduce output in industrial countries. Not only would declines in output in industrial countries bring about hardship in those countries but developing countries would face greater difficulties in exporting to industrial countries to help pay their own higher oil import bills.

Thus, Mr. Witteveen and Mr. van Lennep, as heads of multinational organizations, were deeply worried that the policies to which countries would resort in the acute circumstances of the oil price rise could be exactly the same as they had used in similar circumstances of deflation, unemployment, and balance of payments deficits in the 1930s. With the experience of the lessons learned by economists and by economic policymakers in the 40 years from 1933 to 1973, these officials were determined that countries not make the same mistakes again.

Avoidance of Restrictions and Deflationary Policies

In making alternative policy suggestions to national government officials, Mr. Witteveen first stressed that currency devaluation, internal deflation, and import restraint, the customary and accepted remedies for balance of payments deficits in the 1950s and 1960s, would clearly be wrong in the new changed circumstances affecting the whole world and thus ought to be avoided. If oil importing countries attempted to improve their balance of payments by depreciating their currencies, they would only shift deficits among themselves. For it was unrealistic to expect exchange rate adjustment to make more than a very limited contribution toward reducing the large surpluses of the oil exporting countries. Similarly, trade restrictions or excessive demand deflation would improve one country's balance of payments only by worsening the position of other oil importing countries. If other countries responded by adopting similar policies, there would be

---

[5]See *IMF Survey* (Washington), Vol. 3 (January 21, 1974), pp. 17 and 20–22.

a distortion in the allocation of resources and possibly a cumulative deflationary effect on the world economy. Consequently, oil importing countries, as a group, would have to accept sizable current account deficits. In the course of 1974 the slogan "accept the oil deficit" gradually came into vogue among financial officials.

Following his lead and after many informal conversations among financial officials in late December 1973 and early January 1974, the members of the Committee of Twenty stated in the communiqué issued after their meeting in Rome in January 1974 their serious concerns at the abrupt and significant changes in the world payments structure. They also stressed that countries must avoid policies which would merely aggravate the problems of other countries, emphasizing the importance of avoiding competitive depreciation and the escalation of restrictions on trade and payments and noting that countries should hold close consultations with the Fund on these matters.[6] Five days later, on January 23, the Executive Board took a decision calling on members to collaborate with the Fund and notifying them that the Fund would be consulting them about the policies they were following in the existing circumstances.[7]

An Oil Facility in the Fund

As he spoke out in January 1974, Mr. Witteveen was well aware that warnings against the dangers of competitive exchange depreciation, intensification of restrictions, and deflationary policies were totally insufficient for the problem at hand, which was how to finance the enlarged current account deficits. The means to finance the deficits, of course, existed in the surplus revenues and accumulated funds of the oil exporting countries. The question was how to get these funds recycled in the optimum way.

Officials had recognized almost immediately after the rise in oil prices in December 1973 that recycling petrodollars would probably take place very quickly through the Eurocurrency markets. They had discussed this possibility at a meeting of the deputies of the Group of Ten in December 1973. They realized, too, that some kind of new official facility would take much longer to establish; a relatively lengthy process was inevitable in order to get agreement on any official arrangement. Nevertheless, it was important to try to obtain an official arrangement for recycling petrodollars.

In making the case for an official facility in the Fund, Mr. Witteveen recognized that the private markets, such as the Eurocurrency markets, had a basic role to play in channeling oil revenues from oil exporting to oil importing countries. He was also encouraged by the concrete proposals which officials of Iran and Saudi Arabia immediately began to advance in January 1974 for increasing aid by their governments on concessionary terms, especially to the poorest developing countries. Officials of the OECD were likewise thinking in terms of some official arrangements

---

[6]Communiqué of Committee of Twenty, January 18, 1974, par. 2; Vol. III below, pp. 199–200.
[7]E.B. Decision No. 4134-(74/4), January 23, 1974; Vol. III below, p. 554.

for helping to finance the enlarged deficits of OECD members. Mr. Witteveen noted some difficulties with these prospective private and official arrangements, however. There were distinct limits to the ability of private markets to borrow from oil exporters on short term and relend to oil importers on medium term. The use of private markets would not ensure that the surplus funds of oil exporting countries would find their way to the oil importing countries that needed them most. The new official arrangements proposed by oil producing nations and by the OECD would in all likelihood not be able to furnish substantial amounts until well into 1975. Therefore, he proposed that the Fund introduce a special oil facility. The Fund would obtain funds by borrowing from its oil exporting members and from industrial members with payments surpluses and lending those funds to members with enlarged deficits.

Mr. Witteveen recognized that his proposed oil facility would not provide a permanent solution for financing the extra foreign exchange costs of oil imports and that it certainly could not begin to solve the problems of internal adjustment resulting from the need to pay for, or reduce dependence on, imported oil. He regarded it only as a bridging facility, that is, to help Fund members get through a transition period in which longer-term solutions would be worked out, in order to prevent countries from adopting policies which would be harmful to others or which might bring about recession. With this temporary objective in mind, he envisaged that the oil facility would exist for a maximum of two years, 1974 and 1975. As he made this proposal in January 1974, he was not yet sure how much money he could raise for such a facility.

OBJECTIONS TO AN OIL FACILITY

Even Mr. Witteveen's limited concept met with strong misgivings and outright objections by many financial officials, especially those of the United States. The reactions to the oil crisis of Mr. Shultz, Secretary of the Treasury, and of Mr. Simon, who was at the time Director of the U.S. Federal Energy Office and who was shortly to succeed Mr. Shultz in the U.S. Treasury, were that the world balance of payments situation created by such sudden and large increases in oil prices was unmanageable. In particular, the poorest of the developing countries that had to import oil, such as Bangladesh, India, Pakistan, Sri Lanka, and most African countries, were put in the untenable position of having their already sizable balance of payments deficits still further enlarged by enormous sums. Mr. Shultz and Mr. Simon, as well as other high-ranking officials in President Nixon's Administration who were concerned with problems of energy and of foreign policy, believed that international pressure ought to be brought to bear on the officials of oil exporting countries to induce them "to roll back" some of their recent price increases and that the United States, as a world leader, should exert such pressure. U.S. officials believed that, in any event, if oil consuming nations worked together to cut their imports of crude oil and to increase production of alternative sources of crude oil and of other types of energy, crude oil prices were bound to fall again. They were convinced that there was no serious shortage of supplies of oil in the world, that there was excess capacity in the oil industry, and that price declines would occur in a remarkably short time, within months or at most within a year.

U.S. officials believed, too, that the U.S. Government would lose more of its political leadership in the world if it readily tolerated such sudden increases in the price of oil, resulting from decisions taken more or less unilaterally by the officials of Middle Eastern oil exporting countries, without any negotiation with officials of the large industrial oil importing countries. With these thoughts in mind, U.S. officials viewed Mr. Witteveen's proposal for helping to finance the anticipated large deficits as an acceptance by the international community of the new higher oil prices and as tantamount to underwriting these prices. They were opposed to such acceptance.

Since the enlarged payments deficits resulting from higher prices for oil imports could go on for several years, Mr. Shultz was also worried that many developing countries, having borrowed from the Fund through this proposed oil facility, would be unable to repay. He and other U.S. officials, as well as members of Congress, were concerned that in the event that developing countries were unable to repay the Fund, the U.S. Government might be obliged to vote them grants or other aid. Defaults by developing countries on their debts to the Fund could also create political crises for their governments and thereby have implications for U.S. foreign policy. Moreover, if developing countries could not repay their drawings from the Fund, the concept of the temporary use of the Fund's financial resources and of a revolving fund that was traditionally and legally the basis of the Fund's policies on use of its resources would also be endangered.

Although in general officials of the Federal Republic of Germany did not oppose the proposed oil facility as vigorously as did U.S. officials, Mr. Schmidt, then Minister of Finance, also expressed reservations about the proposal at the Rome meeting of the Committee of Twenty in January. At Executive Board meetings later in 1974, Mr. Schleiminger also indicated that German officials were not yet willing to endorse wholeheartedly the proposed oil facility nor to lend to the Fund for this purpose. German officials were mainly concerned about the Fund's injecting still more liquid resources into the world economy at a time when inflation was continuing to increase.

Some members of the Fund staff as well initially questioned the wisdom of the Managing Director's proposal. As Mr. Witteveen had been Managing Director for only a few months, some members of the staff who had been with the Fund almost since its inception were concerned that he might not have adequately considered the implications of his proposal for the Fund's usual policies and institutional foundations. They questioned, for instance, whether the Fund could help to finance the anticipated immense payments deficits sufficiently to make the associated risk and controversy worthwhile. Financing the large deficits that would occur for most of the Fund's members and that might persist for some years was far beyond the Fund's capability. The staff, therefore, cautioned the Managing Director against borrowing on a substantial scale from a large number of members for such a purpose. They pointed out that except under the General Arrangements to Borrow (GAB), which was a limited arrangement only occasionally used, and the borrowing from Italy in 1966, the Fund had not borrowed from its members. Some staff feared, too, that only members without alternative sources of financing would come to the Fund. The Fund would, in effect, be substituting its own high credit standing in international financial markets for the low credit ratings of many very poor developing members.

Some staff members were concerned that the Fund's regular policies with regard to the use of its resources, tying macroeconomic policies to drawings from the Fund, would be upset; it was unlikely that many conditions could be placed on drawings urgently needed to finance oil deficits. Some of the staff took the position that Fund members ought to begin immediately to adjust their balance of payments in order to reduce their oil imports. They believed that the availability of financing from the Fund on relatively easy terms would delay, or prevent, such adjustment.

Such was the climate of opinion in the first few months of 1974 in which Mr. Witteveen pushed ahead with his proposal for an oil facility. Despite the doubts expressed, Mr. Witteveen remained convinced of the need for an oil facility in the Fund and was determined to proceed. As a pragmatist, he did not want the Fund to remain inactive while the payments problems of members grew inordinately large. He particularly wanted to increase the Fund's financial transactions. Drawings had been declining for several years and in calendar year 1973 had totaled only SDR 730 million, the smallest amount in a decade.

After the Committee of Twenty endorsed his proposal in January 1974, Mr. Witteveen went to Teheran in February to discuss the prospects for Fund borrowing with Iranian officials, including the Shah. He did so not knowing whether his efforts would succeed. Robert S. McNamara, President of the World Bank, also went to Iran at this time to seek funds for the World Bank. From the Managing Director's discussions in Teheran it became evident that, although Iranian officials were more interested in some of Iran's own proposals for helping developing nations, they would be willing to lend substantial amounts to the Fund. The Managing Director's discussions in Teheran also revealed that in borrowing from oil exporting members, the Fund would probably have to pay rates of interest close to commercial interest rates. Since the Fund's charges were normally much lower than commercial rates, the interest rates for borrowing by the Fund would, therefore, be considerably higher than those which the Fund customarily charged its members for drawing from the Fund.

With assurance of some borrowed funds Mr. Witteveen returned to Washington to try to gain support for his facility, particularly from U.S. officials, and to lead the Executive Directors and the staff in shaping the features of the 1974 oil facility.

Gaining U.S. Support

Mr. Witteveen gradually reduced some of the objections of U.S. officials to the facility. He emphasized that there were few alternatives to some form of official financing of the oil deficits of developing countries, which were already experiencing much higher oil bills and would have to borrow from somewhere. The only alternative was for them to curtail their oil imports and submit to corresponding hardships in the form of reduced economic growth, greater unemployment, and even lower living standards. He also suggested to U.S. officials that if he was able to raise the needed funds, they at least let him try an oil facility in the Fund.

In addition, Mr. Witteveen sent to U.S. officials a series of studies prepared by the Fund staff which demonstrated that the Fund's experience had been good with many developing members, including Brazil, Colombia, Indonesia, Korea, Peru, the Philippines, Sierra Leone, Tunisia, Turkey, and Yugoslavia, which had had sizable balance of payments deficits in the past and which had drawn from the Fund; they had been able to repay the Fund within a few years' time. The staff was also optimistic that developing members could over time increase exports sufficiently to enable them to repurchase any purchases made under the oil facility.

The objections of U.S. officials to an oil facility in the Fund were also softened by the attitudes taken by the officials of oil importing developing countries. While U.S. officials had been protesting the rise in prices for oil, partly on behalf of the poor oil importing countries, officials of these countries were not voicing such protests. Identifying with the officials of oil exporting countries, which were also developing countries and fellow members of the Group of Seventy-Seven and the Group of Twenty-Four, officials of non-oil developing countries accepted the increases in oil prices rather quickly. They saw the OPEC moves not as against other developing countries but rather as against the industrial nations, which were by far the largest consumers of oil. To many officials from developing countries, the actions of OPEC looked as if primary producing countries, after centuries of having their national resources developed by the private entrepreneurs of industrial countries, were at last taking charge of their own resources. The moves of OPEC gave to officials of other Third World countries a vision of a fundamental shift in the balance of economic power away from industrial nations and toward developing nations. Hence, rather than objecting to the oil price rises, officials of oil importing developing nations looked for ways of financing the resulting payments deficits. They were vigorous advocates of the Fund's introducing some financial arrangements.

SHAPING THE 1974 FACILITY

Nothing like the oil facility had ever been created in the Fund. A number of procedural, policy, and legal questions had to be answered before the facility could be established. What should the terms and conditions of borrowing be? What types of borrowing agreements should be used? To reduce the need for borrowing, or to get the facility started as soon as possible, should the Fund's regular resources also be drawn upon? If so, to what extent? How much should members be permitted to draw under this new oil facility? How would such drawings affect their right to draw on the Fund's regular resources? What conditions should the Fund attach to a member's use of the facility; that is, what conditionality should apply? What charges should be set for these drawings and how should the Fund handle the problem that the rate of interest the Fund would have to pay on borrowed funds would exceed the Fund's usual charges? Should the usual repurchase provisions apply or should a longer period be allowed in which members could repurchase?

The Managing Director, together with Mr. Dale, who became Deputy Managing Director on March 1, 1974, and the senior staff of the various functional and area departments, drafted features of a facility. These features were discussed in detail at many meetings of the Executive Board in March, April, and May.

Decision to Use Borrowed Funds

Since the Fund's resources had been little drawn upon since 1970, it was possible to use some of the Fund's own resources for the oil facility. The Executive Board, therefore, began its deliberations for the oil facility by thoroughly reviewing the liquidity of the General Account. This review revealed that the Fund's existing holdings of members' currencies were adequate to finance net drawings up to about SDR 5 billion, even without replenishment of the Fund's holdings of currencies through borrowing.

Most Executive Directors objected, however, to using these currency holdings for the oil facility. Some argued that their use would pre-empt these resources for one particular purpose. Messrs. Andreassen and Lieftinck and other members of the Executive Board pointed out that with enlarged payments deficits it could be expected that several members would soon request gold tranche drawings from the Fund. Since these drawings were automatically given, the Fund had to reserve funds for them. Messrs. Kafka and Palamenghi-Crispi also wanted to be sure that enough resources were available in the General Account to finance drawings under the extended facility, which was being proposed and discussed at about the same time. Many Executive Directors stressed that the Fund should avoid use of its own currency holdings for financing transactions under the oil facility because positions in the Fund of individual members should not be altered as a result of transactions under this facility; otherwise, the creditor and debtor positions in the Fund of members would inevitably be changed, as usually occurred when Fund transactions took place. The Executive Board was also at the time considering a change in the method of valuing the SDR, which was still being valued in terms of gold, as described in Chapter 16. Some Executive Directors, especially those appointed or elected by Western European members who favored an upward revaluation of gold, took the occasion to point out that the Fund had only its currency holdings available for use because assets held by the Fund in the form of gold were valued at an artificially low price and hence were abnormally small.

While they did not like using the Fund's currency holdings for the oil facility, Executive Directors were receptive to the idea of the Fund's borrowing to finance the facility and to the idea that the facility would be a floating one. In other words, the holdings of members' currencies that the Fund would acquire in transactions under the oil facility would be notionally segregated from the Fund's other holdings of members' currencies.

Executive Directors liked the idea of a floating facility based on borrowed funds for several reasons. Borrowing did not raise the same problems as did use of the Fund's other assets. Under the arrangement, the Fund would immediately pass to the drawing member the actual currency borrowed, so that the amount and composition of the Fund's holdings of individual members' currencies would not be affected by transactions under the facility. Augmenting the Fund's liquidity by borrowing, rather than through increases in quotas, also would not lead to changes in members' relative positions in the Fund with the consequent changes in voting power, increased drawing rights, and relative shares in any SDR allocations. In addition, unlike replenishment of the Fund's holdings of currencies through the sale of gold or SDRs, borrowing would not cause a permanent shift in the composition of the Fund's assets.

Not only did borrowing get around these problems but it had further advantages. Mr. de Groote, for example, considered it desirable for the Fund to borrow from members not only to augment the moneys available to the Fund but also to increase the participation of the membership in the Fund's operations. Still another reason why Executive Directors preferred the Fund to have separate financing arrangements to handle the oil crisis was the need to preserve the Fund's established policy on conditionality when its regular resources were used.

All in all, most Executive Directors concluded that it was preferable for the Fund to have a separate window with its own financing arrangements to help finance payments deficits associated with the oil price rise. To make it clear that the arrangements for oil were separate from the rest of the Fund's operations, Mr. Lieftinck suggested that the Fund set up an oil account, parallel with the General Account and the Special Drawing Account.

The oil facility was, therefore, to be financed with borrowed funds. Nonetheless, the Executive Board agreed that if necessary the Fund might use a limited amount of its own holdings of currencies until borrowed funds could be made available. The amount was to be roughly equal to the Fund's holdings of certain members' currencies which had not so far been usable in Fund transactions. The Fund held nearly SDR 1 billion in currencies of oil exporting members and of some other members, many of whose currencies had never been used in the Fund's transactions and operations. Under the Articles of Agreement, the Fund could take in repurchases only those currencies that were formally convertible because the member had accepted the obligations of Article VIII. Most members, including several oil exporting members (other than Saudi Arabia), were still under Article XIV, however. On the purchase side, as a matter of practice, the Fund did not use a member's currency in drawings without the consent of that member. The issuer had to stand ready to convert balances of its currency into a reserve currency or to sell its currency for use in discharging a repurchase against the receipt of another currency at appropriate exchange rates. These arrangements had not been made between the Fund and several members which were now major oil exporters.

The Managing Director and the Executive Board believed that the Fund could make the necessary arrangements with the members concerned for use of the Fund's holdings of their currencies. As it turned out, the oil facility did not get under way until borrowed funds were available, so the Fund did not use any of its own holdings of currencies for drawings under the oil facility. Arrangements were made, nonetheless, with a number of oil exporting members, Bahrain, Indonesia, Oman, Qatar, and the United Arab Emirates, to use their currencies in Fund transactions. (Arrangements had been made some years earlier with Kuwait and Venezuela.) These arrangements enabled the Fund to borrow either in U.S. dollars or in a member's own currency. In the financial year which ended on April 30, 1975, the Fund was thus able to use, either for the first time or after a lapse of many years, a number of currencies in its holdings.

Determining the Conditions for Use

Working out the criteria for use of the oil facility necessitated considerably more deliberation by the Executive Board than did the need for borrowing. In keeping with the Fund's long-standing practice of not differentiating its policies by categories of members, it was recognized from the start that the oil facility would have to be open to all members meeting whatever criteria were specified. However, it was assumed, or arranged, that oil exporting members would not use the facility. Mr. Shultz, moreover, assured Mr. Witteveen that although the United States could not lend to the Fund for the oil facility since it continued to be in balance of payments deficit, neither would U.S. officials request a drawing from the Fund under the facility. The implicit understanding between Mr. Witteveen and U.S. officials that the United States would not draw on the oil facility helped the Fund to arrange a facility which, while not of exorbitant size, could be at least nominally open to all members.

Like access to all of the Fund's resources and in line with the Articles that its resources be linked to balance of payments deficits, the drawing member was to have a balance of payments need. In the circumstances of 1974, when all oil importing countries expected to have large payments deficits, however, the requirement of balance of payments need was virtually no requirement at all. What was needed was some way for the Fund to differentiate those members that had fewer means to finance their newly enlarged current account deficits from those members that might be able to reduce their balance of payments need by means other than drawing from the Fund. Industrial members, for instance, were more likely than developing members to receive a reflow of funds from oil exporting countries seeking to invest their enlarged revenues. Some developing members, such as Brazil, were more likely to receive capital inflows from abroad than were other developing members. Some developing members, such as Arab countries that were not oil exporters (for example, Egypt, Jordan, and Syria), were also more likely to receive aid on concessionary terms from their Arab neighbors than were other developing members. The Executive Board accordingly decided to place considerable reliance on an evaluation by the Fund of the balance of payments need of individual members as they requested drawings under the oil facility.

As in the case of other uses of the Fund's resources, a member using the oil facility was also expected to cooperate with the Fund to find appropriate solutions for overcoming its balance of payments deficits. The member was specifically to consult with the Fund during the year and subsequently during the period under which it had drawings outstanding under the facility, either in connection with the regular annual consultations or separately, in order to afford the Fund an opportunity to ascertain whether the drawing member's policies were conducive to balance of payments adjustment and to repurchase. These very general conditions for use of the 1974 oil facility were in lieu of the usual much more specific conditions relating to macroeconomic policies attached to drawings from the Fund. There was thus virtually no conditionality attached to the 1974 oil facility on the grounds that the immediate need of members was too urgent and the situation too unclear to permit working out a full plan for a member to adjust its payments situation to the new higher prices for oil.

One additional condition for access to the oil facility proved important, however. The member was to state that it would refrain from imposing new, or intensifying existing, restrictions on trade without prior consultation with the Fund and would refrain from any additional restrictions on payments without the prior approval of the Fund. (Unlike payments restrictions, trade restrictions could not be made the subject of approval by the Fund.) Prior consultation or prior approval were emphasized because they were considered a more effective deterrent to the imposition of restrictions than were consultation or approval after restrictions had been implemented. The Managing Director, determined to avoid an intensification of restrictions in the new situation, was personally insistent on this condition.

Finding a Formula to Determine Amounts of Access

Another question that involved lengthy discussions in the Executive Board concerned the size of the drawings to be permitted. It seemed advisable to have a general formula by which a member could readily ascertain the maximum amount it was entitled to draw under the facility. The formula suggested by the staff made use of the three elements that seemed important: the increase in oil import costs, the availability of a member's own reserves, and, in line with usual drawings from the Fund, some relation between the size of a member's drawing and its quota in the Fund. A member could draw an amount calculated as (i) the increase in the cost of a member's net imports of petroleum and petroleum products over the costs of its imports of these commodities in 1972, minus (ii) an amount equivalent to 20 percent of its reserves at the end of 1973, subject to (iii) a maximum of 75 percent of its quota in the Fund. The increase in the cost of a member's net imports of petroleum and petroleum products was taken as the increase in the global price of oil from

October 1, 1973 to January 1, 1974, set for this purpose at $5.50 per barrel. To obtain a figure for the cost of a member's net imports of oil prior to the oil price rise, the SDR equivalent of $5.50 per barrel, or SDR 6.6349250 converted at SDR 1 = $1.20635 (the rate between SDRs and the dollar prevailing in the first half of 1974), was to be multiplied by the volume in barrels of the member's net imports (that is, imports less exports) in 1972. The year 1972 was chosen because, at the time, it was the most recent year for which reasonably complete and comparable figures were available; data for 1973 were not then available. Provision for subtracting an amount related to the size of a member's reserves was based on the assumption that a member would be ready to use some of its reserves to help meet the impact on its external payments of the oil price rise. Since use of the Fund's resources was customarily related to the size of the member's quota, the staff suggested 75 percent of quota.

When the Executive Directors discussed the proposed oil facility in the early months of 1974, they had difficulty with the suggested formula. Many Executive Directors elected by developing members were already discouraged by features of the oil facility. Mr. Yaméogo and Mr. Nicol-Cole, for example, foresaw relatively little help from the facility for African members. As they viewed the facility taking shape, the Fund was going to borrow at rates of interest much higher than those prevailing under the Fund's low schedule of charges and so was planning to have relatively high charges. It was likely, too, that in practice some fairly tight macroeconomic policies might be expected by the Fund as a prerequisite for use of the facility. Now, as the discussions in the Executive Board suggested, the proposed formula for determining amounts of access to the facility would be disadvantageous to developing members. Messrs. Amuzegar, Nazih Deif (Egypt), Kafka, and Kharmawan, joined Messrs. Yaméogo and Nicol-Cole in their objections to the formula. They did not like either the use of imports in 1972 as a base or the deduction of an amount equal to 20 percent of a member's reserves. Use of 1972 as a base, they argued, discriminated against members that were developing their economies rapidly and whose imports of oil were rising. Deduction of one fifth of a member's reserves failed to take into account that many developing members needed to husband their reserves to finance imports during periods when export earnings were low. They and the other Executive Directors elected by developing members stressed that the danger of a decline in export earnings of developing members was imminent because 1973 had been a year of extremely high prices for primary products.

Mr. Amuzegar suggested specifically that the 20 percent deduction in the staff formula be reduced to 10 percent, a suggestion with which most Executive Directors and Mr. Witteveen concurred. Mr. Deif circulated to the Executive Directors a paper presenting arguments as to why no formula could apply to all members and why developing members should be allowed greater access than developed members to the facility. Nguyen Huu Hanh (Viet Nam), using statistics for Korea, showed that in instances in which the member had a relatively low quota in the Fund, use of the formula, especially limiting drawings to 75 percent of quota, meant that the Fund would finance only a minimal portion of the member's calculated increased oil import costs.

Some Executive Directors appointed or elected by industrial members were also concerned that under the proposed formula, the bulk of the oil facility might be used by a few industrial members. Mr. Palamenghi-Crispi, for instance, noted that the formula did not take into account the differing abilities of members to cope with oil deficits by means of capital inflows or by borrowing, nor did it allow for the large structural current account deficits which developing members experienced over and above their oil deficits nor for the fact that the reserves of developing members were often used as collateral for borrowing. Mr. Wahl agreed that use of the 1972 figures for oil imports reduced the potential access to the facility of developing members and that for them a 20 percent deduction from reserves was excessive. To overcome these objections, Mr. de Groote proposed that the formula suggested by the staff be revised so that it would emphasize the most pressing needs.

In the decision eventually taken, the Fund was to make detailed assessment of individual members' payments and reserve situations, the formula for access was to be revised, and the Executive Board was to review the facility, including the formula, in September 1974 and again in December 1974. Assessment by the Fund was to establish that the member did have a balance of payments need. The Fund was especially to take into account in the instance of developing members, their success in marshaling concessionary aid and, in the instance of developed members, their ability to attract capital flows from oil exporting nations. A limit of 75 percent of quota was to apply unless an insufficiency of resources for the oil facility required the Fund to apply a lower percentage.

The formula to determine the maximum access of a member to the facility was revised as follows. The 1972 figures were to be used initially, but import data for 1973 were to be used when they became available. The deduction of 20 percent of reserves was reduced to 10 percent. This deduction, moreover, was to be adjusted for variability of exports by a complicated calculation. An amount was to be deducted from the member's reserves at the end of 1973 equal to twice the root mean squared proportional deviation of export values from a centered five-year moving average—using export series generally covering the period 1955–71—multiplied by the SDR value of exports in 1972. If the deduction resulted in a negative figure, the maximum amount that the member could draw under the oil facility was to be equal to the increase in the cost of its imports of petroleum and petroleum products. A member's drawings were not to exceed 35 percent of the amount provided by the formula until the Executive Board had reviewed the amounts available for the facility.

Resources made available under the oil facility were also to be supplementary to any assistance that members might obtain under the Fund's other policies on use of its resources.

ARRANGING TO BORROW FUNDS

Because of the intensive discussions in the Executive Board, by April 1974, when the Managing Director left Fund headquarters for a three-week trip to Middle

Eastern members (other than Iran) to seek funds for the facility, the characteristics of an oil facility were much clearer than when he went to Iran in February. Having lined up financial support from Iran, Mr. Witteveen regarded it as of prime importance to get a commitment from the officials of Saudi Arabia. If Saudi Arabia was willing to lend to the Fund, other Arab members would presumably follow. He was especially hopeful that Saudi Arabian officials would be willing to lend to the Fund. The Fund had the advantage of good, indirect contacts with Saudi Arabia since Ahmed Zaki Saad, a long-time Executive Director in the Fund, was also a Governor of the Fund for Saudi Arabia from 1958 to 1977. Furthermore, Anwar Ali, Director of the Fund's Middle Eastern Department, had for many years been on leave from the Fund staff to serve as Governor of the Saudi Arabian Monetary Agency.

Mr. Witteveen went first to Geneva to talk to Mr. Saad, who had retired there, and next proceeded to Algiers, since Algerian officials were regarded as having special influence with Middle Eastern nations and with the Third World. It was, for instance, at a meeting in Algiers in October 1967 that the Group of Seventy-Seven had adopted the Algiers Charter. Moreover, President Houari Boumédiène of Algeria was in 1974 President of the Non-Aligned Countries, a group of 70 developing countries not allied militarily with either the West or with the East. These countries had met in Algiers in September 1973. President Boumédiène had also initiated the Sixth Special Session of the United Nations General Assembly to consider problems of raw materials. The session was being held in New York in April 1974, just as Mr. Witteveen was seeking to borrow funds for the 1974 oil facility. In this connection President Boumédiène was in the forefront of those pressing for the establishment of "a new system of [international economic] relations based on equality and the common interests of all States," that is, a new international economic order.[8] On May 1, 1974, at the Sixth Special Session, the UN General Assembly adopted two resolutions calling for a new international economic order and setting forth a program of action.[9]

From Algeria, Mr. Witteveen proceeded to Saudi Arabia where he was joined by some members of the Fund staff. His discussions with officials of Saudi Arabia advanced beyond an expression of willingness to lend to the Fund to the terms and conditions of borrowing. It became apparent that, although the Managing Director and staff and many Executive Directors had been thinking in terms of the Fund paying a rate of interest of 5 percent a year (the rate of interest then being discussed for the SDR), officials of Arab nations were thinking in terms of interest rates still closer to prevailing commercial rates of interest of 7 percent a year. Following a virtually firm pledge of funds from Saudi Arabian officials, along with the support he already had from Iranian officials, the Managing Director traveled next to Kuwait, the United Arab Emirates, Lebanon, and Libya. In these countries negotiations were somewhat harder, but eventually he was able to discuss the prospects for borrowing by the Fund and possible amounts, terms, and conditions. In Lebanon, he met with

---

[8]UN General Assembly Document A/9541, February 5, 1974, p. 3.
[9]UN General Assembly Resolutions Nos. 3201 (S-VI) and 3202 (S-VI), May 1, 1974.

several delegations of Middle Eastern countries who were attending the third annual meeting of the Arab Fund for Economic and Social Development.

Upon his return to Washington, Mr. Witteveen reported to the Executive Directors that his trip was rewarding. At an interest rate of 7 percent a year, the Saudi Arabian Monetary Agency was prepared to lend SDR 1 billion in Saudi Arabian riyals, and Kuwait, the United Arab Emirates, and Libya were also prepared to lend to the Fund. In late April Mr. Dale traveled to Nigeria for the same purpose, and in early May Mr. Witteveen went to Venezuela.

Officials of oil exporting members expressed a strong desire that the Fund seek funds from its industrial members as well. They did not want their financing of the new facility to be construed as a penalty for increasing oil prices. Mr. Witteveen, too, wanted to secure funds from industrial members. Not only did he want as large a facility as possible, but he was also eager to have a wide range of lenders. Participation of industrial members in the facility could, he thought, help increase understanding with oil producing nations which would be useful in the difficult financing situation which lay ahead. He went to Europe on May 28–31, 1974 to have conversations, inter alia, about lending to the Fund for the oil facility, with the Ministers of Finance of Belgium, France, the Federal Republic of Germany, Italy, and the Netherlands. He wanted especially to get a contribution from the Federal Republic of Germany since such a contribution would facilitate contributions from Belgium and the Netherlands. However, after Mr. Apel, shortly to become Minister of Finance, and Mr. Pöhl, Under-Secretary, Ministry of Finance, carefully considered the matter with Mr. Schmidt, then Finance Minister and shortly afterward Chancellor, and with officials of the Deutsche Bundesbank, they expressed reluctance to lend to the Fund. They had two reasons. There was the political consideration of why the Federal Republic of Germany should help solve a problem not of its making; and there was the question of what further demands for financial assistance the Federal Republic of Germany might face later in the year from her European partners. German officials, who were always pointing out the inflationary potential of any financial arrangements, were also somewhat concerned that by lending to the Fund's oil facility, they might be underwriting an increase in international liquidity. Consequently, among industrial members, initially only Canada agreed to lend to the Fund for the 1974 facility. Toward the end of 1974, the Managing Director, himself a former official of the Netherlands Government and personally closely identified with the oil facility, was able to get the Netherlands Government to lend SDR 150 million. (As described in the next chapter, several European countries did lend to the Fund for the 1975 facility.)

CHARGES ON USE OF THE FACILITY

The prospect that the Fund would have to pay 7 percent a year on borrowed funds raised problems concerning the Fund's charges. The Fund had traditionally set charges on use of its resources at levels well below commercial rates of interest. As seen in Chapter 16, the schedule of charges in effect in early 1974 had been in effect since May 1, 1963 and had not been substantially altered since 1954. As also seen in Chapter 16, the Executive Board decided in June 1974 to raise the Fund's schedule of charges, effective July 1, 1974, at the time it increased the rate of interest on the SDR and the rate of remuneration on creditor positions in the Fund. The decision in June 1974 to raise the Fund's charges was heavily influenced by the realization that for drawings under the oil facility the Fund would probably have to levy charges close to market rates. The Fund was already operating at a budgetary deficit and if it was going to have an oil facility financed by funds borrowed at market rates of interest, it seemed reasonable for the Fund to cover at least the costs of borrowing. If the Fund "lost money" on drawings under the oil facility, its capacity to finance other drawings would be impaired. The Fund was willing not to try to cover its costs of administering the oil facility.

The idea of the Fund's charging commercial rates of interest was unusual. The Fund's traditionally low charges on use of its resources were justified on the grounds that members should be encouraged to use those resources. The philosophy was that it was preferable for the Fund to have relatively strict conditions on use of its resources and relatively low charges. If the Fund placed both strict conditions and charges close to commercial rates on use of its resources, members would borrow from private banks rather than from the Fund. Over the years, officials from developing members particularly had argued in favor of low charges on use of the Fund's resources. By 1971, however, some Executive Directors appointed or elected by industrial members, especially by European members that were creditors to the Fund, were beginning to come around to the view that the Fund's charges could be set closer to market rates of interest.[10]

When it came time to consider charges on the oil facility, Mr. Witteveen, the staff, and most members of the Executive Board were concerned about the burden on developing members of charges on Fund drawings as high as 7 percent a year. Consequently, a number of questions were examined before agreement was reached on charges for drawings under the oil facility. Could the Fund levy its charges in a different way than usual? (Hitherto, the Fund had based its charges solely on the size of the Fund's holdings of the currency of the member concerned in relation to its quota and the period for which the Fund held those levels of currency. Charges were the same for all members.) Could the Fund, for instance, differentiate its charges by categories of members, giving lower charges to developing members? Or could the Fund vary its charges in accordance with the absolute amounts drawn by members rather than as a percentage of quota? Such an arrangement would give lower charges to developing members which drew lesser absolute amounts. Did the Articles of Agreement require that if relatively high charges were applied to drawings under the oil facility, equally high charges had to be placed on use of the Fund's regular resources?

The Articles of Agreement (Article V, Section 8(c)) specified that charges had to be "uniform for all members." The staff of the Legal Department interpreted this

---

[10]Discussions of the Fund's charges until 1971 can be found in *History, 1945–65*, Vol. II, pp. 428–36, and *History, 1966–71*, Vol. I, pp. 378–81.

provision to mean that different charges could not be applied to different categories of members. Different charges could be established for various types of Fund facilities, however. Thus, there was no legal way that the Fund could offer money to developing members at lower charges than it charged other members. But it was possible to have a separate schedule of charges which applied to a floating facility (a facility that existed independently of the rest of the Fund's resources), such as the oil facility.

The Executive Directors appointed or elected by industrial members favored such an arrangement, that is, a schedule of charges for the oil facility that would reflect the cost to the Fund of borrowing and that would be higher than the Fund's usual charges. Mr. Rawlinson, for example, observed that in supporting the oil facility, the U.K. authorities had assumed that it would be a self-financing operation in which higher rates of charges would prevail than applied to the Fund's regular resources. Charles R. Harley (United States) observed that a separate schedule of charges for the oil facility was preferred by U.S. authorities so that the rate of interest used for Fund borrowings for the oil facility would be disassociated from the considerations which the Fund usually took into account in determining its charges, including the rate of interest on the SDR. Mr. Palamenghi-Crispi observed that it was entirely reasonable to have a relationship between the cost to the Fund of the resources that it would make available and the charges levied for use of those resources.

However, it was recognized by these Executive Directors and by Mr. Witteveen that these high charges would be exceptionally burdensome to many developing members. In order to lower the effective charges on drawings under the oil facility for oil importing developing members, several financial officials, including Mr. Witteveen, decided to try to get agreement on ways to subsidize some of the interest cost of using the oil facility. On the understanding that some kind of subsidy account would eventually be set up, the Executive Board agreed on the schedule of charges for the 1974 oil facility which would work out to an average of 7 percent a year.[11] The schedule of charges is given in Table 5.

Repurchases were to be made in 16 equal quarterly installments starting three years after the drawing was made. Repurchases were thus to be completed seven years after the drawing, compared with five years for other drawings.

THE FACILITY ESTABLISHED

With the features of the facility determined at least for the start of operations, the Executive Board, on June 13, 1974, took a decision establishing an oil facility.[12] Since borrowing arrangements were still being worked out, the Executive Board was to review the decision not later than September 15, 1974 in order to determine

---

[11] A Subsidy Account was set up for the 1975 facility; this Account is described in Chap. 18.
[12] E.B. Decision No. 4241-(74/67), June 13, 1974; Vol. III below, pp. 496–98.

Table 5. Charges on Transactions Effected Under the 1974 Oil Facility

Charges in percent a year,[1] payable on holdings in excess of quota for the period stated

Service charge	0.5
Up to 3 years	6.875
3 to 4 years	7.000[2]
5 to 7 years	7.125

[1]Except for service charge, which was payable once per transaction and was expressed as a percentage of the amount of the transaction.
[2]Point at which consultation between the Fund and the member became obligatory.

whether drawings in excess of 35 percent of the amount produced by the formula would be permitted and to decide on any changes that might be made in the formula. (In August 1974, the Executive Board decided that drawings under the oil facility could be made only after the member had used any gold tranche that it might have.)[13]

Borrowing Agreements

Detailed discussions led to an Executive Board decision, also on June 13, 1974, to permit the Fund to borrow and to an agreement on a standard draft letter to send to members from whom the Fund was borrowing.[14] A loan to the Fund was evidenced by a nonnegotiable instrument. Lenders agreed to make available up to December 31, 1975 either their own currencies, which they agreed to convert into U.S. dollars, or U.S. dollars. All loans were denominated in SDRs.

Unlike the General Arrangements to Borrow, the loans for the oil facility were actual commitments to lend to the Fund up to an agreed amount for the purpose of financing transactions in the facility. The General Arrangements to Borrow, in contrast, were not a line of credit on which the Fund could draw automatically. They represented instead a set of conditional commitments to lend to the Fund; the participants could refuse to do so. Under the agreements for the oil facility, calls could be made on the loans up to the agreed limits when the Fund needed resources to finance specific transactions with a member under the facility. The Fund could also borrow in order to repay another creditor that had made a loan to the Fund for the oil facility and had requested repayments because it had a balance of payments need.

The resulting loan claims on the Fund were transferable, provided prior consent of the Fund had been obtained and the transfer was made on terms and conditions acceptable to the Fund. As with claims on the Fund that members obtained when they lent to the Fund under the General Arrangements to Borrow, the claims that members obtained when they lent to the Fund for the oil facility were

---

[13]E.B. Decision No. 4337-(74/102), August 14, 1974; Vol. III below, p. 498.
[14]E.B. Decision No. 4242-(74/67), June 13, 1974; Vol. III below, pp. 536–38.

highly liquid and were regarded as a primary reserve asset for monetary authorities because they could be quickly mobilized at times of balance of payments need. They were regarded, too, as credit for the purpose of calculating reserve positions in the Fund and for determining the first or second largest amounts of credit extended by members to the Fund which entitled a member to appoint an Executive Director.

Interest was to be paid quarterly by the Fund at an annual rate of 7 percent. In November 1974, in order to permit the Fund to offer members a wider selection of assets for the payment of interest, the Executive Board decided to offer members their own currency, one or several currencies selected from the currency budget, and, wherever appropriate, SDRs. The decision also stipulated that the Fund would normally express a preference for the lender to choose payments in his own currency first, then the currency selected from the currency budget, and finally SDRs.[15]

Further decisions taken in 1977 and 1978 made some modifications in the media to be used for repayments of funds borrowed under these agreements, in repayment provisions, and in the transferability of claims on the Fund arising under these borrowing agreements.[16]

Loans were to be outstanding for between three and seven years, and repayments were to be made in eight equal semiannual installments starting after three years. Earlier repayments were provided for under certain circumstances. For instance, the Fund was to repay its creditor when a member made a repurchase with respect to a drawing made under the oil facility. A creditor might request repayment of all or part of an outstanding loan on a representation that it had a balance of payments need for repayment; in these circumstances the Fund was to give the overwhelming benefit of any doubt to the member. In the case of Canada, where the period of loans was limited by Canadian law, loans were to be repaid in a lump sum not later than five years, or earlier in certain circumstances, from the date of each transfer.

On August 7, after detailed negotiations with prospective lending members, the Fund communicated borrowing agreements to lenders, and the Managing Director was authorized to make calls on these agreements. By August 22, the Fund had entered into borrowing agreements with the governments or the central banks of seven members—Canada, Iran, Kuwait, Oman, Saudi Arabia, the United Arab Emirates, and Venezuela—for a total of just over SDR 2.8 billion. The amounts borrowed from each lender, along with the amounts borrowed for the 1975 oil facility, are given in the next chapter.

The Managing Director continued to seek funds, and in November and December 1974 the Fund concluded borrowing agreements not only with the Netherlands for SDR 150 million but also with Nigeria for SDR 100 million. In total, a little over SDR 3.0 billion was available for the 1974 facility.

---

[15]E.B. Decision No. 4490-(74/140), November 6, 1974; Vol. III below, p. 540.
[16]E.B. Decisions Nos. 5441-(77/84), June 10, 1977, and 5974-(78/190), December 4, 1978; Vol. III below, pp. 542–43.

Drawings Under the Facility

The amounts obtained were less than Mr. Witteveen had originally hoped for. Also, it had taken nearly three quarters of a year for the facility to become operational. To this extent the facility did not fully serve its purpose of helping Fund members finance their 1974 current account deficits.

Despite these setbacks, the oil facility was opened for business at the beginning of September 1974 and members were already requesting drawings. By September 6, nine oil importing developing members—Bangladesh, Chile, Haiti, Kenya, Korea, Pakistan, Sri Lanka, Sudan, and Tanzania—had become the first customers under the new arrangements. By September 29, nine additional members had drawn under the facility, six developing members—Costa Rica, Fiji, Ivory Coast, Madagascar, Panama, and Uruguay—two more developed primary producing members—Greece and Yugoslavia—and one industrial member—Italy. Requests by many other members were in various stages of action. In the last four months of 1974, SDR 1.7 billion was drawn, and in the first six months of 1975, another SDR 800 million, for a total usage of over SDR 2.5 billion under the 1974 facility.[17]

The majority of the drawings under the 1974 oil facility were made by developing members. The only industrial member using the 1974 oil facility was Italy, which drew SDR 675 million in two transactions. Six more developed primary producing countries, Greece, Iceland, New Zealand, Spain, Turkey, and Yugoslavia, drew a total of nearly SDR 800 million; of this, SDR 296 million was drawn by Spain. The remaining SDR 1 billion represented drawings by 33 developing members; India drew SDR 200 million; Chile, Korea, and Pakistan each made drawings of SDR 100 million or more; and Bangladesh, Israel, Sri Lanka, and Uruguay each drew SDR 40 million or more. The drawings of individual members, classified into groups, under both the 1974 and the 1975 oil facilities are given in Table 8 in Chapter 18.

An episode of unusual personal interest to the Managing Director in this period of the Fund's history concerns the drawing by India. Mr. Witteveen visited India in October 1974 where he had discussions with newly appointed Finance Minister, C. Subramaniam, and with S. Jagannathan, Governor of the Reserve Bank of India, and meetings with Prime Minister Indira Gandhi and President Ali Ahmed. The oil facility had just opened for business and Mr. Witteveen suggested informally to Indian officials that India should draw on the Fund's oil facility even though India did not at the time have a balance of payments deficit. His reasoning was that, by having more financial resources, Indian officials could relax some of India's tight restrictions on imports and that additional imports would help foster greater economic growth. Immediately thereafter, before Mr. Witteveen had returned to Washington, India drew SDR 200 million under the oil facility. Subsequently, India was able to import more and to enjoy a faster rate of growth. This episode is

---

[17]Strictly speaking, these amounts should be stated as the equivalent of SDR 1.7 billion, the equivalent of SDR 800 million, and the equivalent of SDR 2.5 billion, since drawings from the Fund were in a parcel made up of several currencies and SDRs. As the constant repetition of the words "the equivalent of" would be tedious, they have been omitted here and in later chapters.

significant in another respect: it belies the criticism sometimes made that Fund officials are unconcerned with economic growth.

These drawings were facilitated by liberalizations put into effect when the Executive Board reviewed the facility in September and December 1974. As a result of the September review, the projected increase in oil export prices was raised, the base date for determining the volume of oil imports was adjusted, drawings were permitted in excess of the 35 percent of the originally computed maximum access for each member, and more generous limits were set.[18] At the December review, the Executive Board decided that members might draw up to the maximum amount of their calculated access, and to give members sufficient time to assess their balance of payments results for 1974, they decided to extend through February 27, 1975 the time by which members' statements of their intentions to draw must be received in the Fund.[19] Intensive effort went into determining the formulas used for maximum access to the oil facility. For example, the staff made numerous calculations to show the results of using different formulas not only when the Executive Board discussed the original facility but also at the time of each review.

■ ■ ■ ■ ■ ■

From the start, the 1974 oil facility proved useful, and the Fund was again providing funds to its members at a critical time for their payments positions. The oil deficits persisted in 1975, and the 1974 facility was followed by another facility for 1975. There were thus two oil facilities. However, because the arrangements for the two facilities were similar, many Fund officials referred to the two facilities in combination, speaking of the Fund's "oil facility."

---

[18]E.B. Decision No. 4393-(74/121), September 20, 1974; Vol. III below, p. 498.
[19]E.B. Decision No. 4529-(74/153), December 6, 1974; Vol. III below, pp. 498–99.

CHAPTER

18

A Second Oil Facility

*A*LTHOUGH THE NEWLY ARRANGED OIL FACILITY had just been put in place when the Governors assembled in Washington at the end of September 1974 for their Twenty-Ninth Annual Meeting, Mr. Witteveen was already advocating another and larger facility for 1975. The world economy was passing through an unusually turbulent period as the largest nonviolent transfer of wealth in human history was taking place, and Mr. Witteveen saw two prime responsibilities for the Fund: to assist all members in devising policies to cope with and adjust to existing circumstances, and to provide many members with financial assistance.

TURBULENT ECONOMIC CIRCUMSTANCES
AND GLOOMY PROSPECTS

Press commentary called the Fund's 1974 Annual Report the gloomiest in the Fund's history. Total output in industrial countries was declining and a further decline was expected. What was to become the deep recession of late 1974 and of 1975 had started. Yet even with the decline in output, inflation had not abated. In many countries it had become virulent, attaining levels considered unacceptable by most governments. What had been called stagflation in the recession of 1969–71, when stagnant economic growth and inflation coexisted for the first time, was being referred to as slumpflation. In addition to recession and inflation, the unusually large disequilibrium in international payments that had been expected was not only materializing but was expected to become even larger as the recession grew deeper. A combined current account deficit of $30 billion was forecast for the non-oil developing countries for 1975, a deficit even bigger than the $21 billion projected for 1974. Many officials doubted that sufficient financing would be available.

By September 1974 it was also widely accepted that the need for recycling petrodollars (the transferring of dollar revenues from oil exporting to oil importing countries) was likely to remain large in 1975. The only question at issue was the extent to which governmental or intergovernmental agencies should supplement the recycling done through private commercial banks. In the course of 1974 private commercial banks of industrial countries had vastly increased their international lending operations. They were successfully channeling enormous sums of money, mainly through Eurocurrency markets, from lenders in oil exporting countries to borrowers in oil importing countries. Moreover, they had extended their operations beyond the private sphere and were lending to governments overseas, including the governments of several developing countries. Lending to governments was a wholly new development in private international banking.

As a result of the greatly increased financing available from commercial banks, the balance of payments problems of both industrial and several oil importing developing countries turned out to be more manageable than expected after the big increases in oil prices had just taken effect. Concern was arising, however, that the commercial banks might be endangering their liquidity positions and becoming overexposed. Oil exporting countries were lending to banks on short term while oil importing countries were borrowing from banks on medium or long term. Such transformation of the maturities of recycled funds by commercial banks could endanger the banks' liquidity positions. Even worse, failure of the German Herstatt Bank in June 1974 enhanced fears, among both private bankers and public officials, that outright widespread failures of commercial banks could occur, as had happened in the 1930s. At a minimum, the recycling operations of private banks could mean that oil exporting countries could be faced with certain risks in channeling their growing volume of funds through private money markets and that oil importing countries could find it increasingly difficult to finance their current deficits by borrowing from private banks.

MR. WITTEVEEN'S PROPOSAL AND GOVERNORS' REACTIONS

To Mr. Witteveen and many other financial officials, these circumstances called for strengthening official ways of financing oil deficits. Therefore, in his opening address to the Governors at the 1974 Annual Meeting, Mr. Witteveen stressed the need for increased official recycling of funds from oil exporters to oil importers and made a strong case for a substantial increase in recycling through the Fund. He argued that, as recycling entered its second year, it was even more important than in the first year to ensure that individual countries start to make adjustments in their balances of payments. Countries had to find ways to reduce rather than to continue to accept their payments deficits. He emphasized that the Fund was uniquely equipped to help countries make these adjustments.[1]

For 1975 Mr. Witteveen wanted an oil facility to which industrial members as well as developing members might have access. He expected that at least Italy and the United Kingdom, among industrial members, might need financial assistance from the Fund in coping with their payments deficits and that the Fund could play a

---

[1]*Summary Proceedings, 1974*, pp. 23 and 26–27.

useful role in working with the officials of these members to devise solutions for these countries' balance of payments deficits. As he put together his proposal in September 1974, he noted that Greece and Yugoslavia had been among the first customers under the 1974 facility. He was thus interested in the prospect that the Fund might help a number of other relatively developed members—Finland, Iceland, New Zealand, Portugal, Spain, and Turkey—to reduce their payments deficits, a sizable portion of which was related to their imports of oil. (Indeed, several of these members later drew even on the 1974 facility.) While he was willing to have the Fund help finance the payments deficits of developing members, he was convinced that the Fund should not become a financier for developing members only. Moreover, with respect to developing members, he stressed that the weaker members that were not in a position to continue paying market-related interest charges or to assume an increasing burden of external debt would, in any event, have to have other sources of official financing beyond those offered by the Fund.

Mr. Witteveen's proposal for a larger oil facility in the Fund for 1975 received the support of several Governors, from both industrial and developing members, at the 1974 Annual Meeting. Officials of the United Kingdom were especially interested in having a sizable oil facility or similar arrangement in the Fund. Mr. Healey, emphasizing that industrial members, as well as developing members, were having serious difficulties financing their large oil-related balance of payments deficits and that these difficulties might last for some years, proposed a more permanent arrangement than the Fund's 1974 oil facility. He advocated the establishment of a mechanism whereby a significant proportion of the surplus revenues of oil exporting countries could be invested in international organizations in exchange for some type of asset issued by the Fund.[2] This proposal was reminiscent of the plans proposed by U.K. officials a decade earlier when the question of ways to augment the supply of international liquidity was being discussed.[3] Officials of other European countries, too, supported the idea of further recycling of petrodollars through the Fund. Emilio Colombo, calling the oil facility one of the best technical instruments devised to reconcile the long-run interests of oil exporters and oil importers, likewise supported the idea of an enlarged facility for 1975. He suggested that in order to raise more money, the Fund might borrow directly on the world's capital markets.[4] Mr. Fourcade endorsed Mr. Healey's suggestion for a more permanent investment-type arrangement, as well as the idea of an enlarged oil facility in the Fund for 1975.[5]

It was primarily the financial officials of the United States, especially Mr. Simon, now Secretary of the Treasury in the new Administration of President Gerald R. Ford, who had reservations about another and still larger oil facility, although Mr. Simon seemed less strongly opposed than he had been to the original

---

[2]Statement by the Governor of the Fund for the United Kingdom, *Summary Proceedings, 1974*, pp. 79–80.

[3]*History, 1966-71*, Vol. I, pp. 19 and 24.

[4]Statement by the Governor of the Fund for Italy, *Summary Proceedings, 1974*, p. 104.

[5]Statement by the Governor of the Fund and the World Bank for France, *Summary Proceedings, 1974*, p. 95.

idea of an oil facility in January–February 1974. Pointing out that the money markets in the United States had been effectively channeling very large sums of money from foreign lenders to foreign borrowers and that the U.S. Government was letting private commercial banks operate freely, Mr. Simon was in favor of letting private markets recycle petrodollars as much as possible. Recognizing the concern that the banking structure might not be able to cope with strains from the large financial flows expected in the period ahead, he expressed confidence that widespread collapse of commercial banks would not occur.[6]

The Annual Meeting ended with the need for official financing still in question; certainly the size of any oil facility in the Fund for 1975 was undetermined. The uncertainty about whether another facility would be set up and about its size was reflected in the communiqué issued by the Interim Committee on October 3, 1974, following its inaugural meeting. In addition to electing John N. Turner, Finance Minister of Canada, as Chairman, members of the new Interim Committee expressed themselves only on the oil facility. Their communiqué stated that the Committee had "reviewed the problem of recycling, and agreed to ask the Executive Directors to consider in this context, as a matter of urgency, the adequacy of existing private and official financing arrangements, and to report on the possible need for additional arrangements, including enlarged financing arrangements through the Fund, and to make proposals for dealing with the problem."[7] In other words, the controversial questions as to whether another oil facility was needed and how large it should be were to be debated and resolved in the Executive Board.

The 1974 Annual Meeting also brought out the lines of policy that officials of oil exporting members were to stress for the next few years. Officials of oil exporting members took the occasion to defend their action in raising crude oil prices. Moreover, they wanted the Fund to borrow much more than had been possible for the 1974 facility from members other than oil exporters with payments surpluses. And officials of Middle Eastern oil exporting members began to press for larger quotas and voting power in the Fund. These three themes were evident, for example, in the remarks of Hushang Ansary.[8]

U.S. PROPOSALS FOR NEW FINANCING MECHANISMS

By November 1974, fear that the private money markets might not be able to recycle petrodollars adequately had grown and there was much more general recognition that official financing arrangements might be needed. It was also becoming more accepted that special financing arrangements would be needed to help some non-oil developing countries which were having a particularly hard time in financing their deficits.

---

[6]Statement by the Governor of the Fund and the World Bank for the United States, *Summary Proceedings, 1974*, pp. 84–85.

[7]Communiqué of Interim Committee, October 3, 1974; Vol. III below, p. 217.

[8]Statement by the Governor of the World Bank for Iran, *Summary Proceedings, 1974*, p. 160.

As 1974 went on, problems associated with higher oil prices provided a greater challenge to U.S. political leadership in the world. Unable to effect a quick reversal of OPEC's decision to raise oil prices, U.S. officials, especially those responsible for foreign policy in general, sought to have the United States organize the industrial nations, as the largest consumers of oil, to take a stand against actions by OPEC. By September the U.S. Administration had begun to form concrete proposals, but these were not made public until November. In an address before the Board of Trustees of the University of Chicago on November 14, Secretary of State Kissinger outlined a strategy for cooperative action by oil importing countries.[9] Dramatizing the political importance of the crisis created by higher oil prices by comparing it with the grave circumstances of World War II, Mr. Kissinger stated that the collective deficit of industrial countries was "the largest in history and beyond the experience or capacity of our financial institutions," and noted that for developing countries, "the rise in energy costs in fact roughly equals the total flow of external aid." Yet 1974 was "only the first year of inflated oil prices." Emphasizing that times of crisis could be times of creativity, Mr. Kissinger stated that in addition to Project Independence (the U.S. program intended to reduce U.S. oil imports and to develop alternative energy sources within the United States) and coordinated efforts by consuming nations to reduce consumption of oil, new official financial arrangements should be established. He announced that the United States proposed the creation of a "common loan and guarantee facility" to provide for distributing up to $25 billion of oil funds in 1975 and a like amount for the next year if necessary. The facility was to be a mechanism for recycling, at commercial interest rates, funds flowing back to the industrial world from the oil producers. Support from the facility was not to be automatic but contingent on "full resort to private financing and reasonable self-help measures" and on measures to lessen dependence on imported oil. This facility was to serve industrial countries. For developing countries, Mr. Kissinger suggested that there might be established a separate "trust fund, managed by the International Monetary Fund," to be financed by contributions by member countries and from sales of gold by the Fund, profits from which might be lent to developing members at rates of interest they could afford. Thus, there emerged the idea of a trust fund, which was subsequently created in the Fund.

Four days after Mr. Kissinger's speech, Secretary of the Treasury Simon, speaking in New York before the National Foreign Trade Convention, elaborated these proposals and the thinking underlying them.[10] Like Mr. Kissinger, Mr. Simon called the situation very serious, stating that "the policies of the oil cartel now pose a fundamental challenge to the economic and political structure which has served the international community for a quarter of a century." Mr. Simon's remarks made it clear, too, that U.S. officials continued to regard existing oil prices as exorbitant and that U.S. policies were based on the belief that crude oil prices would eventually fall

---

[9]This address was reprinted in *Department of State Bulletin* (Washington), Vol. 71 (December 2, 1974), pp. 749–56. Portions quoted here are on p. 749.

[10]Ibid. (December 9, 1974), pp. 794–803. Quoted portions are on pp. 794 and 795.

as world consumption of oil declined and consumers accelerated development of their own sources of energy. "To me, the question is not whether oil prices will fall, but when they will fall."

The essence of the U.S. position was that the price of oil itself, not its immediate repercussions on countries' balance of payments positions, was the real source of trouble in the world economy. To help bring about lower oil prices and to reduce the economic burden of oil imports, major consuming nations should work together to achieve significant reductions in their imports of OPEC oil. By coordinating their policies and actions, the oil importing industrial nations could mold themselves into a combined consumer group to counter the actions of OPEC, whose members were making their decisions collectively. A major new financial mechanism should also be introduced in the OECD to provide stand-by financial assistance for industrial and developed countries. The resources of the International Monetary Fund should be more fully mobilized for all its members. Consideration should also be given to creating a trust fund managed by the International Monetary Fund to help those developing members suffering most and in need of financing on concessional terms. Finally, serious preparations ought to be made for an "eventual dialogue" between the consumer group and producing nations.

Spelling out the details of the proposed "financial safety net" in the OECD, Mr. Simon explained that the facility would have total commitments by all OECD members of $25 billion in 1975, with additional resources provided in subsequent years if needed. The facility was to supplement, not replace, private market channels of financing and other official financing. For this reason, it should do its lending on market-related terms. Decisions on the provision of financial support should be based on the overall economic position of the borrower, not on a single criterion such as oil import bills.

Explaining his reasons for supporting a facility that was to be only for OECD members, Mr. Simon defended the establishment of a new financial mechanism for industrial countries as also in the interest of developing countries. If economic activity could be maintained in industrial countries, developing countries were all the more likely to continue to receive large capital inflows from them. Also, by helping to assure orderly access by industrial countries to the major capital markets and thereby reducing the danger of their competing unduly for the surplus investment funds of the oil exporters, the new financial mechanism for industrial countries would enhance the ability of many developing countries to attract large amounts of capital, certainly all the capital that they could productively employ. Developing countries with the lowest per capita incomes, however, would still require concessional assistance. While most such assistance would be provided by the oil exporting countries, the International Monetary Fund could establish a trust fund financed by contributions from the OPEC and from other sources. Mr. Simon suggested also that the Fund might contribute to such a trust fund the profits derived from the sale of some of its gold holdings in the private market. A trust fund of this nature could offer credit at relatively low cost—perhaps 2 to 4 percent—and on moderately long maturities, thus providing funds to those countries most seriously affected by current problems on terms not needed by other borrowers.

At about the same time, Mr. van Lennep, Secretary-General of the OECD, came up independently with a similar proposal. Under Mr. van Lennep's proposal, instead of each OECD member contributing money to a common fund, there would be a guarantee arrangement administered by the BIS. The BIS might borrow funds in various markets or receive deposits directly from oil surplus countries and lend the funds so acquired to industrial countries against a joint guarantee by the participating OECD countries that the funds would be repaid.

EXECUTIVE BOARD'S CONSIDERATION OF AN OIL FACILITY FOR 1975

These proposals for financial mechanisms through the OECD were made late in 1974 just as the Executive Board started to consider whether an oil facility should be established in the Fund for 1975 and, if so, how large it should be. In their discussions, the Executive Directors took much the same positions as had been expressed by their Governors at the Annual Meeting two months earlier, but, of course, they were now heavily influenced by the enhanced concern of officials in many countries that private recycling facilities might be inadequate for the continuing large payments deficits expected in 1975. Officials of the United Kingdom again pressed for a large facility in the Fund. Mr. Rawlinson explained to the other Executive Directors that the U.K. authorities wanted the Fund's oil facility for 1975 to be multilateral and comprehensive, meaning that it should be available for all members, industrial as well as developing. Both he and Mr. Palamenghi-Crispi believed that eventually the oil facility might have to be merged with the Fund's regular resources, which would then have to be appreciably enlarged through increases in quotas. One of the reasons why the U.K. officials favored a large degree of official financing for oil-related deficits in 1975 was their desire to reserve use of private bank financing for a later period, since they expected that further increases in oil prices might take place.

Mr. Wahl, too, pressed for the rapid establishment of a substantial oil facility for 1975, although French officials did not envision that France itself would use the Fund's oil facility. It was generally expected, however, that Fund members which were former French colonies in the French franc area, such as Benin, Cameroon, the Central African Republic, Chad, Gabon, Ivory Coast, Niger, Senegal, Togo, and Upper Volta, would need considerable financial help from the oil facility. French financial officials usually supported the positions taken by African officials.

Executive Directors elected by developing members welcomed the heightened recognition of the need for larger official financing facilities but insisted that the proposals of Mr. Kissinger and Mr. Simon did not reduce the need for an oil facility in the Fund for 1975. Mr. Kafka, for instance, emphasized that the proposals of U.S. officials took account of the payments deficits of the industrial nations and of the poorest developing countries but did not allow for the deficits or financial problems of the middle group of countries. Countries such as Argentina, Chile, Colombia, Costa Rica, Peru, and Uruguay were neither industrial nor poor. Nevertheless, they needed assistance in financing their payments deficits. As was evident in the principles stated by Mr. Simon, priority was to be given to financing payments deficits through the private sector. Admittedly, many of these middle-income developing countries could borrow from private sources, but that did not rule out the need for some help from the Fund. Moreover, if proposals such as those of Messrs. Kissinger and Simon were substitutes for, rather than complements to, an oil facility in the Fund, they would damage the interests of the middle group of countries. One key source of official financing would no longer be available. Also, obtaining money from the Fund helped middle-income developing countries to borrow from private sources since it made them more creditworthy. Without an oil facility, the access of these countries both to public and private loans would thus become more difficult.

Mr. Kharmawan agreed with Mr. Kafka's views, pointing out the similar need for an oil facility of the middle-income countries in Asia. Mr. Monday, noting that 1975—with floating exchange rates and high oil prices, interest rates, and inflation rates—was going to be an exceptionally difficult year for many developing members, argued for as large a facility in the Fund as possible. He and other Executive Directors elected by developing members were concerned that, with U.S. officials pushing for a relatively small facility, while officials of the United Kingdom and other industrial members advocated use of the facility by industrial members, developing members might receive even less from the 1975 oil facility than they had from the 1974 facility.

Estimating the likely use of a 1975 facility, the staff came up with a facility of about SDR 6–8 billion ($7–9.5 billion). This estimate did not allow for drawings by the five members with the largest quotas: the United States, the United Kingdom, the Federal Republic of Germany, France, and Japan. Should any of these five members draw, a facility of SDR 10 billion or larger would be needed. The staff recommended that the amount of the facility be open-ended, depending on how much could be borrowed.

Arguments Against the Facility by U.S. Officials

U.S. officials opposed such a large facility. Mr. Cross explained to the other Executive Directors the reservations of his authorities. First of all, the U.S. authorities started from the premise that it was not good tactics on the part of oil consuming nations passively to accept higher oil prices and to make arrangements for financing the resulting balance of payments deficits. Financing the deficits did not eliminate the real cost of the increase in prices for oil, that is, the sizable losses in real income experienced by oil importing countries as they transferred additional resources to oil exporting countries. Financing deficits only postponed the impact of those losses. Financing deficits, moreover, meant that individual oil importing nations were accumulating larger and larger external debts which they might never be able to repay. In the view of U.S. authorities, preferable solutions lay in coordinated action by consumer countries to reduce oil imports, which in turn would bring oil prices down again. Excessive amounts of official financing made available relatively easily would inhibit such action and delay measures to reduce oil imports.

Second, U.S. authorities did not like a distinction between the oil-related portion of a country's balance of payments deficits and the rest of its payments deficit. Imports of oil and financial transactions related to oil affected the aggregate of a country's trade, services, and capital so that it was never really possible to identify the portion of a country's balance of payments deficit attributable to higher oil prices. As time went on, it became impossible to separate the oil deficit from the rest of a country's balance of payments deficit. Hence, the Fund did not really determine a member's balance of payments needs or allocate funds accurately if it concentrated on the size of oil-related payments deficits. The Fund's assessment of a member's need for financing should rather be related to the member's overall financial and balance of payments position, as was done when a member drew on the Fund's regular resources. U.S. authorities, consequently, advocated that the Fund move toward greater reliance on drawings under the usual credit tranche policies.

Mr. Cross suggested a number of alternative ways in which the Fund could enlarge access to its regular resources. There would be a temporary "stretching" of the credit tranches; instead of the existing 25 percent of quota for each tranche, perhaps 37.5 percent of quota might be allowed. Waivers could be granted for drawings by members making appropriate use of Fund resources, lifting the limits in relation to quotas that members could draw.[11] The quotas of members in the Fund could be enlarged. Mr. Cross explained that the principal advantage of these alternatives was that they combined recognition of the potential need for substantially greater access to Fund credit in the extraordinary situation existing in 1975 with preservation of the Fund's basic policies on assessment and conditionality. They avoided undue reliance on an inappropriate formula for access to money from the Fund as guided drawings under the 1974 oil facility.

Third, the U.S. authorities had a preference for using private channels for financing deficits to the maximum extent possible. The Fund should not finance deficits that could be handled by private commercial banks.

Possibly another reason U.S. officials opposed an oil facility in the Fund was that they believed that oil imports of the industrial countries were more likely to be reduced through their proposal for the OECD safety net arrangement.

Positions of Other Executive Directors

Most other Executive Directors, however, supported the Managing Director's proposal for a new and larger oil facility in 1975. Executive Directors from other

---

[11]For a discussion of waivers by the Fund, see *History, 1966–71*, Vol. I, p. 322.

industrial members made a number of points to counter the arguments that U.S. officials were making against the facility. Mr. Lieftinck objected to the position of U.S. officials on the grounds that it was contrary to the stance taken in favor of an oil facility by the Committee of Twenty in January 1974 and by the Interim Committee at the 1974 Annual Meeting. Mr. Lieftinck emphasized that the oil facility was a crucial source of assistance for the many members that clearly could not make the necessary adjustments to higher oil prices in the short term. Mr. Wahl commented that he had a great deal of interest in, and sympathy with, the arguments made by Mr. Cross; the concept of an oil deficit was becoming less useful as an analytical tool, and increased conditionality was required to ensure adequate adjustment by countries. However, an identifiable oil-related problem certainly remained and posed difficulties with which the normal facilities of the Fund were not designed to deal. Mr. Kawaguchi explained that the Japanese authorities were also in favor of a continued and expanded oil facility in the Fund for 1975. The Japanese authorities were principally preoccupied with countries that had only limited access to financial markets, in particular the non-oil developing countries. In the view of Japanese officials, the major industrial countries should seek financing primarily through private market sources.

Because of the opposition of U.S. officials to an oil facility, there were intense debates in the Executive Board. Much of the argument for and against the oil facility centered on the extent to which countries should cut their oil imports rather than finance large deficits. The emphasis of U.S. officials on adjustment was unusually strong since the Managing Director and officials of the United Kingdom were advocating a large facility that would accommodate some of the financing needs of industrial and developed members of the Fund, including those of the United Kingdom itself. It was these countries especially that U.S. officials believed ought to curb their imports of crude oil, since they were among the world's largest consumers.

The U.S. view on the need to cut oil imports as an adjustment to higher oil prices had less impact on other financial officials than it might otherwise have had, since the United States produced a sizable percentage of its own oil needs domestically and had much larger reserves of coal and alternative sources of energy than did other countries. Also, the arguments of U.S. officials in international meetings, including those in the Fund, with regard to energy and to oil imports were compromised because at the time the United States was increasing its imports of crude oil and seemed to be doing very little adjusting itself.

These were the positions expressed about a 1975 oil facility in the Fund as the debate went on through November and December 1974. As uneasiness grew that the Eurocurrency markets might not continue to serve as the primary channel of intermediation for funds from oil exporters, support for another oil facility in the Fund gained momentum. When the various proposals for financing oil deficits were discussed by the deputies of the Group of Ten in Paris in November 1974, the deputies of several countries, such as Canada, the Federal Republic of Germany,

Italy, the Netherlands, and Sweden, pointed out that whatever the other merits or demerits of proposals for a safety net for OECD countries, the Fund ought still to have a central role in financing oil deficits. A central role for the Fund meant explicitly that the Fund ought to finance deficits of industrial members as well as those of developing members. A working group of the deputies of the Group of Ten, chaired by Jacques van Ypersele of Belgium, was set up to study the proposals of U.S. officials and of Mr. van Lennep.

Despite the support of many deputies of the Group of Ten for another oil facility in the Fund and because of the reservations advanced by U.S. officials against any facility, both the need for any such facility and its size remained unsettled until the very end of 1974.

RECOMMENDATIONS TO THE INTERIM COMMITTEE AND AGREEMENT BY THE COMMITTEE

Pressed to produce a report to the Interim Committee, scheduled to meet for the second time in mid-January, the Executive Board, after a week of meetings, finally agreed on the afternoon of December 23, 1974 to recommend to the Committee that there be an oil facility for 1975. Access to the facility was again to be determined by a formula which took into account the size of a country's oil imports and its quota in the Fund, as had the formula for access to the 1974 facility. The formula was again complicated.[12] In effect, greater weight was given to a member's quota than in the 1974 facility and somewhat less weight to the increase in oil costs.

Stricter conditionality was also to be applied to use of the 1975 facility, reflecting the position taken by U.S. officials. The member making a drawing was to describe to the Fund its policies to achieve medium-term solutions to its balance of payments problems and to have the Fund assess the adequacy of these policies. The Fund was also to judge the extent to which reserves could be used to meet the member's payments deficit. The member was to describe the measures it had taken, or proposed to take, to conserve oil or to develop alternative sources of energy, although these measures were not subject to the Fund's assessment. As in the 1974 facility, access to the 1975 facility was also to depend on a member's avoidance of the introduction or intensification of restrictions on trade and capital. The management and staff had favored even stricter conditions in the form of quantitative targets for monetary and fiscal policies, as was done when the Fund approved stand-by arrangements. Most Executive Directors did not want to go so far, however.

---

[12]Access, which was to be subject to assessment by the Fund of the member's balance of payments need, was not to exceed the lower of (i) 125 percent of quota, and (ii) 85 percent of the increase in a member's oil import cost, calculated by multiplying the volume of the member's net imports of petroleum and petroleum products in 1972 or 1973 (whichever was higher) by $7.50 per barrel; but (iii) a member's access to the facility was not to be less than one third of the increase in its oil import cost as calculated under (ii) above, nor less than its maximum calculated access under the 1974 facility.

Executive Directors elected by developing members opposed even the degree of conditionality that was worked out.

When it met at its second meeting in Washington on January 15–16, 1975, the Interim Committee agreed that the oil facility should be continued for 1975 on an enlarged basis. But instead of the SDR 6–8 billion talked about earlier, a figure of SDR 5 billion was agreed as the total of loans to be sought by the Managing Director from major oil exporting members and from other members in strong reserve and payments positions. Any unused portion of the loans negotiated in 1974 was also to be available for 1975. In view of the hard debate preceding this agreement, the oil facility was to be kept under constant review. The Fund's regular resources were also to be substantially augmented through an increase in quotas.[13]

Agreement by the Executive Board and by the Interim Committee on an oil facility for 1975 was made possible mainly by paring down the amount involved. But agreement came about, too, because most officials came to believe that some official financing of oil deficits in 1975 was inevitable. Significantly, the ministers and central bank governors of the Group of Ten, meeting in Washington in January 1975 at the same time as the Interim Committee, proposed that a "solidarity fund, a new financial support arrangement" open to the 24 countries of the OECD should be established as soon as possible.[14] This "safety net, to be used as a last resort" was to be about $25 billion.[15] It was politically unwise for the officials of the Group of Ten to agree to provide emergency official financing only for industrial countries and relatively more developed countries and not to find some financing for developing countries. They felt that they had to agree to another facility in the Fund for 1975 available to all Fund members. Indeed, the Group of Twenty-Four, also meeting in Washington in January 1975 just ahead of the Interim Committee meeting, had explicitly supported an oil facility for 1975.

Thus again, as for the 1974 oil facility, substantial debate eventually led to agreement on an oil facility for 1975.

THE FACILITY IN OPERATION

On April 4, 1975, after further discussion of the specific arrangements, the Executive Board took decisions establishing the facility for 1975, setting charges for its use, stating that the gold tranche had to be drawn first, and authorizing the necessary borrowing and payment of interest.[16] The rate of interest was to reflect

---

[13]Communiqué of Interim Committee, January 16, 1975, par. 3; Vol. III below, p. 218.

[14]Australia, Austria, Belgium, Canada, Denmark, Finland, France, the Federal Republic of Germany, Greece, Iceland, Ireland, Italy, Japan, Luxembourg, the Netherlands, New Zealand, Norway, Portugal, Spain, Sweden, Switzerland, Turkey, the United Kingdom, and the United States.

[15]The relevant communiqué of the Group of Ten was reprinted in *IMF Survey* (Washington), Vol. 4 (January 20, 1975), p. 19.

[16]E.B. Decisions Nos. 4634-(75/47), 4635-(75/47), 4636-(75/47), and 4638-(75/47), April 4, 1975; Vol. III below, pp. 499–500, 539, 542, 500.

market conditions more fully than the average rate of 7 percent on funds lent for the 1974 facility, since officials of oil exporting countries considered that the 7 percent a year rate used for the 1974 facility contained a concessionary element. An average rate of 7.25 percent a year was agreed for borrowing for the 1975 facility. Charges for use of the 1975 facility were raised, by ¾ of 1 percent a year, as listed in Table 6 below. The repurchase provisions and the period for which drawings were to be outstanding remained from three to seven years, as under the 1974 facility.

Table 6. Charges on Transactions Effected Under the 1975 Oil Facility

Charges in percent a year[1] payable on holdings in excess of quota, for period stated

Service charge	0.5
Up to 3 years	7.625
3 to 4 years	7.750[2]
5 to 7 years	7.875

[1]Except for service charge, which was payable once per transaction and was expressed as a percentage of the amount of the transaction.
[2]Point at which consultation between the Fund and the member became obligatory.

Between the time of the Interim Committee meeting in January and the Executive Board decision of April, the Managing Director, accompanied by members of the staff, traveled to Iran, Lebanon, Qatar, Saudi Arabia, the United Arab Emirates, and Venezuela, and to the Federal Republic of Germany, the Netherlands, and Switzerland to arrange financial support for the facility. New borrowing agreements were arranged with seven of the nine members that had lent to the 1974 facility: Iran, Kuwait, the Netherlands, Nigeria, Oman, Saudi Arabia, and Venezuela, all major oil exporting countries, except for the Netherlands. (Canada and the United Arab Emirates did not lend for the 1975 facility.) In addition, agreements were concluded with the governments or central banks of six European countries— Austria, Belgium, the Federal Republic of Germany, Norway, Sweden, and Switzerland—and also with the Central Bank of Trinidad and Tobago, making 14 countries which lent to the Fund for the 1975 facility. There were 15 lending institutions since both the Government of Switzerland and the Swiss National Bank lent separately.

Table 7 below lists the amounts borrowed from each lender.

The Managing Director was able to borrow a total of SDR 3.856 billion, over SDR 1 billion less than the SDR 5 billion agreed by the Interim Committee. In addition, however, SDR 464 million was carried over from the 1974 facility, making the total amount available for the 1975 facility SDR 4.320 billion. The Managing Director was authorized to make calls under the agreements as funds were needed and to make arrangements for consultations to agree on the media for interest payments. Also, in 1975 some changes were made in the draft standard letter.[17]

---

[17]E.B. Decision No. 4741-(75/120), July 11, 1975; and E.B. Decisions Nos. 4916-(75/208), 4917-(75/208), 4918-(75/208), and 4919-(75/208), December 24, 1975; Vol. III below, pp. 539–40, 542.

Table 7. Amounts Borrowed by the Fund for the 1974 and 1975 Oil Facilities

(In millions of SDRs)

Lender	For 1974 Facility	For 1975 Facility[1]	Total
Abu Dhabi	100.0	—	100.0
Austrian National Bank	—	100.0	100.0
National Bank of Belgium	—	200.0	200.0
Canada	246.9[2]	—	246.9
Deutsche Bundesbank	—	600.0	600.0
Central Bank of Iran	580.0	410.0	990.0
Central Bank of Kuwait	400.0	285.0	685.0
Netherlands	150.0	200.0	350.0
Nigeria	100.0	200.0	300.0
Bank of Norway	—	100.0	100.0
Central Bank of Oman	20.0	0.5	20.5
Saudi Arabian Monetary Agency	1,000.0	1,250.0	2,250.0
Sveriges Riksbank	—	50.0	50.0
Switzerland[3]	—	250.0[3]	250.0
Central Bank of Trinidad and Tobago	—	10.0	10.0
Central Bank of Venezuela	450.0	200.0	650.0
Total	3,046.9[4]	3,855.5	6,902.4

[1]Totals of agreements concluded in 1975 and 1976.
[2]The SDR equivalent of the Can$300 million which the Government of Canada agreed to lend.
[3]The equivalents of SDR 150 million from Switzerland and SDR 100 million from the Swiss National Bank.
[4]Of which an amount equivalent to SDR 464.077 million was made available for the 1975 facility.

In view of the uncertainty of the demands on and finance for the 1975 facility, access by a member was initially set not to exceed 30 percent of its calculated maximum access. This limit was raised to 50 percent when the Executive Board reviewed the facility in July 1975. Three further reviews of the facility, in November and December 1975 and February 1976, did not change the amount of access. At the review in February 1976, however, it was decided that the final amounts of access should be determined by the Fund after March 12, 1976.[18] (Under the initial decision of April 4, 1975, members were required to submit statements of their intentions to request purchases not later than the close of business on February 27, 1976. The Decision of February 11, 1976 extended this date to March 12, 1976.) At the final review of the facility in March 1976, access was increased to 78.46 percent of the calculated maximum access; the latter figure took account of the funds available for financing the remaining purchases by members that had advised the Fund of their intention to request use of the facility by the prescribed date of March 12, 1976.[19]

---

[18] E.B. Decision No. 4634-(75/47), April 4, 1975, as amended after these reviews; Vol. III below, pp. 499–500.

[19] E.B. Decision No. 4986-(76/47), March 18, 1976; Vol. III below, p. 500.

Drawings Under the Facility

Drawings under the 1975 oil facility came to over SDR 4.3 billion, the full amount available. Two industrial members—the United Kingdom and Italy—drew SDR 1,780 million. The drawing by the United Kingdom for SDR 1,000 million came in December 1975 when the facility was almost ended and it was apparent that sufficient funds for such a transaction would be available. Eight more developed primary producing members drew SDR 850 million. Thirty-six developing members drew nearly SDR 1.5 billion.

In all, between September 1974 and May 1976, when the 1975 facility was ended, 55 members drew a total of SDR 6.9 billion in 156 transactions under the 1974 and 1975 oil facilities. Table 8 lists the drawings of individual members, grouped into broad economic categories.

Table 8. Drawings Under the 1974 and 1975 Oil Facilities

(In millions of SDRs)

Member	Financial Years Ended April 30 1975[1]	Financial Years Ended April 30 1976[2]	Remaining Drawings (May 1976)[2]	Total[3]
All members	2,499.25	3,966.24	436.94	6,902.43
Industrial members	675.00	1,780.24	—	2,455.24
Italy	675.00	780.24	—	1,455.24
United Kingdom	—	1,000.00	—	1,000.00
Other developed members	794.60	851.02	262.75	1,908.37
Finland	—	71.25	115.11	186.36
Greece	103.50	51.75	—	155.25
Iceland	17.20	21.97	—	39.17
New Zealand	109.30	129.37	—	238.67
Portugal	—	114.76	—	114.76
Spain	296.20	275.93	—	572.13
Turkey	113.20	56.62	91.49	261.31
Yugoslavia	155.20	129.37	56.15	340.72
Developing members	1,029.65	1,334.98	174.19	2,538.82
Argentina	—	76.09	—	76.09
Bangladesh	51.50	25.78	14.69	91.97
Burundi	1.20	—	—	1.20
Cameroon	4.62	7.50	4.28	16.41
Central African Republic	3.30	2.66	—	5.96
Chad	2.20	—	—	2.20
Chile	118.50	125.22	—	243.72
Costa Rica	18.84	12.00	6.83	37.67
Cyprus	8.10	14.00	7.97	30.07
Egypt	—	20.19	11.49	31.68
El Salvador	17.89	—	—	17.89
Fiji	0.34	—	—	0.34
Ghana	—	38.60[1]	—	38.60
Grenada	—	0.49	—	0.49
Guinea	3.51	—	—	3.51

347

Table 8 (concluded). Drawings Under the 1974 and 1975 Oil Facilities
(In millions of SDRs)

Member	Financial Years Ended April 30		Remaining Drawings (May 1976)[2]	Total[3]
	1975[1]	1976[2]		
Developing Members (concluded)				
Haiti	4.80	4.14	—	8.94
Honduras	16.78	—	—	16.78
India	200.00	201.34	—	401.34
Israel	62.00	81.25	—	143.25
Ivory Coast	11.17	10.35	—	21.52
Jamaica	—	29.20	—	29.20
Kenya	36.00	24.83	3.10	63.93
Korea	100.00	152.69	—	252.69
Madagascar	14.30	—	—	14.30
Malawi	—	3.73	—	3.73
Mali	5.00	3.99	—	8.99
Mauritania	—	3.39	1.93	5.32
Morocco	—	—	18.00	18.00
Nicaragua	15.50	—	—	15.50
Pakistan	125.00	111.01	—	236.01
Panama	7.37	17.25	—	24.62
Papua New Guinea	—	14.80	—	14.80
Peru	—	52.66	—	52.66
Philippines	—	96.87	55.16	152.03
Senegal	15.52	9.91	—	25.44
Sierra Leone	4.91	4.97	—	9.88
Sri Lanka	43.50	34.13	—	77.63
Sudan	28.71	18.30	—	47.01
Tanzania	31.50	20.61	—	52.11
Uganda	19.20	—	—	19.20
Uruguay	46.58	48.07	—	94.64
Western Samoa	—	0.42	—	0.42
Yemen, People's Democratic Republic of	11.80	4.60	7.42	23.82
Zaïre	—	45.00[1]	32.53	77.53
Zambia	—	18.93	10.79	29.72

[1]Under the 1974 facility.
[2]Under the 1975 facility, except Ghana and Zaïre, which, as noted in footnote 1, were under the 1974 facility.
[3]Components may not add to totals because of rounding of figures for individual members.

As Mr. Witteveen intended, the oil facilities for 1974 and 1975 greatly increased drawings from the Fund and put them again at record levels. To some of the staff, use of the oil facilities at times seemed slower or smaller than might have been expected, causing some staff to wonder whether members really wanted or needed money from the Fund. Relatively slow use of the facility, however, may have resulted from the requirement that members draw only specified portions of their quotas in the Fund. This limitation in effect served as an allocation system. Hence, while some members were not drawing at all, others had drawn their full allotment. As the facilities were periodically reviewed and access to them was increased, further drawings were requested. In the end, all the funds which Mr. Witteveen was able to borrow were used.

In general, almost no conditionality in the form of the macroeconomic policies that the Fund customarily associated with stand-by arrangements was attached to drawings made under the oil facility. As drawings under the oil facilities were requested and approved, governments presented programs to the Fund, but the Fund did not seriously attempt to see that these programs were implemented. In discussions with officials of member governments, the Managing Director and the staff tried to get officials to start thinking in terms of quantitative programs for the longer term in the hope that once this temporary facility had ended members would come to the Fund for additional drawings in the regular credit tranches under stand-by arrangements and would implement programs that would help their balance of payments adjustment. Two instances of this policy were to some extent successful. Italy and the United Kingdom, which had stand-by arrangements approved by the Fund in 1974 and 1975 respectively, not only drew on these stand-by arrangements as well as under the oil facility, but also came to the Fund later in 1976 and 1977 for further stand-by arrangements, as described in later chapters. When developing members drew under the oil facility, the staff also attempted to work with member governments in setting some quantitative limits on the expansion of the money supply and on budgetary expenditures. However, for the most part the oil facility proved to be an unconditional arrangement and did not lead to members requesting first credit tranche drawings under stand-by arrangements.

RESTRICTIONS AVOIDED

One condition required for drawing on the Fund's oil facility proved, nonetheless, to be successfully implemented for nearly all members. That condition was that members refrain from introducing or intensifying their restrictions on trade and capital transactions. Avoidance of restrictions was a primary motive of the Managing Director in originally proposing an oil facility in the Fund. In January 1974, the Committee of Twenty and the Executive Board had taken actions asking members to refrain from restrictions. At its final meeting on June 13, 1974 and in an Appendix to the *Outline of Reform*, the Committee of Twenty had invited members to sign a voluntary declaration concerning trade and other current account measures for balance of payments purposes, and later in June the Executive Directors had established the necessary procedures to implement the declaration. The desire of financial officials that countries avoid resort to restrictions in the new oil crisis was intense.

The voluntary declaration attracted few signatories. By the end of 1974, it had been signed only by Belgium, Botswana, Canada, Denmark, the Federal Republic of Germany, Japan, Liberia, Malawi, Mauritius, the Netherlands, Norway, Oman, and the United States. While 8 of these were large industrial members, the 13 signatories had only about 40 percent of the total voting power in the Fund. Later Austria,

Lebanon, and Lesotho also subscribed. Cameroon, Indonesia, Iraq, Jamaica, Sudan, and Zaïre wrote to the Fund stating that they did not wish to subscribe to the declaration. Several large members, including Australia, France, and the United Kingdom, were concerned, as they had been so often in the past, that the Fund might be extending its authority in matters of trade and usurping the jurisdiction of the GATT. As a result of this concern about Fund jurisdiction, most countries belonging to the OECD did not subscribe. Many developing members did not believe that the pledge, which contained a provision to take account of the special circumstances of developing countries, was applicable to them. The Fund's invitation to members to subscribe to the voluntary declaration was allowed to expire.

In May 1974, a declaration similar to that endorsed by the Committee of Twenty was also adopted by the governments of the countries belonging to the OECD.[20] The idea underlying this pledge against resort to trade restrictions was not merely that the signatory governments were to avoid trade restrictions. That assurance alone was not sufficient. Rather, the objective was to prevent countries from taking advantage of certain legal loopholes in their arrangements with the GATT. Under the usual GATT consultations, a country sought permission to impose restrictions for balance of payments purposes on the grounds of its own balance of payments position. The circumstances of the oil crises were different, however: balance of payments deficits were nearly universal. Virtually all countries could justify restrictions on balance of payments grounds. There could be a "snowballing effect" in which the restrictions imposed by one country would be a precedent for the imposition of restrictions by another country. Hence, the objective of the OECD trade pledge was to persuade all countries from the outset of the oil price rise not to use the legal possibilities open to them under the GATT to impose restrictions.

Although the required number of Fund members did not sign the declaration, an escalation of restrictions on trade and capital movements in the payments crises of 1974 and 1975 was in fact avoided. Most countries did not resort to restrictions on imports or on current invisible transactions as a means of countering their large current account deficits even in 1975 when these deficits became very great. It may well have been unlikely that countries would have rushed into imposing and intensifying restrictions in any event. Once import restrictions had been lifted in the 1960s, there was enormous incentive to keep trade relatively free of restrictions. Domestic consumption and production of most countries depended on continued imports. There was also a desire to keep up imports to restrain increases in domestic prices. And there was genuine concern among financial officials that once any country began seriously to resort to restrictions, other countries might retaliate and restrictions would proliferate. On the positive side, after years of cooperating and meeting in international gatherings to diminish restrictions, officials were eager to continue such cooperation.

---

[20] For a comparison of the declarations of the Fund and of the OECD, see Joseph Gold, "Recent International Decisions to Prevent Restrictions on Trade and Payments," *Journal of World Trade Law* (London), Vol. 9 (January/February 1975), pp. 63–78.

Despite these factors holding back any rush into restrictions, it can be concluded that the Fund's oil facility, the admonitions of the Fund against the use of restrictions, and the strong program of the OECD against restrictions were also important in keeping trade and payments relatively free through the crises years 1974–75.

A SUBSIDY ACCOUNT ESTABLISHED

While the Fund's oil facility was being considered in the first several months of 1974, the international community was made aware of the problems arising in 1974 for some of the poorest developing countries. Several developing countries, especially in Africa and the Middle East, with little domestic industry of their own and low per capita income were still heavily dependent on imports of life-sustaining necessities, such as food and fuel. The Sahelian countries in Africa, for instance, had been experiencing severe drought for a number of years so that their domestic food output was minimal and starvation was prevalent. For many of these countries, imports of petroleum products were also essential; petroleum was used mainly for the internal transportation and distribution of vital commodities, including food. Imports of chemical fertilizers, derived from petroleum products, were also imperative for these countries to maintain even their inadequate levels of food production.

Food prices had already reached high levels in 1972 and 1973. In addition, the cost of capital goods and even of simple manufactured items, such as textiles, imported by these poorer developing countries had been rising for several years. Hence, the announcement in December 1973 of much higher prices for crude oil and consequently for all petroleum products gave rise to concern about the ability of some of the very poor developing countries to pay for essential imports. Their situation could become intolerable.

Accordingly, in May 1974 a United Nations Emergency Operation (UNEO) was set up to seek special emergency contributions to disburse to these countries. UN Secretary-General Kurt Waldheim appointed Raul Prebisch as Special Representative for the UNEO. Staff of the World Bank and of the Fund as well as of other UN agencies were assigned to work with Mr. Prebisch. The Fund sent two staff members to New York in 1974 to work with him for several months.

In these circumstances, when it appeared likely that the charges would be levied on the use of the oil facility at commercial rates of interest, the question arose of subsidizing the purchases made by at least some developing members. This question became more urgent when a facility for 1975 was being considered. At the 1974 Annual Meeting, for instance, Governors of both developed and developing members spoke in favor of a Subsidy Account in the Fund to give relief from high charges to developing members. When the 1975 oil facility was agreed by the Executive Board and endorsed by the Interim Committee, it was on the understanding that such an account would be set up.

351

Use of the UN List of Most Seriously Affected Countries

Although the idea of a Subsidy Account was accepted in principle, it was not easy to establish such an account. There was initial disagreement over which members ought to receive subsidies. Some Executive Directors took the position that it was important for the Fund to retain the practice of treating all its members the same. They argued that distinguishing between industrial, relatively more developed, and developing countries in the Fund membership ought to be avoided. Surely, further distinctions between developing countries on the basis of per capita incomes were spurious. Since per capita income statistics were not very reliable, it was certainly wrong to use them as a basis for distinguishing between members in applying Fund policies.

Although some Executive Directors did not want to distinguish between members, others, especially those elected by African members, insisted on the need for relief from high charges for their countries. Moreover, since members had a vested interest in being on the list to receive subsidies from the Fund, the Executive Directors elected by developing members were deeply concerned about the requirements for being on the list, over which there was extensive debate.

The Fund finally decided to use the list made up in the United Nations through the UNEO. Although not much money was obtained by the UNEO, one of the achievements of the technical staff—an important one so far as the Fund was concerned—was the identification of 41 countries "most seriously affected by the current situation," that is, by the rise in oil prices superimposed on already high prices for food. The countries identified as MSA countries (most seriously affected) had per capita incomes of $400 a year or less in 1971 (many had per capita incomes of $200 a year or less) and were expected to have balance of payments deficits in 1974 and 1975 not smaller than 5 percent of their imports.

These 41 countries became the basis of the Fund's list. Since Cape Verde and Mozambique, which were on the UN list, were not then members of the Fund, 39 Fund members were eligible to receive payments from the Subsidy Account.[21]

The Account in Operation

On this basis, the Executive Board took a decision on August 1, 1975 to establish a Subsidy Account.[22] There was thus established the first facility designed by the Fund specifically to provide financial assistance to a specified list of members. The assets and records of the Account were to be separate from those of the Fund, but, as trustee of the Subsidy Account, the Fund was to administer it. In the usual

---

[21]Afghanistan, Bangladesh, Burma, Burundi, Cameroon, Central African Republic, Chad, Dahomey (Benin), Egypt, El Salvador, Ethiopia, Ghana, Guinea, Guyana, Haiti, Honduras, India, Ivory Coast, Kenya, Khmer Republic (Democratic Kampuchea), Laos (Lao People's Democratic Republic), Lesotho, Malagasy Republic (Madagascar), Mali, Mauritania, Niger, Pakistan, Rwanda, Senegal, Sierra Leone, Somalia, Sri Lanka, Sudan, Tanzania, Uganda, Upper Volta, Western Samoa, Yemen Arab Republic, and the People's Democratic Republic of Yemen.

[22]E.B. Decision No. 4773-(75/136), August 1, 1975; Vol. III below, pp. 500–502.

manner of trustees, the Fund was to solicit contributions to the Account and to make disbursements once the Account was set up.

While the Fund requested contributions from all members not on the MSA list, it expected the contributions to come primarily from oil exporting and industrial countries. Gradually contributions were arranged from 24 members and Switzerland totaling SDR 160.5 million over the life of the Account. As of June 30, 1978, actual contributions amounted to SDR 101 million. The amounts contributed by each of the 25 countries are listed in Table 9.

Of the 39 members eligible to receive funds from the Subsidy Account, only 18 had drawn under the 1975 oil facility. Since drawings on the 1975 oil facility were effected over two financial years of the Fund and could be outstanding for up to seven years after the date of drawing, subsidy payments were expected to be made through eight financial years (1976–83 inclusive).[23] The objective was to reduce the effective rate of annual charge payable on drawings under the 1975 oil facility by about 5 percent a year. In July 1976 the first subsidy payments were made at the rate of 5 percent a year, that is, 5 percent of the average daily balances of the currency of the member held by the Fund in excess of the member's quota which the Fund had acquired as a result of the member's purchases under the 1975 oil facility. The percentage paid was the same for all eligible members.[24] The rate of 5 percent a year was continued for the next two financial years.[25] The effective cost of using the 1975 oil facility for members receiving the subsidy was thus lowered from 7.71 percent to 2.71 percent a year. Table 10 contains the names of the recipient members and the amounts they received in each of these three years.

In November 1978 the decision establishing the Subsidy Account was amended to permit any surplus after payment to the original beneficiaries at the rate of 5 percent to be used to make payments, at a rate not exceeding 5 percent, to seven additional beneficiaries, namely, Grenada, Malawi, Morocco, Papua New Guinea, the Philippines, Zaïre, and Zambia. The addition of these seven members made the list of beneficiaries of the Subsidy Account conform with the list of members that had used the 1975 oil facility that were also eligible for assistance from the Trust Fund.

In summary, although many officials accepted the idea that some relief from what seemed at the time high charges for the use of the 1975 oil facility was desirable for the poorest developing members, the Fund found it difficult to set up and to implement the Subsidy Account. The Executive Directors found it so hard to agree on the selection of members which should be eligible for payments from the Account that the choice of members was made by resorting to the United Nations' list of MSA countries. Moreover, the Managing Director had a difficult time persuading members to contribute to the Account.

---

[23]The Fund's financial year runs from May 1 to April 30.

[24]E.B. Decision No. 5144-(76/102) SA, July 12, 1976; Vol. III below, p. 502.

[25]E.B. Decisions Nos. 5425-(77/79) SA, May 27, 1977 and 5726-(78/59) SA, April 17, 1978; Vol. III below, pp. 502–503.

Table 9. Subsidy Account: Contributions

(In millions of SDRs)

Contributor	Anticipated Total Contributions[1]	Contributions Received as of June 30, 1978
Australia	5.700	3.440
Austria	2.300	2.300
Belgium	5.600	2.240
Brazil	1.850	1.388
Canada	9.500	9.500
Denmark	2.200	0.960
Finland	1.600	0.800
France	12.900	7.527
Germany, Federal Republic of	13.700	6.841
Greece	0.600	0.150
Iran	6.000	4.500
Italy	8.600	8.600
Japan	10.300	4.363
Luxembourg	0.108	0.108
Netherlands	6.000	6.000
New Zealand	1.700	0.607
Norway	2.100	2.100
Saudi Arabia	40.000	19.810
South Africa	1.350	1.350
Spain	3.400	1.470
Sweden	2.800	2.100
Switzerland	3.285	3.285
United Kingdom	12.050	6.692
Venezuela	6.000	4.498
Yugoslavia	0.900	0.675
Total	160.543	101.304

[1]In some cases these amounts were subject to final agreement on amount or on timing, parliamentary approval, and certain conditions. In some cases where contributions were made in installments, budgetary approval was required in each year that a contribution was to be made. SDR amounts might be subject to small adjustments owing to exchange rate changes.

Despite these difficulties, the Subsidy Account was an innovative step in the Fund's evolution. It demonstrated the Fund's ingenuity in implementing its policies in a flexible manner. Unable under its Articles to differentiate the charges levied on use of its resources by categories of members, the Fund was nonetheless able effectively to lower the charges on the 1975 oil facility for those developing members clearly unable to pay them. The Subsidy Account was also the first arrangement in which the Fund distinguished between developing members and other members, and the first arrangement in which accounts were to be kept separate from those for the rest of the Fund's operations and transactions and for which the Fund was to serve as trustee; in this way it laid the basis for establishment, in the next year, of the larger and broader Trust Fund. Both the Subsidy Account and the Trust Fund were sufficiently novel precedents that, when the Articles of Agreement were amended in

Table 10. Subsidy Account: Total Use of 1975 Oil Facility by Most Seriously Affected Members and Subsidy Paid, Financial Years 1976–78

(In millions of SDRs)

Member	Total Use 1975 Oil Facility[1]	Subsidy at 5 Percent for Year Ended		
		April 30, 1976	April 30, 1977	April 30, 1978
Bangladesh	40.47	0.65	2.00	2.02
Cameroon	11.79	0.14	0.59	0.59
Central African Republic	2.66	0.05	0.13	0.13
Egypt	31.68	0.16	1.57	1.58
Haiti	4.14	0.07	0.21	0.21
India	201.34	7.23	10.07	7.46
Ivory Coast	10.35	0.15	0.52	0.52
Kenya	27.93	0.67	1.39	1.40
Mali	3.99	0.01	0.20	0.20
Mauritania	5.32	0.05	0.26	0.27
Pakistan	111.01	2.60	5.55	5.55
Senegal	9.91	0.30	0.50	0.50
Sierra Leone	4.97	0.03	0.25	0.25
Sri Lanka	34.13	0.48	1.71	1.71
Sudan	18.30	0.36	0.92	0.92
Tanzania	20.61	0.68	1.03	1.03
Western Samoa	0.42	0.01	0.02	0.02
Yemen, People's Democratic Republic of	12.02	0.18	0.60	0.60
Total	551.03	13.82	27.51	24.95

[1]Purchases under the 1975 oil facility began in July 1975 and continued until May 1976. The subsidy amounts shown were calculated on the average daily balances of the currency of the member held by the Fund that were outstanding for purchases under the 1975 oil facility during the year and subject to charges.

1978, authority was given to the Fund to administer "resources contributed by members," a power which the Fund did not previously have in such an explicit way.

OUTCOME OF THE 1973 OIL PRICE RISE

The oil crisis that began in December 1973 lasted until the end of 1978. The end of 1978 can be regarded as the cutoff date for what could later be viewed as the "first oil crisis" or a first round of oil price increases. A second oil crisis or second round of price increases occurred at the end of 1978.

In many respects, the economic and financial impact of the first oil crisis of 1973–78, while not to be minimized, proved considerably less troublesome than initially expected. For the most part, after the temporary embargo on supplies to the United States and the Netherlands was lifted in January 1974, oil importing countries experienced no real shortages of oil. Furthermore, after 1974 the size of the disequilibrium in international payments resulting from the quadrupling of oil prices in 1973–74 turned out to be much smaller than had been forecast. Developments both in oil exporting and in oil importing countries worked to diminish this disequilibrium. As an immediate response to their enlarged oil revenues, all major oil exporting countries stepped up their economic development efforts and undertook massive new projects for social improvements. These countries accordingly expanded their imports of goods and services much more than had been projected by even the most optimistic forecasts. During 1974–78 the members of OPEC spent nearly $500 billion on imports of goods and services (excluding income paid to foreign investors), roughly 75 percent of their current earnings from exports. Imports grew by an average of 24 percent a year *in real terms*.

The rate of growth of imports by oil exporting countries was sustained from 1974 onward even though the level of their imports was steadily climbing. Unexpectedly, the most rapid growth of imports of oil exporting countries occurred in countries originally viewed as "low absorbers" of imports because of their relatively sparse population. Saudi Arabia's purchases from abroad, for example, rose at an average annual rate of over 56 percent in value terms (40 percent in real terms) from 1974 to 1978. As had happened in the United States and in Western European countries after World War II, higher per capita incomes quickly led to higher consumption. In particular higher per capita incomes led to greater and more varied consumption of food. Imports of capital goods also went up sharply. In fact, economists realized that they had underestimated the speed with which expanded levels of public expenditure for development programs could be implemented in oil exporting countries and the effect that public expenditures on these programs would have on increasing imports.[26]

Also contributing to smaller balance of payments imbalances than had been forecast were declines in the rate of increase of oil imports by many oil importing countries. France, the Federal Republic of Germany, Italy, and Japan especially reduced the rate at which their imports of oil went up, although a reduced rate of increase of oil consumption and of imports in these countries reflected a much lower rate of growth in their economies as a whole than in earlier years. Total oil consumption of Fund members plus Switzerland increased at an average annual rate of only a little more than 1 percent. In addition, new sources of oil in the North Sea, Mexico, and Alaska were discovered, reducing the need for oil imports from OPEC sources by many countries, including the Netherlands, Norway, and the United Kingdom, and even making them actual or potential oil exporters. As a result of lower demand and enlarged supply, demand for oil from OPEC was virtually unchanged during 1975–78, and oil prices increased by an average of less than 4 percent a year in nominal terms. This increase was less than half the average annual increase in the prices of goods imported by the OPEC, so that by the end of 1978 the

---

[26]Fund staff began to examine the relation between public expenditures in oil exporting countries and imports by these countries. See, for instance, David R. Morgan, "Fiscal Policy in Oil Exporting Countries, 1972–78," *Staff Papers*, International Monetary Fund (Washington), Vol. 26 (March 1979), pp. 55–81.

average terms of trade of the OPEC were nearly 25 percent below the average of these terms in 1974.

As a result of these developments, most industrial countries, except for Italy and the United Kingdom, avoided deep and prolonged balance of payments deficits. By 1978 the industrial countries as a group had again developed large current account surpluses. These surpluses totaled $33 billion, compared with $7 billion in 1976 and $4 billion in 1977. By 1977 even Italy and the United Kingdom swung sharply from balance of payments deficit into surplus. The combined current account surpluses of the major oil exporters had dropped sharply from $68 billion in 1974 to only $6 billion in 1978; they had been $35 billion in 1975, $40 billion in 1976, and $32 billion in 1977. The current account deficits of what the Fund called the more developed primary producers had also been more than cut in half, from $13–15 billion in 1975, 1976, and 1977 to $6 billion in 1978. The current account surpluses of major oil exporting countries and the counterpart of large deficits by oil importing countries thus ceased to dominate the international payments picture by 1978.

Not only were oil-related deficits reduced but financing for payments deficits proved in the end to be readily available. External lending by private commercial banks to the principal industrial countries rose over threefold. Private commercial banks were thus able to recycle vast amounts of petrodollars without becoming illiquid or overexposed and without bank failures. In fact, it was already apparent by the middle of 1975 that investment of the surpluses of oil exporting countries in national and international financial markets together with the expansion of official financing (through both bilateral arrangements and multilateral facilities) was resulting in a satisfactory channeling of funds into the financing of the current account deficits of oil importing countries, including non-oil developing countries. Therefore, no additional official financing mechanisms among the industrial nations were arranged; the financial safety net in the OECD proposed by U.S. officials was never established.

Non-oil developing countries, however, continued to have large current account deficits: $30 billion in 1974, $38 billion in 1975, $26 billion in 1976, $21 billion in 1977, and $31 billion in 1978. But, together with long-term official financing to the most needy of these countries, private bank lending to other developing countries helped substantially to finance these deficits. Not only was financing available but in the face of their enlarged payments deficits from 1974 onward, non-oil developing countries decided to borrow abroad. To deal with the oil crisis of 1973–78, officials of these countries opted to accumulate large external debts rather than endure the more dismal alternative of reducing their economic growth and increasing domestic unemployment. As a consequence, by 1978 many developing countries had a tremendous amount of external debt. Debt servicing of non-oil developing countries began to emerge as a prime concern of all financial officials. In fact, by the end of 1978, concern was more widespread about the precarious finances of many developing countries than it had been at any time since 1950. The main legacy of the 1973 oil price rise was thus the critical problems attending the large external debt of developing members, described in Chapter 48.

SIGNIFICANCE OF THE FACILITY:
A BRIDGE OVER TROUBLED WATER

The amount of money the Fund made available under its oil facility (in effect two facilities) was minute in comparison with the huge current account payments deficits that were eventually financed. But because this money was made available shortly after the start of the oil crisis and continued to be available for about two years until adequate alternative financial arrangements took hold, the Fund's oil facility did, indeed, serve as a bridge, as Mr. Witteveen had wanted, between the old era of cheap oil and energy and the new era of expensive oil and energy.

In addition to serving as a bridge, the Fund's oil facility of 1974 and 1975 was an outstanding achievement in a number of other ways. First, it broke new ground in that the Fund, for the first time, undertook to help finance massive balance of payments deficits prevailing for most of its members. In the past when the question had come up as to whether the Fund could help finance balance of payments deficits prevailing on a worldwide scale, the answer had always been that the Fund's resources were inadequate for broad undertakings. For example, when the Fund was starting operations in 1947, it was decided not to use the Fund's resources to help European countries with payments deficits stemming from their reconstruction needs and efforts.[27] Likewise, from time to time in the 1950s, when officials and economists believed that the United States could again have a depressed economy as it had in the 1930s and that many other countries would then experience depressed exports and payments deficits, it was understood that the Fund should not be the source of major balance of payments financing related to a depressed U.S. economy. The Fund's resources were too small. The oil facility was thus the first time the Fund undertook to participate in the financing of worldwide balance of payments disequilibria.

Second, by realizing at the onset of higher oil prices that huge payments imbalances could endanger the world's liberal trade and payments regime and worsen international recession, Mr. Witteveen helped to make officials in industrial countries more cognizant of the combined inflationary and recessionary implications of higher crude oil prices and to induce these officials to avoid unsatisfactory policies. While public officials of industrial countries were making decisions on which policies to employ, Mr. Witteveen's public statements put officials on notice that the international community was opposed to the use of deflationary policies and of restrictions on trade to deal with higher prices. Thus, Mr. Witteveen deserves credit for heading off policies that might have made the oil price rise much worse than it eventually proved to be.

Third, by proposing the official recycling of petrodollars through the Fund and by instituting one of the first governmental borrowing arrangements with oil exporting countries, Mr. Witteveen demonstrated that officials of all countries were prepared to cooperate in dealing with the payments crisis resulting from the abrupt

---

[27] See *History, 1945–65*, Vol. I, pp. 217–20, and Vol. II, pp. 394–97.

jump in oil prices. At a time when many officials were reacting adversely, he demonstrated the feasibility of handling the rise in oil prices amicably, without conflict between oil importing and oil exporting countries.

Fourth, the institution of official recycling in 1974, and its expansion in 1975, made possible by the Fund's oil facility, lent encouragement to private bankers for the necessary enlargement of private financing arrangements. The Fund's oil facility was a useful forerunner of private financing arrangements.

Fifth, the oil facility was important for the Fund as the organization responsible for international monetary arrangements and for cooperation in the international monetary field. As emergency payments problems erupted in 1974 and 1975, it was essential that the Fund take some action. Already the Fund's influence and functions had been reduced by the collapse of the par value system and the introduction of floating rates earlier in 1973. By the middle of 1973, the Fund's image had also suffered by the failure of world officials to agree on a reformed system. Thus, by introducing the oil facility, Mr. Witteveen pushed the Fund into action on the world's most serious financial problem of 1974 and 1975. The Fund proved to be an instrument of help to a great many of its members in time of serious payments need. The Fund had originally been created to help members finance temporary balance of payments deficits so that they could avoid the imposition of restrictions or of deflationary economic policies. The oil facility served this purpose very well in 1974 and 1975.

Sixth, the oil facility had consequences for the Fund's other financing arrangements. Since charges closer to commercial rates of interest were instituted for drawings under the oil facility, charges close to commercial interest rates were gradually accepted for all Fund transactions. Borrowing agreements on terms more advantageous to the Fund than was the GAB also proved to be possible.

The Oil Facility Viewed Against Later Developments

The revolution in Iran that overthrew the Shah at the end of 1978 caused fresh disruptions in supplies of crude oil. It was expected that the relatively ready supply of oil that had prevailed up until 1978, albeit with higher prices, would change. World shortages of oil were anticipated. In view of actual and expected shortages of oil, OPEC announced at the end of June 1979 a further 24 percent increase in the prices for crude oil, the largest increase in the five and a half years since December 1973. Saudi Arabian light crude oil, for example, went to $18 per barrel and prices for other crude oils went to as high as $23.50 per barrel. In mid-1979 there thus began a second round of oil price increases.

The same problems as had arisen in 1974 were again foreseen. The progress that had been made in improving disequilibria in world payments was expected to be undone, and almost at once. The OPEC surplus, which had nearly disappeared in 1978, was expected to surge to disturbingly large levels in 1979. While officials of the United States planned new measures with enhanced determination to curb rising levels of oil imports by the United States and hoped to reduce the U.S. current account deficit, the OECD countries as a group were expected to move from surplus into deficit. The payments position of non-oil developing countries, already in considerable deficit as a group, was expected to deteriorate much further. Since developing countries already had accumulated overwhelming external debt, there was concern as to how they could service such debt and yet pay still higher oil import bills. Once more world financing needs seemed acute, and once more international monetary arrangements were expected to incur unusual strains.

These developments are beyond the time frame of this History but the coming of a second oil crisis prompted fresh perspectives on the policies devised to weather the first one. In retrospect, it appeared that officials of several oil importing countries, particularly in the United States, and many of the officials of the Fund had assumed in 1974 and 1975 that the sudden jump in crude oil prices announced in 1973 was an unusual, one-time event, a sort of aberration; at the time relatively few officials spoke even privately of the possibility of big jumps in crude oil prices again in the future. The first round of increases in oil prices was thus relatively quickly accepted as needed to make up for the unduly low prices for oil in the past, and a great many officials operated on the assumption that if these price increases for oil were accommodated, the world economy and the international payments system could then again resume their functioning without unduly disruptive international payments disequilibria.

The second round of oil price increases proved the original assumption unfounded. Consequently, some of those officials who had in 1974 and 1975 argued for the need to finance the larger payments deficits were inclined in 1979 to view these earlier policies as misguided. While oil importing countries had financed deficits, they had not taken the measures needed to conserve oil consumption or to develop alternative energy sources. As a result, industrial countries remained excessively dependent on imported oil, and developing countries had external debts so massive as to cause difficult problems of debt servicing and even fears of default. There was no question that basic measures now had to be instituted, and many officials were inclined to think that they had wasted five years of precious time in taking the measures required to adjust to a radically changed world oil situation. The energy crisis thus became severe only after the end of 1978.

There was a significant change in the reactions of officials in international financing organizations, such as the Fund, to the second large price rise in crude oil prices, compared with the 1973–74 price rise. None seriously suggested that the Fund establish another temporary oil facility. As far as Fund financing was concerned, the extended facility and the supplementary financing facility (described in a later chapter) were thought adequate. The energy problem, moreover, was recognized as long term, and it was believed essential that use of the Fund's resources be on conditional terms so as to help members adjust their payments positions. To this end, too, the World Bank started financing projects for exploring for oil in developing countries heavily dependent on imported oil and started planning for a possible energy affiliate.

Harry Dexter White and John Maynard Keynes,
architects of the international monetary arrangements agreed at Bretton Woods

Yousuf Karsh, Ottawa

Pierre-Paul Schweitzer, Chairman of the Executive Board and Managing Director,
September 1, 1963–August 31, 1973

Meeting of the Executive Board, December 1, 1972

Meeting of the Executive Board, January 13, 1975

Kenyatta Conference Center, Nairobi, Kenya,
site of the 1973 Annual Meeting of Board of Governors

Mzee Jomo Kenyatta, President of Kenya, welcoming Governors,
Annual Meeting, Nairobi, September 24, 1973
(Left to right: Robert S. McNamara, President of the World Bank,
George M. Chambers, Governor for Trinidad and Tobago and
Chairman of the Board of Governors, Mrs. Kenyatta, President Kenyatta)

Committee of Twenty, Inaugural Meeting, Washington, September 28, 1972

(above) Ali Wardhana, Chairman, and C. Jeremy Morse, Chairman of Deputies,
discussing *Outline of Reform*, June 13, 1974
(below) H. J. Witteveen and Messrs. Wardhana and Morse
at final press conference, June 13, 1974

CHAPTER
19

An Extended Facility
Established

*E*XTENDED ARRANGEMENTS, comparable to stand-by arrangements
but made under a new extended Fund facility, were introduced in September
1974, as yet another response of the Fund to the lack of agreement on a reformed
international monetary system. The arrangements were accepted, especially by
officials of industrial members, to ameliorate the disappointment of officials of
developing members over the failure of negotiations for reform which meant, among
other things, that no link between allocations of SDRs and development finance
would be established. They were the third type of arrangements the Fund instituted
to widen access of developing members to its resources. Arrangements for the
compensatory financing of export fluctuations had been introduced in 1963,
liberalized and extended in 1966, and arrangements for financing buffer stocks had
been introduced in 1969.

ARGUMENTS FOR A NEW EXTENDED FUND FACILITY

After the staff tentatively suggested in June 1973 that some longer-term use of
the Fund's resources might be introduced, interest by officials of developing
members in some facility in the Fund for extended arrangements developed quickly.
Officials of developing members, convinced that the temporary use of Fund
resources that traditionally governed the Fund's policies did not give them enough
time to change the structure of their economies, wanted to be able to use the Fund's
resources for a more extended period. The Executive Directors for developing
members noted particularly that, after the suggestion for some such facility in mid-
1973, no further action was being taken. By early 1974, Mr. Witteveen was
emphasizing the proposed oil facility and, in the view of some Executive Directors,
was meanwhile delaying consideration by the Executive Board of a possible
extended facility. Mr. Yaméogo in particular pressed for consideration by the
Executive Board of an extended facility. On behalf of the Executive Directors elected

by developing members, in February 1974 he sent to the other Executive Directors a memorandum urging an early resumption of deliberation on an extended Fund facility specifically for developing members.

As the management and staff saw the situation, the Fund had considerable scope to lengthen the time for which its resources were used. Under the Articles of Agreement, the Fund's resources were to be used only temporarily, and from its beginning Fund policies ensured that use of its resources was temporary. The Articles did not define temporary, however. The policy the Fund had followed since the 1950s was that stand-by arrangements, under which regular resources were made available, were normally approved for one year, and repurchases were to be made no later than three to five years after the date of each purchase. Consequently, a member using the Fund's resources usually had a stand-by arrangement on which it was able to draw for up to one year while it adopted policies that would enable it to eliminate its balance of payments deficits and generate a surplus sufficient to repay the Fund within a three-to-five-year period. In practice, members usually repurchased toward the end of this period. Also, the Fund frequently approved a series of successive stand-by arrangements, that is, gave a member one stand-by arrangement after another for several consecutive years. From 1966 to 1974, the Fund approved successive stand-by arrangements for five or more years for Brazil, Burundi, Colombia, Guatemala, Guyana, Haiti, Honduras, Indonesia, Korea, Liberia, Morocco, Panama, the Philippines, Somalia, Tunisia, and Turkey. Before 1966 Colombia and the Philippines, for instance, had had a series of stand-by arrangements for a decade or longer. By having new stand-by arrangements under which further drawings could be made as repurchases due under old stand-by arrangements took place, these members were able effectively to use the Fund's resources for longer than five years, even in the upper credit tranches.

In a paper presented to the Executive Directors in March 1974, the staff first put forward the arguments for a new facility. A succession of one-year stand-by arrangements was inadequate to cope with structural problems. Since stand-by arrangements were approved for only one year, members necessarily oriented themselves toward policies that could be carried out within the year and toward repayment of the Fund within three to five years. Even though the Fund often approved additional stand-by arrangements for members, members could not plan their policies on this assumption. Hence, they could not undertake financial planning that might extend beyond a year. Yet occasionally a member might be able to bring about sustained improvement in its balance of payments if it had a longer time to implement basic changes in its economic and financial policies.

The staff paper also characterized in some detail the situations in which medium-term planning supported by the Fund's resources might be useful and noted how these situations differed from those prevailing when members requested stand-by arrangements. In the first situation distortions in the use of a country's productive resources had developed. A member might be an excellent candidate for an extended arrangement, for example, if it had been pursuing economic and financial policies resulting in misallocations of its productive resources. Distortions in the relative prices of products and in the factors of production may have arisen; the exchange rate may have become overvalued. As a result, productive resources would have been channeled in wrong directions. Investment in export industries, for example, might have been discouraged; domestic industries might have become heavily dependent on imported raw materials or intermediate goods. A member in such a situation could be readily identified. Exports would have become insufficient, imports excessive, and in all probability, the authorities would have been relying on trade and payments restrictions to help balance the external payments accounts.

In these circumstances, a financial stabilization program aimed at bringing about a longer-lasting improvement in the balance of payments would require the member to undertake major changes in, and even reversals of, its economic and financial policies. It would probably have to devalue its exchange rate and liberalize its trade and payments. It would have to make substantial changes in what the Fund commonly referred to as the country's "financial institutions," such as its system of taxation, its tariff structure, and the techniques and agencies used to encourage domestic savings. These changes went beyond agreeing to targets for domestic money and credit expansion or for the budgetary accounts, which were typically involved in the financial stabilization programs associated with stand-by arrangements.

More profound policy changes were necessary in a financial program under an extended arrangement since the objective of such a program was not only to contain inflation and mitigate current pressure on the balance of payments but also to induce a reallocation of real resources. It was necessary, for example, to increase investment in the export sector of the economy so that the member could reinforce improvements in its external payments position stemming from a better control of inflation. Increased investment in exports might well require major changes in financial arrangements, such as tax reform, which would take some years to become fully effective. The staff paper noted that in working with members in implementing tax reform programs the Fund had learned that, even when tax reform programs were well conceived and implemented, several years were required before much larger tax revenues accrued.

There was also an alternative situation in which a member might want to use Fund resources for a period longer than customary, the situation of a low-income country in which domestic investment ought to be increased. While such a member might not necessarily be experiencing immediate pressure on its foreign exchange reserves, it could be regarded as having an inherently unstable balance of payments position because of a weak productive base. This situation was typical of several small developing members. Some of these members, notably in Central America, customarily pursued conservative financial policies, including balanced budgets and relatively tight monetary policies, and usually had realistic exchange rates and virtual balance of payments equilibrium. Hence, for these members, the problem was not excessively expansionary policies. In any event, regardless of the policies pursued, the problem was that the economies of these low-income members were simple, based almost entirely on the export of one or two primary products. The populations of these members suffered from very low per capita incomes, even by the standards of other developing members.

Because the fiscal and credit institutions of such members were generally undeveloped, authorities were unable to mobilize sufficient domestic savings to increase domestic investment. They thus had very little leeway to develop new industries or new types of exports. Yet it was becoming axiomatic that development of new exports was the most effective way to achieve economic growth. Were such countries to increase their investment, they would encounter balance of payments problems by generating additional demand for imports, including consumer imports. Total imports were likely to exceed the imports needed for the new investment projects. Even if development aid was available to cover the foreign exchange cost of new investment projects, the resulting balance of payments deficits could still be unmanageable.

Consequently, these members were obliged either to remain economically stagnated at low levels of per capita income or to start development projects and use restrictions to cope with the accompanying balance of payments deficits. Internal restrictions, such as rationing, as well as external restrictions, such as import controls, might be required. But the Fund's past experience showed that ultimately such restrictions proved detrimental to an expansion of exports that could compete successfully in world markets.

What was necessary was for the Fund to provide financial support for a period long enough to enable the member to develop its monetary and fiscal institutions. The members would then be in a better position to foster domestic investment. Those members that usually pursued orthodox financial policies and appropriate trade and exchange policies would also reap greater benefits from these policies.

In addition to identifying the circumstances warranting extended arrangements, the staff paper cited other advantages of extended arrangements over stand-by arrangements. Financial support from the Fund for a medium-term period could strengthen the hand of the officials of the member concerned as they planned basic changes in economic policies. The implementation of a program involving major shifts in a country's economic and financial policies, including the institution of new fiscal and monetary instruments, such as tax or tariff reforms, required determined leadership. Acceptance of the objectives of the program by the member's main political authorities, often including the political opposition parties, the business community, and the public, was required. It would therefore be of considerable assistance to the government of a member in exerting leadership if the authorities knew that they could rely on Fund support for longer than one year. From this point of view, extended arrangements had an important advantage over the existing technique of successive stand-by arrangements. Still another advantage of extended arrangements cited by the staff was that programs extending beyond one year would enable authorities to give more careful consideration to broad economic objectives, such as the generation of domestic employment. Such objectives could not usually be taken into account in the financial stabilization programs associated with stand-by arrangements.

NATURE OF A PROPOSED EXTENDED FUND FACILITY

In proposing a new extended Fund facility, the management and the staff emphasized that the Fund's regular resources should remain the normal source of Fund support. Extended arrangements would be a supplementary facility for special situations. Traditional stand-by arrangements would be used to meet commonly experienced balance of payments crises; extended arrangements were for members wanting to undertake structural transformations. The extended facility would be a floating facility, alongside other uses of the Fund's resources.

Three considerations suggested that three years should be the maximum time for drawings under an extended arrangement. First, if drawings could take place for three years and repurchases could take place over four to eight years, as the staff was proposing, outstanding drawings under the facility could run for eleven years. Eleven years seemed to be as far as the Fund could go and still regard the use of its resources as temporary, as the Articles of Agreement required. Mr. Schleiminger, among others, objected that even eleven years was long by the standards of lending customary for central banks.

Second, when a member initiated a new economic program, the deficits that affected the balance of payments usually took place in the first year or two before the revamped financial policies and institutions began to have their full impact. By the third year, the new policies should have sufficiently strengthened the external payments position for Fund support to be brought to an end.

Third, if the attack on the member's economic problems was planned to extend beyond three years, political or social pressures or unexpected economic circumstances could evolve which could lead to a slackening of the efforts of the authorities on the agreed program or even to a reversal of policies. It was thus best not to plan a program that extended too far into the future. The staff defined "too far" as longer than three years.

For a member to qualify for an extended arrangement, it should have a specific program. There should be targets for the fiscal position, for export expansion, and for the rate of growth, as well as an agreed understanding of the expected improvements in trade and payments policies. Such specificity was necessary to give direction to the member's policies and to facilitate consultation between the member and the Fund.

It was clear that at the heart of the program a member might arrange with the Fund under an extended arrangement were to be measures affecting the balance of payments. The fiscal, monetary, and exchange policies to be introduced were all designed to strengthen the external payments position. It was definitely not to be a development program of the kind worked out by members with the World Bank. Although there were differences between the Fund's extended facility and the World Bank's loans, the management and staff recognized that the introduction of an extended facility in the Fund, aimed at helping bring about deep-seated structural changes in a member's economy, required greater collaboration between the Fund and the World Bank than that pertaining to the use of the Fund's resources under stand-by arrangements. In working out an extended arrangement with a member, the Fund staff would have to be in close and continuing contact with the staff of the World Bank, particularly on the appropriateness of the financial targets that the member might propose. The Fund staff also would have to draw on the expertise of the World Bank staff concerning the member's development program and priorities. Ways to effect necessary collaboration with the World Bank would have to be worked out as the extended facility was used.

EXECUTIVE BOARD'S CONSIDERATION OF THE FACILITY

When the Executive Board took up consideration of a proposed extended facility in March 1974, it was also considering the proposed oil facility. Several Executive Directors appointed or elected by industrial members were concerned that the Fund's resources might be insufficient for yet another new facility. Mr. Schleiminger, for instance, projecting that the Fund might face increased drawings in the normal credit tranches and in the two existing special facilities (the compensatory financing facility and the buffer stock financing facility), as well as in the proposed oil facility, urged that the Fund defer consideration of an extended facility. Mr. Bryce suggested that the Fund merely lengthen the one-year period involved in stand-by arrangements rather than create a new facility. Although Mr. Brand preferred an extended facility to proposals for a link between SDR allocations and development finance, he agreed with Mr. Bryce that it might be better for the Executive Directors to "feel their way," trying out new programs under existing stand-by arrangements rather than establishing another new facility.

Mr. Kawaguchi took the position that the Fund might not be the most appropriate institution for financing balance of payments difficulties resulting from the implementation of medium-term and long-term programs aimed at generating structural changes in the economies of developing members. Given their experience and expertise in longer-term programs, the World Bank or other development finance institutions might be better qualified for the purpose. Mr. Kawaguchi also questioned whether it was sensible for the Fund to set up so many different facilities each with a specific purpose. It was preferable to consolidate these facilities in one way or another.

All the Executive Directors elected by developing members were, in contrast, very much interested in having the Fund set up an extended facility as soon as possible. Mr. Bueso and Mr. Nicol-Cole argued that detailed specification of the circumstances in which a member might use an extended facility was not necessary.

A greater maladjustment than could be straightened out in the course of one year rather than any particular set of causative factors should be the main criterion for eligibility in conjunction, of course, with the member's willingness to make changes in its economic policies and financial institutions. Mr. Yaméogo considered the situations described by the staff for use of an extended facility inadequate, explaining that the extended facility should encompass additional situations. The Fund could, for instance, assist members with large short-term foreign debts to extend their debt repayments over several years. He also argued that members had to have a longer period in which to pay than the seven or eight years proposed by the management and staff.

Mr. Hanh, noting that developing members needed urgently to readjust their economies to the 1973–74 increases in prices for crude oil, emphasized the unique timeliness of an extended facility. Jahangir Amuzegar (Iran) stressed that if necessary the Fund's liquidity could be enhanced in a number of ways so that it could encompass an extended facility. The Fund could borrow from countries with payments surpluses, as it was doing for the oil facility. Quotas could be substantially enlarged, an enlargement very much favored by oil importing members, who were acutely interested in increasing their combined quotas in the Fund, or the Fund could be transformed into a true world central bank with the right to issue new forms of money. Mohamed Finaish (Libya) shared Mr. Amuzegar's surprise that so many of the Executive Directors appointed or elected by industrial members and by relatively more developed members now hesitated about an extended facility. The same Executive Directors, he said, had been inclined to favor such a facility in 1973 when they had discussed possible link arrangements, and the new oil price rise made such a facility more, not less, urgent.

Other Executive Directors also took a sympathetic attitude toward establishment of an extended facility. Mr. Palamenghi-Crispi, for instance, in keeping with the long-standing position of Italian officials of trying to find more funds to help developing members, argued strongly for an extended facility. He believed also that a large number of members ought to have access to the proposed facility and, like Mr. Yaméogo, was concerned that the staff paper had limited the situations in which the facility might be used. The staff paper, he said, suggested only problem cases. What about the equally important needs of developing members that had avoided getting into circumstances of serious structural maladjustment because they had used good economic management? Were they to be penalized by not being eligible for extended arrangements?

Mr. Lieftinck did not share the concern expressed by many of his colleagues from industrial members about the inappropriateness of the timing of a new facility in the Fund. Nor was he alarmed that the proposed extended facility would place too heavy a burden on the Fund's liquidity, since he took the view that the proposed oil facility ought to be financed out of borrowed resources. He was convinced that there was a gap between the present facilities in the Fund and the normal operations of the World Bank. The Fund financed short-term balance of payments needs and the

World Bank long-term development needs. Neither institution dealt with medium-term financing. Insofar as the Fund was concerned, while it should certainly avoid entering into the financing of development, it should stand ready to assist developing members with balance of payments problems related to their development efforts.

Executive Board Decision

Because of differences of view among the Executive Directors, it was several months before agreement was reached on establishment of an extended facility and the Fund could not include this facility among the announcements of other actions the Fund was taking as the Committee of Twenty ended its work in June 1974. The Executive Board decision on the extended facility came in September 1974.[1] Agreement was facilitated by several factors. First, in the course of 1974 the Fund was assured that it could acquire the resources needed for the oil facility by borrowing. There was no longer any doubt that the Fund's liquidity could accommodate a limited extended facility.

Second, throughout 1974 financial officials were deeply concerned that countries might greatly intensify their trade and exchange restrictions as a result of the large prevalent payments deficits, and several Executive Directors, such as Mr. de Groote, took the occasion to emphasize that an extended Fund facility would enable non-oil developing members to adjust their balance of payments positions over the medium term without intensifying restrictions.

Third, as the Committee of Twenty ended its work in June 1974 without agreeing on a link between allocations of SDRs and development finance, officials of developing members put a great deal of pressure on officials of other members to agree to some kind of special arrangement to increase the access of their countries to the Fund's regular resources. Financial officials of most industrial countries wanted to have some new type of arrangement to offer the developing countries. The extended facility seemed to be the best such arrangement.

Fourth, it was becoming customary for the Fund to inaugurate arrangements on an experimental basis. The oil facility, for instance, was to be periodically reviewed. An extended facility could likewise be set up provisionally and reviewed after a given period.

In the decision establishing the extended facility, a preamble contained a sentence unique to Fund decisions: "The facility, in its formulation and administration, is likely to be beneficial for developing countries in particular." Fund decisions had not previously mentioned developing members.

Under the decision, the Fund was prepared to give special assistance to members to meet balance of payments deficits for longer periods and in amounts larger in relation to quotas than was the practice under existing tranche policies.

---

[1]E.B. Decision No. 4377-(74/114), September 13, 1974; Vol. III below, pp. 503–06.

Such assistance was to take the form of extended arrangements in support of comprehensive programs that included policies of the scope and character required to correct structural imbalances in production, trade, and prices, when the needed improvement in the member's balance of payments could be achieved without policies inconsistent with the purposes of the Fund only over an extended period.

A member was to consult the Managing Director before making a request for an extended arrangement. The Fund had to be satisfied that the solution of the member's balance of payments problem would take longer than the period for which the Fund's resources were available under existing tranche policies. The member was to present a program setting forth the objectives and policies for the whole period of the arrangement and a detailed statement of the policies and measures it intended to pursue in the first 12 months. For each subsequent 12-month period the member was·to present a detailed statement of its progress and of the further policies and measures to be followed, with whatever modifications were needed.

Extended arrangements were to be limited to not more than three years. Each arrangement was to prescribe the total amount and the annual installments available. Drawings were to be phased over the period in which the arrangement was available and to be subject to suitable performance clauses implementing the agreed policies. Drawings outstanding in respect of the extended facility were not to exceed 140 percent of the member's quota or to be allowed to raise the Fund's holdings of the member's currency above 265 percent of the member's quota, apart from holdings obtained by the Fund as a result of purchases under the facilities relating to compensatory financing and buffer stock financing and under the oil facility. Amounts made available under the extended facility were to be repurchased as soon as the member had overcome its balance of payments problems and, in any event, within an outside range of four to eight years after each purchase, normally in 16 equal quarterly installments.

Members were to pay the same charges on amounts purchased under the extended facility as they did for use of the Fund's regular resources. Thus the charges as increased by the Fund's decision of June 13, 1974 (listed in Table 3) were applicable. They were 4 percent a year for the first year that a drawing was outstanding, rising by ½ of 1 percent a year for each succeeding year to 6 percent for drawings outstanding from four to five years, and then, in the instance of the extended facility under which drawings could be outstanding for up to eight years, up to a level of 6.5 percent a year. The only question with respect to charges for use of the extended facility was whether the additional ½ of 1 percent a year should continue to go up for the full period, that is, to 7 percent a year. It was decided that the progression would cease at the beginning of the sixth year at 6.5 percent a year. In 1977, in the course of a broad review of Fund charges, described in Chapter 29, the Executive Board raised the charges on use of the extended facility along with those on regular Fund drawings. Charges were then to range from 4.375 percent a year on drawings outstanding for less than one year to 6.875 percent a year on drawings outstanding from five to eight years.

The Fund was to review the decision on the extended facility in the light of experience and subsequent circumstances when the total amount of purchases that might be made under extended arrangements was equivalent to SDR 2 billion, and in any event not later than July 31, 1976.

THE FIRST EXTENDED ARRANGEMENT: KENYA

Despite the relative speed with which the extended facility was established in 1974, it was not used until ten months later, and by the end of 1978 only six extended arrangements had been approved. Of these, three were approved only in 1978.

The first extended arrangement was that agreed with Kenya in July 1975. The circumstances were a misallocation of real resources resulting from a prolonged use of policies oriented toward import substitution which the Kenyan authorities wanted to reverse.

From 1964, the year following independence, until 1974, Kenya had enjoyed a decade of substantial economic growth. Real gross domestic product increased on average by about 7 percent a year. Both the agricultural and industrial sectors of the economy grew rapidly. In addition, prices were stable, and until 1970 Kenya received large amounts of foreign loans and grants so that it consistently had surpluses in its overall balance of payments. Between 1970 and 1975, however, the balance of payments gradually deteriorated. Periodic deficits emerged, while the occasional surpluses that materialized were made possible only by restrictive monetary policies and the imposition of import and exchange restrictions. To finance recurrent balance of payments deficits, Kenyan authorities turned to using reserves, but by 1975 reserves had declined markedly.

Deterioration in the balance of payments was attributable to the country's industrialization policies, as well as to worsening terms of trade when prices of oil imports rose in 1974–75 and export prices fell following the end of the 1972–73 commodity boom. Since independence industrialization policies had been geared mainly to encourage industries that would supply domestic substitutes for imported consumer goods. Fiscal measures, including tariff protection, and domestic pricing policies had been aimed at fostering investment in manufacturing and construction to the relative neglect of agriculture. Government development expenditure also favored industry. Meanwhile, credit facilities for agriculture, especially for small landholders, remained inadequate. Prices for agricultural products were subject to regulation and held down. Thus, while domestic prices of exported agricultural commodities, such as coffee and tea, reflected world market prices, prices for agricultural products that were for the most part consumed domestically but had a substantial export potential (for example, wheat, maize, and meats) were much lower. In addition to these distortions, there were distortions between the prices of factors of production. Imported capital was relatively cheap. Consequently, capital-intensive rather than labor-intensive production techniques were encouraged. As a result, imports into Kenya of capital goods, as well as of consumer goods, continued to increase, while Kenya's exports did not rise nearly as rapidly. These circumstances were typical of countries pursuing inward-looking rather than outward-looking strategies of development.

A structure of production heavily oriented toward imports, considerable distortion in domestic prices, a slow growth of exports, and an expected further deterioration in the terms of trade all combined to suggest that Kenya's problems were likely to become worse in 1976 and later. The world recession of 1975, moreover, added to Kenya's problems. Accordingly, in July 1975 the Kenyan authorities undertook a three-year program supported by an extended arrangement with the Fund for SDR 67.2 million. Details of the program were worked out after extensive discussions with staff members both of the Fund and of the World Bank.

In May 1975, the World Bank, engaging like the Fund in an innovative undertaking, approved a program loan of $30 million, to be repaid over 25 years, to help Kenya adjust to its deteriorating balance of payments. This loan was to finance imports of essential raw materials and of capital and intermediate goods to help Kenya maintain a reasonable rate of growth while long-term changes were made in its economic structure.

Under the three-year program agreed with the Fund, the Kenyan Government planned to achieve an average annual rate of growth of 5 percent in real gross domestic product during 1975–78, to keep the rate of increases in domestic prices to about half of those in the prices of imports and to eliminate the need for balance of payments assistance after five years. To reach these targets, private consumption was to be contained by taxes that weighed heavily on consumption, by the enforcement of wage guidelines to ensure that the increase in real wages remained below the increase in per capita gross domestic product, and by measures, such as a higher rate of interest, to stimulate savings. The growth of public consumption was also to be restrained, with the Government planning to obtain a surplus of current revenues over current budgetary expenditures large enough to finance at least one third of its increasing capital expenditures. The Government also adopted a budget for the next three years in which the proportion of development expenditures devoted to agriculture, water development, land settlement, and cooperative development was considerably higher than in the past, while the proportion for highway and building construction was lowered.

The program also envisaged a strategy to induce a restructuring of private investment. The Kenyan officials proposed to the other two partner countries in what was then the East African Community—a common market composed of Kenya, Tanzania, and Uganda—that a systematic reform of the customs tariff be undertaken with a view to introducing uniform protective duties on import-competing industries and to levying duties on imports of most capital goods. Under the existing tariff, which taxed most consumer goods at rates between 30 and 50 percent and which permitted most capital goods and industrial inputs to enter free of duty, there was a substantial inducement for producers to undertake capital-intensive and import-intensive production. The proposals for reforming the custom

371

tariff aimed at correcting this situation. The three governments were also studying a modification of the existing regime of investment allowances which in effect gave a subsidy to certain capital goods, thereby encouraging the excessive use of machinery, most of which was imported. The private sector was also to be encouraged, through credit and other policies, to improve repair and maintenance services and to utilize existing productive capacity in order to reduce imports of capital goods.

This overall strategy for changing the structure of production was to be complemented by a credit policy designed to reduce total demand in the medium term, especially for imports, to levels consistent with the balance of payments target. Past developments in Kenya demonstrated that the demand for imports was responsive to monetary and credit policies.

The Kenyan authorities were also planning various institutional changes to strengthen the execution and monitoring of the medium-term program. For example, tax administration, especially of income and sales taxes, was to be improved through a program accelerating the recruitment and training of staff and through a program modernizing procedures and techniques for tax assessment and collection. As another illustration, in view of the need to monitor developments in the external payments position, Kenya was to improve its collection and compilation of balance of payments statistics.

In accordance with the Fund decision establishing the extended facility, Kenya had a 12-month program as well as the three-year program. The 12-month program included wage guidelines, objectives for total domestic credit with separate objectives for the expansion of government credit and of credit to the private sector, budgetary objectives, and a lifting of the government-administered prices for agricultural goods.

In all respects, Kenya's initial undertakings seemed to be consistent with the Fund's concept of what the extended facility was for. As events turned out, the Kenyan authorities used little of the money, drawing only the amount available for 1975, SDR 7.7 million. In 1976 and 1977, because of unexpected upsurges in the prices of coffee and tea, Kenya's two largest exports, the balance of payments turned into substantial surpluses.

Despite the lack of drawings from the Fund, many of the medium-term policies envisaged in the program were effectively implemented in the course of 1976 and 1977. Producer prices for various agricultural products were successively raised, leading to an improvement in the internal terms of trade in favor of agriculture, and government development expenditures were shifted toward agriculture. The exchange rate was depreciated in October 1975, and a wide-ranging import tariff reform was initiated to discourage excessive use of imports and to encourage the use of domestic raw materials and factors of production. Notwithstanding these efforts, the volume of Kenya's nontraditional exports did not grow during the program period. The performance in regard to demand-management policies was mixed.

In 1978 the balance of payments again turned sharply into deficit as export prices declined and imports increased. Hence, after the extended arrangement ended in the middle of 1978, Kenya requested a stand-by arrangement in the first credit tranche, which the Fund granted in November 1978.

Since the extended facility was new and experimental, the management and staff and the Executive Board examined the Fund's experience with this first extended arrangement to draw some conclusions. They agreed that Kenya's circumstances were in accord with the intent of the facility and that Kenya's performance had been satisfactory. They noted, however, that the outcome of the program was heavily influenced by weather conditions and world market prices for Kenya's principal exports. Thus, the first arrangement under the Fund's newly established extended facility once more confirmed the traditional experience of countries dependent on the export of primary products that the basic conditions governing the domestic production of, and the world market prices for, these exports determined the external payments position of these countries much more than did any financial and economic planning.

EXTENDED ARRANGEMENT WITH THE PHILIPPINES

The second extended arrangement, approved in April 1976, was with the Philippines. Like most other developing countries, the economic problems of the Philippines stemmed both from the expansionary fiscal and monetary policies that had been pursued for some years and from structural problems that had gradually emerged by the 1970s. From the early 1950s, growing public expenditures usually exceeded the country's limited capacity to raise tax revenue and the Government frequently ran sizable budget deficits. Budget deficits, moreover, were customarily financed by the banking system, and the Central Bank was unable to pursue an effective monetary policy.

The second part of the Philippine economic problem, like that of other developing countries, was structural. By the 1970s, the Philippines was experiencing marked distortions in its production patterns because of the heavy emphasis placed in earlier years on the development of import-substituting and capital-intensive industries. It was to this structural part of the Philippine economic problem also that the extended arrangement of 1976 was addressed.

The roots of the Philippine structural problem were similar to those of many Latin American countries and not dissimilar to those of Kenya, described above. From the end of World War II and the achievement of political independence until about 1967, the Philippines relied on the development strategy commonly used by developing countries at the time. The strategy, referred to as an inward-looking strategy, encouraged the production of domestic substitutes for imported manufactured consumer goods, such as textiles, clothing, footwear, processed foods, soaps, and paper products. Imports of competing goods were usually restricted to protect infant domestic industries.

The strategy worked well during the 1950s. Domestic production of many finished consumer goods expanded rapidly and real gross domestic product grew on average by 6.5 percent a year. During the 1960s, however, the same problems that many Latin American countries were encountering began to emerge. Once the replacement of imports of relatively simple nondurable consumer goods by domestic products was largely completed, domestic demand did not grow sufficiently to maintain industrial growth at the rates previously achieved. Rates of growth started to decline. Domestic manufacturing remained dependent on imports of raw materials and of intermediate goods, making for a large import content of domestic production. Despite a substantial depreciation of the peso as a result of a floating rate for a time in 1962—from the rate of two pesos per U.S. dollar established in 1946, an exchange rate even incorporated in the Philippine Constitution, to a rate of 3.90 pesos per dollar—export earnings of the Philippines did not grow to any notable degree. Philippine exports continued to consist mainly of traditional primary commodities: coconut products (such as copra), sugar, fruits and vegetables, forest products (such as Philippine mahogany), and copper concentrates. As time went on, balance of payments problems developed as imports, especially of raw materials and of intermediate goods, rose and as exports failed to increase proportionately.

By the middle of the 1960s the limits of growth through the import-substitution strategy had clearly been reached, and a new set of policies was needed to maintain satisfactory growth rates and to keep the external payments position in bounds. Beginning in 1967, the Government consciously reversed its development strategy and adopted a strategy oriented toward the expansion of exports.

Meanwhile, the country's balance of payments situation deteriorated sharply, especially in 1969, an election year, when expansionary monetary and fiscal policies were pursued. To finance the 1969 balance of payments deficit, the Philippines had to engage heavily in foreign borrowing, and external indebtedness suddenly grew to a substantial amount and became a potential problem. Because of the seriousness of the balance of payments situation, following the re-election of President Ferdinand Marcos, additional economic measures were taken, primarily in 1970. A floating exchange rate was introduced which quickly produced an exchange depreciation of more than 60 percent, with the rate reaching close to 6.50 pesos per dollar. Tighter demand-management policies were put into effect, and a comprehensive system of regulation of foreign borrowing was introduced, including a law limiting the amount of debt service payable.

Following the introduction of martial law in 1972, the Government took further economic measures designed to augment tax revenues, increase public expenditure in favor of infrastructure in agriculture, and bring about organizational and institutional improvements in the governmental and financial sectors of the economy. In 1973 a tariff reform was introduced. During all this period (from 1962 onward), the Philippines had a series of consecutive one-year stand-by arrangements with the Fund.

The economic measures taken in 1970–72, together with the boom in world prices for primary commodities in 1972–73, brought about an approximate balance in the Philippine balance of payments in 1970–72 and a surplus in 1973. Also, in 1973 the rate of growth accelerated. However, as a result of the increase in oil prices at the start of 1974 and of the recession in industrial countries, the Philippine economy suffered a serious setback. The balance of payments surplus of 1973 turned into a large deficit and the rate of growth dropped. Moreover, despite the changed emphasis of government policy, manufacturing industries continued to be capital intensive and heavily dependent on imports. Domestic industries, therefore, did not alleviate unemployment in the Philippines nor did they strengthen the balance of payments position, which was expected to worsen as the terms of trade declined still further during the next few years. In these circumstances, it was evident that balance of payments equilibrium in the medium term, that is, through about 1978, could be achieved only by curtailing growth and by resorting to still more import restrictions, unless basic adjustments in policy were made to generate additional domestic savings and effect structural changes.

Against this background, in 1975 the Philippine authorities undertook a thoroughgoing review of development strategy in consultation with the World Bank. In March 1976, they developed a medium-term program for 1976–78, in support of which the Fund granted a second arrangement under the new extended Fund facility. The extended arrangement approved for the Philippines was for SDR 217 million. The program on whose basis the extended arrangement was granted aimed at achieving a more balanced and accelerated economic growth that would also provide social equity and balance of payments viability within a few years without recourse to excessive external borrowing or to new restrictions on imports or current payments. The program contained three macroeconomic targets: an average annual real growth rate of 7 percent, annual average increases in consumer prices of no more than 7 percent, and a gradual reduction in the current account deficit to a manageable level by 1978. It aimed also at achieving a shift from manufacturing industries producing import substitutes to those producing for export and a shift from capital-intensive to employment-intensive production. Supported by an expanding public investment program, greater self-sufficiency in agriculture and energy was also to be attained, as well as a more equitable distribution of income. Despite widespread and extensive unemployment in the Philippines and a recognized need for redistribution of income, the extended Fund facility program did not contain explicit targets for either employment or income distribution.

The objectives of this medium-term program were to be achieved by a mix of policies. Exchange rate policy was to be kept flexible so as to support export expansion, and tariffs were to be "rationalized." Measures to augment private savings, as well as to enlarge tax revenues for the financing of larger public expenditures for investment, were to be introduced. The system of fiscal incentives was to be restructured. Administered prices were to be adjusted so as to reflect market conditions more adequately. Demand-management policies were to be directed toward reducing inflation and containing imports. The annual programs included performance criteria in the form of quantitative limits on credit expansion by the banking system, on expansion of net credit to the public sector, on declines in the net foreign assets of the banking system, which reflected capital flight, and on new foreign borrowing.

As 1978 closed, the Philippine arrangement was nearing an end. The Philippine authorities had purchased the entire amount available under the extended Fund arrangement. The Fund in general regarded the member as having achieved considerable adjustment during the three-year program. While the original targets had not been met, the revised objectives had been attained despite deteriorating external circumstances. Thus, economic growth was maintained at a satisfactory rate, the tax effort was increased, more resources were directed into investment without reducing per capita consumption, increases in domestic prices were relatively moderate, the current account deficit was reduced, and the overall balance of payments position was strengthened.

The use of fiscal policy was regarded as crucial in achieving adjustment. The overall budget deficit was reduced both by restricting public expenditures and by introducing new revenue-generating measures. As noted earlier in this section, the fiscal area was especially in need of strengthening to enable the Government to avoid running budget deficits financed by the banking system. Several packages of new revenue measures were introduced and implemented. These measures yielded substantial additional tax revenue and made feasible much higher levels of public investment. In addition to increasing aggregate revenues, the tax measures made for a more rational and efficient revenue system and for its greater responsiveness to increases in national income. In addition, changes in the incentive system, in administered pricing policies, and in export promotion devices were effectively used to improve resource allocation, especially in expanding nontraditional manufactured exports. The proportion of these exports in total Philippine exports, a significant indicator of the structural changes effected in the Philippine economy, more than doubled, from about 12 percent in 1970–75 to 25 percent in 1978. Nontraditional manufactured products which the Philippines exported by 1978 included textiles, garments, footwear, electrical and electronics equipment, a variety of handicrafts made from local raw materials, chemical products, cement, and furniture made of wood and rattan.

From its experience with the Philippines, the Fund concluded that, as in the instance of Kenya, external factors were decisive in the success of the program. A critical external factor was a sharp fall in the world market price of sugar beginning in 1976. This fall so weakened the Philippine balance of payments position that the Philippine authorities became more determined than ever to develop nontraditional exports. A second external factor helping the program was that the Philippine authorities were able to borrow substantial amounts from the world capital markets at favorable terms. The Managing Director and the staff and the members of the Executive Board also concluded that flexibility was essential in the implementation of a successful extended arrangement. As the Philippine program was implemented, many changes were made in both the program targets and the performance clauses of the arrangement. Members of the Executive Board from developing members, including Ernest Leung (Philippines), Wila D. Mung'omba (Zambia), and Mr. Kharmawan, insisted that flexibility on the part of the Fund was instrumental in making the extended arrangement with the Philippines successful. Meanwhile, officials in the Fund were also beginning to think that for a major external imbalance a period of three years might be relatively short for a country to effect basic changes in its economic structure.

THE EXAMPLE OF MEXICO

The third extended arrangement which the Fund approved was for Mexico. Approved in October 1976, it was to begin in January 1977 and to last for three calendar years. The amount involved was SDR 518 million, equivalent to 140 percent of Mexico's quota, the maximum allowed under the decision, and the same percentage of quota as had been granted to Kenya and the Philippines. The starting date of January 1, 1977 was selected to follow a change in government on December 1, 1976, when President-elect José López Portillo was to take over from President Luis Echeverría, who had been in office since 1970. Since Mr. López Portillo had been Secretary of Finance and Public Credit in President Echeverría's Administration before he had resigned to run for the presidency, he was intimately familiar with the details of Mexico's financial crisis.

The Mexican experience in 1977–79 can be regarded as the most suitable use of the Fund's extended facility. There was a severe crisis of confidence in the currency, resulting from an overextended public budget and a very large budget deficit, aggravated by massive flights of capital out of Mexico. To stem capital flight and loss of reserves, the currency was devalued in September 1976. Following devaluation, there was need for outside financial authorities, such as the Fund, to demonstrate that the Mexican authorities had sufficient foreign exchange resources to hold the new rate. Financial support was necessary for longer than the usual one-year stand-by arrangement in order to give the Mexican authorities time to revamp their fiscal operations thoroughly. To augment revenues they had both to cut expenditures drastically and to introduce new forms of taxation.

Prior to World War II the Mexican economy was based principally on agriculture and mining. After the mid-1950s, however, Mexico became increasingly industrialized because of a growing domestic market, a long-range import substitution policy, and the active promotion of exports of industrial products. During the 1950s the construction, mineral extraction, and manufacturing sectors of the economy provided the dynamism for an overall growth rate of real gross domestic product averaging annually about 5.5 percent. In the 1960s the economy gained still further momentum. Real gross domestic product, spurred by unusual growth in electricity generation, in manufacturing, in construction, and in petroleum production, increased by an average of more than 7 percent a year. Meanwhile the price level remained relatively stable.

Beginning in the 1970s, however, a number of economic problems began to emerge. Acute shortages of domestic supplies arose, including shortages of food. Over the years agriculture had been declining relative to manufacturing, and by the early 1970s, Mexico's official pricing policies for agriculture, combined with unfavorable weather conditions in 1974, resulted in a severe shortage of domestic food crops. Large imports of food became necessary to supplement domestic output. Other supply problems and industrial bottlenecks began to emerge, particularly in the steel industry, in petrochemicals, in cement production, and in the generation of electricity.

Overwhelming budgetary problems developed. A distinguishing feature of the Administration of President Echeverría was its emphasis on redistributing income and on supporting the long-neglected subsistence farming sector. The public sector was assigned a number of new responsibilities and many more state enterprises were created. Emphasis gradually shifted from considerations of economic productivity to considerations of social content, and to an increasing extent the numerous state enterprises were not necessarily run so as to cover their costs of operation. As a result appreciable increases in public expenditures were not offset by increased production. The budget deficit more than tripled and was financed mostly by recourse to the domestic banking system and by borrowing from abroad. This situation caused increasing strain on real resources and unprecedented rates of inflation.

Then came the higher oil prices of 1974 and recession in industrial countries. The recession in general, and in the United States in particular, reduced the export volume of certain products from Mexico and caused a decline in receipts from tourism, border transactions, and remittances of earnings of Mexican workers in the United States. As domestic inflation continued, rising prices led to further and more frequent adjustments of wages, which in turn caused still further inflation. Consequently, the international competitiveness of Mexican goods abroad progressively eroded.

These developments caused a substantial weakening of the Mexican balance of payments position. The current account deficit grew substantially and was financed by heavy foreign borrowing. By 1975 Mexico's external debt reached a total of $15 billion. To reduce the balance of payments deficit, the Mexican authorities resorted to quantitative restrictions on imports, although the traditional freedom that Mexico had usually given to exchange transactions was maintained and exchange controls were avoided.

A major crisis of confidence in the Mexican peso followed. Throughout late 1975 and most of 1976, devaluation was anticipated. There were large flights of capital from Mexico into the United States, accompanied by a growing conversion of peso-denominated financial assets into U.S. dollar-denominated assets. In other words, Mexican citizens preferred to denominate their bank deposits and other assets in dollars rather than in Mexican pesos, a phenomenon termed "dollarization."

In this crisis of confidence in the economy, the Mexican authorities in September 1976 undertook a number of steps, including coming to the Fund for assistance. In a courageous move, they devalued the peso. After more than 22 years of maintaining the same rate for the Mexican peso in terms of U.S. dollars, they decided to allow the peso to float independently. The rate in terms of U.S. dollars per peso immediately depreciated by at least 40 percent. From the Fund, they requested an immediate purchase in the first credit tranche for SDR 134.125 million and an extended arrangement to start on January 1, 1977, subject to approval by the new Government. Mexico had not drawn on the Fund's resources for more than 15 years, since August 1961. The prime objective of the Mexican authorities was to restore confidence at home and abroad. Confidence was a matter of critical importance to a country as heavily dependent on official borrowing in international financial markets as Mexico had become.

The medium-term program developed by the Mexican authorities had five major objectives. The first objective was to resume a rate of real economic growth of about 7 percent a year, the rate attained in the 1950s and 1960s. Such a growth rate was important in order to increase employment, since unemployment had become a critical problem in Mexico. Because increases in employment had not kept pace with increases in the labor force, open unemployment as well as disguised or underemployment had risen appreciably. Open unemployment had risen, for example, from 3.7 percent of the labor force at the end of 1969 to over 6 percent at the end of 1973. Then, when the rate of economic growth dropped, open unemployment increased further, to over 10.5 percent by the end of 1976. Moreover, Mexican authorities estimated that more than 40 percent of the total labor force was underemployed.

The second and third objectives of the program were aimed at the reduction of domestic inflation. The second objective was to raise domestic capital formation to a level consistent with a 7 percent a year growth target. The third objective was to encourage domestic savings to finance such investment with reduced reliance on foreign savings (that is, on borrowing from abroad).

There were two other goals, one for the domestic economy and one for the external economy. For the domestic economy, the goal was to set the stage for a domestic price behavior that permitted a more equitable distribution of income and at the same time preserved the international competitiveness of Mexican goods abroad. For the external economy, the goal was to ensure a balance of payments position that was sustainable over the medium term.

The principal instrument for implementing this program was fiscal restraint. The public sector was to be reduced from 8.2 percent of gross domestic product in 1976 to 2.5 percent in 1979. The number of public sector enterprises was to be reduced and those remaining were to be put on a more efficient basis. Public expenditures were to be cut drastically and measures to enlarge revenues were to be enacted. The program also included pricing policies and wage guidelines to help contain inflation and enhance international competitiveness, as well as monetary measures to stimulate private savings. Given Mexico's external debt position, cautious debt management was also regarded as critical. The program contained projections of key economic variables for the entire period. Ceilings were set on the expansion of net domestic assets of the Bank of Mexico and on the overall deficit of the public sector. With the aim of ensuring an accumulation of net international reserves, the program also included as a performance criterion a clause stating that the increase in net international reserves be no less than the increase in the currency issues of the Bank of Mexico.

As of the end of 1978, the program had been implemented successfully for two years and had begun to produce impressive results. Public sector enterprises had been put on a sound financial basis. "Dollarization" had been reversed. Private financial savings had increased. The rate of economic growth had accelerated. The rate of inflation had declined and the balance of payments position had improved. Confidence in the Mexican economy both at home and abroad had been restored. As a result of its better balance of payments position, in 1978 Mexico repurchased the Fund's holdings of Mexican pesos stemming from Mexico's use of the Fund's resources.

An important factor in the successful implementation of Mexico's medium-term program under the extended arrangement was its success in altering the fiscal situation. The sharp decrease in public expenditures was in fact probably the single most important element in reducing inflation in Mexico and in restoring confidence in the Government's ability to operate its public sector on a sound financial basis. In addition, much larger fiscal revenues did emerge from the measures enacted.

Nonetheless, in the Mexican case, as in the instances of Kenya and the Philippines, the success of the extended arrangement was attributable in considerable part to external factors. While the program was in force, large oil reserves were discovered in Mexico and petroleum emerged as a major source of exports. The new export outlook implied a sizable increase in Mexico's capacity to import and to service external debt so that the country's international creditworthiness was greatly enhanced. The discovery of oil reserves was so significant that the 1978 program under the extended arrangement was modified to accommodate additional investment expenditure in the energy sector, publicly owned in Mexico, that would allow for an accelerated exploitation of the newly discovered oil.[2]

EXTENDED ARRANGEMENTS WITH JAMAICA, EGYPT, AND HAITI

As 1978 ended the extended facility was being used more. In the last months of 1978, the Fund approved three additional arrangements—for SDR 200 million with

---

[2]A brief review of the progress toward adjustment made under the extended arrangement as of early 1978 can be found in Manuel Guitián and Carl-Johan Lindgren, "Mexico's Adjustment Program Shows Success in Reducing Inflation Rate, Payments' Deficit," *IMF Survey* (Washington), Vol. 7 (April 17, 1978), pp. 119–21.

Jamaica in June, with Egypt for SDR 600 million in July, and with Haiti for SDR 32.2 million in October. The amounts approved for Jamaica and Egypt represented 270 percent and 263 percent of their quotas, respectively, almost twice the 140 percent quota specified in the decision establishing the facility.

The economic problems and maladjustments in Jamaica and Egypt and the programs introduced to accompany their extended arrangements were similar to those of Kenya, the Philippines, and Mexico. Large fiscal deficits were being financed by domestic bank credit. Price and cost distortions were widespread as a consequence of heavy subsidies on consumption items and of extensive price controls. Public expenditures and incentives for private industry were biased in favor of capital-intensive and import-intensive investment. An overvalued currency and low procurement prices for agricultural products discouraged agricultural exports. Large balance of payments deficits were causing not only tighter import and payment restrictions but also the accumulation of substantial short-term foreign debt. As balance of payments pressures mounted and domestic bottlenecks increased, economic growth slowed down, and unemployment rose. The oil price increase of 1973–74 and the worldwide recession of 1975 exacerbated these difficulties.

The programs adopted had the same objectives of raising economic growth, lowering unemployment, holding down inflation, and establishing a viable balance of payments position over the medium term, while a liberal exchange and trade system was maintained or restored. To achieve these objectives, first priority was given to measures aimed at removing distortions in relative prices. The most important of these measures was exchange rate devaluation. Other measures included relaxation of price controls, increases in the administered prices for agricultural products, and reduction of consumer subsidies. In order to reduce imports, there were to be measures to promote the use of domestic resources. The objectives of resuming higher rates of economic growth and of restoring balance of payments equilibrium called for increases in investments, coupled with improvements in public sector finances and in the performance of overall savings. To this end, public sector deficits were to be reduced both by increasing revenue and by reducing expenditures, and private saving and investment were to be fostered by measures providing incentives to save and invest. Finally, there were to be measures aimed at reducing the ratio of overall consumption to gross domestic product.

The extended arrangement with Haiti was different. It came within the second category to which the Fund's extended facility could apply, namely, "an economy characterized by slow growth and an inherently weak balance of payments position which prevents pursuit of an active development policy." Haiti had a predominantly agricultural economy, heavily dependent on shifting weather patterns and fluctuations in the world price of coffee, the country's main export. Because of the openness of the economy and its vulnerability to external shocks, economic management had traditionally emphasized fiscal and monetary policies consistent with the maintenance of external payments balance. However, as a majority of the population lived in a rural subsistence economy that generated little or no savings, capital formation had been insufficient to ensure adequate economic growth. Haiti's access to international capital markets was very limited, which also constrained additional domestic investment.

Beginning in 1975, however, with the aid of sizable foreign assistance, the Government embarked upon a major public investment effort in a five-year development plan for 1977–81. To achieve the planned increase in investment, domestic savings, particularly in the public sector, would have to be raised considerably. The authorities recognized that the requisite mobilization of domestic resources required a thorough revamping of the entire fiscal system. They therefore launched a comprehensive program aimed at a complete fiscal reform to be implemented in stages. Fiscal reform was continued in 1976 and 1977 and was a pivotal element in the extended arrangement granted by the Fund in October 1978.

THE FACILITY REVIEWED

When the Executive Board reviewed the extended facility in 1976, the primary concern of most Executive Directors was that it had been used much less than originally expected. The staff had two major explanations why relatively few members had requested extended arrangements. First and foremost, unlike what had been anticipated in 1974 when the facility was created, balance of payments financing had proved readily available for most developing members. The Fund itself had provided members with drawings under the oil facility and with drawings in the first credit tranche and under the liberalized compensatory financing facility. Also, alternative sources of financing to the Fund had been readily obtainable. OPEC provided a new source of payments financing for some developing countries, and the participation of private commercial banks in financing the balance of payments of numerous developing countries had become substantial. These alternative means of financing carried very limited conditionality, and the absence of conditionality seemed to have weighed heavily on the decisions of many developing members to use these alternative sources rather than come to the Fund.

A second reason why the extended facility had been little used was that its use required changes in the operational approach of both member governments and the Fund. An extended program involved issues of broader scope than those normally considered in annual stand-by arrangements. Agencies concerned with investment and pricing policies, such as planning, trade, and agricultural ministries, had to be involved in the programming exercise. It was also necessary for the Fund staff to collaborate closely with the staff of the World Bank. Consequently, working out possible extended arrangements would take time, both on the part of the officials of member governments and on the part of the Fund staff.

Several Executive Directors elected by developing members emphasized another reason why, in their view, the extended facility had not been used more:

the conditionality that the Fund attached to its use was too strict. They stressed that members had to undertake difficult and basic adjustments in their domestic economic policies to receive only a small amount of financial assistance. Mr. Yaméogo concluded that the extended facility needed to be liberalized. He reminded the Executive Directors that the Fund had had a similar experience with the compensatory financing facility. Only two members had drawn under the compensatory financing facility between 1963 when it was first introduced and 1966 when it was liberalized; thereafter drawings under the facility expanded considerably.[3]

In contrast to the Executive Directors from developing members, those appointed or elected by industrial members and by more developed primary producing members regarded the operation of the extended facility as satisfactory. They pointed out that the medium-term programs involved were necessarily far-reaching and complex and that it would take some time before members could plan such programs. They also emphasized that the Fund's extended facility was to be regarded as complementary to, rather than a duplication of, the World Bank's program lending. The Fund should not rush into too many of these arrangements without careful coordination with the World Bank.

After this review, the Executive Board decided to make no changes in the facility but to review it again when the total amount of the purchases that could be made under extended arrangements reached SDR 2 billion.[4] This review came shortly after the end of 1978.[5]

In conclusion, it would seem that as 1978 drew to a close the Fund had not yet had much experience with extended arrangements. There had been only six cases, one of which had not run its full course and three were just getting under way. So far it seemed that external factors had been as important, if not more important, determinants of the success of the programs as had changes in economic policy. Implementation of basic changes in economic policies seemed to require longer than three years. The most important surprise, however, was that the extended facility, heralded as a new longer-term financial arrangement in the Fund to assist its developing members, had not begun a widespread demand for the Fund's resources.

---

[3]See *History, 1966–71*, Vol. I, pp. 263–67.

[4]E.B. Decision No. 5220-(76/144), September 20, 1976; Vol. III below, p. 506.

[5]It was held in June 1979, when the Executive Board once more decided that no modifications in the facility should be made and that the facility should be reviewed again when the possibility of members' access to the supplementary financing facility, just then coming into being, came to an end.

PART FOUR

The Fund in a
Troubled World Economy:
The Setting After 1973

*"Clearly, there can be no stable and
just peace or universal progress
without the solution of pressing
economic problems affecting the vital
interests of numerous countries."*

—Josip Broz Tito, President of Yugoslavia, addressing the
Board of Governors, in Belgrade, October 2, 1979

CHAPTER 20

Shaping Policies Amid a Troubled World Economy

*I*N RETROSPECT, 1973 can be seen as the economic turning point of the 1970s. The problems of inflation and balance of payments disequilibria in industrial countries that had developed in the late 1960s suddenly attained new dimensions. Additional problems of underutilization of productive capacity in industrial countries, much larger payments deficits of non-oil developing countries, and floating exchange rates for the major currencies emerged. In the first half of 1973 gross national product (GNP) deflators for the industrial countries, a measure of inflation, increased on average by over 6 percent (annual rate), more than double the 2.5 percent average of the early 1960s. In the second half of 1973, they averaged 10 percent (annual rate), signaling the onset of double-digit inflation. As the inflationary upsurge of 1973 in industrial countries spread to the more developed primary producing countries and the developing countries, for the first time inflation became a worldwide problem. The unusual coexistence with inflation of underutilization of resources also began late in 1973 with a marked slowdown of output expansion in industrial countries. The growth of real gross national product in industrial countries as a group dropped from an annual rate of 8 percent in the first half of 1973 to about 3 percent in the second half, in contrast to annual growth rates in the 1960s of 4.5–5 percent.

Higher oil prices announced at the end of 1973 were expected to produce unprecedented disequilibria in international payments. The Fund was projecting current surpluses for the oil exporting countries in 1974 of $65 billion, 13 times larger than in 1973, and corresponding deficits for oil importing countries. It was likely that the magnitudes involved would tax the capacity of existing financial institutions and arrangements for recycling funds from countries with surpluses to those with deficits. The oil price increases were also expected to aggravate both inflationary and recessionary trends in the world economy, as both price advances and cutoffs in production were likely.

These new problems, moreover, were emerging shortly after the widespread adoption of floating exchange rates in March 1973. Even in the few months that floating rates had existed, exchange rates had been subject to substantial fluctuations and exchange markets had been highly vulnerable, reacting nervously to unexpected events. With the onset of massive payments disequilibria, there was danger that competitive depreciation and unstable exchange rates could reach the scale of the 1930s.

It was against this background that the Committee of Twenty in January 1974 abandoned its efforts to negotiate a comprehensive reform of the international monetary system in favor of establishing general directions in which the system could evolve, and the Fund took a number of emergency and interim actions, as described in Chapters 15–19. As time passed, problems in the world economy persisted. Only toward the end of the decade policymakers and economists appreciated the pervasive nature of world economic problems and the need for basic structural solutions. Meanwhile, as they resorted to short-term policies, it became evident that precise guidelines for action were more difficult to formulate and the issues remained controversial. As the demand-management and fine-tuning strategies used so successfully in the 1950s and 1960s failed, economists evolved vastly differing theories of appropriate action. From the experiences of the 1970s, policymakers and economists profoundly changed commonly accepted views regarding the role that central authorities should play in the economy and were obliged to re-examine postulates taken for granted during the 1950s and 1960s.

In these circumstances the Fund had to shape its policies from 1974 through 1978. A brief summary of world economic problems from 1974 to 1978, as presented in the Fund's Annual Reports, is thus helpful for understanding the Fund's activities and policies described in subsequent chapters.

THE FUND'S VIEW OF WORLD ECONOMIC PROBLEMS

At mid-1974, the world economy was in the throes of virulent inflation, economic growth was decelerating, and a massive disequilibrium emerged in international payments. Characterizing the situation as "perhaps the most complex and serious set of economic problems to confront national governments and the international community since the end of World War II," the Fund appealed for "international cooperation of a quality rarely achieved in the past."[1] While Fund officials recognized that diagnosis of the balance of expansionary and contractionary forces in the world economy was uncommonly difficult, they considered inflation as the dominant problem, deserving the highest priority. In the first half of 1974 price increases in industrial countries, as measured by the comprehensive GNP deflators, had risen to an overall annual rate of 12 percent, and inflation was also rising in most other countries. Underlying demand still appeared expansionary, and most major countries expected an upturn in real gross national product during the second half of

---

[1] *Annual Report, 1974*, p. 1.

the year, although the possibility of an international recession was not ruled out. In its Annual Report the Fund emphasized that "inflation is a world-wide problem that must be dealt with before it gets further out of hand," and in his opening address to the Board of Governors at the 1974 Annual Meeting on September 30, Mr. Witteveen reiterated the need to bring inflation under control.[2]

As matters developed, judgments about the trend of real economic activity were wide of the mark for most industrial countries. The slowdown that began in 1974 developed into an unexpectedly severe recession, characterized by exceptionally high rates of unemployment. Real gross national product in industrial countries as a group, which had risen steadily by at least 6–7 percent a year in 1972–73, actually fell by an average annual rate of 4–4.5 percent in the second half of 1974 and the first half of 1975. Substantial declines in industrial production took place in nearly all major industrial countries. Unemployment and slack use of productive capacity in the large industrial countries reached levels not experienced since the 1930s. In addition to using official employment statistics, the Fund staff sought to measure economic slack more comprehensively by the concept of a gap between actual and "potential" GNP.[3] The underuse of resources indicated by this staff measure was especially large in the United States and Japan, some 12–14 percent, and ranged from 5 to 8 percent in Canada, France, the Federal Republic of Germany, Italy, and the United Kingdom.

The impact of the recession, like that of the preceding boom and inflation, had radiated to nonindustrial countries, primarily through changes in trade and in associated financial flows but also through worsening terms of trade. The current account situation of the non-oil developing countries, in particular, deteriorated sharply, going from $9 billion in 1973 to $28 billion in 1974, and was projected to reach $35 billion in 1975. The sheer size of the potential aggregate deficit cast doubt on the ability and willingness of the countries concerned to find adequate financing.

Nevertheless, the Fund found encouraging signs. Expansionary policies had been adopted in a number of industrial countries to foster a resumption of economic growth. Progress in stemming inflation had been better than anticipated largely because of the world recession. The problem of financing the external current account deficits associated with the oil price increase proved—again partly because of the recession—less intractable than initially feared. But because prices were still rising in most countries at rates that were high by historical standards, the Fund advised industrial countries to be cautious in taking measures to stimulate their economies for fear of reactivating an inflationary psychology. For the non-oil developing countries, external financing loomed as the critical problem, and the Fund called attention to the urgent need for sizable flows of capital on concessionary terms or of outright grant assistance.

---

[2] *Annual Report, 1974*, p. 9, and *Summary Proceedings, 1974*, p. 19.

[3] Potential GNP purports to measure what an economy would produce if all its resources were "fully" utilized, consistent with reasonable price stability, given existing technology and institutional arrangements.

The year 1975 also saw large changes in the global payments pattern. The current account surplus of the oil exporting countries was sharply reduced, from $67 billion in 1974 to $35 billion in 1975. Although their export earnings were reduced by the recession as well as by oil conservation in importing countries, most oil exporting countries did not have to restrain imports. There was a large swing in the combined current account balance of the industrial countries from a sizable deficit in 1974 to a surplus of about $19 billion in 1975. However, this surplus was quite unevenly distributed. The surpluses of the United States and the Federal Republic of Germany alone exceeded the total. Canada and the United Kingdom in particular had sizable deficits. The current account deficit of the non-oil developing countries reached $38 billion, and they borrowed heavily, as in 1974, as well as reduced their reserves in an effort to sustain import volume in the face of rising costs of manufactured goods, sharply increased oil and food prices, and the weakness in export markets.

By mid-1976 prospects for the world economy, particularly for recovery in the industrial world, seemed brighter. Real gross national product in the industrial countries rose by 6.8 percent in the first half of 1976, and the overall rate of price increase dropped to 6.7 percent. The volume of world trade, which had declined by some 4–5 percent from 1974 to 1975, rose at an annual rate of about 10 percent in the first half of 1976.

By past standards, however, both unemployment and inflation remained exceptionally high for the early phase of a cyclical upswing. Although demand and output were not rising fast enough to reduce unemployment and excess industrial capacity to acceptable levels, the expansion was sufficiently brisk to arouse widespread concern about the danger of renewed acceleration of price increases. The Fund continued to favor cautious management of aggregate demand as essential for bringing down inflation and eliminating inflationary expectations.

For the year 1976, the global pattern of international payments was much improved over what had been expected in 1974 just after the oil price rise. The current account surplus of the major oil exporting countries was $40 billion, down $25 billion from the sudden surplus in 1974, and the combined current account position of the industrial countries was almost in balance. Dramatic reductions had occurred in the oil-related deficits of the United States, the Federal Republic of Germany, and Japan. The other industrial countries, however, continued to run a current account deficit of some $55 billion. The weakness of the Italian and U.K. positions, associated with high rates of domestic inflation, was particularly evident. The current account deficit of the non-oil developing countries, while lower than that of 1975, was still $26 billion, three times larger in nominal terms than it was during the late 1960s and early 1970s. (By mid-1977, the Fund was expressing concern that in meeting the emergency pressures of the period since 1973 many of these countries had relied on external borrowing at rates and costs unsustainable either from their own standpoint or from that of their creditors.)[4]

---

[4]*Annual Report, 1977*, p. 20.

This satisfactory recovery encountered an unexpected and worrisome slow-down in the second half of 1976, setting off a period of slow economic growth in the industrial world. The rate of increase in real gross national product from the first to the second half of 1976 fell to an average of 3 percent. By the second half of 1977, the European industrial countries had lost virtually all their previous upward momentum; only the United States, among the larger industrial countries, was expanding output sufficiently to reduce economic slack. Real gross national product in industrial countries in 1977 increased by only 4 percent a year.

The same sluggish overall growth in the industrial world continued in 1978. According to Fund staff estimates of the gap between actual and potential output, the average degree of underutilization in the manufacturing sector of the seven largest industrial countries (Canada, France, the Federal Republic of Germany, Italy, Japan, the United Kingdom, and the United States) was of the order of 10–11 percent from mid-1977 to mid-1978. Though smaller than that during the recession of 1975, the gap had not narrowed since the first half of 1976. Countries differed, however, in the extent of underutilization of capacity, from almost none in the United States, to a moderate level in the Federal Republic of Germany and Canada, and to very high levels for most other countries. Historically high unemployment persisted—especially in Europe—and the growth of world trade slowed. At the same time, despite some easing of inflation in industrial Europe and Japan, inflation continued to mar the economic performances of many countries, both in the industrial group and especially among the primary producers.

By 1978, the concentration of current account surpluses in a small group of major oil exporting countries had been greatly reduced through the rise in their purchases of foreign goods and services. Moreover, as described in Chapter 18, current account deficits of non-oil producing countries had declined considerably from the alarming levels reached under the combined influence of the 1973–74 oil price increase and the international recession of 1974–75. Financing for the reduced aggregate deficit of those countries was proving more readily available than anticipated two or three years earlier. However, some serious imbalances within the group of industrial countries had arisen. The United States had a current account deficit of $10 billion, while other industrial countries had large surpluses. The Federal Republic of Germany had a surplus of over $13 billion, Italy of more than $9 billion, France of well over $5 billion, and the United Kingdom of nearly $4 billion. Most striking, however, was the strength of the Japanese current account position, which had gone from near balance in 1975 to a surplus of $18 billion in 1978. The annual figures are less revealing than partial-year figures, especially for the United States and Japan. The U.S. current account had shifted steadily from a large surplus in the second half of 1975 ($20 billion at an annual rate) to a large deficit (at an annual rate of $28 billion) in the first quarter of 1978, while the Japanese current account had moved from approximate balance to a surplus of $20 billion (annual rate) over roughly the same period. Moreover, the non-oil developing countries still had a combined deficit in 1978 of over $31 billion.

The problems of the world economy were reflected in the operation of the exchange rate system. In the years reviewed here, there were substantial changes in the structure of exchange rates and significant periodic short-run fluctuations in these rates.

THE FUND'S RESPONSES

The Fund had three primary responses to these difficulties. The first was to enlarge the use of its resources. Following the introduction in 1974 and early 1975 of the oil facility and the extended facility described in earlier chapters, the Fund liberalized its compensatory financing facility at the end of 1975 and from then on approved many more stand-by arrangements. To raise the necessary money, members' quotas in the Fund were enlarged twice within three years, and a supplementary financing facility was introduced, financed with borrowed funds.

As use of its resources increased, the Fund made an important change in its policies. From early 1974 onward, the Fund had emphasized the need for countries to finance oil deficits rather than reduce them, as described in Chapter 17. At the Annual Meeting in Manila in October 1976, the Managing Director observed that the world economy was moving into a situation in which the main danger was no longer a deepening of recession but a resurgence of inflation and that the time had come "to lay more stress on the adjustment of external positions and less emphasis on the mere financing of deficits."[5] The principles discussed in the Executive Board and agreed to by the Interim Committee at its sixth meeting on October 2 could form the basis of adjustment. Briefly, both deficit and surplus countries were to take measures to adjust. Countries in deficit should pursue policies that would restrain domestic demand and permit the shift of resources to the external sector to bring their current account deficits in line with sustainable flows of capital imports and aid. Where necessary, countries with deficits might have to depreciate their exchange rates. Industrial countries with surpluses had to adjust partly by assuring adequate domestic demand, partly by increasing flows of long-term capital exports and development aid, and partly by appreciating their exchange rates.

After 1976, the Fund placed considerably greater emphasis on balance of payments adjustment partly because financing was becoming more difficult and costly, but mainly because adjustment would enhance prospects for a more satisfactory rate of expansion in the world economy without impeding progress toward stability.

The second response of the Fund to the evolving international monetary system was to amend the Articles of Agreement. In July 1974, immediately after the Committee of Twenty ended its work, the staff started to circulate draft amendments to the Executive Directors. Officials of members disagreed on many features of the international monetary arrangements to be included in the amended Articles,

---

[5]Opening Address by the Managing Director, *Summary Proceedings, 1976*, pp. 16–17.

especially arrangements for gold and exchange rates. Inflation and balance of payments disequilibria made agreement even harder to achieve. Some members opposed the legalization of floating rates on the grounds that these rates exacerbated inflation and prevented the reduction of payments deficits; other members disagreed. Some favored arrangements that would enable the use of gold to finance their enlarged payments deficits. Other members opposed such arrangements on the grounds that many countries did not hold gold. Hence, two years were to pass before proposed amendments were ready for submission to the Board of Governors. Meanwhile, in the absence of amended Articles, working out policies for use of the Fund's resources and carrying out the Fund's financial operations and transactions presented challenging difficulties. Until the Second Amendment went into effect in April 1978, the staff was continuously improvising to raise the funds needed for the increased use of resources and to find practical and legally acceptable techniques for disbursing these funds. The gold auctions and the Trust Fund are examples. At the same time experience with ad hoc arrangements and techniques proved useful in the drafting of amendments to the Articles. A number of provisions of the Second Amendment on use of the Fund's resources formalized arrangements already in place.

The Fund's third response was to concern itself more than ever with analyzing and trying to find solutions for world economic problems. To this end, the world economic outlook exercise became one of the Fund's principal activities.[6] The Fund staff also intensified its study of world economic problems, particularly of the causes and process of inflation, its international transmission, and of ways to cope with it.[7]

In 1978 the Fund suggested a strategy of effectively coordinated policies by national governments to restore satisfactory world economic growth and price stability and to improve the functioning of the international adjustment process. Under a medium-term scenario, worked out in the context of the world economic outlook paper of January 1978, the Fund staff showed how the economies of the industrial countries might evolve over the period to 1980 if national policies were to follow an appropriate course.[8] Greater emphasis was to be given to policies to stimulate economic growth by the Federal Republic of Germany and Japan, both with large balance of payments surpluses, so that, together with the United States,

---

[6]The world economic outlook exercise forms the subject of Chapter 40.

[7]See, for example, H. Robert Heller, "International Reserves and World-Wide Inflation," *Staff Papers*, International Monetary Fund (Washington), Vol. 23 (March 1976), pp. 61–87; William H. White, "Improving the Demand-for-Money Function in Moderate Inflation," *Staff Papers*, Vol. 25 (September 1978), pp. 564–607; and George M. von Furstenberg and William H. White, "The Inflation Process in Industrial Countries Individually and Combined," *Kyklos* (Basel), Vol. 33, No. 2 (1980), pp. 261–86. Some of the studies of ways to cope with inflation examined countries' experiences with incomes policies. See, for example, Anne Romanis Braun, "The Role of Incomes Policy in Industrial Countries Since World War II," *Staff Papers*, Vol. 22 (March 1975), pp. 1–36, and "Indexation of Wages and Salaries in Developed Economies," *Staff Papers*, Vol. 23 (March 1976), pp. 226–71; Erich Spitäller, "Incomes Policy in Austria," *Staff Papers*, Vol. 20 (March 1973), pp. 170–202; and Ekhard Brehmer and Maxwell R. Bradford, "Incomes and Labor Market Policies in Sweden, 1945–70," *Staff Papers*, Vol. 21 (March 1974), pp. 101–26.

[8]This scenario is spelled out in *Annual Report, 1978*, pp. 30–33.

which had already been following somewhat expansionary policies but which had a payments deficit, they might help the world economy to grow more rapidly once again.

Supported by the discussion in the Executive Board in favor of such a scenario, Mr. Witteveen undertook to persuade finance ministers and heads of central banks to take the actions suggested when they met as the Interim Committee in Mexico City at the end of April 1978. At the meeting, some Governors endorsed his suggestion. Those from EC countries and Japan, among others, cautioned against it. For three years officials of the Federal Republic of Germany had judged that measures to accelerate domestic growth would not be helpful in bringing about a recovery of the world economy. They felt that inflation must first be slowed down and doubted that expansionary policies would stimulate greater growth in the German economy. Private domestic investment, they argued, was less a function of easy monetary policies than of buoyant demand abroad for German exports. As far as government investment expenditures were concerned, there was little scope for further increase because a modern infrastructure already existed in the Federal Republic of Germany. Moreover, they had reservations about the usefulness of further reductions in taxes as a way to encourage growth. French officials argued that in order to stimulate private investment, emphasis should be placed on restoring business confidence. They believed that sharp declines in the rates for the dollar vis-à-vis the currencies of the EC countries were unfavorably affecting business confidence and private investment and that it was essential for the United States to support the dollar in foreign exchange markets. Japanese authorities argued that they were already doing as much as they could to expand domestic demand, stabilize employment, and cut back Japan's current account surplus.

Despite these reservations, the members of the Interim Committee reached consensus on the general outlines of a coordinated strategy. The Committee emphasized that its implementation should take account of the wide differences in current positions of individual countries and thus lead to a pattern of differentiated growth rates.

The question of an appropriate general strategy was also a preoccupation of the Organization for Economic Cooperation and Development (OECD). At the June 1978 meeting of the OECD Council at the ministerial level, agreement was reached on a strategy broadly similar to that of the Fund. In June 1978 the Annual Report of the Bank for International Settlements favored a concerted international effort to put the world economy back on a more satisfactory path of development. Then at the summit meeting convened in Bonn on July 16–17, the leaders of the seven major industrial countries agreed on a comprehensive strategy covering growth, employment and inflation, international monetary policy, energy, trade, and other issues of particular interest to developing countries.

By the time of the Annual Meeting late in September, although the new Managing Director, J. de Larosière, was able to point to some encouraging developments in the world economy, his emphasis was on continuing problems.

Inflation in most industrial and nonindustrial countries persisted at unacceptable rates. The slow pace of recovery from the world recession of 1974–75 meant that many countries continued to suffer from a substantial underutilization of economic resources, including high levels of unemployment. The international adjustment process was not working satisfactorily and balances of payments on current account of industrial countries were again in serious disequilibrium. As a result, foreign exchange markets for major currencies had become unstable, exacerbating other economic problems. The non-oil developing countries were also encountering difficulties: inadequate real gains in the prevailing low levels of per capita income, external financial problems and burdensome debt positions, adverse impact on export earnings owing to protectionist measures abroad, and problems of exchange rate management arising from the divergent and sometimes rapid movements of exchange rates for major currencies. Thus, as Mr. de Larosière stressed in late 1978, world economic problems continued to make for "a very difficult and potentially dangerous situation."[9]

---

[9]Opening Address by the Managing Director, *Summary Proceedings, 1978,* p. 16.

PART FIVE

Increased Use of Resources

(January 1975–December 1978)

*"The French Revolution of a hundred
and fifty years ago gradually ushered
in an age of political equality, but
the times have changed, and that by
itself is not enough today. The
boundaries of democracy have to be
widened now so as to include
economic equality also. This is the
great revolution through which we
are all passing."*

—JAWAHARLAL NEHRU

CHAPTER
21

Changes in Compensatory
and Buffer Stock Financing

*F*LUCTUATIONS IN COMMODITY PRICES, which had for decades troubled countries producing primary products, were even more troublesome and received greater attention from public officials between 1972 and 1978. Fluctuations in commodity prices were larger than in the previous 30 years: the tremendous upsurge in 1973 and 1974 followed by the deep downswing of 1975, described in earlier chapters, constituted the sharpest reversal of commodity prices since World War II. Pressure on the international community to stabilize export earnings of primary producing countries or compensate them for their losses was greater than ever before. Officials of developing countries, now cooperating in a number of forums, insisted that urgent action be taken.

The "commodities problem" thus began to receive renewed attention in 1975. Much discussion of the problem took place outside the Fund, especially in the United Nations Conference on Trade and Development (UNCTAD) and in the Conference on International Economic Cooperation (CIEC), the "North-South" Conference which opened in Paris at ministerial level on December 16, 1975 and continued until the final meeting, May 30 to June 2, 1977. This discussion influenced the Fund to take action on the two facilities it had established earlier to help deal with unstable prices for primary products, the facilities for the compensatory financing of export shortfalls and for the financing of buffer stocks.

CALLS BEFORE 1975 FOR CHANGING
THE COMPENSATORY FINANCING FACILITY

The compensatory financing facility, introduced in the Fund in 1963, was extended and liberalized in 1966.[1] When it was introduced, the facility was

---

[1]The introduction of the facility was described in *History, 1945–65*, Vol. II, pp. 417–27; subsequent developments through 1971, including the extensions and liberalizations of 1966, in *History, 1966–71*, Vol. I, pp. 261–68.

considered a pioneering achievement, and its extension and liberalization in 1966 were considered innovative. Nevertheless, as a sign of changing times, within three years of its extension and liberalization, several Governors from African and Asian members were already expressing disappointment with the facility and advocating further liberalization.[2] However, when the discussions on overall reform of the international monetary system began late in 1971, officials of developing members became more concerned with finding ways to obtain development finance than with solving problems of commodity prices, especially since these prices were spurting to new high levels in 1972–73. They turned their attention mainly to obtaining agreement on a link between allocations of SDRs and the provision of development finance and to pushing for an extended facility. Not much was said about the compensatory financing facility.

The compensatory financing facility was, however, by no means out of the limelight, nor was it unused. In the financial year ended April 30, 1973, Bangladesh, Chile, Jordan, Cambodia (later Democratic Kampuchea), Peru, Uruguay, Zaïre, and Zambia each made compensatory drawings, for a total of SDR 206 million. In the financial year ended April 30, 1974, Burma, Egypt, Guinea, Guyana, India, Jamaica, the Philippines, and Sri Lanka made compensatory drawings totaling another SDR 212 million. Only in the financial year ended April 30, 1968 had compensatory drawings been larger. By April 30, 1974, Bangladesh and Zambia had both taken advantage of the most important liberalization of 1966, which allowed outstanding drawings under the compensatory financing facility to reach 50 percent of a member's quota rather than 25 percent, the previous limit.

Inasmuch as most commodity prices had never been higher than in 1972–74, this much use of the compensatory financing facility was impressive, although in comparison with the continuing financial needs of developing members, it was minute, as officials of developing members were quick to point out. The third session of UNCTAD in Santiago in April–May 1972 adopted a resolution inviting the Fund "to consider making such adjustments in the terms and conditions governing the use of its compensatory financing and buffer stock financing facilities as would enable developing countries to make more effective use of them."[3] This UNCTAD resolution was followed by requests at the 1972 Annual Meeting by Governors from African and Asian members for a review of the Fund's compensatory financing facility. J.M. Mwanaktwe, for instance, pointed out that while Zambia was grateful for the compensatory financing assistance received in 1971–72, when world copper prices were low and its exports fell following a mine disaster, it had received less than 15 percent of its total export shortfall.[4]

These suggestions of the UNCTAD, together with proposals of Mr. Wardhana with respect to the buffer stock financing facility (considered later in this chapter),

---

[2]*History, 1966–71*, Vol. I, pp. 267 and 281–82.

[3]This resolution was reprinted in *International Financial News Survey* (Washington: International Monetary Fund), Vol. 24 (June 7, 1972), p. 170.

[4]Statement by the Governor of the Fund and the World Bank for Zambia, *Summary Proceedings, 1972*, p. 95.

prompted officials to think about changes that might be made in the Fund's two facilities dealing with primary products. Mr. Witteveen, in his first address to the Governors as Managing Director at the 1973 Annual Meeting in Nairobi, agreed that the Fund's programs for assisting its developing members, including the compensatory financing and buffer stock facilities, ought to be "maintained and strengthened."[5] Messrs. Carli and Duisenberg supported enlargement of compensatory and buffer stock financing.[6] However, except for Kul Sekhar Sharma, little was said about these facilities by the Governors for developing members, probably because prices in world commodity markets were at an all-time high.[7] A year later, interest in compensatory and buffer stock financing had waned. At the 1974 Annual Meeting in Washington attention was given primarily to the balance of payments crisis caused for developing members by the jump in oil prices and to the new oil facility. There was much concern about inflation to the neglect of recession; yet it was only during recession, when commodity prices dropped precipitously, that officials turned their attention to stabilizing these prices.

INTENSIFIED CONCERN WITH COMMODITY PROBLEMS IN 1975

By the middle of 1975, it was clear that the oil facility would expire early in 1976 and that some additional mechanism to channel funds to the non-oil developing members to cope with their massive balance of payments deficits was essential. Since establishment of new facilities took considerable time, and the Fund already had a facility to deal with falling commodity prices, officials inevitably concentrated on reviewing the Fund's compensatory financing facility. The Group of Twenty-Four, meeting in June 1975 in Paris, made specific suggestions for liberalizing the facility. Compensation of export shortfalls should take place as they occurred, not many months thereafter. Coverage should be expanded to include services as well as merchandise exports. The period for repayment ought to be lengthened. The Group of Twenty-Four, arguing that the sharp deterioration in the terms of trade of developing countries was due more to declines in their export prices than to increases in prices for their imports, including oil, also emphasized the need for measures to safeguard in real terms the export earnings of developing countries. The Group suggested that the facility should take account of increases in the prices of imports as well as of shortfalls in exports. The Group of Twenty-Four also called for a number of specific actions by international organizations with regard to buffer stocks, including action by the Fund to improve its facility.[8] Meeting a few days

---

[5]Opening Address by the Managing Director, *Summary Proceedings, 1973*, p. 23.

[6]Statements by the Governor of the World Bank and Alternate Governor of the Fund for Italy and the Governor of the World Bank for the Netherlands, *Summary Proceedings, 1973*, pp. 69 and 123.

[7]Statement by the Governor of the Fund for Nepal, *Summary Proceedings, 1973*, p. 315.

[8]Communiqué of Intergovernmental Group of Twenty-Four on International Monetary Affairs, June 9, 1975, pars. 10 and 19; Vol. III below, pp. 640–41.

later, also in Paris, the Interim Committee requested the Executive Directors to consider appropriate modifications in the Fund's facilities for the compensatory financing of export shortfalls and for financing buffer stocks, and the Development Committee urged not only the Fund but also the World Bank to study ways and means of helping to finance commodity stabilization schemes.[9]

Background for Action by Financial Officials

The concern of the Group of Twenty-Four, the Interim Committee, and the Development Committee with commodity problems reflected the increasing attention devoted to commodity problems in nearly all international forums in 1975. Concern intensified because the balance of payments situation of non-oil developing countries, faced not only with higher oil import costs but also with lower volumes of exports and sharply falling commodity prices because of world recession, became desperate. In 1975, the UNCTAD Committee on Commodities, meeting in Geneva, the Group of Seventy-Seven, meeting in Dakar, the OECD High-Level Group on Commodities, meeting in Paris, the European Economic Community, and the United Nations all addressed declining commodity prices. The UNCTAD initiated a proposal for an Integrated Program for Commodities, a proposal that was debated and discussed for the next several years. The program aimed at "insuring just and stable markets for a comprehensive range of commodities of export interest to developing countries." The rationale for an integrated program was that the simultaneous stabilization of the prices of 10 or 12 commodities was more cost-effective in producing orderly commodity markets and stable prices than past efforts of trying to obtain commodity agreements for a number of commodities individually. The proponents of the integrated program, primarily officials of the Group of Seventy-Seven, were frustrated with previous international agreements for commodity price stabilization for individual commodities because it had been possible to work out such agreements between producers and consumers for only a few commodities, such as coffee, cocoa, tin, and sugar.

Discussions of commodity problems among European officials and officials of developing countries led to the Lomé Convention, signed in Lomé, Togo, on February 28, 1975. This Convention was a five-year accord between members of the European Community (EC) and 44 African, Caribbean, and Pacific (ACP) countries covering trade relations, financial assistance, and industrial cooperation.[10] All

---

[9]Communiqués of Interim Committee, June 11, 1975, par. 8, and Development Committee, June 13, 1975; both in Vol. III below, pp. 222 and 581–84.

[10]The 44 developing countries that signed the Lomé Convention with the European Community in February 1975 were 35 African countries (Benin, Botswana, Burundi, Cameroon, Central African Republic, Chad, Congo, Ethiopia, Equatorial Guinea, Gabon, The Gambia, Ghana, Ivory Coast, Kenya, Lesotho, Liberia, Madagascar, Malawi, Mali, Mauritania, Mauritius, Niger, Nigeria, Rwanda, Senegal, Sierra Leone, Somalia, Sudan, Swaziland, Tanzania, Togo, Uganda, Upper Volta, Zaïre, and Zambia), 6 countries in the Caribbean (Bahamas, Barbados, Grenada, Guyana, Jamaica, and Trinidad and Tobago), and 3 countries in the Pacific (Fiji, Tonga, and Western Samoa). Originally Guinea-Bissau and Guinea were also to sign the Convention but at the last moment they did not.

exports from the ACP nations, except for a number of agricultural products subject to the Community's common agricultural policy and representing less than 1 percent of the Community's imports from the ACP, were allowed to enter the EC free of customs duties and of quotas. No reciprocity was required of the ACP. The EC also committed itself to help the ACP nations expand exports by giving them technical assistance in promotional activities.

Over $4 billion in financial aid was to go to the ACP nations, about 85 percent in grants and loans, over a five-year period. This amount included $400 million to finance the stabilization of export earnings from a number of primary products when prices for these products fell. Thus, the compensatory financing scheme administered by the EC, known as the STABEX scheme (for the stabilization of export earnings), was inaugurated. The third feature of the Convention, industrial cooperation, was to consist of technical assistance aimed at broadening the industrial base of the ACP.

Commodity problems were also a prime topic at the Seventh Special Session of the UN General Assembly held from September 1–16, 1975. The debate in the session was whether emphasis should be placed on an integrated commodity program with financing mechanisms for building up buffer stocks, as proposed by the UNCTAD, or on compensatory financing of shortfalls in export income, as the Fund was doing with the compensatory financing facility and the EC was doing to some extent through the STABEX scheme. The final resolution of the United Nations was a compromise. At the insistence of the developing countries, an integrated commodity program and the feasibility of indexation schemes linking developments in the prices of exported commodities to the prices of manufactured goods imported by developing countries were to be taken up by the fourth session of UNCTAD (UNCTAD IV) to be held in Nairobi in May 1976. The topic of compensatory financing, especially an examination of the possibility of liberalizing and expanding compensatory financing, was to be taken up by the Fund.

Discussions in the Fund

This was the background against which the Group of Twenty-Four, meeting in June 1975, made the specific suggestions for liberalizing the compensatory financing facility described above. It was the background against which the Interim Committee, also meeting in June 1975, had requested the Executive Directors to consider appropriate modifications of the Fund's facility for the compensatory financing of export fluctuations. And it was the background against which the Development Committee, meeting the same month, had welcomed the request.

Early in 1975 the Executive Directors began their many meetings to consider modifications of the compensatory financing facility. By August they were considering a staff paper suggesting specific modifications. Meeting at the end of August in Washington just before the 1975 Annual Meeting, the Group of Twenty-Four once again urged a substantial improvement of the compensatory financing facility. The Interim Commitee, meeting on August 31, 1975, urged the Executive Directors to complete their work on changing the facility. The Development Committee, meeting on September 3–4, 1975, gave special attention to commodity price fluctuations and to their consequences on export earnings of developing countries.[11] Clearly, all financial officials seemed to be ready for some change in the Fund's compensatory financing arrangements, and the atmosphere for liberalizing the arrangements was favorable.

At the 1975 Annual Meeting, Governors enthusiastically supported the idea of improving the facility. In his opening address as a co-chairman of the Board of Governors, Gumersindo Rodríguez, Governor of the World Bank for Venezuela, for instance, emphasized that improvement of the compensatory financing and buffer stock financing facilities of the Fund was important for easing the fundamental problem which traditionally beset developing countries.[12] Mr. Wardhana presented a strong case for tackling fluctuations in primary product prices; schemes could be introduced both to limit price fluctuations and to compensate countries for export earnings losses caused by such fluctuations.[13] Mwai Kibaki, Chong Hon Nyan, Aumua Ioane, Victor Castillo, Arthur D. Hanna, and J.F. Abela, among other Governors from developing members, lent their support to Mr. Wardhana's arguments.[14] Mr. Hanna urged that compensatory financing be extended to cover receipts from invisibles, pointing out that receipts from tourism and remittances from immigrant workers were the prime source of foreign exchange earnings for many members and that these receipts, like receipts from commodity exports, were subject to cyclical variation. Among Governors from industrial members and more developed primary producing members, Emilio Colombo, Jean-Pierre Fourcade, and W.G. Hayden also supported "more extensive and more flexible" compensatory financing through the Fund.[15]

PROPOSALS BY OFFICIALS OF THE UNITED STATES

Any important change in the Fund's compensatory financing arrangements depended heavily on the attitude of U.S. officials, however, who in principle strongly opposed international commodity agreements. Embarrassed that other industrial countries, especially Belgium, France, Italy, the Netherlands, and

---

[11]See communiqués of Group of Twenty-Four, August 30, 1975, Interim Committee, August 31, 1975, and Development Committee, September 4, 1975; all in Vol. III below, pp. 642–44, 222–25 and 584–85.

[12]*Summary Proceedings, 1975*, p. 13.

[13]Statement by the Governor of the Fund for Indonesia, *Summary Proceedings, 1975*, p. 82.

[14]Statements by the Governor of the Fund and the World Bank for Kenya, speaking on behalf of African Governors; the Governor of the World Bank for Malaysia; the Governor of the Fund and the World Bank for Western Samoa; the Governor of the Fund for Bolivia, speaking on behalf of Latin American countries; the Governor of the Fund and the World Bank for the Bahamas, speaking on behalf also of Barbados, Guyana, Jamaica, and Trinidad and Tobago; and the Governor of the Fund for Malta, *Summary Proceedings, 1975*, pp. 146, 166, 200, 210, 214, and 243.

[15]Statements by the Governor of the Fund for Italy, the Governor of the Fund and the World Bank for France, and the Governor of the Fund and the World Bank for Australia, *Summary Proceedings, 1975*, pp. 42, 99, and 128.

Sweden, appeared more sympathetic than the United States to the special problems of developing countries, U.S. officials wanted to offer proposals. Mr. Kissinger and Mr. Simon under President Ford's direction had already, in November 1974, come up with a proposal for a Trust Fund financed in part by sale of some of the Fund's gold to provide highly concessional balance of payments financing for the poorest developing countries. At the opening of the Seventh Special Session of the UN General Assembly in New York, on September 1, 1975, speaking on behalf of Mr. Kissinger, the U.S. Representative to the United Nations, Daniel P. Moynihan, set forth details of proposals that Mr. Kissinger and Mr. Simon had worked out with President Ford.[16] He called for a "development security facility" in the International Monetary Fund to meet the needs of developing nations suffering from sharp fluctuations in export earnings. This development security facility would replace the Fund's compensatory financing facility. At the 1975 Annual Meeting, Mr. Simon explained that the Trust Fund that U.S. officials had proposed the year before could be broadened to provide grants to the poorest developing countries experiencing export shortfalls.[17] The suggestion that compensatory financing be accomplished through a new Trust Fund had been made by Mr. Pöhl of the Federal Republic of Germany at the meeting of the Development Committee in June 1975.

In making suggestions alternative to liberalizing the Fund's existing compensatory financing facility, officials of both the United States and the Federal Republic of Germany were trying to circumvent the demand for greater financial assistance by officials of many developing countries which had had relatively high incomes and high growth rates for nearly a decade, such as Argentina, Brazil, Romania, and Yugoslavia. U.S. and German officials wanted to confine any balance of payments assistance to the poorest developing countries. But the uniformity principle inherent in the Fund's Articles of Agreement and in all the Fund's policies precluded differentiation between members in any schemes instituted in the Fund. Accordingly, U.S. officials came up with ideas such as the Trust Fund or a "development security facility" that were separate in structure and organization from the International Monetary Fund but were still administered by it, and in which arrangements could be instituted for the benefit of only a limited number of poor developing countries.

In late 1975, however, when agreement on a Trust Fund was not readily forthcoming, U.S. officials proposed specific changes to liberalize the Fund's existing compensatory financing facility.

Operation of the Compensatory Financing Facility Prior to 1975

The changes proposed by U.S. officials and the modifications subsequently made in the facility are more clearly understood if seen in light of how the compensatory financing facility operated just prior to the changes.

---

[16]Published as "Global Consensus and Economic Development," in *Department of State Bulletin* (Washington), Vol. 73 (September 22, 1975), pp. 429–30.

[17]Statement by the Governor of the Fund and the World Bank for the United States, *Summary Proceedings, 1975*, p. 113.

The facility was established to provide additional assistance from the Fund to members experiencing balance of payments deficits arising from shortfalls in their export earnings. The assistance was additional in the sense that drawings made under the facility did not affect the amounts that a member could draw under its gold tranche or its credit tranches or from other special facilities of the Fund. Compensatory drawings, like credit tranche drawings, were financed from the Fund's own resources; charges and repurchase provisions were the same as for credit tranche drawings. Purchases under the facility were, however, subject to limitations depending on a member's quota. Except for shortfalls resulting from disasters or major emergencies, net drawings in any 12-month period could not exceed 25 percent of the member's quota and outstanding drawings under the facility could not exceed 50 percent of quota. Moreover, the sum of the outstanding drawings under the compensatory and the buffer stock facilities together could not exceed 75 percent of the member's quota.

The conditionality associated with compensatory drawings was light. The Fund had to be satisfied that the shortfall in export earnings was short term and largely attributable to circumstances beyond the member's control and that the member would cooperate with the Fund to find, where required, appropriate solutions for its balance of payments difficulties. Like all other drawings, compensatory drawings required that the member have a balance of payments need in order to be eligible to draw from the Fund.

Since the facility was to finance "shortfalls from a medium-term trend in export earnings," inevitably the size of any export shortfall and of the medium-term trend (called the trend value) had to be determined. The medium-term trend in export earnings from which the shortfall was measured was defined as "a five-year moving average of exports centered on the shortfall year." (In other words, exports for the two years prior to the shortfall and for the two years after the shortfall as well as exports during the shortfall year were taken into account.) This medium-term trend, or moving average, was estimated by the Fund staff partly by use of a general formula that the staff had developed to cover the two years preceding the shortfall and the shortfall year and partly by making a judgmental forecast for exports for the two years after the shortfall.[18]

One of the liberalizations of 1966 was that in calculating export shortfalls, greater weight was to be given to judgmental forecasts of a country's export performance than to use of a general formula. When a country had a rising trend of exports, explicit account was to be taken of this fact in calculating any export shortfall. In effect, if the exports of a country were no longer increasing at the rate prevailing in the past, a shortfall in exports could be presumed to exist. The margin of subjectivity was limited, however, by the specification of lower and upper limits to the judgmental forecasts. The average value of export earnings during the two post-shortfall years could not be estimated at less than the value of export earnings during the shortfall year or at more than 10 percent above the average value of export

---

[18]This formula was explained in *History, 1945–65*, Vol. II, p. 423.

earnings during the pre-shortfall years. These forecasting limits set corresponding limits to the permissible estimates of the export shortfall.

In order to make the compensation as timely as possible, the 1966 decision also prescribed the shortfall year as the latest 12-month period for which customs data were available, provided that the interval between the end of the shortfall year and the time of the request did not exceed 6 months. In addition, the 1966 decision contained a provision linking repurchases of compensatory drawings more closely to the recovery of a member's exchange earnings rather than making such repurchases subject to the usual three-to-five-year rule. The Fund could recommend that repurchases be made earlier if the member had excess exports as calculated by the Fund.[19]

Details of U.S. Proposals

The proposals made by the United States in September 1975 for liberalizing the compensatory financing facility were based on the analysis by the Fund staff of three principal constraints on access to the existing facility. As explained above, the limited use that could be made of judgmental forecasts restricted the size of the export shortfall for which members could be compensated. A member could draw no more than 25 percent of its quota in any 12-month period under the facility. Outstanding compensatory drawings by a member could not exceed 50 percent of its quota.

Accordingly, U.S. officials proposed that the method of calculating compensable export shortfalls be changed so as to raise the forecast limit from 10 percent to 20 percent, that the annual access to the facility be raised from 25 to 50 percent of quota, that the 75 percent of quota limit on both compensatory and buffer stock drawings be eliminated, and that the total amount that a member might draw under the compensatory financing facility be increased to 75 percent of quota. With respect to the last suggestion, U.S. officials were prepared to permit outstanding compensatory drawings of up to 100 percent of quota, but only on the provision that consensus could be reached among Executive Directors that the facility would be used only by developing members and not by the more developed primary producing members, such as Australia, Iceland, New Zealand, South Africa, and others.

DISCUSSION OF POSSIBLE CHANGES
IN THE FACILITY AND A NEW DECISION

The Executive Board's discussions of what to do about the compensatory financing facility went on for several months in 1975. While nearly all Executive Directors agreed that more provision for compensatory financing of fluctuations of export earnings was needed, a number of questions had to be answered before they

---

[19]A description of the way in which this repurchase provision worked can be found in *History, 1966–71*, Vol. I, pp. 262–63.

could agree on the specific action to take. Some questions were quite technical. Others were concerned with the relation between the compensatory financing facility of the Fund and the Fund's regular policies on use of its resources.

The following questions were to be answered. Instead of liberalizing the existing compensatory financing facility, should the new Trust Fund, then also being discussed, be broadened to include compensatory financing assistance for those developing members with the lowest per capita incomes, as had been proposed by Mr. Pöhl and which was acceptable to U.S. officials? If the existing compensatory financing facility was to be substantially liberalized, should its use be limited to developing members as suggested by U.S. officials or should the facility continue to be open to all primary producers, including more developed primary producing members? Should the method used for calculating export shortfalls be revised so that shortfalls could be regarded as taking place even if export earnings did not actually fall but rather did not grow at a normal rate? Should the method of calculating export shortfalls be revised to take into account the effects of inflation on the nominal values of export earnings? In other words, could export shortfalls be presumed to take place even if the nominal values of export earnings were rising because of continuously rising price levels? Should export shortfalls be measured in real terms rather than in value terms so as to help members keep up the purchasing power for buying imports as proposed by officials of some developing members? If export shortfalls were to be measured in real terms, what deflator ought to be used? For example, should indexation be used to measure export shortfalls as was proposed by the UNCTAD.[20] Should the compensatory financing facility be extended to cover shortfalls in receipts from invisibles, such as tourist receipts and remittances from laborers who had gone abroad to work? Or should the facility be retained as originally designed to serve the needs of members heavily dependent on "primary product exports"? Apart from the philosophy involved, were statistics even adequate for the inclusion of invisibles?

How many liberalizations could be made in the compensatory financing facility without causing excessive drawings on the Fund and jeopardizing the Fund's liquidity? To what extent would liberalization of compensatory drawings, which were subject to low conditionality, endanger the Fund's policies on conditionality in the credit tranches? What particular financial policies could be regarded as policies which the member was taking to cooperate with the Fund to find appropriate solutions for its balance of payments problems? To what extent should members drawing under the compensatory financing facility commit themselves to avoid resort to restrictions on trade and payments, a commitment which the Fund especially emphasized?

As they debated these questions, the Executive Directors appointed or elected by industrial members, in general, held different positions from the Executive Directors elected by developing members. Messrs. Cross, Lieftinck, and Pieske wanted to retain the original concept of compensatory financing. The Fund was

---

[20]See UNCTAD, *Indexation: Report by the Secretary-General of UNCTAD*, UNCTAD Document TD/B/563 (Geneva, July 7, 1975).

merely to help members suffering from a temporary shortfall of exports of primary products to finance a transition. The facility was not intended to ensure members a certain level of purchasing power for imports or to protect them against changes in their terms of trade. Nor was the compensatory financing facility, or even the buffer stock facility for that matter, intended to help stabilize the prices of primary products in world markets. These Executive Directors, moreover, wanted to ensure that any modifications in the compensatory financing facility would not reduce use of the Fund's resources in the regular credit tranches and the application of the policy conditions usually associated with use of resources in the credit tranches.

Mr. Kharmawan and other Executive Directors elected by developing members, on the other hand, in line with the discussions going on in the UNCTAD and elsewhere, were very much concerned about commodity prices and, since the Fund's compensatory financing facility was the major financial arrangement in the commodity field, wanted to extend it as far as possible. Among the Executive Directors appointed or elected by industrial members, Mr. Wahl gave most support to the developing members.

Agreement to liberalize the compensatory financing facility eventually came about at the very end of 1975. By then, many developing members were experiencing large balance of payments deficits, and financial officials, especially those of France, the Federal Republic of Germany, and the United States, wanted to find some way of channeling more funds to them after the expiration of the oil facility. Meeting at 8 p.m. on December 23, 1975 for the third time that day, the Executive Board finally agreed to an overall new decision on compensatory financing of export fluctuations; the changes were too extensive merely to amend the decisions of 1963 and 1966.[21]

Elements of the Decision of December 1975

The principal changes made in the compensatory financing facility by the decision of December 1975 involved the maximum entitlement in terms of quota that a member might draw and the method of calculating export shortfalls. The limit on drawings during a 12-month period was increased from 25 percent of a member's quota to 50 percent; the maximum amount that might be outstanding was raised from 50 percent to 75 percent of quota; and the joint limit of 75 percent of quota that previously applied to purchases under both the compensatory and the buffer stock facilities was removed. The method of calculating export shortfalls was changed so that calculated shortfalls would be larger and so that a member could receive assistance early in the shortfall year. The upper and lower limits on export forecasts for the two post-shortfall years were eliminated. Also, what was called an early drawing procedure was introduced: export shortfalls could be based on partially estimated data for up to six months of the shortfall year. This provision was designed (i) to improve the timeliness of assistance through the possibility of a

---

[21]E.B. Decision No. 4912-(75/207), December 24, 1975; Vol. III below, pp. 506–08.

drawing being made before the end of the shortfall year, and (ii) to extend the possible use of the facility to members previously denied access to it because their trade data were more than six months in arrears. Even for a member with customs data only three months in arrears, nine months would elapse between the middle of the shortfall year and the time of the drawing.

As protection against exaggerated shortfall estimates, a special repurchase provision was included in the early drawing procedure. The member had to specify in its request for a drawing under the compensatory financing facility that it would repurchase promptly any excess amounts drawn if it had been overcompensated because of an underestimation of its export earnings during the shortfall year. Members whose customs data for trade were late also benefited from a provision in the 1975 decision by which ordinary drawings made up to 18 months before the request could be reclassified as compensatory; formerly ordinary drawings made only in the previous 6 months could be so reclassified.

As had happened in most other decisions of the Executive Board after 1972, especially when agreement had been hard to achieve and when changes in the Fund's financial operations were being introduced, the Executive Directors made provision for a review of the decision in the near future. The Fund was to review the formula for computing the export shortfall no later than March 31, 1977 and to review the decision as a whole when experience and developing circumstances made this desirable. The decision was to be reviewed in any event whenever drawings in any 12-month period exceeded SDR 1.5 billion or outstanding drawings exceeded SDR 3.0 billion. In addition, the upper limit of 75 percent of quota applied since the buffer stock facility was introduced in 1969 to combined drawings under the compensatory financing facility and the buffer stock facility was eliminated.

UPSURGE IN COMPENSATORY DRAWINGS

Liberalization of the compensatory financing facility at the end of 1975 came at a uniquely opportune time for both the Fund and its members. Use of the Fund's resources was greatly expanded and the facility gave non-oil developing members access to badly needed funds. The year 1974 had been exceptionally good for members exporting primary products: relatively few had an export shortfall. The next year was unusually poor for primary product exporters: two thirds of them experienced export shortfalls. The substantial upsurge in compensatory drawings expected after the liberalizations in the facility of December 1975 thus quickly materialized. In the first four months of 1976 alone, Argentina, the Central African Republic, Iceland, Ivory Coast, Mauritania, Morocco, New Zealand, the Philippines, Romania, Sierra Leone, Tanzania, Turkey, Uganda, Uruguay, and Zaïre all made compensatory drawings. By April 30, 1976, compensatory drawings for the Fund's financial year 1975/76 amounted to a record SDR 828 million. The total amount of compensatory drawings outstanding on April 30, 1976 came to over SDR 1.2 billion.

Compensatory drawings were so numerous that by May 1976, less than six months after the decision of 1975, the Executive Directors already had to review it. They quickly decided to make no changes.[22] They reasoned that any changes that liberalized the facility further would be unfair to members that had already made drawings and that any changes restricting the facility would be unfair to members whose requests for drawings were still being processed. Although the Executive Directors elected by developing members took the position that increased use justified the liberalization already undertaken and that further liberalization should be considered, some Executive Directors appointed or elected by industrial members, noting the large drawings made by more developed primary producing members, such as Australia, New Zealand, and South Africa, believed that the compensatory financing facility was already more liberal in practice than had been intended.

In the next financial year ended April 30, 1977 compensatory drawings doubled the record amount of the previous year, reaching more than SDR 1,750 million. Australia made the largest purchase, for SDR 332.5 million. Egypt, Malaysia, Mexico, New Zealand, Pakistan, and South Africa also made purchases each in the range of SDR 90–185 million. By April 30, 1977, total compensatory drawings outstanding were at nearly SDR 2.7 billion. Outstanding purchases by 7 members— Bangladesh, Chile, Egypt, Jamaica, New Zealand, Zaïre, and Zambia—amounted to 75 percent of their quotas, the maximum amount that could be outstanding under the facility. In the 16 months after the liberalizations of December 1975, 50 members had made compensatory drawings for a total of SDR 2.4 billion, an amount twice that drawn in the more than 13 years since the facility was established in 1963. The compensatory financing of export shortfalls had become one of the Fund's principal activities.

In view of the continued large volume of compensatory drawings in 1976 and the early part of 1977, the Executive Board again reviewed the facility in March 1977. Once more, the Executive Directors decided not to make any changes in the facility but agreed to review it again before March 31, 1979, if drawings under it exceeded SDR 1.5 billion in any 12-month period or if outstanding purchases exceeded SDR 4.0 billion.[23]

Commodity prices improved during 1976, however, and, following the relatively heavy use of the compensatory financing facility from January 1976 to April 1977, purchases subsequently fell. Compensatory drawings in the financial year ended April 30, 1978 declined to SDR 322 million, as purchases were made by only 9 members, Barbados, Fiji, Mauritius, Portugal, Romania, Spain, Tunisia, Turkey, and Zaïre.

Table 11 lists the members making compensatory drawings in the financial years covered in this History, 1972 to 1978, and the total amounts drawn in these 7 years.

---

[22]E.B. Decision No. 5088-(76/77), May 21, 1976; Vol. III below, p. 508.
[23]E.B. Decision No. 5348-(77/33), March 11, 1977; Vol. III below, p. 508.

Table 11. Drawings Under the Compensatory Financing Facility, Financial Years 1972–78

(In millions of SDRs)

Member	Drawings
More Developed Primary Producing Members	1,191.50
Australia	332.50
Greece	58.00
Iceland	11.50
New Zealand	151.50
Portugal	87.75
Romania	142.50
South Africa	160.00
Spain	98.75
Turkey	149.00
Non-Oil Developing Members	2,357.86
Africa	*462.10*
Cameroon	17.50
Central African Republic	5.10
Chad	6.50
Congo	6.50
Gambia, The	3.50
Guinea	6.00
Ivory Coast	26.00
Kenya	24.00
Mauritania	6.50
Mauritius	11.00
Morocco	56.50
Sierra Leone	12.50
Tanzania	21.00
Togo	7.50
Tunisia	24.00
Uganda	20.00
Zaïre	113.00
Zambia	95.00
Asia	*746.56*
Bangladesh	101.56
Burma	21.50
Fiji	6.50
India	62.00
Kampuchea, Democratic	12.50
Korea	40.00
Lao People's Democratic Republic	6.50
Malaysia	93.00
Pakistan	117.50
Papua New Guinea	10.00
Philippines	116.25
Sri Lanka	59.75
Thailand	67.00
Viet Nam	31.00
Western Samoa	1.50

Table 11 (*concluded*). Drawings Under the Compensatory Financing Facility,
Financial Years 1972–78

(*In millions of SDRs*)

Member	Drawings
Non-Oil Developing Members (*concluded*)	
Latin America and the Caribbean	*863.15*
Argentina	284.00
Barbados	6.50
Chile	158.00
Dominican Republic	21.50
Guyana	15.00
Jamaica	39.75
Mexico	185.00
Panama	18.00
Peru	92.25
Uruguay	43.15
Middle East	*286.05*
Cyprus	13.00
Egypt	141.00
Israel	65.00
Jordan	7.35
Sudan	44.70
Syrian Arab Republic	12.50
Yemen, People's Democratic Republic of	2.50
TOTAL	3,549.36

Not only was the compensatory financing facility commonly used after 1975 but in the context of continued concern about the commodities problem, it was, as in earlier years, intensively analyzed by the Fund staff. The staff ascertained, for example, the extent to which the upsurge in drawings in 1976 and 1977 was attributable to the liberalization of 1975 as distinct from the effects of the 1974–75 recession. The staff also studied the cyclical pattern of compensatory drawings, the extent to which shortfalls in the export earnings of individual members were attributable to worldwide factors (such as variations in the import demand linked with the business cycle in industrial countries and changes in the rate of inflation in world trade) rather than to events specific to each country (such as natural disasters or crop failures). In addition, the staff compared the Fund's facility with the operations of the STABEX, the compensatory financing scheme administered by the EC.[24]

---

[24]The Fund published several of these studies, along with descriptions of how the compensatory financing facility operated. See the following articles by Louis M. Goreux, "Compensatory Financing: The Cyclical Pattern of Export Shortfalls," *Staff Papers*, International Monetary Fund (Washington), Vol. 24 (November 1977), pp. 613–41; "The Use of Compensatory Financing," *Finance & Development* (Washington), Vol. 14 (September 1977), pp. 20–24; "Recovery of Commodity Prices Is Expected to Slow Compensatory Drawings This Year," *IMF Survey*

DISCUSSION OF FURTHER LIBERALIZATION
OF THE COMPENSATORY FINANCING FACILITY

Even after the Fund's decision of 1975, proposals for the stabilization of commodity prices and for further liberalization of the Fund's compensatory financing facility persisted. When the members of the Group of Twenty-Four met in Kingston, Jamaica, in January 1976, they noted that the liberalization of the compensatory financing facility, just agreed to by the Executive Board, fell short of the expectations of developing members. The Group of Twenty-Four suggested specifically once again that the facility provide for the calculation of export shortfalls in real terms, for the inclusion of invisible receipts, especially from tourism and workers' remittances, and for a lengthening of the repayment period. The group noted that members in the Caribbean area had special interest in the inclusion of tourist receipts, and that several labor-exporting countries, such as Egypt, Greece, India, Pakistan, the Philippines, and Turkey, were interested in the inclusion of emigrant workers' remittances to their home countries.

The Group of Seventy-Seven, meeting in Manila in January and February 1976, shaped "the Manila Charter," which included an integrated program of commodity stabilization agreements with a "common fund," initially of $3 billion but with another $3 billion on call to finance buffer stocks in ten basic commodities. This integrated program for commodities with a common fund became the centerpiece of the proposals of officials of developing countries for a new international trade and monetary regime. UNCTAD IV in Nairobi in May 1976 adopted a resolution calling for establishment of a common fund under the Integrated Program for Commodities.[25] At their meeting in Manila on October 1–2, 1976, the Group of Twenty-Four urged the implementation of such a common fund, a call that was repeated at the 1975–77 Conference on International Economic Cooperation (CIEC).[26] This Conference resulted, among other things, in the establishment of commissions on energy, raw materials, development, and financial affairs. Agreement was reached in principle on the establishment of a common fund for raw materials and of a special program for low-income countries. The purposes, objectives, and provisions of the common fund were to be further negotiated in the UNCTAD.

The CIEC also asked the Development Committee to continue to study

---

(Washington), Vol. 6 (March 7, 1977), pp. 66–69; and *Compensatory Financing Facility*, IMF Pamphlet Series, No. 34 (Washington: International Monetary Fund, 1980). Annex IV of the latter contained a comparison of the compensatory financing scheme (STABEX) administered by the European Community and the Fund's compensatory financing facility and described the changes in STABEX when the Lomé Convention of 1975 was extended for another five years (1980–84) under the 1979 Lomé Convention, pp. 80–84.

[25]This program was briefly described in *IMF Survey* (Washington), Vol. 6 (July 4, 1977), pp. 220–23.

[26]Representatives of Algeria, Argentina, Australia, Belgium, Brazil, Cameroon, Canada, Denmark, Egypt, France, the Federal Republic of Germany, India, Indonesia, Iran, Iraq, Ireland, Italy, Jamaica, Japan, Luxembourg, Mexico, the Netherlands, Nigeria, Pakistan, Peru, Saudi Arabia, Spain, Sweden, Switzerland, the United Kingdom, the United States, Venezuela, Yugoslavia, Zaïre, and Zambia all took part.

stabilization of export earnings. Subsequently, at its meeting in Washington on September 25, 1977, the Development Committee recognized the importance of effective international action to offset the adverse effects on members of instability in export earnings and decided to review the adequacy of existing facilities and the need for improvements.

As a basis for this examination, the Development Committee invited the Fund and the World Bank to prepare a staff study on these matters and to submit it, together with such comments and recommendations as the Executive Directors might wish to make, to the Committee for its consideration. Consequently, in 1978 a study was prepared jointly by the staffs of the Fund and the World Bank, with the participation of the Executive Secretary of the Development Committee. The staffs of the Fund and the World Bank consulted with the staffs of the UNCTAD and the EC and were in contact with the authorities of Sweden that had presented specific ideas at the CIEC for the stabilization of export earnings. This study was discussed in the Executive Boards of both the Fund and the World Bank. Insofar as the Fund was concerned, the Executive Directors agreed that the Fund's compensatory financing facility played a crucial role in dealing with the problem of the stabilization of export earnings, particularly since the liberalization of that facility in 1975. In considering how further to deal with prices of primary products, they concentrated on further liberalization of that facility.

Specific additional liberalizations of the facility had been suggested by Governors at the 1976 Annual Meeting. Marie-Christiane Gbokou, for example, speaking on behalf of the African Governors, advocated the inclusion of invisible receipts.[27] Sir Veerasamy Ringadoo complained that 40 percent of the drawings in 1976 had been made by more developed primary producing members, compared with an average of 10 percent during the period 1963–75, and that a member with a history of a high export growth rate had a better chance of qualifying for the facility than a member with low export growth rates. He urged, therefore, that the facility be revised to enable members to draw on the Fund either for export volume shortfalls or for export price declines.[28] A.H. Jamal, Bernal Jiménez M., speaking as the representative of the Latin American Governors, and George F. Hosten urged the inclusion of income from tourism.[29]

Some of these suggestions, such as the inclusion of receipts from invisibles, met with a favorable response from Executive Directors. Executive Directors held differing views, however, on two suggestions made by the staff in the study— increasing access to the facility by an additional tranche, from 75 percent of quota to 100 percent, and use of a geometric average, as against the arithmetic average then used, in the calculation of the five-year averages for exports against which export

---

[27]Statement by the Governor of the Fund for the Central African Republic, *Summary Proceedings, 1976*, p. 125.

[28]Statement by the Governor of the Fund for Mauritius, *Summary Proceedings, 1976*, p. 142.

[29]Statements by the Governor of the Fund and the World Bank for Tanzania, the Governor of the Fund for Costa Rica, and the Governor of the Fund and the World Bank for Grenada, *Summary Proceedings, 1976*, pp. 151, 172, and 232.

shortfalls were measured. Geometric averages give a more accurate measure of the shortfall, since the rate of inflation and hence nominal export earnings tend to increase geometrically (at a constant *rate*) rather than arithmetically (by a constant *amount*). Most Executive Directors opposed other changes in the facility such as calculations of export shortfalls in real terms, inclusion in the coverage of the facility of fluctuations in the cost of cereal imports, adoption of the equivalent of first credit tranche conditionality for drawings beyond 50 percent of quota, and a subsidy account to offset part of the cost of using the facility by low-income members. A summary of the Executive Board discussion, together with the staff study, was sent to the Development Committee in August 1978.

After considering the staff study and the summary of the Executive Board discussion at its meeting in Washington on September 23, 1978, the Development Committee expressed a strong desire to see the Fund's compensatory financing facility further liberalized and invited the Executive Board to consider this possibility.

The request of the Development Committee was supported by pleas from many Governors at the 1978 Annual Meeting for liberalization of the compensatory financing facility. Cesar E.A. Virata, for example, as Chairman of the Development Committee, called the attention of the Governors to the Committee's endorsement of proposed improvements in the Fund's compensatory financing facility.[30] Likewise, Tengku Razaleigh Hamzah, Chairman of the Boards of Governors and hence Chairman of the 1978 Annual Meeting, stressed that the Fund should further develop the policies and procedures of its buffer stock and compensatory financing facilities.[31] Hamed El-Sayeh advocated altering the compensatory financing facility so that it would be activated not only when an export shortfall gave rise to a balance of payments deficit but also when export earnings of a specific commodity declined, regardless of the country's overall balance of payments situation. He also urged lifting the limit on drawings as a percent of a member's quota, lengthening the period before repurchase was required, changing the method of calculating export shortfalls, and taking into account increases in the volumes and prices of imports needed by developing countries.[32]

As 1978 came to a close, the staff was studying these various suggestions preparatory to the Executive Board's next review of the compensatory financing facility, scheduled for March 1979.[33]

---

[30]*Summary Proceedings, 1978*, p. 116. For the report to the Boards of Governors of the Bank and the Fund of the Joint Ministerial Committee of the Boards of Governors on the Transfer of Real Resources to Developing Countries (Development Committee), see Vol. III below, pp. 611–17.

[31]Opening Address by the Chairman of the Boards of Governors, the Governor of the Fund and the World Bank for Malaysia, *Summary Proceedings, 1978*, p. 11.

[32]Statement by the Governor of the World Bank for Egypt, *Summary Proceedings, 1978*, p. 166.

[33]This review was to lead in August 1979 to another new decision of the Executive Board on the compensatory financing facility which liberalized the facility still further. Invisibles were to be covered; geometric averages, rather than arithmetic averages, were to be used to calculate export

CHANGES IN BUFFER STOCK FINANCING

Officials of developing members were also eager to revise the Fund's facility for financing buffer stocks.[34] This facility had been used very little. After the Executive Board decided in November 1970 that members could use the facility for financing contributions to the international tin buffer stocks established under the Fourth International Tin Agreement, the first use approved for the new facility, five tin-producing members, Bolivia, Indonesia, Malaysia, Nigeria, and Thailand, purchased SDR 20 million in financial year 1971/72. In the next financial year, three of these members, Bolivia, Indonesia, and Nigeria, purchased another SDR 5 million for the same purpose. In May 1975, the Fund approved another purchase by Bolivia (for SDR 4.7 million) to finance further contributions to tin buffer stocks. The total of such purchases under the buffer stock facility was thus only SDR 30 million. The Executive Board had also decided in April 1973 that members could draw under the buffer stock facility in connection with their loans to the International Cocoa Council to establish a buffer stock of cocoa.[35] But cocoa prices remained high and no use was made of the buffer stock facility for this purpose.

Because of this meager use, officials of developing members considered that the Fund's buffer stock financing facility should be redesigned. At the 1972 Annual Meeting, for example, Shehu Shagari and Serm Vinicchayakul suggested review of the buffer stock arrangements.[36] In the course of the deliberations of the Committee of Twenty in early 1973, proposals for liberalizing both the compensatory financing facility and the buffer stock facility were submitted to the deputies of that Committee by the staff of the UNCTAD and by the constituency composed of Southeast Asian members, that is, Burma, Fiji, Indonesia, Cambodia (later Democratic Kampuchea), Korea, the Lao People's Democratic Republic, Malaysia, Nepal, the Philippines, Singapore, Thailand, and Viet Nam. Several of these members were also major producers of tin, to which the buffer stock facility applied, as well as of other raw materials, such as rubber, palm oil, and timber, for which buffer stock arrangements were wanted but on which agreement had not been possible. Mr. Wardhana, representing the Asian constituency, presented specific proposals to the Committee of Twenty. He suggested that the Fund directly finance buffer stocks and that the limit of 50 percent of quota on drawings that a member could make under the buffer stock facility and of 75 percent of quota for both buffer stock and compensatory drawings be raised.

---

shortfalls; the Fund was prepared to authorize drawings under the facility of up to 100 percent of quota; and the provision that compensatory drawings could not exceed a net amount of more than 50 percent of a member's quota in any 12-month period was abolished. (E.B. Decision No. 6224-(79/135), August 2, 1979, superseding E.B. Decision No. 4912-(75/207), December 24, 1975, as revised by E.B. Decision No. 5348-(77/33), March 11, 1977.) This 1979 decision was reprinted in *IMF Survey* (Washington), Vol. 8 (August 20, 1979), p. 253.

[34]The introduction of this facility in the Fund in 1969 was described in *History, 1966–71*, Vol. I, pp. 269–84.

[35]E.B. Decision No. 3933-(73/42), April 23, 1973; Vol. III below, pp. 509–10.

[36]Statements by the Governor of the Fund for Nigeria and the Governor of the World Bank for Thailand, *Summary Proceedings, 1972*, pp. 163 and 294.

In June 1973 the Executive Directors, eager to retain their authority vis-à-vis the Committee of Twenty particularly with regard to policies concerning use of the Fund's resources, took up these questions. They reviewed the proposals made by the staff of the UNCTAD and by Mr. Wardhana, now advanced by Mr. Kharmawan and Mr. Hanh. No major revisions came out of the Executive Board's discussion, however. Many Executive Directors favored raising the limits on drawings under the buffer stock facility that a member could make in relation to its quota. But the majority of the Executive Directors did not want the Fund to go much further; particularly they did not want the Fund to get into the business of stabilizing prices in the world's commodity markets by directly financing buffer stocks.

New Proposals for the Facility in 1975

A few months after the 1974 Annual Meeting, when commodity prices began to drop precipitously and improvements in the Fund's compensatory facility were being suggested, new proposals were also made for changing the buffer stock facility. Mr. Wardhana, Minister of Finance of Indonesia, now a member of the Interim Committee, submitted a detailed memorandum to the Interim Committee at its second meeting in January 1975 outlining possible improvements in both the compensatory financing and the buffer stock facilities. Since the Articles of Agreement were to be redrafted in any event, Mr. Wardhana suggested two amendments with regard to buffer stocks. One would enable the Fund to make direct loans to international organizations to assist in financing international buffer stocks. (Otherwise, the Fund provided assistance only to members so that they could contribute to buffer stocks.) The other would enable the Fund to permit purchases under the existing buffer stock financing facility to "float alongside the reserve tranche," that is, it would allow a member with a reserve tranche position in the Fund to draw on the buffer stock facility and still retain its reserve tranche position. Drawings under the compensatory financing facility could already float alongside the reserve tranche.[37] Drawings under both facilities already floated alongside the credit tranches.

Mr. Wardhana's plea in the Interim Committee on behalf of the Southeast Asian constituency for changes in the Fund's two facilities dealing with primary products, and especially for the Fund directly to finance buffer stocks rather than indirectly through assistance to members, was repeated in the Development Committee by Chong Hon Nyan, Deputy Minister of Finance of Malaysia, when the

---

[37]After being amended in 1969, the Articles of Agreement permitted drawings under the compensatory financing facility to float alongside what was then called the gold tranche ("reserve tranche" in the Second Amendment) because the term "gold tranche" purchase was defined in such a way that compensatory drawings were explicitly excluded. Article XIX(j) thus read as follows: "Gold tranche purchase means a purchase by a member of the currency of another member in exchange for its own currency which does not cause the Fund's holdings of the member's currency to exceed one hundred percent of its quota, provided that for the purposes of this definition the Fund may exclude purchases and holdings under policies on the use of its resources for compensatory financing of export fluctuations." The buffer stock facility was not in existence when the First Amendment to the Articles of Agreement, and this definition, were drafted.

Development Committee held its second meeting in January 1975. In both Committees, the proposal of the Southeast Asian constituency drew a sympathetic response from officials of other developing members. The Interim Commitee, therefore, explicitly asked the Executive Directors to consider possible improvements in these facilities and to study the possibility of an amendment to the Articles of Agreement that would permit the Fund to provide assistance directly to international organizations accumulating buffer stocks of primary products.[38]

After the Executive Directors began in April 1975 to hold meetings to consider modifications of both the compensatory financing facility and the buffer stock facility, they soon took up the proposals for direct financing of buffer stocks by the Fund and for having buffer stock drawings by members float alongside the reserve tranche. Mr. Kharmawan, following up on Mr. Wardhana's proposals, argued that because of the constraints imposed members did not use the buffer stock facility. Drawings could not float alongside the reserve tranche and were subject to the requirement that the member have a balance of payments need. Unless members had severe balance of payments deficits and few foreign exchange reserves, they were expected to finance contributions to buffer stocks out of their own resources. As a minimum change, buffer stock drawings should float alongside the reserve tranche as did compensatory drawings.

The proposal of Indonesian officials that the Fund undertake the direct financing of buffer stocks—that is, lending to agencies that were building buffer stocks—was supported by Messrs. Deif, Gavaldá, Roberto Guarnieri (Venezuela), Kafka, and Yaméogo. Executive Directors from industrial members, however, raised questions strongly implying that they could not support the Fund's direct involvement in building buffer stocks. Noting that the U.S., U.K., and Canadian Governments were conducting a plenary review of their policies on primary commodities, Messrs. Cross, Rawlinson, and Reynolds doubted that the Fund should become involved in general international policies with regard to commodities. Messrs. Pieske and Schneider expressed outright opposition to the Fund's direct lending to other agencies for buffer stocks. They argued that, as in the past, the Fund should lend only to members. Members that borrow from the Fund should have a definite balance of payments need. Financial assistance from the Fund should be temporary and conditional. Members, not other international agencies, should remain responsible for repaying the Fund.

After this discussion, the Executive Directors reported back to the Interim Committee in time for the Committee's next meeting in June 1975. They explained that the proposal to enable the Fund to make direct loans to buffer stock agencies, while supported by a number of Executive Directors, raised misgivings in the minds of many other Executive Directors. These misgivings concerned the departure from the Fund's principles if the Fund was to start lending to entities other than member governments or was to circumvent the requirement that a country experience a balance of payments need to obtain Fund assistance. They also concerned the

---

[38]Communiqué of Interim Committee, January 16, 1975, par. 7; Vol. III below, p. 219.

possible involvement of the Fund in the management of international buffer stocks of a number of commodities, an activity which took the Fund far afield from its monetary role. However, inasmuch as the commodities problem was very much in the forefront of discussions in international agencies, the Executive Directors told the Interim Committee that they would keep the matter on their agenda. Meanwhile, most Executive Directors favored an amendment to the Articles of Agreement that would enable the Fund to permit the buffer stock financing facility to float alongside the reserve tranche.

At its June meeting, the Interim Committee agreed that after amendment of the Articles of Agreement, drawings under the buffer stock facility would not reduce a member's reserve position in the Fund.[39] This provision already applied to drawings under the compensatory financing facility. In July 1975 the Executive Directors agreed to a draft amendment on this point.

Further Developments in the Buffer Stock Facility

There were further developments in the buffer stock facility. The decision of 1969 introducing the facility was altered to accord with the new decision on the compensatory financing facility, by removing the joint limit of 75 percent of quota that previously applied to purchases under the two facilities.[40] On July 1, 1976 the Fifth International Tin Agreement provisionally entered into effect for five years, replacing the Fourth International Tin Agreement, which expired on June 30, 1976. Just before the new Agreement went into effect, the Executive Board decided that the Fund would meet members' requests for assistance up to the full amount of their compulsory contributions to the tin buffer stock to be established under the new agreement.[41] But in the financial years 1976/77 and 1977/78 no member requested assistance from the Fund under this facility. World market prices for tin, like those for cocoa, remained above the levels at which stocks could be purchased under the terms of the agreement, and the manager of the tin buffer stock made no calls on participants other than for their initial compulsory contributions.

In December 1977, the Executive Board decided that members could use the buffer stock facility to help finance special stocks of sugar to be set up under the 1977 International Sugar Agreement, adopted by the United Nations Sugar Conference on October 7, 1977 and provisionally in force beginning January 1, 1978. This decision was novel in that although the basic policy of the Fund and the criteria applied by the Fund related to contributions by members for the purchase of internationally owned stocks, the Sugar Agreement provided for stocks that were nationally owned although controlled internationally by the International Sugar Organization. The Agreement aimed at stabilizing prices between 11 and 21 U.S.

---

[39]Communiqué of Interim Committee, June 11, 1975, par. 8; Vol. III below, p. 222.

[40]E.B. Decision No. 2772-(69/47), June 25, 1969, as amended by E.B. Decision No. 4913-(75/207), December 24, 1975; Vol. III below, p. 509.

[41]E.B. Decision No. 5127-(76/91), June 23, 1976; Vol. III below, p. 510.

cents a pound by regulating the flow of exports to the free market (as defined) through export quotas and buffer stock operations. The Fund's assistance was not to exceed the value of the special sugar stocks calculated at the floor price under the agreement of 11 U.S. cents a pound or at the average market price on which these stocks were constituted if the market price was below the floor price. It was to be complementary to loans from the International Sugar Organization.[42] In December 1978 the Philippines made the first drawing under this arrangement.

---

[42]E.B. Decision No. 5597-(77/171), December 16, 1977; Vol. III below, pp. 510–12.

CHAPTER
22

The Fund as Lender:
an Overall Picture

*D*RAWINGS FROM THE FUND greatly increased in the period reviewed in this History and put the Fund in the forefront as a lending institution. Drawings were made under the newly introduced oil facility, the extended facility, the substantially liberalized compensatory financing facility, and the buffer stock facility, described in foregoing chapters. Moreover, in the seven years from 1972 to 1978, the Fund approved over 100 stand-by arrangements. Many members also drew all or part of their gold tranches.[1]

This chapter presents a very brief overview of the aggregate use of the Fund's resources from 1972 to 1978. Much of the material is in statistical tables. In addition to drawings, members received money from the Fund in other ways and received allocations of SDRs, but amounts for these transactions are not included in the figures given in this chapter. Later in this History there is a discussion of the aggregate amounts of money made available by the Fund in all forms, including allocations of SDRs, distributions of gold, and loans from the Trust Fund.

TOTAL DRAWINGS

In the seven financial years from May 1, 1971 to April 30, 1978, total drawings from the Fund under its various facilities amounted to SDR 23.4 billion. Of this sum, drawings under the oil facility accounted for the largest amount, SDR 6.9 billion. Another sizable proportion of total drawings in these years consisted of drawings in the gold tranche, amounting to SDR 5.4 billion. Seven of the main industrial members (Denmark, France, the Federal Republic of Germany, Italy, the Netherlands, the United Kingdom, and the United States) as well as a number of more developed primary producing members (Finland, New Zealand, South Africa,

---

[1]Drawings in the gold tranche were purchases from the Fund which did not increase the Fund's holdings of a member's currency to more than 100 percent of the member's quota after allowances for excluded holdings.

423

Spain, Turkey, and Yugoslavia), and many developing members drew on their gold tranches in the Fund. Drawings under the gold tranche by industrial members were relatively large since countries of the EC used their net positions in the Fund to settle liabilities under the European narrow margins arrangement. Drawings under stand-by arrangements came to another SDR 6.3 billion.

Aggregate figures for the seven years beginning May 1, 1971 and ending April 30, 1978 are not really indicative of the increase in drawings, since most drawings were concentrated in the last four years. From May 1, 1971 to April 30, 1974, drawings from the Fund were small, totaling only SDR 4.3 billion. Drawings from the Fund by type of drawing for each of the financial years from 1972 to 1978 are given in Table 12 below.

This table shows that in the four years from May 1, 1974 to April 30, 1978, drawings totaled SDR 19.1 billion. In one financial year alone, that ended on April 30, 1976, nearly SDR 6.6 billion was drawn from the Fund. In the previous financial year, over SDR 5 billion had been drawn.

USE OF STAND-BY ARRANGEMENTS

Apart from the oil facility, most drawings took place under stand-by arrangements. In the seven calendar years ended in 1978, the Fund approved 111 stand-by arrangements with 54 members, for a total amount of SDR 9,806 million. Stand-by arrangements with Italy and the United Kingdom (two with each) accounted for more than half of the amount authorized—SDR 5,510 million of the SDR 9,806 million. The first stand-by arrangement with Italy, approved in April 1974 (the first ever with Italy) was for SDR 1,000 million; the second, approved in April 1977, was for SDR 450 million. The first stand-by arrangement for the United Kingdom approved in the seven-year period ended in 1978 (the tenth arrangement for that member) was for SDR 700 million, approved in December 1975; the second of this period, approved in January 1977, was for SDR 3,360 million.

Six members for which nine stand-by arrangements were approved in these seven years for a total of SDR 1,029 million were classified by the Fund for statistical purposes as more developed primary producing members: Finland, Portugal, Romania, South Africa, Spain, and Turkey. The stand-by arrangements approved for Portugal and Romania were the first for those two members. All other stand-by arrangements approved during 1972–78 (totaling SDR 3,267 million) were for 46 developing members. Bangladesh, the Congo, Fiji, Gabon, The Gambia, Grenada, Israel, Kenya, Madagascar, Mauritania, Mauritius, Nepal, Tanzania, Thailand, Western Samoa, and Zambia all had stand-by arrangements for the first time although some of them, such as Israel and Thailand, had been members of the Fund for many years.

The largest single stand-by arrangements approved for developing members were for Argentina (SDR 260 million in August 1976), Zambia (SDR 250 million in April 1978), Peru (SDR 184 million in September 1978), Egypt (SDR 125 million in

Table 12. Drawings from the Fund, by Type of Drawing, Financial Years 1972–78

(In millions of SDRs)

Type of Drawing[1]	1972	1973	1974	1975	1976	1977	1978	Total[2]
Gold tranche drawings[3]	1,576.50	641.00	607.47	981.45	1,324.12	160.61	135.69	5,426.84
Credit tranche drawings:								
Under stand-by arrangements	220.44	212.78	179.25	1,297.70	303.86	2,210.43	1,922.68	6,347.14
Direct drawings in credit tranches	44.50	110.00	59.50	306.05	157.10	159.59	14.13	850.87
Drawings under:								
Compensatory financing facility	167.00	206.35	211.50	18.00	827.75	1,752.75[4]	321.75	3,505.10[5]
Buffer stock facility	20.05	5.30	—	—	4.66	—	—	30.01
Extended Fund facility	•	•	•	—	7.70	190.00	108.75	306.45
Oil facility	•	•	•	2,499.25	3,966.24	436.94	—	6,902.43
Total[2]	2,028.49	1,175.43	1,057.72	5,102.45	6,591.42	4,910.33	2,503.01	23,368.85

[1] A dot (•) indicates that the facilities did not exist in that year. A dash (—) indicates that no drawings were made.
[2] Components may not add to totals because of rounding.
[3] When the Second Amendment became effective on April 1, 1978, the term "gold tranche" was changed to "reserve tranche."
[4] In addition, the following amounts purchased within credit tranches during the financial year ended April 30, 1976 totaling the equivalent of SDR 39.56 million were reclassified as having been made under the compensatory financing decision: Bangladesh—SDR 19.06 million, Pakistan—SDR 18 million, and the People's Democratic Republic of Yemen—SDR 2.5 million.
[5] Because of reclassification of credit tranche drawings as compensatory financing drawings in financial years 1972 and 1977, the grand total of compensatory financing drawings should be SDR 3,549.36 million and the grand total of credit tranche drawings correspondingly reduced.

425

April 1977), Pakistan (SDR 100 million in May 1972), and Sri Lanka (SDR 93 million in December 1977). The largest aggregate amounts approved under stand-by arrangements in the seven years 1972–78 for developing members were for Argentina, Pakistan, and Peru. A number of developing members—Guyana, Haiti, Korea, Liberia, Pakistan, Panama, and the Philippines—had a succession of one-year stand-by arrangements, signaling fairly regular support from the Fund during these years.

Table 13 gives a complete listing of all the members for which the Fund approved stand-by arrangements and the amounts authorized from 1952, when stand-by arrangements were first inaugurated, until the end of 1978. In this table a brief statistical history of the Fund's stand-by arrangements since 1952 can be seen. It is noteworthy that a substantial proportion of the stand-by arrangements that the Fund approved since 1952 were with members in Latin America and the Caribbean.

Table 13. Stand-By Arrangements Approved, 1952–78

(In millions of SDRs)

Member	Date of Inception[1]	Amount of Arrangement	Member	Date of Inception[1]	Amount of Arrangement
Afghanistan	June 1965	6.75	Brazil	June 1958	37.50
	Aug. 1966	8.00		May 1961	160.00
	July 1968	7.00		Jan. 1965	125.00
	Oct. 1969	12.00		Feb. 1966	125.00
	June 1973	10.00		Feb. 1967	30.00
	July 1975	8.50		April 1968	87.50
				April 1969	50.00
Argentina	Dec. 1958	75.00		Feb. 1970	50.00
	Dec. 1959	100.00		Feb. 1971	50.00
	Dec. 1960	100.00		Mar. 1972	50.00
	Dec. 1961	100.00			
	June 1962	100.00	Burma	Nov. 1969	12.00
	May 1967	125.00		Feb. 1973	13.50
	April 1968	125.00		Nov. 1974	31.50
	Aug. 1976	260.00		May 1977	35.00
	Sept. 1977	159.50		July 1978	30.00
Australia	May 1961	100.00	Burundi	Jan. 1965	4.00
Bangladesh	June 1974	31.25		Mar. 1966	5.00
	July 1975	62.50		Mar. 1967	6.00
				Mar. 1968	6.00
Belgium	June 1952	50.00		April 1969	4.00
				June 1970	1.50
Bolivia	Nov. 1956	7.50		June 1976	6.50
	Dec. 1957	3.50			
	May 1959	1.50	Chile	April 1956	35.00
	July 1961	7.50		April 1957	35.00
	Aug. 1962	10.00		April 1958	10.00
	Sept. 1963	10.00		April 1959	8.10
	Sept. 1964	12.00		Feb. 1961	75.00
	Sept. 1965	14.00		Jan. 1963	40.00
	Dec. 1966	18.00		Feb. 1964	25.00
	Dec. 1967	20.00		Jan. 1965	36.00
	Jan. 1969	20.00		Mar. 1966	40.00
	Jan. 1973	27.30		Mar. 1968	46.00

Table 13. (*continued*). Stand-By Arrangements Approved, 1952–78

(*In millions of SDRs*)

Member	Date of Inception[1]	Amount of Arrangement	Member	Date of Inception[1]	Amount of Arrangement
Chile (*concluded*)	April 1969	40.00	El Salvador	Dec. 1967	10.00
	Jan. 1974	79.00	(*concluded*)	July 1969	17.00
	Mar. 1975	79.00		Dec. 1970	14.00
Colombia	June 1957	25.00		Sept. 1972	8.75
	June 1958	15.00	Fiji	Nov. 1974	3.25
	Oct. 1959	41.25	Finland	Dec. 1952	5.00
	Nov. 1960	75.00		Mar. 1967	93.75
	Jan. 1962	10.00		June 1975	95.00
	Jan. 1963	52.50			
	Feb. 1964	10.00	France	Oct. 1956	262.50
	Jan. 1966	36.50		Jan. 1958	131.25
	April 1967	60.00		Sept. 1969	985.00
	April 1968	33.50	Gabon	May 1978	15.00
	April 1969	33.25			
	April 1970	38.50	Gambia, The	May 1977	2.53
	April 1971	38.00	Ghana	May 1966	36.40
	May 1972	40.00		May 1967	25.00
	June 1973	20.00		May 1968	12.00
Congo	Jan. 1977	4.70		May 1969	5.00
Costa Rica	Oct. 1961	15.00	Grenada	Sept. 1975	0.50
	Dec. 1962	11.60		June 1976	0.23
	Feb. 1965	10.00	Guatemala	June 1960	15.00
	Mar. 1966	10.00		Aug. 1961	15.00
	Aug. 1967	15.50		Jan. 1966	15.00
	July 1976	11.60		April 1967	13.40
Cuba	Dec. 1956	12.50		April 1968	10.00
				Aug. 1969	12.00
Dominican Republic	Dec. 1959	11.25		Dec. 1970	14.00
	Aug. 1964	25.00		Mar. 1972	9.00
Ecuador	June 1961	10.00	Guyana	Feb. 1967	7.50
	June 1962	5.00		Feb. 1968	4.00
	July 1963	6.00		Mar. 1969	4.00
	July 1964	13.00		April 1970	3.00
	July 1965	12.00		May 1971	4.00
	July 1966	13.00		May 1972	2.80
	April 1969	18.00		May 1973	4.00
	Sept. 1970	22.00		May 1974	5.00
	July 1972	16.50		June 1975	5.00
Egypt	May 1962	42.50		June 1976	7.25
	May 1964	40.00		Aug. 1978	6.25
	April 1977	125.00	Haiti	July 1958	5.00
El Salvador	Oct. 1958	7.50		Oct. 1959	4.00
	Oct. 1959	7.50		Oct. 1960	6.00
	Oct. 1960	11.25		Oct. 1961	6.00
	July 1961	11.25		Oct. 1962	6.00
	Sept. 1962	11.25		Oct. 1963	4.00
	Sept. 1963	5.00		Oct. 1964	4.00
	Oct. 1965	20.00		Oct. 1965	4.00

427

Table 13 (*continued*). Stand-By Arrangements Approved, 1952–78

(*In millions of SDRs*)

Member	Date of Inception[1]	Amount of Arrangement	Member	Date of Inception[1]	Amount of Arrangement
Haiti (*concluded*)	Oct. 1966	4.00	Japan	Jan. 1962	305.00
	June 1970	2.20		Mar. 1964	305.00
	June 1971	3.00	Kenya	Nov. 1978	17.25
	July 1972	4.00			
	July 1973	4.00	Korea	Mar. 1965	9.30
	Aug. 1974	4.00		Mar. 1966	12.00
	Aug. 1975	4.75		Mar. 1967	18.00
	Aug. 1976	6.88		April 1968	25.00
	Aug. 1977	6.90		April 1969	25.00
				Mar. 1970	25.00
Honduras	Nov. 1957	3.75		Jan. 1971	25.00
	Jan. 1959	4.50		Jan. 1972	30.00
	Mar. 1960	7.50		April 1973	20.00
	May 1961	7.50		May 1974	20.00
	June 1962	7.50		Oct. 1975	20.00
	July 1963	7.50		May 1977	20.00
	Aug. 1964	7.50			
	Jan. 1966	10.00	Liberia	June 1963	5.70
	Jan. 1968	11.00		June 1964	4.40
	Feb. 1969	11.00		June 1965	4.00
	June 1971	15.00		June 1966	6.00
	June 1972	15.00		June 1967	4.40
				June 1968	3.20
Iceland	Feb. 1960	5.62		June 1969	2.00
	Feb. 1961	1.62		June 1970	2.00
	Mar. 1962	1.62		Mar. 1972	4.00
				May 1973	4.00
India	Mar. 1957	72.50		Aug. 1974	4.00
	July 1962	100.00		Jan. 1976	5.00
	July 1963	100.00			
	Mar. 1965	200.00	Madagascar	Dec. 1977	9.43
Indonesia	Aug. 1961	41.25	Mali	July 1964	9.90
	Aug. 1963	50.00		Aug. 1967	6.50
	Feb. 1968	51.75		Aug. 1968	5.00
	April 1969	70.00		Oct. 1969	3.00
	April 1970	46.30		July 1971	4.50
	April 1971	50.00			
	April 1972	50.00	Mauritania	May 1977	4.71
	May 1973	50.00	Mauritius	Feb. 1978	7.97
Iran	May 1956	17.50	Mexico	April 1954	50.00
	Oct. 1960	35.00		Mar. 1959	90.00
				July 1961	90.00
Israel	Nov. 1974	32.50	Morocco	Nov. 1959	25.00
	Feb. 1975	32.50		Sept. 1965	45.00
	Oct. 1976	29.25		Sept. 1966	50.00
				Oct. 1967	50.00
Italy	April 1974	1,000.00		Oct. 1968	27.00
	April 1977	450.00		Dec. 1969	25.00
				Mar. 1971	30.00
Jamaica	June 1963	10.00			
	Aug. 1977	64.00	Nepal	Feb. 1976	4.50

Table 13 (*continued*). Stand-By Arrangements Approved, 1952–78

(*In millions of SDRs*)

Member	Date of Inception[1]	Amount of Arrangement	Member	Date of Inception[1]	Amount of Arrangement
Netherlands	*Sept. 1957*	*68.75*	Peru (*concluded*)	*Mar. 1962*	*30.00*
				Mar. 1963	*30.00*
New Zealand	*Oct. 1967*	*87.00*		*Mar. 1964*	*30.00*
Nicaragua	*Nov. 1956*	*3.75*		*April 1965*	*30.00*
	Oct. 1957	*7.50*		*Mar. 1966*	*37.50*
	Sept. 1958	*7.50*		*Aug. 1967*	*42.50*
	Nov. 1960	*7.50*		*Nov. 1968*	*75.00*
	Mar. 1963	*11.25*		*April 1970*	*35.00*
	April 1964	*11.25*		*Nov. 1977*	*90.00*
	Mar. 1968	*19.00*		*Sept. 1978*	*184.00*
	May 1969	*15.00*	Philippines	*April 1962*	*40.40*
	Aug. 1970	*14.00*		*April 1963*	*40.40*
	Feb. 1972	10.75		*April 1964*	*40.40*
Pakistan	*Dec. 1958*	*25.00*		*April 1965*	*40.40*
	Mar. 1965	*37.50*		*April 1966*	*26.70*
	Oct. 1968	*75.00*		*Jan. 1967*	*55.00*
	May 1972	100.00		*Mar. 1968*	*27.50*
	Aug. 1973	75.00		*Feb. 1970*	*27.50*
	Nov. 1974	75.00		*Mar. 1971*	*45.00*
	Mar. 1977	80.00		May 1972	45.00
Panama	*July 1965*	*7.00*		May 1973	45.00
	May 1968	*3.00*		July 1974	38.75
	Jan. 1969	*3.20*		May 1975	29.06
	Feb. 1970	*10.00*	Portugal	April 1977	42.40
	Mar. 1971	*14.00*		June 1978	57.35
	June 1972	9.00	Romania	Oct. 1975	95.00
	Aug. 1973	9.00		Sept. 1977	64.13
	Oct. 1974	9.00	Rwanda	*April 1966*	*5.00*
	Nov. 1975	9.00		*April 1967*	*2.00*
	April 1977	11.25		*April 1968*	*3.00*
	June 1978	25.00		*April 1969*	*2.00*
Paraguay	*July 1957*	*5.50*	Sierra Leone	*Nov. 1966*	*7.50*
	July 1958	*1.50*		*Jan. 1968*	*3.60*
	Aug. 1959	*2.75*		*Mar. 1969*	*2.50*
	Oct. 1960	*3.50*		June 1977	9.02
	Dec. 1961	*5.00*			
	Nov. 1964	*5.00*	Somalia	*May 1964*	*4.70*
	Sept. 1966	*7.50*		*Jan. 1965*	*5.60*
	Jan. 1968	*8.00*		*Jan. 1966*	*2.80*
	Jan. 1969	*7.50*		*Jan. 1967*	*5.00*
Peru	*Feb. 1954*	*12.50*		*Jan. 1968*	*7.00*
	Feb. 1955	*12.50*		*Jan. 1969*	*6.00*
	Feb. 1956	*12.50*		*Jan. 1970*	*3.98*
	Feb. 1957	*12.50*			
	Feb. 1958	*25.00*	South Africa	*April 1958*	*25.00*
	Mar. 1959	*13.00*		*July 1961*	*75.00*
	Mar. 1960	*27.50*		Jan. 1976	80.00
	Mar. 1961	*30.00*		Aug. 1976	152.00

Table 13 (*concluded*). Stand-By Arrangements Approved, 1952–78

(In millions of SDRs)

Member	Date of Inception[1]	Amount of Arrangement	Member	Date of Inception[1]	Amount of Arrangement
Spain	*Aug. 1959*	*25.00*	Uganda	*July 1971*	*10.00*
	Aug. 1960	*25.00*	United Kingdom	*Dec. 1956*	*738.53*
	Feb. 1978	143.19		*Dec. 1957*	*738.53*
Sri Lanka	*June 1965*	*30.00*		*Dec. 1958*	*738.53*
	June 1966	*25.00*		*Aug. 1961*	*500.00*
	May 1968	*19.50*		*Aug. 1962*	*1,000.00*
	Aug. 1969	*19.50*		*Aug. 1963*	*1,000.00*
	Mar. 1971	*24.50*		*Aug. 1964*	*1,000.00*
	April 1974	24.50		*Nov. 1967*	*1,400.00*
	Dec. 1977	93.00		*June 1969*	*1,000.00*
Sudan	*Sept. 1966*	*28.50*		Dec. 1975	700.00
	Sept. 1967	*10.00*		Jan. 1977	3,360.00
	Dec. 1968	*12.00*	United States	*July 1963*	*500.00*
	Mar. 1972	40.00		*July 1964*	*500.00*
	Aug. 1973	24.00	Uruguay	*June 1961*	*30.00*
	Aug. 1974	24.00		*Oct. 1962*	*30.00*
Syrian Arab Republic	*May 1960*	*7.50*		*June 1966*	*15.00*
	Mar. 1962	*6.60*		*Mar. 1968*	*25.00*
	Mar. 1964	*18.50*		*May 1970*	*13.75[2]*
Tanzania	Aug. 1975	10.50		June 1972	20.00
Thailand	July 1978	45.25		May 1975	17.25
Tunisia	*Oct. 1964*	*14.25*		Aug. 1976	25.00
	Nov. 1965	*5.60*		Sept. 1977	25.00
	Dec. 1966	*9.60*	Venezuela	*April 1960*	*100.00*
	Dec. 1967	*9.61*	Western Samoa	Nov. 1975	0.50
	Jan. 1969	*6.00*		Jan. 1977	0.59
	Jan. 1970	*7.50*		Feb. 1978	0.73
Turkey	*Jan. 1961*	*37.50*	Yugoslavia	*Jan. 1961*	*30.00*
	Mar. 1962	*31.00*		*July 1965*	*80.00*
	Feb. 1963	*21.50*		*Jan. 1967*	*45.00*
	Feb. 1964	*21.50*		*Feb. 1971[3]*	*51.75*
	Feb. 1965	*21.50*		*July 1971*	*83.50*
	Feb. 1966	*21.50*	Zaïre	*July 1967*	*27.00*
	Feb. 1967	*27.00*		Mar. 1976	40.96
	April 1968	*27.00*		April 1977	45.00
	July 1969	*27.00*	Zambia	May 1973	19.00
	Aug. 1970	*90.00*		July 1976	62.00
	April 1978	300.00		April 1978	250.00

[1]Stand-by arrangements approved before 1972 are in italics; stand-by arrangements approved in 1972–78 are in roman.

[2]After being fully utilized, the stand-by arrangement with Uruguay was augmented by $13.75 million because of repurchases in October and November 1970. The full amount of these augmentations was also utilized, and the stand-by arrangement was again augmented in May 1971 by $9.5 million because of repurchases.

[3]Canceled by Yugoslavia in July 1971 when a stand-by arrangement for a larger amount was arranged.

Many members did not draw the full amounts authorized for them under stand-by arrangements. Some never really intended to draw on these arrangements. They wanted them because stand-by arrangements with the Fund helped them to formulate and implement financial programs and to maintain international recognition of their creditworthiness. Brazil was such a member, for example.[2] Other members failed to observe the specified performance criteria, and their right to draw under the arrangements was suspended. Members which for one reason or another did not draw at all on at least one of the stand-by arrangements that they had concluded with the Fund in 1972–78 included not only Brazil but also Colombia, Costa Rica, Finland, Fiji, Guatemala, Guyana, Haiti, Honduras, Indonesia, Korea, Liberia, Panama, the Philippines, Tanzania, and Uruguay. Although they used some of the authorized amounts, many other members did not draw the full amounts allowed. These members included Italy and the United Kingdom, as well as Argentina, Bolivia, Burma, Chile, Egypt, Haiti, Israel, Jamaica, Korea, Nicaragua, Pakistan, the Philippines, Sri Lanka, Sudan, and Uruguay. As a result, actual drawings under stand-by arrangements constituted only about 25 percent of total drawings from the Fund during 1972–78.

DISTRIBUTION OF DRAWINGS BY GROUPS OF MEMBERS

Statistics relating to the distribution of total drawings by members indicate that of the SDR 23.4 billion of total drawings in the seven financial years ended on April 30, 1978, nearly SDR 10.2 billion was drawn by industrial members, SDR 4.5 billion by more developed primary producing members, and SDR 8.7 billion by non-oil developing members. Of the amount drawn by industrial members, well over one third (SDR 3.7 billion) was accounted for by drawings in the gold tranche; the rest, nearly SDR 6.5 billion, represented drawings by Italy and the United Kingdom. In contrast, only a relatively small proportion of the drawings made by more developed primary producing members and by non-oil developing members represented drawings in the gold tranche; most drawings by these members were under stand-by arrangements, the oil facility, and the compensatory financing facility.

Table 14 gives statistics for total drawings from the Fund in the seven financial years 1972–78 by major economic groupings of members, listing gold tranche drawings separately.

Among industrial members, the largest drawings were made by Italy and the United Kingdom. Among the 11 more developed primary producing members which drew from the Fund in 1972–78, SDR 250 million or more was drawn by 10 of them, in order of descending magnitude, by Spain, South Africa, Turkey, Yugoslavia, New Zealand, Romania, Australia, Greece, Portugal, and Finland. Among the non-oil developing members, the largest amounts drawn—SDR 150 million or

---

[2]The Fund's stand-by arrangements with Brazil from 1966 to 1971 were described in *History 1966–71*, Vol. I, pp. 360–63.

more—were, in order of descending magnitude, by Argentina, India, Pakistan, the Philippines, Chile, Mexico, Egypt, Korea, Israel, Bangladesh, Zaïre, Peru, Sri Lanka, Uruguay, Zambia, Sudan, and Morocco. Table 15 lists the amounts drawn by each member in each of the seven financial years 1972–78.

Table 14. Use of Fund Resources, by Economic Groups, Financial Years 1972–78

(*In millions of SDRs*)

Economic Group[1]	Gold Tranche Drawings	Other Drawings	Total Drawings
Industrial members	3,668	6,496	10,164
More developed primary producing members	545	3,915	4,460
Major oil exporting members	80	7	87
Non-oil developing members	1,134	7,524	8,658
Total	5,427	17,942	23,369

[1]For names of members comprising each of these groups, see fn. 11 in Chap. 2.

Table 15. Drawings from the Fund, Financial Years 1972–78[1]

(In millions of SDRs)

	1972	1973	1974	1975	1976	1977	1978	Total[2]
Industrial Members								
Denmark	—	—	—	85.3	—	—	—	85.3
France	—	—	138.0	—	78.3	—	—	216.3
Germany, Federal Republic of	—	—	19.6	123.5	30.4	8.3	41.1	222.9
Italy	—	—	—	1,942.8	780.2	—	90.0	2,813.0
Netherlands	—	—	280.4	—	—	—	—	280.4
United Kingdom	—	583.6	—	—	1,700.0	1,700.0	1,250.0	5,233.6
United States	1,312.0	—	—	—	—	—	—	1,312.0
Total[2]	1,312.0	583.6	438.0	2,151.6	2,588.9	1,708.3	1,381.1	10,163.6
More Developed Primary Producing Members								
Australia	—	—	—	—	—	332.5	—	332.5
Finland	—	—	—	—	135.0	115.1	—	250.1
Greece	—	—	—	138.0	86.2	58.0	—	282.3
Iceland	—	—	—	28.7	33.5	—	—	62.2
New Zealand	—	—	—	159.9	230.4	50.5	—	440.7
Portugal	—	—	—	—	144.0	58.5	75.6	278.2
Romania	•	—	95.0	—	135.0	55.0	72.5	357.5
South Africa	—	—	—	—	171.2	349.0	123.0	643.2
Spain	—	—	—	413.6	275.9	—	98.8	788.3
Turkey	15.0	15.0	—	151.0	132.1	91.5	161.2	550.8
Yugoslavia	88.5	—	—	185.2	129.4	56.2	—	474.2
Total[2]	103.5	15.0	95.0	1,076.3	1,472.7	1,166.2	531.2	4,460.0

Table 15 (continued). Drawings from the Fund, Financial Years 1972–78[1]

(In millions of SDRs)

	1972	1973	1974	1975	1976	1977	1978	Total[2]
Major Oil Exporting Members								
Indonesia	3.8	1.8	—	—	80.0	—	—	85.6
Nigeria	0.8	0.7	—	—	—	—	—	1.5
Total[2]	4.6	2.5	—	—	80.0	—	—	87.1
Non-Oil Developing Members								
Africa								
Burundi	—	—	—	3.3	—	—	—	3.3
Cameroon	—	—	—	11.5	7.5	21.8	—	40.8
Central African Republic	—	—	—	3.9	7.8	—	—	11.6
Chad	—	—	—	5.0	—	6.5	—	11.5
Comoros	•	•	•	•	•	•	0.5	0.5
Congo	—	—	—	—	—	8.5	8.0	16.5
Equatorial Guinea	—	1.0	—	—	—	—	1.8	2.8
Gambia, The	—	—	—	—	—	5.2	—	5.2
Ghana	—	—	—	—	51.9	—	—	51.9
Guinea	—	—	6.0	6.2	—	—	8.7	20.9

								Total
Ivory Coast	—	—	—	21.9	36.4	—	—	58.3
Kenya	—	—	—	60.3	32.5	27.1	—	120.0
Liberia	1.0	2.8	—	—	—	4.6	—	8.4
Madagascar	—	—	—	19.3	—	—	9.4	28.8
Malawi	—	—	—	—	7.5	—	5.4	12.9
Mali	4.5	—	—	5.0	4.0	—	—	13.5
Mauritania	—	—	—	1.0	12.0	1.9	4.7	19.7
Mauritius	—	—	—	5.5	—	—	16.5	22.0
Morocco	8.2	—	—	—	125.7	18.0	—	152.0
Rwanda	—	2.1	—	—	—	—	—	2.1
Senegal	—	—	—	20.3	9.9	—	—	30.2
Sierra Leone	—	—	—	11.1	12.0	5.5	7.0	35.6
Somalia	—	—	—	—	—	—	4.8	4.8
Sudan	15.0	17.5	19.0	65.7	18.3	26.7	—	162.2
Swaziland	—	0.2	0.5	—	—	—	—	0.6
Tanzania	—	—	—	52.5	41.6	4.7	—	98.8
Togo	—	—	—	—	—	7.5	—	7.5
Tunisia	—	—	—	—	—	—	24.0	24.0
Uganda	16.5	—	—	19.2	20.0	—	—	55.7
Zaïre	—	28.2	—	28.3	101.5	73.5	33.2	264.8
Zambia	38.0	19.0	19.0	—	56.9	57.3	—	190.2
Subtotal	83.2	70.8	44.5	340.1	545.4	268.8	124.0	1,476.8

Table 15 (continued). Drawings from the Fund, Financial Years 1972–78[1]

(In millions of SDRs)

	1972	1973	1974	1975	1976	1977	1978	Total[2]
Non-Oil Developing Members (continued)								
Asia								
Afghanistan	—	—	7.5	2.5	8.5	—	—	18.5
Bangladesh	•	62.5	1.1	82.1	88.6	56.2	—	290.4
Burma	6.5	13.5	15.0	24.0	—	—	35.0	94.0
China	59.9	—	—	30.0	29.9	—	30.0	149.7
Fiji	—	—	—	2.6	—	—	8.4	11.0
India	—	—	138.2	435.0	201.3	—	—	774.5
Kampuchea, Democratic	12.5	6.2	—	—	—	—	—	18.8
Korea	7.5	—	—	140.0	152.7	49.0	—	349.2
Lao People's Democratic Republic	—	—	—	—	6.5	3.2	—	9.8
Malaysia	11.7	—	—	—	—	93.0	—	104.7
Nepal	—	—	—	—	—	7.6	—	7.6
Pakistan	—	84.0	60.0	174.0	152.0	99.5	80.0	649.5
Papua New Guinea	•	•	•	•	19.8	10.0	—	29.8
Philippines	15.0	35.0	38.8	40.0	203.4	145.2	108.8	586.1
Sri Lanka	32.2	—	24.5	50.5	44.9	15.8	55.0	223.0
Thailand	2.2	—	—	—	—	67.0	—	69.2
Viet Nam	—	—	—	—	—	46.5	—	46.5
Western Samoa	—	—	—	—	1.8	1.0	—	2.8
Subtotal	147.4	201.2	285.0	980.7	909.4	594.0	317.2	3,435.1

Latin America and the Caribbean

Argentina	179.2	110.0	—	15.2	406.1	159.5	—	870.1
Barbados	—	—	—	—	—	3.5	3.0	6.5
Bolivia	6.0	21.0	—	—	4.7	—	—	31.6
Chile	77.5	41.0	39.5	178.0	125.2	79.0	—	540.2
Colombia	30.0	—	—	—	—	—	—	30.0
Costa Rica	6.0	—	—	21.5	12.0	6.8	—	46.3
Dominican Republic	—	—	—	10.8	10.8	36.5	—	58.0
Ecuador	—	15.2	2.6	—	—	17.6	—	35.4
El Salvador	—	8.8	—	22.4	—	—	—	31.2
Grenada	•	•	•	•	1.5	0.2	—	1.7
Guyana	4.0	—	9.6	—	—	22.2	—	35.8
Haiti	—	—	3.7	8.5	8.4	3.0	—	23.5
Honduras	—	—	—	23.0	—	—	—	23.0
Jamaica	—	13.3	32.0	—	42.5	26.5	19.2	133.4
Mexico	—	—	—	—	—	516.9	—	516.9
Nicaragua	4.0	—	12.0	15.5	—	—	—	31.5
Panama	—	—	—	16.4	17.2	18.0	—	51.6
Peru	—	61.5	—	—	128.0	61.5	10.0	261.0
Trinidad and Tobago	—	6.6	—	—	—	—	—	6.6
Uruguay	9.5	22.2	16.4	65.3	91.2	—	—	204.6
Subtotal	316.2	299.4	115.7	376.6	847.5	951.3	32.2	2,939.0

437

Table 15 (concluded). Drawings from the Fund, Financial Years 1972–78[1]

(In millions of SDRs)

	1972	1973	1974	1975	1976	1977	1978	Total[2]
Non-Oil Developing Members (concluded)								
Middle East								
Bahrain	•	—	—	—	—	5.0	—	5.0
Cyprus	—	—	—	14.6	14.0	21.0	—	49.6
Egypt	32.0	—	47.0	40.0	20.2	105.5	105.0	349.7
Israel	—	—	32.5	107.0	101.2	77.0	—	317.8
Jordan	4.5	2.8	—	—	—	—	—	7.4
Syrian Arab Republic	25.0	—	—	—	—	—	12.5	37.5
Yemen, People's Democratic Republic of	—	—	—	15.6	11.8	13.2	—	40.6
Subtotal	61.5	2.8	79.5	177.2	147.3	221.6	117.5	807.4
Total Non-Oil Developing Members	608.4	574.3	524.7	1,874.6	2,449.7	2,035.7	590.8	8,658.2
GRAND TOTAL[2]	2,028.5	1,175.4	1,057.7	5,102.5	6,591.4	4,910.3	2,503.0	23,368.8

[1] A dot (•) indicates that the country was not a member at the time; a dash (—) indicates that no drawing was made.
[2] Components may not add to totals because of rounding of figures for individual members.

CHAPTER 23

Stand-By Arrangements
with an Industrial Member:
Italy

*T*HE YEAR 1973 was a watershed in the economic history of the countries of Western Europe. Until 1973, except for a downturn in 1969 and 1970, most Western European countries had enjoyed consistently rapid rates of economic expansion since the early 1950s. These years of expansion were, however, already coming to an end before the oil price increases of 1973.

The Western European countries differed in the timing of their reactions to the slowdown in their postwar economic growth. The Federal Republic of Germany was the first to gear its policies to a lower rate of growth. German authorities staunchly believed that they should not pursue expansionary monetary and fiscal policies despite declines in economic activity. They consequently resisted the suggestions of some officials and economists in 1974 and 1975 that they pursue expansionary policies as part of a strategy of "locomotive economies" in which the three largest industrial countries—the United States, the Federal Republic of Germany, and Japan—were urged to expand their domestic economies so as to help pull the rest of the world out of recession. The German position was that as long as inflation was accelerating, lower rates of economic growth in industrial countries would have to be accepted. They applied these policies to their own economy and advocated them to officials of other industrial countries. They recognized that their policies entailed some domestic unemployment but were prepared to accept this as the price for maintaining price stability. A number of smaller countries, such as Austria, Belgium, the Netherlands, and Switzerland, whose economies are closely tied to that of the Federal Republic of Germany, followed more or less similar policies.

Italy and the United Kingdom followed a different policy course until the late 1970s. Both countries continued to pursue expansionary policies after 1973 in an effort to maintain employment and to stimulate sluggish economic activity. They pursued these policies despite accelerating inflation and deterioration in the current account positions in their balances of payments. France and the Scandinavian countries followed policies between the two extremes. They tried to pursue some policies that helped adjust their balance of payments positions and others that stimulated higher rates of domestic economic growth and reduced unemployment.

The consequences of these different reactions to the slowdown of economic growth rates after mid-1973 quickly became apparent. By 1974, Italy and the United Kingdom were experiencing the highest inflation rate among industrial countries. Their current account deficits were large and recurrent pressures in exchange markets were leading to a sizable depreciation of the lira and of the pound sterling. To cover their payments deficits they had to borrow abroad extensively, and by 1977 both were in what was regarded by their own and by Fund officials as extreme difficulty.

The Federal Republic of Germany in contrast had very large current account surpluses (generally considered too large even by German officials, but reduced in 1978), a rate of growth that was regarded as "reasonable," and a very low inflation rate (only 2.5 percent for 1978). In effect, officials of the Federal Republic of Germany seemed to have proved their argument, at least regarding their own economy, that high growth rates were not sustainable without persistent policies to restrain inflation.

French officials tried to combine both balance of payments adjustment and a reasonable rate of growth, and their management of the economy worked adequately well. In the second half of the 1970s, France experienced sizable balance of payments deficits, which were however easily financed in international capital markets.

Of course all European countries benefited from the determination of officials of the United States from 1974 onward to keep up domestic employment by pursuing expansionary policies. Since these policies were pursued when the Federal Republic of Germany and Japan were following policies of restraint, they led to large U.S. current account deficits and to a progressive weakening of the dollar vis-à-vis the major European currencies, especially the deutsche mark. A considerable amount of dollars flowed into the Federal Republic of Germany in these years, and intervention in foreign exchange markets by German officials was vast.

To help finance their balance of payments deficits, the authorities of Italy and of the United Kingdom had substantial recourse to the Fund from 1974 through 1977. Both drew on the oil facility and had large stand-by arrangements. In the course of their stand-by arrangements, both greatly adapted their economic and financial policies to the new realities of slower economic growth. By 1978 Italy and the United Kingdom were experiencing less inflation and balance of payments pressure than in the previous several years.

PRELUDE TO THE ITALIAN STAND-BY ARRANGEMENTS

The stand-by arrangements that the Fund approved for Italy in the 1970s were special in a number of respects. The stand-by arrangement of April 1974 was the first for Italy, although Italy at the time had been a member of the Fund for 27 years. Italy had drawn upon the Fund only in 1964 and in 1970, and both drawings were in the gold tranche.

Italy was also the first member to come to the Fund for a stand-by arrangement following the announcement of higher oil prices at the end of 1973. The new circumstances meant prodigious rises in external deficits by the standards of the previous 20 years. Not only were officials of member governments faced with the most difficult policy choices since the reconstruction days following World War II, but Fund officials, too, were seeking to identify the appropriate extent and means of external adjustment in a world environment dominated by higher oil prices.

Moreover, Italy requested a stand-by arrangement equivalent to SDR 1,000 million, the largest that the Fund had approved in the nearly five years since it approved stand-by arrangements for France and the United Kingdom in 1969. The stand-by arrangement approved for Italy in 1974 was also special in that it was followed by a second arrangement three years later, in April 1977. The Fund's relations with Italy in this period thus form an important part of the Fund's history of the 1970s.

The Fund's negotiations with Italian officials in the 1970s and the resulting conditions associated with the two stand-by arrangements are illustrative of the process of the Fund's negotiations, of the way in which conditions are established, and of subsequent reviews of the situation. Moreover, the details of the stand-by arrangements approved for Italy (and of the stand-by arrangements approved for the United Kingdom described in the next chapter) are especially interesting in that they contradict the criticism sometimes leveled at the Fund that the conditions attached to stand-by arrangements for industrial members are less stringent than those for developing members.

THE STAND-BY ARRANGEMENT OF 1974

A group of Italian officials, who had attended a conference in Washington of officials from large oil consuming countries called by U.S. officials to consider the implications of the jump in oil prices, came to the Fund's headquarters from February 11 to 16, 1974 to discuss a request for a stand-by arrangement of SDR 1,000 million. This amount was the size of Italy's quota in the Fund, so that if Italy made full use of its gold tranche and purchased the full amount under the proposed stand-by arrangement, the Fund's holdings of lire would reach 200 percent of quota, the maximum then permitted under the Articles of Agreement without a waiver by the Fund. The Italian team was headed by Guido Carli, Governor of the Bank of Italy; the Fund staff team by L. Alan Whittome, Director of the European Department. Francesco Palamenghi-Crispi, Executive Director for Italy, took part in the meetings. By the end of the six days of negotiations, a draft stand-by arrangement, a draft letter of intent, and a draft memorandum of understanding had been initialed.

Review of the Economic Situation

The review of recent economic developments customary in negotiations for stand-by arrangements made it apparent that, beginning in the middle of 1972, there had been a startling reversal of Italy's domestic and external position from its position in the previous three years. As described in Chapter 4, since 1969 Italy had been suffering from virtual economic stagnation, especially as a result of depressed private investment, and because of low domestic demand had been experiencing sizable current account surpluses offset by large net capital outflows. When these capital outflows became excessive late in 1972 and early in 1973, Italian authorities had been forced to introduce a floating rate for the lira, putting Italy, along with Canada and the United Kingdom, among the first major industrial members to have recourse to a floating rate.

In the second half of 1972, however, the Italian economy started to recover, and in 1973 real GNP rose by 5 to 5½ percent. Moreover, in contrast to other periods of economic expansion since World War II, when exports had led economic growth, the current recovery was led by a rapid growth of internal demand. The long-awaited revival of fixed private investment finally occurred and, reaching some 7 percent in 1973, exceeded expectations.

Almost at once the recovery imposed strains on Italy's economy, as evidenced by rising costs and prices and, even more, by a sudden, large deterioration in the balance of payments position. In 1973 the current account had shown a deficit of $3 billion, reflecting both a lack of expansion of exports, in contrast to the steady growth of Italy's exports in earlier years, and an increase of imports. The poor performance of exports was partly the result of shortages of supplies of exportable goods because of strikes in key export industries early in 1973. Moreover, the Italian economy was operating at full capacity and increasing output was difficult in many export industries. Rapidly rising domestic demand was also pulling resources away from exports. At the same time, as a result of rising internal demand, imports had gone up 11 percent in volume. Imports in value terms were much higher too as prices of imports went up both because of steep increases in the prices of imported goods expressed in foreign currency and because of the effects of the depreciation of the lira following its floating at the beginning of 1973. Despite substantial official intervention in the exchange market, the lira had depreciated about 14 percent on a trade-weighted basis between December 1971 and December 1973.

In addition to the current account deficit, receipts from tourism and remittances from workers abroad, two usually abundant sources of foreign exchange earnings, were underrecorded. To finance the external deficit, Italian public companies had been encouraged to resort to extensive borrowing, called "compensatory borrowing," in international capital markets. Gross official reserves were about $5.5 billion, with gold valued at the official price of SDR 35 an ounce. But inasmuch as special borrowing for balance of payments purposes since June 1972 also amounted to some $5.5 billion, the net reserve position was zero.

The review of Italy's situation revealed, too, that inflationary pressure was increasing. Labor costs were rising sharply because of earlier strikes and because of contracts concluded earlier in 1973 calling for higher wages. Prices were also rising, as were inflationary expectations. Financial policies had been clearly expansionary. The treasury deficit in 1973 had grown to more than 7 percent of GNP, and the rate of increase in domestic credit had accelerated from 17 percent in 1971 to 21 percent in 1972 to 27 percent in 1973. The strong expansion of demand in the second half of 1972 and in 1973 revealed that, notwithstanding the near stagnation of economic activity in preceding years, there was little spare capacity in Italy's economy.

The Italian representatives, moreover, expected little improvement in 1974. Although exports were likely to rise—by the second half of 1973 they were already rising at a seasonally adjusted annual rate of about 14 percent while the effective depreciation of the lira had substantially maintained the competitiveness of Italy's exports—rising real domestic demand was likely to cause an even greater increase in the volume of imports, and import prices were also expected to show a further sharp increase.

In these already adverse circumstances Italy confronted the first oil price increase. The situation was suddenly grave. Italy ranked among the largest users of oil in the industrial world, both in absolute and in relative terms. Nearly 80 percent of Italy's primary energy requirements was accounted for by oil, the bulk of which was imported. Its degree of dependence on imported oil was about equal to that of Japan and considerably greater than that of most other Western European countries.

The objective of the Italian authorities was to eliminate the non-oil portion of the current account deficit at the latest by the end of 1975. In the meantime, they expected that the non-oil current account deficit for 1974 would be reduced because the increase in oil prices itself, like an equivalent increase in indirect taxes, would have a deflationary impact on domestic output. The increase in real GDP in 1974 was expected to level off at about 4 percent instead of the 6 percent otherwise projected. The non-oil current account deficit for 1974 might accordingly be some Lit 1,000 billion (approximately $1.5 billion), only half the current account deficit in 1973. They projected the oil-related portion of the current account deficit at Lit 3,600 billion (roughly $5.5 billion).

The Program Agreed

The staff approached the negotiations in a spirit of accommodation. Like the Italian authorities, they preferred to avoid an overly deflationary approach in dealing with Italy's external payments problems, especially since the Italian economy was just emerging from three years of slow growth and a decade of inadequate capital formation. The staff agreed that elimination of the non-oil portion of the current account deficit no later than the end of 1975 was an acceptable short-term objective. They believed, however, that in the medium term it was important for Italy to achieve current account balance. While it might make sense for Italy at this stage of its economic development to run a current account deficit, a continuing deficit was not feasible because a net inflow of capital into Italy had not proved sustainable. The problem had usually been to prevent capital outflows. Balance in the current account in the medium term also seemed consistent with maintaining an appropriate rate of economic growth.

After agreement had been reached on objectives, the negotiators focused on the financial program that would best help to promote these objectives. Agreement was reached on use of a ceiling on "comprehensive credit expansion," a concept that included the nonbank public's holding of bonds and bills and hence was a broader aggregate than that of domestic credit expansion (DCE) customarily used by the staff. Because of the particular characteristics of Italy's banking system, the Italian representatives believed that a ceiling on DCE alone might unduly restrict the flow of funds to private industry. In a period of rising interest rates, the general public might switch out of bonds and into bank deposits; hence, though the volume of bank deposits would expand, total credit available to finance industry would not be enlarged.

The Italian officials proposed a financial program based on a projected increase in money supply, broadly defined, of 18.5 percent in 1974, compared with 21.5 percent in 1973. This rate of increase in the aggregate money supply exceeded that expected in gross national product, but the relationship between the two rates was in line with those recorded during past periods of credit stringency. One third of the projected credit expansion was to finance the treasury deficit.

The staff argued for more restrictive ceilings both in order to ensure sufficient progress in 1974 toward eliminating the non-oil current account deficit in 1975 and to strengthen the credibility of the program and thus promote a capital inflow. In the end the ceilings agreed were in between the initial positions of the Italian representatives and the staff, but the Italian authorities undertook to include in the letter of intent a commitment to an active interest rate policy to support the credit restraint effected through credit ceilings.

Separate ceilings for credit expansion were fixed for intervening quarterly periods. It was agreed also that the credit ceiling would be reviewed in July 1974. Should the oil-related portion of the current account deficit turn out to be lower than that being forecast, there would be less drain on domestic liquidity and the agreed credit ceiling would be more permissive than had originally been thought appropriate; hence the agreed credit ceiling might have to be lowered.

In essence, the program relied on monetary restraint. However, some fiscal measures were to be designed to ensure that the treasury deficit would stay within the agreed limit of Lit 9,200 billion, the amount estimated by Italian officials as the borrowing requirement of the Treasury for 1974. These measures included a prepayment of income taxes intended to bolster revenue in 1974 by about Lit 5,000 billion.

A statement on exchange rate policy was also agreed and put into the letter of intent. This statement was based on the understanding that the Italian authorities regarded the current effective exchange rate for the lira as adequate to ensure Italy's competitiveness in world markets, that is, that they would not engage in competitive depreciation, but at the same time they would continue to let the rate for the lira move sufficiently to maintain the country's competitiveness.

The staff also obtained a commitment from the Italian authorities that they would not introduce new restrictions on payments or transfers or new multiple currency practices on current international transactions or new restrictions on imports. The Managing Director and the staff needed especially to be reassured on these points since, as described in Chapter 17, the Fund was placing considerable emphasis on the avoidance of restrictions following the emergence of large oil deficits. When the Italian representatives indicated that, in a further effort to reduce capital outflows, they intended to review the regulations governing allocations of exchange to tourists, the staff expressed the strong hope that any changes would not involve restrictions on current payments. The Italian representatives agreed to include in the letter of intent an assurance that the Government did not intend to refuse any bona fide applications for exchange by tourists. (At the time of the negotiations the Italian authorities maintained a dual exchange market but this dual market was abolished shortly thereafter, in March 1974.)

One problem remained to be settled. At the start of the negotiations, the staff had informed the Italian representatives that, as was customary in Fund programs, drawings under the stand-by arrangement would have to be phased. Given Italy's urgent need for financing, it was agreed that the authorities would draw Italy's super gold tranche and gold tranche positions, along with the first credit tranche available under the stand-by arrangement, immediately upon approval of the stand-by arrangement by the Executive Board.

On the basis of these detailed agreements, the Managing Director and the staff believed that the Italian Government had a credible program that would allow them to recommend that the Executive Board approve the requested stand-by arrangement. The program and the stand-by arrangement were seen as holding actions to buy time in which to make more fundamental adjustments in the Italian economy.

A Fall of Government but the Stand-By Arrangement Still Stands

When the Italian team returned to Rome, disagreement in the Cabinet about the terms of the program negotiated with the Fund contributed to the resignation of Ugo La Malfa, Minister of the Treasury, and to the fall of the Cabinet. The Government was a coalition of political parties that had come into power, offering "a new opening to the left," and the Budget Minister, the Minister of the Treasury, and the Finance Minister, each of a different party, shared responsibility for economic policy. The political parties had differing points of view. The Socialist Party, for example, favored expansionary policies to help promote high rates of growth and employment, while the Republican Party, to which Mr. La Malfa belonged, favored anti-inflationary policies to help stem price increases and advances in labor costs.

445

As a new Cabinet was being formed, Mr. Palamenghi-Crispi was able to inform the Managing Director that his authorities still regarded the letter of intent already prepared as reasonable, given the Fund's existing policies. Both Mr. Palamenghi-Crispi and Mr. Witteveen agreed that renegotiation would be extremely difficult. A few weeks later, on March 28, 1974, Emilio Colombo, Mr. La Malfa's successor as Minister of the Treasury, sent a letter to Mr. Witteveen formally requesting the one-year stand-by arrangement for SDR 1,000 million. The letter of intent and the terms of the stand-by arrangement were exactly those negotiated in February.

In considering Italy's request for the stand-by arrangement, on April 10, 1974, the Executive Directors supported the strategy of the Italian authorities. In general, they agreed with the staff that, while the Italian authorities needed measures to strengthen Italy's balance of payments and to contain inflationary pressure, a heavily deflationary package was neither feasible nor desirable. They agreed, too, that the oil-related part of the current account deficit ought to be financed rather than be adjusted to, while the reverse was true of the non-oil-related part of the current account deficit. Mr. Lieftinck, in particular, raised questions that reflected increasing concern in the international financial community about Italy's deep-seated economic problems. Since there was heavy pressure from trade unions for the maintenance of real wages, backed up with the threat of strikes, how could the Italian Government best restrain the spiral of rising prices and labor costs? How was Italy going to reorient private spending so as to reduce consumption and facilitate the expansion of exports necessary for Italy eventually to pay for its oil imports?

At the time, the Executive Directors were also concerned about the Fund's limited holdings of usable currencies, especially since they expected many requests for drawings. Many Executive Directors elected by developing members or having developing members in their constituencies, concerned that other industrial members might also request large stand-by arrangements or drawings, wanted to make sure that the Fund would still have enough money left for developing members. Since this stand-by arrangement was the first with an industrial member since 1969, some Executive Directors elected exclusively by developing members were particularly vigilant in comparing the conditions of the stand-by arrangement approved for Italy with those of stand-by arrangements approved for developing members. They found that the conditions for Italy were considerably more stringent than those for developing members.

After this discussion in the Executive Board, the stand-by arrangement was approved. The phasing of drawings specified that drawings under the stand-by arrangement could not exceed SDR 400 million until August 15, 1974 or SDR 700 million until February 17, 1975.

PROBLEMS ARISE BUT THE PROGRAM IS ACHIEVED

In the next several months, Mr. Witteveen, the staff, and the Executive Directors kept in close contact with the Italian authorities and with subsequent economic developments in Italy, both through annual consultations under Article VIII and through the reviews of performance required by the stand-by arrangement. Italy's political situation remained delicate. The new coalition Government formed in February 1974 to replace the fallen coalition Government itself resigned in June, only to resume office again a few days later.

When the staff reviewed the economic situation in Rome in late June and early July 1974, it was clear that the Italian authorities had been carrying out the agreed program. Ceilings had been placed on lending by banks, short-term interest rates had risen from 11 percent to 17 percent, and long-term interest rates had gone up from 8 percent to 11 percent. The total financing requirement of the Treasury had also been kept within the agreed ceiling. Nonetheless, the balance of payments deficit in the first half of 1974 was much larger than expected. The current account deficit was running at an annual rate of about Lit 6,400 billion ($9.8 billion), nearly twice the amount projected, and the overall deficit was running at about Lit 7,000–8,000 billion ($11–12 billion).

To finance the external deficit, the Italian authorities had engaged in extensive borrowing abroad and had used some of Italy's gross reserves. The deficit had also caused the lira to depreciate further. Moreover, because of the large payments deficit, in May the Italian authorities had introduced a temporary import deposit requirement and a regulation limiting the amount of foreign exchange permitted to Italians traveling abroad. The former was a monetary measure, intended to help absorb excessive liquidity in the domestic economy; the latter was a restriction, intended as a check against illegal capital outflows. More importantly, the Italian authorities had also introduced a restrictive fiscal program. Charges for several public services, certain social security contributions, and taxes, mostly indirect, were raised. The new fiscal package was expected to yield about Lit 1,200 billion in calendar 1974, reducing the expected treasury deficit for the year to Lit 8,000 billion from the Lit 9,200 billion quoted in the letter of intent. Because of the new measures, the treasury deficit for 1975 was also expected to be about Lit 600 billion lower than otherwise. As Mr. Palamenghi-Crispi later emphasized to his colleagues on the Executive Board, the introduction of a fiscal program of such magnitude constituted a major policy shift for Italy, one which would have been regarded as "unthinkable" only a few months before.

Because the oil-related portion of the current account deficit projected for the year ending March 31, 1975 was now revised downward, at the review of the program in July 1974 the staff and the Italian authorities reached an understanding that the comprehensive credit ceiling for the 12-month period ending March 31, 1975 would be lowered, as provided in the letter of intent. The quarterly credit ceilings were adjusted accordingly. While staff members were concerned about the possible deflationary impact of the new fiscal measures, they were convinced that both the fiscal and the monetary measures were needed for the Italian authorities to correct the large external deficit and to get the acute inflationary pressures and expectations under control.

447

These were the circumstances when the Executive Board held the 1974 Article VIII consultation and its first review and consultation under the stand-by arrangement in August 1974. The introduction of the import deposit requirement in May had the effect of suspending the right to draw under the stand-by arrangement because of the performance criterion specifying that the Italian authorities would not impose restrictions on payments and transfers for current international transactions. At the Executive Board's review in August 1974, however, the Italian authorities assured the Fund that they would terminate the import deposit scheme not later than March 31, 1975, the end of the stand-by arrangement program. Moreover, the new fiscal package made it possible for Italian officials to eliminate the scheme. Accordingly, the Executive Board took a decision permitting Italy to go ahead with any purchases that might be made through December 31, 1974 under the stand-by arrangement.

In August and September Italy made substantial use of the Fund. In August it drew SDR 268 million in the gold tranche and SDR 250 million in the first credit tranche, the first drawing made under the stand-by arrangement. In September, it drew another SDR 450 million under the stand-by arrangement and another SDR 262.5 million under the oil facility. In November, it drew a further SDR 412.5 million under the oil facility.

Outcome of the Program

When the Fund undertook its next review under the stand-by arrangement, at the end of December 1974, it was again apparent that the Italian authorities were not only observing the credit ceilings but that credit expansion in the nine months to December 1974 was substantially below the ceiling set for December 31. Moreover, the new Government formed in November under Premier Aldo Moro (in which Mr. Colombo retained the office of Minister of the Treasury) was reaffirming Italy's intention to remain within the ceilings for the duration of the stand-by arrangement.

It was evident that the strong fiscal action taken in May was proving very effective, and that Italy's economic situation was turning around at a speed which few observers would have predicted only six months earlier or, insofar as the external accounts were concerned, would have dared to hope. After a rise of 3.4 percent in the first half of 1974, domestic demand in the second half of the year had fallen by an annual rate of 6–7 percent, with sharp declines occurring both in fixed investment and consumption. The most recent projections showed such an improvement in the non-oil current account deficit in the third quarter of 1974 that it was likely that the deficit would be eliminated in the fourth quarter of 1974. The objective of the Italian program would thus be accomplished a year ahead of schedule. Moreover, in the third quarter of 1974, owing to leads and lags in favor of Italy, the capital account was in substantial surplus. This shift reflected partly the effects of the import deposit scheme and partly the sharp rise of interest rates in Italy, where the prime rate had reached 19 percent. The Italian authorities had continued to manage the exchange rate policy in a flexible manner, allowing an effective (trade-weighted) depreciation of the lira of 11 percent from February 1973 to the end of the year and of 22 percent in the course of 1974. This depreciation broadly offset the differential increase in domestic costs and prices between Italian and foreign manufactured goods.

In view of Italy's policies and of the restated intention of the Italian authorities to abolish the travel restriction as soon as possible and to terminate the import deposit scheme not later than March 31, 1975, the Executive Board, early in January 1975, took a decision that no further understandings were necessary for any purchases that might be made under the stand-by arrangement. Early in 1975, the Italian authorities drew the remaining SDR 550 million under the stand-by arrangement.

The stand-by arrangement ended on March 31, 1975. Actual credit expansion during the year ending on that date did not exceed the limits envisaged under the program, as amended in June 1974. In fact, the actual domestic financial policy carried out was considerably more restrictive than the Fund would have required. On March 21, 1975, Mr. Colombo cabled Mr. Witteveen to inform him that the import deposit requirement was being abolished on March 24, 1975.

From the viewpoint of external adjustment, the stand-by arrangement had been very successful. The current account deficit in the second half of 1974 declined to SDR 2.4 billion, just over half the amount in the first half of 1974, and the objective of Italian officials of achieving equilibrium in the non-oil current account was attained in the fourth quarter of 1974, a year earlier than expected. Autonomous capital movements, negative to the extent of SDR 1 billion in the first half of 1974, yielded an inflow of SDR 1.6 billion in the second half of 1974, notwithstanding yet another political crisis in October 1974. Italy could thus dispense with further borrowing in the Eurocurrency market. With the aid of drawings from the Fund and a loan to the Bank of Italy by the Deutsche Bundesbank of $2 billion against gold collateral, gross official reserves had risen to SDR 5.7 billion at the end of 1974, about 18 percent of imports for that year.

RECESSION, REFLATION, AND RENEWED DIFFICULTIES

The balance of payments improvement obtained with the stabilization program turned out to be short-lived, however, and by January 1976, Italian authorities were informally exploring with the Fund staff the terms on which another stand-by arrangement might be negotiated. A complicated sequence of events underlay this unexpected reversal.

The astonishingly rapid balance of payments adjustment of the second half of 1974 had been achieved at the cost of a sizable fall in domestic demand (especially in the demand for accumulation of inventories) and in output. By early 1975 unemployment was up to about 5 percent of the labor force and would have been higher except for an increase in partial employment. The economic downturn of the second half of 1974 continued into the middle of 1975, and by then Italy's own recessionary tendencies were being compounded by the impact of the worldwide recession of 1974–75. The recession in Italy consequently became deeper than in any industrial country. The low point was reached in the third quarter of 1975 when GDP fell further, to nearly 6½ percent below the previous peak.

Despite depressed demand conditions, in February 1975 workers received large wage increases as a result of the revision and extension of coverage of the indexation mechanism used to adjust wages to increases in the cost of living. In consequence, real contractual wages in Italy's manufacturing industries rose by nearly 10 percent between the fourth quarter of 1974 and the fourth quarter of 1975. Since productivity also declined as production slowed down, unit labor costs in manufacturing industries rose by nearly 33 percent in domestic currency; relative to major trading partners and adjusted for changes in exchange rates, unit labor costs rose by some 18 percent, signifying a marked loss in Italy's competitiveness in world markets.

Despite the sharp increase in wages, in the face of mounting political pressure to check the rise in unemployment, Italian authorities abruptly changed their financial policies in August 1975 by adopting a major reflationary program. Public expenditures were increased, raising the treasury borrowing requirement from the Lit 10,000 billion forecast in mid-1975 to an actual Lit 14,000 billion by the end of the year. Monetary policy was also eased. After expanding by only Lit 10,700 billion in the first half of 1975, domestic credit increased by nearly twice that amount, Lit 20,500 billion, in the second half of 1975. The treasury deficit accounted for a substantial portion of the increase in credit expansion. By the end of 1975, the money supply (M_2)was over 23 percent higher than at the end of 1974, and interest rates had fallen sharply. Liquidity was also boosted by a large refinancing of export credits by the Bank of Italy. The ceilings on domestic credit expansion agreed with the Fund in August 1975, when Italy drew SDR 780.24 million under the 1975 oil facility, as well as the ceilings that had been agreed with the European Community, were greatly exceeded.

Since the reflationary policies of 1975 could to some extent be considered a reaction to the deflationary policies of 1974, it could be argued that the very success of the program introduced by the Italian authorities while the 1974 stand-by arrangement was in effect contributed to the problems arising in 1975 and 1976.

By late 1975, Italy was once again experiencing serious difficulties in its external accounts. The need to restock after the earlier drawing down of inventories had produced a strong upturn in domestic demand. This upturn, superimposed on the abrupt change in financial policy, the earlier wage increases, and the deterioration of Italy's competitive position in world markets, quickly produced adverse effects on the balance of payments. By late 1975, capital inflows were reversed and the current account, in surplus even through the third quarter of 1975, shifted back into deficit. Foreign exchange reserves fell from SDR 2.6 billion at the end of 1974 to SDR 1.1 billion (less than 5 percent of imports) at the end of 1975.

Large capital outflows, augmented by the uncertainties associated with the likelihood of an early election in June, widely believed about to result in a major political realignment in the Government, led to more major exchange rate crises for the lira in January 1976 and again in March and April 1976. Despite massive new borrowing and heavy intervention, the effective exchange rate for the lira, 20 percent below the level of February 1973, depreciated by a further 16 percent during the first four months of 1976. To counteract speculative pressure on the lira, on May 6 the Italian authorities introduced a 50 percent deposit requirement on most purchases of foreign exchange.

A SECOND STAND-BY ARRANGEMENT

Meanwhile, in January 1976, Italian officials started to inquire about another stand-by arrangement in the amount of SDR 530 million. Exploratory talks by Italian representatives with Fund staff were held in Washington. Mr. Whittome was again head of the Fund staff team; Mr. Palamenghi-Crispi again attended the discussions. These talks suggested that agreement would not be easy to reach on a comprehensive stabilization program that would provide a sustained improvement in Italy's economic performance. Discussions and negotiations between Italian officials and the staff went on intermittently for well over a year before a stand-by arrangement was finally approved in April 1977, and a program was gradually put together.

After the exploratory talks in January, Mr. Whittome led a staff team to Rome in March 1976 to discuss the policies the Italian officials had in mind. The negotiations had the added complexity that Italian officials were simultaneously negotiating with officials from the EC for a prospective loan of $1,000 million.

Mr. Whittome and other staff dealing with Italy were of the view that while adverse developments in the world economy, especially the widespread recession of 1974–75, had magnified Italy's economic problems, "the erratic and unsatisfactory performance" of Italy's economy since 1973 was mainly the result of recent domestic economic policies designed with only short-term objectives in mind and subject to abrupt reversals. In the staff's view, the Italian miracle of the 1950s and 1960s seemed to have ended, and since 1969 Italy had been encountering basic problems causing economic stagnation. Hence what Italy needed were policies of a longer-term nature aimed at resolving these basic problems.[1] Moreover, certain institutional arrangements, such as the wage indexation system by which wage increases were tied fairly fully to increases in the cost of living, the *scala mobile*, and the system by which an enlarged public sector financed a sizable range of Italian enterprises and activities, inhibited the ability of Italian authorities to pursue adequate macroeconomic policies. Therefore, as a precondition for another stand-by arrangement, a comprehensive program would have to be negotiated which, while ensuring the

---

[1] For a brief study of some of these basic problems by the staff that the Fund later published, see Hans O. Schmitt, "Sources of Growth: A Search for the Lost 'Italian Miracle,'" *IMF Survey* (Washington), Vol. 6 (February 21, 1977), pp. 62–64.

451

adoption of appropriate short-term fiscal, monetary, and other policies, would also begin to tackle some of the more basic institutional problems, such as the wage indexation scheme and the deficit of the enlarged public sector.

While the importance of tackling Italy's basic economic problems had become progressively more apparent to the Italian authorities as well as to the Fund staff, the Italian authorities were not quite ready for a comprehensive program. Early elections were anticipated in June, and it was widely believed that the election would result in a major political realignment of the Government. In these circumstances, once the EC loan was arranged in March 1976, the Italian authorities held off on further talks with the Fund.

The minority Government which emerged from the election in June governed only with the support of a coalition of parties, including the Communist Party. Inheriting a difficult economic situation and unable to introduce a comprehensive program, starting in mid-1976 the Government adopted a step-by-step approach to economic stabilization. Allowed to float, the lira depreciated by over 21 percent in relation to the U.S. dollar in the course of the year. Interest rates were again raised sharply, reserve requirements on bank deposits were increased, and, to mop up liquidity in the domestic economy, the 50 percent deposit requirement introduced in May was extended to practically all purchases of foreign exchange. A special temporary levy was also imposed on payments in foreign exchange. In addition, when the lira was again under heavy pressure in exchange markets in September and October, the authorities took a series of tax measures and raised the prices charged by state-owned enterprises. As a result of all these measures, the external current account reverted to a position of near equilibrium in the second half of 1976 while the capital account and the overall balance moved into substantial surplus.

The Italian authorities viewed a number of these measures as stopgap measures. Meanwhile, the Minister of the Treasury, Gaetano Stammati, sought domestic political support for a comprehensive economic stabilization program. He believed that help from outside institutions, such as the Fund, would help get a comprehensive program enacted.

Italian officials had held some informal discussions on this matter in Rome with officials of the Treasury of the United States. Mr. Stammati, together with Mr. Ossola from the Bank of Italy, also met informally with Mr. Witteveen and Mr. Whittome in Manila early in October during the 1976 Annual Meeting. Italian officials met again with the Fund staff later in October, the discussions being held in Paris so that they could be kept secret in the event that the negotiations broke down. Lamberto Dini, who had succeeded Mr. Palamenghi-Crispi as the Executive Director for Italy, participated in both series of discussions.

Throughout the discussions with Italian officials in 1976, the staff spent a long time, including many hours working with the Italian Treasury, assembling data on the finances of the public sector. The staff wanted particularly to obtain data to show operation of the finances of the consolidated public sector on a cash flow basis (in contrast to an appropriations or accrual basis) and to make projections for the financial accounts of the public sector for the immediate future. The staff also held many discussions with Italian officials on the system of wage indexation.

Following the meetings with the Managing Director and the staff in Manila and in Paris in October 1976, Italian officials issued a communiqué announcing a stabilization program and indicating that the program was supported by the Fund staff. Shortly thereafter the Prime Minister, Giulio Andreotti, presented the program to the Italian Parliament.

In the last few months of 1976 the Italian authorities also held informal talks with officials of the Federal Republic of Germany about the terms of assistance from the Fund. When Prime Minister Andreotti was in Washington on a state visit early in December, he met with Mr. Witteveen to review the status of various Italian measures and of the possible stand-by arrangement. Mr. Witteveen agreed with the staff that because the wage indexation system caused wages to respond rapidly and almost fully to increases in domestic prices, it reinforced and perpetuated inflation as well as seriously undermined the effectiveness of the major instruments of economic policy that might be used in Italy, such as changes in the exchange rate, in indirect taxes, and in the prices charged by public enterprises. Mr. Witteveen consequently stressed to Mr. Andreotti the need for a satisfactory modification of the system as a condition for a stand-by arrangement with the Fund. Changes in the wage indexation system were politically difficult since labor unions strongly opposed any change. However, Mr. Andreotti assured Mr. Witteveen that the proposed changes had the support of some Italian officials, that legislation on this subject was in progress in the Italian Parliament, and that Italian employers and labor union officials continued to discuss ways to limit increases in labor costs.

Added insight into the thoughts of Italian officials at the time comes from Mr. Andreotti's published diary. In December 1976 Mr. Andreotti recorded that he discussed with President Ford and Secretary of State Kissinger "the IMF's conditions for the loan" and expressed the hope that Mr. Witteveen, himself a former high-ranking political figure in the Netherlands, would understand that Italian officials "cannot be asked to do the impossible" and that "were Italy to collapse both politically and economically, Italy would not be the only loser." The diary also makes it clear that Mr. Witteveen reconfirmed that funds were available for the loan but only on condition that the Italian Government implement its program immediately and with secure guarantees, that is, with at least a guarantee of nonbelligerence on the part of labor unions. Mr. Andreotti noted further that earlier programs in Italy had always remained less than half completed and that "the Fund does not mix with politics."[2]

At the start of 1977, negotiations between the Fund and the Italian Government became still more intense. In January, the Managing Director had informal discussions with Paolo Baffi, Governor of the Bank of Italy, while they were in Basle for a regular monthly meeting of the central bank governors of the large industrial

---

[2] Giulio Andreotti, *Diari, 1976–1979: gli anni della solidarietà* (Milan: Rizzoli, 1981), pp. 56 and 57.

countries. Mr. Witteveen wanted to ascertain, in particular, the status of negotiations between the Government and labor unions on possible modifications of the wage indexation system. By February the Italian authorities had made what the Fund management and staff regarded as commendable progress toward achieving the targets for monetary and fiscal policies that Fund officials considered reasonable and they had made a considerable political effort to modify the wage indexation system. Since even after protracted discussions with labor unions and the employers' associations, it was proving impossible for the Government to secure a basic modification of the system, the Managing Director and the staff were seeking a compromise on a less ambitious target, especially as agreement with the Fund on a program was becoming increasingly important to Italian officials. (From an entry in Mr. Andreotti's diary of February 22, 1977, it would appear that officials of the EC were also making a Fund loan a prerequisite to further financial assistance to Italy from the EC.)[3]

The Italian authorities agreed to take a number of measures designed to hold down increases in labor cost during the program period. These increases, together with the further tightening of financial policies during the previous several months, were regarded by the Managing Director and the staff as an adequate basis for a program supported by the Fund. Accordingly, on April 6, 1977, Mr. Stammati wrote to the Managing Director formally requesting a stand-by arrangement for an amount of SDR 450 million for the 18-month period to December 31, 1978.

THE FINAL PROGRAM

The program, supported by the stand-by arrangement, set as its main objectives (i) a deceleration of the rate of inflation to 15 percent during 1977, 13 percent in the 12 months to March 1978, and to no more than 8 percent during 1978 as a whole, and (ii) an improvement in the current account of the balance of payments from a deficit of Lit 2,343 billion in 1976 to a surplus of Lit 500 billion in the year to March 1978, an amount considered consistent with a current account deficit of Lit 500 billion in calendar 1977 and a surplus of some Lit 1,000 billion or more in 1978. It was accepted that the pursuit of such targets was likely to entail a continued slowdown of demand and output in the short run, but it was hoped that the easing of external constraint and the decline of inflation would allow a resumption of sustained growth, led by exports and investment, over the medium term. Along with measures for demand management over the short term, the program accordingly contemplated a number of steps aimed at changing some of the more fundamental and troublesome features of the Italian economy. Thus, the program sought specifically not only to limit domestic credit expansion but also to reduce the deficit of the enlarged public sector, to modify the system of wage indexation, and to maintain Italy's competitiveness in world markets.

---

[3] Ibid., p. 82.

Starting with monetary policy, quarterly ceilings were set on domestic credit expansion over the year to the end of March 1978. A preliminary ceiling of Lit 30,000 billion was also set for the calendar year 1978 as a whole, subject to later review with the Fund. The appropriate level of interest rates was left unspecified. In effect, credit ceilings were calculated on the basis of a somewhat smaller decline in the velocity of circulation of money than had prevailed in the recent past.

With regard to fiscal policy, the program reflected in part the belief that the deterioration of Italy's public finances since the early 1970s was a major threat to the attainment of internal and external balance in Italy's economy. The public sector deficit had escalated rapidly as a result of (i) a sluggish growth of tax receipts, reflecting lags in collections and a high degree of evasion, (ii) a policy of delaying adjustments in the prices of public services, and especially (iii) a rapid and largely uncontrolled growth of public expenditure, in particular by local authorities and by institutions responsible for social security benefits.

The program approached on two levels the task of reversing these trends. First, quarterly ceilings were set to reduce the treasury deficit from Lit 15,000 billion in 1976 to Lit 13,100 billion in 1977, with a further reduction planned for 1978, subject to later reviews with the Fund. Second, a ceiling of Lit 16,450 billion for 1977 was specified for the deficit of the enlarged public sector, defined to include the Treasury, local authorities, social security institutions, and the state-owned electricity company (ENEL). Subject to review with the Fund, the enlarged public sector deficit was not to exceed Lit 14,450 billion in 1978. Because various tax measures had already been enacted, no more were required, but it was understood that further increases in revenue or cuts in expenditure would be required to ensure observance of the specified ceilings. In addition to these short-term measures, the program envisaged a number of steps designed to bring about a lasting improvement in the public finances, including tighter control by the Treasury over expenditure by other public bodies, better collection and reporting of data on fiscal developments, and more realistic pricing policies for public services.

With regard to wage and price policy, steps had already been taken in late 1976 and early 1977 (i) to reduce the coverage of the wage indexation system by excluding severance and seniority bonuses, (ii) to change the commodity composition of the index, and (iii) to require by law that cost of living increases for wage earners with incomes above certain levels be paid wholly or partly in nonnegotiable five-year treasury bonds. In addition, the program provided for quarterly ceilings on the cost of living indicator to which wages were indexed (*indice sindacale*) through April 1978, with the understanding that if such ceilings for price increases were broken, the Italian authorities would take further steps to modify the wage indexation mechanism in collaboration with the trade unions and the management of Italy's industries. Until the wage indexation system could be modified in a more comprehensive manner, a part of the social security contributions made by employers was put into the government budget in order further to moderate increases in labor costs.

455

With regard to exchange rate policy, following the sharp depreciation of the lira in 1976, the Italian authorities aimed at broadly stabilizing the effective exchange rate in 1977. A tight monetary policy and relatively high interest rates were intended to play a major role in preventing any further rapid fall in the exchange rate of the lira. At the same time, the authorities were determined to maintain, without imposing restrictions, the competitive position both at home and abroad of internationally traded goods and services produced by Italy and to confine intervention in the foreign exchange market to operations designed to minimize disruptive short-term fluctuations in the exchange rate.

In addition to these performance clauses in an agreed program, the stand-by arrangement contained clauses for phasing the amounts that could be purchased while the stand-by arrangement was in force. Purchases were not to exceed SDR 90 million until December 1, 1977, SDR 150 million until June 1, 1978, and SDR 300 million until December 1, 1978.[4]

EXECUTIVE BOARD APPROVAL

When the Executive Directors considered the 1977 Article VIII consultation simultaneously with the request for a stand-by arrangement on April 25, 1977, they generally agreed with the management and staff's assessment of the Italian situation and with the program. Many Executive Directors, including William S. Ryrie (United Kingdom), who a few months earlier had himself been through negotiations for a stand-by arrangement, described in Chapter 24, commended the Italian authorities and the Managing Director and staff on the outcome of these difficult and lengthy negotiations. In their view, the program appeared well balanced and well suited to the realities of the Italian situation. The shift of the Italian authorities from primary emphasis on monetary policy to emphasis on much tighter fiscal policy was, in many Executive Directors' view, especially laudable. The Executive Directors for other industrial members specifically relayed to Lamberto Dini, Italy, their congratulations on the intention of Italian authorities to take profound measures aimed at the heart of Italy's persistent balance of payments problem. They were impressed especially that the Italian authorities intended to give priority to gaining more effective control over the national budget, the budgets of local governments, and the finances of the many public enterprises. They recognized the political difficulties involved in such measures.

Most Executive Directors regretted, however, as had the staff, that the Italian authorities could not make more substantial changes in the wage indexation system

---

[4] Mr. Andreotti's diary indicates that, as of the middle of March, some ministers in the Italian Cabinet were concerned about "the harsh conditions," but on April 6, the Italian Parliament approved the wage provisions, so that the Italian authorities were in a position to send the letter of intent to the Fund. Entry of March 18, 1977, p. 88, and entry of April 6, 1977, p. 93.

so as to weaken further the link between price increases and wage adjustments. Noting that the rate of increase in GDP since 1974 had averaged only 2 percent a year, Mr. de Groote stressed that the structural reforms called for by the program were essential so that Italy could again enjoy a higher but sustainable rate of economic growth and a reduction in unemployment.

Executive Directors elected by developing members again carefully scrutinized the stand-by arrangement with Italy for precedents it might set for stand-by arrangements with developing members. Mr. Al-Atrash expressed concern that this stand-by arrangement contained conditions that were too specific and too strict for most developing members. He, like some other Executive Directors, objected especially to the use of rises in the general price index as a performance criterion even if, as the staff explained, price increases were being used only as a "test statistic," that is, as a way to reopen talks about wage indexation should increases in prices be excessive. Mr. Al-Atrash stressed that as the price level was not a phenomenon under the direct control of governmental authorities, governments could not really commit themselves to such a performance criterion.

After discussion, the Executive Directors approved the stand-by arrangement and, in the context of the Article VIII consultation, the continuation of the restriction on exchange available for travel.

Financing and Use of the Arrangement

To finance Italy's purchases under the stand-by arrangement, the Fund arranged to borrow SDR 337.5 million from eight of the ten participants in the General Arrangements to Borrow (GAB): Belgium, Canada, the Deutsche Bundesbank, France, Japan, the Netherlands, the Sveriges Riksbank, and the United States. Italy, of course, and the United Kingdom, also in acute balance of payments difficulties, were not called upon. In addition, arrangements were made with the Swiss National Bank for a loan to the Fund in U.S. dollars equivalent to SDR 37.5 million, and purchases of up to SDR 75 million were to be financed from the Fund's own resources.

In May 1977, Italy purchased SDR 90 million under the stand-by arrangement. By June 1, 1978, when the Fund was to review the arrangements for financing purchases under the stand-by arrangement, Italy had not drawn any further amounts. In the interim, the Italian authorities had repurchased the Fund's holdings of Italian lire (excluding holdings resulting from purchases under the oil facility) so that the Fund's lira holdings were only 87 percent of Italy's quota. Italy thus had a gold tranche which exceeded the total amount authorized by the stand-by arrangement, so that it would have been in a position to make purchases from the Fund without challenge or without meeting the performance criteria specified in the stand-by arrangement. Since the Fund's liquidity in the meantime had also improved, the Fund could finance any future purchases under the stand-by arrangement from its own resources and had no need to call on the GAB.

PERFORMANCE UNDER THE STAND-BY ARRANGEMENT

In the first year of the program, performance exceeded expectations with respect to both the external account and inflation. The current account showed a surplus of over Lit 2,000 billion in calendar 1977 and of over Lit 3,000 billion in the program year, the 12 months ended in March 1978, six times the program target of Lit 500 billion. While this surprisingly big improvement in Italy's external account was partly the result of a stronger than expected performance of exports, in value terms, it was primarily the result of an unanticipated gain in the terms of trade, particularly as the U.S. dollar depreciated in exchange markets beginning in late 1977 and continuing through most of 1978.

Italy's external current account balance was also favorably affected by unexpectedly sharp increases in net invisible receipts, as previously concealed capital outflows through tourists' and emigrants' transactions were reversed. The capital account itself also improved markedly as Italy's enterprises, faced with tight domestic credit conditions, ample liquidity abroad, and a strengthening of the lira, relied increasingly on borrowing abroad. The Italian authorities took advantage of this capital inflow to reconstitute foreign exchange reserves, and gross official reserves rose by over $3.7 billion in the course of 1977. By intervening heavily in the foreign exchange market, the Italian authorities also prevented a substantial *appreciation* of the lira vis-à-vis the dollar after mid-1977, although the lira continued to depreciate vis-à-vis stronger European currencies.

With regard to inflation, the rate of increase in consumer prices declined slightly faster than projected during 1977, primarily because import prices rose more slowly than before, and by April 15, 1978 the general price index was below the ceiling specified in the program agreed with the Fund.

The improvement in the external accounts continued in 1978. The current account surplus grew to Lit 5,308 billion, far in excess of the program target. However, the deceleration of increases in prices largely came to an end in 1978. The rate of inflation, while considerably lower on average than in 1977, stabilized at around 12 percent, a substantially higher rate than that targeted in the program. Partly as a result of the stabilization program, the rate of growth of GDP fell from nearly 6 percent in 1976 to 2 percent in 1977. In 1978 real GDP grew by 2.7 percent on average but the rate of increase was markedly accelerating in the course of the year.

The sharp improvement in the current account and, to a lesser extent, in inflation occurred even though the performance criteria pertaining to the treasury deficit, the enlarged public sector deficit, and domestic credit expansion contained in the program were generally not observed, in some instances by substantial amounts. Although preliminary data did not indicate a breach of ceilings on the first test date (June 30, 1977), no drawings were made under the stand-by arrangement beyond the first installment, as already mentioned, and even that drawing was repurchased in July 1978. The Italian authorities did not seek any waiver or modification of the performance criteria nor were any formal new understandings sought with the Fund for the period April 1–December 31, 1978.

To conclude, the program was successful insofar as the immediate stabilization objectives were concerned, but the Italian authorities had less success in implementing those features of the program aimed at tackling some of the longer-term structural problems in Italy's economy. Little progress was made, for example, toward redirecting resources from private and public consumption to productive investment: real gross fixed investment stagnated in 1977 and even declined in 1978, and the ratio of public expenditures to GDP continued to increase rapidly. Moreover, the main factors underlying the escalation of public expenditures in the 1970s went largely uncorrected. Finally, the program did not succeed in substantially modifying the wage indexation system. The moderation of import prices, together with the absence of contractual wage increases, helped to reduce the pressures making for rising labor costs; hence Italian officials and employers felt less of a sense of urgency to modify the wage indexation system, particularly as labor unions continued to be strongly opposed to modifications.[5]

At the Annual Meeting in September 1978, Filippo Maria Pandolfi, who had become Minister of the Treasury earlier in 1978, referred in his speech to the persisting need in Italy for "a radical change ... to correct slowly but steadily the structural conditions of the economy."[6]

---

[5] Other versions of developments in Italy's economy in these years and of the negotiations between Italian officials and the Fund management and staff from 1974 to 1977, written outside the Fund and not necessarily endorsed by Fund officials, are those of Luigi Spaventa, "Two Letters of Intent: External Crises and Stabilization Policy, Italy, 1973–77," in *IMF Conditionality*, John Williamson, ed. (Washington: Institute for International Economics, 1983), and of John R. Hillman, "The Mutual Influence of Italian Domestic Politics and the International Monetary Fund," *Fletcher Forum* (Medford, Mass., Winter 1980), pp. 1–22.

[6] Statement by the Governor of the Fund for Italy, *Summary Proceedings, 1978*, p. 39.

CHAPTER
24

Stand-By Arrangements with an Industrial Member: the United Kingdom

*E*VEN BEFORE THE OIL PRICE RISE late in 1973, the Fund staff considered the problems of the U.K. economy basic and in need of resolution over the long term. The ups and downs in the U.K. balance of payments and reserve position that had led to the devaluation of the pound sterling in 1967, followed by the swing to large payments surpluses in 1970 and 1971, and then the sudden reversal of the external position, culminating in the floating of the pound sterling in the middle of 1972, were symptomatic of longer-run problems.

NATURE OF ECONOMIC PROBLEMS

The unexpectedly slow growth in real output after 1968 and the rising level of unemployment beginning in 1971 (described in Chapter 3) also continued into 1973 and 1974. By 1974 it was apparent that for over a decade real gross domestic product in the United Kingdom had been increasing at a much lower rate than that of the six other major industrial countries. The Fund staff attributed this slow growth to a variety of factors, all of which were difficult to correct: an antiquated industrial structure, trade union and management practices, low profit margins, high interest rates, high marginal income tax rates, and a relatively low rate of capital formation. The low rate of capital formation was of particular concern to the Fund staff because it contributed to a loss of U.K. exports in world markets and to a prolonged weakness in the U.K. external position. The share of U.K. exports of manufactures in the total exports of manufactures of the 11 largest countries, for instance, had declined from 15.5 percent in 1962 to 8.8 percent in 1974.

As the Fund staff in 1974 and 1975 looked back at the economic policies of the United Kingdom over the previous ten years, it seemed that the U.K. policymakers had been trying to avoid the Scylla of balance of payments deficits and pressure on

461

sterling and the Charybdis of excessively high levels of underutilized capacity and unemployment. Efforts to increase investment and raise the level of growth usually led, and usually very rapidly, to unmanageably large balance of payments deficits and to flights from sterling. But then tightening demand-management policies to regain confidence in sterling led quickly to a sharp slowdown of domestic output. In seeking a solution, U.K. officials since 1964 had alternated between expansionary and contractionary policies. They seemed to be locked into a series of deflationary policies followed by expansionary policies, so-called stop and go policies.[1]

In this pattern, after the crisis of June 1972, which had led to the floating of the pound sterling, planned budgetary expenditures were cut and an incomes policy was introduced to curb inflation. A temporary standstill on pay, prices, rents, and dividends was put into effect to give the Government time to introduce more lasting wage and price controls. Statutory pay controls were then introduced but they were replaced in July 1974 by voluntary wage restraints.

Although incomes policy was gaining wide public acceptance and trade union leaders and officials of industry were increasingly aware of the need to make substantial sacrifices to cure the basic economic problems of the United Kingdom, the Fund management and staff and many Executive Directors remained concerned about a number of elements in the U.K. economy. Were the needs of the private sector being crowded out by the claims on domestic savings of the public sector? Was not the public sector borrowing requirement (PSBR), that is, the borrowing needed to finance the budgetary deficits of the public sector, too large in relation to gross national product? The PSBR covered more activities than the customary budgetary deficit. It included the central government budget, the budgets of local governments, the capital borrowing needs of nationalized industries and public corporations, and even some borrowing by the government sector for on-lending to the private sector. The relatively large PSBR of the United Kingdom highlighted some basic and increasingly debated questions about the economies of industrial countries. Could governments continue to support the wide range of social welfare programs that had come into being since World War II? Were large government claims on the economy retarding private investment? And in the case of the United Kingdom where many industries had been nationalized after World War II, could government-owned industries be run in the same efficient and profitable way as private industry?

There were problems about monetary policy, too. Interest rates had to be sufficiently low to accommodate private borrowers for domestic investment, but yet sufficiently high to attract enough capital inflows from abroad to help support the pound sterling in the exchange markets. The high proportion of output going to consumption and the low proportion going to investment also suggested an

---

[1]For a brief staff study published by the Fund analyzing why the period after World War II did not produce an "economic miracle" in the United Kingdom, as it did in other European countries, see Hans O. Schmitt, "Labor Shortage, Excess Demand Hindered Postwar Growth of U.K.," *IMF Survey* (Washington), Vol. 6 (June 6, 1977), pp. 162–64.

underlying structural problem. Because of changes toward greater equality in the distribution of income, consumption in the United Kingdom was being stimulated and represented a very high proportion of the increased real output. The re-emergence of a trade deficit in 1972 caused still further concern about U.K. exports. The United Kingdom had a long history of large surpluses on invisible transactions owing to the country's large shipping interests and to the long-standing and well-established financial and insurance activities of the City of London. Although these surpluses on invisible transactions continued, the customary deficit on trade in the U.K. accounts was becoming so large that it could not possibly be covered by the surplus on invisible transactions. Furthermore, although U.K. officials had been able to finance external payments deficits by letting balances of pounds sterling held by foreign entities accumulate and by some borrowing abroad without high interest rates, the risk that foreign entities would be unwilling to hold ever larger amounts of pounds sterling was growing. Moreover, the cost of borrowing abroad was rapidly increasing.

The concerns of Fund officials about the U.K. economy were justified by late 1973. There was again a large deterioration in the U.K. current account, which developed a deficit of nearly £1.5 billion for 1973 as a whole. After a current account surplus of more than £1 billion in 1971, the current account had been barely balanced in 1972, and now again showed a sizable deficit. The overall balance of payments was not yet in crisis because the capital account swung from deficit into surplus in 1973, the U.K. Government had no difficulty in borrowing abroad on medium term to cover its current account deficit, and foreign holders were willing to accumulate larger balances of pounds sterling. But any of these elements could quickly change.

Impact of the Oil Crisis

The crisis caused by the announcement of higher oil prices in 1973 was superimposed on several already existing difficulties. In conducting the Article VIII consultations in mid-1974, the Executive Directors, the Managing Director, and the staff, noting that the U.K. officials were planning to finance their oil deficit and to refrain from imposing payments restrictions—in accord with Mr. Witteveen's suggestions of the previous January—were cautious in their assessment of the situation. The prospects for oil from the North Sea had considerably brightened the outlook for the U.K. external accounts. Many members of the Executive Board from industrial members stressed, however, that the United Kingdom had to deal with its basic problems. It had particularly to develop better incentives for private investment and to increase exports. Executive Directors from developing members were struck by the similarity of the basic economic problems of the United Kingdom and those of developing members. It was difficult to reconcile a sustainable balance of payments position with a moderately high rate of economic growth. The economy was vulnerable to economic events abroad; a large percentage of output went into consumption, and there was need to divert resources from consumption to investment so as to enlarge productive capacity. More of the economy needed to be

463

oriented toward exports, and reliance on imports needed to be reduced. All these goals, moreover, had to be accomplished without excessive budget deficits since budgetary deficits contributed to inflation, making exports uncompetitive in world markets and causing exchange rate depreciation.

By the time of the next Article VIII consultation in June 1975, the world recession was at its deepest point, greatly reducing the volume of U.K. exports. The deficit on current account in 1974 more than doubled from 1973, to £3.4 billion, and although U.K. officials were still able to finance it, especially since the governments and private entrepreneurs of oil exporting countries were willing to accumulate balances of pounds sterling, balance of payments management was obviously becoming more difficult. In addition, unemployment was steadily increasing and inflation was escalating; the consumer price index, for instance, had risen progressively from an annual rate of increase of 10.6 percent in December 1973 to 21.7 percent in April 1975, by far the highest rate of inflation among the industrial countries. Business profits and investment had fallen sharply.

THE 1975 STAND-BY ARRANGEMENT

In these circumstances Denis Healey, Chancellor of the Exchequer in the Labour Government of Prime Minister James Callaghan, informally approached the Managing Director in late November 1975 with a request to purchase SDR 1,000 million under the 1975 oil facility and a request for a stand-by arrangement for SDR 700 million. The requested stand-by arrangement was for 25 percent of the U.K. quota of SDR 2.8 billion and was in the first credit tranche. In requesting both an oil purchase and a first credit tranche stand-by arrangement, U.K. officials were doing as many members did in the course of 1975. Since use of the 1975 oil facility was subject to first credit tranche conditionality, also asking for a first credit tranche drawing or stand-by arrangement allowed members to obtain more money from the Fund without their having to fulfill additional conditions. Moreover, the Fund customarily approved requests for direct drawings or stand-by arrangements in the first credit tranche. From the Fund's point of view, the policies and conditions to which the member subscribed for a purchase under the oil facility were likely to be taken more seriously both by the government and by the Fund if they were related to use of the Fund's regular resources. The Fund staff also believed that they could more readily persuade officials to think in terms of a program to adjust their oil-related balance of payments deficits if these officials had a customary stand-by arrangement with the Fund as well as a drawing on the temporary oil facility.

The immediate circumstance that precipitated the U.K. request for Fund assistance was, as in the previous requests from the United Kingdom, a decline in the rate for the pound sterling. The deficit on current account was actually lower in 1975: it was £1.7 billion, half the deficit of 1974. The trade balance improved because of a favorable shift in the terms of trade when world commodity prices fell in 1975 and because of a large drop in imports into the United Kingdom as a result of depressed domestic demand and of the depletion of inventories of fuels and industrial materials. The surplus on invisible transactions also continued to be large.

Despite the improved current account position, U.K. officials had a problem with the overall external payments situation. Instead of accumulating further holdings of pounds sterling, as they had been doing, the governments and private entrepreneurs of oil exporting countries began to sell large amounts of pounds sterling. As a result, the United Kingdom's gross official reserves declined by about SDR 1,000 million, despite further foreign currency borrowing by the public sector of some SDR 1.4 billion. Sterling was repeatedly under pressure. By December 17, 1975, the day before Mr. Healey formally wrote to the Managing Director requesting the stand-by arrangement, the rate for the pound sterling was 30 percent lower in effective trade-weighted terms than it had been at the end of 1971. Declines in the rate reflected concern about inflation in the United Kingdom (the consumer price index for 1975 as a whole rose by 25 percent as against less than 10 percent in the major industrial countries taken collectively) and about the prospects for U.K. exports and investment.

The policies that the Government had been using since April 1975 to reduce the rate of inflation were spelled out in the letter of intent sent to the Fund along with the request for the purchase under the oil facility and for the stand-by arrangement. The Chancellor of the Exchequer had introduced into the budget for 1975/76 a series of tax increases intended to prevent a further rise in the PSBR in terms of its relation to national income. More significantly, to ensure that public expenditure plans were strictly adhered to, the Government, for the first time, was making extensive use of cash limits on public spending programs. The main element of the counterinflationary policy, however, was incomes policy. Strict limits of £6 on weekly wage increases were to be implemented in cooperation with the trade union movement.

The Fund staff assessed the U.K. situation and policies in this way. Since the reduction in 1975 in the U.K. current account deficit was mainly attributable to a decline in domestic output and a drawing down of inventories of imported items, it might not last and, in any event, the achievement of the Government's longer-term economic goals was still a long way off. Meanwhile, the policies taken were appropriate to the United Kingdom's problems and were in fact already having some success by the end of 1975. The Fund, therefore, ought to approve the transactions requested.

When the Executive Board, working right up to the last day of an exceptionally busy year, considered the U.K. requests on December 31, 1975, William S. Ryrie, Executive Director appointed by the United Kingdom, emphasized that had the cost of imported oil not gone up, the United Kingdom would not have had great difficulty financing its balance of payments deficit. Authorities of the United Kingdom had wanted to avoid Draconian measures to curb their payments deficits, partly because of political differences in the United Kingdom as to how far the authorities ought to go with deflationary policies that increased unemployment and reduced the real income of the work force, and partly in line with the request of

Mr. Witteveen and the Committee of Twenty in January 1974 for countries to avoid excessive deflation. Hence, U.K. officials were only now, in the latter part of 1975, beginning to take strong domestic measures aimed at correcting payments imbalances. Mr. Ryrie agreed with the Fund management and staff that the actions of his Government met first-tranche conditions for using the oil facility and for the requested stand-by arrangement.

The Executive Directors wholly supported the proposed use of the Fund's resources. Members of the Executive Board from virtually all members commended the U.K. authorities on their political courage. The U.K. authorities were taking measures in two critical areas, public expenditure and incomes policy. Policies which implied a fall in real wages and allowed considerable unemployment to develop were difficult for a government to take. The Executive Directors were pleased that, for the first time, an incomes policy was being consistently applied in a major industrial member. Nearly all Executive Directors insisted that the U.K. authorities had to have a "firm policy of restraint and cautious demand management" if they were to reduce a rate of inflation in the United Kingdom greatly exceeding that of most other industrial countries. Several Executive Directors elected by developing members, although recognizing the legitimacy of the United Kingdom's request for use of the Fund's resources, were nevertheless concerned that the large drawings involved would leave less for drawings by developing members.

Both the drawing on the oil facility and the stand-by arrangement were approved. On January 16, 1976 the United Kingdom purchased the full amount of its gold tranche, equivalent to SDR 700 million. On January 23, 1976 it purchased the SDR 1,000 million under the oil facility. On May 12, 1976, it purchased the SDR 700 million available under the stand-by arrangement.

THE 1977 STAND-BY ARRANGEMENT: CIRCUMSTANCES

After the transactions approved in December 1975, Mr. Witteveen and the staff kept in frequent informal contact with Mr. Healey, with Gordon Richardson, Governor of the Bank of England, and with other high-level financial officials, including Sir Derek Mitchell and Sir Douglas Wass, and with Mr. Ryrie. In March 1976 there was once again sudden, unexpected, and unexplained pressure on the pound sterling, and despite substantial intervention in exchange markets by the Bank of England and consequent large losses of reserves, the rate for the pound dropped to $1.92, breaking what had seemed to be a psychological barrier of $2. It was difficult for the U.K. authorities to know what to do. On the one hand, the decline in the value of the pound helped to make U.K. exports more competitive in world markets and helped to counter the effects of relatively high inflation in the United Kingdom. On the other hand, the decline in the value of sterling could have adverse effects on the confidence of major holders of pounds. These holders seemed willing to hold on to their balances even with the rate dropping slightly provided they were convinced that the U.K. Government was not deliberately engineering a lower rate.

The problem was how to determine an appropriate rate. No time period in the economic history of the United Kingdom since World War II could be regarded as a suitable benchmark for an "equilibrium rate for the pound," a rate which would foster sufficient exports, allow the U.K. economy to grow at a reasonable rate, and maintain current account equilibrium.

As the rate for the pound sterling declined further in May 1976, to ensure confidence in sterling and to prevent another balance of payments crisis coming from capital outflows, the Bank of England in June secured a six-month stand-by credit from the central banks of other industrial countries and from other monetary institutions for up to $5.3 billion. Up to $1 billion was to be made available by the U.S. Federal Reserve System, up to $1 billion by the U.S. Treasury, up to $800 million by the Deutsche Bundesbank, up to $600 million by the Bank of Japan, up to $300 million each by the Bank of France and the Bank of Canada, and the remainder by Switzerland and the Bank for International Settlements. Use of this external credit facility was to be as limited as possible. It was intended to give the U.K. authorities time to put into effect monetary and fiscal policies that would again encourage inward rather than outward capital flows. Meanwhile, the U.K. authorities had committed themselves firmly to refrain from any general use of import restrictions. This credit was arranged on the understanding that within six months, that is, by December 1976, the U.K. Government would have obtained a stand-by arrangement with the Fund.

By August 1976, U.K. officials and the Fund management and staff were engaged in secret exploratory discussions about a stand-by arrangement. Since U.K. officials expected that they could not deliver the necessary forecasts of economic developments until late October, it seemed to the Fund staff even in August that any stand-by arrangement could not be in place until late December at the earliest. In August and early September, informal discussions took place on possible amounts of an arrangement. Because of the Fund's decision of January 1976 to enlarge by 45 percent the amounts that could be drawn under credit tranches, the United Kingdom could have a stand-by arrangement up to 245 percent of quota. An amount of SDR 4,060 million, less the SDR 700 million of the first credit tranche already drawn, or SDR 3,360 million, could thus be involved. It was by no means certain, however, that the Executive Board would approve such a large amount. Much depended on the policy package that could be put together.

At the time, despite the decline in the rate for the pound sterling, the outlook for the U.K. economy seemed better than it had for many years. The domestic economic measures taken in 1975 were proving successful; voluntary agreement restraining pay increases was proving especially helpful in reducing the rate of increase in money wages. The current account deficit was also lower. With a lower rate of inflation, a successful incomes policy, and a tolerable payments position, it appeared that the U.K. authorities were finally in a good position to work on the structural problems of the economy. Since the world economy was itself beginning to recover from the 1974–75 recession and world trade was again expanding, it seemed the U.K. economy might have an opportunity to achieve the real expansion of exports so lacking in the past.

The crucial problem was that exchange markets for sterling remained unsettled. The rate for sterling continued to decline. At the end of July 1976, just before the exploratory talks with the Fund began, the dollar-sterling rate was $1.7865, a depreciation on an effective trade-weighted basis of nearly 40 percent in the four and a half years since the Smithsonian agreement. To make matters worse, as had happened in earlier years, any action taken by the U.K. authorities to stimulate domestic investment was immediately translated into pressure on the rate for sterling. A lowering of the minimum lending rate early in 1976, for instance, had created the impression that the U.K. authorities were deliberately letting the pound depreciate to help U.K. exports and touched off further speculation.

By the end of September the outlook for the U.K. economy was again becoming clouded. Industrial output was rising very little; prices were once more beginning to accelerate, but, most serious of all, sterling remained under intense pressure. While U.K. officials continued to advise the Managing Director of their intended policies to restrain fiscal and monetary expansion, exchange markets became chaotic. The dollar-sterling spot rate dropped to $1.68 per pound on September 27, 1976 and to $1.63 per pound on September 28, 1976, just as the 1976 Annual Meeting was about to open in Manila. On September 28, Mr. Healey announced that he was informing the Managing Director of the Fund of his intention to apply for a stand-by arrangement in the remaining credit tranches, an announcement aimed at instilling confidence in sterling and restoring order to the exchange markets. Mr. Witteveen, en route to Manila, was informed in advance of this announcement. Because of the emergency, Mr. Healey and Mr. Richardson remained in London, and their absence from the Annual Meeting meant that Mr. Witteveen was unable to talk directly to them at that time about the terms of a stand-by arrangement. The lack of frank, face-to-face talks at this stage may have added to the difficulty of later negotiations.

THE 1977 STAND-BY ARRANGEMENT: NEGOTIATIONS

After the Managing Director and the staff returned to Washington from Manila and discussed informally their attitudes toward the U.K. situation, a staff mission headed by Mr. Whittome went to London in November. To the staff it appeared that the desperate weakness of the pound sterling late in 1976 might have come from fears that foreign official holders of sterling balances would sell off these balances if they believed that the U.K. Government was not doing enough to stimulate economic growth through exports and investment and would therefore have to resort to import controls and to even more stringent controls on capital movements. An even gloomier view suggested that the social and political framework of the United Kingdom was under such heavy pressure that the Government's ability to take decisions was impaired. The Fund management and staff considered these views exaggerated, noting that in July 1976, the Government had imposed cash limits on public sector expenditure, that the rate of increase in wage settlements was declining, and that interest rates had been raised.

The atmosphere in London was tense. In order to reduce encounters between the Fund staff and reporters, U.K. officials registered the staff in a hotel under assumed names. Although the intention was innocent enough, reporters later interpreted it as part of a desire by Fund staff to "slip quietly and secretly into London to urge tough policies."

It was also evident that there would be no easy agreement on policies needed to support the requested stand-by arrangement, despite the pressure of trying to have the stand-by arrangement in place by the end of the year. Mr. Healey had stated that he believed existing U.K. policies would suffice as a basis for a stabilization program and had so indicated to the Managing Director. Consequently, when the staff arrived in London, they met with officials who were not allowed to discuss any change in U.K. policies. In the view of U.K. officials, the economy had been doing well earlier in the year, and only the sudden pressure on sterling presented a problem. Hence, all that was needed was an announcement by the Fund of financial support so that confidence in sterling would be quickly restored. Several politicians and economists, including members of Mr. Callaghan's Cabinet, in the long-standing Keynesian tradition of the United Kingdom, insisted on budgetary policies that would maintain high levels of employment and would continue to finance social welfare programs. They strongly criticized Mr. Healey for the cuts he had already made in public expenditure. To cope with the balance of payments deficit and stem the decline in the pound sterling, these advocates of expansionary measures favored direct controls on imports, if needed.

U.S. officials, such as Mr. Simon and Mr. Burns, and officials of the Federal Republic of Germany, such as Mr. Schmidt, Mr. Pöhl, and Mr. Emminger, held more conservative views.[2] Since they were market oriented and favored private enterprise, they tended to be critical of the inflationary consequences of "British socialism." As they saw it, the social welfare programs financed by the U.K. Government were no longer affordable and, by draining funds from private investment, were harmful to the private sector and to U.K. exports. As some politicians and officials in the United Kingdom shared this point of view, long debates were inevitable. Mr. Callaghan himself was in a difficult position because as Chancellor of the Exchequer he had presided over the devaluation of the pound sterling in November 1967 and as a result had been forced to resign.

---

[2]As Fund officials negotiated with U.K. officials, the latter also consulted U.S. and German officials. An unusually detailed newspaper account (which of course is not endorsed by Fund officials), describing how the policies of Prime Minister Callaghan were shaped amid the domestic political debate within the United Kingdom and the influence of high-level political figures in the United States and the Federal Republic of Germany, can be found in a three-part article by Stephen Fay and Hugo Young, "The Day the £ Nearly Died," *Sunday Times* (London), May 14, 21, and 28, 1978, Part 1, pp. 33–35, Part 2, pp. 33–35, and Part 3, pp. 33–34.

The Managing Director and the staff believed that the authorities of the United Kingdom would be best advised to introduce strong constraints on the money supply and on the budget deficit so as to help restore confidence in the pound sterling. Regardless of their own views, however, they were well aware that the large stand-by arrangement requested by the United Kingdom, going to 245 percent of quota, was imperative to stabilize sterling and needed the support of the international community. To gain this support, U.K. officials would have to embark on a strong anti-inflationary program. In October, Lord Cromer, former Governor of the Bank of England, had pointed out to the House of Lords that the United Kingdom was no longer dealing with foreign private bankers but with foreign official financiers. He noted that the resources requested from the Fund derived from the official reserves of Fund members that had managed their resources more prudently and, as a result, the Fund was likely to ask for the adoption of policies that the United Kingdom should in its own interest be implementing in any event.

Mr. Richardson likewise tried to line up public support for whatever conditions might be necessary to get the stand-by arrangement approved. Speaking at the Lord Mayor's Dinner to the Bankers and Merchants of the City of London on October 21, 1976, he supported establishing publicly announced monetary targets, the domestic credit expansion goals for which the Fund was well known. An article by Economics Editor Malcolm Crawford in the *Sunday Times* on October 24 added to the tension, however, by reporting the alleged terms of a $3.9 billion stand-by arrangement as agreed by the International Monetary Fund and the U.S. Treasury. Among the terms reported was an agreement to let the rate for the pound drop further, from the $1.64 then prevailing, to $1.50. The rate immediately started to fall in exchange markets and the Fund had to issue denials of the *Sunday Times*'s story.

Negotiations between the Fund management and staff and U.K. officials were protracted. The staff team stayed in London from the first week in November until the middle of December, three times longer than the customary two-week period for such negotiations. Nonetheless, an appalling time constraint played on both parties, since the United Kingdom had to be able to draw under the Fund's arrangements by the end of December in order to repay its drawings on the six months' agreement with the industrial countries. Officials of the United States and the Federal Republic of Germany remained in close touch with officials of the United Kingdom. Following his defeat in the election of November 1976, President Ford took considerable interest in the question of sterling during his remaining days in office until January 20, 1977. Officials of the United States and of the Federal Republic of Germany were relying on the Fund management and staff to assess the specific measures needed and to get U.K. officials to agree to them, thus putting the Fund in a key role in financial negotiations with the U.K. Government. U.S. Treasury officials, especially Mr. Simon, Secretary, and Edwin H. Yeo III, Under Secretary for Monetary Affairs, had come to regard the Fund as the only multicountry instrument that could make a serious attempt to lend on conditional terms and that might persuade a country to adopt the policies it recommended. The Fund's reputation was generally good, as were the relations between the Managing Director and staff and senior U.K. financial officials.

The Managing Director and staff insisted on acting independently in the Fund's negotiations with the United Kingdom and were determined not to be unduly influenced by officials of other industrial countries. Maintaining this independence was at times difficult, particularly as U.K. officials persistently tried to soften the positions of the Fund management and staff indirectly by requesting U.S. and German officials to persuade the Fund not to be "too tough." Arthur F. Burns, however, stressing that it was important that the "rule of law" be observed for all Fund members, helped the Managing Director resist such pressure.

The Fund staff aimed at ensuring that U.K. officials had in place a set of policies that promised a deceleration of inflation and a sufficient improvement in the balance of payments to enable the country to concentrate on its structural economic problems. Debate centered primarily on the size of the public sector borrowing requirement for 1977/78 and 1978/79 and on the target for domestic credit expansion. Fund officials at first urged a borrowing requirement of £6.5–7.0 billion for 1977/78, while U.K. officials were forecasting the need for £8 billion, if not more. Fund officials also wanted the domestic credit expansion to be about £1–2 billion less than U.K. officials estimated would develop under existing policies. The size of an initial drawing under a stand-by arrangement was also debated. U.K. officials understandably wanted to be able to have as large a "front-loading" as possible, while the Fund management and staff considered about SDR 1 billion more appropriate as a first drawing under the stand-by arrangement.

At the end of November, the positions of the Fund staff and of the U.K. officials were still far apart. At the suggestion of Mr. Witteveen, the staff mission remained in London and let the negotiations proceed slowly to give U.K. officials time to come to an agreed position among themselves. The Fund staff continued to insist that an acceptable policy package be put together that would justify a stand-by arrangement of 245 percent of quota. The Fund management and staff were more or less concurrently negotiating with the officials of Italy for the 1977 stand-by arrangement described in Chapter 23. In fact, Mr. Whittome, Director of the European Department, was the main negotiator for the Fund with regard to both Italy and the United Kingdom. Thus, it was extremely important that the Fund officials not weaken the policies expected of the United Kingdom. Otherwise the policies expected of Italy might also have to be weakened.

At one point, Mr. Whittome returned to Fund headquarters to seek the support of Mr. Witteveen. The U.K. Cabinet was about to decide on the policies that the Government should take. Some U.S. officials and the Fund staff team considered it essential for the Managing Director to meet with the Prime Minister before the Cabinet meeting to elicit his support for macroeconomic policies in preference to use of restrictions on imports. By this time, Mr. Healey himself favored reducing the public sector borrowing requirement and wanted assurance of the Prime Minister's support. U.S. Treasury authorities transmitted to Mr. Witteveen President Ford's belief that it would be desirable for Mr. Witteveen, in the interest of the international community, to go to London to help persuade Mr. Callaghan to support a reduction in the public sector borrowing. Mr. Witteveen was asked to keep secret President Ford's request. He was fully aware that such a trip was risky and would have to be secret or the negotiations between the Fund and the United Kingdom could be in jeopardy. In these circumstances, he felt that he could not even inform the Executive Board in advance of his travel, as was customary.

When Mr. Witteveen arrived at Downing Street on December 1, 1976, U.K. officials had on the table a copy of the charter of the GATT. Apparently they were seriously considering imposing import restrictions. Mr. Witteveen pointed out to Mr. Callaghan the disadvantages both for the U.K. and the world economy of using import restrictions to cut the U.K. payments deficit as a means of restoring confidence in the pound sterling. They discussed possible adjustment measures. The four key men, Mr. Witteveen and Mr. Whittome from the Fund and Mr. Callaghan and Mr. Healey from the United Kingdom, continued talks over lunch. Afterwards, just before the Cabinet was to meet, Mr. Callaghan finally agreed to support a reduction of the public sector borrowing requirement. Although this reduction was not as large as that proposed by the staff, it was, nonetheless, substantial. After Mr. Callaghan made known his position, the Cabinet agreed. Mr. Healey was especially pleased with the successful outcome of Mr. Witteveen's trip and told him so.

Mr. Witteveen managed to elude reporters at Heathrow Airport. The Executive Board, however, presented more of a problem. While it was informed that Mr. Witteveen would be unavailable for the usual scheduled Executive Board meeting, it was not given the correct explanation. When the Executive Directors learned that Mr. Witteveen had been in London, many were annoyed, not because of his role in the negotiations but because they felt that they had been misled.

In a written memorandum, Mr. Witteveen explained the circumstances as "exceptional and compelling" and defended the secrecy of his trip as "necessary to avoid any publicity around my visit." While he could understand that his action "may have left an unfavorable impression with some Executive Directors," he hoped that he could count "on their understanding particularly because of the need for quick action in order to help resolve some extremely difficult problems in a negotiation of crucial importance." This event was to color Mr. Witteveen's relations with the Executive Board for the rest of his term.

The details of a policy package and of a stand-by arrangement were finally worked out by the weekend of December 11–12, 1976. The Managing Director was later to compliment Mr. Whittome for conducting "the largest, longest, most difficult, and, perhaps, most momentous negotiation in the history of the Fund" and to send a special memorandum to the members of the mission complimenting them for their work "conducted under the most intense glare of public and political interest of any mission in the Fund's experience."

Arrangements were made to enable Mr. Healey to reveal the U.K. measures to Parliament before formal Executive Board approval was secured, although Executive

Directors were told informally of the main lines of the agreement. On Wednesday, December 15, Mr. Healey presented the essential features of the agreement with the Fund to the House of Commons. On the same day he also sent a formal letter to the Managing Director requesting a stand-by arrangement for up to SDR 3,360 million to be extended over two years, the first two-year stand-by arrangement that the Fund approved.

The forecasts for the public sector borrowing requirement for £10.5 billion for 1977/78 and for £11.5 billion for 1978/79 were to be reduced to £8.7 billion in 1977/78 and to somewhat less in 1978/79, or from 9 percent of GDP in the 1976/77 budget to about 6 percent in 1977/78 and just over 5 percent in 1978/79. The needed fiscal adjustment was to come mainly from savings in public expenditure, which was to be cut by £1–1.5 billion in each of the next fiscal years. These cuts were to be across the board. The system of cash limits, introduced a year earlier, which had effectively held spending in real terms in check, was to be applied to two thirds of public expenditure. To increase revenues, indirect taxes were to be increased and the Bank of England was to sell its shares in the British Petroleum Company. Essential monetary targets for domestic credit expansion were to be formulated in accordance with the Fund's usual requirements. Domestic credit expansion was to be kept to £9 billion in fiscal year 1976/77, to £7.7 billion in fiscal 1977/78, and to about £6 billion in fiscal 1978/79. These rates of expansion were equivalent to 24 percent of sterling M_3, the broadly defined money stock that included time deposits as well as the normal components of M_1, the traditional concept of "money supply," that is, currency and demand deposits, at the beginning of 1976/77, 18 percent of sterling M_3 at the beginning of 1977/78, and 13 percent of sterling M_3 at the beginning of 1978/79.

Incomes policy was also to be continued. The voluntary incomes policy in force for the previous 18 months had been fully complied with, even though the agreements provided for pay increases significantly below the current rate of inflation. Discussions on pay policy between the Government, the Trades Union Congress, and the Confederation of British Industries were going forward so that incomes policy would continue along the lines of the previous voluntary wage restraint. In fact, the main instrument of counterinflation policy during 1977 was to be agreement with the trade unions on voluntary wage restraint. Take-home pay, that is, income from wages and salaries after taxes and other deductions, was expected to fall by about 7.5 percent in real terms by mid-1977 and possibly by as much as 10 percent during the year.

THE STAND-BY ARRANGEMENT
APPROVED BY THE EXECUTIVE BOARD

The Executive Directors took up the U.K. request for a stand-by arrangement on January 3, 1977. The phased amount to be available to the United Kingdom in the first year, calendar year 1977, was to be SDR 1,950 million, while SDR 1,410 million was to be available for 1978. The Managing Director proposed to activate the General Arrangements to Borrow for an amount of SDR 2,860 million, with the balance, SDR 500 million, to come from the Fund's own resources.

The Executive Directors unanimously supported the U.K. request. Many Executive Directors believed that the U.K. situation would quickly improve, and they again commended the U.K. officials for their courageous fiscal and incomes policies. Mr. Whitelaw, for instance, pointed out that the U.K. Government had had to bear the stigma of taking advice publicly from an international institution, obviously a difficult thing to do for the "once grand lady of international finance." The U.K. Government had also faced internal political pressures as it cut back on public expenditures and risked higher unemployment when unemployment was already twice the level of two years before and gross national product was 10 percent below its potential. Mr. Kafka wondered whether the considerable fall in real wages implicit in the current agreement with trade unions would be tolerable. Did the policy give due regard, he questioned, to wage differentials between different groups of wage earners? Was it compatible with adequate incentives to produce? Mr. Kharmawan, after observing that it was difficult to promote social justice and a redistribution of income without at the same time increasing total national income, commended the U.K. authorities for rejecting the easy solution for improving the balance of payments, that of introducing direct controls on imports. These controls would have had especially adverse effects on developing members seeking to increase their exports.

Mr. de Groote noted the special role that the Fund had performed in the process. The size of the proposed stand-by arrangement and the extent of the commitments undertaken by the U.K. authorities demonstrated the necessary function of the Fund as a central financial intermediary between countries in surplus and those in deficit and as "the supervisory authority of the adjustment process." Mr. de Groote noted, too, that the discussions with the United Kingdom also reaffirmed the validity of the Fund's procedures under which the Managing Director and staff had full responsibility for negotiations. Direct involvement of the Executive Directors would have made an agreement almost impossible because it would have deprived the Chancellor of the Exchequer of the climate of secrecy that he needed to elicit the support of some of his colleagues and of "some other elements of the population in London." Mr. de Groote regretted, however, that the Executive Directors were apprised of the negotiations only at a very late stage, that an agreement on the financing of the stand-by arrangement through the GAB was reached before a meeting of the Group of Ten, and that it did not include some of the smaller members participating in the GAB.

Several Executive Directors were concerned about the implications of the U.K. stand-by arrangement for the Fund's liquidity. If the full amount available under the stand-by arrangement was drawn, outstanding drawings by the United Kingdom would exceed SDR 5 billion, or one third of total outstanding drawings by all Fund members. Messrs. Al-Atrash, Amuzegar, and Guarnieri, Executive Directors elected by developing members, called attention to the unprecedented efforts and flexibility of the Managing Director and the staff in their negotiations with U.K. officials and voiced the hope that "other requests would receive the same treatment."

After a full day of discussions, the Executive Board approved the stand-by arrangement.

AGREEMENT ON STERLING BALANCES

Concurrently with the stand-by arrangement with the Fund, the U.K. Government arranged an agreement on balances of pounds sterling held abroad by official entities. U.K. officials had been discussing for many months such an agreement with officials of the other nine countries in the Group of Ten and of Switzerland. The elements of the agreement were finally put in place at a meeting of the central bank governors of the major industrial countries at the Bank for International Settlements (BIS) in Basle on January 10, 1977, one week after the stand-by arrangement with the Fund was approved. Mr. Witteveen attended the meeting at the invitation of Jelle Zijlstra, President of the Netherlands Bank, who was Chairman of the central bank governors.

The agreement provided for a $3 billion facility furnished by the several participating central banks and the BIS, with the BIS as administrator. Drawings under the facility depended on two conditions: that the United Kingdom should continue to be eligible to draw under its stand-by arrangement of January 3, 1977 with the Fund and that sterling balances held abroad by official entities not exceed $6.75 billion net of public sector foreign currency borrowing, unless the participating central banks agreed that the excess was temporary. This amount was the level of officially held balances of sterling on December 8, 1976. The facility was to be available for two years, roughly for the calendar years 1977 and 1978, but extendable, subject to agreement, for a third year.

The facility was intended to help reduce the use of the pound as a reserve currency. It was to support an orderly reduction over a period of two to three years in the balances of sterling held in the official reserves of governments and central banks abroad, down to the amounts needed as working balances. The United Kingdom undertook to secure such a reduction by the sale of foreign currency bonds of five to ten years' maturity and by other appropriate means and to exercise restraint with respect to future increases in balances of sterling held by private entities.

The Managing Director of the Fund was asked to undertake an unusually important role in monitoring the agreement. The U.K. Government was to review regularly with the Managing Director and with the governors of the participating central banks the progress made in meeting U.K. commitments. If the right of the United Kingdom to draw on the stand-by arrangement with the Fund was interrupted, the Managing Director was to notify the BIS. In addition, the Managing

Director was to make a judgment about the extent to which the U.K. Government was fulfilling its undertakings with respect to official balances of pounds sterling and to notify the BIS of his findings. If, in the opinion of the Managing Director, any of these commitments were not being adequately fulfilled, the eligibility of the U.K. Government to draw on the facility could be suspended and the amounts already drawn would have to be repaid within a certain period.

This role of the Managing Director was subject to approval by the Executive Board. Mr. Witteveen was himself enthusiastic about the novel and important functions for the Managing Director, which he regarded as a position of honor and trust. The Executive Directors were also pleased with this unusual request for the services of the Managing Director. Inevitably, they had some questions since this request represented the breaking of new ground for the Fund. They wondered, for example, whether Mr. Witteveen was being asked to give opinions in a personal capacity, or as Managing Director, or because he was Managing Director but would not be acting in that capacity. But the Executive Board also wanted to respond positively to the request and worked out relatively quickly the necessary procedural and legal details. The agreement on balances of pounds sterling went into force on February 8, 1977 and the Executive Board approved the role of the Managing Director on March 28, 1977.

THE U.K. CRISIS RESOLVED

A few days after the stand-by arrangement was approved, the U.K. Government, in accordance with a prior understanding with the Fund, purchased SDR 1 billion. In May and again in August the agreed phased amounts, SDR 320 million each time, were drawn. This total of SDR 1,640 million was financed wholly by Fund borrowing under the GAB and from the Swiss National Bank. Thereafter, no further drawings were made because of the rapid improvement in the U.K. balance of payments position.

Immediately after the stand-by arrangement was approved, much to the pleasant surprise of U.K. and Fund officials, confidence in the pound was restored and the U.K. Government had resounding success in meeting short-term problems. Huge inflows of capital took place both into sterling and into the gilt-edged bonds offered for sale by the Government in accordance with the agreement on sterling balances. Figures tell the story graphically. In January 1977, for example, short-term capital inflows amounted to $2,000 million, some $500 million larger than even the most optimistic forecasts. When Mr. Witteveen visited London a short time later, U.K. officials were informally asking him how much to let sterling appreciate. The program was clearly enormously successful.

Under the stand-by arrangement, the U.K. Government consulted periodically with the Executive Board to review the performance of the U.K. economy. In July 1977 the annual Article VIII consultation was held as well. By this time, the U.K. authorities had been able to reduce the public sector deficit considerably below the level of a year earlier and, for the first time in many years, to reduce the actual total of public expenditures. Mr. Ryrie told the other Executive Directors that in the second half of fiscal 1976/77 public sector borrowing was £2.4 billion below the limit agreed under the stand-by arrangement and domestic credit actually contracted by £0.4 billion, compared with a ceiling in the memorandum of understanding permitting an expansion of £4.5 billion. Cash limits on large sectors of both central and local government public expenditure were especially effective in keeping down total public expenditures. Incomes policy was also a success, as reflected in a fall in the year-on-year increase in average earnings from 26.5 percent in July 1975 to 8.5 percent two years later.

These achievements provided the underpinning for a recovery of confidence in the pound that gathered momentum as operators in exchange markets came to comprehend the determination of the U.K. authorities to implement appropriately restrained financial plans. Excessive monetary expansion was stopped and the return of confidence brought a decline in interest rates, a rapid recovery of foreign exchange reserves, and an appreciation in the exchange rate. In mid-1977 the United Kingdom even made its first repurchase under the stand-by arrangement.

After consultation with the staff, the U.K. authorities proposed in December 1977 that the quantitative performance criteria relating to the public sector borrowing requirement and to domestic credit expansion be extended to mid-1978. The authorities proposed also to consult and reach understandings with the Fund before the end of June 1978 on the limits on the borrowing requirement and on credit expansion for the remaining period of the stand-by arrangement. In the meantime, the U.K. authorities would not request purchases under the stand-by arrangement above the first credit tranche. The Executive Board agreed to these proposals on January 13, 1978, when the full-scale review of the stand-by arrangement after one year's operation took place. By that time, the massive inflow of capital and the growth of short-term reserves from $4.1 billion to $20.6 billion began to pose a dilemma for U.K. officials: they had to choose between maintaining the competitive gains associated with the earlier devaluation of the pound and preserving the autonomy of monetary policy. They gave priority to the latter, a choice welcomed by Fund officials.

In May 1978 staff discussions took place for the first consultation under the new Article IV held with the United Kingdom. The public sector borrowing requirement for 1977/78, subject under the stand-by arrangement to a ceiling of £8.7 billion, turned out to be only £5.6 billion, 4 percent of gross national product. In the 12 months to April 19, 1978, domestic credit expansion amounted to £4.4 billion, about £1.6 billion below the ceiling agreed under the stand-by arrangement. The staff team also initiated consultations with the U.K. authorities regarding performance criteria for the remaining period of the stand-by arrangement. The Chancellor of the Exchequer again proposed quarterly limits for public sector borrowing and domestic credit expansion, and the Executive Board agreed to these limits.

The current account also moved into surplus and gross official reserves increased by almost SDR 10 billion in the two years 1977 and 1978. After a short lag, moreover, the performance of the real economy distinctly improved. Private investment in manufacturing rose sharply (by 9 percent in 1977 and 6 percent in 1978), and by 1978 the annual rate of increase in consumer prices was reduced by half (from 16 percent to 8 percent), close to the average for industrial countries. Also, for the first time in several years, the share of U.K. manufactures in world exports increased.

In September 1977, in March 1978, and in September 1978, after consultation with the Fund staff, U.K. authorities, and officials of other participating central banks, the Managing Director reported in Basle to the governors of those banks on the progress made by the Government of the United Kingdom in performing its undertakings under the arrangements for sterling balances. The central bank governors agreed with the Managing Director's judgment that the U.K. authorities were making reasonable efforts to close the gap between official holdings of balances of pounds sterling and the working balances needed to meet trade and other commitments.

As of the end of 1978, the stand-by arrangement had to be termed a success. Some members of the Executive Board went so far as to label it "the most successful ever implemented." The stand-by arrangement expired on January 2, 1979 and the arrangements on sterling balances on February 7, 1979.

SIGNIFICANCE FOR THE FUND OF THE STAND-BY ARRANGEMENTS WITH ITALY AND THE UNITED KINGDOM

The stand-by arrangements approved for Italy and the United Kingdom in 1974–77 were important for the Fund in several respects.

First, the Managing Director and staff of the Fund bore the brunt of the negotiations. Although the highest-ranking officials of other large industrial countries, especially of the Federal Republic of Germany and of the United States, were consulted directly by officials of Italy and the United Kingdom, the hard decisions on the ingredients of the stabilization programs and the performance clauses of the stand-by arrangements were worked out with the Fund management and staff. This procedure represented a notable advance for the Fund from the 1950s when the main features of financial programs were worked out first between officials of large industrial members, particularly with the U.S. Government, and then presented to the Fund for more or less pro forma approval.

Second, stringent terms were agreed upon, especially in the stand-by arrangements of 1977. The government authorities involved, without question, considered themselves "pushed" by the Fund's officials. In this respect, the Fund had come a long way since the first drawing by the United Kingdom in 1956 and even since the stand-by arrangements of 1964 and 1967, which involved much less negotiation of terms and policies.

Third, for the first time in the Fund's history, and probably in international monetary history, stabilization programs deliberately involved negotiations between government officials and leaders of labor unions and of industry. It was no longer possible for a government of a large industrial member, faced with serious inflation, to secure financial assistance from the Fund without a commitment not only on the usual credit and fiscal policies but also on incomes policy.

Fourth, the stabilization programs and stand-by arrangements agreed upon required actual cuts in consumption and real income. In the 1950s and 1960s, when the economies of industrial countries were growing rapidly in real terms, anti-inflationary programs usually meant the adoption of policies which slowed, but did not reverse the rapidly increasing growth of consumption and real income. In the 1970s, however, serious anti-inflationary efforts, even in the large industrial countries, as evidenced by the experiences of Italy and the United Kingdom, meant an actual lowering of existing standards of living. It is no wonder that negotiations between Fund officials and officials of member governments became increasingly politically sensitive and controversial.

Fifth, the results of the programs for Italy and the United Kingdom demonstrated that programs worked out with the Fund can be remarkably and quickly effective. Moreover, the improvements in the economies of Italy and the United Kingdom continued until the world economy encountered new difficulties following the second round of oil price increases in mid-1979, when changed external conditions meant that each country had to undertake further measures of adjustment. While structural problems persisted in the economies of both Italy and the United Kingdom after the expiration of the 1977 stand-by arrangements, by 1978 the economies of both countries were in a better financial position to undertake the adjustments needed to deal with the structural problems.

Sixth, while most of the Fund's "customers" were developing members, the Fund still had two large industrial members as customers. This meant that the Fund was maintaining its financial functions vis-à-vis all its members, both industrial and developing.

CHAPTER
25

Conditionality: A Disputed
Issue Arises

CONDITIONALITY BECAME A FAMILIAR TERM in the international
financial lexicon after 1975. It refers to the conditions that the Fund attaches
to use of its resources and came under mounting and intense criticism in the second
half of the 1970s. When Fund officials undertook to defend the Fund's policies,
discussions about conditionality, even within the Fund, aroused deep-seated
emotions.

The same degree of conditionality did not apply to all uses of the Fund's
resources. By the middle of 1974 policy governing use of these resources was no
longer as monolithic as it had been in earlier years. The Fund had developed a
number of "windows," called facilities, from which a member might request
drawings. There was a compensatory financing facility, a buffer stock financing
facility, an oil facility, and an extended facility. A supplementary financing facility,
which had a different character, was yet to come. Different conditions applied to
each facility. The compensatory financing facility and the oil facility, for instance,
were subject to what some Executive Directors and staff regarded as mild or modest
conditionality, and others regarded as "virtually no conditionality." Drawings
within the gold tranche (that is, drawings which raised the Fund's holdings of a
member's currency to not more than its quota) were made legally automatic when
the First Amendment was approved in 1969. After 1968, drawings or stand-by
arrangements in the first credit tranche (that is, drawings, except for those explicitly
excluded, which raised the Fund's holdings of a member's currency above 100
percent but not above 125 percent of its quota) were subject to what Fund officials
regarded as only moderate conditionality. More stringent conditions applied to other
stand-by arrangements, that is, those under which members used the Fund's
resources in amounts which went beyond the gold (reserve) tranche and the first
credit tranche into the upper credit tranches.

This chapter explains the Fund's conditions and describes criticisms of those
conditions. Chapter 26 explains how the Fund answered these criticisms.

EVOLUTION OF CONDITIONALITY PRIOR TO THE 1970s

The conditions governing use of the Fund's resources have a long history. They were intensively debated even before the Fund was established. John Maynard Keynes and Harry Dexter White held contrasting views on the attitude the Fund should have toward members' requests to draw. Mr. White was convinced that the Fund must have the power to question any request in order to prevent unjustified drawings, which in the circumstances of 1945 meant drawings in U.S. dollars, and to require that repayment should take place at a set time. Mr. Keynes sought to ensure that members would have the right to draw automatically and that repayment should follow when the balance of payments deficit for which the drawing was made was reversed. This difference of view found expression in the original Articles. The provisions governing use of resources were general and permissive, yet gave the Fund power to interpret these provisions and to declare a member ineligible to use its resources.[1]

In 1946 the Executive Directors discussed the provisions of the Articles extensively and in 1948 took decisions interpreting them.[2] The issue between "automaticity" and "conditionality," however, continued to divide the Executive Board for several years. Officials of Canada and the United Kingdom pressed for automaticity, while U.S. officials staunchly insisted that the Fund had to devise some form of placing conditions on drawings.[3] In the meantime, for a number of reasons, the Fund did not evolve a general policy on use of its resources until 1952. In fact, after April 1948, the "ERP decision" placed a virtual freeze on drawings.[4]

By 1952 Fund officials wished to develop a general policy on use of resources. World trade and payments were still shackled by exchange controls, restrictions, and inconvertible currencies, and Fund officials developed the idea that use of the Fund's resources could be tied to members taking measures that would improve their balance of payments positions sufficiently to enable them to relax their payments restrictions and exchange controls and to move closer to convertibility of their currencies. Members might be more willing to lift restrictions if assured that they could have recourse to the Fund if lifting restrictions should result in unmanageable current account deficits.

---

[1]The debates of 1943–44 on the right to draw and the resulting Articles are described in *History, 1945–65*, Vol. I, pp. 67–77 and 101–103, and Vol. II, pp. 381–84.

[2]These decisions—E.B. Decision No. 284-4, March 10, 1948, and E.B. Decision No. 287-3, March 17, 1948—were reproduced in *History, 1945–65*, Vol. III, pp. 227 and 228.

[3]The debates in the Executive Board concerning automaticity versus conditionality in the Fund's first few years have been described in *History, 1945–65*, Vol. I, pp. 151–52, 189, 223, 242, 244–46, 276, 280–82, 330, and 599, and Vol. II, pp. 390–97 and 522. Frank A. Southard, Jr., Executive Director for the United States in these years, has also briefly described some of these debates in his *The Evolution of the International Monetary Fund*, Essays in International Finance, No. 135, Princeton University (Princeton, New Jersey, 1979), pp. 16–20.

[4]On April 5, 1948, the Fund took a decision limiting use of the Fund's resources during the period of the European Recovery Program (ERP), better known as the "Marshall Plan." See *History, 1945–65*, Vol. I, pp. 219–20.

The Rooth Plan for use of the Fund's resources—named after Ivar Rooth, the second Managing Director—became the basis for the landmark decision of February 1952. Members could count on "receiving the overwhelming benefit of any doubt" for drawings in the gold tranche, thereby instituting automaticity for these drawings. In the absence of such automaticity, members who had put part of their gold reserves in the Fund were worse off than nonmembers who had no restriction on use of their gold reserves. Drawings beyond the gold tranche were not to remain outstanding beyond the period reasonably related to the payments problem for which the drawing was originally made. The Fund's determination of whether to grant a member's request to draw was to depend on whether the payments problem was temporary and whether the member's policies were adequate to overcome the problem within such a period. Thus, drawings from the Fund were explicitly related to a member's policies. To preserve the revolving character of the Fund, repurchases, for which previously there was no time limit, were normally to be made after three years and within five years at the maximum. In addition, by suggesting that members might not want to draw immediately but could ensure themselves that they might be able to draw within a subsequent 6 to 12 months, the 1952 decision contained the germ of the stand-by arrangement. With this decision, the Fund for the first time had a general policy on use of its resources.[5]

In the following six to seven years, the Fund gained experience with the new policy. To implement it, a general framework was used and no fixed model or preset techniques were imposed on members to eliminate restrictions. Rather, Fund staff talked to members about their domestic inflation and balance of payments problems and discussed with them how they would get rid of restrictions and move toward the Fund's objectives. Gradations of conditionality were also worked out. Liberal treatment was applied to requests for drawings in the first credit tranche while more rigorous expectations for corrective policies were applied to requests for drawings in the upper credit tranches. By the mid-1950s Fund officials felt comfortable with the policy.

Conditionality Incorporated into Stand-By Arrangements

The stand-by arrangement at first lent a degree of automaticity to use of the Fund's resources: having initially qualified for use of the Fund's resources, a member would be assured of use of those resources for a time without having to meet further conditions. Since the decision of 1952 tied the use of the Fund's resources to the attainment of the Fund's objectives, particularly to eliminating restrictions, and since stand-by arrangements were increasingly used, the argument over automaticity and conditionality eroded.

---

[5]The 1952 decision on use of the Fund's resources and the preceding discussions in the Executive Board have been described in *History, 1945–65*, Vol. I, pp. 276–82 and 321–26, and Vol. II, pp. 399–403. The decision itself was reproduced in Vol. III, pp. 228–30. The decision is also described in Southard (cited in fn. 3 above), pp. 17–18.

Along with greater use of stand-by arrangements, there was greater use also of stabilization programs primarily to help the management and staff determine whether they could recommend the stand-by arrangement to the Executive Board. The Fund gradually developed methodology and criteria for judging the monetary, fiscal, and exchange rate policies that constituted acceptable stabilization programs. By the end of the 1960s the programs went into considerable detail by covering not only the total supply of money but also the sources of expansion of money and quasi-money, as well as the structure of interest rates and interest rate policies. Often they also covered the management of cash balances and of domestic public debt, and other monetary activities.[6]

As time passed, the stand-by arrangement became the principal vehicle by which members drew on the Fund's resources. Drawings without stand-by arrangements became unusual.[7] Furthermore, the question arose as to how the Managing Director and the staff could review, or monitor, performance to ensure that the member would actually achieve its objectives under the agreed program and be in a position to repurchase from the Fund within three to five years. The idea of monitoring the performance of members was reinforced by a growing conviction in the 1950s and early 1960s on the part of the Managing Director and staff and of the Executive Directors from industrial and relatively more developed members that countries, especially developing countries, ought to have "monetary discipline." Per Jacobsson, Managing Director, had made his reputation as an advocate of strong anti-inflationary policies in Western Europe as far back as World War I, and he in particular urged developing countries to pursue strict monetary discipline and fiscal restraint. He urged such policies especially on Latin American members whose rates of inflation were much higher than those in Europe.[8]

Just as monetary data and targets were helpful for deciding a member's initial eligibility for a stand-by arrangement, so were they helpful for monitoring a member's performance. Initially the use of monetary data and targets did not reflect belief in monetarist doctrines. The staff analyzed balance of payments developments and the effectiveness of measures to reduce payments deficits, especially of exchange devaluation, in terms of the elasticity-absorption approach being developed in the Fund at the time, as described in Chapter 5. Monetary data and targets supplemented this analysis by providing simple aggregate measures easily available from members' statistics for determining the direction in which an economy was moving. In the late 1960s, however, monetarism was increasingly advanced as an economic doctrine, and more of the Fund staff and more Executive Directors came to believe in a causal connection between monetary targets and the achievement of balance of payments goals. The ascendancy of monetarism as a doctrine and the refinement of economic models lent credibility to the Fund's technique, based on

---

[6]The origin and evolution of stabilization programs until 1971 can be found in *History, 1945–65*, Vol. II, pp. 492–510, and *History, 1966-71*, Vol. I, pp. 363-66.

[7]See *History, 1966–71*, Vol. I, pp. 320–22 and 338.

[8]Mr. Jacobsson's economic views have been described by his daughter, Erin E. Jacobsson, in *A Life for Sound Money: Per Jacobsson, His Biography* (Oxford: Clarendon Press, 1979).

monetary statistics, of identifying a member's eligibility for a stand-by arrangement and of monitoring its performance.

The policies and targets included in stabilization programs were eventually integrated with the clauses and performance criteria of stand-by arrangements. Protective clauses were written into stand-by arrangements to permit interruption of a member's automatic right to draw if it failed to observe established performance criteria. In this way conditionality was explicitly written into stabilization programs and into stand-by arrangements.

Conditionality Incorporated into the Articles

The concepts of conditional and unconditional liquidity were refined in the course of extensive discussions of international liquidity in the 1960s, and the distinction between them was incorporated into the Articles of Agreement in 1969 when the First Amendment became effective.[9] Unconditional liquidity was to take the form of SDR allocations. The rest of the Fund's resources—except for purchases in the gold tranche which the Articles of Agreement made legally automatic—were to be used only on a conditional basis. Several amendments emphasized that the use of the Fund's resources had to be temporary, that the Fund's policies had to ensure that the use of resources was temporary, and that the member's policies should assist it to solve its balance of payments problem.[10]

These amendments were not intended to introduce new policies nor to make the rules governing the use of the Fund's resources more restrictive. The Fund's policies had already been going in the direction taken by the amendments. But conditionality as a feature of the Articles was put beyond controversy. The provisions of the amended Articles were included at the insistence of officials of the EC countries. It is noteworthy that these officials had earlier supported automaticity in the use of the Fund's resources. By the 1960s, however, the currencies of the Fund's European members were being heavily used in drawings. As a consequence, when the Articles were amended in 1969, European officials reversed their position and became the staunchest advocates of conditionality.[11]

APPLYING CONDITIONALITY

In 1968 the Executive Board reviewed the terms of stand-by arrangements. This review was prompted by the concern of several Executive Directors elected by

---

[9]See *History, 1966–71*, Vol. I, p. 23.

[10]These amendments are described in *History, 1966–71*, Vol. I, pp. 255–59.

[11]Further discussion of the evolution of the Fund's policy on drawings and of conditionality can be found in *History, 1945–65*, Vol. II, pp. 390–410 and 522–41, in Joseph Gold, *Conditionality*, IMF Pamphlet Series, No. 31 (Washington: International Monetary Fund, 1979), pp. 1–13, and in Manuel Guitián, *Fund Conditionality: Evolution of Principles and Practices*, IMF Pamphlet Series, No. 38 (Washington: International Monetary Fund, 1981).

developing members that the terms of the stand-by arrangement for the United Kingdom in 1967 were considerably more lenient than those customarily approved for developing members. These Executive Directors particularly objected to the absence of phasing in the stand-by arrangements approved for the United Kingdom. The outcome of the review guaranteed for all members uniform treatment taking the form of a substantial liberalization of stand-by arrangements that did not go beyond the first credit tranche. For such arrangements, there was to be no phasing of the amounts that might be drawn and no clauses requiring the observance of performance criteria.[12] Because of this liberalization, most stand-by arrangements requested by developing members for several years after 1968 were concentrated in the first credit tranche.

Policies Applied After 1968

The stabilization programs and the performance clauses and criteria worked out and agreed after 1968 between officials of member governments and the Fund continued to evolve. These programs were developed on a case-by-case basis by the Managing Director and staff and approved by the Executive Board. The fiscal criteria specified in the performance clauses of stand-by arrangements were changed. Performance clauses that set limits on the size of the budget deficit or that called for new revenue measures or the tightening of specific expenditures were, for the most part, dropped. After 1968 fiscal performance criteria of this type were used only with the three industrial members, France, Italy, and the United Kingdom, which had stand-by arrangements from 1969 to 1978. Instead, the fiscal performance criterion usually took the form of a subceiling on the expansion of domestic bank credit to the government for financing a budget deficit, which was additional to the ceiling on total bank credit expansion. The staff preferred use of this subceiling to outright limitations on expenditures or on the size of the deficit partly for technical reasons. Monetary data were available more promptly than fiscal data and could be interpreted with greater precision. In addition, credit ceilings were less likely to convey the impression that the Fund was judging the member's social and economic priorities reflected in its public sector operations.[13]

The change in form of the fiscal performance criteria did not mean that the Fund paid less attention to a member's fiscal performance. On the contrary, fiscal performance clauses in the form of ceilings on domestic bank credit expansion to the government were included in nearly all the financial programs in the upper credit tranches agreed after 1968. Between 1973 and 1978, only six programs in the upper

---

[12]The review of policies on use of resources in 1968 has been described in *History, 1966–71,* Vol. I, pp. 343–48.

[13]The use of fiscal performance clauses in stand-by arrangements in the 1970s was described in W.A. Beveridge and Margaret R. Kelly, "Fiscal Content of Financial Programs Supported by Stand-By Arrangements in the Upper Credit Tranches, 1969–78," *Staff Papers,* International Monetary Fund (Washington), Vol. 27 (June 1980), pp. 205–49.

credit tranches did not include a fiscal performance clause. This represented something of a shift in the Fund's past policy. Traditionally, inclusion of a fiscal performance clause was regarded as unnecessary when past fiscal performance had been good and when there was confidence that adequate fiscal adjustment had been made or would be made during the period of the program. For programs with members whose nongovernment sector had little or no access to bank credit, the Fund took the view that developments in the financial accounts of the public sector could be monitored adequately through a single performance clause on overall bank credit.

After 1973, however, a consensus grew among Fund officials that the problems of rapidly accelerating inflation, of much higher costs for energy, and of much larger balance of payments deficits could be resolved only if the budgetary deficits of most members were reduced. Consequently, reliance on fiscal performance clauses in stand-by arrangements was intensified.

Since 1968 exchange rate policy also had become a more important part of the Fund's conditionality, and "balance of payments tests" to judge the appropriateness of exchange rate policy were increasingly used in financial programs. Three such tests were devised. One applied where a unitary fluctuating rate existed. The test took the form of limiting sales of exchange in the exchange market, or, more often, of requiring authorities to maintain a minimum level of reserves so as to force the member to take action to correct its deficit. If the member could not use more reserves to finance deficits, it was obliged either to devalue its exchange rate or to restrict domestic credit expansion. A second test was for cases in which the exchange rate was periodically adjusted (a flexible rate). Exchange depreciation was to keep pace roughly with movements in domestic prices relative to foreign prices so as to maintain the country's competitive position, or where the currency was greatly overvalued, with domestic prices alone. A third applied where two or more rates prevailed, usually one fixed rate and another free market rate (a dual system). The test here combined features of the other two tests described above: agreed amounts of reserves had to be accumulated by specified dates and limits were set on sales of foreign exchange in the free market. Some staff, especially in the Western Hemisphere Department, believed that these policies provided exchange rate flexibility and enabled members to simplify their exchange systems and meet their targets for building reserves, and facilitated an understanding between the Fund and members on how and when to alter exchange rates. Gradually, however, these balance of payments tests were given up. The main requirement then usually imposed on members was that they could not introduce or tighten restrictions on imports.

Another development in financial programs after 1968 was the greater inclusion as performance criteria of policy statements regarding the management of external debt as well as limits on external debt. Although fewer than one fourth of

487

the programs adopted between 1958 and 1967 contained declarations of policy on external debt, almost two out of every three programs agreed from 1967 to 1970 and over 80 percent of the programs agreed from 1971 to 1973 contained such declarations. By 1973 more than three quarters of the programs agreed set quantitative limits to foreign indebtedness, and in most stand-by arrangements these limits were specified as performance criteria. From 1974 to 1978, use of performance criteria relating to external indebtedness became the norm for stand-by arrangements in the upper credit tranches. Special attention was usually given to external debt with short-term maturities. Frequently one, or in some instances two, subceilings on short-term debt were specified within the overall debt ceiling. Debt limits most commonly covered only borrowing by the public sector, but as time went on, some stand-by arrangements also contained limits on new external borrowing incurred by the private sector.

Initially, limitations on external debt were incorporated into stand-by arrangements in order to reinforce limits placed on domestic credit expansion. Since foreign borrowing could be substituted for domestic borrowing, the staff believed that it was imperative to limit foreign borrowing; otherwise domestic credit ceilings could be evaded. By the 1960s, limitations on external debt were used more commonly as part of balance of payments management. After 1971, when a staff survey showed that extensive recourse to short-term and medium-term borrowing was a major factor in the emergence of debt servicing difficulties for several members, some of the staff came to believe that effective procedures were needed for keeping track of the contracting of external debt. They also believed that where servicing of external debt obligations comprised a substantial claim on the country's foreign exchange or budgetary resources, financial programs worked out with the Fund ought to include performance criteria governing the appropriate management of external debt.

These elements formed a major part of the Fund's policy on conditionality as it had developed by the second half of the 1970s. By 1978 additional performance criteria or conditions were occasionally used. For example, in some programs the elimination of subsidies for basic food items was included. Not only was this considered helpful in cutting budgetary expenditures but, by permitting high prices for foodgrains, it was considered a price incentive to farmers to increase production. More commonly, a member was expected to adopt such measures as exchange rate depreciation, liberalization of trade and payments, enactment of revenue measures, or adjustment of the prices charged by public enterprises before its request for a stand-by arrangement was presented to the Executive Board. The staff believed that prior actions of this type, especially when the member had long delayed instituting policies for balance of payments adjustment, were essential to enable the Managing Director to recommend the member's request for a stand-by arrangement to the Executive Board.

In brief, by the 1970s the Fund's conditions had become specific and quantitative. Furthermore, since officials and technicians of many members that requested stand-by arrangements, especially in Africa, the Caribbean, and in the Indian and Pacific Oceans, were inexperienced in developing financial programs, the Fund staff in effect wrote many of the programs. Accordingly, to an ever greater extent, it appeared as though the Fund—and particularly the Fund staff—were "imposing" conditions.

ENVIRONMENT IN WHICH CRITICISM OF CONDITIONALITY AROSE

After 1973 when members, especially non-oil developing members, began in greater numbers to request stand-by arrangements in the upper credit tranches, these conditions were subjected to mounting criticism. In fact, by 1978 attacks on the Fund's conditionality had become vitriolic. World economic circumstances and the political environment after 1973 were especially conducive to interest in, and criticisms of, the Fund's conditionality. The unprecedentedly large and widespread balance of payments deficits had somehow to be financed. While most industrial and relatively more developed members and even several non-oil developing members with good credit standing and good banking contacts could obtain financing of these deficits from commercial banks or through the Eurocurrency market, these sources of funds were closed to many non-oil developing members. Once the Fund's oil facility expired early in 1976, official sources of balance of payments and of development financing also became more scarce.

In addition, except for Italy and the United Kingdom, which had stand-by arrangements in the early part of 1977, it was developing members that were most affected by and concerned with the Fund's conditionality. Many developing members, especially the smaller newly independent nations, were sensitive in all their relations, but especially in their relations with creditors. They did not want to be pressured into accepting stringent conditions. Moreover, as developing countries became economically and politically more powerful in the 1970s and pressed after 1973 for a new international economic order and for larger receipts of the world's real resources, it was inevitable that they would turn to the Fund as a sizable source of financial resources and that they would request a re-examination of the terms on which the Fund's resources were available to them.

In this context, the Fund's conditionality was bound to be subjected to attack. For the first time, the Fund was being judged as "a lending institution" primarily for developing countries, a role not originally intended for it. Without an agreed code of conduct for international monetary behavior, and with the severe needs of many non-oil developing members for balance of payments financing, the Fund was in a position where its regulatory functions were minimal and its financial functions at a maximum. Consequently, although the Fund had meanwhile developed other functions, such as technical assistance, the initial concept of the Fund as an institution to monitor members' exchange rates and restrictions with a revolving pool of resources to assist it in keeping exchange rates stable and international

489

payments free from restrictions tended to be overlooked. Instead, attention turned to the Fund as a source of financing for countries having a difficult time raising money elsewhere. The terms or conditions on which the money was available became subject to intense scrutiny.

MOUNTING CRITICISM

Strong criticism of the Fund's conditionality was expressed by the Governors of several non-oil developing members at the Thirty-First Annual Meeting, in Manila in October 1976. This criticism coincided with the Managing Director's call for greater emphasis on adjustment of balance of payments deficits and less emphasis on the financing of deficits. Speaking on behalf of the Governors of several African members, Marie-Christiane Gbokou urged the Fund to review the conditions attached to use of the extended facility.[14] Most other Governors went further and asked for a review of the conditions governing use of all the Fund's facilities.[15]

At the Thirty-Second Annual Meeting, held in Washington in October 1977, when the supplementary financing facility was being proposed as a way for the Fund to obtain resources to help finance stand-by arrangements in the upper credit tranches, the Governors of African, Asian, and Latin American members again voiced complaints about the Fund's "strict conditionality." Governors for African members, for example, noting especially the little use that had been made of the extended facility in the three years since it had been established, urged the Fund to be more flexible. Noting that developing members were not making much use of the Fund's regular resources under either stand-by or extended arrangements, they argued that less strict conditions were needed if developing countries were to make greater use of the Fund's resources.[16] Emphasizing that the Brazilian authorities did not oppose, indeed supported, the principle of conditionality for use of the Fund's resources, Mario Henrique Simonsen also urged that the criteria governing conditionality be reviewed. The Brazilian authorities, he stated, wanted to see the conditions to be applied in stand-by arrangements become "more predictable and more uniform."[17]

By the time of the 1978 Annual Meeting, held in Washington in September, even more Governors spoke against conditionality as it was applied in practice. The

---

[14]Statement by the Governor of the Fund for the Central African Republic, *Summary Proceedings, 1976*, p. 125.

[15]Statements by the Governor of the World Bank for Malaysia, the Governor of the Fund for Guinea, the Governor of the World Bank for Nepal, the Governor of the World Bank for Pakistan, the Governor of the World Bank for Bangladesh, and the Governor of the Fund and the World Bank for Sri Lanka, *Summary Proceedings, 1976*, pp. 136, 145, 163, 168, 199, and 203.

[16]Statements by the Governor of the World Bank for Algeria, the Governor of the World Bank for Egypt, and the Governor of the Fund for Mauritius, *Summary Proceedings, 1977*, pp. 118, 149, and 177.

[17]Statement by the Governor of the Fund and the World Bank for Brazil, *Summary Proceedings, 1977*, p. 91.

Group of Twenty-Four expressed concern, for instance, "at the multiplicity of performance criteria."[18] Several Governors for developing members urged the Fund to loosen the conditions governing use of its resources. "The stiffness of conditionality attaching to Fund drawings," stated H.M. Patel, "and the widespread feeling among developing countries that they are discriminated against in this respect are matters which merit serious attention."[19]

Specific Criticism

By 1978 strong criticism of the Fund's conditionality was being voiced in public and in private by officials of developing members and by some economists and staff of other international institutions.[20] They complained that conditions applied by the Fund were too strict or unduly severe, implying that the conditions went beyond those needed for the Fund to ensure repurchase within the specified time. "Too strict" meant that the conditions involved making major changes in a member's basic policies within too short a time. "Unduly severe" meant that the Fund's conditions were excessively deflationary. These conditions were said to provoke unacceptable unemployment and to reduce to intolerable levels the real income and consumption of important sectors of the economy of a country requesting a stand-by arrangement. Critics cited budget cuts in essential social programs, such as subsidies on basic food items for the urban poor. These criticisms increased after riots in the streets of Cairo in January 1977 following cuts made by the Egyptian Government in the budget for food subsidies were widely reported in the press.

In other instances, too, when authorities of member governments found themselves unable to cope with the political pressure that arose following agreement with the Fund, governments fell and cabinet ministers resigned. The Fund was subsequently criticized for paying insufficient attention to the political difficulties members faced in initiating the required policy reforms. A few political scientists went further and contended that, since only dictatorial regimes could carry out the drastic deflationary programs requested by the Fund, the Fund was inevitably forced to support "repressive regimes in Third World countries." Whether or not they accepted these arguments, many officials commented that the fundamental policy changes that the Fund required for stand-by arrangements in the upper credit tranches were unduly severe in relation to the limited amounts of money that the Fund could make available to the member.

The Fund's conditions were also criticized on the grounds that they were too monetarist. By placing so much importance on limits on total domestic credit expansion as well as on bank credit expansion to the public sector, the Fund's

---

[18]Communiqué of Group of Twenty-Four, September 22, 1978, par. 12; Vol. III below, p. 656.

[19]Statement by the Governor of the Fund and the World Bank for India, *Summary Proceedings, 1978*, p. 73.

[20]See, for example, the report, *The Balance of Payments Adjustment Process in Developing Countries: Report to the Group of Twenty-Four*, UNDP/UNCTAD Project INT/75/015 (New York, January 1979).

conditions, it was said, reflected monetarist explanations of inflation and of balance of payments deficits, explanations which were debated and criticized by economists themselves and were not generally accepted.

A related criticism of the Fund's conditionality was that the methodology and techniques used by the staff in determining credit ceilings were too standardized and did not take adequate account of the differing economic and social situations of members. Officials of many developing members complained that the models used by the staff had been planned initially for the economies of industrial members and were inapplicable to developing members. The policy recommendations made by the Fund were said to be based on "faith in the working of the price mechanism as an allocation of resources." Critics complained that, while changes in relative prices might quickly generate more efficient production in market-oriented industrial economies with sufficient resource mobility, they had slower and far less predictable effects in developing economies, which had market deficiencies, narrow production bases, and shortages of essential factors of production. Indeed, some developing countries were not market oriented but rather centrally planned economies.

Critics argued, too, that policies based on the price mechanism were regressive. Adjustment of the exchange rate and of prices charged by public utilities and enterprises, as well as reduction in budget subsidies, depressed real wages or the standard of living of the poorest groups in developing members, accentuating unequal distribution of income and conflicting with the promotion of social equity. Here, the staff of the Fund was faulted even by the staff of its sister organization, the World Bank. In the late 1970s, the World Bank began to emphasize a "basic needs approach" to economic development. With the slogan of helping "the poorest of the poor," World Bank loans were increasingly directed to projects for supplying food and other necessities for subsistence and for making the distribution of income in the poorest developing members less unequal.[21] The financial policies for balance of payments adjustment advocated by the Fund were said by some staff of the World Bank to counter the aims of their own programs.

The emphasis given to depreciation of the exchange rate was also of concern. Rather than easing the task of coping with balance of payments deficits, exchange rate devaluation was said to make it more difficult. Depreciation had an immediate impact on domestic inflation, while the supply responses necessary to achieve the desired expansion of exports and substitution of imports took a long time to materialize. Critics stated that balance of payments deficits of developing members should be reduced by a series of direct measures aimed at increasing domestic production rather than by exchange rate changes. They contended, too, that exchange rate devaluation was a general policy instrument and consequently did not permit selectivity in the control of imports, particularly in distinguishing imports for essential consumption and investment from those for luxury consumption.

---

[21]For a short description of the basic needs strategy see Paul Streeten, "From Growth to Basic Needs," *Finance & Development* (Washington), Vol. 16 (September 1979), pp. 28–31.

With its emphasis on restraint of current demand in dealing with balance of payments problems, conditionality was criticized for compromising economic growth. Insufficient attention was paid, so critics said, to working out longer-run structural changes in a member's economy, such as developing new export industries or making existing industries more efficient.

Even the style of operation of the Fund staff was criticized. The staff was said to be in effect running the countries that had stand-by arrangements with the Fund. These feelings were accentuated by press reports describing in detail the political difficulties of members in reaching and observing understandings with Fund staff. These press reports often suggested that economic policies were strongly influenced, if not dictated, by Fund staff, thus touching on sensitive issues of national pride and sovereignty. Some officials of developing members felt that stand-by arrangements were paternalistic. Use of Fund resources, it was said, had become such a traumatic experience that members with access to other funds hesitated to subject themselves to the Fund's conditions. Along these lines the Fund's policies were said to be inconsistent. Policies applied to various members were said to be different because of the size of the member, with larger members receiving less strict treatment than smaller members, and because of differing attitudes of individuals on the Fund staff.

Many of these criticisms were summed up by Ronnie de Mel at the 1978 Annual Meeting:

> It is not in dispute that Fund resources in the upper credit tranches should be conditional. Nor the fact that Fund conditionality could improve the effectiveness of Fund credit. But we also feel that Fund conditionality, as it has been applied so far, should be reappraised with a view to making it more flexible. The types of performance criteria have multiplied in recent years. They relate to prices, interest rates, exchange rates, subsidies, protectionism, and foreign borrowing. Naturally, these have given the impression that stabilization programs are increasingly fashioned in such a way as to give the Fund controlling power over the functioning of the economy of the country concerned. Performance criteria should be limited to those having a direct bearing on the balance of payments. Above all, the stabilization programs should not worsen income distribution, should not be contrary to the satisfaction of basic human needs, and should not undermine the basic features of the economic organization desired by the member country. Above all, conditionality should take greater account of political and social realities in the countries concerned, a criterion that has already been enshrined in the Articles.[22]

Multiplier Effects of the Fund's Conditions

Attacks on the Fund's conditionality became especially acute in 1977 when officials of private commercial banks began to make a stand-by arrangement with the Fund a prerequisite for their lending to a country. A close tie between the willingness of commercial banks to lend to a country and the country's having a stand-by arrangement with the Fund became almost standard after commercial banks encountered repayment problems with Zaïre in 1976 and 1977. When it

---

[22]Statement by the Governor of the Fund and the World Bank for Sri Lanka, *Summary Proceedings, 1978*, p. 157.

seemed likely that Zaïre could not repay its debt to commercial banks, commercial bank officials worked out an ingenious solution. Rather than have Zaïre declare a legal default, a "standstill operation" would be mounted in which commercial banks would not lend to the country, but at the same time the country would not be repaying past debt. This solution meant that a country which was not "in good standing" with banks was nonetheless not formally declared in default, but it raised the question of how commercial bank officials could judge which countries were creditworthy. Commercial bank officials were beginning to be more familiar with Fund parlance and policy, and the test which they devised to judge the creditworthiness of a country was whether it could meet the conditions needed for a stand-by arrangement with the Fund in the upper credit tranches. This test induced private commercial banks to have prospective borrowing countries obtain the stamp of approval of the Fund by obtaining a stand-by arrangement in the upper credit tranches. Once a stand-by arrangement with the Fund was used to attest to a country's creditworthiness, the conditions for a stand-by arrangement were more intensely debated. To make their requests more acceptable to outside lenders, officials of developing members understandably pressed for "more flexible," meaning "more lenient," conditions for stand-by arrangements.

A response by officials of industrial and relatively more developed members to such criticisms was to be expected. These members drew infrequently on the Fund and conceived of themselves as putting up the bulk of the Fund's resources for the developing members to draw. As the Fund's policies came under more strident attack, response by Fund officials also became essential. This response is discussed in the next chapter.

CHAPTER 26

Conditionality:
the Fund Answers

*D*EFENSE OF THE FUND'S CONDITIONS by officials of many members
and by officials of the Fund was inevitable. Beginning with the 1976 Annual
Meeting, when conditionality was first disputed, several Governors from industrial
and more developed primary producing members emphasized the need for "strict
conditionality." What was becoming a North-South polarization on a number of
topics relating to the international monetary system was reflected in comments
about the Fund's conditionality. Supporting Mr. Witteveen's call for shifting
emphasis from financing external deficits to adjustment through changes in internal
economic policies, Phillip Lynch was blunt. Developing countries especially needed
to adjust to reduce their balance of payments deficits. If the international aid that
they received was used only to finance their payments deficits and not to reallocate
their domestic economic resources in response to higher costs for energy, that aid
would have been largely frittered away. In the long term, private financial
institutions and donor countries would "lose their enthusiasm for providing aid on
such a basis." Developing countries had to realize that "the capacity of the industrial
countries to aid the development process—whether through the international
lending institutions or in other ways—has been weakened by the circumstances."[1]

By the time of the 1977 Annual Meeting, several Governors of industrial
members were adamant that adjustment was essential and that use of the Fund's
resources ought to be subject to conditions sufficient to bring about such adjustment.
W. Michael Blumenthal, Secretary of the Treasury under President Jimmy Carter,
stressed that current account positions had to be brought into line with sustainable
capital flows and that financing by the Fund should support programs that would
correct the payments problems of borrowers, not postpone their resolution. "It is not
a matter of whether the Fund attaches conditions, but what kind."[2] Robert Boulin,

---

[1]Statement by the Governor of the World Bank for Australia, *Summary Proceedings, 1976,*
pp. 182–84.

[2]Statement by the Governor of the Fund and the World Bank for the United States, *Summary
Proceedings, 1977,* p. 66.

expressing his disappointment that progress toward balance of payments adjust-ment had been very little and less than expected, regarded appropriate domestic policies in particular as essential to a restoration of external equilibrium and stressed that the supplementary financing facility then being proposed ought to have "adequate" conditions.[3]

Hans Apel also wanted conditionality to be strict. The officials of the Federal Republic of Germany, he stated, trusted the Fund's ability to take due account of any member's particular economic situation. There was no reason to believe that in negotiating with borrowers the Fund would impose policy conditions that countries would find impossible to meet. He advocated, in fact, that instead of distributing the general quota increase under the Seventh General Review evenly over all four credit tranches, those tranches whose use was tied to stricter conditionality be expanded more than proportionately.[4]

Denis W. Healey, then Chairman of the Interim Committee, seeking a compromise position, suggested further discussions in the Executive Board and in the Interim Committee of the conditions attached to drawings from the Fund. He noted that it was no good increasing the Fund's resources, as was then being considered, if those who needed them most were unable to accept the conditions for their use.[5]

REPLIES OF MR. WITTEVEEN AND OTHER FUND OFFICIALS

In his concluding remarks at the 1977 Annual Meeting, and in the other public speeches early in 1978 prior to his leaving the Fund, Mr. Witteveen also undertook to defend the Fund's conditionality. At the 1977 Annual Meeting, he explained that when officials of a member approached the Fund for a drawing in the higher credit tranches—and under the proposed supplementary facility—the member was usually in a very difficult external payments situation. Such a situation had to be remedied whether the member drew on the Fund or not. Indeed, the availability of finance from the Fund allowed the member to make the necessary adjustments less abruptly and with less adverse impact on its own economy and fewer adverse effects on other countries. For these reasons, the basic principles of conditionality had to remain an integral part of the Fund's operations.[6]

Just prior to his departure from the Fund, Mr. Witteveen, in May 1978, again spoke at length about conditionality.[7] The Fund's conditionality was not a quid pro

---

[3]Statement by the Governor of the Fund for France, *Summary Proceedings, 1977*, p. 80.

[4]Statement by the Governor of the World Bank for the Federal Republic of Germany, *Summary Proceedings, 1977*, p. 94.

[5]Statement by the Governor of the Fund for the United Kingdom, *Summary Proceedings, 1977*, p. 62.

[6]Concluding Remarks by the Managing Director, *Summary Proceedings, 1977*, pp. 215–16.

[7]"Financing the LDCs: The Role of Public and Private Institutions," an address by the Managing Director at the 1978 Euromarkets Conference in London, May 8, 1978; published in *IMF Survey* (Washington), Vol. 7 (May 22, 1978), pp. 145–50.

quo for its financial assistance; on the contrary, it was "an essential complement" to the assistance the Fund provided. Without conditionality, financial assistance could not be used to its maximum potential advantage, and without assistance, the process of adjustment would be much more painful. Conditionality was based on the simple premise that, except in a few situations, it was unwise and, in the end, not even feasible to finance balance of payments deficits over a protracted period without taking corrective measures. It was essential to counter the belief that the Fund's conditionality involved policy measures that countries in balance of payments difficulties could otherwise do without; no country could use reserves or borrow indefinitely to finance sizable deficits.

The components of conditionality, Mr. Witteveen emphasized, were inevitably controversial. Control of inflation and the effectiveness of monetary policy, such as the responsiveness of savings to higher interest rates, the efficacy of exchange rate depreciation in inducing changes in trade flows, and the responsiveness of farmers to price incentives were debated among economists. Dealing with inflation and balance of payments difficulties necessarily meant cutting back, at least temporarily, on real incomes; there were understandable fears on the part of each sector of a society that it might have to assume a disproportionate share of the burden of this cutback. Such matters were highly charged politically.

With regard to the criticism that the Fund's conditions were too severe, Mr. Witteveen pointed out that all too many members came to the Fund only when their economic situations had become desperate. It had become common for members to perceive the Fund as "the lender of last resort," approaching it only when all alternative sources of financing had been exhausted. Under such circumstances, it was inevitable that corrective measures were severe. Such situations made the Fund's conditionality appear harsh. The initial purpose of a stand-by arrangement—as a precautionary device to assure the availability of financing—had been lost sight of. Members should come to the Fund at an earlier stage of their difficulties.

To answer the criticism that Fund staff were controlling the economies of members, Mr. Witteveen pointed out that the performance criteria in the economic policy programs supported by the Fund usually related to the broadest possible economic aggregates that sufficed for the achievement of balance of payments adjustment. The Fund avoided taking a view on the appropriate distribution of the burden of adjustment as between the various sectors of an economy. For example, if an improvement in the government budgetary position was an ingredient of the program, as was frequently the case, the performance criterion related to the extension of bank credit to the government rather than to specific measures to increase revenues or cut expenditures. Similarly, performance criteria did not give specific prices for individual commodities but dealt rather with overall prices, like exchange rates and interest rates.

In justifying the Fund's emphasis on exchange rate depreciation, Mr. Witteveen emphasized that under the Second Amendment of the Articles of

Agreement that had come into effect in the previous month, members were obliged to ensure that their exchange rates were not set at levels that would impede effective balance of payments adjustment; the Fund was required to oversee the observance by each member of this obligation. Beyond this obligation an exchange rate change was the simplest and least painful of the alternative measures to revitalize a foreign trade sector of a country when its domestic prices and costs were substantially out of line with those in trade partners or competitor countries. The alternative of domestic deflation alone was far more costly in output and employment. The alternative of restrictions on trade and payments might hold down imports but did little to encourage exports; indeed, it served to discourage them insofar as it raised the input costs of exporters without increasing their returns. Attempts to overcome this difficulty by subsidizing exports, together with restrictions on imports, resulted over time in an excessively complex system of controls and subsidies and induced producers to try to obtain administrative favors rather than to develop markets, improve products, or reduce costs. A realistic exchange rate, moreover, was not merely an instrument for balancing the external accounts but also a powerful instrument of development policy. By appropriately pricing capital goods which developing countries import, a correct exchange rate encouraged the substitution of labor for capital and thus helped to promote employment, one of the most important policy objectives of developing countries.

Mr. Witteveen also explained how the Fund management and staff viewed the controversial subject of cuts in the budget for subsidies on basic food items. When such subsidization was done through the government budget, he said, the Fund usually pointed out to the officials of members the budgetary problems that such subsidies could create, but accepted their continuation if they were an important part of the social program of the government and it was clearly understood that the burden of such a subsidy was being borne by some sector of society. Experience had shown, moreover, that when other prices were rising, low prices for basic foods were a disincentive to their production so that output remained low. It might be preferable therefore to eliminate subsidies and raise wages.

Additional Replies to Criticism

There were a number of further replies, usually expressed informally, to the mounting criticism of the Fund's conditionality. Many regarded the criticism as unfair. Often, cabinet ministers and other high-level officials genuinely saw the need to take strong policies, but since such policies were unpopular, they found it politically expedient publicly to blame the Fund for these policies. The Fund was thus made the whipping boy, performing the role as a service to members in the interest of appropriate policies. Defenders of the Fund's policies realized too that some officials of developing members were voicing criticism from which they might otherwise have refrained because in the political circumstances of a North-South dialogue developing members were eager to have a unified position that differed from that of officials of industrial members.

Fund officials had replies to other criticism, too. They elaborated Mr. Witteveen's point that it was neither desriable nor feasible for a member to finance balance of payments deficits over an unduly protracted period without reducing or eliminating the underlying causes of the deficits. If these deficits were merely suppressed by resorting to restrictions or if they were merely financed, they were likely to reappear, perhaps in a more acute form, thus compounding the severity of the required adjustment measures. That the principal determinants of the balance of payments difficulties were exogenous did not diminish the need for taking corrective measures. The fundamental question of whether adjustment was required did not depend on the identification of the causes of the payments imbalance but on whether the imbalance was temporary and self-reversing within a reasonable time. If the imbalance was soon reversible, adequate temporary financing was all that was required. But if the imbalance was not transient and self-reversing, there was no alternative to adjustment.

A further defence was that the staff did not rely on any particular model or standard approach. Indeed, given the number of Fund members, with their widely differing economic structures and systems, stages of development, and problems, it would be impossible to envisage a single model of adjustment that could apply to all. Fund officials especially emphasized that the conditions that the Fund was applying in 1977 and 1978 reflected crises: relatively harsh conditions had to be used when members had few, if any, alternative means of finance and came to the Fund as lender of last resort. Such conditions could not be taken as a guide in less desperate circumstances. Defenders of the Fund's conditionality believed, too, that underuse of the Fund's resources was attributable not to the Fund's conditionality but primarily to the ready availability of other sources of finance.

There were still other defenses of the Fund's conditionality. A stable economy and a sustainable balance of payments position were prerequisites to economic growth. Use of credit ceilings did not necessarily reflect belief in monetarist doctrines but rather served as neutral aggregate indicators of economic performance. While the Fund gave due recognition to the relationship between monetary factors in a member's economy and developments in its balances of payments, its approach took into account all facets of economic policies bearing on the supply of, and demand for, the member's economic resources. It was Fund policy to leave decisions on the details of the execution of policy measures (for example, how credit should be rationed, specific tax and subsidy measures applied, and where public expenditures should be reduced) to the authorities of the member concerned. To do otherwise would involve the Fund directly in microeconomic policy measures closely related to the member's social and political choices.

Another important defense of the Fund's conditionality was the success attained with previous stabilization programs. A study by the Fund staff of the performance of net foreign assets, prices, and the level of economic activity resulting from adjustment programs supported by stand-by arrangements in the upper credit tranches in 1963–72, for instance, concluded that the vast majority of programs had been successful. Programs which failed did so mainly because of fiscal problems, and, in particular, because the limits on credit expansion to the public sector had not been observed. Admittedly, an increasing number of the programs implemented from 1973 to 1977 did not achieve their objectives. Lack of success, however, arose not from use of the wrong type of programs but rather from insufficient stabilization efforts or from uncontrollable factors affecting the member's balance of payments, such as the recession of 1975, the sharp declines in prices of many primary commodities, and higher prices for oil.[8]

The various defenses notwithstanding, the conditions associated with use of the Fund's resources remained a prime issue in international discussions, and in accordance with Mr. Healey's suggestion at the 1977 Annual Meeting, in 1978 the Executive Board undertook to review the entire subject.

POSITIONS OF EXECUTIVE DIRECTORS FROM DEVELOPING MEMBERS

The review by the Executive Board of conditions on stand-by arrangements in the upper credit tranches got under way in 1978, following a formal request by the members of the Interim Committee at their tenth meeting in April. This was the first broad review of the policies governing use of the Fund's resources that the Executive Directors had undertaken since 1968. The 1978 review went on intermittently for eight months, until March 2, 1979 when a new Executive Board decision was taken.

For nearly a year, the Executive Directors reviewed the Fund's experience with the application of conditionality. They discussed the objectives of financial programs, the policies and the criteria that the Fund had been using, and the many criticisms and defenses of the Fund's policies.

Shortly after the review started, J. de Larosière succeeded Mr. Witteveen as Managing Director. When the Governors again assembled in Washington, for their Thirty-Third Annual Meeting, September 25–28, 1978, Mr. de Larosière made clear his position on this controversial subject. He very much wanted to help the non-oil developing members in the troubled world economy, but at the same time he stressed that the Fund had to apply meaningful conditions. He also stated that the Fund must act fairly and evenhandedly.[9] The subject of conditionality was now so

---

[8]This study was published as Thomas M. Reichmann and Richard T. Stillson, "Experience with Programs of Balance of Payments Adjustment: Stand-By Arrangements in the Higher Credit Tranches, 1963–72," *Staff Papers*, International Monetary Fund (Washington), Vol. 25 (June 1978), pp. 293–309. A short article on this subject covering 1973–75 is that of Thomas M. Reichmann, "The Fund's Conditional Assistance and the Problems of Adjustment, 1973–75," *Finance & Development* (Washington), Vol. 15 (December 1978), pp. 38–41. Later studies by the staff of Fund-supported stabilization and adjustment programs undertaken in the 1970s include Donal J. Donovan, "Real Responses Associated with Exchange Rate Action in Selected Upper Credit Tranche Stabilization Programs," *Staff Papers*, Vol. 28 (December 1981), pp. 698–727 and his "Macroeconomic Performance and Adjustment Under Fund-Supported Programs: The Experience of the Seventies," *Staff Papers*, Vol. 29 (June 1982), pp. 171–203.

[9]Opening Address by the Managing Director, *Summary Proceedings, 1978*, pp. 19–20.

sensitive that most Governors from industrial members refrained from commenting on it at the 1978 Annual Meeting, although Hans Matthöfer did emphasize that German officials insisted on an element of "reasonable conditionality." Any weakening of conditionality, he thought, would harm both the Fund and borrowing countries by discouraging private and official lenders.[10]

The difficult task of working out new policies was left to the Executive Directors. To some extent, the views expressed by the Executive Directors had already been voiced by their Governors at the 1976 and 1977 Annual Meetings. But additional points were brought out as well in the discussions.

The nine Executive Directors elected exclusively by developing members emphasized how the world economic environment of 1978 had changed since the last review of policies on use of resources and the general feeling of dissatisfaction and distrust among officials of developing members with the application by the Fund of its conditionality. They stressed, however, that developing members were not opposed to conditionality as such; on the contrary, they had always supported conditionality because it served a useful and necessary role in their efforts to stabilize their economies. Problems existed not because of the existence of conditionality, but because the application of conditionality in the previous few years had been wrong. Conditionality seemed to involve the Fund's requesting an excess of policy measures in an attempt to obtain a swift and complete reorientation of economies. Furthermore, the standards used in applying conditionality were not uniform among members, nor were the conditions that the Fund applied flexible or well understood. The Executive Directors from developing members were convinced, too, that the lack of requests from developing members for use of the Fund's resources was almost entirely attributable to the Fund's conditionality.

They favored the change proposed by the management and staff that stand-by arrangements be granted for two-year or even three-year periods instead of the customary one-year period and that greater use be made of review clauses. These clauses required a periodic review of the member's economic situation before it could draw further, as had been done in the stand-by arrangement approved for the United Kingdom in 1969.[11] The staff suggested that review clauses might also be used for other members. But Executive Directors elected by developing members were not at all certain that they favored this idea. In fact, the review clause technique was not used even for the United Kingdom in the stand-by arrangement of 1977, as was seen in Chapter 24.

The Executive Directors elected by developing members also welcomed recognition by the management and staff that a longer time for balance of payments adjustment was needed. To support their argument, they cited the position taken by

---

[10]Statement by the Governor of the World Bank for the Federal Republic of Germany, *Summary Proceedings, 1978*, p. 34.

[11]See *History, 1966–71*, Vol. I, pp. 348–51.

Mr. Matthöfer at the 1978 Annual Meeting that the Federal Republic of Germany needed ample time to rid itself of its chronic trade surpluses. Mr. Matthöfer had stated explicitly that "an economy which for more than two decades became accustomed to produce external surpluses cannot easily adjust to current account equilibrium. As everywhere, structural changes take time and organizational imagination."[12] Officials of developing members argued that if the Federal Republic of Germany needed time for adjustment, developing members certainly did.

Several Executive Directors argued for even more changes in the Fund's conditionality than the two proposed by the management and staff. Mr. Kharmawan, for example, wanted the Fund to drop performance criteria relating to the budget of a member. He argued that a country's budget was an especially sensitive document and the product of compromises between many ministries, setting out the government's economic priorities. The Fund "ought not to meddle" in those compromises and priorities. Eduardo Mayobre (Venezuela), as well as Mr. Kharmawan, objected to prior conditions for a stand-by arrangement as the staff paper suggested. Such prior conditions would undo the liberalization in force for the past ten years of stand-by arrangements in the first credit tranche. Mr. Mayobre also wanted a considerable reduction of performance criteria and a change in their orientation. When it negotiated with officials of a member government, the staff should not go into policies outside direct control of the government, such as wage and price policies. Balance of payments adjustment programs should give more weight to the general trend of the economy and less to the attainment of particular quantitative monetary targets. Ceilings on external debt should take into account the significant difference between long-term and short-term debt. Mr. Mayobre argued, too, for a close involvement of the Executive Board in the application of the Fund's policies to particular countries by having the Executive Board set up specific guidelines and constraints.

Mr. Kafka observed that the complaint most frequently heard was that the Fund's balance of payments adjustment programs neglected social and political, as against economic, factors. A related but rarely voiced complaint, he thought, was that the Fund used "an almost medieval bargaining technique in negotiating programs," that is, it tried to extract maximum concessions from members though it should aim at offering a member various choices on how to obtain balance of payments adjustment. He also believed that coordination by the management and staff was inadequate to ensure that the programs used in different members were sufficiently similar. The style of negotiation and the tone in which reports were written differed even within a given area department; yet style and tone had a lot to do with members' reactions to the Fund's conditions and with the reactions of outside lenders.

---

[12]Statement by the Governor of the World Bank for the Federal Republic of Germany, *Summary Proceedings, 1978*, p. 32.

Mr. Al-Atrash believed that the impression of toughness of the Fund's conditionality was attributable to its being so far reaching. Conditionality, as currently applied, was not confined only to ceilings on net domestic credit expansion and to measures in trade and exchange; it included measures involving wages, interest rates, and domestic prices, especially restructuring and decontrolling some prices. He agreed, too, with Mr. Mayobre and others that the Executive Board ought to have a larger role in the application of conditionality to individual members. As it was, conditions were not approved ex ante by the Executive Board, that is, before the program was finalized; they were determined by the management and staff and approved only ex post by the Executive Board through its approval of the final stand-by arrangement.

Samuel Nana-Sinkam (Cameroon) felt that the letters of intent had a contractual flavor which many developing members did not like. They were inclined to fear that if they could not keep their economic policy undertakings, they would be regarded as breaking their international obligations. In effect, their "track record" would have been tarnished.

Others observed that credit squeezes in the private sector of the economies of developing countries were hard on domestic enterprises. As a result, large foreign multinational companies with ready access to credit abroad were likely to gain larger footholds in the manufacturing industries of developing countries. Often the Fund's conditionality meant that members had to take domestic measures to cope with balance of payments deficits deriving from external factors. Not all balance of payments deficits were attributable to inappropriate domestic policies, yet the Fund's conditionality implied that they were.

Festus G. Mogae (Botswana) and other Executive Directors believed that an initial depreciation of the exchange rate received undue emphasis. He expressed doubt about the effectiveness of exchange rate depreciation, particularly in developing countries that exported primary commodities. He and others contended in particular that staff reports did not always sufficiently explain how the "appropriate exchange rate" for a member was determined.

POSITIONS OF EXECUTIVE DIRECTORS FROM INDUSTRIAL AND DEVELOPED MEMBERS

Most Executive Directors appointed or elected by industrial members and by more developed primary producing members wanted to retain conditionality fairly much in its existing form but were open to suggested changes. Generally, they believed that when a member made purchases from the Fund in the upper credit tranches, it had to do so in support of fairly specific financial policies that gave substantial assurance to the Fund that the member would achieve a viable balance of payments position within a reasonable time.

They defended their views with a number of specific arguments. Messrs. Pieske and Gerhard Laske (Federal Republic of Germany) stressed that conditionality had been central to the Fund's activities for more than two and a half decades and that it was difficult to conceive of an alternative. The concept of balance of payments adjustment incorporated in the principles of conditionality was, in their view, "appropriate and workable." Moreover, the Fund's experience with conditionality had been good and amply justified continuing with the well-tested practices of the past. The European Community had followed the Fund in devising policies to promote balance of payments adjustment in its own members. Messrs. Pieske and Laske, like many other members of the Executive Board, believed strongly that it was not so much the Fund's conditionality as the ready availability of nonconditional funds from other sources, particularly from the international credit and capital markets, that explained the limited use of stand-by arrangements in upper credit tranches when balance of payments deficits were widely prevalent. They believed, too, that the seeming harshness of the Fund's conditions was due largely to the tardiness with which members approached the Fund. The solution was not to change the Fund's conditions but to encourage members to come to the Fund at an early stage of their external payments problems when adjustment measures could be less demanding.

Sam Y. Cross (United States), too, suggested that the Fund, by and large, had been acting correctly. He stressed that it was essential to maintain the institutional integrity of the Fund and the World Bank, with the Fund concentrating on balance of payments financing for relatively short-term adjustment and the Bank on other forms of financing for economic development on a longer-term basis. Therefore, while Fund assistance and adjustment programs supported by stand-by arrangements might be made for a little longer period than one year and could perhaps extend to three years, stand-by arrangements should not extend too far into the future.

In a separate statement, Mr. Cross also explained the position of the U.S. Government on performance criteria in stand-by arrangements. Such criteria should be broad, aiming at correcting an economy and avoiding intervening in members' decisions on how to allocate expenditures. Also, while the U.S. Government in no way wanted to dilute or subordinate the fundamental objectives of economic stabilization and balance of payments adjustment intended by the financial programs that the Fund supported by stand-by arrangements, it considered other objectives important as well. Programs for balance of payments adjustment should foster in the country concerned a broader base of productive investment and employment. They should help productive activities which could lead to a better allocation of productive resources and meeting of basic human needs, such as those for food and shelter.

Bernard J. Drabble (Canada), observing that much of the use of the Fund had taken place through low conditional channels, such as the oil facility, the compensatory financing facility, and drawings in the first credit tranche, argued that any comprehensive assessment of conditionality should include appraisal of the contribution low conditional resources had made to the adjustment process. Most of the so-called harshness of conditionality arose, he believed, because members delayed until they were in dire straits before requesting Fund assistance.

Mr. Dini also supported appropriate conditionality but believed that the financial programming techniques used by the Fund needed to be improved. They were biased toward rapid balance of payments adjustment at the expense of growth and employment. Would it not be possible, he asked, to devise a balance of payments measure similar to the concept of the full-employment balanced budget, in which medium-term external equilibrium was defined in such a way as to include potential economic growth?

Mr. Wahl pointed out that slowdowns in economic growth were unfortunately unavoidable when a member was faced with serious payments disequilibria. He stated that the French authorities favored enlarging the amount of money the Fund could make available when conditions were being satisfied. Pendarell Kent (United Kingdom) also favored this suggestion so that conditionality would not be too high for "meager assistance," but supported the existing characteristics of conditionality as reflecting long years of experience.

A few members of the Executive Board vigorously supported the Fund's conditionality as it had been applied. Noting that a number of members had developed "an allergy" to the Fund's conditionality, Mr. Schneider believed that the Fund's conditionality was only what a country should do anyway sooner or later, with or without the help of the Fund, if it wanted to restore a viable payments position. Conditionality was more than just a safeguard for the temporary use of the Fund's resources. It was an "indirect trade-off" for creditor members who placed a portion of their reserves at the disposal of the Fund at low interest rates in the hope that this contribution would enhance the international adjustment process. Mr. Schneider stressed especially that drawings changed the reserve positions of members in the Fund. In effect, when a member used the Fund's resources, it was using the reserves of another member. This use had to be temporary and had to be conditional. The Fund was not "a lending institution."

Masanao Matsunaga (Japan) took the view simply that without conditionality, there "need be no Fund," as unconditional assistance was available from the private banking community. Mr. Whitelaw agreed and made the further point that if conditionality was weakened, the case against higher charges on Fund resources would be correspondingly weakened. He still favored as low charges as possible.

In general, most Executive Directors from industrial and more developed primary producing members were willing to accept two-year stand-by arrangements, or occasionally three-year arrangements, as proposed by the staff, if they did not become the norm. They also preferred continuing the use of performance criteria to substituting review clauses and stressed the need for a more active policy of providing information to a wider public about the Fund's conditionality. Such explanations would, they believed, be the most effective way to reduce the heavy criticism to which the Fund was subjected.

NEW GUIDELINES ESTABLISHED

After these extensive discussions, the Executive Board, on March 2, 1979, adopted a decision which set forth new guidelines on conditionality.[13] Several guidelines were not new. Rather they clarified practices and policies that had gradually emerged in the Fund's operations since 1968. Nevertheless, some were sharpened, a few features were added to accommodate the views of developing members, and the Executive Directors were given closer participation in the negotiating process.

While the one-year stand-by arrangement remained the norm, stand-by arrangements for up to three years could be approved. Phasing and performance clauses were to be omitted in stand-by arrangements that did not go beyond the first credit tranche, but included in all other stand-by arrangements, although these clauses would be applicable only to purchases beyond the first credit tranche. The major liberalization of the 1968 review was thus reaffirmed. Limits on performance criteria were emphasized. They were normally to be confined to macroeconomic variables and those necessary to implement specific provisions of the Articles. Explicit provision was made for preconditions. The Managing Director could ask a member to adopt some corrective measures *before* he recommended that the Executive Board approve the stand-by arrangement, but he was to keep the Executive Directors informed of the progress of negotiations with the member.

Members were to be encouraged to come to the Fund for assistance before their payments difficulties became acute and they needed to undertake drastic reforms. The Fund was to help members identify impending economic difficulties. To take account of criticism that the Fund neglected relevant considerations when it devised adjustment programs, the Fund was to pay due regard to domestic social and political objectives, economic priorities, and circumstances of members, including the causes of their balance of payments problems. The Managing Director was to coordinate staff work to ensure nondiscriminatory treatment of members. Significantly, the word "nondiscriminatory" replaced the Fund's customary word "uniform."

Should a member be unable to formulate an essential feature of a program as a performance criterion at the beginning of a program year because of substantial uncertainties over major economic trends, the Fund might review the situation and, if appropriate, revise the performance criteria. But the member was to be guarded

---

[13]E.B. Decision No. 6056-(79/38), March 2, 1979, *Selected Decisions of the International Monetary Fund and Selected Documents*, (hereafter referred to as *Selected Decisions*), Tenth Issue (Washington, April 30, 1983), pp. 20–23.

against the possibility that such a review would amount to a total renegotiation by a provision specifying that the Managing Director would inform Executive Directors of the subject matter of the forthcoming review.

The decision also made it explicit that stand-by arrangements are not international agreements and therefore language with a contractual connotation was to be avoided in stand-by arrangements and letters of intent.[14] This provision met the criticism that some creditors interpreted failure to observe performance criteria as a serious departure from agreed international rules of behavior.

A few Executive Directors elected by developing members regarded the March 1979 decision as a new approach. They thought that the staff would have to offer members alternative programs for the achievement of balance of payments adjustment. Most Executive Directors and staff, however, viewed the guidelines as a restatement of past policy. Some regarded such a restatement as favorable: the conditionality that the Fund had been applying was correct and was vindicated by the new guidelines. Others regarded the restatement of past policy unfavorably: they had hoped for "constructive, positive change." They criticized, for example, the customarily used performance criteria as too simple and the balance of payments tests as too mechanical, precluding deeper assessment of exchange rate policy. They questioned the need for, and the value of, placing limits on new foreign borrowing on the grounds that Fund assistance should be aimed at re-establishing a member's creditworthiness so as to enable it to borrow abroad and not at preventing such borrowing. In any event, when members came to the Fund for financial resources as a last resort, other lenders had usually already stopped lending to the country anyway, so that there was no need for the Fund to limit the incurrence of additional debt.

Thus, the decision of March 1979 by no means laid to rest arguments and debates about conditionality, even within the Fund itself. Moreover, in the circumstances of 1973–78, when many developing members were able to borrow from private commercial banks, there was yet another problem concerning requests for use of the Fund's resources. To some extent, only members unable to raise money from private sources were requesting aid from the Fund. Consequently, something of a stigma attached to use of the Fund: the authorities of some members without access to private markets feared that a request for use of the Fund's resources might be construed by outside lenders as an inability of the member to secure funds elsewhere. Use of the Fund thus might reduce rather than enhance a member's creditworthiness.

Conditionality would certainly require much rethinking in the near future.[15]

---

[14]Discussion of this point can be found in Joseph Gold, *The Legal Character of the Fund's Stand-By Arrangements and Why It Matters*, IMF Pamphlet Series, No. 35 (Washington: International Monetary Fund, 1980).

[15]Shortly after the end of the period described here, public as well as internal discussion of the Fund's conditionality became even more common. See, for example, Sidney Dell, *On Being Grandmotherly: The Evolution of IMF Conditionality*, Essays in International Finance, No. 144, Princeton University (Princeton, New Jersey, 1981), and Bahram Nowzad, *The IMF and Its Critics*, Essays in International Finance, No. 146 (Princeton, New Jersey, 1981).

PART SIX

Arranging for an Increased Use of Resources

(1974–1978)

"As currency difficulties have become more acute, unilateral action by each country to preserve its own self-interest has been a setback to the cause of world cooperation and the brotherhood of man."

—Mzee Jomo Kenyatta, addressing the Board of Governors, in Nairobi, September 24, 1973

CHAPTER

27

Quotas Enlarged

Q UOTAS CONTINUED TO BE INTEGRAL to the Fund's financial
structure in the years 1972–78. Upon joining the Fund each member was
assigned a quota and was required to pay a subscription equal to that quota. Until
the Second Amendment of the Articles of Agreement became effective on April 1,
1978, subscriptions were customarily to be paid partly in gold and partly in the
member's own currency, the gold portion normally amounting to 25 percent of the
member's quota. The aggregate of quotas was the principal determinant of the
volume of currencies and of gold (or after April 1978 of other primary reserve assets)
available to the Fund, although the Fund had access to additional resources by
borrowing. The size of the quota was the main factor affecting the contribution of a
member to the Fund's resources, the amount that the member might draw from the
Fund, the member's voting rights, and, for a member that was a participant in the
Special Drawing Rights Department, its allocation of SDRs.[1] Consequently, every
member was vitally interested in the size of its quota both in absolute terms and
relative to the quotas of other members.

Periodically, as required by the Articles of Agreement, general reviews of
quotas took place. On the occasion of general reviews, not only were there general
increases in quotas but there were also special increases in the quotas of a number of
individual members. Because special increases changed the relative position of
members within the Fund's quota structure, they usually provoked even more
debate and negotiation than did the size of the general increase.

Quotas were subjected to increasing scrutiny, debate, and negotiation in the
seven years ended in 1978 for two main reasons. First, the industrial members,
which had the largest quotas, were for the first time since World War II in financial
straits and were much less inclined than in earlier years to contribute money to
international organizations, including the Fund.

Second, there was a sharpened focus on the relative shares of different
members and of different groups of members in total Fund quotas. The Federal

---

[1] The term Special Drawing Rights Department was used after the Second Amendment
became effective on April 1, 1978. Previously the term Special Drawing Account was used. See also
Chap. 36.

Republic of Germany, some other European members, and Japan argued for larger quotas on the basis of their ever-growing volumes of trade. After the oil price rises and the emergence of large payments surpluses by oil exporting countries, major oil producing members expected that their quotas would be substantially enlarged. The developing members, as a group, insisting on a greater role in the decision-making process of all international forums, also wanted a larger collective share in Fund quotas. However, while these members as a group all sought larger relative shares in Fund quotas, other industrial members and the relatively more developed primary producing members were reluctant to see any reduction in their relative shares because changes in quotas had direct consequences for voting power in the Fund and for representation on the Executive Board. These conflicts of interest meant that agreement on quotas was hard to achieve.

In addition, since gold was being phased out of the international monetary system, the Fund had to take crucial decisions about the form in which subscriptions resulting from higher quotas were to be paid, especially that portion formerly paid in gold.

But before turning to discussion of these problems regarding quotas in 1972 to 1978, a brief review of the developments of earlier years in Fund quotas and in the quota formula used might be helpful.

GENERAL QUOTA INCREASES
BEFORE THE SIXTH GENERAL REVIEW

By early 1974, when the Sixth General Review of Quotas began, total Fund quotas were just over SDR 29 billion (approximately $35 billion), making the Fund five times the size it was when the Articles of Agreement were signed on December 31, 1945.[2] The growth in quotas came from increased membership, numerous increases in quotas of individual members, and from three general increases in quotas. In accordance with the requirement of the original Articles that the Fund conduct reviews of quotas every five years, the Fund had held four quinquennial reviews from 1950 to 1965. The review conducted in 1969–70 was the Fifth General Review. The amendment of the Articles in 1969 made it explicit that general reviews of quotas were to take place at intervals of "not more than five years." In other words, quota reviews could be conducted more frequently than every five years. Quinquennial reviews thus became general reviews.

The First and Second Quinquennial Reviews, in 1950 and 1955, did not result in general increases in quotas mainly because the Fund's existing resources had been virtually unused, and the United States and the United Kingdom, the two members

---

[2]Total quotas of the 44 members that had been at Bretton Woods—excluding the U.S.S.R., which did not sign the Articles—as decided at Bretton Woods and listed in Schedule A to the Articles of Agreement, came to $7.6 billion.

with the largest quotas, did not want to commit more money to the Fund. With a continuous expansion of membership, the total of Fund quotas, nonetheless, gradually increased and, as of the end of 1955, came to $8.5 billion.

The first general increase in quotas came in 1959 when, in response to questions that arose in 1958 about the adequacy of international liquidity, quotas of all members were raised by 50 percent. In addition, larger selective quota increases were given to Canada, the Federal Republic of Germany, and Japan to reflect their faster-growing trade and economic strength relative to that of other members. Hence, when the Third Quinquennial Review took place a year later, in 1960, the Executive Board decided that no further general revision of quotas was necessary. As of December 31, 1960, total quotas came to $14.7 billion.

After nearly two years of deliberation, the Fourth Quinquennial Review in 1965–66 resulted in another round of general quota increases, this time of 25 percent plus special increases for 16 members. As of April 30, 1966, total quotas came to $19.4 billion. The Fifth General Review, in 1969–70, resulted in another overall quota increase. After two years of discussion, an increase in the size of the Fund of the absolute amount of $7.6 billion was agreed upon. The proposed new quotas offered at least a 25 percent increase to all members, except the United Kingdom, which received an increase of less than 15 percent, China, which received no increase, and several members that received percentage increases higher than 25 percent. As of December 31, 1971, total quotas stood at $28.8 billion.[3]

Experience with these five reviews of quotas suggested some lessons. The basic consideration in obtaining members' agreement on quota increases was the need for the Fund to have larger resources. Usually the Fund needed larger resources because of the continuous growth in the volume and value of international trade and because of the reduction in the real value of the Fund's existing resources as a result of a continuous rise in world prices. However, in each review from 1959 on, some currently prevailing factor bearing on the need for greater Fund resources was a major determinant of the decision to increase quotas. In the general quota increase of 1959, the possible need for more funds following members' relaxation of import controls in the 1950s and the assumption of convertibility obligations in 1958 were decisive. Officials believed that members might call on the Fund more readily if they could no longer have recourse to import restrictions and exchange controls when they encountered balance of payments deficits. In the general quota increase of 1964–65, what was decisive was the increased mobility of short-term capital. Officials believed that the Fund might have to assist members faced with sudden large drains on their reserves because of capital flight. In the quota increase of 1970–71, the advent of SDRs in the international monetary system had to be taken into account.

---

[3]The four Quinquennial Reviews of Quotas and the gradual increase in quotas for individual members from 1945 to early 1966 are described in *History, 1945–65*, Vol. I, pp. 267–68, 389–91, 446–52, 536–40, and 574–86; Vol. II, pp. 349–63 and 378–80; and *History, 1966–71*, Vol. I, pp. 32–34 and 306–308. The Fifth General Review and the gradual increase in quotas for individual members from 1966 to 1971 are described in *History, 1966–71*, Vol. I, pp. 287–308.

Since SDRs represented unconditional liquidity, the Fund's need for an adequate supply of conditional liquidity, provided by the Fund's regular resources, was a prime factor in securing agreement on a general increase in quotas.

In the end, however, the final determinant of the size of any general increase in Fund quotas was agreement by member governments, especially of the major industrial members, on the amounts they would be willing to contribute to an enlarged Fund. Until the First Amendment in 1969, decisions for general increases in quotas required the support of members having 80 percent of total voting power. In 1969, this figure was raised to 85 percent. In the Fourth and Fifth Reviews of Quotas, the large industrial members used the forum of the Group of Ten to reach agreement on the size of a general increase in Fund quotas. In other words, they went outside the Fund's usual procedures.

CALCULATING QUOTAS BEFORE THE SIXTH GENERAL REVIEW

Since the late 1960s some Governors and Executive Directors for developing members had complained of the way in which Fund quotas were calculated, and as 1971 ended the Fund committed itself to an extensive review of this methodology.[4] In the years 1972–78 much more attention was paid to the way quotas were calculated, and for the first time the staff sent to the Executive Board detailed explanations of the methodology used. From these explanations, it is possible to trace the evolution of the Fund's "quota formula."

Criticism centered on the so-called Bretton Woods formula used as the starting point in determining the initial quotas of the 44 countries at Bretton Woods. This formula contained figures for national income, foreign exchange reserves, and foreign trade.[5] However, quotas had never been determined entirely by the Bretton Woods formula. Even at Bretton Woods the quotas yielded by the formula were only preliminary and were still negotiated so that substantial differences existed between the quotas calculated according to the formula and the actual quotas listed in Schedule A to the original Articles. On the whole, members took smaller quotas because of the gold subscription requirement and the absence of a legal right to draw automatically amounts equivalent to their gold subscriptions.

To keep quota calculations for new members roughly comparable with those of the original members, the Bretton Woods formula was used as a basis for calculating the initial quotas of another 27 countries that joined the Fund from January 1946 to September 1958. Again, there were substantial differences between the quotas calculated by use of the formula and the initial quotas actually agreed. In many instances new members preferred to take smaller initial quotas than the calculations indicated.

---

[4]*History, 1966–71*, Vol. I, pp. 303–305.
[5]The Bretton Woods formula and the reasons for its use are described in *History, 1945–65*, Vol. I, pp. 94–98, and Vol. II, p. 351.

By September 1958, virtually all large countries were members of the Fund. With a few exceptions, the next applicants for membership were small and newly independent countries for which use of the Bretton Woods formula for calculating initial quotas was inappropriate. Not only were data before World War II for the trade and national income of these relatively small countries unavailable but by this time it was also apparent that the Bretton Woods formula yielded initial quotas that were too small for them. Hence, the Fund relied on the special policy on small quotas introduced in 1955 under which both new and existing members were assured of a minimum quota.[6] For new members that would have initial quotas beyond the minimum quota under the small quota policy, the economic size of the country was compared with that of existing members and their quotas were aligned accordingly. Calculations based on the Bretton Woods formula figured in the end result only indirectly inasmuch as the quotas of the members used for purposes of comparison had been determined partly on the basis of the formula.

Further deviation from the Bretton Woods formula took place in 1959 when increases in selective quotas for several members were determined with little reliance on the formula. Instead, use was made of the criteria of the total level of trade and of the growth of trade, especially the growth after the pre-1939 levels used in the Bretton Woods formula. Both criteria were taken into account since calculations using levels of trade alone yielded large quotas for small developing members while calculations based on growth of trade yielded large quotas for the industrial members. By using both criteria the Fund tried to give larger quotas to developing members.

Although they recognized that trade data were simple and readily available, the staff was not satisfied with the use of trade data for determining the selective increases in quotas in 1959. Trade data were not good approximations for external transactions on current account nor indicative of the instability of a member's foreign trade, and did not take international capital transactions into account. All these factors bore on a country's need to draw on the Fund. Also, trade data did not necessarily produce quota increases closely related to the Fund's need for overall liquidity or for certain currencies. Furthermore, a structure of overall Fund quotas resulting from the use of data for members' shares in total world trade differed from that resulting from the use of data for growth in trade since 1939, and it was impossible to decide which of the two trade criteria should be given greater weight.

For these reasons, in preparing for the compensatory financing decision of 1963 and before the Fourth Quinquennial Review of Quotas of 1964, the staff undertook a revision of the Bretton Woods formula and developed a number of alternative formulas. The Bretton Woods formula was modified by changing the original concept of variability of exports that favored the industrial and more developed primary producing members. By eliminating the influence of trends in exports, this bias in quota calculations in favor of industrial and more developed primary producing members was lessened. The Bretton Woods formula was reduced by

---

[6]See *History, 1945–65,* Vol. I, pp. 390–91, 450, and 540.

515

reducing all the weights in the formula; the lower weights selected were those which yielded calculated quotas that were closely in line with the Fund's actual size at that time.

In addition to modifying and reducing the Bretton Woods formula, the staff developed 15 alternative formulas by changing the weights given to the different variables in the Bretton Woods formula. The weight for reserves was eliminated, the weight given to national income was reduced, and the weights given to trade and to variability of exports were increased. The extent to which the weights could be changed was limited by the need to produce calculated quotas with a reasonable relation to existing quotas. Thus, the Bretton Woods formula could not be entirely eliminated without adverse effects on the existing quotas of the large members, particularly the United States. In setting the initial quota of the United States, national income and reserves had played an unusually large role compared with trade and variability of trade, and the size of the quota of the United States was a significant element in the Fund's whole quota structure.

Of the 15 formulas, six retained the multiplicative factor of the Bretton Woods formula: the sum of the variables was multiplied by the ratio of exports to national income. The other nine formulas were linear, that is, no multiplication was applied.

The number of formulas for quota calculations indicated the difficulty of deriving a single formula that would produce reasonable quota calculations for all members, while account was still taken of the existing structure of Fund quotas and the desirability of proceeding slowly with shifts in that structure. To narrow the range of choice, five formulas were selected: the Bretton Woods formula as modified and reduced, two nonlinear formulas, and two linear formulas. In this way two basically different types of formulas were composed. The Bretton Woods type of formula gave larger quotas to export-oriented members (given the same size of national income) and gave weight to the size of a member's exchange reserves. The other four formulas gave more weight to the variability of exports and none to reserves. These two types of formula effectively included in calculations of quotas a number of considerations.

The staff made quota calculations for each member using all five formulas. In fact, ten calculations were made for each member, one using trade data, that is, exports and imports as in the Bretton Woods formula, and another using current account data, that is, total current receipts and payments, thereby taking advantage of the improvements that had occurred since 1944 in reporting balance of payments data. The ten calculations were then averaged to obtain a range for a potential quota. One end of the range was derived from averaging the two calculations using the modified and reduced Bretton Woods formula. The other end of the range was derived by taking an average of the lowest two calculations resulting from the four reweighted formulas using export and import data and an average of the two lowest calculations of the same four formulas using data for current receipts and payments and then averaging these two averages; this procedure had the effect of taking account of invisible payments and receipts to the extent of only half their actual size.

The calculation of a range for a member's quota emphasized that no single quota calculation was appropriate; rather there was a zone within which an appropriate quota might be established after other relevant factors were taken into account. The staff obtained a single calculated quota by using the higher of the potential range.

Thus, by the mid-1960s the staff was computing a "calculated quota" for each member. In the Sixth and Seventh General Reviews in the 1970s, as described below, these calculated quotas were used heavily in determining selective increases in quotas.

SIXTH GENERAL REVIEW BEGINS

Under the Articles of Agreement, the Sixth General Review of Quotas had to be completed before February 9, 1975, five years after the Fifth General Review. The customary Committee of the Whole on Review of Quotas, that is, a committee of all the Executive Directors with the Managing Director as Chairman had to be constituted a year in advance, not later than February 9, 1974. It was already anticipated that the three main issues that would arise in the Sixth General Review would be difficult to resolve. The first concerned the size of the total increase. Mr. Witteveen, supported by officials of the developing members and to some degree of France, Italy, and the United Kingdom, wanted an increase as large as 70–100 percent. Borrowing, as was being done for the oil facility, was regarded as an unusual and temporary way for the Fund to augment its funds, and Mr. Witteveen expected huge demands on the Fund's resources, especially after the oil facility expired. Officials of the industrial members which had to furnish most of the money were much less certain that such a large boost in the Fund's resources was necessary.

The second issue concerned the distribution of quota increases among members. It was generally understood that the relative share in total Fund quotas of the major oil exporting members as a group would have to be substantially enlarged, probably doubled, from the existing 4.5 to 5 percent to nearly 10 percent of the total. There was, accordingly, the further question of how to apportion quota increases among the individual major oil exporting members. But much more difficult questions concerned which categories of members, industrial or more developed primary producing or non-oil developing members, would have to undergo reductions in their shares in total Fund quotas, and the extent of such reductions.

The third issue involved the mode of paying for increased subscriptions to the Fund resulting from the increases in quotas. Inasmuch as the possibility of phasing gold out of the international monetary system in the provisions of the amended Articles was then being discussed, the Fund could not automatically require the traditional payment of 25 percent in gold.[7] The Fund thus had to decide how the

---

[7]Discussions in 1974 and 1975 about the role of gold in the international monetary system and final agreement on the provisions included in the amended Articles are described in Chaps. 31, 32, 35, and 36.

former gold portion of subscriptions should be paid. Should it be paid in SDRs? If so, would not the Fund become overloaded with SDRs? Should not the Fund, therefore, require members to pay the former gold portion in foreign exchange, that is, in national currencies used as reserve currencies? Or could the Fund go to the extreme and permit the entire subscription to be paid in a member's own currency? How could the Fund ensure that all members' currencies would be usable in the Fund's transactions? In the past, some members had been unwilling to make the necessary arrangements for converting their national currencies into currencies that were more customarily used in international financial transactions. This made some national currencies unusable in the Fund's transactions.

A further question concerned the legal status of the gold subscription. Since payment in gold of a portion of the subscription was required under the existing Articles, which were unlikely to be quickly amended, when could quota increases that did not involve gold payments legally take effect?

Contrasting Views

From the first meeting of the Committee of the Whole on Review of Quotas, in April 1974, it was apparent that Executive Directors held contrasting views on at least the first two issues. As expected, the nine Executive Directors elected exclusively by developing members unanimously favored a large increase in Fund quotas and endorsed the 70–100 percent increase recommended by the Managing Director which would raise the Fund from SDR 29 billion to SDR 50 billion or more. Their argument was simply that the Fund needed greatly enlarged resources to help members finance the huge balance of payments deficits that were emerging in 1974 and were likely to continue for some years.

Members of the Executive Board elected by developing members, moreover, insisted that there should be no decrease in the collective share of the non-oil developing members to accommodate the larger share of the major oil producing members. To achieve larger quotas for individual non-oil developing members, Mr. Kafka urged the staff to make quota calculations not only on the basis of the formulas used in the Fourth and Fifth General Reviews but also on the basis of the incremental approach suggested by Ricardo Arriazu (Argentina) in the course of the Fifth General Review.[8] Messrs. Kharmawan and Prasad pointed out that, despite attempts by the Fund to increase the quotas of developing members, the proportion of these quotas in total Fund quotas had remained more or less the same since the Bretton Woods Conference. The relative share of these quotas was more important now because they were the basis for allocations of SDRs. The share in Fund quotas of the industrial and more developed primary producing members would have to bear the full brunt of the decline needed to permit oil producers to have a larger share.

Messrs. Cross and Schleiminger, and to some extent Mr. Kawaguchi, took positions opposite to those of the Executive Directors from developing members

---

[8]*History, 1966–71*, Vol. I, pp. 304–305.

both on the size of the general increase and on the distribution of increases. They were against a large general increase. Mr. Schleiminger took the position often expressed by officials of the Federal Republic of Germany: the action was wrong because it would be inflationary. He argued that world reserves had doubled since the Fifth General Review of Quotas and that the Fund should not add to the "excess liquidity." Because of their fear of inflation, the authorities of the Federal Republic of Germany, noting also the relatively little use made of the Fund's resources since 1970, would have been content with no increase at all in Fund quotas. The U.S. position against a large general increase was based on the belief that members could readily meet their balance of payments financing needs by recourse to private banks.

The majority of officials of the EC countries took a middle position on the size of any quota increase; they favored what they termed a "fairly sizable increase in the Fund," to SDR 40–45 billion. Mr. Lieftinck, speaking personally, reiterated his long-standing concern that an appropriate balance was needed between conditional and unconditional liquidity.[9] Although total liquidity in the world economy had increased since the Fifth General Quota Review, conditional liquidity, as represented by Fund quotas, had not. Conditional liquidity did not have the same implications for global inflation as did unconditional liquidity. Hence, Mr. Lieftinck took issue with the position of Mr. Schleiminger and of other German officials that the expansion of world liquidity precluded the need for an increase in Fund quotas. On the contrary, there was a good case for an increase in conditional liquidity. Mr. Wahl, expressing the French position on the need to revalue gold at higher prices, observed that the size of the Fund would not have to be enlarged by the SDR 20 billion proposed by the Managing Director if the Fund's gold holdings were revalued at prices related to those in private gold markets.

While the desirability of substantially enlarging—probably doubling—the share in total quotas of the major oil exporting members was agreed on, views differed markedly even among the Executive Directors from industrial and more developed primary producing members on how the corresponding reduction in the shares of other members should be accomplished. U.S. officials, including Mr. Cross, believed that the shares of all other groups of members should be proportionately reduced. However, inasmuch as officials of non-oil developing members were insisting that the aggregate share of non-oil developing members not be reduced, U.S. officials held the view that, as a minimum, the reduction in relative positions ought to be shared proportionally among all the countries of the OECD, except for the United Kingdom, which had already indicated its willingness to let its share drop more than that of other industrial members.

Officials of other industrial members and of more developed primary producing members did not accept this position of U.S. officials. Some industrial members, such as the Federal Republic of Germany and Japan, had shown the largest rates of economic advance among the Fund's membership and believed it inappropriate that

---

[9]Mr. Lieftinck's earlier concerns on this subject were described in *History, 1966–71*, Vol. I, pp. 26–27, 109, and 112.

their share in an enlarged Fund should fall. Furthermore, in the past some of these members had forgone quota increases that had been indicated by the staff's calculations on the basis of the formulas. Officials of these members, especially of Japan, even went further than objecting to a proportionate reduction. They wanted the quotas for their countries to be increased more than those of other industrial members. Calling attention to an imbalance between the quota structure of the Fund and the relative economic strength of members which ought to form the basis for calculating voting power in the Fund, Mr. Kawaguchi wanted a thoroughgoing examination of the functions of quotas in the Fund and of the formulas by which quotas were determined.

Mr. Kawaguchi, as well as Mr. Bryce and other Executive Directors from industrial members, also opposed the trend of using quotas for a host of new purposes. They noted that quotas already influenced the size of SDR allocations. The quotas of several members were also being used to determine the relative weights of currencies in the basket for valuing the SDR. It was likely that the quotas of developing members would be used to determine the amounts they would receive from profits on gold sales through the Trust Fund, then being discussed. The use of quotas for these additional purposes made negotiating and determining quotas all the harder. Mr. Schleiminger explained that the officials of the Federal Republic of Germany were at ease about their relative quota, as they had been in previous quota reviews. They realized that room for plausible changes in the quota structure was comparatively limited, that the Fund had never automatically applied quota calculations, or the formulas on which they were based, and that "enlightened discretion" was the usual basis on which quotas were determined.

Officials of other industrial members insisted that their country's position in the Fund relative to the positions of certain other countries, as judged by their respective quotas, should be broadly maintained. A few statistics make graphic the inflexibility of members' positions. Officials of the Federal Republic of Germany preferred to have a quota that retained Germany at about 5.5 percent of total Fund quotas. French officials wanted France to have a quota equivalent to at least 5 percent of total Fund quotas. Japanese officials wanted to continue to have a quota for Japan at least equal to a little over 4 percent of total Fund quotas. Officials of Sweden and Norway, whose quotas had been lagging behind their relative increases in foreign trade and national income, wanted relative increases in the Swedish and Norwegian quotas. Also, the nine Fund members that belonged to the EC wanted to be assured of retaining seven seats on the Executive Board. The ten more developed primary producing members also insisted on protection from any decline in their shares in Fund quotas. Officials of Romania and Yugoslavia argued that, for this purpose, their countries should be regarded as developing countries, as were Argentina, Brazil, and Mexico.

The positions of officials from non-oil developing members and from the more developed primary producing members meant that the 14 industrial members as a group would have to bear the whole weight of enabling the major oil exporters to double their share. But resistance by some industrial members against decreasing their own shares meant that the full brunt of any decrease would fall on a few industrial members, especially on the United States.

There was yet another complication, however. U.S. officials insisted that they did not want to have much, if any, reduction in the existing share of the U.S. quota. The U.S. quota was 22.95 percent of the total, which gave the United States 20.80 percent of total voting power in the Fund. The view of U.S. officials was that the United States needed to have a little protection from possible erosion of its quota to below the critical 20 percent of voting power by which the United States retained a veto over those Fund decisions which required an 80 percent voting majority. Although a special majority of 85 percent of voting power for certain decisions had been introduced in the Articles at the time of the First Amendment in 1969, an 80 percent majority still applied to some important actions, such as members' acceptance of amendments to the Articles. U.S. officials did not want to be in a position where they could be overridden by the rest of the Fund membership. They pointed out that the gradual addition of new members to the Fund would automatically reduce the proportion of the U.S. quota in total Fund quotas. They noted, moreover, that it was probable that the Government of the People's Republic of China would soon represent China in the Fund and obtain a substantially enlarged quota, which would also reduce the relative share of the U.S. quota. Hence, U.S. officials argued that the United States needed some margin to retain at least 20 percent of voting power. U.S. officials argued, too, that lowering the voting power of the United States to below 20 percent of the total might well lower the commitment to the Fund by the U.S. government and even by the U.S. public at large, which would be contrary to the interests of the Fund itself.

The constraint placed on the quota exercise of not letting the share of the United States in Fund quotas fall below 21 or 22 percent was serious. The scope for maneuvering needed to satisfy all parties was considerably narrowed.

PRINCIPLES AGREED AND DISCUSSIONS CONTINUE IN THE EXECUTIVE BOARD

After months of discussion of these issues in the Executive Board, the Interim Committee, at its second meeting, in January 1975, agreed on the principles for the Sixth General Review of Quotas. Fund quotas were to be increased by 32.5 percent and rounded up to SDR 39 billion, an increase of SDR 10 billion. Since this was well below the increase favored by many officials, including Mr. Witteveen, an effort was made to moderate disappointment, especially by officials of developing members. It was agreed that the Seventh General Review would take place in three years rather than in the usual five. In effect, deliberations for the Seventh General Review would immediately follow those for the Sixth General Review. The Interim Committee also agreed that the quotas of the major oil exporters were to be substantially increased by doubling their share as a group in the enlarged Fund and that the collective share of all other developing members was not to be allowed to fall below its existing level. The Executive Directors were requested to work out as promptly as possible the resulting increases in quotas for individual members.[10]

It was apparent that more time would be needed not only to work out quotas for individual members but also to decide on the mode of payment for subscriptions. As many members were unable to pay in gold, most Executive Directors supported an amendment of the Articles of Agreement to give members the option to use other media for the payment of the former gold portion of increased subscriptions. Many Executive Directors believed that members should be permitted to pay in SDRs. This solution was not sufficient either, as many developing members held small amounts of SDRs and a few members, as nonparticipants in the Special Drawing Account, had no SDRs. There was concern about whether many members would be able to pay higher subscriptions in *any* type of primary reserve asset, especially if much higher quotas were agreed for them. A number of Executive Directors therefore argued that members be permitted to pay the entire subscription in their own national currencies.

Use of national currencies, however, raised problems for the Fund. Some national currencies were not usable in the Fund's transactions unless the issuing members were willing to agree on arrangements to convert the Fund's holdings of their currencies into foreign exchange. Moreover, some members of the Executive Board were concerned about the quality of the Fund's assets. Mr. Lieftinck suggested that members be required to pay 10 or 15 percent of their subscription in SDRs. Mr. Wahl suggested that members have the option to pay in gold but at a price related to the market price for gold.

Because the deadline of February 1975 for the completion of the quota review was nearing, the Board of Governors was asked to adopt a resolution merely noting that the quota review was in progress. About a month was to pass before the resolution was adopted.[11]

Discussions Continue in the Executive Board

Working out the distribution of the SDR 10 billion quota increase among over 130 individual members proved difficult and time-consuming. It was in fact to take a year. Some Executive Directors began to press for solutions. Mr. Drabble, like Mr. Bryce before him, indicated the willingness of the authorities in his constituency to compromise and of the Canadian authorities not to be excessively concerned with Canada's relative quota in the total of Fund quotas. Mr. Palamenghi-Crispi indicated that the Italian authorities were also prepared to accept a lower share in Fund quotas. Mr. de Groote suggested that instead of waiting for political authorities to agree, as in the past, the management and staff propose quotas that could serve as

---

[10]Communiqué of Interim Committee, January 16, 1975, par. 5; Vol. III below, pp. 218–19.

[11]Resolution No. 30-1, March 4, 1975; (reproduced in report of the Executive Directors to the Board of Governors, February 19, 1976), Vol. III below, pp. 245–51.

the basis for agreement. Executive Directors for developing members suggested that China be included in the quota calculations for the group of developing members, although it was not so treated in previous quota reviews. China had not taken up any previous quota increases and China's original quota of SDR 550 million was still large in comparison with the quotas of many developing members. Including China as a developing country in the calculations would permit its allocation to be distributed among other developing members, thereby giving them somewhat larger quotas than might otherwise be possible.[12]

To help determine in some objective way which members' quotas might be regarded as out of line with the quotas of other members, and by how much, the staff for the first time in a general quota exercise used the concept of "calculated quotas." Previously, calculated quotas, determined according to the formulas described earlier in this chapter, had been circulated to the Executive Board primarily for information. They had not been much used in determining quotas for individual members, although they gave some support to suggested selective quota increases. Now, in the Sixth General Review, the staff went further, comparing calculated quotas with actual quotas for all members to reveal differences between the two.

To indicate how the total increase of SDR 10 billion in Fund quotas might be distributed among all members, the staff made numerous calculations. In most calculations, industrial members, more developed primary producing members, major oil producing members, and non-oil developing members were treated as separate categories. But in some calculations the 14 industrial members and the 10 more developed primary producing members were treated as a single group, in accordance with the U.S. position that all 24 members of the OECD experience equiproportional reductions in the share of their quotas in total Fund quotas. In still other calculations, at least some general increase—5, 10, 15, 16.25, 20, or 22 percent—in the quotas of all members was assumed, while amounts remaining of the total SDR 10 billion were distributed in the form of special quota increases. Alternative calculations were made in which no general increase for all members was assumed; the entire SDR 10 billion was distributed among all members on the basis of the relation between calculated and actual quotas. Some calculations put limits on the extent to which the quota of any particular country might be increased; other calculations did not. In addition, the staff made calculations on the basis of the incremental approach that Mr. Arriazu had developed a few years earlier and that had been recommended by several Executive Directors from Latin American members.

In this way, quotas were eventually agreed for the major oil exporters, but no agreement was reached on the quotas of other members. To break the stalemate on individual members, there was an unusual amount of behind-the-scenes activity. For the first time in a quota review exercise, several Executive Directors came forward with their own informal suggestions to the Managing Director and staff on how to calculate quotas for the industrial members. Mr. Lieftinck, for instance,

---

[12]See fn. 6 in Chap. 2, p. 35 above, and fn. 34 below.

supported for the 14 industrial members calculations that reduced the share of the United States in total Fund quotas significantly below the critical 21–22 percent desired by U.S. officials. Accordingly, unlike in previous quota reviews where resolution of differences was left to the officials of the industrial countries themselves, the Managing Director and staff and the individual Executive Directors appointed or elected by the large industrial members exchanged many internal memoranda and held many informal bilateral conversations on ways to resolve the question of quota increases for the industrial members.

In order to overcome the opposition of U.S. officials to reducing the percentage of voting power of the United States below 20 percent, the Executive Board discussed the possibility of raising the special voting majority required for certain decisions of the Board of Governors from 80 percent to 85 percent. Such a change would lower the critical percentage needed by the United States to retain a veto power from 20 percent to 15 percent. As described in Chapter 36, when the Articles of Agreement were amended, the special voting majority needed for several decisions was raised to 85 percent.

With regard to the mode of payment for the increased subscriptions, further discussion in the Executive Board yielded greater progress toward agreement. Most Executive Directors agreed that insofar as 25 percent of the increase in subscriptions was concerned—formerly payable in gold—the member should have the widest available choice of media, that is, SDRs, the member's own currency, or the currency of a member that was a net creditor to the Fund, subject, of course, to the concurrence of the issuers of these currencies. Most Executive Directors also believed that any amounts of the member's own currency paid in excess of 75 percent of quota should not be subject to the usual repurchase provision applicable if the Fund held excessive amounts of a member's currency. The Articles of Agreement would have to be amended accordingly. In this way, members could effectively pay their entire subscription in their own currencies.

SIXTH GENERAL REVIEW CONCLUDED

While these discussions were continuing in the Executive Board, the Interim Committee met again, in June 1975, in Paris. The Committee noted that progress had been made in reaching agreement on quota increases for some individual members and agreed that, subject to amendment of the Articles, members should be given an option of paying 25 percent of the increase in SDRs, in the currencies of certain other members subject to their concurrence, or in their own currency. The balance of the increase would be paid as in the past in the member's own currency. The Committee also recommended that a member should not be obliged to repurchase the amounts of its own currency paid in excess of 75 percent of the increase in its quota. In addition, the Interim Committee asked the Executive Directors to prepare for consideration by the Board of Governors at its Annual Meeting in September 1975 a resolution that would include proposed increases in the quotas of individual members and provisions on the payment of corresponding subscriptions on the basis of understandings reached in June.[13] Thus, only limited progress had been made in resolving the issues in the Sixth General Review of Quotas, although discussions had been going on for nearly a year and a half. The Executive Directors had to go back to work on the quotas of individual members other than the major oil producers.

As the time approached for the 1975 Annual Meeting, the Executive Directors were still not in a position to submit to the Board of Governors a final report on the quotas of all individual members. Potential quotas were agreed for 111 members, that is, for 13 "other developed and more advanced developing countries," for 13 "major oil exporting countries," and for 85 "other developing countries." But no potential quotas were agreed for the 14 industrial members.

On Sunday, August 31, 1975, just as the Annual Meeting was to begin, the finance ministers and governors of the central banks of the largest industrial members, meeting as the Group of Ten, finally agreed to a schedule of quotas for the 14 industrial members. The quotas agreed meant that the share of the 14 industrial members as a group in the total of Fund quotas would drop from 63 percent to 59 percent. This decline was sufficient to accommodate a doubling of the share in Fund quotas of the major oil producing members from 5 percent to 10 percent. The relative share of the quotas of other developed members could remain unchanged at roughly 9 percent and that of the non-oil developing members 22–23 percent. The share of the United States would decline from nearly 23 percent to a little over 21 percent, the share of the United Kingdom would go down from not quite 10 percent to under 8 percent, France's share would decline slightly from just over 5 percent, and Austria, Canada, Denmark, Italy, and Norway would receive quota increases that would also give them lower shares in the Fund. On the other hand, relatively larger quota increases would go to Belgium, the Federal Republic of Germany, Japan, the Netherlands, and Sweden so that their shares in Fund quotas would all go up, but only slightly. Compromise had been the order of the day for officials of all 14 industrial members. The way was now paved for completion of the Sixth General Review of Quotas. The Interim Committee, meeting on the same day, formally noted the agreement on increases in the quotas of almost all members.[14]

There were still problems to be resolved, however, that were to require the attention of the Executive Directors for the next few months. A number of members, such as Australia, Chile, Colombia, New Zealand, and Yugoslavia, considered the quotas proposed for them too low; adjustment in these quotas therefore had to be made and agreed.

Outcome of the Review

The arithmetic of the final list of quotas determined under the Sixth General Review was considerably more complicated than in previous quota reviews. For the

---

[13]Communiqué of Interim Committee, June 11, 1975, par. 9; Vol. III below, p. 222.
[14]Communiqué of Interim Committee, August 31, 1975, par. 5; Vol. III below, pp. 223–24.

first time a general review of quotas resulted in various groups of members being treated differently. Indeed, differential treatment had been explicitly rejected as recently as 1969 at the time of the Fifth General Review.[15] In the Sixth General Review, members classified as industrial countries and as other developed countries received a 7.5 percent general increase, but a 45 percent limit was applied to increases in the quotas of any industrial member. Of the total SDR 10 billion increase in the Fund, SDR 4.36 billion represented a general increase in the quotas of industrial members and SDR 500 million in special increases. Members classified as major oil exporters received a general increase of 20 percent in their quotas plus SDR 2.1 billion in special increases. Members classified as non-oil developing countries received a general increase of 21 percent, and 17 members received special increases as well.[16] Among non-oil developing members the relative positions of Argentina, Bangladesh, Burma, Colombia, Egypt, Ghana, India, Pakistan, and Sri Lanka declined.

The Interim Committee, meeting in Jamaica in January 1976, endorsed the recommendations in the draft report to the Board of Governors.[17] The report, with an accompanying draft resolution to be submitted to the Governors, was then finished by the Executive Directors and sent to the Governors on February 19, 1976. The resolution was adopted by the Board of Governors on March 22, 1976.[18]

The Governors' resolution provided that the increased quotas would not become effective until members having not less than three fourths of total quotas on February 19, 1976 had consented to them and paid their subscriptions. Since the first general increase in quotas in 1959, Governors' resolutions on general increases in quotas had provided that the proposed increases in quotas would become effective only when members holding a specified proportion of total quotas had consented to them and paid their subscriptions.[19] This policy was followed to ensure that quotas were increased both for members likely to use the Fund's resources and for members whose increased subscriptions provide the Fund with the bulk of the money needed to finance these uses. Otherwise, the increase in the Fund's resources might be insufficient to meet members' additional requests for drawings.

The resolution adopted for the Sixth General Review also provided that the increased quotas would not become effective until the Second Amendment went into force. This provision was necessary because, until the Articles were amended, members could not use SDRs and members' currencies to pay their subscriptions as was to be permissible under the Sixth General Review. While this provision was

---

[15]*History, 1966–71,* Vol. I, pp. 293–94.

[16]The Bahamas, Bahrain, Brazil, Chile, Guatemala, Israel, Ivory Coast, Jamaica, Kenya, Korea, Lebanon, Malaysia, Mexico, Panama, Singapore, Viet Nam, and Zambia. Bahrain was classified as a non-oil developing country because it did not satisfy the criteria used by the Fund to classify it as a major oil exporter.

[17]Communiqué of Interim Committee, January 8, 1976, par. 2; Vol. III below, pp. 225–26.

[18]This report, with an annex listing proposed quotas, and Resolution No. 31-2 are in Vol. III below, pp. 245–51.

[19]See *History, 1945–65,* Vol. I, pp. 450 and 585.

needed legally, it was also included as a matter of policy: to induce members to take the necessary steps to accept the Second Amendment.

In addition, within six months of the resolution's adoption a member was to make arrangements satisfactory to the Fund for the use of its currency in the Fund's operations and transactions. The provision was inserted in the resolution so that when members paid subscriptions in their own currencies, the Fund could be assured that it would be able to use these currencies. While the Fund could request members to make the necessary arrangements, it could not oblige them to do so. As described in later chapters, provisions were included in the Second Amendment which made arrangements by members to convert their currencies when their currencies were purchased from the Fund by other members mandatory.

Even after the proposed increases in quota were agreed, it was to take an unusually long time for members to consent to these increases. By early March 1977, a year after the resolution was approved, only Bolivia, Saudi Arabia, and the United States had consented to the proposed increases in their quotas. By November the list had grown to 48 but it still was far from complete. While the list now included 7 industrial members (Canada, Denmark, the Netherlands, Norway, Sweden, the United Kingdom, and the United States), 14 other industrial, developed, and more advanced developing members were still missing. Because members with relatively large quotas were delaying action, many more developing members with small quotas had to consent before the increases could go into effect. The delay was not very serious because the new quotas could not become effective even if the required number of members consented to them until the proposed Second Amendment was approved, and acceptances of the Second Amendment were also proceeding slowly.

On April 1, 1978, when the Second Amendment became effective, 86 members having 78.65 percent of total quotas had consented to the increases, which went into effect for all members that had consented and paid. Other members had up to May 1, 1978 to do so. The Executive Board later extended this period, first to June 12, 1978, then to August 7, 1978, and finally to October 31, 1978. By October 31, 1978, all eligible members except Democratic Kampuchea had consented to the increases and the Fund's total quotas reached SDR 39 billion. (No quota increase had been granted to China; hence, that country was not an "eligible" member.) The Sixth General Review of Quotas was now completed and in effect. The full process had taken approximately five years. By that time, Mr. Witteveen had been gone from the Fund for several months.

TEMPORARY ENLARGEMENT OF CREDIT TRANCHES

Although he had not expected such a long delay, Mr. Witteveen had, of course, anticipated some delay in implementing the quota increases of the Sixth General Review. Consequently, while final agreement on the quotas of the Sixth General Review was being worked out, he proposed in November 1975 an unusual technique for increasing members' access to the Fund's resources under their existing quotas. The proposal was temporarily to widen each credit tranche by one half so that each tranche would be equivalent to 37.5 percent of quota instead of the customary 25 percent.

When the Executive Directors considered this proposal in informal session, most were receptive to some such change. The Executive Directors elected exclusively by developing members wanted the tranches to be widened even further. Mr. Kafka, for instance, pointing out that most developing members used only their first credit tranche since drawings in that tranche were subject to relatively low conditionality, argued that the first credit tranche be made equal to 100 percent of existing quotas or to 75 percent of the prospective quotas under the Sixth General Review. He was prepared to see this substantial widening of the credit tranches even if it necessitated more borrowing by the Fund. Mr. Kafka's suggestion was supported by Messrs. Kharmawan, Monday, Nana-Sinkam, Suarez, W. M. Tilakaratna (Sri Lanka), and Ryrie.

Mr. Pieske and Mr. Cross, however, were concerned about what was emerging as a new concept, the Fund's liquidity.[20] If large industrial members such as Italy or the United Kingdom could draw on the Fund, potential access to existing resources under widened credit tranches might well exceed the Fund's supply of usable currencies. In any event, in their view the Fund already had adequate arrangements to meet members' needs.

Despite the concerns of the officials of the Federal Republic of Germany and the United States, Mr. Witteveen, cognizant that the oil facility would expire at the beginning of 1976 and eager to find an alternative way of enabling members to draw substantial amounts from the Fund, pushed his proposal. Supported by the nine Executive Directors elected exclusively by developing members and by Messrs. Lieftinck and Whitelaw, who had developing members in their constituencies, as well as by Mr. Åsbrink and Mr. Ryrie, he obtained the Executive Directors' concurrence to put the matter before the Interim Committee when it met in January 1976.

The Interim Committee was sharply divided. Developing members took a position similar to that of Mr. Kafka—that there should be an especially large widening of the first credit tranche where moderate conditionality applied. Industrial members resisted a larger widening of the first credit tranche on the grounds that it would compromise the Fund's main function of inducing members to achieve balance of payments adjustment. If the Fund weakened its conditionality and its role in balance of payments adjustment, industrial members might cease to regard the Fund as an organization that served their interests as well as the interests of developing members. Industrial members might then be less willing to enlarge the Fund's resources and the Fund would be weakened for all members.

Against the background of the protracted negotiations in the Sixth General Review of Quotas, just concluded, and the obvious reluctance of industrial members

---

[20]The evolution of this concept is described in Chap. 30.

to agree to a general increase larger than 25 percent, their argument was accepted. The Interim Committee agreed that, until the Second Amendment and the new quotas went into effect, the size of each credit tranche should be increased by 45 percent, an amount somewhat smaller than Mr. Witteveen's initial suggestion. Each tranche was thus made equal to 36.25 percent of quota and total access under the credit tranches increased from 100 percent to 145 percent of quota.[21] Conditionality was to remain unchanged. Because the Interim Committee was an advisory body only, the topic was returned to the Executive Board which took the necessary decision on January 19, 1976.[22]

SEVENTH GENERAL REVIEW BEGINS

Disappointed that the Sixth General Review of Quotas had produced so much argument and so little additional money, Mr. Witteveen was already pressing the Governors at the 1976 Annual Meeting in Manila to get on with the Seventh General Review. "I attach particular importance to the fact that the Seventh General Review of Quotas will be accelerated and is to be concluded by February 1978, two years ahead of the usual schedule." Emphasizing the need for adjustment of payments deficits rather than for continuously financing them, he stressed "the crucial importance of having a Fund that is adequate in size to perform its adjustment role effectively."[23] In his concluding remarks, he repeated "High priority will be given to initiation of the Seventh General Review of Quotas."[24] In February 1977, in accordance with the usual procedure, the Executive Board set up a Committee of the Whole on Seventh General Review of Quotas, a year in advance of when the review was to be completed, to begin deliberations.

The Managing Director advocated a substantial general quota increase for the Seventh General Review, as he had for the Sixth. The staff paper presented to the Executive Board suggested an increase of the order of 75–100 percent, which would bring the Fund close to SDR 80 billion. The paper argued that Fund quotas had become inadequate in relation to the size of world trade and even more in relation to the size of members' current account balance of payments deficits. Aggregate quotas had fallen steadily to about 4 percent of annual world imports, compared with 8–12 percent in the 1960s and 10–14 percent in the 1950s. In relation to current account deficits which were greatly enlarged, quotas had become seriously inadequate.

As in the Sixth General Review, it was quickly apparent that agreement on a very sizable increase in quotas was going to be difficult, if not impossible. Most members of the Executive Board, from industrial as well as from developing members supported the increase recommended by the Managing Director. One of

---

[21]Communiqué of Interim Committee, January 8, 1976, par. 6(b); Vol. III below, pp. 226–27.
[22]E.B. Decision No. 4934-(76/5), January 19, 1976; Vol. III below, p. 495.
[23]Opening Address by the Managing Director, *Summary Proceedings, 1976*, p. 20.
[24]Concluding Remarks by the Managing Director, *Summary Proceedings, 1976*, p. 245.

their main arguments was similar to his. The relatively small existing quotas were a major deterrent to the officials of many members considering coming to the Fund for financial assistance. These officials were reluctant to undertake the fundamental reorientation of their policies required by the Fund's financial programs if they received in exchange only small amounts of money. Members of the Executive Board who supported a large increase in quotas had other arguments for enlarging the Fund. A substantial increase in quotas was needed to help the Fund scale down its current borrowing and put the Fund in a better position to borrow in the future. It was also essential to maintain the level of the Fund's resources at adequate levels so as to uphold confidence in the Fund by both users and lenders. It was, furthermore, imperative to enlarge the Fund to enable the Fund better to fulfill its financial functions, which were increasingly being taken over by private commercial banks.

Messrs. Cross, Drabble, and Pieske favored a much smaller increase in quotas, perhaps 25–33 percent, and cited several considerations to justify this position. Because of the widened tranche policy, members had increased access to the Fund as a proportion of their existing quotas. Alternative sources of balance of payments finance were readily available through private channels. Members had not been using Fund resources in the upper credit tranches even under existing quotas. The increased flexibility of exchange rates helped to correct balance of payments deficits, thereby reducing the need for financing. As Mr. Cross noted, many members had been slow in consenting even to the quota increases assigned to them under the Sixth General Review, so that it was not at all assured that members would readily consent to much larger increases in quotas under the Seventh General Review. Fund officials had to be realistic, he said, and face up to the political difficulties confronting officials in many industrial countries in obtaining large amounts of money for the Bretton Woods institutions. Mr. Matsunaga expressed the Japanese position in favor of a 50 percent increase.

A few Executive Directors believed that they could go along with an overall increase on the order of 30 percent on the understanding that the Eighth General Review would be completed two years after the completion of the Seventh General Review; in this respect, they considered any quota adjustments proposed in the Seventh General Review supplementary to those agreed in the Sixth General Review. The Sixth and Seventh General Reviews could be considered as a unit, raising the total size of the Fund by about 60 percent. Some Executive Directors believed that they could agree to an overall quota increase of 40 percent provided that the Eighth General Review would be completed within three years after the Seventh General Review. A considerable number of Executive Directors, however, were strongly of the view that the Eighth General Review should not be conducted in less than five years after completion of the Seventh General Review.

The question of the distribution of quota increases among members, which had delayed agreement in the Sixth General Review and which many officials had hoped would not come up again in the Seventh General Review, did re-emerge. Again this question of possible selective increases in quota was controversial. U.S. officials, in particular, maintained that any quota increases under the Seventh General Review ought to be equiproportional to the quotas agreed under the Sixth General Review. There should be no further changes in the relative positions of members. But officials of other members, including several industrial members that had received special increases in the Sixth General Review, such as the Federal Republic of Germany and Japan, argued that special adjustments should again be made for members whose quotas were "seriously out of line with their relative positions in the world economy." Officials of these members which wanted special quota increases argued, too, that emphasis should be placed on increasing those quotas which would strengthen the Fund's liquidity. This argument was intended to imply that, in the second half of the 1970s, the Fund was in greater need of deutsche mark, Japanese yen, and the currencies of some of the major oil producing nations than it was of dollars or pounds sterling, currencies crucial to the Fund in previous years. The position of the authorities of the Federal Republic of Germany was that selective quota adjustments would have to be considered if the general increase in quotas was to exceed 25–30 percent.

Difficulties in Reaching Agreement

When the Interim Committee met in Washington in April 1977, the only conclusion reached was that "there should be an adequate increase in the total of quotas pursuant to the Seventh General Review."[25] With the 1977 Annual Meeting and the next meeting of the Interim Committee approaching in September, Mr. Witteveen held a number of informal bilateral talks with Executive Directors. In September 1977 he took the unusual step of putting forward a draft report of the Executive Directors to the Interim Committee based on his assessment of the views of the Executive Directors obtained through these talks. Although the Executive Directors found this procedure somewhat disconcerting, they agreed to the report inasmuch as it reflected their persisting differences of view.

Just before the Annual Meeting, it appeared that a breakthrough might be forthcoming. At a meeting of the finance ministers of the EC countries, officials of the Federal Republic of Germany agreed to accept an overall increase in Fund quotas of 50 percent, provided that the increase was proportionately larger in the higher tranches where use was tied to stricter conditionality. Specifically, total quotas could go up from SDR 39 billion to SDR 58 billion, provided SDR 10 billion was marked for the first credit tranche, and SDR 16 billion for each of the second, third, and fourth tranches. This proposal was acceptable to officials of the other EC countries, and at the 1977 Annual Meeting Mr. Apel made such a suggestion to the other Governors.[26]

Agreement was not at hand, however. After the 1977 Annual Meeting, Mr. Witteveen held many informal discussions with Executive Directors and with

---

[25]Communiqué of Interim Committee, April 29, 1977, par. 4; Vol. III below, pp. 231–32.

[26]Statement by the Governor of the World Bank for the Federal Republic of Germany, *Summary Proceedings, 1977*, p. 94.

officials of their governments, either by telephone or when he visited their countries. He was determined to find a consensus both on the size of an overall increase and on any selective increases. He concluded that little progress could be made, at least until officials of the U.S. Administration decided on the size of the general increase that they would support. U.S. officials were unable to decide on an increase that they could recommend to the U.S. Congress, since members of Congress were having long debates over the proposed supplementary financing facility (discussed in Chapter 28 below).

Mr. Witteveen then temporarily suspended discussions on the Seventh General Review of Quotas and turned his attention instead to the supplementary financing facility. In the meantime, since the Executive Directors were not in a position to make recommendations to the Board of Governors on the Seventh General Review of Quotas by the agreed date of February 9, 1978, they so notified the Board of Governors. In late March and early April 1978, the Committee of the Whole resumed its meetings in preparation for the tenth meeting of the Interim Committee scheduled for April 29–30 in Mexico City.

In order to advance the discussions, the staff circulated "calculated quotas" for all members and this time made greater use of the concept of calculated quotas for suggesting actual quotas. For the first time, the Managing Director and the staff placed heavy emphasis on calculated quotas as a way to help measure how much a member's actual quota could be regarded as deviating from a quota that reflected its relative strength in the world economy, that is, the "out of lineness" of any particular quota. A calculation was made for each member to indicate the "excess" of its calculated quota from its actual quota. This excess was expressed not in absolute amounts but as a percentage of the quota agreed in the Sixth General Review. Members with the largest excess (indicating high calculated quotas compared with their actual quotas) included nine major oil exporting members—Iran, Iraq, Kuwait, Libya, Nigeria, Oman, Qatar, Saudi Arabia, and the United Arab Emirates—and the Federal Republic of Germany, Japan, Korea, Lebanon, the Netherlands, Singapore, and Sweden. At the opposite end, the members with the lowest excess (indicating low calculated quotas compared with their actual quotas or even actual quotas which exceeded calculated quotas) were Afghanistan, Bangladesh, Burma, India, Pakistan, Sri Lanka, Sudan, Uganda, and a number of African members with relatively small quotas.

As might be expected, these calculations of the relationship between calculated quotas and actual quotas elicited a great deal of debate in the Executive Board about the formulas underlying them and the use to be made of them. Mr. Matsunaga, for example, strongly supported the calculations as corroborating the belief of the Japanese authorities that a sizable selective increase in Japan's quota was warranted. Most of the Executive Directors who had non-oil developing members in their constituencies, as well as Mr. Wahl, taking into account the interests of French-speaking African members, called for reconsideration of the formulas. The relative share of the quotas of non-oil developing members would go down substantially.

Even the staff, which had first introduced the modified and reduced Bretton Woods formula in 1963–64 as a way to increase the relative share in Fund quotas of the smaller and developing members with a tendency toward balance of payments deficits, had not expected this result. Using the same formulas in the Seventh General Review yielded relatively low quotas for the small non-oil developing members because the largest increases in trade in the 1970s among non-oil developing members were by small countries that had developed balance of payments surpluses.

Apart from the formulas used, the big question concerned the extent to which the excess of a member's calculated quota over its actual quota should determine its eligibility for a selective quota increase. While Executive Directors for major oil exporting members and for Japan supported the use of calculated quotas to determine selective quota increases, other Executive Directors did not. Messrs. Cross, Dini, Drabble, Frede Hollensen (Denmark), Laske, and Ryrie, in particular, all favored equiproportional increases in quotas, with only a very few selective quota increases. Mr. Laske agreed that there should be only a few selective quota increases on the assumption that the general increase would not exceed 25–30 percent. Most Executive Directors from industrial members were especially opposed to selective increases for the Federal Republic of Germany and Japan. Mr. Dini perhaps best expressed the reasons for this opposition. Giving the Federal Republic of Germany and Japan special quota increases was, in his view, tantamount to granting premiums to those members that had failed to adjust their balance of payments position to the changed world situation after the rise in oil prices. These industrial members were still running very large current account surpluses, seriously aggravating the adjustment problems of other industrial members and of the non-oil developing members.

At their meeting in Mexico City at the end of April, the members of the Interim Committee continued to reflect the diversity of view of the Executive Directors. But they also expressed their disappointment at the delay; after more than a year and a half of discussion, agreement on the Seventh General Review of Quotas had still not been reached.[27]

There was also a question about the form in which the additional subscriptions should be paid. Was not the mode of payment of the Sixth General Review too lenient? Should not members be required to pay a certain proportion of their higher subscriptions—say, 25 percent—in SDRs or in the currencies of other members as specified?

AGREEMENT REACHED

The time approached for the 1978 Annual Meeting and for the eleventh meeting of the Interim Committee. Mr. Witteveen had meanwhile left the Fund. The

---

[27]Communiqué of Interim Committee, April 30, 1978, par. 6; Vol. III below, pp. 237–38.

Executive Directors were considering the possibility of new allocations of SDRs, and since the considerations governing both SDR allocations and quota increases were closely interconnected, it seemed timely to settle the Seventh General Review of Quotas. The new Managing Director, Mr. de Larosière, accordingly sent to the Executive Directors an aide-mémoire proposing a solution to the quota exercise. Noting that there was an enhanced need for the Fund to furnish credit in world markets and that the ratio between Fund quotas and world imports had gone down considerably, Mr. de Larosière recommended that there now be a general quota increase of 50 percent (SDR 19.5 billion) and that no further general adjustment in quotas would take place for five years. With regard to selective increases, he suggested that selective quota increases be limited to 11 developing members, using the criterion that only those members with a calculated quota four times greater than the actual quota be offered selective increases. He provided detailed supporting evidence for these special increases.[28]

Most Executive Directors repeated their previous stance. Mr. Cross, for instance, noted that in the meantime the Fund's own financial position had improved. It held more usable currencies, it held SDR 1 billion in SDRs, and the supplementary financing facility would soon be in place. Drawings had also fallen and repurchases had risen sharply. In these circumstances, there was hardly a strong case for an increase in quotas. Mr. Pieske had similar arguments against a 50 percent general increase. The Executive Directors again sent to the Interim Committee a report reflecting these differences.

To the surprise of most officials, however, the members of the Interim Committee, meeting in Washington just before the Annual Meeting, agreed on a 50 percent general increase for all members, except China and Democratic Kampuchea, and on selective increases for 11 developing members, Iran, Iraq, Korea, Kuwait, Lebanon, Libya, Oman, Qatar, Saudi Arabia, Singapore, and the United Arab Emirates.[29]

On this basis the final report of the Executive Directors was submitted to the Board of Governors on October 27, 1978. The quota increases were to become effective when members having not less than three fourths of the total of quotas on November 1, 1978 consented to increases in their quotas. However, if the new quotas would become effective between July 1, 1980 and October 5, 1980, the effective date was to be postponed. In this way, the new quotas would not go into effect during, or shortly before, the 1980 Annual Meeting when the next election of Executive Directors was scheduled to take place. In earlier quota reviews new quota increases had also been postponed until after the election of Executive Directors so as to delay the consequences for the composition of the Executive Board.[30] A member was to be able to consent to an increase in its quota any time on or before November 1, 1980, but the Executive Directors could extend this period.

---

[28]The aide-mémoire, dated August 4, 1978, is in Vol. III below, pp. 253–56.
[29]Communiqué of Interim Committee, September 24, 1978, par. 6; Vol. III below, pp. 241–42.
[30]See *History, 1966–71*, Vol. I, pp. 298–300.

The mode of payment for higher subscriptions was different from that of the Sixth General Review. Participants in the Special Drawing Rights Department were to pay 25 percent of the increase in their quotas in SDRs. A nonparticipant was to pay 25 percent in the currencies of other members specified by the Fund, subject to their concurrence. The balance of the increase in quota was to be paid in a member's own currency.

If all members accepted increases in their quotas to the maximum amounts proposed, total quotas in the Fund would rise from SDR 39 billion to SDR 58.6 billion. After the adoption by the Board of Governors of the resolution on the Seventh General Review, the Executive Board would not propose a general adjustment of quotas for five years.

After nearly two years of discussion, the resolution on the Seventh General Review of Quotas was adopted by the Board of Governors on December 11, 1978.[31] Members would now have to consent to the individual quotas proposed for them. In view of the prolonged discussions involved in the quota review and the length of time it had taken members to agree to quota increases under the Sixth General Review, the prospect that members would accept these additional quota increases quickly was not favorable.[32] It was becoming apparent that expansion of the Fund's resources through increases in quotas was becoming politically much more difficult than it had been in the past.

QUOTAS OF MEMBERS JOINING THE FUND, 1972–78

In addition to the two general reviews of quotas conducted in the seven years from 1972 to 1978 and the resulting increases, total Fund quotas were increased by the initial quotas assigned to the 18 countries that joined the Fund in these years. Although the majority of these new members had very small initial quotas, Bangladesh and Romania were assigned initial quotas of SDR 125 million and SDR 190 million, respectively, so that this source of quotas came to another SDR 450 million. Moreover, the quotas of the oil producing countries of Qatar and the United Arab Emirates were substantially enlarged in the Seventh General Review so that aggregate quotas proposed for the new members following the Seventh General Review came to over SDR 1 billion.

---

[31]The report, dated October 25, 1978, and Resolution No. 34-2 are in Vol. III below, pp. 256–63.

[32]The increase in quotas under the Seventh General Review did not come into effect until November 29, 1980 when 127 members representing 75.15 percent of total Fund quotas as of November 1, 1978 had consented to the proposed increases in their quotas. By December 12, 1980, two additional members had also consented to the increases, leaving only four members—Iran, Lesotho, Oman, and the United States—that had not yet done so. It was significant that the United States, the member with the largest single quota and the single most important contributor to the Fund since its establishment, had not yet consented to the proposed increase in its quota. Within the next few days, however, legislative action was completed in the U.S. Congress and the Fund was notified by the United States of the acceptance of its quota increase.

Table 16 lists the 18 members that joined the Fund from 1972 to 1978, the dates on which they became members, the size of their initial quotas, and the size of the quotas proposed for them under the Seventh General Review. The quotas of all members on April 30, 1973 (the end of the first financial year covered in this History) and on December 31, 1978 (the cutoff date of this History) are given in Table 18 at the end of this chapter.

Table 16. Quotas of Members Joining the Fund, 1972–78

Member	Date Membership Became Effective	Initial Quota	Quota Proposed Under Seventh General Review
		(In millions of SDRs)	
Bahamas	August 21, 1973	20.0	49.5
Bahrain	September 7, 1972	10.0	30.0
Bangladesh	August 17, 1972	125.0	228.0
Cape Verde	November 20, 1978	2.0	3.0
Comoros	September 21, 1976	1.9	3.5
Djibouti	December 29, 1978	3.8	5.7
Dominica	December 12, 1978	1.9	2.9
Grenada	August 27, 1975	2.0	4.5
Guinea-Bissau	March 24, 1977	3.2	5.9
Maldives	January 13, 1978	0.7	1.4
Papua New Guinea	October 9, 1975	20.0	45.0
Qatar	September 8, 1972	20.0	66.2
Romania	December 15, 1972	190.0	367.5
São Tomé and Principe	September 30, 1977	1.6	3.0
Seychelles	June 30, 1977	1.0	2.0
Solomon Islands	September 22, 1978	2.1	3.2
Suriname	April 27, 1978	25.0	37.5
United Arab Emirates	September 22, 1972	15.0	202.6

DISTRIBUTION OF QUOTAS AMONG MEMBERS

The question of the relative distribution of quotas among individual members and among the groups of members in different economic categories was raised much more sharply in the Sixth and Seventh General Reviews of Quotas than in the three decades since Bretton Woods. It is interesting, therefore, to trace some of the changes in the distribution of quotas from 1945 to 1978. In these years there had been significant changes in the relative positions in Fund quotas of individual members, especially in the position of individual industrial members, and there had been some changes in the relative positions of different groups of members.

Changes in Different Groupings of Members

Table 17 gives the percentages of total Fund quotas for various economic categories of members on December 31, 1945, when the Fund was created, and just after the quota increases approved under the Fourth, Fifth, and Sixth General Reviews went into effect. Also shown are the percentages of total quotas for these categories resulting from the quotas proposed in the Seventh General Review.

Table 17. Percentages of Total Fund Quotas of Members, Classified by Economic Category, 1945–78

	December 31, 1945 (Original Membership)	April 30, 1966 (After Fourth Quinquennial Review)	December 31, 1971 (After Fifth General Review)	December 31, 1978 (After Sixth General Review)	Quotas Proposed in Seventh General Review
Total	100	100	100	100	100
Industrial Members	70	64	63	59	59
Of which:					
United States	(36)	(27)	(23)	(21)	(21)
United Kingdom	(17)	(12)	(10)	(8)	(8)
Other industrial members	(17)	(25)	(30)	(30)	(30)
More Developed Primary Producing Members	9	9	9	9	9
Developing Members	21	27	28	32	32
Of which:					
Major oil exporters	(1)	(4)	(5)	(10)	(10)

As can be seen from the table, the share of industrial members as a group declined from 70 percent in 1945 to 59 percent in 1978, with the decline being taken up by an increase in the share of developing members, which rose from 21 percent in 1945 to 32 percent in 1978; the share of the more developed primary producing members remained roughly the same, just over 9 percent. The brunt of the decline in the share of industrial members in total Fund quotas was in the shares of the two members with the largest quotas, the United States and the United Kingdom. The share of the United States was reduced from 36 percent in 1945 to 21 percent in 1978, and the share of the United Kingdom was reduced from 17 percent to 8 percent. Quotas of the United States and the United Kingdom, which had made up more than half of the Fund's total quotas in 1945, were accordingly only a little over one fourth of total quotas after the Sixth General Review. The quotas of the other industrial members went through a reverse development, nearly doubling, from 17 percent in 1945 to 30 percent in 1978. Most of the decline in the relative quotas of the United States and the United Kingdom was thus taken up by increased relative quotas for the 12 other industrial members, as a group.[33]

---

[33] Austria, Belgium, Canada, Denmark, France, the Federal Republic of Germany, Italy, Japan, Luxembourg, the Netherlands, Norway, and Sweden.

Part of the jump in the share of other industrial members in Fund quotas came in the late 1940s and early 1950s when several large industrial countries that had not been original members—Austria, the Federal Republic of Germany, Italy, Japan, and Sweden—joined the Fund. But beyond that, the group of other industrial members continued to achieve a growing proportion of aggregate quotas through selective increases in quotas as the economies of Western European countries and of Japan gradually recovered after World War II and continued to expand. By the end of 1978, the quota of the Federal Republic of Germany had become the third largest in the Fund, accounting for 5.5 percent of total Fund quotas, against 3.8 percent in 1955; the quota of Japan had become the fifth largest, accounting for 4.25 percent of total Fund quotas, against 2.9 percent in 1955; and the quota of Italy had become the seventh largest, at 3.18 percent of the total. Quotas granted over the years to Austria, Belgium, Canada, Denmark, Luxembourg, Norway, and Sweden were also sufficiently large so that these members retained their relative shares in aggregate quotas.

The largest increase in relative quotas among developing members up to 1978 was in the share of the major oil exporters as a group, especially following the Sixth General Review. From the time of Bretton Woods their share as a group went up more than tenfold, from less than 1 percent in 1945 to 10 percent in 1978.[34]

Some Remaining Issues

Two issues concerning the structure of Fund quotas were being debated as 1978 ended: the relative position of individual members and the relative position of developing members as a group in total Fund quotas. From the narrative in this chapter, one can derive an observation about each of these issues.

With regard to the first issue, changes in the structure of quotas among members brought about by the Sixth General Review seemed profound when they were agreed in 1975 and 1976. With regard to the second issue, when the Fund undertook the Sixth General Review in 1974–75, one of the first major decisions made was to protect the relative position of developing members as a group. As noted earlier, in January 1975 the Interim Committee agreed that the relative share in Fund quotas of non-oil developing members collectively was not to go down in order to accommodate the increased share that was to go to oil exporting members, thereby ensuring that the relative share of all developing members was to be enlarged. This decision was taken more than five years before the Brandt Commission argued for increased shares in Fund quotas of developing members.

Despite the changes of the Sixth and Seventh General Reviews, the differences between calculated quotas and actual quotas remained sizable. Officials of members with calculated quotas much in excess of their actual quotas, such as some oil producing countries, continued to press for larger relative quotas in the Fund.

---

[34]When the Government of the People's Republic of China assumed the representation of China in the Fund in April 1980, the quota for China was raised from SDR 550 million to SDR 1.2 billion under the Sixth General Review and to SDR 1.8 billion under the Seventh General Review, giving China the eighth largest quota in the Fund.

Officials of developing members as a group also continued to press for a larger proportion of total Fund quotas, particularly since the voting system in the Fund was one of weighted voting, determined largely by quotas. Officials of some industrial members, especially the Federal Republic of Germany and Japan, whose trade had expanded unusually rapidly and which were running balance of payments surpluses, so that the Fund was making heavy use of its holdings of their currencies, also wanted to have relatively larger quotas in the Fund. The problem in granting these desires for larger relative quotas was that major changes in the relative quota structure would upset the original and long-standing quota structure of the Fund, including relative voting power. Such changes were necessarily political, involving the question as to the members, or groups of members collectively, that would control the Fund. They also had an important financial aspect involving how much money the Fund would receive and in what currencies.

The Seventh General Review of Quotas ended on a note that recognized this situation. The report stated that after quota increases under the Seventh General Review had gone into effect, the Executive Board was to review the customary method of calculating quotas. In the Eighth General Review of Quotas the Executive Board was directed to examine the relative quotas of members in relation to their relative positions in international trade and finance explicitly in order to adjust their relative quotas in the Fund. At the same time, since changes in the Fund's structure of quotas had implications for appointing or electing Executive Directors, attention was also to be paid to the desirability of having "an appropriate balance in the composition of the Executive Board." In effect, what was not accomplished by changing the distribution of relative quotas in the Fund by the Sixth and Seventh General Reviews was left for the Eighth General Review.

Table 18. Quotas of Fund Members, 1973 and 1978

(In millions of SDRs)

	April 30, 1973[1]	December 31, 1978[2]
Industrial Members		
Austria	270.0	330.0
Belgium	650.0	890.0
Canada	1,100.0	1,357.0
Denmark	260.0	310.0
France	1,500.0	1,919.0
Germany, Federal Republic of	1,600.0	2,156.0
Italy	1,000.0	1,240.0
Japan	1,200.0	1,659.0
Luxembourg	20.0	31.0
Netherlands	700.0	948.0
Norway	240.0	295.0
Sweden	325.0	450.0
United Kingdom	2,800.0	2,925.0
United States	6,700.0	8,405.0
Total	18,365.0	22,915.0
More Developed Primary Producing Members		
Australia	665.0	790.0
Finland	190.0	262.0
Greece	138.0	185.0
Iceland	23.0	29.0
Ireland	121.0	155.0
Malta	16.0	20.0
New Zealand	202.0	232.0
Portugal	117.0	172.0
Romania	190.0	245.0
South Africa	320.0	424.0
Spain	395.0	557.0
Turkey	151.0	200.0
Yugoslavia	207.0	277.0
Total	2,735.0	3,548.0
Major Oil Exporting Members		
Algeria	130.0	285.0
Indonesia	260.0	480.0
Iran	192.0	660.0
Iraq	109.0	141.0
Kuwait	65.0	235.0
Libya	24.0	185.0
Nigeria	135.0	360.0
Oman	7.0	20.0
Qatar	20.0	40.0
Saudi Arabia	134.0	600.0
United Arab Emirates	15.0	120.0
Venezuela	330.0	660.0
Total	1,421.0	3,786.0

Table 18 (*continued*). Quotas of Fund Members, 1973 and 1978

(*In millions of SDRs*)

	April 30, 1973[1]	December 31, 1978[2]
Non-Oil Developing Members		
Africa		
Benin	13.0	16.0
Botswana	5.0	9.0
Burundi	19.0	23.0
Cameroon	35.0	45.0
Cape Verde	•	2.0
Central African Republic	13.0	16.0
Chad	13.0	16.0
Comoros	•	2.3
Congo	13.0	17.0
Djibouti	•	3.8
Equatorial Guinea	8.0	10.0
Ethiopia	27.0	36.0
Gabon	15.0	30.0
Gambia, The	7.0	9.0
Ghana	87.0	106.0
Guinea	24.0	30.0
Guinea-Bissau	•	3.9
Ivory Coast	52.0	76.0
Kenya	48.0	69.0
Lesotho	5.0	7.0
Liberia	29.0	37.0
Madagascar	26.0	34.0
Malawi	15.0	19.0
Mali	22.0	27.0
Mauritania	13.0	17.0
Mauritius	22.0	27.0
Morocco	113.0	150.0
Niger	13.0	16.0
Rwanda	19.0	23.0
São Tomé and Principe	•	2.0
Senegal	34.0	42.0
Seychelles	•	1.3
Sierra Leone	25.0	31.0
Somalia	19.0	23.0
Sudan	72.0	88.0
Swaziland	8.0	12.0
Tanzania	42.0	55.0
Togo	15.0	19.0
Tunisia	48.0	63.0
Uganda	40.0	50.0

Table 18 (*continued*). Quotas of Fund Members, 1973 and 1978

(*In millions of SDRs*)

	April 30, 1973[1]	December 31, 1978[2]
Non-Oil Developing Members (*continued*)		
Africa (*concluded*)		
Upper Volta	13.0	16.0
Zaïre	113.0	152.0
Zambia	76.0	141.0
Subtotal	1,161.0	1,572.3
Asia		
Afghanistan	37.0	45.0
Bangladesh	125.0	152.0
Burma	60.0	73.0
China	550.0	550.0
Fiji	13.0	18.0
India	940.0	1,145.0
Kampuchea, Democratic	25.0	25.0
Korea	80.0	160.0
Lao People's Dem. Rep.	13.0	16.0
Malaysia	186.0	253.0
Maldives	•	0.9
Nepal	12.4	19.0
Pakistan	235.0	285.0
Papua New Guinea	•	30.0
Philippines	155.0	210.0
Singapore	37.0	49.0
Solomon Islands	•	2.1
Sri Lanka	98.0	119.0
Thailand	134.0	181.0
Viet Nam	62.0	90.0
Western Samoa	2.0	3.0
Subtotal	2,764.4	3,426.0
Latin America and the Caribbean		
Argentina	440.0	535.0
Bahamas	•	33.0
Barbados	13.0	17.0
Bolivia	37.0	45.0
Brazil	440.0	665.0
Chile	158.0	217.0
Colombia	157.0	193.0
Costa Rica	32.0	41.0
Dominica	•	1.9
Dominican Republic	43.0	55.0

Table 18 (*concluded*). Quotas of Fund Members, 1973 and 1978

(*In millions of SDRs*)

	April 30, 1973[1]	December 31, 1978[2]
Non-Oil Developing Members (*concluded*)		
Latin America and the Caribbean (concluded)		
Ecuador	33.0	70.0
El Salvador	35.0	43.0
Grenada	•	3.0
Guatemala	36.0	51.0
Guyana	20.0	25.0
Haiti	19.0	23.0
Honduras	25.0	34.0
Jamaica	53.0	74.0
Mexico	370.0	535.0
Nicaragua	27.0	34.0
Panama	36.0	45.0
Paraguay	19.0	23.0
Peru	123.0	164.0
Suriname	•	25.0
Trinidad and Tobago	63.0	82.0
Uruguay	69.0	84.0
Subtotal	2,248.0	3,117.9
Middle East		
Bahrain	10.0	20.0
Cyprus	26.0	34.0
Egypt	188.0	228.0
Israel	130.0	205.0
Jordan	23.0	30.0
Lebanon	9.0	12.0
Syrian Arab Republic	50.0	63.0
Yemen Arab Republic	10.0	13.0
Yemen, People's Dem. Rep. of	29.0	41.0
Subtotal	475.0	646.0
Total	6,648.4	8,762.2
GRAND TOTAL	29,169.4	39,011.2

[1]A dot (•) indicates that the country was not a member on that date.
[2]These quotas were those actually in effect on December 31, 1978, after the Sixth General Review of Quotas. The quotas proposed under the Seventh Review that were approved on December 11, 1978 under Resolution No. 34–2 are listed in Vol. III, pp. 261–63.

CHAPTER 28

A Supplementary
Financing Facility

SUPPLEMENTARY FINANCING was Mr. Witteveen's answer to the anticipated delay in getting quotas enlarged. He proposed that the Fund temporarily borrow from any member in a position to lend to "supplement" the funds that the
Fund could make available to members under existing quotas. This was an
innovative and imaginative idea, although for the Fund to augment its own
resources by borrowing was not new. The Fund had already done so through the
General Arrangements to Borrow and for the oil facility. What was new was that the
Fund was to borrow not for exceptional circumstances, but because its own quotas
and resources were insufficient, albeit temporarily. By proposing that the Fund
borrow for a supplementary financing facility, Mr. Witteveen was giving importance
to borrowing as a means of obtaining money for the Fund. The Fund was becoming a
major financial intermediary, borrowing from some members to lend to others.

The proposal for a supplementary financing facility was so identified with
Mr. Witteveen that it was originally referred to as the "Witteveen facility."

WORKING OUT THE PROPOSAL AND GAINING SUPPORT

Mr. Witteveen, surveying the situation at the end of 1976, feared that the Fund
would run short of resources. Drawings in 1976 were nearing SDR 7 billion, largely
because drawings under the compensatory financing facility both by developing
members and by the more developed primary producing members were numerous
after the liberalization of the facility in December 1975. The extended facility that had
been introduced in 1974 was also beginning to be used. In addition, Italy and the
United Kingdom were deep in discussions with Fund officials for stand-by
arrangements totaling close to SDR 4 billion. Many more members were expected to
turn to the Fund for stand-by arrangements. The Fund's oil facility had expired, and
public officials and senior officers of commercial banks were concerned, just as they
had been in late 1974 and in 1975, that the private banking system could no longer
make extensive credit available.

The increases agreed under the Sixth General Review would augment the Fund's total quotas by only SDR 10 billion. In any event, the prospect for making these quota increases effective quickly was already dim. Members were slow in consenting to the increases and equally slow in approving the Second Amendment necessary for these quota increases to take effect. While the Seventh General Review of Quotas, just getting under way, was likely to yield a larger general increase, getting agreement on those quota increases and on making them effective could take close to two years, as had happened in the Fourth, Fifth, and Sixth General Reviews of Quotas.

In proposing the supplementary financing facility in February 1977, Mr. Witteveen wished to make it possible for a member to draw on the credit tranches in amounts well beyond the limit of 245 percent of quota, agreed in January 1976, which temporarily extended the previous limit of 200 percent of quota. In certain circumstances, access to the supplementary credit alone might be a multiple of a member's quota, depending on the Fund's judgment of the member's need for financing. Conditionality in the first tranche and in the upper credit tranches would be maintained. Following the pattern proposed for the stand-by arrangement with the United Kingdom being discussed at the end of 1976, stand-by arrangements were to be agreed for two years rather than for the traditional one year. Charges for use of supplementary credit would be high enough to give the Fund a margin of income over the interest it would have to pay for borrowing the funds. Mr. Witteveen assumed that, as in the instance of the oil facility, the Fund would .have to pay market rates of interest on borrowed funds.

Borrowing would take place under lines of credit that the Fund would seek to establish with governments or central banks of members in strong external payments positions that could readily lend to the Fund in case of need. Repurchases might have to be effected over a longer period than the customary three to five years, and probably up to seven years as in the oil facility. The arrangement would be temporary, terminating when the increase in quotas under the Seventh General Review became effective. Mr. Witteveen wanted the facility to be large enough that confidence in the Fund and in the financial system could be maintained. If the facility was too small, heavy use might give both public and private financial officials the impression that the Fund was becoming illiquid or unable adequately to respond to requests for drawings. Such an impression could destabilize exchange rates or cause panic among private bankers. As lender of last resort, the Fund had to be regarded as commanding resources commensurate with its needs. Although Mr. Witteveen initially had in mind a target of some SDR 14 billion for the supplementary financing facility, he later revised this figure down to $10 billion (about SDR 8.5 billion). He proposed to borrow about half from major oil producing members and half from industrial members.

Reactions

By the time the Executive Board discussed his proposal in mid-April 1977, Mr. Witteveen, accompanied by a few staff members, had already visited Riyadh and Kuwait City to discuss with Saudi Arabian and Kuwaiti officials the possibility of borrowing for this supplementary financing facility and had ascertained their willingness. Many Executive Directors were receptive to his proposal and had a number of reasons for supporting the facility, depending on their points of view. First, the Fund's liquidity was inadequate. Second, in accordance with the function established in connection with the oil facility, the Fund *should* serve as a financial intermediary between members with large payments surpluses and those with large deficits. Channeling greater financial assistance through the Fund, which helped members adopt appropriate policies, helped balance of payments adjustment so that imbalances in world payments would gradually be reduced. It was imperative for members to reduce their payments deficits because the foreign debt that could be accumulated was limited.

Third, the credit that the Fund could provide had declined steeply over time, especially relative to members' external payments imbalances. Many members were making little use of the Fund because of the limited amounts of money that the Fund could make available. As noted in the previous chapter, public officials were reluctant to undertake the politically unpopular austerity programs needed for balance of payments adjustment and required as a condition for financial support from the Fund if in return they obtained only limited financial assistance. It was therefore urgent that the Fund find ways for members to draw supplementary amounts substantially larger than the limit at that time of 245 percent of quota. Fourth, the Fund was in a good position to borrow. It could readily establish lines of credit, and with the experience gained from the GAB and the oil facility, it could negotiate borrowing arrangements reasonably favorable to the Fund.

These Executive Directors also had ideas about specific features they preferred in any new borrowing arrangements. In particular, borrowing arrangements should be more convenient than those of the GAB, under which minor amendments, as well as renewal, had to be approved by all ten participants and involved cumbersome and time-consuming parliamentary procedures in some participating countries. For this reason, bilateral borrowing arrangements between the Fund and individual lending governments or central banks, such as had been used for the oil facility, were decidedly preferable to any general borrowing arrangements with a group of countries. The Fund should assure its lenders that they would receive in exchange claims against the Fund that could be considered liquid reserve assets comparable to creditor positions in the Fund. The facility should be open-ended so that other countries could lend to the Fund if improvements in their balance of payments and reserve positions permitted them to do so.

Messrs. Cross and Matsunaga, however, were uneasy about the proposed supplementary financing facility. They were concerned that the Managing Director might be exaggerating the need for the Fund to enlarge its role in financing balance of payments deficits. In their view, the bulk of payments deficits was being financed by private credit and should continue to be so financed. They regarded the Fund's role as not to replace private financing with official financing but to safeguard the international monetary system from excessive instability. Mr. Whitelaw, moreover, cautioned the Executive Directors against proposing features for the supplementary financing facility that might make members reluctant to use it. Some Executive Directors favored upper credit tranche conditionality. Others wanted to set charges higher than market-related interest rates to allow the Fund a service charge. Still others suggested that members draw on their regular second, third, and fourth credit tranches before having access to the supplementary financing facility. Were the facility to have all these features, Mr. Whitelaw asked, what incentive would there be for members to use it? Despite their differences, the Executive Directors were able to agree on a report to the Interim Committee outlining the main features of a supplementary credit facility. These features related to the size of a facility (about SDR 14 billion), its open-endedness (additional members could lend to the Fund for the facility), the magnitude of access to the facility, conditionality and charges associated with its use, the repayment period, and provisions for ensuring that the claims of lenders were sufficiently liquid.

When the deputies of the Group of Ten met in April 1977, most supported the proposed supplementary financing facility, some warmly. A few were concerned about the relation between the proposal for supplementary financing in the Fund and an earlier proposal for a financial support fund in the OECD (the "safety net" proposal), which staff members of the OECD had been pushing.[1] The administration in the United States had changed in January 1977 when Jimmy Carter became President, and U.S. officials were more willing to work with the Fund than they had been for several years. The U.S. deputies endorsed the creation of a new financial arrangement in the Fund rather than in the OECD for a number of reasons. Unlike the financial support fund, proposed by the previous U.S. Administration and to be financed by borrowing from private markets, the Fund's proposal for a supplementary financing facility involved borrowing almost equal amounts from members of OPEC and from industrial members. Participation by OPEC was a virtual precondition to selling any plan to officials of industrial countries. Officials of those industrial countries, especially of the Federal Republic of Germany and of the United States, that would have to provide most of the funds for any financial arrangement argued that OPEC ought to be the mainstay of the balance of payments support needed by oil importing countries since the decision by OPEC to raise oil prices created the excessive deficits in the first place.

U.S. officials favored the Fund plan rather than the OECD plan for other reasons as well. The Fund plan covered developing members as well as industrial and relatively more developed members. It was politically important that any plan for financing payments deficits provide some help for non-oil developing countries. Otherwise the United States in particular, with the largest payments deficit among the industrial countries, might appear self-serving in advocating a plan applicable only to industrial and relatively more developed countries. At the same time, the Fund needed a broad arrangement that would also provide financing to industrial

---

[1] This proposal for a financial support fund in the OECD was described in Chap. 18.

countries; the Fund must not seem to be evolving into an aid agency for developing countries. In addition, the financial support fund of the OECD had come to be adversely perceived as a "bailing out" operation for private commercial banks, in which official funds would help countries repay debts owed to commercial banks. Members of the U.S. Congress, which had to authorize U.S. participation in either plan, especially perceived the financial support fund in this way.

Support of U.S. officials in the Group of Ten advanced the supplementary financing facility. One result of the Fund's supplementary financing facility was that the financial support fund in the OECD, extensively discussed in 1975 and 1976, never came into being. This was an understandable disappointment to Mr. van Lennep, who had initiated the idea independently of U.S. officials, worked hard in developing the plan, and hoped that the OECD would, for the first time, have ample funds available to it.

To advance the discussions, on April 27, 1977, the evening before the meeting of the Interim Committee in Washington, Mr. Witteveen held an informal dinner meeting with the finance ministers and governors of the central banks of countries that he had approached about extending lines of credit to the Fund. The Interim Committee endorsed the proposed supplementary financing facility, welcomed the willingness of countries to lend to the Fund, and urged the Managing Director to complete, as soon as possible, his discussions with potential lenders on terms, conditions, and amounts. The Committee also requested the Executive Directors to take the necessary steps to make the supplementary financing facility operative as soon as possible.[2]

A UNIQUE MINISTERIAL MEETING

Agreement on the concept of a supplementary financing facility was easy. How to raise the money was more difficult. Despite general skepticism that adequate funds would be forthcoming, Mr. Witteveen persisted. Of the initiatives that he took in his term as Managing Director, none was more audacious than his request to the finance ministers and governors of central banks of the 13 members expected to lend for the supplementary financing facility to meet with him in Paris to discuss the terms and conditions of the loans. The meeting was planned for Saturday, August 6, 1977. Belgium, Canada, the Federal Republic of Germany, Iran, Japan, Kuwait, the Netherlands, Nigeria, Qatar, Saudi Arabia, the United Arab Emirates, the United States, and Venezuela were invited. Representatives of the Swiss National Bank also participated. The list of members not invited was interesting. France, Italy, Sweden, and the United Kingdom, which were members of the Group of Ten and which customarily took part in discussions of world economic and financial problems, were not invited. Adding affront to this exclusion was the invitation to many developing countries not previously represented at such gatherings: Iran, Kuwait, Nigeria,

---

[2]Communiqué of Interim Committee, April 29, 1977, par. 3; Vol. III below, p. 231.

Qatar, Saudi Arabia, and Venezuela. The composition of the invitees exemplified a shift in world economic power. The Executive Directors of some members not included in the Paris meeting protested to the Managing Director, warning him to avoid the emergence of "a permanent creditors' club."

An aide-mémoire, based on discussions by the Executive Directors about the borrowing arrangements for the facility and its operational features, served as a basis for discussion with the potential lenders. It explained the suggested period of commitment, the relation to regular tranche drawings from the Fund, the conditionality for supplementary credit, the denomination of loans, the interest rate, the transferability of the loan claims on the Fund, charges, and the repayment period.

At the meeting, which involved lengthy morning and afternoon sessions, it was agreed that supplementary credit should be available "in an equitable manner" to meet the needs of members facing difficult payments problems. "A fair and substantial share" of supplementary credit was to be used to assist developing or nonindustrial members, but was not to be made available in such a way that "too large a proportion would be used by only a few members," a subtle reference to Italy and the United Kingdom that had used sizable amounts of the oil facility and had been recipients a few months earlier of large stand-by arrangements. This understanding and language were used to compensate officials of Saudi Arabia and other Fund members for the rejection of their proposal that borrowings by the Fund should be used exclusively for the benefit of developing members. To ensure that the needs of many members were met, it was agreed that the use of supplementary credit was to be the subject of a report after one year.

The interest rate payable to creditors was a subject of intense discussion and negotiation. Some industrial countries were willing to accept a modest discount from the rate on five-year U.S. Treasury bills, but OPEC members favored a premium. A reasonable compromise was agreed upon. An initial rate of 7 percent would apply until June 30, 1978. For each period of six months thereafter, the interest rate was to be the average yield for that period for U.S. Government securities with five years to run, rounded upward to the nearest ⅛ of 1 percent. The amounts each country would lend received even greater attention. As the discussion progressed, representatives slipped from the meeting to telephone higher officials in their governments for agreement on how much could be committed.

The amount committed was expected to reach at least SDR 8.435 billion and possibly exceed SDR 8.6 billion ($10 billion), Mr. Witteveen's target. While commitments were reasonably firm, in some instances they had to be confirmed at the cabinet level or ratified by legislative bodies.

All in all, the response was heartening. Mr. Witteveen's efforts were crowned with success. In one day, he had managed to borrow $10 billion on terms that involved only commercial considerations, that is, without political concessions, such as changes in Fund quotas or a restriction reserving the use of borrowed resources to developing members. When he reported to the Executive Board a few days later that the $10 billion seemed to be in hand, he was unanimously congratulated by the

Executive Directors. A few weeks later, at the 1977 Annual Meeting, he was also to receive the grateful accolades of Governors from both industrial and oil importing developing members.

THE FACILITY AGREED

Although several Executive Directors observed that the finance ministers of a few creditor members had usurped one of the main functions of the Executive Board, making policy on use of the Fund's resources, the Executive Directors adopted on August 29, 1977 two decisions agreeing to the supplementary financing facility. One decision established the facility; the second set out the borrowing arrangements.[3]

Under the decision establishing the facility, a member contemplating use of the Fund's resources in the three credit tranches beyond the first (that is, in the upper credit tranches) that would include supplementary financing was to consult the Managing Director before making a request. The request was to be met only if the Fund was satisfied: (i) that the member needed financing that exceeded the amount available in its four credit tranches, and its problem required a relatively long period of adjustment and a maximum period for repurchase longer than the three to five years under the credit tranche policies; and (ii) that the member's program would be adequate for the solution of its problem and compatible with the Fund's policies on the use of its resources in the upper credit tranches or under the extended Fund facility.

Supplementary financing was to be available only if the Fund had approved a stand-by arrangement in the upper credit tranches, or beyond, or an extended arrangement in support of an agreed program. The stand-by or extended arrangement was to be in accordance with the Fund's policies on conditionality, phasing, and performance criteria. The period of a stand-by arrangement approved under the decision was normally to exceed one year and might extend up to three years in appropriate cases. The period of an extended arrangement was to be in accordance with the decision setting up the extended facility, described in Chapter 19 above.

The amounts available to a member under a stand-by or extended arrangement were to be apportioned in a complicated way between the Fund's ordinary resources and the amounts obtained by supplementary financing. So long as the size of the first credit tranche remained at 36.25 percent of a member's quota, that is, until the Second Amendment of the Articles of Agreement became effective, the use of the first credit tranche was not to be accompanied by any use of the supplementary financing facility. For drawings in each of the three upper credit tranches, supplementary financing up to 34 percent of a member's quota could be available. After the temporary enlargement of the first credit tranche had lapsed, a member could draw under the supplementary financing facility an amount equivalent to

---

[3]E.B. Decisions Nos. 5508-(77/127) and 5509-(77/127), August 29, 1977; Vol. III below, pp. 512–15, 550.

12.5 percent of its quota along with the unused portion of its first credit tranche and 30 percent of its quota along with each of the upper credit tranches. In special circumstances, drawings might be made beyond the upper credit tranches, but these drawings were to be made wholly under the supplementary financing facility. For drawings under an extended arrangement, supplementary financing was to be available in an amount not exceeding 140 percent of a member's quota. Drawings under an extended arrangement were to be financed with the Fund's ordinary resources and with supplementary credit in a ratio of one to one.

The objectives of the intricate provisions on amounts were to ensure that a member (i) would not unfairly use ordinary resources, thus avoiding use of borrowed resources, and (ii) would not repurchase in respect of borrowed resources ahead of ordinary resources. Rules were adopted to achieve equity and uniformity for all members.

Furthermore, the decision provided that in exceptional circumstances supplementary financing might be available under a stand-by arrangement even though the credit tranches had been used in full, or under an extended arrangement even though the limit of 140 percent of quota had been reached and the cumulative amounts of supplementary financing available in respect of the credit tranches and the limit of 140 percent of quota had been utilized. No limitation was placed on supplementary financing not associated with the credit tranches or with the limit of 140 percent of quota. The supplementary financing facility defined certain uses of the Fund's resources under the policy in terms of quota, but it was recognized that a member's needs might be too large and uncertain for a definition of this kind. The policy therefore permitted uses that were not defined in terms of quota and was the first that was open-ended in this sense.

To the extent that a drawing under the supplementary financing facility was financed with ordinary resources, it was subject to the same practices on periodic charges and repurchases that applied to a drawing in the credit tranches or under the extended Fund facility. To the extent that a drawing was made with supplementary financing, it was to be repurchased in equal semiannual installments that began not later than three and one-half years after the drawing and was to be completed not later than seven years after the drawing.

The claims on the Fund that creditors received were to be what Mr. Witteveen called "desirable international reserve assets, with an attractive rate of interest and a high degree of liquidity."[4] They were encashable on demand by the Fund if the creditor represented that it had a balance of payments need. Without prior reference to the Fund, lenders could transfer these claims to any other lender, to any Fund member, or to other official entities at prices agreed between the transferor and the transferee.

The decision establishing the supplementary financing facility was to be reviewed not later than two years after the facility came into existence or when the

---

[4]Opening Address by the Managing Director, *Summary Proceedings, 1977,* p. 19.

Seventh General Review of Quotas became effective. The facility was to become effective on the date on which borrowing agreements by the Fund and lenders to the facility were completed for a total of at least SDR 7.75 billion, including at least six agreements in an amount of not less than SDR 500 million each. The rationale of this timing was to make certain that the United States obtained from Congress the necessary authority to participate. U.S. officials had successfully pressured the officials of the other lending countries to obtain authority to participate in the supplementary financing facility and then, as we shall see later in this chapter, had difficulty in obtaining from Congress the necessary authority. A report on the use of supplementary financing was to be made one year after the facility became effective.

In September 1977 the Executive Board set the charges on the Fund's holdings of currencies resulting from drawings under the supplementary financing facility. Members would pay the rate of interest that the Fund had to pay on its borrowed funds (plus the usual service charge of ½ of 1 percent of the amount of the transaction) plus an additional ⅕ of 1 percent a year for drawings outstanding for up to three and one-half years plus a further ⅛ of 1 percent a year for drawings outstanding for more than three and one-half years. The resulting schedule is shown in Table 19 below.

Prior to the Second Amendment, the Articles of Agreement required that charges take the form of a progression of at least three steps, depending on the length of time drawings were outstanding. Consequently, the decision on the charges for the supplementary financing facility called for a further charge of ⅛ of 1 percent a year for drawings outstanding for more than four and one-half years, that is, the rate of interest paid by the Fund plus 0.450 percent. This third-layer charge was made inapplicable, however, by a provision of the decision stating that until the Articles were amended, the charges on drawings under the supplementary financing facility were not to exceed the rate of interest paid by the Fund plus 0.325 percent. Hence, in Table 19, three steps of charges are listed, but the charge for drawings outstanding from three and one-half to four and one-half years and the

Table 19. Charges on Transactions Effected Under the Supplementary Financing Facility Prior to the Second Amendment

Charges in percent a year[1] payable on holdings for period stated	
Service charge	0.5
Up to 3½ years	Rate of interest paid by the Fund plus 0.20 percent
3½ to 4½ years	Rate of interest paid by the Fund plus 0.325 percent
Over 4½ years	Rate of interest paid by the Fund plus 0.325 percent

[1]Except for service charge, which was payable once per transaction and was expressed as a percentage of the amount of the transaction.

applicable charge for drawings outstanding for more than four and one-half years are the same.

In order to implement the supplementary financing facility, the Executive Board also took a decision in November 1977, setting forth in detail the form of the stand-by arrangement and the form of the extended arrangement to be used when these arrangements provided for supplementary financing.[5]

DELAY IN PUTTING THE FACILITY INTO OPERATION

The United States, the second largest contributor to the facility, was among the creditors that had to obtain approval of its legislature to lend money to the Fund. Under Section 5 of the Bretton Woods Agreements Act, as amended, the U.S. Congress had to authorize the Secretary of the Treasury to make available the SDR 1,450 million for the supplementary financing facility to which Mr. Blumenthal had tentatively agreed on behalf of the U.S. Government; the Congress then had to appropriate the money.

As President Carter told the Governors on September 26 at the opening session of the 1977 Annual Meeting, the U.S. Administration fully supported the new facility.[6] U.S. officials submitted the request for approval of the money for the supplementary financing facility to Congress in September 1977, as soon as possible after the Executive Board had taken the decisions establishing the facility. Anticipating reluctance by some members of Congress to approve money for the Fund, Administration officials took the position that the transaction with the Fund was unlike other expenditures for foreign aid and was more in the nature of an exchange of monetary assets. The United States provided dollars to the Fund and in return received claims on the Fund. These claims increased the automatic drawing rights of the United States on the Fund, forming part of the U.S. reserve position in the Fund. They were also highly liquid claims that could readily be transferred should the U.S. Government later need the money. Thus, the money lent to the Fund was part of the international reserves of the United States.

Members of Congress were cool to this line of argument. They debated the Administration's request for funds for the supplementary financing facility with virtually the same detailed scrutiny as they did requests for all foreign aid, which was becoming an unpopular cause. Several members of Congress and several witnesses called to testify in the hearings customarily preceding U.S. legislation were, moreover, strongly opposed to the U.S. Government giving more money to the Fund. Different groups had different reasons for objecting to the Fund. Some members of Congress and some witnesses took what was regarded as a conservative line with regard to social and economic issues. In general, they preferred as little use of government institutions and regulations as possible, including regulation through

---

[5]E.B. Decision No. 5585-(77/161), November 30, 1977; Vol. III below, p. 518.
[6]Address by the President of the United States, *Summary Proceedings, 1977*, p. 2.

international governmental institutions, and favored reliance on private entities and markets instead. Hence, they questioned the extent to which the Fund should assist its members in financing their payments deficits. Could not private commercial banks adequately finance the payments deficits of other countries? Was not the U.S. economy suffering because private banks were lending abroad in huge amounts at high interest rates and hence were not lending enough for domestic investment? Did not continuing payments deficits by countries abroad increase the likelihood of default to U.S. banks, so that there was danger of commercial bank failures? Was it not better for the Fund to borrow in private capital markets than from its member governments and their central banks?

Some members of Congress, angry at "the OPEC cartel" for raising prices for crude oil, insisted that OPEC finance the greater bulk of the resulting balance of payments deficits of the non-oil developing countries. They wanted to reject participation by the United States in the supplementary financing facility to force OPEC to provide the needed financing directly to oil importing countries and to accept the risk involved in this financing.

Members of Congress and some of the witnesses testifying at the hearings who regarded themselves as liberals on social and economic issues had quite different misgivings about the Fund and its policies. They saw the Fund as an advocate of excessively austere financial and economic policies, such as balancing governmental budgets at the expense of necessary social welfare programs. They worried that social welfare programs would be cut at the expense of desperately poor consumers in poor developing nations. They raised questions about the effects of the Fund's stabilization programs on the ability of developing members to finance basic human needs. Some members of Congress even suggested that the Executive Director for the United States submit regular reports to Congress evaluating the effects of the monetary and fiscal policies worked out with members in their stand-by arrangements with the Fund on satisfying basic human needs in developing members.

Some members of Congress also raised questions about the Fund's attitude toward the political circumstances in members to which the Fund lent money. Inasmuch as the Fund extended funds to Third World countries on the basis of economic considerations and customarily did not take the political character of governments into account, some members of Congress were concerned about "the Fund's support of repressive governments." Some of these members of Congress wanted the Fund to include human rights as a consideration in the policies governing use of its resources and urged that human rights be taken into account whenever any drawing was made from the Fund. As a compromise among members of Congress so that U.S. participation in the supplementary financing facility could be obtained, a provision was included in the Bretton Woods Agreements Act requiring the Secretary of the Treasury to make an annual report on the subject of human rights insofar as the policies of international organizations were concerned.[7]

---

[7]Sec. 31 of Public Law 435, 95th Cong., October 10, 1978, 92 Stat. 1051.

Members of Congress of all political persuasions questioned the salaries of the staffs of the Fund and the World Bank.

The process of prior Congressional approval for the funds needed for the U.S. contribution to the supplementary financing facility was thus prolonged. From these discussions Fund officials feared that the institution was losing some of its support and goodwill on Capitol Hill and with the U.S. public. Both conservatives and liberals seemed to be increasingly critical of the Fund's policies.[8]

The delay of over six months in getting the facility into operation after the decision on its establishment caused members of the Interim Committee, meeting in Mexico City in April 1978, to express their concern: "In view of the need of a number of members for prompt financial assistance on the scale envisaged by the supplementary financing facility, the Committee urged that all necessary steps be taken for bringing the facility into operation at the earliest possible date."[9] The delay also had consequences for other discussions in the Fund in 1977 and 1978. During the consideration of the Seventh General Review of Quotas, for example, U.S. officials were so concerned about the debate in Congress over the supplementary financing facility that they hesitated for many months before indicating the size of a general quota increase that they could support.

In the end, however, supporters of the Fund in the U.S. Administration, among members of the U.S. Congress, and among the witnesses called to testify won approval of U.S. participation in the supplementary financing facility. On October 25, 1978, 13 months after the initial request of the Administration, Secretary of the Treasury Blumenthal informed Mr. de Larosière that the legislation necessary for the United States to participate in the facility for $1,832 million (SDR 1,450 million) had been enacted into law.

Despite U.S. participation, the facility was still not ready for operation because sufficient funds were not yet available from other members. The SDR 700 million expected from Iran, which was supposed to be the fourth largest contributor, was not forthcoming because of the revolution in that country. In addition, among the other participants at the Paris meeting, Abu Dhabi and Saudi Arabia lent less to the Fund for the facility than had been expected, and Qatar did not participate. Hence, the supplementary financing facility was not yet in existence as 1978 ended.

The facility came into existence shortly thereafter, however. To help acquire the amounts needed, the Fund appealed to other countries and obtained small amounts from Austria and Guatemala. The facility entered into force on February 23, 1979, when the Austrian National Bank agreed to lend SDR 50 million to the Fund and joined 12 other members or institutions that had concluded agreements to lend

---

[8]See U.S. Congress, Senate, Committee on Foreign Relations, Subcommittee on Foreign Economic Policy, *The Witteveen Facility and the OPEC Financial Surpluses: Hearings*, 95th Cong., 1st Sess. (Washington: Government Printing Office, 1978).

[9]Communiqué of Interim Committee, April 30, 1978, par. 7; Vol. III below, p. 238.

to the Fund, raising the total to SDR 7,754 million to finance transactions under the facility. The agreement with Guatemala for SDR 30 million was concluded on April 16, 1979, raising the total amount available to SDR 7,784 million. The 14 individual lenders and the amounts committed (in millions of SDRs) were as follows:

Abu Dhabi	150	Central Bank of Kuwait	400
Austrian National Bank	50	The Netherlands Bank	100
National Bank of Belgium	150	Central Bank of Nigeria	220
Canada	200	Saudi Arabian Monetary Agency	1,934
Deutsche Bundesbank	1,050	Swiss National Bank	650
Banco de Guatemala	30	United States	1,450
Japan	900	Central Bank of Venezuela	500
		Total	7,784

Participation in the financing of the facility remained open to other lenders with strong external payments and reserve positions.

CHAPTER

29

Charges, Repurchases, Currencies, and the Fund's Liquidity

*T*RANSFORMATION OF THE FUND into a more complex financial institution by increasing the number of facilities under which members might draw and by making the Fund a major financial intermediary led to complications in the Fund's charges, its policies on repurchases, the currencies used in its transactions and operations, and even in determining the amount of current funds it had available. Temporary policies and practices were introduced pending the amendment of the Articles of Agreement. Many of these policies and practices, originally introduced by decision of the Executive Board, were subsequently made part of the amended Articles by the Second Amendment.

CHARGES UNTIL 1974

Until June 1974 the charges the Fund levied on use of its resources were simple. A one-time service charge was applied when a member entered into a stand-by arrangement or drew from the Fund, and periodic charges on balances of a member's currency in excess of its quota held by the Fund were calculated according to a single schedule. Since December 1951, the service charge on drawings had been only ½ of 1 percent, the lowest level possible under the original Articles. Although the Fund was permitted to levy a service charge on gold tranche drawings as well as on other drawings, in 1969 it decided to eliminate this charge in order to improve the reserve status of members' gold tranche positions in the Fund. The Fund also levied a charge for stand-by arrangements of ¼ of 1 percent on the amount of the arrangement, but offset this charge against the service charge. The schedule of periodic charges was unusual in that it progressed both with the size of the Fund's holdings of a currency in relation to a member's quota (that is, by tranche) and with the length of time that drawings were outstanding. Under the original Articles, there had to be a progression of charges (a schedule of charges) because there had to be a level of Fund holdings of a member's currency at which the Fund consulted with the member on ways to reduce its holdings of the member's currency, and a level at

559

which, if the Fund and the member failed to agree, the Fund might apply penalty rates "as it deems appropriate." Charges were payable in gold, except that, when a member's monetary reserves were less than one half its quota, it might pay in gold only that proportion of the charges due which its reserves bore to one half its quota, and the balance could be paid in its own currency.

While the Executive Directors could change the schedule of periodic charges by a three-fourths majority of total voting power, they rarely did so. Between 1945 and 1965, the schedule was altered only three times, on December 1, 1951, on January 1, 1954, and on May 1, 1963. The changes made in 1963 were so minor that virtually the same schedule existed from January 1, 1954 onward. From 1966 to 1973 annual reviews took place, but each time the Executive Board decided to retain the existing schedule.

Since the days of Bretton Woods, Executive Directors had held various views on how high the Fund's charges ought to be. Several Directors from industrial members that provided the bulk of the Fund's resources had consistently argued that the Fund's charges should be related to the rates of interest prevailing in short-term money markets. Others, mainly from developing members but also a few from industrial and more developed primary producing members, believed that the Fund's charges should be deliberately kept low to provide members with low-cost funds and to induce them to come to the Fund as a way to encourage them to institute financial stabilization policies and to correct their balance of payments deficits. Between 1956, when the first large drawing by the United Kingdom took place, and August 1971, the Fund was solvent, running budget surpluses and adding to reserves. Although charges on use of its resources were the Fund's only source of income, the Fund's budgetary situation was not a weighty determinant of the level of charges, and officials who favored low charges succeeded in keeping them low. Consequently, the rates of charges in the schedule still applicable early in 1974 ranged from an initial 2 percent a year to a maximum of 5 percent a year.[1]

INCREASES IN 1974

In June 1974, these simple charges came to an end. No longer was there only a single schedule of charges. As the Fund introduced special facilities, such as the 1974 oil facility, the 1975 oil facility, and the supplementary financing facility, all based on borrowed funds, separate schedules of charges were applied to drawings under each facility; other schedules were applied to drawings from the Fund's regular resources and were changed twice between 1974 and 1978.

The first increase in charges during these years, noted in Chapter 16, came in June 1974 when charges were raised mainly to help the Fund cover additional

---

[1]Further information on the Fund's charges from 1945 to 1971 can be found in the earlier Histories. See *History, 1945–65*, Vol. I, for example, pp. 84–86, 103–104, 229–30, 321–23, 371–72, 417, 457–60, 527–30, and 562, and Vol. II, pp. 428–36; and *History, 1966–71*, Vol. I, pp. 378–81 and pp. 385–92.

operational expenses incurred by raising the rate of interest on the SDR and consequently the rate of remuneration. Other circumstances also suggested the need to raise charges at that time. Interest rates in short-term money markets had risen considerably since 1963 without a corresponding increase in the Fund's charges. The charges on the newly introduced oil facility, financed by borrowed funds, were to be close to commercial interest rates and consequently considerably higher than those in the Fund's prevailing schedule. Drawings had been increasing after the 1968 review by the Executive Board of the Fund's policies on use of its resources, but charges had not been subsequently re-examined. After 1969 the Fund had operational as well as administrative expenditures since it had to pay remuneration to members with net creditor positions in the Fund. At the same time, other decisions, such as making gold tranche drawings automatic and eliminating the service charge on these drawings, reduced the Fund's income.

With a new schedule of charges effective July 1, 1974, two schedules of charges were applicable to use of the Fund's resources. The older, lower schedule, ranging from zero to 5 percent a year, continued to apply to balances of members' currencies that the Fund held as a result of drawings effected between May 1, 1963 and June 30, 1974 (Table 3 in Chapter 16). The new, higher schedule, ranging from 4 to 6 percent a year, applied to currency balances that the Fund held as a result of drawings effected after July 1, 1974 (Table 4 in Chapter 16). When the decision was taken in June 1974 to introduce a higher schedule of charges, the Executive Directors had considered the desirability of making all the Fund's holdings of currencies subject to the new schedule and of eliminating the former schedule. They decided against such action for two reasons. It would deviate from past practice: the Fund had always applied a revised schedule of charges only to drawings made *after* the new schedule of charges was adopted. It would be bad policy: to apply the new schedule to holdings of currency from past drawings was to change the financial terms on which members had made earlier drawings. According to the legal staff, however, if the Executive Board gave notice in advance that the Fund's holdings of a member's currency might be subjected to higher charges, a revised schedule of higher charges could apply to holdings of a member's currency resulting from earlier drawings. The purpose of notice was to avoid retroactivity, which applied, in the absence of notice, to higher charges. (Lower charges could be applied without notice because they were beneficial for members.)

Accordingly, in June 1974, the Executive Board took a decision so notifying members.[2] The decision related to all revisions of charges, increases or decreases.

INCREASES IN 1977

In April 1977 the schedule of charges was again revised upward. The rates of charge were raised, though slightly, from a schedule with an initial charge of 4 percent a year, ranging to a maximum of 6 percent, to a schedule that ranged from an

---

[2]E.B. Decision No. 4239-(74/67), June 13, 1974; *Selected Decisions*, 10th Issue, p. 110.

initial charge of 4.375 percent a year to a maximum of 6.375 percent. The service charge, applied to all drawings except for those in the gold tranche, remained at 0.5 percent of the transaction. This schedule is given in Table 20.

Table 20. Charges on Transactions Effected from July 1, 1974

Charges in percent a year[1] payable on holdings in excess of quota, for period stated

Service charge	0.5
Up to 1 year	4.375
1 to 2 years	4.875
2 to 3 years	5.375
3 to 4 years	5.875[2]
4 to 5 years	6.375

[1]Except for service charge, which was payable once per transaction and expressed as percentage of amount of transaction.
[2]Point at which consultation between the Fund and the member became obligatory.

Since members had been notified that higher charges could be applied to the Fund's currency holdings resulting from earlier drawings, the new schedule was applied to the Fund's holdings of all currencies from drawings undertaken from July 1, 1974 onward, except for drawings made under the oil facilities. This action eliminated the schedule of charges introduced on July 1, 1974 (Table 4 in Chapter 16). The long-standing schedule of May 1963 to June 1974 (Table 3 in Chapter 16) was still applicable to use of the Fund's ordinary resources, but was to be gradually phased out.

The schedule of charges for use of the extended facility was adapted to accommodate the longer period for which drawings under extended arrangements could be outstanding: a charge of 6.875 percent a year was to apply to drawings outstanding from five to eight years. In July 1975 the charge of ¼ of 1 percent a year imposed on extended arrangements (as on stand-by arrangements) was to be payable in advance on the amount that could be purchased during that year.

Charges were raised in 1977 because the average cost of money obtained by the Fund, notably the rate of remuneration, was gradually rising and because since 1971 the Fund's budget had been in deficit. Although the schedule of charges had been raised in June 1974, the increase proved insufficient to restore an adequate spread between charges and remuneration. Of special concern by 1977 was the persistence of budget deficits, though from 1974 onward both the volume of drawings and the Fund's operational income from charges were at their highest levels ever.

While the Fund is not a commercial institution and is not expected to maximize profits, neither can it operate year after year with budget deficits. It needs income to cover interest costs on borrowing, to cover remuneration and administrative expenses, and to add to its reserves. Since the Fund was becoming a borrowing, as well as a lending, institution, its financial soundness was becoming a salient consideration in world financial markets. A number of dilemmas had to be resolved before the budgetary problem could be solved. The rate of remuneration paid to members with net creditor positions in the Fund was a decisive factor determining what the Fund charges ought to be: charges could be kept low if the rate of remuneration was low. The rate of remuneration could not be too low, however, as it had to be at least somewhat comparable to market rates of interest if members were to provide the Fund with their currencies. Similarly, rates of interest on the SDR comparable to market rates were essential if members were to continue to allow themselves to be designated as holders of more SDRs than they were obliged to hold.

The rate that the Fund paid for remuneration and as interest on the SDR could, some officials argued, be somewhat lower than the interest rate that the Fund paid for borrowed funds. The Fund was likely to have to pay a higher rate on borrowed funds because borrowing agreements were voluntary and unrelated to members' quotas in the Fund. Moreover, claims on the Fund resulting from borrowing agreements were less liquid than claims resulting from members having a net creditor position in the Fund or from holding SDRs. At the same time, the gap between interest rates on borrowed funds and rates of remuneration and interest on the SDR could not be unreasonably large. Consequently, there were limits to how low the rate of remuneration could be. Any decision about how to fix the rate of remuneration and the rate of charges was made more difficult by the general reluctance of Executive Directors to raise the Fund's charges.

To meet the Fund's need for income without raising charges, the Executive Directors in 1977 considered a number of alternatives. They considered reintroducing a service charge on drawings in the gold tranche but rejected the idea because, after much effort member governments had been persuaded to regard their gold tranche positions in the Fund as genuine and unconditional reserve assets, and to levy a service charge on use of these positions was a step backward. They considered investing some of the Fund's reserves, but until the Articles of Agreement were amended, the Fund had limited authority in this regard. In any event, such investment would not provide sufficient income for even a small budget surplus in the financial years 1978 and 1979.

After considerable discussion, the Executive Directors agreed in April 1977 to raise charges a little (by only 0.375 percent a year), as described above, and to take a number of related decisions to strengthen the Fund's income from charges. First, a way was found to eliminate gradually the long-standing schedule of charges applied to currency balances acquired by the Fund prior to July 1, 1974 (Table 3 in Chapter 16). The method traditionally used by the Fund to calculate the amount of currency holdings subject to charges was based on the LIFO (last in, first out) principle. When a member repurchased its currency, the Fund cancelled the portions of currency holdings that it had most recently acquired. This method best measured the extent to which the member had been using the Fund's resources continuously and the period over which such use had been made. Because of this method of applying repurchases to the currency balances subject to the highest charges, a member that had made drawings after July 1, 1974 could still pay charges under the previous schedule that were no higher than the 5 percent a year maximum prevailing since 1963. Because these members were paying charges even lower than the existing rate of remuneration, the Fund was losing money by holding their currencies. Consequently, the Executive Board decided in 1977 to apply reductions in the Fund's holdings of currency (other than holdings resulting from the use of the extended facility and the oil facility) first to the holdings of currency still subject to the pre-July 1974 schedule.

Another decision taken in April 1977 to strengthen the Fund's income from charges required members to pay charges promptly after the end of the quarter to which they related rather than allowing a grace period of 30 days. This change brought the receipt of charges by the Fund more closely in line with the Fund's practices of paying interest to members promptly after the end of each quarter and of paying remuneration promptly after the end of each financial year.

A third decision relating to charges taken in April 1977 was, when the Second Amendment became effective, to exclude for the purpose of determining the member's reserve tranche the Fund's holdings of a member's currency as a result of drawings under the two oil facilities. This decision meant that the Fund's holdings of such currency would be subject to the charges applicable to the oil facility even when these holdings fell below the level of a member's quota. Previously, a certain amount of these holdings had fallen into the reserve tranche, and although the Fund had been receiving no income from charges on these holdings, it had continued to pay interest on that amount to the members from which it had borrowed.

The central decision of April 1977 with respect to charges also provided that, if the margin of the initial rate of charge above the rate of remuneration was reduced to less than ¼ of 1 percent or was increased to more than 1 percent because of changes in the rate of remuneration, the Fund's financial position, the rate of remuneration paid to creditors, and the initial rate of charge would be promptly reviewed. The rate of remuneration and the initial rate of charge were thus to be linked in a way that would trigger a review of the Fund's basic financial situation. At such a review, the Executive Board could change either the rate of remuneration or the initial rate of charge, but the budgetary problem could not continue without some action being taken. Some Executive Directors were unhappy with a decision that linked remuneration and charges, but consideration of the Fund's financial position left them little choice. The decision of April 1977 on charges was also to be reviewed if the Fund's annual income substantially exceeded its annual expenses.

OTHER DEVELOPMENTS IN CHARGES

From April 1977 to the end of 1978, the Executive Board took several other decisions relating to charges. In November 1977, the customary charge levied on a stand-by arrangement was adapted to the possibility that after January 1977 stand-by arrangements might last for up to three years. The charge of ¼ of 1 percent a year, previously levied on the full amount that could be drawn under a stand-by arrangement payable for the whole period of the arrangement at the time the stand-by arrangement was entered into, which went up to a maximum of ½ of 1 percent as a member drew under the stand-by arrangement, would instead be payable at the beginning of each 12-month period of a stand-by arrangement on that part of the total amount of the arrangement not yet drawn. When the member made a drawing under the arrangement, the amount of the stand-by charge was reduced, through a refund, by the proportion that the amount of the drawing bore to the total amount that could be drawn under the stand-by arrangement. In the absence of this decision a member could have been placed in a position of having paid a stand-by arrangement charge of ¾ of 1 percent for a three-year arrangement but of receiving credit for only ½ of 1 percent even though the full amount of the stand-by arrangement had been drawn.

The Executive Board temporarily adopted, effective April 21, 1978, a higher schedule of charges to apply to holdings of a member's currency acquired not later than June 30, 1979 under the credit tranches that raised the Fund's holdings above 200 percent of quota (excluding balances acquired under special facilities and under the extended facility) and to currency holdings under the extended facility in excess of 140 percent of a member's quota. This schedule (Table 21 below) resulted from the application to the supplementary financing facility of the charges described in the previous chapter. It seemed essential to maintain equity between the charges on the supplementary financing facility and those for use of the Fund's regular resources and to have a higher schedule of charges for exceptional use of the Fund's resources. Higher charges were also thought to encourage members to repurchase outstanding drawings as soon as possible. This decision was to be reviewed before December 31, 1978.

Table 21. Charges on Transactions Effected in Excess of 200 Percent of Members' Quotas Under Stand-By Arrangements or in Excess of 140 Percent of Quotas Under the Extended Fund Facility

Charges in percent a year[1] payable on holdings for period stated	
Service charge	0.5
Each six months	Average yield to constant five-year maturity of U.S. Government securities, rounded to next 0.25 percent, plus 0.25 percent

[1] Except for service charge, which was payable once per transaction and expressed as percentage of amount of transaction.

In December the Executive Board decided that this schedule would apply only until the supplementary financing facility came into effect. This occurred on February 23, 1979.

In brief, as 1978 came to an end, four principal developments in the Fund's charges had taken place. First, charges had become complicated. Seven schedules were in effect, applicable to different segments of the Fund's holdings of a member's currency. Consequently, officials of members had a difficult time knowing what charges they had to pay on their use of the Fund's resources or how they could best minimize these charges. Second, the rates of charge for use of the Fund's resources were concessional, and the degree of concessionality was becoming larger. Third, the level of charges was affected more closely than in the past by the Fund's budgetary position. The Fund was increasingly faced with the dilemma of avoiding budget deficits while still paying an adequate rate of remuneration and trying to retain a concessional schedule of charges. Despite this dilemma, the Fund's charges had been relatively stable, having been adjusted only twice. Fourth, debate about the structure and level of the Fund's charges was growing more intense and involved. Many officials, including some of the Fund staff, believed that charges had to be much higher while others continued to resist any substantial increase in the Fund's charges. The relationship of the Fund's charges to market rates of interest and the rate of remuneration paid by the Fund, the extent to which the Fund's rates of charges should incorporate concessional (subsidy) elements, and the question of whether the rates of charges should be inversely related to the degree of conditionality associated with use of the Fund's resources would all have to be resolved.

REPURCHASES

Repurchases are the reverse of purchases. Using gold, SDRs, or the currency of another member, as specified by the Fund, the member buys back from the Fund excess amounts of its own currency that the Fund holds as a result of the member's earlier purchases of other currencies.

As noted in Chapter 2, ad hoc arrangements had to be made to effect repurchases after August 15, 1971, including special arrangements for the U.K. repurchase in 1972. Between 1972 and 1978 other ad hoc and temporary arrangements were also made. In 1973, for example, the Executive Board decided that if an obligation to repurchase included an amount of gold equal to less than one standard bar, such an amount should not be collected.[3] Since amounts of gold not exceeding one standard bar could be regarded as minimal, the decision to waive these amounts did not materially affect the Fund's gold position but enabled the Fund to avoid the administrative costs and inconvenience to itself and to members of collecting these amounts. Mr. Wahl dissented from the decision on the grounds that the Fund should not forgo any receipt of gold until the entire problem of gold payments to the Fund, then being debated, was resolved. Another example was that at least until the problem of gold was resolved, members could repay repurchase obligations in SDRs

---

[3]E.B. Decision No. 4087-(73/105), November 9, 1973; Vol. III below, p. 523.

rather than in gold. Payment in SDRs rather than in gold was not a final discharge of the obligation to pay gold. The interim payment was to be subject to the provisions of the Second Amendment.

Another development in the years 1972–78 was the gradual extension of repurchase obligations. As members found it hard to repay in three years under the usual three-to-five-year rule, more members were permitted to complete repurchase in installments over five years. As a matter of general policy, repurchase obligations were extended over longer periods than in the past; new facilities had especially long periods for repurchases. Under the oil facility repurchases were to take place in 16 equal quarterly installments not later than seven years after the drawing, and repurchases under the extended facility were to take place in 12 equal installments within four to ten years after the drawing.

The Fund gradually permitted a member undertaking a repurchase, or when its equivalent, a sale of its currency by the Fund, occurred, to attribute the reduction in the Fund's holdings of its currency to holdings under any facility. In the past, reductions in the Fund's holdings of a member's currency resulting from the discharge of a repurchase obligation not identified with a particular drawing and reductions resulting from sales of a member's currency were attributed to the member's drawing having the earliest commitment for repurchase. Only if a member made a voluntary repurchase was it free to attribute the resulting reduction in the Fund's holdings of its currency to any drawing it desired. Voluntary repurchases were all that were not obligatory. There were few voluntary repurchases.

To put all members on an equal footing and to accommodate members' desire to choose repurchases they preferred to discharge so as to take advantage of the different periods of use and different rates of charge of new facilities in the Fund, the Executive Directors agreed in March 1977, as a matter of practice, to allow a member to specify the drawing to which it wished to attribute the reduction in the Fund's holdings of its currency, even when the repurchase was mandatory. If a member wished to attribute a repurchase to a drawing for which the Fund had borrowed and the attribution differed from the original practices, the Fund was to request the lenders to accept the new attribution; otherwise, repayment was to be made in accordance with the original schedule. If there had been recourse to the General Arrangements to Borrow, the matter was to be brought to the Executive Board for decision.

Magnitude of Repurchases

In two of the seven financial years reviewed here—1971/72 and 1977/78—repurchases were the largest ever in the Fund's history, SDR 3.1 billion and SDR 4.5 billion. Because they exceeded drawings by a considerable amount, there was a net inflow in those years of money from members back to the Fund.

The magnitude of repurchases was attributable to repurchases by industrial members. In the financial year 1971/72 (the year ended on April 30, 1972) repurchases by France and the United Kingdom accounted for SDR 2.5 billion, and in the financial year 1977/78 (the year ended on April 30, 1978) repurchases by the United Kingdom and Italy accounted for SDR 2.6 billion. In fact, for the seven-year period as a whole, repurchases by industrial members, almost entirely by the three mentioned above, accounted for more than half of total repurchases, SDR 5.7 billion out of SDR 11.2 billion. In other financial years, however, 1974/75 for instance, total repurchases were the smallest in many years. For the seven-year period, total repurchases of SDR 11.2 billion were somewhat less than half the amount of total drawings, so that there was a net outflow of money from the Fund. Table 22 below shows drawings and repurchases for each of the seven financial years 1971/72 to 1977/78. That repurchases were very much larger than drawings in the financial year ended on April 30, 1978 was of particular significance. The Fund was about to embark on a major review of its conditionality, as described in Chapter 26, and the Executive Directors and the Managing Director and staff could not help being aware that there was at the time a net transfer of money from members to the Fund rather than the other way round.

Repurchases were, of course, widely distributed among members, but there were concentrations among some members too. The non-oil developing members as a group were making substantial repurchases and several individual countries among them, including Argentina, Bangladesh, Chile, India, Pakistan, and the Philippines, were repaying the Fund by sizable amounts. Table 23 lists the amounts of repurchases by each member, grouped into economic categories.

Table 22. Total Drawings and Repurchases, Financial Years 1972–78

(In millions of SDRs)

	Drawings[1]	Repurchases[2]
1972	2,028.5	3,122.3
1973	1,175.4	540.3
1974	1,057.7	672.5
1975	5,102.4	518.1
1976	6,591.4	960.1
1977	4,910.3	868.2
1978	2,503.0	4,485.0
Total[3]	23,368.8	11,166.5

[1]Includes drawings in the reserve tranche that were not subject to repurchase.
[2]Includes repurchases that reduced the Fund's holdings of members' currencies below the amounts originally paid on subscription account and repurchases of members' currencies paid in settlement of charges. Excludes sales of currencies of members held by the Fund in excess of 75 percent of quota, as a result of previous drawings; these sales had the effect of repurchase.
[3]Components may not add to totals because of rounding of figures for individual years.

Table 23. Repurchases by Members, Grouped by Economic Category,[1] Financial Years 1972–78

(In millions of SDRs)

	1972	1973	1974	1975	1976	1977	1978	Total[2]
Industrial Members								
Denmark	38.8	—	—	—	—	3.9	—	42.7
France	983.8	—	—	—	—	—	—	983.8
Italy	—	—	—	—	—	—	1,308.6	1,308.6
Luxembourg	0.7	—	—	—	—	—	—	0.7
United Kingdom	1,564.4	—	—	—	396.3	—	1,310.0	3,270.7
United States	—	—	110.1	—	—	—	—	110.1
Total	2,587.7	—	110.1	—	396.3	3.9	2,618.6	5,716.6
More Developed Primary Producing Members								
Australia	—	—	—	—	—	—	85.6	85.6
Greece	—	—	—	—	—	—	77.1	77.1
Iceland	—	—[3]	—	—	—	—	1.0	1.0
New Zealand	—	—	—	—	—	—	18.3	18.3
Portugal	—	—	—	—	—	—	4.0	4.0
Romania	—	—	—	—	—	—	55.0	55.0
South Africa	—	—	—	—	—	75.0	85.0	160.0
Turkey	117.3	—	9.6	—	—	—	37.8	164.7
Yugoslavia	20.0	15.0	51.7	51.8	21.8	—	114.7	275.0
Total	137.3	15.0	61.3	51.8	21.8	75.0	478.5	840.7
Major Oil Exporting Members								
Indonesia	21.0	38.0	103.7	36.4	10.0	—	65.0	274.1
Iran	13.2	34.7	—	—	—	—	—	47.9
Iraq	—	17.2	10.0	—	—	—	—	27.2
Nigeria	3.1	3.1	17.7	—	—	—	—	23.9
Total	37.3	93.0	131.4	36.4	10.0	—	65.0	373.1

Table 23 (continued). Repurchases by Members, Grouped by Economic Category,[1]
Financial Years 1972–78

(In millions of SDRs)

	1972	1973	1974	1975	1976	1977	1978	Total[2]
Non-Oil Developing Members								
Africa								
Botswana	—	—	—	—	—	—	0.6	0.6
Burundi	5.1	2.1	1.6	0.2	—	—	4.8	13.8
Cameroon	—	—	—	—	—	—	2.3	2.3
Central African Republic	0.1	0.1	0.1	0.1	1.5	—	0.3	2.2
Chad	0.1	0.6	1.2	2.3	0.1	—	1.6	5.9
Comoros	•	—	•	•	•	0.5	—	0.5
Congo, People's Republic of	0.1	0.1	0.1	0.1	0.1	—	3.3	3.8
Equatorial Guinea	—	—	—	—³	1.8	—	—	1.8
Gabon	—³	—³	—³	—³	—³	—	—	—
Gambia, The	0.1	0.1	0.1	0.1	1.2	—	—	1.6
Ghana	25.6	12.7	6.7	2.7	1.7	—	—	49.4
Guinea	—	0.7	1.9	5.5	—	—	1.7	9.8
Guinea-Bissau	•	•	•	•	•	—	0.8	0.8
Ivory Coast	—	—	—	—	—	24.2	10.0	34.2
Kenya	—	—	—	—	22.6	—	37.4	60.0
Lesotho	0.1	0.1	0.2	0.2	0.6	—	—	1.2
Liberia	4.3	1.8	1.4	1.4	1.9	1.3	—	12.1
Madagascar	—	—	—	—	—	—	8.8	8.8
Malawi	0.2	0.2	1.8	—³	—	—	—	2.2
Mali	5.2	0.7	1.2	1.2	2.2	3.0	0.3	13.8
Mauritania	0.1	0.1	0.1	0.6	1.6	—	—	2.5
Mauritius	0.6	—	3.0	—	5.5	—³	—	9.1
Morocco	45.8	18.2	—³	—³	—³	—	—	64.0
Niger	—³	—³	—³	—³	—³	—	—	—³
Rwanda	5.0	—	—	—	2.1	—	—	7.1

Country								Total
São Tomé and Príncipe	•	•	•	•	•	•	0.4	0.4
Senegal	0.3	0.3	0.3	0.6	—	—	1.0	2.5
Seychelles	•	•	•	•	•	•	0.1	0.1
Sierra Leone	—	—[3]	1.2	0.2	—	—	2.1	3.5
Somalia	—[3]	—	—[3]	—[3]	0.3	—	0.5	0.8
Sudan	15.6	15.6	8.1	3.6	9.6	20.0	19.4	91.9
Swaziland	0.1	0.1	0.4	0.7	0.4	1.0	—[3]	2.7
Tanzania	—	—	3.6	—	—	—	24.0	27.6
Tunisia	4.5	14.6	—	—	—	—	—	19.1
Uganda	—	—	—	1.3	10.1	5.1	—	16.5
Upper Volta	1.1	0.6	0.1	—	—	—	—	1.8
Zaïre	—	—	—	—	5.7	22.6	—	28.3
Zambia	—	—	—	19.0	19.0	19.0	19.0	76.0
Subtotal	114.0	68.7	33.1	39.8	88.0	96.7	138.4	578.7
Asia								
Afghanistan	4.8	4.0	5.0	6.0	2.0	9.3	9.2	40.3
Bangladesh	•	—	—	—	28.3	33.0	38.6	99.9
Burma	5.0	10.0	8.5	9.0	4.0	7.1	7.9	51.5
China[4]	—	—	—	59.9	—	—	30.0	89.9
Fiji	—	—	—	—	3.6	—	—	3.6
India	—[3]	—	—	—	62.0	230.0	281.2	573.2
Korea	—	—	7.5	—	—	20.0	27.6	55.1
Lao People's Democratic Republic	—	—	—	—	—	—	0.4	0.4
Malaysia	—[3]	—	7.2	—	—	85.7	—	92.9
Nepal	—[3]	—	—	—	—	—	3.1	3.1

Table 23 (concluded). Repurchases by Members, Grouped by Economic Category,[1] Financial Years 1972–78

(In millions of SDRs)

	1972	1973	1974	1975	1976	1977	1978	Total[2]
Non-Oil Developing Members (concluded)								
Asia (concluded)								
Pakistan	0.9	25.9	40.9	10.9	25.9	59.0	87.2	250.7
Papua New Guinea	•	•	5.0	•	5.0	—	5.0	10.0
Philippines	28.5	31.0	56.0	33.7	26.6	38.8	38.8	253.4
Sri Lanka	24.2	28.8	13.3	22.6	19.3	17.7	23.7	149.6
Thailand	—	2.1	—	—	—	—	—	2.1
Western Samoa	—	—	—	—	—	0.5	0.7	1.2
Subtotal	63.4	101.8	138.4	142.5	176.7	501.1	553.0	1,676.9
Latin America and the Caribbean								
Argentina	—	—	—	110.0	126.0	48.0	320.4	604.4
Bahamas	•	•	5.0	—	—[3]	—	—[3]	5.0
Barbados	—	—	—	—	1.2	—	—	1.2
Bolivia	4.0	10.0	3.6	2.4	9.2	13.9	2.8	45.9
Chile	39.5	1.5	—	39.5	23.8	84.8	79.5	268.6
Colombia	33.5	47.0	39.3	—[3]	—	—	—	119.8
Costa Rica	0.3	—	—	2.4	2.4	3.0	4.2	12.3
Dominican Republic	7.7	2.0	13.5	—	10.7	—	—	33.9
Ecuador	8.2	21.3	7.6	2.6	—	—	—	39.7
El Salvador	5.0	8.2	8.8	4.5	5.1	—	21.6	53.2
Grenada	•	•	•	•	0.5	—	—	0.5
Guatemala	3.0	6.0	—	—	—	—	—	9.0
Guyana	0.1	2.6	2.1	8.6	3.2	—	—	16.6
Haiti	3.0	1.1	0.9	0.4	3.8	3.7	3.3	16.2
Honduras	—	—	6.2	—	—	—	12.5	18.7

Jamaica	3.7	—	5.5	13.3	13.2	—	—	35.7
Mexico	—	—	—	—	—	—	92.5	92.5
Nicaragua	6.6	6.8	11.0	4.0	5.2	—	6.7	40.5
Panama	—	—	1.0	—	—	6.8	2.9	10.5
Peru	30.7	25.9	61.5	—	—	—	—	118.1
Trinidad and Tobago	—	—	—	11.3	4.4	—	—	15.7
Uruguay	5.2	22.4	16.5	17.3	25.9	4.3	21.6	113.2
Subtotal	150.5	154.8	182.5	216.3	234.6	164.5	568.0	1,671.2
Middle East								
Cyprus	—	—	—	—	—	—	7.0	7.0
Egypt	27.2	36.2	4.7	17.2	20.2	22.0	28.0	155.5
Israel	—	65.0	—	—	—	—	27.1	92.1
Jordan	—	—	5.8	1.6	—	—	—	7.4
Syrian Arab Republic	4.8	4.8	4.8	12.5	12.5	5.4	—	44.8
Yemen Arab Republic	—	1.0	—	—	—	—	—	1.0
Yemen, People's Democratic Republic of	—	—	—	—	—	—	1.5	1.5
Subtotal	32.0	107.0	15.3	31.3	32.7	27.4	63.6	309.3
Total	359.9	432.3	369.3	429.9	532.0	789.7	1,323.0	4,236.1
GRAND TOTAL[2]	3,122.2	540.3	672.1	518.1	960.1	868.6	4,485.1	11,166.5

[1] A dot (·) indicates that the country was not a member at the time; a dash (—) indicates that no repurchases were made.
[2] Components may not add to totals because of rounding of figures for individual members.
[3] Less than SDR 50,000.
[4] See fn. 6 in Chap. 2.

CURRENCIES USED: POLICIES UNTIL 1971

One of the most complicated subjects with respect to the Fund's transactions was the determination of the particular currencies to be used in purchases (drawings) and repurchases.

Until August 15, 1971, the currencies used in the Fund's transactions were selected on the basis of guidelines set forth in an Executive Board decision of July 1962.[4] Under this decision, the chief determinants of the currencies to be used were the balance of payments and reserve positions of individual members and the Fund's holdings of each member's currency compared with its quota. The economic concept involved was that reserves should flow, through the Fund, from members with strong balance of payments and reserve positions to members with weak ones. Ideally, each member's reserve position in the Fund should move in parallel with movements in its gross reserves. These economic considerations were overridden, however, by legal constraints in the original Articles of Agreement protecting the composition of the Fund's holdings of currencies and by attention to members' attitudes toward use of their currencies by the Fund. On the repurchase side, usable currencies were limited under the Articles to the currencies of those members that had assumed the obligations of Article VIII (and hence had convertible currencies) and that the Fund did not hold in amounts above 75 percent of the member's quota. Balances of a nonconvertible currency could, however, be "deemed" to be convertible and hence acceptable in repurchase. This deeming took place for a number of currencies, as noted later in this chapter. On the purchase side, as a matter of practice, the Fund traditionally did not allow a member's currency to be drawn without the member's agreement.

Following the decision of 1962, the staff gradually assumed the responsibility of drawing up for each quarter of the financial year a "currency budget," that is, a proposed list of the currencies to be used in purchases and repurchases with amounts suggested for each currency. In drawing up this list, the staff tried to equalize the ratios between members' reserve positions in the Fund and their gross holdings of gold and foreign exchange. Purchases were distributed over the list of currencies of members with strong balance of payments and reserve positions in proportion to their gross holdings of gold and foreign exchange. Repurchases were distributed in proportion to their reserve positions in the Fund. The rationale of this procedure was that when currencies were purchased, the Fund's holdings of them declined, and when currencies were used in repurchases, the Fund's holdings of them were replenished; these movements were reflected in converse movements in the members' reserve positions in the Fund. A distribution of repurchases in proportion to members' reserve positions in the Fund thus tended to counterbalance the cumulative net use of currencies in purchases, leading to a gradual harmonization of the ratios between members' reserve positions in the Fund and their holdings of gold and foreign exchange.

---

[4]E.B. Decision No. 1371-(62/36), July 20, 1962; *History, 1945–65*, Vol. III, pp. 235–38.

In applying guidelines for determining currency budgets, the staff did not use a precise formula, but adapted the guidelines to fit changing circumstances. The amounts derived from calculations were often modified by taking into account members' economic positions, the attitudes of members toward having their currencies used in the Fund's transactions, and the composition of the Fund's currency holdings. The proposed currency budgets were submitted to the Executive Board for approval but only after consultations were held with individual Executive Directors to obtain their concurrence in the amounts proposed for the currencies of their countries. Whenever there were unusually large drawings and repurchases, such as those by the United Kingdom and the United States, the currencies to be used were determined outside the currency budget.

The number of currencies included in the currency budget was gradually enlarged. By 1971, 24 currencies were being used in drawings. The number of currencies used for repurchases remained considerably smaller than that for drawings; some countries whose currencies were used for drawings had not yet accepted the obligations of Article VIII so that their currencies were ineligible for use in repurchases, while changes in members' balance of payments and reserve positions severely limited the number of currencies used in repurchases. In December 1969 the Executive Board approved the use of SDRs for members' repurchases from the Fund. SDRs were not included in the currency budget because they were not currency, but members could opt to repurchase with SDRs instead of with the currencies listed in the budget and did so to a considerable extent in 1970 and 1971. In September 1971, the Executive Board agreed that SDRs held by the Fund in its General Account could be used in purchases in place of currencies.[5]

CURRENCIES USED: POLICIES AFTER
AUGUST 15, 1971

These policies on selection of currencies came to an abrupt end after the suspension of official convertibility of the dollar into gold by the United States on August 15, 1971. With the end of dollar convertibility and the prospect that the dollar price of gold would be raised, certain members with super gold tranche positions in the Fund were reluctant to have these positions (which represented primary reserve assets) diminished through use of their currency in repurchase, while members with liabilities to the Fund saw advantage in their discharge. Consequently the staff had to make ad hoc arrangements to enable repurchases to take place in late 1971 and to enable a large repurchase by the United Kingdom in April 1972.

Throughout 1972, the Fund's operations continued on the basis of such turnstile arrangements. To achieve an equitable distribution of changes in net

---

[5]Further details on the Fund's policies with regard to the currencies used in drawings and repurchases through the end of 1971 can be found in *History, 1945–65*, Vol. II, pp. 448–59 and *History, 1966–71*, Vol. I, pp. 322–29.

creditor positions and to even out the effects of the Fund's transactions on the composition of members' reserves, the currencies used in drawings were limited in practice to those acceptable by the Fund in repurchases. This procedure meant that less emphasis was placed on equalizing the reserve positions in the Fund of creditor members relative to their holdings of gold and foreign exchange. In March 1972 the number of currencies included in these turnstile arrangements was increased. Austrian schillings, Italian lire, and Japanese yen could be used in drawings and repurchases (in addition to Canadian dollars, deutsche mark, and French francs), while pounds sterling could be used in drawings.

In the next several years, when purchases started to exceed repurchases, however, the staff had to devise a number of temporary policies and procedures for the currencies to be used in the Fund's transactions. This task became especially difficult as the volume of transactions swelled. During 1973 the procedure was resumed of determining the amounts of currencies to be used in drawings in accordance with the member's holdings of gold and foreign exchange and the amounts of currencies for use in repurchases in accordance with the member's reserve position in the Fund. This procedure tended to equalize, for the currencies to which it was applied, the cumulative use of members' currencies relative to their holdings of gold and foreign exchange. The use of Belgian francs, Mexican pesos, and Netherlands guilders in repurchases was, however, to a large extent balanced by use of these currencies in drawings.

From time to time several modifications to these practices were introduced to avoid running down the Fund's holdings of currencies too quickly and to avoid undue use of strong creditor currencies in repurchases. In the financial year 1974/75, for example, the Fund began to sell extensively (that is, to use in members' purchases) currencies of members with debtor positions in the Fund (that is, currencies of which the Fund's holdings were in excess of 75 percent of the member's quota). A sale of currency held above that level reduced the member's indebtedness to the Fund and had the effect of substituting for repurchases. This practice explained why, in 1974/75, total repurchases, which amounted to only SDR 518 million, were the smallest amount for any financial year since 1966/67. Eventually, the currencies of more members with debtor positions were included in the currency budget. In the financial year 1976/77, for instance, the CFA franc (Upper Volta), the Cyprus pound, the Nicaraguan córdoba, the Papua New Guinea kina, the Salvadoran colón, and the Uruguayan new peso were included in the currency budget for the first time. Nevertheless the sale by the Fund of currencies of debtor members had to proceed carefully, in consultation with the member, because such sales were equivalent to requiring the members concerned to repay their indebtedness.

When the Fund's holdings of particular currencies were reduced to very low levels, both in absolute amounts and in relation to members' quotas, the Fund put great emphasis on protecting its holdings of these currencies and much less emphasis on members' reserves. In effect, the Fund concentrated on selling the currencies of members with strong external positions whose currencies it held in relatively large amounts. This practice led in 1974/75, for instance, to the more extensive use of U.S. dollars, French francs, and Japanese yen than would have been the case had the Fund continued to sell currencies in proportion to members' reserves.

The number of currencies that could be used became critical in 1972–78. For the currency of a member to be used in drawings, that member had to make arrangements for converting the amounts of its currency received by other members in drawings from the Fund into currencies that the drawing members could use. If a drawing member received, for instance, Bahrain dinars, the Government of Bahrain had to have in place arrangements whereby the drawing member might readily exchange Bahrain dinars for U.S. dollars, pounds sterling, or other currency customarily used in exchange markets and in the settlement of international transactions.

Under the original Articles of Agreement, members were not legally obliged to make such conversion arrangements. Conversion arrangements were based on a member's willingness to collaborate with the Fund. While many members were willing to collaborate with the Fund in exchanging their currencies for more usable currencies, some were not, especially since they might then have to keep on hand such usable currencies and even possibly forgo interest on some of their reserves. The reluctance of members to exchange their currencies for the currencies common to international transactions limited the Fund's use of certain currencies.

From 1974 onward the Managing Director and the staff continuously engaged in persuading a number of members to make the necessary arrangements for converting balances of their currencies purchased from the Fund so as to enlarge the number of currencies that the Fund could use in its drawings. On the occasion of the Sixth General Review of Quotas in 1976, the Board of Governors' resolution provided that members would have to make arrangements satisfactory to the Fund for use of their currencies in the operations and transactions of the Fund.

Gradually, as many more members made conversion arrangements, more currencies could be used in the Fund's currency budget. In the financial year 1974/75, for instance, the currencies used either for the first time or after a lapse of many years were Argentine pesos, Bahrain dinars, Ecuadoran sucres, Indonesian rupiah, Kuwaiti dinars, Malaysian ringgit, rials Omani, Qatar riyals, Spanish pesetas, U.A.E. dirhams, and Venezuelan bolívares. By the end of the financial year 1976/77, significant progress had been made in extending the list of usable currencies. A total of 101 members had completed the necessary arrangements for exchanging their currencies into alternative, more commonly used currencies. Included for the first time in the currency budget in the financial year 1976/77, for instance, were Colombian pesos, Guatemalan quetzales, Luxembourg francs, Nigerian naira, Paraguayan guaraníes, Saudi Arabian riyals, and Yemen rials. In order to extend further the number of currencies that could be used in repurchases, the Fund deemed a number of balances of currencies of members having Article XIV status as convertible for the purpose of accepting them in repurchase. The currencies were those of Brazil, Colombia, Indonesia, Malta, Nigeria, Spain, Trinidad and Tobago, and Venezuela.[6]

The increase in the number of usable currencies and the expansion in the use of the Fund's resources led to a greater dispersion and absolute increase in members' net creditor positions in the Fund. Members' net creditor positions rose from SDR 2.4 billion on April 30, 1975 to SDR 3.7 billion on April 30, 1976 and to SDR 6.3 billion on April 30, 1977. Many more members, including developing members such as Brazil, Colombia, Guatemala, Malta, Nigeria, Trinidad and Tobago, and Upper Volta, became net creditors in the Fund. The increase in the number of usable currencies notwithstanding, the Fund's holdings of U.S. dollars still represented a large proportion—50–60 percent—of the Fund's holdings of usable currencies, and the currencies of a few creditor members made up nearly 90 percent of the total.

Use of SDRs in Drawings

In March 1977 the Executive Board decided to include SDRs in the currency budget for purchase by members drawing on the Fund. Members obtaining SDRs in this way might hold the SDRs or use them to acquire currency in a transaction with designation. This decision came about because the Fund's holdings of SDRs in its General Account were increasing and were expected to increase further, while its holdings of usable currencies were decreasing. An Executive Board decision of August 1976 that enabled participants in the Special Drawing Account to obtain SDRs from other participants in certain categories of transaction by agreement among themselves, rather than from the General Account, had had the effect of decreasing the inflow into the Fund of usable currencies and of increasing the Fund's holdings of SDRs. During the period August 1976 to April 1977, for instance, participants obtained SDRs totaling SDR 153 million from other participants in transactions by agreement; most of these SDRs might otherwise have been acquired from the Fund's General Account with currencies acceptable to the Fund. The Fund's holdings of SDRs in the General Account also increased because members that had no need to reconstitute their SDR holdings paid their charges to the Fund in SDRs.

As a result, the holdings of SDRs in the Fund's General Account more than doubled in the financial year 1976/77, from SDR 310 million to SDR 771 million. At the same time, the continued heavy use of the Fund's resources brought sharp reductions in the Fund's holdings of usable currencies. These holdings dropped from SDR 10 billion in April 1975 to SDR 7.2 billion in April 1976 and to SDR 4.5 billion in April 1977. The staff argued that the inclusion of SDRs in the currency budget on a regular basis would have several advantages. It would alleviate the shortage of usable currencies. It would promote the role of the SDR as a means of payment as well as conserve the Fund's holdings of usable currencies. And prior to

---

[6]After Venezuela accepted the obligations of Article VIII on July 1, 1976, its currency became fully usable for repurchase even in the absence of this decision.

the coming into effect of the Second Amendment when the quarterly currency budget and the quarterly designation plan for SDRs would be considered simultaneously and when the currencies of all members would be freely usable, it would mean that those members included in designation plans for SDRs but not in currency budgets (because arrangements had not been completed regarding the usability of their currencies in Fund transactions) were also indirectly included in the currency budget. This arrangement was fairer to those members whose currencies were in the currency budget.

The substitution of SDRs for currency was subject to agreement by the participants purchasing SDRs, who could use SDRs immediately, if they so desired, to obtain currency through a transaction with designation. In the 1977/78 financial year, the amount of SDRs included for sales in the four quarterly currency budgets averaged about SDR 300 million per budget, or 37 percent of the total budgeted sales of currencies and SDRs. Actual sales of SDRs through the currency budget amounted to 33 percent of total sales. The inclusion of SDRs in the budget meant that the name "currency budget" would have to be changed to "operational budget."

Further Techniques with Regard to Currency Policy

By 1977/78 the Fund was heavily financing drawings through sales of SDRs. Nevertheless, the Fund also sold the currencies of several members whose balance of payments and reserve positions had improved and which wished to reduce their indebtedness to the Fund not only by making repurchases but also by having their currencies sold. In the financial year 1976/77, and again in 1977/78, the Fund agreed with certain creditor members whose currencies were not generally usable in Fund transactions, on the sale of their currencies to the equivalent of the amount of gold that the Fund distributed to them under its policies regarding gold distribution.[7] Moreover, in accordance with established practice, large individual drawings, such as those of the United Kingdom in 1977/78, were not included in the operational budget, but were agreed on the basis of special consultations with Executive Directors.

In brief, the Fund's tight liquidity position, especially from 1974 to 1977, and the absence of amended Articles meant that the staff had continuously to innovate procedures for the currencies to be used in drawings and repurchases.

Currency policy was finally to prove somewhat easier in the financial year ended April 30, 1978 when the Fund's liquidity underwent its first large overall improvement since 1974/75. The volume of usable currencies held by the Fund more than doubled during the year, to about SDR 11.2 billion. This increase followed the substantial volume of net repurchases (SDR 2 billion) and of the inflow of currencies and SDRs that arose from members paying the increase in their subscriptions to which they had consented under the Sixth General Review of Quotas (SDR 2.7 billion). In fact, as members continued to pay their subscriptions under the Sixth

---

[7]See Chap. 34.

General Review, the Fund's holdings of usable currencies rose to SDR 14.5 billion by the end of June 1978.

Moreover, when the Second Amendment became effective in April 1978, provisions entered into force regarding the usability of the Fund's holdings of the currencies of all members, as discussed in Chapter 38. This development made it possible to add to the total of usable currencies the equivalent of about SDR 1 billion in currencies not previously used by the Fund or sold only on an irregular basis in limited amounts. Nonetheless, the Fund's holdings of only 11 creditor currencies totaled about 85 percent of all usable currencies at the end of April 1978, with the U.S. dollar representing 50 percent of the total.

Table 24 below lists the currencies in which drawings (other than those under the oil facility) and repurchases were made during the financial years 1972–78 and the amounts of gold and SDRs used. Forty-six currencies were used in drawings, almost double the number used in 1966–71.

The number of currencies (24) used for repurchases in 1972–78 was only about half that used for drawings, but was still larger than the number of currencies used

Table 24. Drawings and Repurchases in Currencies, SDRs, and Gold, Financial Years 1972–78

(In millions of SDRs)

	Drawings[1]	Repurchases
Algerian dinars	1.0	—
Argentine pesos	33.3	—
Australian dollars	53.0	97.9
Austrian schillings	237.1	115.3
Bahrain dinars	7.0	—
Belgian francs	1,037.2	815.0
Brazilian cruzeiros	93.3	11.7
Canadian dollars	686.0	727.5
Colombian pesos	39.7	—
CFA francs (Niger)	1.0	—
CFA francs (Upper Volta)	1.5	—
Danish kroner	111.3	13.2
Deutsche mark	2,646.8	1,843.7
Ecuadoran sucres	10.0	—
Ethiopian birr	0.5	—
Fiji dollars	2.0	—
French francs	1,158.8	546.3
Guatemalan quetzales	4.5	—
Indonesian rupiah	20.0	—
Iranian rials	21.5	—
Iraqi dinars	1.0	—
Irish pounds	57.4	14.0
Italian lire	113.8	142.0
Japanese yen	1,567.7	865.9
Kuwaiti dinars	51.0	10.3

Table 24 *(concluded)*. Drawings and Repurchases in Currencies, SDRs, and Gold, Financial Years 1972–78

(In millions of SDRs)

	Drawings[1]	Repurchases
Luxembourg francs	4.0	—
Malaysian ringgit	14.2	—
Malta pounds	10.7	1.1
Mexican pesos	—	17.5
Netherlands guilders	1,183.9	733.6
Nigerian naira	11.5	—
Norwegian kroner	136.4	70.1
Paraguayan guaraníes	2.0	—
Pounds sterling	524.5	10.0
Qatar riyals	12.0	2.7
Rials Omani	3.0	—
Saudi Arabian riyals	38.0	—
South African rand	11.0	0.2
Spanish pesetas	27.7	4.5
Swedish kronor	175.2	82.5
Trinidad & Tobago dollars	2.0	—
U.A.E. dirhams	11.0	1.0
U.S. dollars	4,381.7	2,268.1
Uruguayan new pesos	5.0	—
Venezuelan bolívares	223.8	80.6
Yemen rials	3.0	—
Total in currencies	14,737.0	8,474.6
SDRs	1,729.4	1,979.3
Gold	—	512.1
Total[2]	16,466.4	10.966.0

[1]Exclusive of drawings under the oil facility for which different arrangements applied.
[2]Components may not add to totals because of rounding of figures for individual members.

for repurchases in 1966–71. Nevertheless, nearly SDR 2 billion of the SDR 11 billion of repurchases was effected in SDRs, and the bulk of other repurchases was effected in seven currencies, U.S. dollars, deutsche mark, Japanese yen, Belgian francs, Netherlands guilders, Canadian dollars, and French francs.

THE FUND'S LIQUIDITY

The foregoing description of the implementation of currency policy suggests how difficult it was in 1972–78 to gauge the Fund's ability to meet demands on its resources. It was nevertheless imperative for the Executive Directors and for the Managing Director and staff, especially of the Treasurer's Department, to be able to assess this ability accurately so that decisions about prospective new borrowings or requests for further increases in members' quotas could be taken "in light of the facts." To help this assessment, the staff of the Treasurer's Department gradually evolved the concept of the Fund's liquidity.

The concept of the Fund's liquidity was essentially that of the relationship between the Fund's readily usable assets and the demands that might be made on them. It differed from the "Fund's financial position," which referred to the total income and expenditures of the Fund, both operational and administrative, that is, to the Fund's budget, discussed in the next chapter.

In assessing the Fund's liquidity, both the Fund's readily available assets and its liquid liabilities had to be added up and their adequacy appraised. On the side of readily available assets, the Fund had, of course, its own resources derived from members' subscriptions. Initially these resources were in the form of gold and members' currencies. After 1969 they were also in the form of the SDRs held in the General Account, obtained when members settled their obligations to the Fund, such as charges and repurchases, in SDRs. To give an indication of magnitudes, at the end of 1978 the Fund's own resources in gold, currencies, and SDRs totaled a little over SDR 44 billion. Holdings of members' currencies were SDR 39 billion; holdings of approximately 118 million ounces of gold, valued at SDR 35 an ounce, came to a little over SDR 4 billion, and holdings of SDRs were a little over 1 billion. If the Fund's gold holdings were valued at the market price for gold at the end of 1978, they would have been the equivalent of SDR 22 billion. But they were not so valued.[8]

All these ready assets did not have the same degree of usability or liquidity, however. While the Fund's gold holdings were an important part of its assets, providing the Fund's creditors considerable confidence, they could not be considered immediately usable. Decisions about the Fund's gold were difficult and, until the Second Amendment, there were many legal constraints on what the Fund could do with its gold. The Fund's holdings of SDRs, on the other hand, were readily available to finance the Fund's transactions and operations. They could be sold directly to members making drawings on the Fund, and the recipients could, if they wished, use them immediately to acquire foreign exchange. Alternatively, the Fund itself could sell SDRs to acquire currency that could be provided to a member making a drawing. But, despite their usability, because the Fund's holdings of SDRs were small, they were not an important element in the Fund's liquidity as of the end of 1978.

---

[8]Because of the definition of the SDR, the official price of gold in terms of SDRs remained at SDR 35 an ounce, although the official price of gold in dollars after the two devaluations of the dollar rose to $38 an ounce in December 1971 and $42 in February 1972. Under the Articles of Agreement as amended in 1969, the value of the SDR was set as equal to US$1 *with gold content of the weight and fineness in effect on July 1, 1944.* The SDR was thus not devalued in terms of gold when the U.S. dollar was devalued in terms of gold. The Fund's gold holdings continued to be valued at SDR 35 an ounce rather than at the market price for gold because the Fund's equivalent liabilities to the members which had contributed the gold in the first place—members' reserve (gold) tranche positions in the Fund—were also valued at SDR 35 an ounce. The valuation and enlargement of reserve tranche positions in accordance with the market price of gold would unduly reduce the relative size of credit tranche positions and cause other complications for the Fund's transactions and operations.

It was thus the Fund's holdings of currencies that generally provided the bulk of the Fund's readily available resources. Nonetheless, as the previous section indicates, until the Second Amendment went into effect, the Fund's ability to use all these currencies was also a complex matter. In addition to its own resources, the Fund's ready assets included its access to borrowed money. The amounts available under the GAB, under the borrowing agreements for the oil facility, and under the borrowing agreements for the supplementary financing facility could all be considered part of the Fund's liquid assets.

Against these assets were the Fund's liabilities. The most liquid liabilities were immediately encashable claims of members, that is, members' reserve tranche positions in the Fund and their loan claims on the Fund derived from borrowing by the Fund. The Fund had to be in a position to finance at once any reserve tranche drawings and to redeem any loan claims. Sizable amounts were involved. As of the end of 1978, for example, readily encashable claims amounted to close to SDR 15 billion, reserve tranche positions being SDR 8.5 billion and loan claims being SDR 6.4 billion. The rest of the Fund's liquid liability was in the form of the Fund's need to finance drawings in the credit tranches and under its various special facilities.

In order to judge the adequacy of the Fund's readily available assets in the light of these liquid liabilities, the extent to which members were likely to request drawings had to be forecast. Here it was necessary to judge many factors. Possible demands for the encashment of reserve tranche positions or of loan claims on the Fund depended, for example, on developments in the balances of payments of the members that held them, the composition of the reserves of these members, and the attractiveness of liquid claims on the Fund as reserve assets. Possible requests for use of the Fund's resources in the credit tranches or under the Fund's various special facilities were even harder to gauge. These requests were influenced in varying degrees by the conditionality attached to the different facilities, by the levels of the Fund's charges, and by alternative financing available to members.

In other words, in order to determine the adequacy of the Fund's assets or liquidity, some judgment had to be made about the distribution among members of balance of payments surpluses and deficits, changes in members' reserve levels, the willingness of members to finance their deficits by using their reserve positions in the Fund or by drawing on Fund credit, and the willingness of creditors to increase their reserve positions in the Fund, including lending to the Fund. The concept of the Fund's liquidity was accordingly complex, involving many elements of judgment. The concept was also dynamic. It varied over time as the character of the Fund's operations changed. The introduction of new facilities or the establishment of new means of financing changed the ingredients making up the Fund's liquidity. Moreover, once assessment of the Fund's liquidity had been made, the position could change rapidly. A large drawing, such as that by the United States in November 1978, could suddenly and drastically reduce the Fund's holdings of usable currencies and place the Fund in the position of being unable to use its holdings of the currency of the drawing country, U.S. dollars in this case. It was therefore exceedingly difficult for the staff to make assessments of the Fund's liquidity with any degree of firmness even for as short a time as a year ahead.

Table 25 and Table 26 below indicate the kind of tables that the staff used to analyze the Fund's liquidity and to present relevant data to the Executive Board; these tables usually provided data for the variables used for several previous years. Table 25 lists the absolute magnitudes for quotas, usable currencies, holdings of SDRs, holdings of gold, the amounts available under borrowing arrangements, the size of reserve positions in the Fund, and the use of Fund credit at the end of each of the years 1972–78. From this table it can be determined, for example, that, as of the end of 1977, the Fund's total readily available assets (total quotas, holdings of SDRs, and amounts available under borrowing arrangements) were SDR 35.4 billion to finance possible liquid claims (use of Fund credit and reserve positions in the Fund) of over SDR 31 billion. Usable currencies were only SDR 6 billion. The Fund's liquidity was distinctly better as of the end of 1978. The three sources of readily available assets of SDR 45.7 billion were available to finance possible Fund credit and reserve positions of just over SDR 25 billion; usable currencies were SDR 10 billion.

Table 25. Factors Relevant to the Fund's Liquidity, 1972–78

(In billions of SDRs)

	As of December 31						
	1972	1973	1974	1975	1976	1977	1978
Total quotas	29.2	29.2	29.2	29.2	29.2	29.2	39.0
Usable currencies[1]	5.3	10.0	13.1	9.1	5.6	6.1	10.2
U.S. dollars	—	5.0	5.2	4.8	2.9	3.2	—
Holdings of SDRs	0.6	0.5	0.5	0.6	0.7	1.2	1.2
Holdings of gold	5.4	5.4	5.4	5.4	5.2	4.6	4.1
Amounts available under borrowing arrangements	5.8	5.6	6.9	6.9	6.3	5.0	5.5
GAB	5.8	5.6	5.5	5.5	6.3	4.8	5.3
Oil facility	—	—	1.3	1.4	—	—	—
Other	—	—	—	—	—	0.2	0.2
Use of Fund credit[2]	1.1	1.0	3.7	7.4	12.7	13.3	10.3
Compensatory financing facility	0.4	0.5	0.5	0.7	2.7	2.8	2.9
Oil facility	—	—	1.7	4.8	6.7	6.4	5.0
Reserve positions in the Fund	6.3	6.2	8.8	12.6	17.7	18.1	14.8
Reserve tranche positions	6.3	6.2	7.1	7.9	11.0	9.9	8.5
Loan claims	—	—	1.7	4.8	6.7	8.2	6.4

[1] The total of the Fund's holdings of currencies of all members listed in the currency budget at the end of each year, except for the currencies of members whose holdings by the Fund were in excess of quota.
[2] Use of Fund's resources other than in the reserve tranche.

Table 26 lists a number of ratios used by the staff in assessing the Fund's liquidity and the actual figures for these ratios as of the end of each year, 1972–78. Again, the tight liquidity position of the Fund in some years and its easing in others can be seen in these ratios. As of the end of 1977, for example, the use of Fund credit was 46 percent of members' quotas. Usable currencies were only 34 percent of members' total reserve positions in the Fund. These ratios improved greatly in 1978. The use of Fund credit was only 26 percent of the quotas of all members and usable currencies were 69 percent of members' total reserve positions in the Fund. As 1978 ended, the Fund staff was still developing the concept of the Fund's liquidity.

Table 26. Ratios of Fund Liquidity, 1972–78

(In percentages)

	As of December 31						
	1972	1973	1974	1975	1976	1977	1978
Use of Fund credit as percentage of quotas of all members							
Total Fund credit	4	4	13	26	43	46	26
Compensatory financing facility	1	2	2	2	9	10	8
Oil facility	—	—	6	16	23	22	13
Use of Fund credit as percentage of quotas of all members using Fund credit							
Total Fund credit	38	35	68	118	113	118	86
Compensatory financing facility	13	16	10	11	24	24	24
Oil facility	—	—	31	75	60	57	42
Usable currencies as percentage of							
Reserve tranche positions	84	161	184	115	51	62	121
Total reserve positions (including loan claims)	84	161	148	72	32	34	69

Other Developments
in the Fund's Finances

T HE FUND DEVELOPED VARIOUS NEW FACILITIES and new ways of raising money during 1972–78, as just recounted. The same years also witnessed further developments with respect to the General Arrangements to Borrow, the rate of remuneration paid to members with net creditor positions in the Fund, the Fund's maintenance of the value of its holdings of members' currencies, and its budget.

THIRD RENEWAL OF THE
GENERAL ARRANGEMENTS TO BORROW IN 1975

The General Arrangements to Borrow (GAB), renewed for the second time in 1970, were due to expire in October 1975, and, to renew the Arrangements again, the necessary decisions by the Executive Board and the Group of Ten had to be taken a year in advance.[1] Accordingly, in early 1974 the Fund management and staff started to re-examine the GAB.

The GAB, while providing the Fund with needed moneys, had been controversial from the start. They were exclusive arrangements, open in principle to all of the ten participants but distinctly limited to the ten participants. They were not a line of credit under which the Fund could draw automatically but rather a set of conditional commitments by the participants to lend to the Fund; participants could refuse to lend to the Fund. The participants thus retained a kind of veto power over the economic program of a member requesting a drawing from the Fund if that drawing required that the Arrangements be used. In effect, what had developed over time was that the Fund management and staff tried to satisfy in advance the positions of the other nine participants in the Arrangements with respect to the economic

---

[1] The negotiation of the GAB in the early 1960s was described in *History, 1945–65*, Vol. I, pp. 507–16 and Vol. II, pp. 373–77 and 519–21; the first renewal in 1965 in *History, 1945–65*, Vol. I, pp. 567–70, and the second renewal in 1970 in *History, 1966–71*, Vol. I, pp. 370–74.

program of the member requesting a drawing before asking that the GAB be activated. At times, officials of the drawing member itself directly consulted officials of at least some of the other participants in the GAB while negotiations with Fund officials were going on.

The Arrangements were unpopular with officials except those of the ten largest industrial countries also because they had led to the formation of the Group of Ten. The need for the participants to consult each other whenever the Fund asked to borrow under the Arrangements meant that the ten countries had to organize themselves in order to decide how to respond to the Fund's requests. For this purpose, the finance ministers and the governors of the central banks of each of the ten participating countries—20 officials in all—began to assemble regularly as the Group of Ten and soon became an independent body deliberating many of the same topics as the Executive Board. This was resented by officials of other countries, and Per Jacobsson, then Managing Director, who negotiated the Arrangements, was subsequently faulted for relinquishing a vital part of the Fund's authority. Some officials objected particularly that Mr. Jacobsson had given substantial power over the Fund's decisions to officials of continental European countries, which included six of the ten countries in the Group of Ten.[2]

At the time of the second renewal of the GAB little change had been effected in the Arrangements. The management and staff looked to the third renewal, however, as offering better prospects for change. At that time, they were also working out the features of the borrowing arrangements for the 1974 oil facility, designing agreements which gave the Fund more freedom and flexibility than did the GAB. Consequently, some of the staff contemplated proposing "radical revisions" in the GAB: increasing the amount of loans that each participant was willing to make; increasing the number of currencies that each participant would lend beyond the existing arrangement that provided for each participant to lend only its own currency; ending the restriction on use of the Arrangements for drawings only by the ten participants; widening the circumstances for which the Fund could borrow under the Arrangements beyond the necessity to "forestall or cope with an impairment of the international monetary system"; and changing the charge of ½ of 1 percent on transfers by participants, the way the rate of interest paid on borrowings was determined, and the requirement for the Fund to use gold to pay interest and the transfer charge to participants.

The staff was by no means agreed, however, on whether the GAB should be so extensively amended. Some argued that since even the limited amendments proposed in 1969 had been rejected after debate in the Executive Board and in the Group of Ten, only the most essential revisions ought to be proposed. This view prevailed. The management decided that inasmuch as the Fund needed the GAB and a thoroughgoing review might provoke opposition and involve protracted negotiations, it was best to propose only the minimum modifications necessary to make renewal acceptable to both the Fund and the participants.

---

[2]A defense of Mr. Jacobsson's actions is given by Erin E. Jacobsson in *A Life for Sound Money* (cited in fn. 8 of Chap. 25 above), pp. 358–85.

The Group of Ten, noting at their meeting in Washington on September 29, 1974 that "this means of reinforcing the Fund's lending capacity could be of great value in the coming years," agreed to renew the Arrangements for a further period of five years from October 24, 1975, subject to some amendments needed to bring the operational provisions up to date.[3]

The Executive Board agreed on October 23, 1974 that the Fund was willing to renew the GAB, with a minimum of change, for another five years, until October 23, 1980.[4] Two noteworthy modifications concerned the rate of interest to be paid on borrowing and the media in which interest and the transfer charges were to be made. The 1½ percent annual rate of interest prevailing since 1962 was dropped. The Fund was now to pay interest at rates equal to those levied periodically on the holdings of a member's currency resulting from the drawings for which the Fund had borrowed, but in any event at a rate not less than 4 percent a year. (The Fund was to continue to pay a transfer charge of ½ of 1 percent on the amount borrowed.)

The Executive Directors had discussed whether the maximum interest rate should be higher than 4 percent a year. Since the Fund's charges had just recently been raised to start at 4 percent a year, the Executive Directors were concerned over the loss for the Fund's budget that would be incurred by paying an interest rate higher than 4 percent on borrowings under the GAB. At best, the Fund would receive no net income from a transaction for which it borrowed (since the rate of interest paid on the amounts borrowed was equal to the initial charge levied on drawings). For any drawings in the reserve tranche for which it borrowed, the Fund would incur a loss (since the Fund would have to pay interest on the amounts borrowed but did not levy a charge for drawings in the reserve tranche).[5]

Payments for interest, charges, and repayments of indebtedness no longer had to be made in gold but could also be made in SDRs, in the currency of the lender, and in other currencies that were convertible in fact.[6] While some Executive Directors would have preferred use of SDRs in lieu of gold, instead of in addition to gold, others wanted to retain the possibility of using gold, since the gold problem was at the time still unresolved.

Although participants had six months, until April 23, 1975, to notify the Fund of their concurrence in these amendments to the GAB, they had all done so by January 8, 1975. The Swiss Federal Council again agreed to extend its association with the GAB for another five years, until October 23, 1980.[7]

---

[3]Communiqué of Group of Ten, par. 2; Vol. III below, p. 632.

[4]E.B. Decision No. 4421-(74/132), October 23, 1974; *Selected Decisions*, 8th Issue, pp. 112–13.

[5]At the time of this discussion in 1974, the term gold tranche was still used.

[6]"Currency convertible in fact" is a concept that evolved in Fund usage to refer to currencies that were actually fully convertible and not just convertible in the legal sense that the issuing members had assumed the obligations of Article VIII of the Fund's Articles of Agreement. The term was invented to take care of the Japanese yen, and then incorporated in the GAB. When SDRs were introduced in 1969, the term was used to specify the currencies that would be made available in exchange for SDRs. See *History, 1966–71*, Vol. I, pp. 168–69 and 373, and Joseph Gold, *The Fund's Concepts of Convertibility*, IMF Pamphlet Series, No. 14 (Washington, 1971), pp. 37–58.

[7]E.B. Decision No. 4858-(75/172), November 5, 1975; Vol. III below, p. 534.

FURTHER DEVELOPMENTS IN THE GAB

In addition to the third renewal in 1975, other developments in the GAB took place during 1972–78. For the first time since the Arrangements went into effect, the amount to be lent to the Fund changed. With preliminary negotiations going on in late 1976 with officials of Italy and the United Kingdom about possible stand-by arrangements with the Fund, Mr. Witteveen asked Japanese officials for an enlargement of Japan's commitment under the GAB. In November 1976, the Executive Board and the ten participants formally agreed on an increase in the amount of Japan's commitment, from ¥ 90 billion (approximately SDR 265 million) to ¥ 340 billion (approximately SDR 1 billion).[8] This increase enlarged the size of the GAB from SDR 5.5 billion at the time of the third renewal to SDR 6.2 billion at the end of 1976; Switzerland committed Sw F 865 million (about SDR 200 million) as of the end of 1976.

Activation of the GAB took place three times in 1972–78. In December 1976, as described in Chapter 24, the Fund arranged to borrow SDR 2,560 million under the GAB to help finance the SDR 3,360 million stand-by arrangement with the United Kingdom. The Fund called on eight of the ten participants, all except the United Kingdom and Italy, which was then also experiencing severe balance of payments problems. In April 1977 the Fund again used the GAB to arrange borrowings of SDR 337.5 million from the same eight participants to help finance the SDR 450 million stand-by arrangement with Italy, described in Chapter 23. Actual borrowing by the Fund in January and May 1977 for these stand-by arrangements amounted to SDR 1,285 million. The largest amounts were provided by the United States (SDR 448 million), the Deutsche Bundesbank (SDR 389 million), and Japan (SDR 276 million), with considerably smaller amounts provided by the other participants. In the financial year ended April 30, 1978, the Fund again borrowed SDR 583 million under the GAB to help finance drawings by the United Kingdom and SDR 82.5 million to help finance a drawing by Italy. These were the last borrowings in connection with the stand-by arrangements for the United Kingdom and Italy.

In November 1978, however, the Fund again turned to the GAB, borrowing SDR 777 million (SDR 583 million from the Deutsche Bundesbank and SDR 194 million from Japan) to finance the reserve tranche drawing of $3 billion (about SDR 2.22 billion) undertaken by the United States (described in Chapter 44). This was the first activation of the GAB for a drawing by the United States, although the possibility of the United States drawing on the Fund had been a principal inducement for the Fund to undertake the General Arrangements in the first place.

In 1978 several provisions of the GAB were altered to make them conform to the provisions of the Second Amendment of the Fund's Articles of Agreement. The changes included some formal changes, such as the replacement of references to the U.S. dollar in terms of gold of the weight and fineness in effect on July 1, 1944 by references to the SDR and the deletion of all other references to gold. There were also

---

[8]E.B. Decision No. 5249-(76/154), November 5, 1976; Vol. III below, p. 536.

some substantive changes, such as making repayments of borrowings by the Fund conform to the amended provisions of the Articles about repurchases. Changes were limited, however. The deputies of the Group of Ten had agreed in April 1977 that changes should be limited to those required to make the GAB conform to the amended Articles. Unlike other decisions taken to implement the Second Amendment, decisions about the GAB had to be approved by all ten participants before any change could take effect. Changes agreed in the Executive Board had also to be considered by each of the participants. This process took from early 1977 until August 11, 1978, when the Fund was notified of concurrence in the changes by all ten participants.[9]

A re-examination of the GAB by the Group of Ten was requested by the finance ministers and governors of the central banks of the ten participating countries who met in Mexico City on April 29, 1978. They instructed their deputies to re-examine the role of the GAB, including the question of the amounts committed by each participant. In June, Karl Otto Pöhl, Deputy Governor of the Deutsche Bundesbank, who had just been elected Chairman of the deputies of the Group of Ten, sent a list of questions to all deputies. In preparing the draft report for discussion by the deputies in September, Mr. Pöhl drew on the replies to these questions as well as on a technical paper prepared by the Fund staff that commented on the size of the GAB. This paper pointed out that, if the commitments by the ten participants to lend under the GAB were restored to their original size relative to the aggregate size of the Fund—about 60 percent of the quotas of the ten participants and about 40 percent of Fund quotas—the Arrangements would have to be more than doubled from SDR 6.5 billion to SDR 15 billion. The staff paper also pointed out that the relative shares of the participants would also have to be changed to reflect changes in their economic and financial positions since 1962. The paper stressed that, in the absence of an appropriate increase in the GAB, the Fund's liquidity could be impaired were any of the ten participants to draw on the Fund.

The draft report, discussed at a meeting of the deputies in Paris on September 8, 1978, concluded, however, that except for possible minor changes, the provisions of the GAB should remain as they were. The deputies felt that, although some reasons for establishing the GAB were no longer relevant and fundamental changes had emerged in the international monetary system in the last decade (including the rapid expansion of the Eurocurrency markets, the transition to general floating of exchange rates, and the establishment of SDRs), the Fund might still become short of usable currencies and unable to meet large drawings by the countries of the Group of Ten. The GAB should therefore continue. The majority of the deputies still believed that activation of the GAB should be restricted to circumstances in which the Fund needed additional resources "to forestall or cope with an impairment of the international monetary system," although some deputies now believed that the Fund's recourse to the GAB need not be so limited. Concluding

---

[9]The text of the GAB as amended is contained in E.B. Decision No. 1289-(62/1), January 5, 1962, as amended by Decisions Nos. 1362-(62/13), July 9, 1962; 1415-(62/47), September 19, 1962; 4421-(74/132), October 23, 1974; and 5792-(79/144), June 2, 1978; Vol. III below, pp. 527–34.

that a major reason for the effective functioning of the GAB had been "the cohesion of the participants," they favored retaining the provision of the GAB requiring agreement by all participants before any new participants were accepted. Although they were aware that closer cooperation and consultation among all the Fund's major creditors, including the oil importing countries, might be desirable insofar as the Fund's operations were concerned, most deputies did not favor widening the existing Group of Ten.

When they reviewed the size of the GAB, most deputies, for a variety of reasons, advocated no change in total commitment or in the commitments of individual participants. Some deputies believed that the amounts then in effect were generally satisfactory. Others believed that while some increase might be advisable, the Group of Ten would not agree on the size of any increase. Still others believed that parliaments or other legislative bodies, particularly the U.S. Congress, would be reluctant to approve larger amounts.

Given the deputies' opposition to change in the GAB, the Fund management and staff realized they could do little to influence the conclusions of the deputies' report to the finance ministers and governors of central banks. The report consequently recommended postponing consideration of any substantive amendments to the GAB at least until the fourth renewal in 1980.

The Group of Ten endorsed the report in September 1978. One change recommended by the deputies was accepted: the liquidity of the claims on the Fund that participants received under the GAB should be enhanced to make them comparable with claims lenders were to receive who lent to the Fund under the supplementary financing facility.[10]

BILATERAL BORROWING FROM SWITZERLAND

On the occasion of the large stand-by arrangements for the United Kingdom and for Italy in 1977, the Fund borrowed bilaterally from Switzerland in arrangements entirely separate from Switzerland's association with the GAB, in much the same way as the Fund had borrowed bilaterally from Italy in 1966 on the occasion of the drawing by the United States.[11] The Swiss National Bank put at the disposal of the Fund, in U.S. dollars, the equivalent of SDR 300 million to finance drawings by the United Kingdom and the equivalent of SDR 37.5 million to finance drawings by Italy.[12] Some, but not all, of the provisions of the two loan agreements were similar

---

[10]In March 1979 the claims under the GAB were made comparable with those arising under the supplementary financing facility when the Executive Board decided to allow the transfer, under certain conditions and terms, of all or part of the claims of GAB participants and the Swiss National Bank.

[11]*History, 1966–71*, Vol. I, pp. 376–77.

[12]E.B. Decisions Nos. 5288-(76/167), December 22, 1976 and 5387-(77/61), April 25, 1977; see also E.B. Decisions Nos. 5306-(77/2), January 3, 1977, 5331-(77/15), January 31, 1977, and 5488-(77/116), August 1, 1977, concerning the media in which the Fund was to pay interest and transfer charges. These five decisions are in Vol. III below, pp. 543–46, 549–50.

to the provisions for the GAB. One provision that was not similar to the GAB was that Switzerland was required to lend if the Fund asked to borrow. Under the GAB, Fund requests to borrow could be refused. The Fund actually borrowed SDR 154 million under this bilateral arrangement with the Swiss National Bank.

■   ■   ■   ■   ■   ■

In the years reviewed here, the Fund became a large-scale borrower. Under the oil facility, the supplementary financing facility, the GAB, and bilateral borrowing arrangements with Switzerland, the Fund put itself in a position to add substantially to its own resources by borrowing. From April 1974, when the first borrowing arrangements were being worked out for the oil facility, to the end of April 1978, the close of the last financial year covered here, the Fund borrowed or made arrangements to borrow the equivalent of SDR 18.9 billion. This amount was equal to about 65 percent of the Fund's quotas just prior to the quota increases under the Sixth General Review. As of April 30, 1978, the amount of outstanding borrowing by the Fund was equivalent to SDR 8.1 billion, about 25 percent of the Fund's quotas on that date. This borrowing was all from official sources, namely, the Fund's member governments or their central banks. The Fund had not yet considered borrowing from private sources, although a few officials from Fund members were suggesting this possibility.

CHANGES IN THE RATE OF REMUNERATION

As the Fund started to borrow from its members at market rates of interest, as the rate of interest on the SDR was raised from 1½ percent to as high as 5 percent a year, and as the rate of interest on borrowings under the GAB was raised to at least 4 percent a year, it was inevitable that the rate of remuneration paid to members with net creditor positions in the Fund would be increased as well. All these transactions created "Fund-related reserve assets held by members." Net creditors were members which, until the Second Amendment, had what was called a super gold tranche position in the Fund, that is, the Fund held the member's currency in amounts less than 75 percent of its quota. (A debtor position was the difference between 75 percent of quota and the Fund's holdings of a member's currency when these holdings exceeded 75 percent of quota.) In effect, the member was making its currency available to the Fund for use by other members. Creditor members were thereby in effect extending money or usable liquidity to the Fund just as were members which lent to the Fund through borrowing agreements (and received market-related rates of interest) and members which held SDRs in excess of their net cumulative allocations (and received interest on such holdings).

Reasons for a Split Rate of Remuneration

The rate of remuneration was linked under the Articles of Agreement as amended in 1969 to the rate of interest on the SDR. When the rate of interest on the

SDR was raised in June 1974 from 1½ percent to 5 percent a year, the rate of remuneration was also increased. At that time, whether remuneration had to be uniform for all members in net creditor positions was questioned. It was decided that the Executive Directors could establish different rates of remuneration for different brackets of net creditor positions. The wording "a rate uniform for all members" (Article V, Section 9) permitted distinctions in establishing rates of remuneration provided that the rates applied to all members within the same bracket without discrimination, just as it permitted different schedules of charges for different facilities. Consequently, when the Executive Board increased the rate of remuneration in June 1974, a split rate of remuneration was adopted. In order to mitigate the consequences of higher rates of remuneration on the Fund's operational expenditure and hence on the Fund's budgetary deficits or on any needed increase in the Fund's schedule of charges, a basic rate of remuneration of 5 percent a year, the same as the rate of interest on the SDR, was given to creditor positions where the Fund's holdings of a member's currency were below 50 percent of quota; a lower rate of remuneration, half the basic rate, or 2.5 percent a year, was given to creditor positions where the Fund's holdings of a member's currency were between 50 and 75 percent of quota. If the Fund's net income permitted, the lower rate was to be increased.

Since the new higher rates of remuneration and interest on the SDR were intended to reflect current market rates of interest, the decision of June 1974 provided that both the rates of remuneration and of interest on the SDR were to remain at 5 percent a year for only six months, from July 1, 1974 to December 31, 1974. After this period, both rates were to be reviewed every six months, in January and July, and adjusted according to a weighted average of the rates of interest on five money market instruments, one each in the United States, the United Kingdom, the Federal Republic of Germany, France, and Japan. If the combined market rate on these five money instruments was below 9 percent, the rates of remuneration and of interest on the SDR were to be reduced below 5 percent by three fifths of the difference between the combined market rate and 9 percent. If the combined market rate was above 11 percent, the rates of remuneration and of interest on the SDR were to be increased above 5 percent by three fifths of the difference between the combined market rate and 11 percent.

The assumption underlying this formula was that while the rate of remuneration should approximate current market rates of interest, it should nonetheless be below those rates. Moreover, the need for a split rate of remuneration was considered temporary, to apply for only two years. Fund officials anticipated that the amended Articles of Agreement would alleviate some of the adverse consequences on the Fund's budget of requiring that the rate of remuneration be equal to the rate of interest on the SDR. For example, when quotas were increased, members would pay subscriptions in SDRs in lieu of gold, and the Fund would earn interest on the SDRs it received. Furthermore, under the amended Articles the Fund would be given authority to invest some of its reserves in interest-earning assets, so that the Fund's entire income would not then be so dependent on charges. The provisions of the decision of June 1974 were to be reviewed after two years and were to lapse in the absence of a further decision.

Developments After June 1974

After reviewing the two rates of remuneration in December 1974, the Executive Directors decided not to change them. By the next review, six months later, rates in the short-term money markets had been falling because of the prevailing world recession, and the formula adopted in June 1974 yielded a rate of remuneration of 3.75 percent. The Executive Directors were divided on whether to reduce the rate of remuneration and were hesitant to call for a vote, which was the only way the existing rate could be retained. Realizing they could not reach agreement, they postponed the review that was to have been completed by the end of June 1975.

When they took up the issue in the first week of July, the depth of their division became apparent. Several Executive Directors did not like automatic use of the formula agreed in June 1974. They complained that use of the formula produced rates of remuneration and of interest on the SDR that were too low by the standards of the market and certainly low in comparison with the interest rates that the Fund had to pay on funds borrowed for the oil facility. They considered it decidedly unfair for the Fund to pay 7 or 7.25 percent a year on funds borrowed from members with balance of payments surpluses and only 3.75 percent a year on creditor positions in the Fund or on members' holdings of SDRs in excess of their net cumulative allocations. Other Executive Directors, on the other hand, wanted to use some formula, otherwise they would go on debating and never reach agreement on these rates. Because of the need to take some decision, use of the formula won out, and on July 7, 1975 the Executive Board adopted a decision unifying the two rates of remuneration at 3.75 percent a year for the next six months. Because of the size of the net creditor positions subject to the previous split rates of 5.0 and 2.5 percent a year, unification of the two rates of remuneration actually increased the average rate of remuneration paid by the Fund.

At the next six-month review of the rate of remuneration, in December 1975, the formula produced a rate of remuneration (and an interest rate on the SDR) of only 3.5 percent a year. Again the strong predilection of many of the Executive Directors to use the formula induced the Executive Board to reduce the rate of remuneration in line with the results obtained by the formula. Mr. de Groote, Mr. Whitelaw, and other Executive Directors again expressed concern that, if the rate of remuneration remained relatively low, the monetary authorities of members with large creditor positions in the Fund and with holdings of SDRs above 100 percent of their cumulative allocations might develop unfavorable attitudes toward reserve assets in these forms, thereby making it harder for the Fund to get members to consent to increases in their quotas or to agree to hold excess amounts of SDRs.

June 1976, the time of the next six-month review of the rate of remuneration and the rate of interest on the SDR, was also time for the review of the original June

1974 decision about how the SDR was valued in terms of a basket of currencies. The decision of June 1974 had specified a review of all three elements two years later. Since several Executive Directors, in the meantime, had asked for a review of the procedures and the formula used in determining the rates of interest on the SDR and of remuneration, a thoroughgoing re-examination of the June 1974 decision was conducted in June 1976. After this re-examination, the formula for determining the rate of remuneration was changed to relate the rate more closely to changes in the rates of short-term money in world markets. The rate of remuneration was to be determined for each calendar quarter, instead of for six-month periods. Furthermore, it was to be equal to three fifths of the weighted average of the daily interest rates on specific money instruments of the same five major countries—France, the Federal Republic of Germany, Japan, the United Kingdom, and the United States—rounded to the nearest ¼ of 1 percent. To make the formula more current, the weighted average of the five short-term interest rates was to be calculated for the six-week period ending on the fifteenth day of the last month before the calendar quarter for which the rate of remuneration was determined. According to the revised formula, the rate of remuneration for the calendar quarter beginning on July 1, 1976 was to be 3.75 percent a year, slightly higher than the 3.25 percent that the previous formula would have yielded. This new decision was to be reviewed in three years.[13]

The rates of remuneration that prevailed from May 1969, when remuneration was first introduced in the Fund, until the last quarter of 1978 are listed in Table 27.

MAINTAINING THE VALUE
OF THE FUND'S CURRENCY HOLDINGS

Provisions for maintaining the value of the Fund's holdings of members' currencies were integral to the original Articles of Agreement. Article IV, Section 8 provided that the "gold value" of the Fund's assets was to be maintained whenever there was a change in the par value or foreign exchange value of the currency of any member, a provision sometimes referred to as the gold clause. This provision was intended to ensure that the Fund neither suffered loss nor reaped profit in the event of a change in the value of any currency it held. Another objective was implicit, to enable the Fund to continue to conduct its operations and transactions at realistic exchange rates. The obligation to maintain the value of the Fund's holdings of a member's currency in terms of gold rested on both the Fund and the issuer of the currency. On devaluation, the member issuing the currency was to pay more currency to the Fund; on revaluation, the Fund was to return currency to the issuer.

In accordance with this provision, until 1971 the Fund maintained the value of its currency holdings when the par values of currencies changed. Computations of

---

[13]The Rules and Regulations governing remuneration, Rules I-10 and T-1(b), (c), and (d), are in Vol. III below, pp. 467, 480.

Table 27. Rates of Remuneration, 1969–78

Period	Percent a Year
May 1, 1969–June 30, 1973	1.50
Six months beginning:	
July 1, 1974	5.00[1]
January 1, 1975	5.00[1]
July 1, 1975	3.75
January 1, 1976	3.50
Quarter beginning:	
July 1, 1976	3.75
October 1, 1976	4.00
January 1, 1977	4.00
April 1, 1977	3.75
July 1, 1977	3.50
October 1, 1977	3.50
January 1, 1978	3.50
April 1, 1978	3.75
July 1, 1978	3.75
October 1, 1978	4.00

[1] From July 1, 1974 through June 30, 1975, the basic rate of remuneration of 5.0 percent a year applied to creditor positions of up to 50 percent of quota; a lesser rate of remuneration, 2.5 percent a year, was applied to creditor positions that were between 50 and 75 percent of a member's quota. In July 1975, these two rates of remuneration were unified at 3.75 percent a year.

the value of various currencies for the purposes of the Fund's operations and transactions were made on the basis of members' par values. Par values were customarily expressed directly in terms of gold or indirectly in terms of the U.S. dollar of the weight and fineness of gold in effect on July 1, 1944. The relationship to the dollar was used because of the obligation the United States had undertaken to maintain the value of its currency in relation to gold by being willing to buy gold from the monetary authorities of other members at the fixed official price of $35 an ounce and because many members expressed the values of their currencies in terms of the dollar.

Even the original Articles of Agreement, based as they were on par values, nonetheless provided explicitly for maintenance of the value of the Fund's holdings of a member's currency if that currency was allowed to float. The depreciation (or appreciation) of a floating currency was to be measured by reference to its actual gold value, determined by the rate of exchange between the currency in its main market and the U.S. dollar. (The staff interpreted the Articles as also implicitly referring to appreciation.)

As early as 1954, the Fund found it needed a general policy for maintaining the value of its currency holdings of what were then called fluctuating currencies and for computing the exchange rates used for operations and transactions in those currencies. At the time there was a suspicion that sterling might be floated. Further problems arose because since 1949 Peruvian soles had fluctuated freely in the markets and because the Canadian dollar had floated since 1950. The decision the Executive Board adopted in 1954 was based on the principles just described: adjustments were to be made to maintain the gold value of the Fund's holdings of a currency that was fluctuating, and the Fund's operations and transactions involving that currency were to take place at a realistic exchange rate. The decision aimed to ensure that equivalent exchange value would be maintained over time and uniform value made available to a member drawing from the Fund whatever the currency in which an operation or transaction was conducted. In August 1961 the 1954 decision was amended to cover sales of gold by the Fund in exchange for Canadian dollars when the Fund undertook currency replenishment activities, and in December 1961 an amendment covered borrowing by the Fund of Canadian dollars and repayment of any sums borrowed under the General Arrangements to Borrow then being negotiated.[14]

New Problems After 1971

Following the suspension of official dollar convertibility in August 1971, much more extensive problems of exchange rate valuation arose. The Executive Board's decisions of January and May 1972 about the exchange rates to be used for computations and adjustment of the Fund's holdings of currencies enabled the Fund to continue its operations and transactions fairly much on the basis of par values or of central rates. On the occasion of the next devaluation of the U.S. dollar, in February 1973, the Fund immediately put the prospective new par value for the dollar in terms of SDRs into effect for purposes of valuing other currencies.

With the introduction of floating rates in March 1973, much more serious problems arose. Since the Fund was using the SDR defined in terms of gold after March 1972 as the basis of its accounts, for expressing the value of its assets, and for expressing exchange rates, these asset valuations and exchange rate problems could not be resolved until agreement was forthcoming on how to value the SDR. After the method of valuing the SDR with reference to a basket of currencies was agreed in June 1974, the decision on computations and adjustment of the Fund's holdings of currencies of May 1972 was modified. Another modification specifying when and how adjustments in the Fund's currency holdings were to be made was taken in May 1975. More modifications were made in May 1976. The decision of May 1972, with the modifications of June 1974, May 1975, and May 1976, permitted the Fund to conduct operations and transactions and regularly to adjust the value of its currency holdings. Basically, exchange rates for currencies were determined in relation to the SDR whose value was determined in turn on the basis of the currency basket.

---

[14]More information on the history of maintaining the value of the Fund's currency holdings when currencies were floated can be found in *History, 1945–65*, Vol. II, pp. 165–67, and in Joseph Gold, *Maintenance of the Gold Value of the Fund's Assets*, IMF Pamphlet Series, No. 6 (Washington, 2nd ed., 1971).

DEVELOPMENTS IN THE FUND'S BUDGET

The Fund's budgetary situation, or financial position, was an altogether different concept from that of its liquidity position. While the Fund's liquidity referred to its liquid assets and liabilities and its ability to meet current claims by members on these assets, the Fund's financial position referred to its own current operating and administrative budget. The Fund's financial position (budgetary situation) underwent significant changes in the years 1972–78.

Until 1971 the Fund's budgetary income was derived almost solely from the charges it levied on use of its resources. Interest on the SDRs that the Fund held in its own General Account did not exist until 1969, and the Fund's income from this source in the first few years that the SDR existed was minute. Income from charges on drawings rose more or less with the size of the Fund: when quotas were increased and drawings expanded, the Fund's income climbed. After the first big drawing by the United Kingdom in 1956 and the upsurge in the Fund's income as a result of the charges received on this drawing, the Fund's income was more than adequate to cover administrative expenses, including financing a new headquarters building in 1958. The Fund had no operational expenses in the sense of having to pay for the money it acquired through its own resources until 1969 when it began to pay remuneration to members with creditor positions. Budget surpluses were placed into a General Reserve and, beginning in 1967, distributions of net income were made to members for the next four financial years. Despite these distributions, the General Reserve attained a level as of April 30, 1971 of over $375 million. After 1956 the Fund had also been receiving income from investments it made in short-term securities of the U.S. Treasury. Income from these investments was about $40–60 million each financial year. The Fund credited this investment income to a Special Reserve as a contingency against administrative deficits, and as of April 30, 1971 the Special Reserve totaled over $400 million.[15]

Emergence of a Deficit

This solvent position, as well as the character of the Fund's budgetary accounts, started to change in August 1971. Diminished drawings in 1970 and 1971 reduced income from charges, and the cash financing of another headquarters building then being constructed threw the budget into deficit in the financial year 1971/72 for the first time in 14 years. In the financial years 1971/72 and 1972/73 the deficits were relatively small and were considered temporary. It was thought that deficits would be eliminated as soon as drawings picked up and the new building was paid for. It was not until late 1973 that Fund officials came to view the budget deficit as serious and to expect the deficits to persist for some years. By then, it was apparent that several recent decisions pertinent to the Fund's financial operations

---

[15]For further information on the Fund's budgetary situation in 1945–71, the reader is referred to *History, 1945–65*, Vol. II, pp. 363–73 and *History, 1966–71*, Vol. I, pp. 383–92.

were threatening the Fund's budgetary solvency. The decision in 1969 to pay remuneration to members with net creditor positions in the Fund introduced operational expenses into the Fund's budget. In the financial years 1970–74, remuneration ran at about SDR 27 million to SDR 37 million a year. This amount almost equaled the Fund's total administrative expenditures. Other decisions of 1969 and 1970 lowered the Fund's income, such as the elimination of the service charge on drawings in the gold tranche and the disinvestment of the income-earning investments in U.S. Government securities.[16] Aggravating the budgetary situation were the decisions of the Executive Board, at each annual review of the Fund's charges until 1973, to retain the same low schedule of charges in effect since 1963, despite the Fund's growing expenses and loss of income from other sources.

The Fund's budgetary situation worsened still further after the rate of remuneration was increased from 1½ percent to 5 percent a year in June 1974. In the financial year ended April 30, 1975, remuneration paid to creditor members doubled, to SDR 62 million. In the next financial year, it went up to SDR 104 million, twice the size of the Fund's administrative expenditures. By the financial years 1977 and 1978, remuneration was running at over SDR 200 million a year, three times administrative expenditures, despite a continuous rise in the latter.

Although the Fund had raised its charges in June 1974, it was suffering from the sharp rise in the average cost of funds it obtained relative to the average rate of charge it received. Between April 1974 and January 1977, the average cost of funds (excluding interest on borrowing by the Fund), that is, the rate of remuneration, rose from 1.5 percent to 3.8 percent, while the average rate of charges on balances of currencies held in excess of quota rose from 2.85 percent to 4.2 percent. The margin between the two was thus only 0.4 percent in January 1977, compared with 1.35 percent in April 1974. In June 1974, when remuneration was raised, so were charges, but in July 1975, when the split rate of remuneration was ended, raising the average rate of remuneration, charges were not adjusted. In fact, between September 30, 1976 and April 1, 1977, when charges were raised again, the rate of remuneration of 4.0 percent a year was the same as the initial rate of charge. Hence, no income was earned in the first year that the Fund held balances of a member's currency in excess of its quota (except for a onetime service charge of ½ of 1 percent on drawings in the credit tranche). As noted in the previous chapter, this situation prompted the Executive Directors to raise the Fund's charges in April 1977 and to link the initial rate of charge with the rate of remuneration and with a review of the Fund's financial position.

The sizable reserve tranche drawings made by members after 1974 also increased operational expenses. Reserve tranche drawings produce no income since no charges are levied on them, but these drawings usually expand the net creditor positions on which the Fund has to pay remuneration. (These drawings meant that the Fund sold U.S. dollars, deutsche mark, or Japanese yen, for instance, so that its holdings of these currencies went down, giving the members that issued these

---

[16]*History, 1966–71*, Vol. I, pp. 383–85.

currencies larger creditor positions in the Fund.) Over the ten years from 1967 to 1977, for example, outstanding reserve tranche drawings accounted for about 45 percent of total outstanding drawings and were a major reason why average creditor positions, on which remuneration was paid, exceeded average debtor positions on which charges were paid. The combination of a small and diminishing margin between the rate of initial charge and the rate of remuneration and the excess of creditor balances over debtor balances meant that though the Fund's operational income (almost entirely from charges, with only small amounts coming from interest on the Fund's holdings of SDRs) was sufficient to cover operational expenses (remuneration plus transfer charges and interest on the Fund's indebtedness), it was insufficient to meet administrative expenses as well. Consequently, from 1971/72 to 1976/77, the Fund ran budget deficits ranging from SDR 2.9 million (in 1975/76) to SDR 37.2 million (in 1973/74).

After charges were raised in April 1977, the Fund's budgetary situation improved. Income from charges rose enough so that for the financial year ended April 30, 1978, the Fund's net operational income doubled and the total budget was again in surplus, to the extent of SDR 27.5 million. The provisions of the Second Amendment were also expected to improve the Fund's budgetary position. Since currency balances acquired by the Fund under various facilities rather than as a result of regular drawings could float alongside the reserve tranche, they were subject to charges. (Previously, some of these currency balances were in the reserve tranche and hence not subject to charges.)

Growth and New Concepts

Apart from the emergence of a deficit, the Fund's budget changed in other ways after 1971. The Fund gradually received somewhat larger income from interest on its holdings of SDRs in the General Resources Account, previously called the General Account. By the financial year 1978 this interest income reached nearly SDR 40 million. The most striking change, however, was an enormous expansion in the size of the Fund's operational income and expenses. As the Fund's operations under its various facilities expanded, as the Fund borrowed large amounts to finance facilities, and as the Fund paid market rates of interest on these borrowings and levied charges to cover these interest payments, its operational budget increased severalfold. Income from charges, for example, rose over twelvefold, from SDR 65 million in financial year 1972 to SDR 800 million in financial year 1978. On the expense side, transfer charges and interest paid on the Fund's indebtedness leaped. They went from a little over SDR 1 million in financial year 1972 and zero in financial years 1973 and 1974 to SDR 541 million in financial year 1978. These tremendous increases in the Fund's operational income and expenses made the Fund's administrative expenditures (although expanding from SDR 36 million in financial year 1972 to SDR 66 million in financial year 1978) a relatively small part of the Fund's budget.

Table 28 below summarizes the Fund's income and expenses and the resulting net deficit or surplus for each of the financial years 1972–78.[17]

In short, as 1978 came to a close, the Fund's accounts were very much larger and more complex than ever before. The rates of remuneration paid, the initial rate of charge, and the budgetary position were integrally linked not only financially but, as will be seen in Part Eight, even legally under the Articles of Agreement following the Second Amendment.

Because the Fund's financial situation was growing complex, the staff continuously developed new concepts and new calculations to assess the situation. In addition to the concept of the Fund's liquidity, the staff developed concepts on, for instance, the "average annual rate of charge" and the "average annual rate of remuneration and interest on borrowings, net of interest on SDR holdings." These concepts measured the average charges levied by the Fund on use of its resources compared with the average cost to the Fund of raising money through increases in members' quotas or through borrowing from member governments. A concept was also developed and calculated for the spread between these two concepts, that is, the "spread between the combined average annual rate of charge and the combined average annual rate of expense." At first these concepts were used internally in the Fund, but they were published in the Annual Reports for 1977 and 1978.

■ ■ ■ ■ ■ ■

In 1972–78, the Fund's accounts evolved beyond their early simplicity in the Fund's first quarter century. More important, the decisions needed to help keep the Fund solvent had also become much more difficult. They no longer concerned merely the size of administrative expenses, the schedule of charges, and the relatively small investments in U.S. Government securities. Decisions now had to be taken concerning the extent to which the rate of remuneration and the rate of interest on the SDR, as well as the schedule of charges, should reflect rates in short-term money markets; the amount of borrowing in which the Fund should engage; and the extent to which the Fund should cover its current expenses by charges alone. The study of these technical questions relating to the Fund's operations involved increased attention from not only the staff but also the Executive Directors, who had to take decisions on all these matters.

---

[17]Detailed information, including statistical tables, on the Fund's budget for the financial years 1972–78 can be found in the Fund's *Annual Reports*.

Table 28. The Fund's Budget: Income and Expenses, Financial Years 1972–78[1]

(In millions of SDRs)

	1972	1973	1974	1975	1976	1977	1978
Operational income							
Operational charges[2]	3.0	3.2	2.5	21.0	26.6	24.4	13.2
Periodic charges[3]	62.0	28.2	28.2	124.4	408.5	727.3	786.6
Interest on holdings of SDRs	7.2	10.2	7.8	21.1	20.8	23.0	39.8
Total operational income	72.2	41.6	38.5	166.5	455.9	774.6	839.6
Deduct: operational expenses							
Remuneration	30.5	29.3	27.2	62.4	104.1	226.9	200.9
Transfer charges and interest on indebtedness	1.2	—	—	69.2	303.4	500.7	540.7
Total operational expenses	31.8	29.3	27.2	131.6	407.5	727.6	741.6
NET OPERATIONAL INCOME	40.5	12.2	11.2	34.9	48.4	47.1	98.0
Expenses[4]							
Administrative budget expenses[5]	36.0	38.7	42.5	44.8	52.5	60.8	65.9
Fixed property expenses	17.7	–4.8[6]	5.9	–0.3	–0.9	—	—
Amortization of past service liabilities	—	—	—	—	—	4.4	4.4
Total expenses[4]	53.7	34.0	48.4	44.6	52.3	65.3	70.5
Excess of (expenses) or income	(13.3)	(21.7)	(37.2)	(9.7)	(2.9)	(18.2)	(27.5)

[1] Components may not add to totals because of rounding of figures for individual items.
[2] Service charges and charges on stand-by and extended arrangements.
[3] Charges on the Fund's holdings of currencies in excess of quotas.
[4] Other than the operational expenses deducted from operational income above.
[5] Includes the administrative costs purely of the IMF. Amounts received by the General Resources Account from assessments levied on participants for the expenses of operating the Special Drawing Account and the Trust Fund are not included in these figures.
[6] Represents the sale of the Fund's former headquarters building for SDR 21.2 million from which fixed property expenses of SDR 16.4 million have been deducted. Also in other years any gains from the sale of property have been combined with fixed property expenses.

603